STRATEGY FORMULATION AND IMPLEMENTATION

—

TASKS OF THE GENERAL MANAGER

FIFTH EDITION

ARTHUR A. THOMPSON, JR.

A.J. STRICKLAND III

BOTH OF

THE UNIVERSITY OF ALABAMA

IRWIN

HOMEWOOD, IL 60430

BOSTON, MA 02116

Sponsoring editor: Karen L. Johnson
Developmental editor: Elizabeth Rubenstein
Project editor: Waivah Clement
Production manager: Bette K. Ittersagen
Designer: Tara L. Bazata
Art manager: Kim Meriwether
Artist: Arcata Graphics, Kingsport
Compositor: Weimer Typesetting Co., Inc.
Typeface: 10.5/12 Palatino
Printer: Von Hoffmann Press, Inc.

Library of Congress Cataloging-in-Publication Data

Thompson, Arthur A., 1940-
  Strategy formulation and implementation : tasks of the general
manager / Arthur A. Thompson, Jr. [and] A.J. Strickland III.—5th
ed.
      p.   cm.
  ISBN 0-256-09718-6
  1. Management.   I. Strickland, A. J. (Alonzo J.)   II. Title.
HD31.T4886   1992
658.4′012—dc20   91–28706

Printed in the United States of America
2 3 4 5 6 7 8 9 0 VH 9 8 7 6 5 4 3 2

Preface

Our goal in preparing this fifth edition of *Strategy Formulation and Implementation* has been to effectively present what every manager needs to know about crafting and implementing business strategies. The revisions and enhancements extend from cover to cover. We have "internationalized" the entire treatments of strategic analysis and strategy formation, devoting much more space to global competition, multinational strategies, and strategic alliances. There are new sections dealing with best-cost producer strategies, the concept of strategic intent, core competencies, profit sanctuaries, economies of scope, company values and codes of ethics, incentive compensation, and employee training, plus 25 new Illustration Capsules and 7 new readings. A new series of "margin notes" puts the spotlight on key concepts and the "principles" of strategic management. Throughout, the presentation reflects new contributions to strategic thinking, a straightforward conceptual framework, and a sharp focus on analytical techniques.

A RUNDOWN ON THE NEW FEATURES

Ongoing advances in the literature of strategic management mandate important edition-to-edition revisions to keep the content close to the cutting edges of both theory and practitioner experience. While the chapter organization of this edition parallels the last, we have instituted numerous changes in coverage and emphasis:

- Chapters 1 and 2 feature new discussions of a company's need for both strategic objectives and financial objectives, the role each has in the strategic management process, and the tradeoffs between actions to strengthen long-term competitive position and actions to improve short-term financial performance.
- There are two new sections in Chapter 2 detailing how ethics, values, and social responsibility considerations shape the choice of strategy.

- The chapter-length treatment of industry and competitive analysis has been streamlined, simplified, and made applicable to any market situation, whether local, national, or global. The conceptual framework weaves together all the basic tools for evaluating a company's external situation—key industry characteristics, driving forces, Porter's model of competition, competitor analysis and strategic group mapping, key success factors, and industry attractiveness.

- The strategic role and relevance of a company's *core competencies* have been woven into the discussions of company strengths, crafting strategy around what a company does best, and building a capable organization (Chapters 2, 4, and 9).

- To help distinguish between good and bad strategies, we've added a section on the tests of a winning strategy (Chapter 2).

- A much revised chapter on strategy and competitive advantage presents the whole gamut of strategic options—striving for low-cost leadership, becoming a best-cost producer, differentiation, focusing, offensive strategies, defensive strategies, and vertical integration. There is a new section on the dynamics of achieving a sustainable competitive advantage.

- Chapter 6, "Matching Strategy to the Situation," surveys the major strategic options and generic types of industry environments and company situations. The new centerpiece of this chapter is the coverage given to strategies for competing in international and global markets. There are sections covering multicountry (or *multidomestic*) competition versus global competition, the pros and cons of strategic alliances, the difference between a multicountry strategy and a global strategy, the ways to achieve competitive advantage with a global strategy, and how global competitors can build profit sanctuaries and use cross-subsidization to outcompete domestic competitors.

- To draw together the main lessons from the three-chapter module on business strategy, we've added a summary section that presents 13 "commandments" for successful strategy-making in single-business enterprises (Chapter 6).

- The chapter on corporate diversification strategies contains new treatments of (1) how to test whether diversification builds shareholder value, (2) the roles of cost-sharing and skills transfer in creating competitive advantage via diversification, and (3) the relationships between strategic fit, economies of scope, and competitive advantage. How diversified multinational enterprises can rely upon *economies of scope* and cross-subsidization to gain competitive advantage over single-business domestic firms is prominently featured in Chapter 7.

- In Chapter 8, there is more methodological detail in the explanations of how to compare industry attractiveness and business-unit strength in diversified companies.

- Chapter 10 includes a new section on establishing ethical standards and values, a second new section on enforcing ethical behavior, and a third new section on the CEO's role in setting an ethical example.

- There is enhanced coverage of how corporate social responsibility and corporate citizenship enter into the tasks of establishing a mission

(Chapter 2) and putting together a culture-shaping statement of corporate values and beliefs (Chapter 10).

- Greater emphasis has been placed on the role of employee training in the strategy implementation process (Chapter 9) and on using incentive compensation approaches to strengthen employee commitment to strategy implementation (Chapter 10).

- A visible addition to all the chapters is the series of margin notes highlighting basic concepts, major conclusions, and "core truths" about strategic behavior in competitive markets. Many of these notes represent an effort to distill the presentation into concise "principles" and kernels of wisdom. Our purpose in preparing the margin notes was to put added stress on important points and help readers become more rigorous strategic thinkers.

In making these changes, however, we've continued to keep the spotlight trained squarely on the strategy-related tasks of managers, the methods of strategic analysis, and the making of good strategic decisions. Senior managers (major department heads and up) are cast firmly in the twin roles of chief strategy-maker and chief strategy-implementer, charged with presiding over insightful strategic analysis, formulating and reviewing strategic-action plans, and leading the process of strategy implementation and execution in their respective areas of responsibility. Every key aspect of strategic management is examined—defining the business, setting strategic and financial objectives, conducting industry and competitive analysis, doing company situation analysis, evaluating diversified business portfolios, checking the various generic corporate and business-strategy options, probing for sustainable competitive advantage, building a capable organization, shaping the corporate culture, creating strategy-related administrative fits, and exerting strategic leadership.

On the whole, we think you will find the treatments of the material very current and comfortably mainstream. Because we've put more effort into improving clarity and style than in any previous edition, we also believe you will find the content of this fifth edition crisply and forcefully presented.

THE READING SELECTIONS

As with the last edition, we have included a set of readings to complement the chapter discussions. The readings serve three purposes: to add detailed coverage of several important, newly published topics; to provide modest exposure to the strategic management literature; and to respond to the requests of users who, as a regular practice, assign articles from current journals to their classes. We have chosen nine readings for this edition; two are holdovers from the prior edition and seven are new.

The first reading, by Henry Mintzberg on "Crafting Strategy," won a best article award in the *Harvard Business Review*; it stresses the very important point that strategy is more often crafted as events unfold than formulated by strict, preconceived design. It provides a marvelous insight into where strategy comes from and how it takes shape. The second reading is by C. K. Prahalad and Gary Hamel on the subject of "Strategic Intent"; it also won a best article award in the *Harvard Business Review* for its innovative discussion of how global competitors approach strategic thinking, strategic objectives, and crafting long-range strategies. They stress why companies need to set challenging strategic objectives and why it is crucial to strive constantly to build and strengthen the company's long-term competitive position. Prahalad and Hamel's article is one of those landmark articles that every student of strategic management needs to read. We suggest assigning these first two readings following coverage of Chapters 1 and 2.

We've included four readings to accompany our three-chapter coverage of strategic analysis in single-business enterprises. The first of these is David Aaker's article on "Managing Assets and Skills: The Key to Sustainable Competitive Advantage." Aaker's thesis is that long-term success entails creating, managing, and exploiting assets and skills that rivals find difficult to match or counteract. The next two readings are taken from Ira Magaziner and Mark Patinkin's fascinating and insightful book on *The Silent War: Inside the Global Business Battles Shaping America's Future*. Both are about strategy and competition in global markets. One concerns Samsung's strategic drive to become a major player in the world microwave industry and the other describes GE's strategic efforts to restore its competitiveness in the refrigerator business. The two Magaziner-Patinkin readings are fascinating studies in global competition; they convey what it will take for U.S. companies to compete effectively in world markets as well as anything we've seen. The fourth article relating to business strategy describes how Honda tailors its strategy to fit the special circumstances of the host country markets where it competes; this article is especially good for better understanding the differences between a global strategy and a multicountry strategy (a topic covered at some length in Chapter 6).

Michael Porter's article on "From Competitive Advantage to Corporate Strategy" accompanies the two-chapter module on strategic analysis in diversified companies. This article won the McKinsey award as the best *Harvard Business Review* article during 1987. It presents significant research findings about the success and failure of corporate diversification strategies and provides some important prescriptions for making diversification work to greater advantage.

The last two readings deal with strategy implementation and should be read in conjunction with Chapters 9 and 10. One is excerpted from Wess Roberts' book on *Leadership Secrets of Attila the Hun*; it presents a series of proverbs, advice, and basic truths about managing people and exercising leadership. The other is by Charles O'Reilly on the role and importance of a strategy-supportive corporate culture.

We think you will find these nine readings well worth covering. Given that their number is limited, these readings should not be burdensome or cause readers to become bogged down in excessive detail. All nine articles are eminently readable and well matched to the chapter discussions.

ADDITIONAL PEDAGOGICAL FEATURES

As in previous editions, all the chapters incorporate the liberal use of examples and references to the strategic successes and failures of companies—what has worked, what hasn't, and why. The use of boxed Illustration Capsules to further highlight "strategy in action" was well received in earlier editions and has been continued. Twenty-five of the 28 capsules are new to this edition.

Together, the examples and the capsules keep the bridge between concept and actual practice always open, giving the reader a stronger feel for how strategic analysis concepts and techniques are utilized in real-world management circumstances.

We've also included an appendix giving students positive direction in case methods pedagogy and offering suggestions for approaching case analysis. In our experience, many students are unsure about what they are to do in preparing a case, and they are certainly inexperienced in analyzing a company from a "big picture" or strategic point of view. The appendix discussion is intended to provide explicit guidance and to focus student attention on the traditional analytical sequence of (1) identify, (2) evaluate, and (3) recommend. There is also a table on how to calculate and interpret key financial ratios, a discussion of how to prepare a case for oral class discussion, and guidelines for doing a written case analysis.

THE BUSINESS STRATEGY GAME OPTION

This fifth edition has an optional supplement called *The Business Strategy Game*. It is a PC-based simulation exercise that gives players hands-on experience in crafting strategies and analyzing markets from a strategic perspective. Version one of *The Business Strategy Game*, introduced two years ago, was very well received and provoked renewed interest in PC-based simulations. The second version, which is an integrated companion to this edition, has new features that make use of a simulation exercise in the strategy course even more appealing. Based on our experience of having used a simulation game every semester for the past 15 years, we are convinced that simulation games are the *single best exercise* available for helping students pull the pieces of the business puzzle together and giving them an integrated, capstone experience.

The Value a Simulation Adds

First and foremost, the exercise of running a simulated company over a number of decision periods helps develop students' business judgment. They learn about risk-taking. They have to react to changing market conditions, study the actions of competitors, and weigh alternative courses of action. They get valuable practice in spotting market opportunities, evaluating threats to their company's well-being, and assessing the long-term consequences of short-term decisions. And by having to live with the decisions they make, they experience what it means to be accountable and responsible for achieving satisfactory results. All this has a positive and meaningful impact on students' business acumen and managerial judgment.

Second, students learn an enormous amount from working with the numbers, exploring options, and trying to unite production, marketing, finance, and human resource decisions into a coherent strategy. The effect is to help students integrate a lot of material, look at decisions from the standpoint of the company as a whole, and see the importance of thinking strategically about a company's competitive position and future prospects. Since a simulation game is, by its very nature, a hands-on exercise, the lessons learned are forcefully planted in students' minds: the impact is far more lasting than what is remembered from lectures. Third, students' entrepreneurial instincts blossom as they get caught up in the competitive spirit of the game. The resulting entertainment value helps maintain an unusually high level of student motivation and emotional involvement in the course throughout the term.

We think you will find *The Business Strategy Game* a welcome course option. It will add a dimension to your course that can't be matched by any other teaching-learning tool. Moreover, with the aid of today's high-speed personal computers and the technical advances in software capability, there's minimal gear-up time on the instructor's part. You'll find that the time and effort required to administer *The Business Strategy Game* is well within tolerable limits.

About the Simulation

The product for *The Business Strategy Game* is athletic footwear—chosen because it is a product students personally know about, buy themselves, and wear regularly. The industry setting is global—companies can manufacture and sell their brands in the United States, Europe, or Asia. Competition is head-to-head; each team of students must match its strategic wits against the other company teams. Companies can focus their efforts on one geographic market or two or all three; they can establish a one-country production base or they can manufacture in all three of the geographic markets. Demand conditions, tariffs, and wage rates vary from area to area.

The company that students manage has plants to operate, a work force to compensate, distribution expenses and inventories to control, capital expenditure decisions to make, marketing and sales campaigns to wage, sales forecasts to consider, and changes in exchange rates, interest rates, and the stock market to take into account. Students must evaluate whether to pursue a low-cost producer strategy, a differentiation strategy, or a focus strategy. They have to decide whether to produce "off-shore" in Asia where wage rates are very low or whether to avoid import tariffs and transocean shipping costs by having a producing base in every primary geographic market. And they must endeavor to maximize shareholder wealth via increased dividend payments and stock price appreciation. Each team of students is challenged to use its entrepreneurial and strategic skills to become the next Nike or Reebok and ride the wave of growth to the top of the worldwide athletic footwear industry.

There's a built-in planning and analysis feature that allows students to (1) craft a five-year strategic plan, (2) make five-year financial projections, (3) do all kinds of "what-iffing," (4) assess the revenue-cost-profit consequences of alternative strategic actions, and (5) develop a tentative five-year set of decisions (in effect, a five-year strategic plan) which can easily be revised and updated as the game unfolds. A special "Calc" feature allows all the number-crunching to be done in a matter of seconds.

The Business Strategy Game can be used with any IBM or compatible PC with 640K memory and it is suitable for both senior-level and MBA courses. The game is programmed to accommodate a wide variety of computer setups as concerns disk drives, monitors, and printers.

Features of the Second Edition

This latest version of *The Business Strategy Game* makes things easier and better for both the players and the game administrator:

- No longer is access to Lotus 1-2-3 (or any other spreadsheet software) required as a supporting tool for either players or game administrators. By completely eliminating the need for any kind of outside software supplement, we've cast aside a requirement that complicated the procedures and that proved inconvenient for some and burdensome for others.

- We've enhanced the visual appeal of the screens by using color throughout (something that will be appreciated by those with color monitors).

- The scoring algorithm has been reworked to include a "power rating" for each company's strategy. In addition, the stock price performance measure has been replaced with a stock value measure (stock price × number of shares outstanding) to create a more inclusive measure of how successful the players have been in boosting shareholder value.

- The *Player's Manual* now has an index, and those parts of the manual that students found unclear have been rewritten to improve the explanations of how things work.

- We've recast the treatment of exchange rate fluctuations to impact costs rather than profits—the effect is to make the decision-making implications of exchange rate fluctuations more straightforward and understandable to students.

- A new manufacturing decision variable has been added to give companies another option for increasing the efficiency of existing plants over time. By making expenditures for *production methods improvement,* company managers can reduce production run set-up costs, cut supervision costs, and boost worker productivity.

- The company operations reports provide more extensive cost analysis figures, and the Footwear Industry Report provides more complete financial information for each company.

- Based on the experiences and suggestions of users, we've added print options for both dot-matrix and laser printers and reprogrammed several things to reduce the potential for glitches (disk problems and disk errors). We've improved the procedures for processing decisions and done all kinds of behind-the-scenes programming to make things run faster and more trouble-free on almost any kind of IBM or 100 percent-IBM compatible computer setup. Both players and game administrators will find Version 2.0 more user-friendly in virtually every respect.

At the same time, though, we've retained the features that made Version 1.0 so popular:

- Everything is done on disks. Students enter their decisions on disks and, during processing, a complete set of industry and company results is written back on the disks. It takes only a few minutes to collect the disks and return them. A printout of the industry scoreboard and a printout of the instructor's report are automatically generated during processing.

- Decisions can be processed in 40 minutes (less than 25 minutes on a fast PC); simple procedures allow most or all of the processing to be delegated to a student assistant.
- Students will find it convenient and uncomplicated to use the PC to play *The Business Strategy Game* even if they have had no prior exposure to PCs; *no programming of any kind is involved* and full instructions are presented in the *Player's Manual* and on the screens themselves.
- A scoreboard of company performance is automatically calculated each decision period. Instructors determine the weights to be given to each of six performance measures—revenues, after-tax profits, return on stockholders' investment, stock value, bond rating, and strategy rating; the overall performance score can be used to grade team performance.
- An *Instructor's Manual* describes how to integrate the game into your course, provides pointers on how to administer the game, and contains step-by-step processing instructions.

INSTRUCTOR SUPPLEMENTS

Adopters of this edition can obtain an *Instructor's Manual* containing suggested course outlines and a test bank of over 850 multiple choice and essay questions; a computerized test bank for generating examinations is also available. In addition, there's a set of color transparencies of the figures and selected tables in the 10 text chapters plus a manual of over 450 transparency masters that thoroughly cover the text presentation and support the instructor's lectures on the material.

ACKNOWLEDGMENTS

We have benefited from the help of many people during the evolution of this book. Our intellectual debt to those academics, writers, and practicing managers upon whose works and experiences we have drawn will be obvious to any reader familiar with the literature of strategic management; we have endeavored to acknowledge their specific contributions in our many footnote references and in the list of suggested readings at the end of each chapter. Students, adopters of previous editions, and reviewers have kindly offered an untold number of insightful comments and helpful suggestions for improving the manuscript.

Naturally, as custom properly dictates, we are responsible for whatever errors of fact, deficiencies in coverage or in exposition, and oversights that remain. As always, we value your recommendations and thoughts about the book. Your comments regarding coverage and content will be most welcome, as will your calling our attention to specific errors. Please write us at P.O. Box 870225, Department of Management and Marketing, the University of Alabama, Tuscaloosa, Alabama 35487-0225.

Arthur A. Thompson, Jr.
A. J. Strickland III

Contents

P A R T

III

APPENDIX:
A GUIDE TO CASE ANALYSIS 427

THE CONCEPTS AND TECHNIQUES OF STRATEGIC MANAGEMENT

CHAPTER

1

The Strategic Management Process

"Cheshire Puss," she [Alice] began . . . "would you please tell me which way I ought to go from here?"
"That depends on where you want to get to," said the cat.
Lewis Carroll

My job is to make sure the company has a strategy and that everybody follows it.
Kenneth H. Olsen
CEO, Digital Equipment Corp.

A strategy is a commitment to undertake one set of actions rather than another.
Sharon M. Oster
Professor, Yale University

This book is about the managerial tasks of crafting and implementing company strategies. *An organization's strategy consists of the moves and approaches devised by management to produce successful organization performance.* Strategy, in effect, is management's game plan for the business. Managers develop strategies to guide *how* an organization conducts its business and *how* it will achieve its target objectives. Without a strategy, there is no established course to follow, no roadmap to manage by, no cohesive action plan to produce the intended results.

Crafting and implementing a strategy for the business are *core* management functions. Among all the things that managers do, few affect organizational performance more lastingly than how well the management team handles the tasks of charting the organization's long-term direction, developing effective strategic moves and approaches, and then executing the strategy in ways that produce the intended results. Indeed, *good strategy and good implementation are the most trustworthy signs of good management.*

There is strong reason to associate "good management" with how well managers develop and execute strategy. Managers cannot be awarded a top grade for designing shrewd strategies but failing to carry them out well—weak implementation opens the door for organizational performance to fall short of full potential. Competent execution of a mediocre strategy scarcely qualifies managers for a gold-star award either. But powerful execution of a powerful strategy is a proven recipe for business success—the instances where a company with a well-conceived, well-executed strategy is unable to build a leading market position are few and far between. The standards for judging whether an organization is well managed, therefore, are grounded in good strategy-making *combined* with good strategy execution. The better conceived an organization's strategy and the more flawless its execution, the greater the chance that the organization will be a peak performer in its industry.

To qualify as excellently-managed, an organization must exhibit excellent execution of an excellent strategy.

However, superior strategy-making and strategy-implementing don't *guarantee superior organizational performance continuously*. Even well-managed organizations can hit the skids for short periods because of adverse conditions beyond management's ability to foresee or react to. But the bad luck of adverse events never excuses weak performance year after year. It is management's responsibility to adjust to negative conditions by undertaking strategic defenses and managerial approaches that can overcome adversity. Indeed, the essence of good strategy-making is to build a position strong and flexible enough to produce successful performance despite unforeseeable and unexpected external factors.

THE FIVE TASKS OF STRATEGIC MANAGEMENT

The strategy-making, strategy-implementing function of managers consists of five interrelated components:

1. *Developing a concept of the business and forming a vision of where the organization needs to be headed*—in effect, infusing the organization with a sense of purpose, providing long-term direction, and establishing a *mission*.
2. *Converting the mission into specific performance objectives.*
3. *Crafting a strategy* to achieve the targeted performance.
4. *Implementing and executing the chosen strategy* efficiently and effectively.
5. *Evaluating performance, reviewing the situation, and initiating corrective adjustments* in mission, objectives, strategy, or implementation in light of actual experience, changing conditions, new ideas, and new opportunities.

Figure 1–1 shows a model of the process. Together, these five components define what we mean by the term *strategic management*. Let's explore this basic conceptual model in more detail to set the stage for the chapters that follow.

Developing a Vision and a Mission

The foremost direction-setting question senior managers of any enterprise need to ask is "What is our business and what will it be?" Developing a carefully reasoned answer to this question pushes managers to consider what the

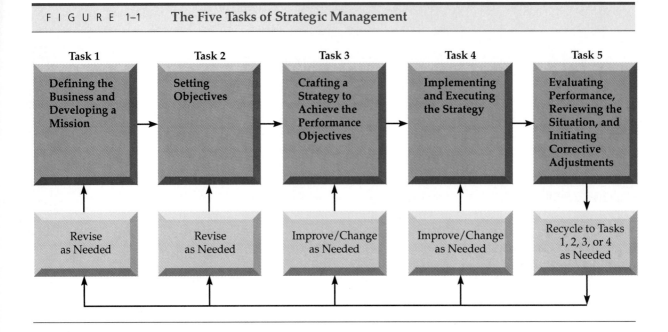

FIGURE 1–1   **The Five Tasks of Strategic Management**

organization's business makeup should be and to develop a clearer vision of where the organization needs to be headed over the next five to ten years. Management's answer to "What is our business and what will it be?" begins the process of carving out a meaningful direction for the organization to take and of establishing a strong organizational identity. Management's vision of what the organization seeks to do and to become is commonly termed the organization's *mission*. A mission statement establishes the organization's future course and outlines "who we are, what we do, and where we're headed." In effect, it sets forth the organization's intent to stake out a particular business position. Some examples of *company mission statements* are presented in Illustration Capsule 1.

Setting Objectives

The purpose of setting objectives is to convert the statement of organizational mission and direction into specific performance targets, something the organization's progress can be measured by. Objective-setting implies challenge, establishing a set of desired outcomes that require stretch and disciplined effort. The challenge of trying to close the gap between actual and desired performance pushes an organization to be more inventive, to exhibit some urgency in improving both its financial performance and its business position, and to be more intentional and focused in its actions. Setting *challenging but achievable* objectives thus helps guard against complacency, drift, internal confusion over what to accomplish, and status quo organizational performance. The set of objectives management establishes should ideally embrace a time horizon that is both near-term and far-term. *Short-range objectives* spell out the immediate improvements and outcomes management desires. *Long-range*

ILLUSTRATION CAPSULE
1

EXAMPLES OF COMPANY MISSION STATEMENTS

Presented below are seven actual company mission statements:

Otis Elevator

Our mission is to provide any customer a means of moving people and things up, down, and sideways over short distances with higher reliability than any similar enterprise in the world.

Deluxe Checks

The mission of Deluxe Checks is to provide all banks, S&L's, and investment firms with error-free financial instruments delivered in a timely fashion.

McCormick & Company

The primary mission of McCormick & Company is to expand our worldwide leadership position in the spice, seasoning, and flavoring markets.

Hewlett-Packard Company

Hewlett-Packard is a major designer and manufacturer of electronic products and systems for measurement and computation. HP's basic business purpose is to provide the capabilities and services needed to help customers worldwide improve their personal and business effectiveness.

The Saturn Division of General Motors

To market vehicles developed and manufactured in the United States that are world leaders in quality, cost, and customer satisfaction through the integration of people, technology, and business systems and to transfer knowledge, technology, and experience throughout General Motors.

Public Service Company of New Mexico

Our mission is to work for the success of the people we serve by providing our CUSTOMERS reliable electric service, energy information, and energy options that best satisfy their needs.

American Red Cross

The mission of the American Red Cross is to improve the quality of human life; to enhance self-reliance and concern for others; and to help people avoid, prepare for, and cope with emergencies.

Source: Company annual reports.

objectives prompt managers to consider what they can do *now* to enhance the organization's strength and performance capabilities over the long term.

Objective-setting is required of *all managers.* Every unit in an organization needs concrete, measurable performance targets indicating its contribution to the organization's overall objectives. When organizationwide objectives are broken down into specific targets for each unit and lower-level managers are held accountable for achieving them, a results-oriented climate emerges, with each part of the organization striving to achieve results that will move the whole organization in the intended direction.

Two types of performance yardsticks are called for: *financial objectives* and *strategic objectives.* Financial objectives are needed because acceptable financial performance is critical to preserving an organization's vitality and well-being. Strategic objectives are needed to provide consistent direction in strengthening a company's overall business position. Financial objectives typically focus on such measures as earnings growth, return on investment, and cash flow. Strategic objectives, however, relate more directly to a company's overall competitive situation and involve such performance yardsticks as growing faster than the industry average and making gains in market share, overtaking key competitors on product quality or customer service, achieving lower overall costs than rivals, boosting the company's reputation with customers, winning

---

Strategic Management Principle
Strategic objectives are, at the very least, coequal in importance to financial objectives.

ILLUSTRATION CAPSULE
2

EXAMPLES OF CORPORATE OBJECTIVES
Nike, La-Z-Boy, Owens-Corning, and McCormick & Company

Nike's Objectives (as stated in 1987)

- Protect and improve NIKE's position as the number one athletic brand in America, with particular attention to the company's existing core businesses in running, basketball, tennis, football, baseball, and kid's shoes and newer businesses with good potential like golf and soccer.
- Build a strong momentum in the growing fitness market, beginning with walking, workout, and cycling.
- Intensify the company's effort to develop products that women need and want.
- Explore the market for products specifically designed for the requirements of maturing Americans.
- Direct and manage the company's international business as it continues to develop.
- Continue the drive for increased margins through proper inventory management and fewer, better products.

La-Z-Boy's Objectives (as stated in 1990)

- To position La-Z-Boy as a full-line furniture manufacturer.
- To strengthen La-Z-Boy's brand name image with American families and businesspeople.
- To improve the quality of the company's distribution network.
- To expand production capacity and make it more efficient.
- To continue to gain financial strength.

Owens-Corning's Objectives (as stated in 1990)

- To anticipate our customers' requirements and provide them with the products which meet their market, quality, and service needs.
- To maintain our number one market positions through continued leadership in technology, manufacturing, and marketing.
- To maximize cash flow for continued debt reduction.
- To focus on operating profit improvements through productivity programs and focused market development.
- To make the most of the talents of our people and provide them with the opportunity and training to reach their full potential.

McCormick & Company's Objectives (as stated in 1990)

- Improve the returns from each of our existing operating groups—consumer, industrial, food service, international, and packaging.
- Dispose of those parts of our business which do not or cannot generate adequate returns or do not fit with our business strategy.
- Make selective acquisitions which complement our current businesses and can enhance our overall returns.
- Achieve a 20% return on equity.
- Achieve a net sales growth rate of 10% per year.
- Maintain an average earnings per share growth rate of 15% per year.
- Maintain total debt to total capital at 40% or less.
- Pay out 25% to 35% of net income in dividends.

Source: Company annual reports.

a stronger foothold in international markets, exercising technological leadership, and developing attractive growth opportunities. Strategic objectives make it explicit that management not only must deliver good financial performance but also must deliver on strengthening the organization's long-term business and competitive position.

Examples of the kinds of strategic and financial objectives companies set are shown in Illustration Capsule 2.

Crafting a Strategy

Strategy-making brings into play the critical managerial issue of *how* to achieve the targeted results in light of the organization's situation and prospects. Objectives are the "ends," and *strategy* is the "means" of achieving them. In effect, strategy is a management tool for achieving strategic targets. The task of forming a strategy starts with hard analysis of the organization's internal and external situation. Armed with an understanding of the "big picture," managers can better devise a strategy to achieve targeted strategic and financial results.

Definitionally, *strategy is the pattern of organizational moves and managerial approaches used to achieve organizational objectives and to pursue the organization's mission.* The pattern of moves and approaches already taken indicates what the prevailing strategy is; the planned moves and approaches signal how the prevailing strategy is to be embellished or changed. Thus, while strategy represents the managerial game plan for running an organization, this plan does not consist of just good intentions and actions yet to be taken. An organization's strategy is nearly always a blend of prior moves, approaches already in place, and new actions being mapped out. Indeed, the biggest part of an organization's strategy usually consists of prior approaches and practices that are working well enough to continue. An organization's strategy that is mostly new most of the time signals erratic decision-making and weak "strategizing" on the part of managers. Quantum changes in strategy can be expected occasionally, especially in crisis situations, but they cannot be made too often without creating undue organizational confusion and disrupting performance.

An organization's strategy for achieving its performance objectives consists of actions and approaches already in place and scheduled for continuation, supplemented with new actions just underway and additional future moves being mapped out.

Strategy and Entrepreneurship Crafting strategy is an exercise in *entrepreneurship.* Some degree of venturesomeness and risk-taking is inherent in choosing among alternative business directions and devising the next round of moves and approaches. Managers face an ever-present entrepreneurial challenge keeping the organization's strategy fresh, responding to changing conditions, and steering the organization into the right business activities at the right time. Consideration of strategy changes thus cannot and should not be avoided. Often, there is more risk in coasting along with the status quo than there is in assuming the risk of making strategic changes. When managers become reluctant entrepreneurs, they get complacent about current strategy and become overly analytical or hesitant to make strategic decisions that blaze new trails. How boldly or cautiously managers push in new directions and how vigorously they initiate actions for boosting organizational performance are good indicators of their entrepreneurial spirit.

All managers, not just senior executives, need to exercise entrepreneurship in strategy-making. Entrepreneurship is involved when a district customer service manager crafts a strategy to cut the response time on service calls by 25 percent and commits $15,000 to equip all service trucks with mobile telephones. Entrepreneurship is involved when a warehousing manager develops a strategy to reduce the error frequency on filling orders from 1 error per every hundred orders to 1 error per every thousand orders. A sales manager exercises strategic entrepreneurship in deciding to run a special advertising promotion and cut sales prices by 5 percent. A manufacturing manager exercises strategic entrepreneurship in deciding to source an important component from a lower-priced South Korean supplier instead of making it in-house.

Strategy-making is fundamentally an entrepreneurial activity—risk-taking, venturesomeness, business creativity, and an eye for spotting emerging market opportunities are all involved in crafting a strategic action plan.

Strategy-making is not something just top managers do; it is something all managers do—every manager needs an entrepreneurial game plan for the area he/she is in charge of.

A company's strategic action plan is dynamic, undergoing continuous review, refinement, enhancement, and occasional major revision.

Why Strategy Is Constantly Evolving   From the perspective of the whole organization, the task of "strategizing" is always an ongoing exercise.[1] "The whats" of an organization's mission and long-term objectives, once chosen, may remain unaltered for several years. But "the hows" of strategy evolve constantly, partly in response to an everchanging external environment, partly from managers' efforts to create new opportunities, and partly from fresh ideas about how to make the strategy work better. On occasion, quantum changes in strategy emerge when a big strategic move is put to test in the real world or when crisis strikes and managers see that the organization's strategy needs radical reorientation. Refinements and additions, interspersed with periodic quantum leaps, are a normal part of managerial "strategizing."

Because strategic moves and new action approaches are made in an ongoing stream, an organization's strategy forms over a period of time and then reforms, always consisting of a mix of holdover approaches, fresh actions in process, and unrevealed moves being planned. Aside from crisis situations (where many strategic moves are often made quickly to produce a substantially new strategy almost overnight) and new company start-ups (where strategy exists mostly in the form of plans and intended actions), a company's strategy is crafted in bits and pieces as events unfold and as managerial experience accumulates. Everything cannot be planned out in advance, and even the best-laid plans must be responsive to changing conditions and unforeseen events. Strategy-making thus proceeds on two fronts—one proactively thought through in advance, the other conceived in response to new developments, special opportunities, and experiences with the successes and failures of prior strategic moves, approaches, and actions. Figure 1–2 depicts the kinds of actions that form a company's strategy.

Strategy and Strategic Plans   The three tasks of defining the business, setting objectives, and crafting a strategy all involve direction-setting. Together, they specify where the organization is headed and how management intends to achieve the targeted results. Together, they constitute a *strategic plan*. In some companies, especially large corporations committed to regular strategy reviews and formal strategic planning, the strategic plan is explicit and written (although parts of the plan may be omitted if they are too sensitive to reveal before they are actually undertaken). In other companies, the strategic plan is not put on paper but rather exists in the form of understandings among managers about what is to be carried over from the past and what new actions are to be taken. Organizational objectives are the part of the strategic plan that are most often written and circulated among managers and employees.

Illustration Capsule 3 presents an outline of Sara Lee Corporation's mission, objectives, and strategies as an example of how the three direction-setting steps join together.

---

[1]Henry Mintzberg, "Crafting Strategy," *Harvard Business Review* 65, no. 4 (July–August 1987), pp. 66–75; and James B. Quinn, *Strategies for Change: Logical Incrementalism* (Homewood, Ill.: Richard D. Irwin, 1980), chap. 2, especially pp. 58–59.

F I G U R E 1–2   **The Components of Company Strategy**

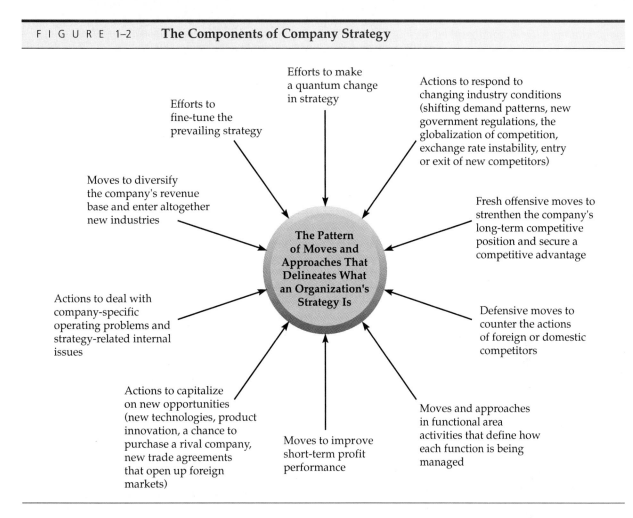

Efforts to make a quantum change in strategy

Efforts to fine-tune the prevailing strategy

Actions to respond to changing industry conditions (shifting demand patterns, new government regulations, the globalization of competition, exchange rate instability, entry or exit of new competitors)

Moves to diversify the company's revenue base and enter altogether new industries

Fresh offensive moves to strenthen the company's long-term competitive position and secure a competitive advantage

The Pattern of Moves and Approaches That Delineates What an Organization's Strategy Is

Actions to deal with company-specific operating problems and strategy-related internal issues

Defensive moves to counter the actions of foreign or domestic competitors

Actions to capitalize on new opportunities (new technologies, product innovation, a chance to purchase a rival company, new trade agreements that open up foreign markets)

Moves to improve short-term profit performance

Moves and approaches in functional area activities that define how each function is being managed

---

Strategy Implementation and Execution

The strategy-implementing function consists of seeing what it will take to make the strategy work and to reach the targeted performance on schedule—*the skill comes in knowing how to achieve results.* The job of implementing strategy is primarily an action-driven *administrative task* that cuts across many internal matters. The principal administrative aspects associated with putting the strategy into place include:

- Building an organization capable of carrying out the strategy successfully.
- Developing budgets that steer resources into those internal activities critical to strategic success.
- Motivating people in ways that induce them to pursue the target objectives energetically and, if need be, modifying their duties and job behavior to better fit the requirements of successful strategy execution.
- Tying the reward structure tightly to the achievement of the targeted results.

Strategy implementation is fundamentally an administrative activity—organizing, budgeting, motivating, culture-building, supervising, and leading are all part of "making it happen" and achieving the intended strategic and financial outcomes.

ILLUSTRATION CAPSULE
3

SARA LEE CORPORATION: MISSION, OBJECTIVES, AND STRATEGY

In a recent annual report, the management of Sara Lee Corporation set forth the company's mission, objectives, and strategy:

Mission

Sara Lee Corporation's mission is to be the leading brand-name food and consumer packaged goods company with major market share positions in key consumer markets worldwide.

We manufacture and market high-quality, marketing-sensitive products with growth potential. These products, which are sold through common distribution channels, include

- Packaged food products,
- Food products and services for the foodservice industry,
- Consumer personal products, and
- Household and personal care products.

Objectives

Size alone—that is, being the largest by some quantitative measure—does not define leadership. We aspire to be a larger company only to the extent that size and scale contribute to achieving more important measures of pre-eminence.

First, and above all, the leading company must be an outstanding financial performer for its stockholders. We must produce dependable and consistent financial returns which rank high in absolute terms as well as relative to our peer competitors.

Second, our product positions must be very high quality, compete in significant market segments, and command exceptionally strong market shares.

Third, our management people and processes must be of the highest caliber and appropriate to the times.

And fourth, we must be recognized as a corporation with an especially high sense of responsibility to our employees and public constituencies.

Corporate Strategies

1. Invest to accelerate internal growth. Direct and focus investment spending on strategic opportunities to build share and to accelerate unit volume growth in key product positions.
2. Develop the lowest cost position in all product categories. Emphasize and measure operating efficiencies and cost structures in all areas of the corporation to reduce costs consistently and to increase return on sales without sacrificing quality.
3. Make acquisitions. Acquire businesses which fit Sara Lee Corporation's strategic focus and which provide increased opportunity for growth consistent with our mission.
4. Leverage brand names and strategically link businesses for synergy. Generate growth by building and extending brand positions, and improve returns by strategically combining divisions and developing synergies among businesses.
5. Pursue cross-channel distribution for established products, brands and positions. Increase unit volume and return on sales with cross-channel distribution.

Source: 1987 Annual Report.

- Creating a work environment conducive to successful strategy implementation.
- Installing strategy-supportive policies and procedures.
- Developing an information and reporting system to track progress and monitor performance.
- Exerting the internal leadership needed to drive implementation forward and to keep improving on how the strategy is being executed.

The administrative aim is to create "fits" between the way things are done and what it takes for effective strategy execution. The stronger the fits, the better the execution of strategy. The most important fits are between strategy and organizational capabilities, between strategy and the reward structure, between strategy and internal policies and procedures, and between strategy and the organization's culture (the latter emerges from the values and beliefs shared by organizational members and from management's human relations practices). Fitting the ways the organization does things internally to what it takes for effective strategy execution is what unites the organization firmly behind the accomplishment of strategy.

The strategy-implementing task is easily the most complicated and time-consuming part of strategic management. It cuts across virtually all facets of managing and must be initiated from many points inside the organization. The strategy-implementer's agenda for action emerges from careful assessment of what the organization must do differently and better to carry out the strategic plan proficiently. Each manager has to think through the answer to "What has to be done in my area of responsibility to carry out my piece of the overall strategic plan and how can I best get it done?" How much internal change is needed to put the strategy into effect depends on the degree of strategic change, whether internal practices deviate very far from what the strategy requires, and how well strategy and organizational culture already match. As needed changes and actions are identified, management must supervise all the details of implementation and apply enough pressure on the organization to convert objectives into actual results. Depending on the amount of internal change involved, full implementation can take several months to several years.

Evaluating Performance, Reviewing the Situation, and Initiating Corrective Adjustments

None of the previous four tasks are one-time exercises. New circumstances always crop up that make corrective adjustments desirable. Long-term direction may need to be altered, the business redefined, and management's vision of the organization's future course narrowed or broadened. Performance targets may need raising or lowering in light of past experience and future prospects. Strategy may need to be modified because of shifts in long-term direction, because new objectives have been set, or because of changing conditions in the environment.

The search for even better strategy execution is also continuous. Sometimes an aspect of implementation does not go as well as intended and changes have to be made. Progress typically proceeds unevenly—faster in some areas and slower in others. Some tasks get done easily; others prove nettlesome. Implementation occurs through the pooling effect of many administrative decisions about how to do things and how to create stronger fits between strategy and internal operating practices. Budget revisions, policy changes, reorganization, personnel changes, culture-changing actions, and revised compensation practices are typical ways of trying to make the chosen strategy work better.

A company's mission, objectives, strategy, or approach to strategy implementation is never final; evaluating performance, reviewing changes in the surrounding environment, and making adjustments are normal and necessary parts of the strategic management process.

WHY STRATEGIC MANAGEMENT IS AN ONGOING PROCESS

Because each one of the five tasks of strategic management requires constant evaluation and a decision whether to continue with things as they are or to make changes, *the process of managing strategy is ongoing.* Nothing is final—

all prior actions are subject to modification as conditions in the surrounding environment change and ways to improve emerge. Strategic management is a process filled with constant motion. Changes in the organization's situation, either from the inside or outside or both, constantly drive strategic adjustments. This is why, in Figure 1–1, we refer to recycling.

The task of evaluating performance and initiating corrective adjustments is both the end and the beginning of the strategic management cycle. The march of external and internal events guarantees revision in the four previous components will be needed sooner or later. It is always incumbent on management to push for better performance—to find ways to improve the existing strategy and how it is being executed. Changing external conditions add further impetus to the need for periodic revisions in a company's mission, performance objectives, strategy, and approaches to strategy execution. Adjustments usually involve fine-tuning, but occasions for a major strategic reorientation do arise—sometimes prompted by significant external developments and sometimes by sharply sliding financial performance. Strategy managers must stay close enough to the situation to detect when changing conditions require a strategic response and when they don't. It is their job to read the winds of change, recognize significant changes early, and capitalize on events as they unfold.[2]

Characteristics of the Process

Although the tasks of developing a mission, setting objectives, forming a strategy, implementing and executing the strategic plan, and evaluating performance constitute the elements of the strategic management function, actually performing these five tasks is not so cleanly divided and neatly sequenced. There is much interplay among the five tasks. For example, considering what strategic actions to take raises issues about whether and how the strategy can be satisfactorily implemented. Deciding on a company mission shades into setting objectives for the organization to achieve (both involve directional priorities). To establish challenging but achievable objectives, managers must consider both current performance and the strategy options available to improve performance. Deciding on a strategy is entangled with decisions about long-term direction and whether objectives have been set too high or too low.

Second, the five strategic management tasks are not done in isolation. They are carried out in the midst of all other managerial responsibilities—supervising day-to-day operations, dealing with crises, going to meetings, preparing reports, handling people problems, and taking on special assignments and civic duties. Thus, while the job of managing strategy is the most important function management performs insofar as organizational success or failure is concerned, it isn't all managers must do or be concerned about.

Third, strategic management makes erratic demands on a manager's time. An organization's situation does not change in an orderly or predictable way. The events that prompt reconsideration of strategy can build quickly or gradually; they can emerge singly or in rapid-fire succession; and the implications they have for strategic change can be easy or hard to diagnose. Hence strategic

---

[2]Mintzberg, "Crafting Strategy," p. 74.

issues and decisions take up big chunks of management time some months and little or none in other months. As a practical matter, there is as much skill in knowing *when* to institute strategic changes as there is in knowing *what* to do.[3]

Last, the big day-in, day-out time-consuming aspect of strategic management is trying to get the best strategy-supportive performance out of every individual and trying to perfect the current strategy by refining its content and execution. Managing strategy is mostly improving bits and pieces of the strategy in place, not developing and instituting radical strategic changes. Excessive changes in strategy can be disruptive to employees and confusing to customers, and they are usually unnecessary. Most of the time, there's more to be gained from improving execution of the present strategy. Persistence in trying to make a sound strategy work better is often the key to managing the strategy to success.

WHO ARE THE STRATEGY MANAGERS?

An organization's chief executive officer is the most visible and important *strategy manager*. The CEO, as captain of the ship, bears full responsibility for leading the tasks of formulating and implementing the strategic plans of the whole organization, even though many other managers have a hand in the process. The CEO functions as chief direction-setter, chief objective-setter, chief strategy-maker, and chief strategy-implementer for the total enterprise. What the CEO views as important usually moves to the top of every manager's priority list, and the CEO has the final word on big decisions.

Vice presidents for production, marketing, finance, human resources, and other functional departments have important strategy-making and strategy-implementing responsibilities as well. Normally, the production VP oversees production strategy; the marketing VP heads up the marketing strategy effort; the financial VP is in charge of financial strategy; and so on. Usually, functional vice presidents are also involved in proposing and developing key elements of the overall strategy, working closely with the CEO to hammer out a consensus and make certain parts of the strategy more effective. Only rarely does a CEO personally craft all the key pieces of organization strategy.

But managerial positions with strategy-making and strategy-implementing responsibility are by no means restricted to these few senior executives. *Every manager is a strategy-maker and strategy-implementer for the area he/she has authority over and supervises.* Every part of a company—business unit, division, operating department, plant, or district office—has a strategic role to carry out. And the manager in charge of that unit, with guidance from superiors, usually ends up doing some or most of the strategy-making for the unit and implementing whatever strategic choices are made. However, managers farther down in the managerial hierarchy have a narrower, more specific strategy-making/strategy-implementing role than managers closer to the top.

Another reason lower-echelon managers are strategy-makers and strategy-implementers is that the more geographically scattered and diversified an organization's operations are, the more impossible it becomes for a few senior executives to handle all the strategic planning that needs to be done. Managers

All managers are involved in the strategy-making and strategy-implementing process.

---

[3]Ibid., p. 73.

in the corporate office don't know all the situational details in all geographical areas and operating units to be able to prescribe appropriate strategies. Usually, they delegate some of the strategy-making responsibility to the lower-level managers who head the organizational subunits where specific strategic results must be achieved. Delegating a lead strategy-making role to those managers who will be deeply involved in carrying it out in their areas fixes accountability for strategic success or failure. When the managers who implement the strategy are also its architects, it is hard for them to shift the blame or make excuses if they don't achieve the target results.

In diversified companies where the strategies of several different businesses have to be managed, there are usually four distinct levels of strategy managers:

- *The chief executive officer and other senior corporation-level executives* who have primary responsibility and personal authority for big strategic decisions affecting the total enterprise and the collection of individual businesses the enterprise has diversified into.

- *Managers who have profit-and-loss responsibility for one specific business unit* and who are delegated a major leadership role in formulating and implementing strategy for that unit.

- *Functional area managers within a given business unit* who have direct authority over a major piece of the business (manufacturing, marketing and sales, finance, R&D, personnel) and whose role it is to support the business unit's overall strategy with strategic actions in their own areas.

- *Managers of major operating departments and geographic field units* who have front-line responsibility for developing the details of strategic efforts in their areas and for implementing and executing the overall strategic plan at the grassroots level.

Single-business enterprises need no more than three of these levels (business-level strategy managers, functional area strategy managers, and operating-level strategy managers). In a large single-business company, the team of strategy managers consists of the chief executive, who functions as chief strategist with final authority over both strategy and its implementation; the vice presidents in charge of key functions (R&D, production, marketing, finance, human resources, and so on); plus as many operating-unit managers of the various plants, sales offices, distribution centers, and staff support departments as it takes to handle the company's scope of operations. Proprietorships, partnerships, and owner-managed enterprises, however, typically have only one or two strategy managers since in small-scale enterprises the whole strategy-making/strategy-implementing function can be handled by just a few key people.

Managerial jobs involving strategy formulation and implementation abound in not-for-profit organizations as well. For example, a multicampus state university has four strategy-managing levels: (1) the president of the university system is a strategy manager with broad direction-setting responsibility and strategic decision-making authority over all the campuses; (2) the chancellor for each campus customarily has strategy-making/strategy-implementing authority over all academic, student, athletic, and alumni matters, plus budgetary, programmatic, and coordinative responsibilities for that campus; (3) the academic deans have lead responsibility for charting future direction at the college level, steering resources into high-demand programs and out of low-demand programs, and otherwise devising a collegewide plan to fulfill the college's teaching-research-service mission; and (4) the heads of various academic departments are strategy managers with first-line strategy-making/strategy-implementing responsibility for the department's under-graduate and graduate program offerings, faculty research efforts, and all other activities relating to the department's mission, objectives, and future direction. In federal and state government, heads of local, district, and regional offices function as strategy managers in their efforts to respond to the needs and situations of the areas they serve (a district manager in Portland may need a slightly different strategy than a district manager in Orlando). In municipal government, the heads of various departments (fire, police, water and sewer, parks and recreation, health, and so on) are strategy managers because they have line authority for the operations of their departments and thus can influence departmental objectives, the formation of a strategy to achieve these objectives, and how the strategy is implemented.

Managerial jobs with strategy-making/strategy-implementing roles are thus the norm rather than the exception. The job of crafting and implementing strategy touches virtually every managerial job in one way or another, at one time or another. Strategic management is basic to the task of managing; it is not something just top-level managers deal with.[4]

The Role and Tasks of Strategic Planners

If senior and middle managers have the lead roles in strategy-making and strategy-implementing in their areas of responsibility, what should strategic planners do? Is there a legitimate place in big companies for a strategic planning department staffed with specialists in planning and strategic analysis? The answer is yes. But the planning department's role and tasks should consist chiefly of helping to gather and organize information that strategy managers need, establishing and administering an annual strategy review cycle whereby all strategy managers reconsider and refine their strategic plans, and coordinating the process of reviewing and approving the strategic plans developed for all the various parts of the company. Strategic planners are valuable because they help managers at all levels crystallize the strategic issues that ought to be addressed; in addition, they can provide data, help analyze industry and competitive conditions, and distribute information on the company's strategic performance. But strategic planners should *not* make strategic decisions, prepare strategic plans (for someone else to implement), or make strategic action recommendations that usurp the strategy-making responsibilities of managers in charge of major operating units.

When strategic planners are asked to go beyond providing staff assistance and actually prepare a strategic plan for management's consideration, either of two adverse consequences may occur. First, some managers will gladly toss tough strategic problems in their areas onto the desks of strategic planners to

Strategic Management Principle
Strategy-making is not a proper task for strategic planners.

---

[4]Since the scope of a manager's strategy-making/strategy-implementing role varies according to the manager's position in the organizational hierarchy, our use of the word "organization" includes whatever kind of unit the strategy manager is in charge of—an entire company or not-for-profit organization, a business unit within a diversified company, a major geographic division, an important functional area within a business, or an operating department or field unit reporting to the functional area head. It should be clear from the context of the discussion whether the subject applies to the total enterprise or to most or all management levels.

let the planners do their strategic thinking for them. The planners, not knowing as much about the situation as managers do, are in a weaker position to design a workable action plan. And they can't be held responsible for implementing what they recommend. Giving planners responsibility for strategy-making and line managers responsibility for implementation makes it hard to fix accountability for poor results. It also deludes line managers into thinking they don't have to be personally involved in crafting a strategy for their own organizational unit or in finding strategic solutions to strategic problems in their area of responsibility. The hard truth is that strategy-making is not a staff function, nor is it something that can be handed off to an advisory committee of lower-ranking managers. Second, when line managers have no ownership stake in or personal commitment to the strategic agenda proposed by the planners, they give it lip service, make a few token implementation efforts, and quickly get back to "business as usual," knowing that the formal written plan concocted by the planners does not match their own "real" managerial agenda. The written strategic plan, because it lacks credibility and true top-management commitment, soon collects dust on managers' shelves. The result is that few managers take the work product of the strategic planning staff seriously enough to pursue implementation—strategic planning comes to be seen as just another bureaucratic exercise.

Either consequence renders formal strategic planning efforts ineffective and opens the door for a strategy-making vacuum conducive to organizational drift or to fragmented, uncoordinated strategic decisions. The odds are then heightened that the organization will have no strong strategic rudder and insufficient top-down direction. The flaws in having staffers or advisory committees formulate strategies for areas they do not manage are: (1) they can't be held accountable if their recommendations don't produce the desired results since they don't have authority for directing implementation, and (2) what they recommend won't be well accepted or enthusiastically implemented by those who "have to sing the song the planners have written." But when line managers are expected to be the chief strategy-makers and strategy-implementers for the areas they head, it is their own strategy and their own implementation approach that are being put to the test of workability. They are likely to be more committed to making the plan work (their future careers with the organization are at more risk!), and they can be held strictly accountable for achieving the target results in their area.

The Strategic Role of the Board of Directors

Since lead responsibility for crafting and implementing strategy falls to key managers, the chief strategic role of an organization's board of directors is to see that the overall task of managing strategy is adequately done.[5] Boards of directors normally review important strategic moves and officially approve the strategic plans submitted by senior management—a procedure that makes the board ultimately responsible for the strategic actions taken. But directors rarely can or should play a direct role in formulating strategy. The immediate task of directors in ratifying strategy and new direction-setting moves is to ensure that all proposals have been adequately analyzed and

---

[5]Kenneth R. Andrews, *The Concept of Corporate Strategy*, 3rd ed. (Homewood, Illinois: Richard D. Irwin, 1987), p. 123.

considered and that the proposed strategic actions are superior to available alternatives; flawed proposals are customarily withdrawn for revision by management.[6] The longer-range task of directors is to evaluate the caliber of senior executives' strategy-making and strategy-implementing skills. The board must determine whether the current CEO is doing a good job of strategic management (as a basis for awarding salary increases and bonuses and deciding on retention or removal) and evaluate the strategic skills of other senior executives in line to succeed the current CEO.

THE BENEFITS OF A "STRATEGIC APPROACH" TO MANAGING

The message of this book is that doing a good job of managing inherently requires doing a good job of strategic management. Today's managers have to think strategically about their company's position and about the impact of changing conditions. They have to monitor the external situation closely enough to know *when* to institute strategy change. They have to know the business well enough to know *what kind* of strategic changes to initiate. Simply said, the fundamentals of strategic management need to drive the whole approach to managing organizations.[7] The chief executive officer of one successful company put it well when he said:

> In the main, our competitors are acquainted with the same fundamental concepts and techniques and approaches that we follow, and they are as free to pursue them as we are. More often than not, the difference between their level of success and ours lies in the relative thoroughness and self-discipline with which we and they develop and execute our strategies for the future.

The advantages of first-rate strategic thinking and conscious strategy management (as opposed to freewheeling improvisation, gut feel, and drifting along) include (1) providing better guidance to the entire organization on the crucial point of "what it is we are trying to do and to achieve," (2) making managers more alert to the winds of change, new opportunities, and threatening developments, (3) providing managers with a rationale to evaluate competing budget requests for investment capital and new staff—a rationale that argues strongly for steering resources into strategy-supportive, results-producing areas, (4) helping to unify the numerous strategy-related decisions by managers across the organization, and (5) creating a more *proactive* management posture and counteracting tendencies for decisions to be reactive and defensive.[8]

The fifth advantage of being proactive rather than merely reactive is that trail-blazing strategies can be the key to better long-term performance. Business history shows that high-performing enterprises often *initiate* and *lead*, not just *react* and *defend*. They launch strategic *offensives* to secure sustainable competitive advantage and then use their market edge to achieve superior financial

---

[6]Ibid.

[7]For a lucid discussion of the importance of the strategic management function, see V. Ramanujam and N. Venkatraman, "Planning and Performance: A New Look at an Old Question," *Business Horizons* 30, no. 3 (May–June, 1987), pp. 19–25; and Henry Mintzberg, "The Strategy Concept: Another Look at Why Organizations Need Strategies," *California Management Review* 30, no. 1 (Fall 1987), pp. 25–32.

[8]Kenneth R. Andrews, *The Concept of Corporate Strategy*, rev. ed. (Homewood, Ill.: Richard D. Irwin, 1980), pp. 15–16, 46, 123–29; and Seymour Tilles, "How to Evaluate Corporate Strategy," *Harvard Business Review* 41, no. 4 (July–August 1963), p. 116

performance. Aggressive pursuit of a creative, opportunistic strategy can propel a firm into a leadership position, paving the way for its products/services to become the industry standard.

A RECAP OF IMPORTANT TERMS	We conclude this introductory overview by defining key terms that will be used again and again in the chapters to come:

Organization mission—management's customized answer to the question "What is our business and what will it be?" A mission statement broadly outlines the organization's future direction and serves as a guiding concept for what the organization is to do and to become.

Performance objectives—the organization's targets for achievement.

Financial objectives—the targets management has established for the organization's financial performance.

Strategic objectives—the targets management has established for strengthening the organization's overall position and competitive vitality.

Long-range objectives—the results to be achieved either within the next three to five years or else on an ongoing basis year after year.

Short-range objectives—the organization's near-term performance targets; the amount of short-term improvement signals how fast management is trying to achieve the long-range objectives.

Strategy—the managerial action plan for achieving organizational objectives; strategy is mirrored in the *pattern* of moves and approaches devised by management to produce the targeted outcomes. Strategy is the *how* of pursuing the organization's mission and achieving the desired objectives.

Strategic plan—a statement outlining an organization's mission and future direction, near-term and long-term performance targets, and strategy in light of the organization's external and internal situation.

Strategy formulation—the entire direction-setting management function of conceptualizing an organization's mission, setting performance objectives, and crafting a strategy. The end product of strategy formulation is a strategic plan.

Strategy implementation—the full range of managerial activities associated with putting the chosen strategy into place, supervising its pursuit, and achieving the targeted results.

In the chapters to come, we will probe the strategy-related tasks of managers and the methods of strategic analysis more intensively. When you get to the end of the book, we think you will see that two factors separate the best-managed organizations from the rest: (1) superior strategy-making and entrepreneurship, and (2) competent implementation and execution of the chosen strategy. There's no escaping the fact that the quality of managerial strategy-making and strategy-implementing has a significant impact on organization performance. A company that lacks clear-cut direction, has vague or undemanding objectives, or has a muddled or flawed strategy is a company whose performance is probably suffering, whose business is at long-term risk, and whose management is less than capable.

Andrews, Kenneth R. *The Concept of Corporate Strategy.* 3rd ed. Homewood, Ill.: Richard D. Irwin, 1987, chap. 1.

Gluck, Frederick W. "A Fresh Look at Strategic Management." *Journal of Business Strategy* 6, no. 2 (Fall 1985), pp. 4–21.

Hax, Arnoldo C., and Nicolas S. Majluf. *The Strategy Concept and Process: A Pragmatic Approach* (Englewood Cliffs, N.J.: Prentice Hall, 1991), chaps. 1 and 2.

Kelley, C. Aaron. "The Three Planning Questions: A Fable." *Business Horizons* 26, no. 2 (March–April 1983), pp. 46–48.

Kotter, John P. *The General Managers.* New York: Free Press, 1982.

Levinson, Harry, and Stuart Rosenthal. *CEO: Corporate Leadership in Action.* New York: Basic Books, 1987.

Mintzberg, Henry. "The Strategy Concept: Five Ps for Strategy." *California Management Review* 30, no. 1 (Fall 1987), pp. 11–24.

_____. "The Strategy Concept: Another Look at Why Organizations Need Strategies." *California Management Review* 30, no. 1 (Fall 1987), pp. 25–32.

_____. "Crafting Strategy." *Harvard Business Review* 65, no. 4 (July–August 1987), pp. 66–75.

Quinn, James B. *Strategies for Change: Logical Incrementalism.* Homewood, Ill.: Richard D. Irwin, 1980, chaps. 2 and 3.

Ramanujam, V., and N. Venkatraman. "Planning and Performance: A New Look at an Old Question." *Business Horizons* 30, no. 3 (May–June 1987), pp. 19–25.

Yip, George S. "Who Needs Strategic Planning?" *Journal of Business Strategy* 6, no. 2 (Fall 1985), pp. 22–29.

SUGGESTED
READINGS

The Three Strategy-Making Tasks
Developing a Mission, Setting Objectives, and Forming a Strategy

—

Management's job is not to see the company as it is . . . but as it can become.
John W. Teets
CEO, Greyhound Corp.

—

Without a strategy the organization is like a ship without a rudder, going around in circles. It's like a tramp; it has no place to go.
Joel Ross and Michael Kami

—

You've got to come up with a plan. You can't wish things will get better.
John F. Welch
CEO, General Electric

—

In this chapter, we provide a more in-depth look at each of the three strategy-making tasks: defining the business and developing a mission, setting performance objectives, and crafting a strategy to produce the desired results. We also examine the nature of strategy-making at each managerial level in the organizational hierarchy and discuss the four basic ways managers perform the strategy-making task.

DEVELOPING A MISSION: THE FIRST DIRECTION-SETTING TASK

Management's vision of what the organization is trying to do and to become over the long term is commonly referred to as the organization's *mission*. A *mission statement* specifies what activities the organization intends to pursue and what course management has charted for the future. It outlines "who *we* are, what *we* do, and where *we* are headed." Mission statements are thus personalized in the sense that they set an organization apart from others in its industry and give it its own special identity, character, and path for development. For example, the mission of a globally active New York bank like Citicorp has little in common with that of a locally owned small town bank even though both are in the banking industry. Without a concept of what the organization should and should not do and a vision of where the organization needs to be going, a manager cannot function effectively as either leader or strategymaker. There are three distinct aspects to the task of developing a company mission:

- Understanding what business a company is really in.
- Deciding when to change the mission and alter the company's strategic course.
- Communicating the mission in ways that are clear, exciting, and inspiring.

Effective strategic leadership starts with a concept of what the organization should and should not do and a vision of where the organization needs to be headed.

Understanding and Defining the Business

Deciding what business an organization is in is neither obvious nor easy. Is IBM in the computer business (a product-oriented definition) or the information and data processing business (a customer service or customer needs type of definition) or the advanced electronics business (a technology-based definition)? Is Coca-Cola in the soft-drink business (in which case its strategic vision can be trained narrowly on the actions of Pepsi, 7Up, Dr Pepper, Canada Dry, and Schweppes)? Or is it in the beverage industry (in which case management must think strategically about positioning Coca-Cola products in a market that includes fruit juices, alcoholic drinks, milk, bottled water, coffee, and tea)? This is not a trivial question for Coca-Cola. Many young adults get their morning caffeine fix by drinking cola instead of coffee; with a beverage industry perspective as opposed to a soft-drink industry perspective, Coca-Cola management is more likely to perceive a long-term growth opportunity in winning youthful coffee drinkers over to its colas.

Defining what business an organization is in requires taking three factors into account:[1]

1. Customer needs, or *what* is being satisfied.
2. Customer groups, or *who* is being satisfied.
3. The technologies used and functions performed—*how* customers' needs are satisfied.

A company's business is defined by what needs it is trying to satisfy, by which customer groups it is targeting, and by the technologies it will use and the functions it will perform in serving the target market.

Defining a business in terms of what to satisfy, who to satisfy, and how the organization will go about producing the satisfaction adds completeness to the definition. It also directs management to look outward toward customers and markets as well as inward in forming its concept of "who we are and what we

---

[1]Derek F. Abell, *Defining the Business: The Starting Point of Strategic Planning* (Englewood Cliffs, N.J.: Prentice Hall, 1980), p. 169.

ILLUSTRATION CAPSULE
4

CIRCLE K's MISSION STATEMENT

We believe our primary business is not so much retail as it is service oriented.

Certainly, our customers buy merchandise in our stores. But they can buy similar items elsewhere, and perhaps pay lower prices.

But they're willing to buy from Circle K because we give them added value for their money.

That added value is service and convenience.

Our Mission

As a service company, our mission is to:

Satisfy our customers' immediate needs and wants by providing them with a wide variety of goods and services at multiple locations.

Our Customers

We will not place a limit on the conveniences we offer customers.

They buy at Circle K much differently than at a supermarket. They come to our stores for specific purchases, which they make as quickly as possible. They want immediate service and are willing to pay a premium for it.

Our Stores

We will build our stores at locations most accessible to our customers.

We will organize our merchandise to (1) facilitate quick purchases and (2) encourage other purchases.

We will maintain our stores so they will always be brightly lit, colorful, clean, and comfortable places for our customers and our employees.

Our Goods and Services

We will not be one store—but a dozen stores in one.

We are a gas station, a fast-food restaurant, a grocery store, drugstore, liquor store, newsstand, video rental shop, small bank—and more.

Source: 1987 Annual Report.

do."[2] A good example of a business definition that incorporates all three aspects is a paraphrase of Polaroid's business definition during the early 1970s: "perfecting and marketing instant photography to satisfy the needs of more affluent U.S. and West European families for affection, friendship, fond memories, and humor." For years, McDonald's business definition has centered on "serving hot, tasty food quickly in a clean restaurant for a good value" to a broad base of customers worldwide (McDonald's now serves over 25 million customers daily at some 14,000 restaurants in over 40 countries). Illustration Capsule 4 describes how Circle K, the second largest convenience store retailer in the United States, views its mission and business.

The Polaroid, McDonald's, and Circle K examples all adhere closely to the three necessary components of a mission statement: the specific needs served by the company's basic product(s) or service(s), the targeted customer groups, and the technology and functions the company employs in providing its product/service. It takes all three to define what business a company is really in. Just knowing what products or services a firm provides is never enough. Prod-

---

[2]There is a tendency sometimes for companies to view their mission in terms of making a profit. However, profit is more correctly an *objective* and a *result* of what the company does. Missions based on making a profit are incapable of distinguishing one type of profit-seeking enterprise from another—the mission and business of Sears are plainly different from the mission and business of Delta Airlines, even though both endeavor to earn a profit.

ucts or services per se are not important to customers; what turns a product or service into a business is the need or want being satisfied. Without the need or want there is no business. Customer groups are relevant because they indicate the market to be served: the geographic area to be covered and the types of buyers the firm is going after. Technology and functions performed are important because they indicate how the company will satisfy customers' needs and how much of the industry's production chain its own activities will span. For instance, a firm can be *specialized*, participating in one aspect of the whole industry's production chain, or *fully integrated*, operating in all parts of the industry chain. Circle K is a specialized firm operating only in the retail end of the chain; it doesn't manufacture the items it sells. Major international oil companies like Exxon, Mobil, and Chevron, however, are fully integrated; they lease drilling sites, drill wells, pump oil, transport the oil in their own ships and pipelines to their own refineries, and sell gasoline and other refined products through their own distributors and service stations. Because of the disparity in functions performed and technology employed, the business of a retailer like Circle K is much narrower and quite different from a fully integrated enterprise like Exxon. Between these two extremes, firms can stake out *partially integrated* positions, participating only in selected stages of the industry. So one way of distinguishing a firm's business, especially among firms in the same industry, is by looking at which functions it performs in the chain and how far its scope of operation extends across the industry.

A Broad or Narrow Business Definition?   A small Hong Kong printing company that defines its business broadly as "Asian-language communications" gains no practical guidance in making direction-setting decisions; with such a definition the company could pursue limitless courses, most well beyond its scope and capability. To have managerial value, mission statements and business definitions must be narrow enough to pin down the real arena of business interest. Otherwise they cannot serve as boundaries for what to do and not do and as beacons of where managers intend to take the company. Consider the following definitions based on broad-narrow scope:

Broad Definition	Narrow Definition
Beverages	Soft drinks
Footwear	Athletic footwear
Furniture	Wrought iron lawn furniture
Global mail delivery	Overnight package delivery
Travel and tourism	Ship cruises in the Caribbean

Broad-narrow definitions are relative, of course. Being in "the furniture business" is probably too broad a concept for a company intent on being the largest manufacturer of wrought iron lawn furniture in North America. On the other hand, soft drinks has proved too narrow a scope for a growth-oriented company like Coca-Cola, which, with its beverage industry perspective, acquired Minute-Maid and Hi-C (to capitalize on growing consumer interest in fruit juice products) and Taylor Wine Company (using the California Cellars brand to establish a foothold in wines).[3] The U.S. Postal Service operates with a broad definition—providing global mail delivery services to all types of senders. Federal Express, however, operates with a narrow business definition based on handling overnight package delivery for customers who have unplanned emergencies and tight deadlines.

Diversified companies have broader missions and business definitions than single-business enterprises.

Diversified firms have more expansive business definitions than single-business enterprises. Their mission statements typically use narrow terms to define current customer-market-technology arenas but are open-ended and adaptable enough to incorporate expansion into desirable new businesses. Alcan, Canada's leading aluminum company, used this type of language in its mission statement:

> Alcan is determined to be the most innovative diversified aluminum company in the world. To achieve this position, Alcan will be one, global, customer-oriented enterprise committed to excellence and lowest cost in its chosen aluminum businesses, with significant resources devoted to building an array of new businesses with superior growth and profit potential.

Morton-Thiokol, a substantially more diversified enterprise, used simultaneous broad-narrow terms to define its business:

> We are an international, high-technology company serving the diverse needs of government and industry with products and services ranging from massive solid rocket motors to small ordnance devices, from polymers to disc brake pads, from heavy denier yarns to woven carpet backing, from snow-grooming vehicles to trigger sprayers.

John Hancock's mission statement communicates a shift from its long-standing base in insurance to a broader mission in insurance, banking, and diversified financial services:

> At John Hancock, we are determined not just to compete but to advance, building our market share by offering individuals and institutions the broadest possible range of products and services. Apart from insurance, John Hancock encompasses banking products, full brokerage services and institutional investment, to cite only a few of our diversified activities. We believe these new directions constitute the right moves . . . the steps that will drive our growth throughout the remainder of this century.

Where Entrepreneurship Comes In

A member of Maytag's board of directors summed it up well when commenting on why the company acquired a European appliance-maker and shifted its long-term focus to include international markets as well as domestic ones: "Times change, conditions change." The swirl of new events and altered circumstances make it incumbent on managers to continually reassess their company's position and prospects, always checking for *when* it's time to steer a new course and adjust the mission. The key question here is "What new directions should we be moving in *now* to get ready for the changes we see coming in our business?" Repositioning an enterprise in light of emerging developments

---

[3]Coca-Cola's foray into wines evidently was not successful enough; the division was divested about five years after initial acquisition.

lessens the chances of getting caught in a poor market position or being dependent on the wrong business at the wrong time. For example, Philip Morris, the leading U.S. manufacturer of cigarettes, in anticipation of long-term deterioration in the demand for tobacco products, positioned itself as a major contender in the food products industry by acquiring two of the largest manufacturers, General Foods and Kraft. Many U.S. companies are broadening their missions geographically and forming joint ventures with European companies to try to capitalize on the dismantling of trade barriers in the European Community in 1992 and the opening of markets in Eastern Europe.

Good entrepreneurs are alert to changing customer wants and needs, customer dissatisfaction with current products and services, emerging technologies, changing international trade conditions, and other important signs of growing or shrinking business opportunity. Appraising new customer-market-technology developments ultimately leads to entrepreneurial judgments about which of several roads to take. A strategy leader must peer down each of the roads, evaluate the risks and prospects of each, and make direction-setting decisions to position the enterprise for success in the years ahead. *A well-chosen mission prepares a company for the future.* Many companies in consumer electronics and telecommunications, believing that their future products will incorporate microprocessors and other elements of computer technology, are expanding their missions and establishing positions in the computer business to have access to the needed technology. Numerous companies in manufacturing, seeing the swing to internationalization and global competition, are broadening their missions from serving domestic markets to serving global markets. Coca-Cola, Kentucky Fried Chicken, and McDonald's are pursuing market opportunities in China, Europe, Japan, and the Soviet Union. Japanese automobile companies are working to establish a bigger presence in the European car market. CNN, Turner Broadcasting's successful all-news cable channel, is pushing hard to become the first global all-news channel. Thus, a company's mission always has a time dimension; it is subject to change whenever top management concludes that the present mission is no longer adequate.

> *The entrepreneurial challenge in developing a mission is to recognize when emerging opportunities and threats in the surrounding environment make it desirable to revise the organization's long-term direction.*

Communicating the Mission

How to phrase the mission statement and communicate it to lower-level managers and employees is almost as important as the soundness of the mission itself. A mission statement phrased in words that inspire and challenge can help build committed effort from employees, thus serving as a powerful motivational tool.[4] Bland language, platitudes, and motherhood-and-apple-pie-style verbiage should be scrupulously avoided. Companies should communicate their mission in words that induce employee buy-in and convey a sense of organizational purpose. In organizations with freshly changed missions, executives need to provide a convincing rationale for the new direction; otherwise a new mission statement does little to change employees' attitudes and behavior or to win their commitment—outcomes that make it harder to move the organization down the chosen path.

---

[4]Tom Peters, *Thriving on Chaos* (New York: Harper & Row, 1988), pp. 486–87.

ILLUSTRATION CAPSULE
5

NOVACARE'S BUSINESS MISSION AND VISION

NovaCare is a fast-growing health care company specializing in providing patient rehabilitation services on a contract basis to nursing homes. Rehabilitation therapy is a $10 billion industry, of which 35% is provided contractually; the contract segment is highly fragmented with over 1,000 competitors. In 1990 NovaCare was a $100 million company, with a goal of being a $275 million business by 1993. The company stated its business mission and vision as follows:

> NovaCare is people committed to making a difference . . . enhancing the future of all patients . . . breaking new ground in our professions . . . achieving excellence . . . advancing human capability . . . changing the world in which we live.
>
> We lead the way with our enthusiasm, optimism, patience, drive and commitment.
>
> We work together to enhance the quality of our patients' lives by reshaping lost abilities and teaching new skills. We heighten expectations for the patient and family. We rebuild hope, confidence, self-respect and a desire to continue.
>
> We apply our clinical expertise to benefit our patients through creative and progressive techniques. Our ethical and performance standards require us to expend every effort to achieve the best possible results.
>
> Our customers are national and local health care providers who share our goal of enhancing the patients' quality of life. In each community, our customers consider us a partner in providing the best possible care. Our reputation is based on our responsiveness, high standards and effective systems of quality assurance. Our relationship is open and proactive.
>
> We are advocates of our professions and patients through active participation in the professional, regulatory, educational and research communities at national, state and local levels.
>
> Our approach to health care fulfills our responsibility to provide investors with a high rate of return through consistent growth and profitability.
>
> Our people are our most valuable asset. We are committed to the personal, professional and career development of each individual employee. We are proud of what we do and dedicated to our Company. We foster teamwork and create an environment conducive to productive communication among all disciplines.
>
> NovaCare is a company of people in pursuit of this Vision.

Source: Company annual report.

A well-worded mission statement creates enthusiasm for the future course management has charted; the motivational goal in communicating the mission is to challenge and inspire everyone in the organization.

The best mission statements use simple, concise terminology; they speak loudly and clearly, generate enthusiasm for the firm's future course, and encourage personal effort and dedication from everyone in the organization. They need to be repeated over and over in a challenging, convincing fashion. A short, clear, often-repeated, inspiring mission statement has the power to turn heads in the intended direction and begin a new organizational march. As this occurs, the first step in organizational direction-setting has been completed successfully. Illustration Capsule 5 illustrates an inspiration-oriented mission statement.

A well-conceived, well-said mission statement has real managerial value: (1) it crystallizes top management's own view about the firm's long-term direction and makeup, (2) it helps keep the direction-related actions of lower-level managers on the right path, (3) it conveys an organizational purpose and identity that motivates employees to do their best, (4) it helps managers avoid either visionless or rudderless management, and (5) it helps an organization prepare for the future.

ESTABLISHING OBJECTIVES: THE SECOND DIRECTION-SETTING TASK

Establishing objectives converts the mission and directional course into designated performance outcomes. Objectives represent a managerial commitment to produce specified results in a specified time. They spell out *how much* of *what kind* of performance *by when*. They direct attention and energy to what needs to be accomplished.

The Managerial Value of Establishing Objectives

Unless an organization's mission and direction are translated into *measurable* performance targets, and managers are pressured to show progress in reaching these targets, an organization's mission statement is just window-dressing. Experience tells a powerful story about why objective-setting is a critical task in the strategic management process: *Companies whose managers set objectives for each key result area and then aggressively pursue actions calculated to achieve their performance targets are strong candidates to outperform the companies whose managers operate with hopes, prayers, and good intentions.*

For performance objectives to have value as a management tool, they must be stated in *quantifiable* or measurable terms, and they must contain a *deadline for achievement*. This means avoiding statements like "maximize profits," "reduce costs," "become more efficient," or "increase sales" which specify neither how much or when. Spelling out organization objectives in measurable terms and then holding managers accountable for reaching their assigned targets within a specified time frame (1) substitutes purposeful strategic decision-making for aimless actions and confusion over what to accomplish and (2) provides a set of benchmarks for judging the organization's performance.

Objectives are a managerial commitment to achieve specific performance targets by a certain time.

What Kinds of Objectives to Set

Objectives are needed for each *key result* that managers deem important to success.[5] Two types of key result areas stand out: those relating to *financial performance* and those relating to *strategic performance*. Achieving acceptable financial performance is a must; otherwise the organization's survival ends up at risk. Achieving acceptable strategic performance is essential to sustaining

Strategic Management Principle
Every company needs to establish both strategic objectives and financial objectives.

---

[5]The literature of management is filled with references to *goals* and *objectives*. These terms are used in a variety of ways, many of them conflicting. Some writers use the term *goals* to refer to the long-run results an organization seeks to achieve and the term *objectives* to refer to immediate, short-run performance targets. Some writers reverse the usage. Others use the terms interchangeably. And still others use the term *goals* to refer to broad organizationwide performance targets and the term *objectives* to designate specific targets set by subordinate managers in response to the broader, more inclusive goals of the whole organization. In our view, little is gained from semantic distinctions between *goals* and *objectives*; the important thing is to recognize that the results an enterprise seeks to attain vary both in scope and in time perspective. Nearly always, organizations need to have broad and narrow performance targets for both the near term and long term. It is inconsequential which targets are called "goals" and which are called "objectives." To avoid a semantic jungle, we will use the single term *objectives* to refer to the performance targets and results an organization seeks to attain. We will use the adjectives *long-range* (or long-run) and *short-range* (or short-run) to identify the relevant time frame, and we will try to describe objectives in words that indicate their intended scope and level in the organization.

and improving the company's long-term market position. Specific kinds of financial and strategic performance objectives are shown below:

Financial Objectives	Strategic Objectives
• Faster revenue growth	• A bigger market share
• Faster earnings growth	• A higher, more secure industry rank
• Higher dividends	• Higher product quality
• Wider profit margins	• Lower costs relative to key competitors
• Higher returns on invested capital	• Broader or more attractive product line
• Stronger bond and credit ratings	• A stronger reputation with customers
• Bigger cash flows	• Superior customer service
• A rising stock price	• Recognition as a leader in technology and/or product innovation
• Recognition as a "blue chip" company	
• A more diversified revenue base	• Increased ability to compete in international markets
• Stable earnings during recessionary periods	• Expanded growth opportunities

Illustration Capsule 6 provides a sampling of strategic and financial objectives of some well-known corporations.

Strategic Objectives versus Financial Objectives: Which Take Precedence? Although both financial and strategic objectives carry top priority because of their key results character, a dilemma arises when tradeoffs must be made between actions to boost short-term financial performance and efforts to build a stronger business position for the long term. Managers with strong financial instincts often focus on short-term financial performance at the expense of actions with a longer-term and more uncertain market and competitive payoff. This is especially true when an organization's financial performance is poor. Yet, once an organization's financial results are healthy enough to avert crisis, the objective of building a stronger competitive position for the long term outweighs better financial payoffs in the short term. A company that consistently passes up opportunities to strengthen its long-term competitive position (opting instead for immediate improvements in its financial performance) risks diluting its competitiveness, losing momentum in its markets, and impairing its ability to stave off market challenges from ambitious rivals. The risks are especially great when a company has growth-minded competitors who place more value on achieving long-term industry leadership than on current profits. Competitors who will accept lower prices and lower profit margins for long periods in return for annual gains in market share can in time build a leading market position at the expense of companies that are preoccupied with their short-term profitability. One need look no further than the long-range strategic efforts of Japanese companies to gain market ground on their more profit-centered American and European rivals to appreciate the pitfall of letting short-term financial objectives dominate the strategic objective of building a sustainable competitive position.

The Concept of Strategic Intent   A company's strategic objectives are important for another reason—they delineate its *strategic intent* to stake out a partic-

ILLUSTRATION CAPSULE
6

STRATEGIC AND FINANCIAL OBJECTIVES OF WELL-KNOWN CORPORATIONS

Ford Motor Company:	To be a low-cost producer of the highest quality products and services that provide the best customer value.
Federal Express:	To continue the expansion of Federal Express's global network linking key markets around the world by merging dissimilar networks, providing service to additional countries, increasing the number of flight destinations, expanding our fleet of aircraft, opening new hubs, and adding U.S. gateways for the distribution of packages and freight.
Eastman Kodak:	To be the world's best in chemical and electronic imaging.
Alcan Aluminum:	To be the lowest cost producer of aluminum and to outperform the average return on equity of the Standard & Poor's Industrial Stock Index.
General Electric:	To become the most competitive enterprise in the world by being number one or number two in market share in every business the company is in.
Apple Computer:	To offer the best possible personal computing technology, and to put that technology in the hands of as many people as possible.
Atlas Corporation:	To become a low-cost, medium-size gold producer, producing in excess of 125,000 ounces of gold a year and building gold reserves of 1,500,000 ounces.
Quaker Oats Company:	To achieve return on equity at 20 percent or above, "real" earnings growth averaging 5 percent or better over time, be a leading marketer of strong consumer brands, and improve the profitability of low-return businesses or divest them.

Source: Company annual reports.

ular business position.[6] The strategic intent of a large company may be to exercise industry leadership on a national or global scale. The strategic intent of a small company may be to dominate a market niche and gain recognition as an up-and-coming enterprise. The time horizon underlying the concept of strategic intent is long term. Companies that rise to prominence in their markets almost invariably begin with strategic intents that are out of proportion to their immediate capabilities and market positions. But they set ambitious long-term strategic objectives and then pursue them relentlessly, sometimes even obsessively, over a 10- to 20-year period. In the 1960s, Komatsu, Japan's leading earth-moving equipment company, was less than one-third the size of Caterpillar, had little market presence outside Japan, and depended on its small bulldozers for most of its revenue. Komatsu's strategic intent was to "encircle Caterpillar" with a broader product line and compete globally against Caterpillar. By the late 1980s, Komatsu was the industry's second-ranking company, with a strong sales presence in North America, Europe, and Asia plus a product line that included industrial robots and semiconductors as well as a broad array of earth-moving equipment.

Often, a company's strategic intent takes on a heroic character, serving as a rallying cry for managers and employees alike to go all out and do their very

Basic Concept
A company exhibits strategic intent *when it relentlessly pursues a long-term strategic objective and concentrates its actions on achieving that objective.*

---

[6]The concept of strategic intent is described in more detail in Gary Hamel and C. K. Pralahad, "Strategic Intent," *Harvard Business Review* 89, no. 3 (May–June 1989), pp. 63–76. This section draws on their pioneering discussion.

best. Canon's strategic intent in copying equipment was to "beat Xerox." The strategic intent of the U.S. government's Apollo space program was to land a person on the moon ahead of the Soviet Union. Wal-Mart's strategic intent has been to "overtake Sears" as the largest U.S. retailer. In such instances, strategic intent signals a deep-seated commitment to winning—unseating the industry leader, remaining the industry leader (and becoming more dominant in the process), or otherwise beating long odds to gain a significantly stronger business position. A capably managed enterprise whose strategic objectives go well beyond its present reach and resources is potentially a more formidable competitor than a company with modest strategic intent.

Long-Range versus Short-Range Objectives   An organization needs both long-range and short-range objectives. Long-range objectives serve two purposes. First, setting performance targets five or more years ahead raises the issue of what actions to take *now* in order to achieve the targeted long-range performance *later* (a company can't wait until the end of year 4 of its 5-year strategic plan to begin building the competitive market position it wants to have in year 5!). Second, having explicit long-range objectives pushes managers to weigh the impact of today's decision on longer-range performance. Without the pressure to make progress in meeting long-range performance targets, it is human nature to base decisions on what is most expedient and worry about the future later. The problem with short-sighted decisions, of course, is that they put a company's long-term business position at greater risk.

Short-range objectives spell out the immediate and near-term results to be achieved. They indicate the *speed* at which management wants the organization to progress as well as the *level of performance* being aimed for over the next two or three periods. Short-range objectives can be identical with long-range objectives any time an organization is already performing at the targeted long-term level. For instance, if a company has an ongoing objective of 15 percent profit growth every year and is currently achieving this objective, the company's long-range and short-range profit objectives coincide. The most important situation where short-range objectives differ from long-range objectives occurs when managers are trying to elevate organizational performance and cannot reach the long-range/ongoing target in just one year. Short-range objectives then serve as stairsteps for reaching the ultimate target.

The "Challenging but Achievable" Test

Company performance targets should be challenging but achievable.

Objectives should not represent whatever levels of achievement management decides would be "nice." Wishful thinking has no place in objective-setting. For objectives to serve as a tool for *stretching* an organization to reach its full potential, they must meet the criterion of being *challenging but achievable*. Satisfying this criterion means setting objectives in the light of several important "inside-outside" considerations:

- What performance levels will industry and competitive conditions realistically allow?
- What results will it take for the organization to be a successful performer?
- What performance is the organization capable of *when pushed*?

To set challenging but achievable objectives, managers must judge what performance is possible in light of external conditions and what performance the organization is capable of achieving. The tasks of objective-setting and strategy-making often become intertwined at this point. Strategic choices, for example, cannot be made in a financial vacuum; the money has to be available to execute whatever strategy is chosen. Consequently, decisions about strategy are contingent on setting the organization's financial performance objectives high enough to (1) execute the chosen strategy, (2) fund other needed actions, and (3) please investors and the financial community. Objectives and strategy also intertwine when it comes to matching the means (strategy) with the ends (objectives). If a company can't achieve established objectives by following its current strategy (either because the objectives are unrealistic or because the strategy is), the objectives or the strategy need adjustment to produce a better fit.

The Need for Objectives at All Management Levels

For strategic thinking and strategy-driven decision-making to penetrate the organizational hierarchy, performance targets must be established not only for the organization as a whole but also for each of the organization's separate businesses and product lines down to each functional area and department within the business-unit/product-line structure.[7] Only when every manager, from the chief executive officer to the lowest level manager, is held accountable for achieving specific results in their units is the objective-setting process complete enough to ensure that the whole organization is headed down the chosen path and that each part of the organization knows what it needs to accomplish.

The objective-setting process is more top-down than it is bottom-up. To see why strategic objectives at one managerial level tend to drive objectives and strategies at the next level down, consider the following example. Suppose the senior executives of a diversified corporation establish a corporate profit objective of $5 million for next year. Suppose further, after discussion between corporate management and the general managers of the firm's five different businesses, that each business is given the challenging but achievable profit objective of $1 million by year-end (i.e., if the five business divisions contribute $1 million each in profit, the corporation can reach its $5 million profit objective). A concrete result has thus been agreed on and translated into measurable action commitments at two levels in the managerial hierarchy. Next, suppose the general manager of business unit X, after some analysis and discussion with functional area managers, concludes that reaching the $1 million profit objective will require selling 100,000 units at an average price of $50 and producing them at an average cost of $40 (a $10 profit margin × 100,000 units = $1 million profit). Consequently, the general manager and the manufacturing manager may settle on a production objective of 100,000 units at a unit cost of $40. The general manager and the marketing manager may agree on a sales objective of 100,000 units and a target selling price of $50. In turn, the marketing manager may break the 100,000-unit sales objective into unit sales targets for each sales territory, each item in the product line, and each salesperson.

---

[7]Peter F. Drucker, *Management: Tasks, Responsibilities, Practices* (New York: Harper & Row, 1974), p. 100. See also Charles H. Granger, "The Hierarchy of Objectives," *Harvard Business Review* 42, no. 3 (May–June 1963), pp. 63–74.

A top-down approach of establishing performance targets is a logical way to divide organizationwide targets into pieces that lower-level units and managers are responsible for achieving. Such an approach also provides a valuable degree of *unity* and *cohesion* to the objective-setting and strategy-making occurring in different parts of the organization. Generally speaking, organizationwide objectives and strategy need to be established first so they can *guide* objective-setting and strategy-making at lower levels. Top-down objective-setting and strategizing steer lower-level units toward objectives and strategies that take their cues from those of the total enterprise. When objective-setting and strategy-making begin at the bottom levels of an organization and organizationwide objectives and strategies reflect the aggregate of what has bubbled up from below, the resulting strategic action plan won't be consistent, cohesive, or coordinated. Bottom-up objective-setting, with no guidance from above, nearly always signals an absence of strategic leadership on the part of senior executives.

CRAFTING A STRATEGY: THE THIRD DIRECTION-SETTING TASK

Organizations need strategies to guide *how* to achieve objectives and *how* to pursue the organization's mission. Strategy-making is all about *how*—how to reach performance targets, how to outcompete rivals, how to seek and maintain competitive advantage, how to strengthen the enterprise's long-term business position. An organization's overall strategy and managerial game plan emerge from the *pattern* of actions already initiated and the plans managers have for making fresh moves. In forming a strategy out of many possible options, the strategist forges responses to market change, seeks new opportunities, and synthesizes different approaches taken at various times in various parts of the organization.[8]

An organization's strategy evolves over time. One would be hard pressed to find a company whose strategy was conceived in advance and followed exactly for a sustained time period. As a rule, companies revise their strategies in response to changes inside the company or in the surrounding environment. The unknowable or unpredictable character of competition and market change make it impossible to anticipate and plan for everything in advance. There is always something new to react to and some new strategic window opening up. This is why the task of strategizing is always ongoing, involving continuous review and reconsideration and fresh strategic initiatives to embellish or modify the current strategy.

As we emphasized in the opening chapter, strategy-making is not just a task for senior executives. In large, diversified enterprises, decisions about what approaches to take and what new moves to initiate involve corporate senior executives, heads of business units and product divisions, heads of major functional areas within a business or division (manufacturing, marketing and sales, finance, human resources, and the like), plant managers, product managers,

---

[8]Henry Mintzberg, "The Strategy Concept II: Another Look at Why Organizations Need Strategies," *California Management Review* 30, no. 1 (Fall 1987), pp. 25–32.

T A B L E 2–1	**The Strategy-Making Hierarchy**	*(Who has primary responsibility for what kinds of strategy actions)*

Strategy Level	Primary Strategy-Development Responsibility	Strategy-Making Functions and Areas of Focus
Corporate strategy	CEO, other key executives (decisions are typically reviewed/approved by boards of directors)	• Building and managing a high-performing portfolio of business units (making acquisitions, strengthening existing business positions, divesting businesses that no longer fit into management's plans) • Capturing the synergy among related business units and turning it into competitive advantage • Establishing investment priorities and steering corporate resources into businesses with the most attractive opportunities • Reviewing/revising/unifying the major strategic approaches and moves proposed by business-unit managers
Business strategies	General manager/head of business unit (decisions are typically reviewed/approved by a senior executive or a board of directors)	• Devising moves and approaches to compete successfully and to secure a competitive advantage • Forming responses to changing external conditions • Uniting the strategic initiatives of key functional departments • Taking action to address company-specific issues and operating problems
Functional strategies	Functional managers (decisions are typically reviewed/approved by business-unit head)	• Crafting moves and approaches to support business strategy and to achieve functional/departmental performance objectives • Reviewing/revising/unifying strategy-related moves and approaches proposed by lower-level managers
Operating strategies	Field-unit heads/lower-level managers within functional areas (decisions are reviewed/approved by functional area head/department head)	• Crafting still narrower and more specific approaches/moves aimed at supporting functional and business strategies and at achieving operating-unit objectives

district and regional sales managers, and lower-level supervisors. In diversified enterprises, strategies are initiated at four distinct organization levels. There's a strategy for the company and all of its businesses as a whole (*corporate strategy*). There's a strategy for each separate business the company has diversified into (*business strategy*). Then there is a strategy for each specific functional unit within a business (*functional strategy*)—each business usually has a production strategy, a marketing strategy, a finance strategy, and so on. And, finally, there are still narrower strategies for basic operating units—plants, sales districts and regions, and departments within functional areas (*operating strategy*). Single-business enterprises have only three levels of strategy-making (business strategy, functional strategy, and operating strategy) unless diversification into other businesses becomes an active consideration. Table 2–1 highlights which level of management usually has lead responsibility for which level of strategy and indicates the kinds of strategic actions that distinguish each of the four strategy-making levels.

FIGURE 2–1   **Identifying the Corporate Strategy of a Diversified Company**

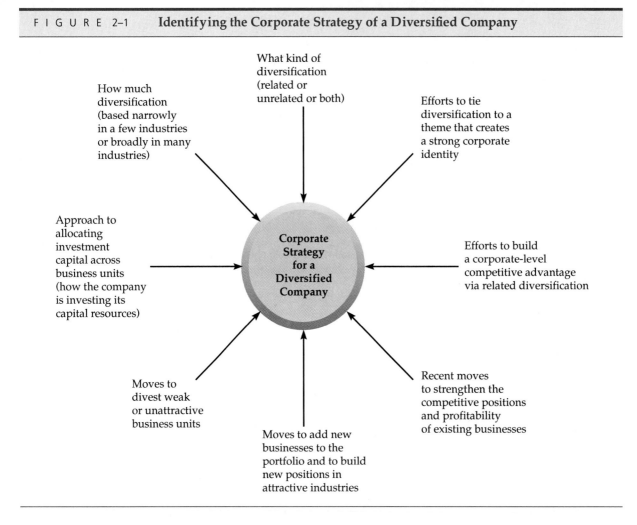

Corporate Strategy

Basic Concept
Corporate strategy
*concerns a diversified
company's moves to
establish business
positions in different
industries and the actions
and approaches it uses
in managing its
diversified businesses.*

Corporate strategy is the overall managerial game plan for a diversified company. Corporate strategy extends companywide—an umbrella over all businesses that a diversified company is in. It consists of the moves made to establish business positions in different industries and the approaches used to manage the company's group of businesses. Figure 2–1 depicts what to look for in profiling a diversified company's corporate strategy. Crafting corporate strategy for a diversified company involves four kinds of initiatives:

1. *Making the moves to accomplish diversification.* The first concern in diversification is what the portfolio of businesses should consist of—specifically, what industries to diversify into and whether to enter those industries by starting a new business or acquiring a company already in the industry (an established leader, an up-and-coming company, or a troubled company with turnaround potential). This piece of corporate strategy establishes whether diversification is based narrowly in a few industries or broadly in many industries, and it shapes how the company will be positioned in each of the target industries.

2. *Initiating actions to boost the combined performance of the businesses the firm has diversified into.* As positions are created in the chosen industries, corporate strategy-making concentrates on ways to get better performance out of the business-unit portfolio. Decisions must be reached about how to strengthen the long-term competitive positions and profitabilities of the businesses the corporation has invested in. Corporate parents can help their business subsidiaries be more successful by financing additional capacity and efficiency improvements, by supplying missing skills and managerial know-how, by acquiring another company in the same industry and merging the two operations into a stronger business, and/or by acquiring new businesses that strongly complement existing businesses. The overall plan for managing a group of diversified businesses usually involves pursuing rapid-growth strategies in the most promising businesses, keeping the other core businesses healthy, initiating turnaround efforts in weak-performing businesses with potential, and divesting businesses that are no longer attractive or that don't fit into management's long-range plans.

3. *Finding ways to capture the synergy among related business units and turn it into competitive advantage.* When a company diversifies into businesses with related technologies, similar operating characteristics, the same distribution channels, common customers, or some other synergistic relationship, it gains competitive advantage potential not open to a company that has diversified into totally unrelated businesses. With related diversification companies can usually transfer skills, share expertise, or share facilities across businesses, thereby reducing overall costs, strengthening the competitiveness of some of the corporation's products, or enhancing the capabilities of particular business units— any of which can represent a significant source of competitive advantage. The greater the relatedness among the businesses of a diversified company, the greater the opportunities for skills transfer and/or sharing across businesses and the bigger the window for creating competitive advantage. Indeed, what makes related diversification so attractive is the synergistic *strategic fit* across related businesses that allows company resources to be leveraged into a combined performance *greater* than the units could achieve operating independently. The 2 + 2 = 5 aspect of strategic fit makes related diversification a very appealing strategy for boosting corporate performance and shareholder value.

4. *Establishing investment priorities and steering corporate resources into the most attractive business units.* A diversified company's different businesses are usually not equally attractive from the standpoint of investing additional funds. Corporate executives need to rank the attractiveness of investing more capital in each business so they can channel resources into areas where earnings potentials are higher. Corporate strategy may include divesting businesses that are chronically poor performers or those in an unattractive industry. Divestiture frees up unproductive funds for redeployment to promising businesses or for financing attractive new acquisitions.

FIGURE 2–2   **Identifying Strategy for a Single-Business Company**

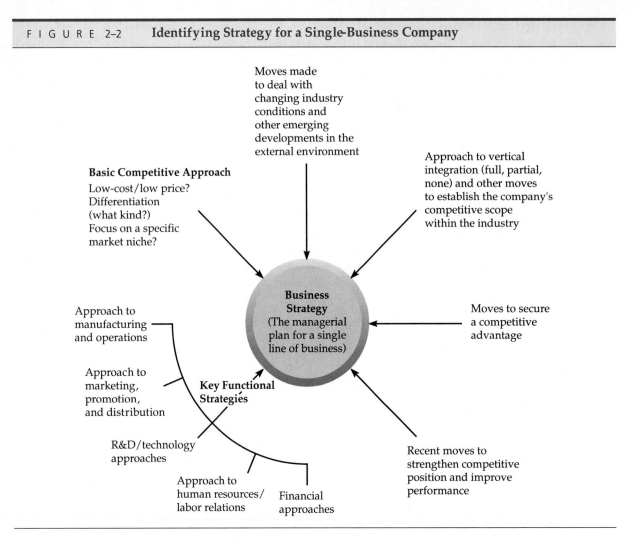

Corporate strategy is crafted at the highest levels of management. Senior corporate executives normally have lead responsibility for devising corporate strategy and for synthesizing whatever recommendations bubble up from lower-level managers. Key business-unit heads may also be influential, especially in strategic decisions affecting the businesses they head. Major strategic decisions are usually reviewed and approved by the company's board of directors.

Business Strategy

The term *business strategy* (or business-level strategy) refers to the managerial game plan for a single business. It is mirrored in the pattern of approaches and moves management devises to produce successful performance in *one specific line of business*. The various elements of business strategy are shown in Figure 2–2. For a stand-alone single-business company, corporate strategy and business strategy are one and the same since there is only one business to form a strategy for; the distinction between corporate strategy and business strategy is relevant only when diversification enters the firm's picture.

The central thrust of business strategy is how to build and strengthen the company's long-term competitive position in the marketplace. Toward this end, business strategy is concerned principally with (1) forming responses to changes underway in the industry, the economy at large, the regulatory and political arena, and other relevant areas, (2) crafting competitive moves and market approaches that can lead to sustainable competitive advantage, (3) uniting the strategic initiatives of functional departments, and (4) addressing specific strategic issues the business faces.

Clearly, business strategy encompasses whatever moves and new approaches managers deem prudent in light of competitive forces, economic trends and market developments, buyer demographics, new legislation and regulatory requirements, and other broad external factors. *A good strategy is well matched to the external situation*; as the external environment changes in significant ways, adjustments in strategy eventually become desirable. Whether a company's response to external change is quick or slow tends to be a function of how long events must unfold before managers can assess any implications for the business and how much longer it takes them to form a strategic response. Some external changes, of course, require little or no response, while others call for significant strategy alterations. On occasions, external factors change in ways that pose a formidable strategic hurdle—for example, cigarette manufacturers face a tough challenge holding their own against the mounting antismoking campaign.

What separates a powerful business strategy from a weak one is the strategist's ability *to forge a series of moves and approaches capable of producing sustainable competitive advantage.* With a competitive advantage, a company has good prospects for above-average profitability and success in the industry. Without competitive advantage, a company risks being outcompeted by stronger rivals and locked into mediocre performance. Crafting a business strategy that yields sustainable competitive advantage has several facets: deciding where a firm has the best chance to win a competitive edge, developing product/service attributes that have strong buyer appeal and set the company apart from rivals, and neutralizing the competitive moves of rival companies. A company's strategy for competing is typically both offensive and defensive—some aggressive actions amount to direct attacks on competitors' market positions; others neutralize fresh moves made by rivals. The three basic competitive approaches are: (1) striving to be the industry's low-cost producer (thereby aiming for a cost-based competitive advantage over rivals); (2) pursuing differentiation based on such advantages as quality, performance, service, styling, technological superiority, or unusually good value; and (3) focusing on a narrow market niche and winning a competitive edge by doing a better job than rivals of serving the special needs and tastes of buyers in the niche.

Internally, business strategy involves taking actions to develop the skills and capabilities needed to achieve competitive advantage. Successful business strategies usually aim at building the company's competence in one or more core activities crucial to strategic success and then using the core competence as a basis for winning a competitive edge over rivals. A *core competence* is something a firm does especially well in comparison to rival companies. It thus

Basic Concept
Business strategy concerns the moves and the approaches crafted by management to produce successful performance in one line of business; the central business strategy issue is how to build a stronger long-term competitive position.

Strategic Management Principle
A business strategy is powerful if it produces a sizable and sustainable competitive advantage; it is weak if it produces no advantage or results in competitive disadvantage.

represents a source of competitive strength. Core competences can relate to R&D, mastery of a technological process, manufacturing capability, sales and distribution, customer service, or anything else that is a competitively important aspect of creating, producing, or marketing the company's product or service. *A core competence is a basis for competitive advantage because it represents specialized expertise that rivals don't have and can't readily match.*

On a broader internal front, business strategy must also aim at uniting strategic initiatives in the various functional areas of business (purchasing, production, R&D, finance, human resources, sales and marketing, and distribution). Strategic actions are needed in each functional area to *support* the company's competitive approach and overall business strategy. Strategic unity and coordination across the various functional areas add power to the business strategy.

Business strategy also extends to action plans for addressing any special strategy-related issues unique to the company's competitive position and internal situation (such as whether to add new capacity, replace an obsolete plant, increase R&D funding for a promising technology, or reduce burdensome interest expenses). Such custom-tailoring of strategy is one of the reasons every company in an industry has a different business strategy.

Lead responsibility for business strategy falls in the lap of the manager in charge of the business. Even if the business head does not personally wield a heavy hand in the business strategy-making process, preferring to delegate much of the task to others, he or she is still accountable for the strategy and the results it produces. The business head, as chief strategist for the business, has at least two other responsibilities. The first is seeing that supporting strategies in each of the major functional areas of the business are well-conceived and consistent with each other. The second is getting major strategic moves approved by higher authority (the board of directors and/or corporate-level officers) if needed, and keeping them informed of important new developments, deviations from plan, and potential strategy revisions. In diversified companies, business-unit heads may also have to ensure that business-level objectives and strategy conform to corporate-level objectives and strategy.

Functional Strategy

Functional strategy refers to the set of strategic initiatives taken in one part of a business. A company needs a functional strategy for every major functional activity—an R&D strategy, a production strategy, a marketing strategy, a customer service strategy, a distribution strategy, a finance strategy, a human resources strategy, and so on. Functional strategies add detail to business strategy and govern *how* functional activities will be managed. A company's marketing strategy, for example, represents the managerial game plan for running the marketing part of the business. The primary role of a functional strategy is to *support* the company's overall business strategy and competitive approach. Another role is to create a managerial roadmap for achieving functional area performance objectives. Thus, functional strategy in the production/manufacturing area represents the game plan for *how* manufacturing activities will be managed to support business strategy and achieve manufacturing objectives. Functional strategy in the finance area consists of *how* financial activities will be managed in supporting business strategy and achieving specific financial objectives.

Lead responsibility for strategy-making in functional areas is normally delegated to the functional area heads, unless the business-unit head decides to exert a strong influence. In crafting strategy, a functional department head ideally works closely with key subordinates and often touches base with the heads of other functional areas and the business head. Coordinated and mutually supportive functional strategies are essential for the overall business strategy to have maximum impact. Plainly, a business's marketing strategy, production strategy, finance strategy, and human resource strategy should be working in concert rather than at cross-purposes. Coordination across functional area strategies is best accomplished during the deliberation stage. If inconsistent functional strategies are sent up the line for approval, it is up to the business head to spot the conflicts and get them resolved.

Operating Strategy

Operating strategies concern the even narrower strategic initiatives and approaches for managing key operating units (plants, sales districts, distribution centers) and for handling daily operating tasks with strategic significance (advertising campaigns, materials purchasing, inventory control, maintenance, shipping). Operating strategies, while of lesser scope than the higher levels of strategy-making, add relevant detail and completeness to the overall business plan. Lead responsibility for operating strategies is usually delegated to operating-level managers, subject to review and approval by higher ranking managers.

Even though operating strategy is at the bottom of the strategy-making hierarchy, its importance cannot be minimized. For example, a plant that fails to achieve production volume, unit cost, and quality targets can undercut sales and profit objectives and wreak havoc with the whole company's strategic efforts to build a quality image with customers. One can't always judge the importance of a strategic initiative by the managerial level where it originated.

Operating managers are part of an organization's strategy-making team because numerous operating-level units have strategy-critical performance targets and need to have strategic action plans in place to achieve them. A regional manager needs a strategy customized to the region's particular situation and objectives. A plant manager needs a strategy for accomplishing the plant's objectives, carrying out the plant's part of the company's overall manufacturing game plan, and dealing with any strategy-related problems at the plant. A company's advertising manager needs a strategy for getting maximum audience exposure and sales impact from the ad budget. The following two examples illustrate how operating strategy supports higher-level strategies.

- A company with a low-price, high-volume business strategy and a need to achieve low manufacturing costs launches a companywide effort to boost worker productivity by 10 percent. To contribute to this objective: (1) the manager of employee recruiting develops a strategy for interviewing and testing job applicants that weeds out all but the most highly motivated, best-qualified candidates; (2) the manager of information systems devises a way to use technology to boost the productivity of office workers; (3) the employee benefits manager devises an improved incentive-compensation plan to reward manufacturing

Basic Concept
Operating strategy concerns the game plan for managing key organizational units within a business (plants, sales districts, distribution centers) and for handling strategically significant operating tasks (materials purchasing, inventory control, maintenance, shipping, advertising campaigns).

employees for increased output; (4) the purchasing manager launches a program to obtain new efficiency-increasing equipment faster and easier.

- A distributor of plumbing equipment emphasizes quick delivery and accurate order-filling as keystones of its customer service approach. To support this strategy, the warehouse manager (1) develops an inventory-stocking strategy that allows 99 percent of all orders to be completely filled without back ordering any item and (2) institutes a warehouse staffing strategy that allows any order to be shipped within 24 hours.

Uniting the Strategy-Making Effort

Strategic Management Principle

Companies can't create unified objectives and strategies if each manager has objective-setting and strategy-making autonomy.

The previous discussion underscores that *an organization's strategic plan is a collection of strategies* devised by different managers at different levels in the organizational hierarchy. The larger the enterprise, the more points of strategic initiative it has. Management's direction-setting effort is not complete until managers unify the separate layers of strategy into a coherent, supportive pattern. Ideally the pieces and layers of strategy should fit together like the pieces of a picture puzzle. Unified objectives and strategies don't emerge from an undirected process where managers at each level set objectives and craft strategies *independently*. Indeed, functional and operating-level managers have a duty to set performance targets and invent strategic actions that will help achieve business objectives and make business strategy more effective.

Consistency between business strategy and functional/operating strategies comes from organizationwide allegiance to business objectives.

Harmonizing objectives and strategies piece-by-piece and level-by-level can be tedious and frustrating, requiring numerous consultations and meetings, annual strategy review and approval processes, trial and error, and months (sometimes years) of consensus-building. The politics of gaining strategic consensus and the battle of trying to keep all managers and departments focused on what's best for the total enterprise (as opposed to what's best for their departments or their careers) are often big obstacles in unifying the layers of objectives and strategies.[9] Gaining broad consensus is particularly difficult when there is ample room for opposing views and disagreement. It is not unusual for discussions about the organization's mission and basic direction, what objectives to set, and what strategies to employ to provoke heated debates and strong differences of opinion.

Figure 2–3 portrays the networking of objectives and strategies down through the managerial hierarchy. The two-way arrows indicate that there are simultaneous bottom-up and top-down influences on the objectives and strategies at each level. These vertical linkages, if managed in a way that promotes coordination, can help unify the objective-setting and strategy-making activities of many managers into a mutually reinforcing pattern. The tighter coordination is enforced, the tighter the linkages in the objectives and strategies of the various organizational units. Tight linkages safeguard against organizational units straying from the direction top management has charted.

---

[9]Functional managers can sometimes be more interested in doing what is best for their own areas, in building their own empire, and in consolidating their personal power and influence than they are in cooperating with other functional managers to unify behind the overall business strategy. As a consequence, it's easy for functional area support strategies to conflict, thereby forcing the general manager to spend time and energy refereeing differences and building support for a more unified approach.

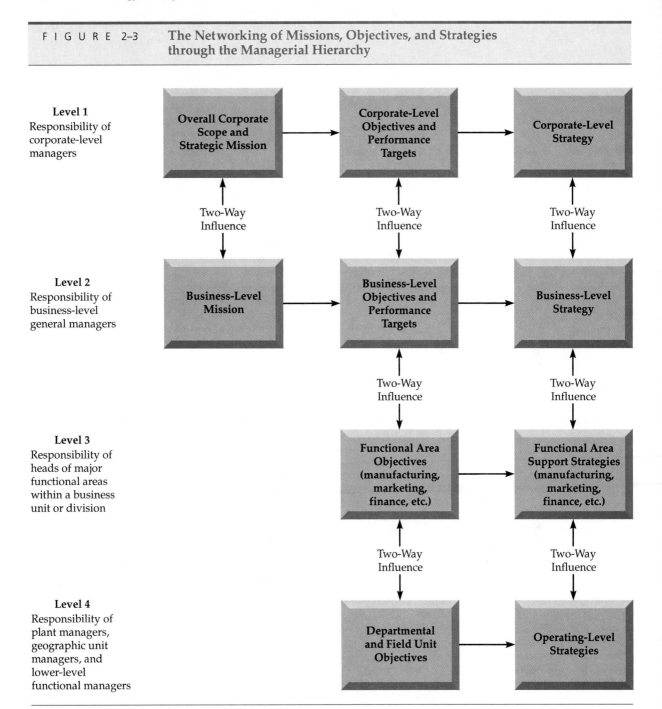

F I G U R E 2–3   **The Networking of Missions, Objectives, and Strategies through the Managerial Hierarchy**

As a practical matter, however, corporate and business missions, objectives, and strategies need to be clearly outlined and communicated down the line before much progress can be made in objective-setting and strategy-making at the functional and operating levels. Direction and guidance needs to flow from the corporate level to the business level and from the business level to the functional and operating levels. The strategic disarray that occurs in an organization when senior managers don't exercise strong top-down direction-setting and strategic leadership is akin to what would happen to a football team's offensive performance if the quarterback decided not to call a play for the team, but instead, gave each player the latitude to pick whatever play he thought would work best at his respective position.

THE FACTORS THAT SHAPE STRATEGY

Many factors enter into the forming of a company's strategy. Figure 2–4 is a simple model of the primary factors that shape the choice of a strategy. The interplay of these factors is frequently complex and always industry- and company-specific. No two strategic choices are made in exactly the same context; the situational factors always differ, if only slightly. This is why managers need to assess all the various situational factors, both external and internal, before they begin crafting strategy.

Societal, Political, Regulatory, and Citizenship Considerations

Societal, political, regulatory, and citizenship factors limit the strategic actions a company can take.

What an enterprise can and cannot do strategywise is always constrained by what is legal, by what is in compliance with government policies and regulations, by what is considered socially acceptable, and by what constitutes community citizenship. Outside pressures also come from other sources—special interest groups, the glare of investigative reporting, a fear of unwanted political action, and the stigma of negative opinion. Societal concerns over health and nutrition, alcohol and drug abuse, hazardous waste disposal, sexual harassment, and the impact of plant closings on local communities have impacted many companies' strategies. American concerns over the growing volume of foreign imports and political debate over whether to impose tariffs and import quotas to help reduce the chronic U.S. trade deficit have been key factors in the strategic decisions of Japanese and European companies to locate plants in the United States. Heightened awareness of the dangers of cholesterol has driven food products companies to substitute low-fat ingredients despite extra costs.

More and more companies now consider societal values and priorities, community concerns, and the potential for onerous legislation and regulatory requirements when analyzing their external situation. Intense public pressure and adverse media coverage have made such a practice prudent. The task of making an organization's strategy "socially responsible" means (1) conducting organizational activities within the bounds of what is considered ethical and in the general public interest; (2) responding positively to emerging societal priorities and expectations; (3) demonstrating a willingness to take action ahead of regulatory confrontation; (4) balancing stockholder interests against the larger interests of society; and (5) being a "good citizen" in the community.

The concept of corporate social responsibility is showing up in company mission statements. John Hancock, for example, concludes its mission statement with the following sentence:

> In pursuit of this mission, we will strive to exemplify the highest standards of business ethics and personal integrity; and shall recognize our corporate obligation to the social and economic well-being of our community.

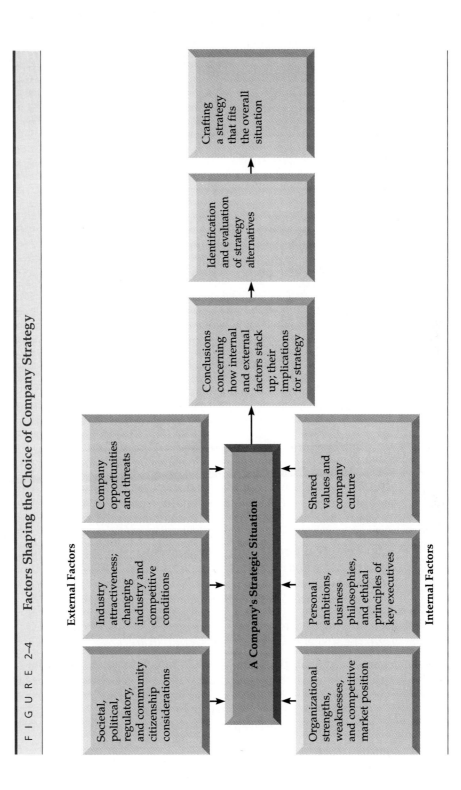

F I G U R E   2-4   Factors Shaping the Choice of Company Strategy

External Factors

Societal, political, regulatory, and community citizenship considerations

Industry attractiveness; changing industry and competitive conditions

Company opportunities and threats

A Company's Strategic Situation

Conclusions concerning how internal and external factors stack up; their implications for strategy

Identification and evaluation of strategy alternatives

Crafting a strategy that fits the overall situation

Organizational strengths, weaknesses, and competitive market position

Personal ambitions, business philosophies, and ethical principles of key executives

Shared values and company culture

Internal Factors

Union Electric, a St. Louis–based utility company, includes the following statement in its official corporate policy:

> As a private enterprise entrusted with an essential public service, we recognize our civic responsibility in the communities we serve. We shall strive to advance the growth and welfare of these communities and shall participate in civic activities which fulfill that goal . . . for we believe this is both good citizenship and good business.

Illustration Capsule 7 describes Anheuser-Busch's efforts to be socially responsible.

Industry Attractiveness and Competitive Conditions

Strategic Management Principle

A company's strategy ought to be closely matched to industry and competitive conditions.

Industry attractiveness and competitive conditions are big strategy-determining factors. A company's assessment of the industry and competitive environment directly affects how it should try to position itself in the industry and what its basic competitive strategy approach should be. When a firm concludes its industry environment has grown unattractive, and it is better off investing company resources elsewhere, it may craft a strategy of disinvestment and abandonment. When competitive conditions intensify significantly, a company must respond with strategic actions to protect its position. Fresh moves on the part of rival companies, changes in the industry's price-cost-profit economics, and new technological developments can alter the requirements for competitive success and mandate that a firm reconsider its strategy. A strategist, therefore, has to be a student of industry and competitive conditions.

Specific Company Opportunities and Threats

Strategic Management Principle

A well-conceived strategy aims at capturing a company's best growth opportunities and defending against external threats to its well-being and future performance.

The particular business opportunities a company has and the threats to its position that it faces are key influences on strategy. Strategy needs to be deliberately crafted to capture some or all of a company's best growth opportunities, especially the ones that can enhance its long-term competitive position and profitability. Likewise, strategy should be geared to providing a defense against external threats to the company's well-being and future performance. For strategy to be successful, it has to be well matched to company opportunities and threats.

Organizational Strengths, Weaknesses, and Competitive Capabilities

Strategic Management Principle

A company's strategy ought to be grounded in what it is good at doing (i.e., its organizational strengths and competitive capabilities) and avoid what it is not so good at doing (i.e., its organizational and competitive weaknesses).

Experience shows that in matching strategy to a firm's internal situation, management should build strategy around what the company does well and avoid strategies whose success depends heavily on something the company does poorly or has never done at all. In short, *strategy must be well matched to company strengths, weaknesses, and competitive capabilities.* Pursuing an opportunity without the organizational competences and resources to capture it is foolish. An organization's strengths make some opportunities and strategies attractive; likewise its internal weaknesses and its present competitive market position make certain strategies risky or even out of the question.

ILLUSTRATION CAPSULE
7

SOCIAL RESPONSIBILITY EFFORTS AT ANHEUSER-BUSCH

In a recent annual report, Anheuser-Busch described three main areas in which it was exercising social responsibility:

Alcohol Issues—Anheuser-Busch has long believed it is in the company's best interest, and in the interest of society as a whole, to play an important role in the fight against the abuse of alcoholic beverages. Although the company's efforts were already the most extensive in the brewing industry, in 1989 Anheuser-Busch created a Department of Consumer Awareness and Education to (1) educate consumers and servers of alcohol about the appropriate use of its products and (2) aggressively defend the right of brewers and beer consumers to make and enjoy beer without the fear of being stigmatized. One of the current activities of this department was an expanded "Know When to Say When" advertising campaign featuring well-known sports celebrities. In addition, Anheuser-Busch supported scientific research into the causes and possible cures of alcoholism and alcohol abuse. More than $15 million was contributed in 1989 to such organizations as the Alcoholic Beverage-Medical Research Foundation in Baltimore, Md., and the Alcohol Research Center at UCLA.

Minority Development—Anheuser-Busch supports minority organizations engaged in economic development, cultural heritage, education and leadership development. As the founder and national sponsor of the Lou Rawls Parade of Stars telethon, Anheuser-Busch commissioned a traveling exhibit to commemorate this television special's 10th anniversary and its success in raising more than $75 million since 1980. The company also contributed $15 million in 1989 to the National Hispanic Scholarship Fund to support its development and scholarship efforts. Anheuser-Busch is the NHSF's largest corporate supporter.

Community Support—Anheuser-Busch tries to enrich the communities in which it operates breweries and other major facilities by supporting local nonprofit organizations such as the United Way, social service agencies, arts and cultural groups, health care institutions, youth groups and colleges and universities. In addition, through the Anheuser-Busch Employee Volunteer Grant Program, the company recognizes its employees who actively volunteer their services to nonprofit organizations by making grants to these organizations. The company also has an employee Matching Gift program for educational institutions.

Source: 1989 Annual Report.

One of the most pivotal strategy-shaping internal considerations is whether a company has or can build the core strengths or competences needed to execute the strategy proficiently. An organization's core strengths—the things it does especially well—are an important strategy-making consideration because of (1) the skills and capabilities they provide in capitalizing on a particular opportunity, (2) the competitive edge they may give in the marketplace, and (3) the potential they have for becoming a cornerstone of strategy. The best path to competitive advantage is found where a firm has core strengths in one or more of the key requirements for market success, where rivals do not have matching or offsetting competences, and where rivals can't develop comparable strengths except at high cost and/or over an extended period of time.[10]

Even if an organization has no outstanding core competences (and many do not), it still must shape its strategy to suit its particular skills and available

---

[10]David T. Kollat, Roger D. Blackwell, and James F. Robeson, *Strategic Marketing* (New York: Holt, Rinehart & Winston, 1972), p. 24.

resources. It never makes sense to develop a strategic plan that cannot be executed with the skills and resources a firm is able to muster.

The Personal Ambitions, Business Philosophies, and Ethical Beliefs of Managers

Managers' personal ambitions, business philosophies, and ethical beliefs are usually woven into the strategies they craft.

Managers do not dispassionately assess what strategic course to steer. Their decisions are often influenced by their own vision of how to compete and how to position the enterprise and by what image and standing they want the company to have. Both casual observation and formal studies indicate that managers' ambitions, value, business philosophies, attitudes toward risk, and ethical beliefs have important influences on strategy.[11] Sometimes the influence of the manager's personal values and experiences is conscious and deliberate; at other times it is unconscious. As Professor Andrews has noted in explaining the relevance of personal factors to strategy, "People have to have their hearts in it."[12]

Several examples of how business philosophies and personal values enter into strategy-making are particularly noteworthy. Japanese managers are strong proponents of strategies that take a long-term view and that aim at building market share and competitive position. In contrast, some corporate executives and Wall Street financiers have drawn criticism for overemphasizing short-term profits at the expense of long-term competitive positioning and for being more attracted to strategies involving a financial play on assets (leveraged buyouts and stock buybacks) rather than using corporate resources to make long-term strategic investments. Japanese companies also display a different philosophy regarding the role of suppliers. They prefer to establish long-term partnership arrangements with key suppliers to improve the quality and reliability of component parts and to reduce inventory requirements. In the United States and Europe the prevailing managerial philosophy has been to play suppliers off against one another, doing business on a short-term basis with whoever offers the best price and delivery.

Attitudes toward risk also have a big influence on strategy. Risk-avoiders favor "conservative" strategies that minimize downside risk, have a quick payback, and produce sure short-term profits. Risk-takers lean more toward opportunistic strategies where bold moves can produce a big payoff over the long term. Risk-takers prefer innovation to imitation and strategic offensives to defensive conservatism.

Managerial values also shape the ethical quality of a firm's strategy. Managers with strong ethical convictions take pains to see that their companies observe a strict code of ethics in all aspects of the business. They expressly forbid such practices as accepting or giving kickbacks, badmouthing rivals' products, and buying political influence with political contributions. Instances

---

[11]See, for instance, William D. Guth and Renato Tagiuri, "Personal Values and Corporate Strategy," *Harvard Business Review* 43, no. 5 (September–October 1965), pp. 123–32; Kenneth R. Andrews, *The Concept of Corporate Strategy*, 3rd ed. (Homewood Ill.: Richard D. Irwin, 1987), chap. 4; and Richard F. Vancil, "Strategy Formulation in Complex Organizations," *Sloan Management Review* 17, no. 2 (Winter 1986), pp. 4–5.

[12]Andrews, *The Concept of Corporate Strategy*, p. 63.

where a company's strategic actions run counter to high ethical standards include charging excessive interest rates on credit card balances, employing bait-and-switch sales tactics, continuing to market products suspected of having safety problems, and using ingredients that are known health hazards.

The Influence of Shared Values and Company Culture on Strategy

An organization's policies, practices, traditions, philosophical beliefs, and ways of doing things combine to give it a distinctive culture. A company's strategic actions typically reflect its cultural traits and managerial values. In some cases a company's core beliefs and culture even dominate the choice of strategic moves. This is because culture-related values and beliefs become so embedded in management's thinking and actions that they condition how the enterprise responds to external events. Such firms have a culture-driven bias about how to handle strategic issues and what kinds of strategic moves it will consider or reject. Strong cultural influences partly account for why companies gain reputations for such strategic traits as technological leadership, product innovation, dedication to superior craftsmanship, a proclivity for financial wheeling and dealing, growth through acquisitions, a strong people-orientation, or unusual emphasis on customer service and total customer satisfaction.

A company's values and culture sometimes dominate the kinds of strategic moves it will consider or reject.

In recent years, more companies have begun to articulate the core beliefs and values underlying their business approaches. One company expressed its core beliefs and values this way:

> We are market-driven. We believe that functional excellence, combined with teamwork across functions and profit centers, is essential to achieving superb execution. We believe that people are central to everything we will accomplish. We believe that honesty, integrity, and fairness should be the cornerstone of our relationships with consumers, customers, suppliers, stockholders, and employees.

IBM's founder, Thomas Watson, once stated, "We must be prepared to change all the things we are in order to remain competitive in the environment, but we must never change our three basic beliefs: (1) respect for the dignity of the individual, (2) offering the best customer service in the world, and (3) excellence." For nearly a century, AT&T's value system has emphasized (1) universal service, (2) fairness in handling personnel matters, (3) a belief that work should be balanced with commitments to family and community, and (4) relationships (from one part of the organization to another). AT&T's management views these values as essential in a technologically dynamic, highly structured company. Both the IBM and AT&T value systems are deeply ingrained and widely shared by managers and employees. Whenever this happens, values and beliefs become more than an expression of nice platitudes; they become a way of life within the company.[13]

---

[13]For more details, see Richard T. Pascale, "Perspectives on Strategy: The Real Story behind Honda's Success," in Glenn Carroll and David Vogel, *Strategy and Organization: A West Coast Perspective* (Marshfield, Mass.: Pitman Publishing, 1984), p. 60.

LINKING STRATEGY WITH ETHICS

Strategy ought to be ethical. It should involve rightful actions, not wrongful ones, or it won't pass the test of moral scrutiny. This means more than conforming to what is legal. Ethical and moral standards go beyond the prohibitions of law and the language of "thou shalt not" to the issues of *duty* and the language of "should do and should not do." Ethics concerns human duty and the principles on which these duties rest.[14]

Every business has an ethical duty to each of five constituencies: owners/shareholders, employees, customers, suppliers, and the community at large. Each of these constituencies affects the organization and is affected by it. Each is a stakeholder in the enterprise, with certain expectations as to what the enterprise should do and how it should do it.[15] Owners/shareholders, for instance, expect a return on their investment. Even though individual investors differ in their preferences for profits now versus profits later, their desire to take risks, and their willingness to exercise social responsibility, business executives have a moral duty to profitably manage the owners' investment.

A company's duty to employees arises out of respect for the worth and dignity of individuals who devote their energies to the business and depend on the business for their economic well-being. Principled strategy-making requires that employee-related decisions be made equitably and compassionately, with concern for due process and for the impact that strategic change has on employees' lives. At best, the chosen strategy should promote employee interests in areas such as wage and salary levels, career opportunities, job security, and overall working conditions. At least, the chosen strategy should not disadvantage employees. Even in crisis situations where adverse employee impact cannot be avoided, businesses have an ethical duty to minimize whatever hardships have to be imposed in the form of workforce reductions, plant closings, job transfers, relocations, retraining, and loss of income.

A company's duty to the customer arises out of expectations that attend the purchase of a good or service. Inadequate appreciation of this duty has led to product liability laws and a host of regulatory agencies to protect consumers. All kinds of strategy-related ethical issues still arise here, however. Should a seller inform consumers *fully* about the contents of its product, especially if it contains ingredients that, though officially approved for use, are suspected of having potentially harmful effects? Is it ethical for the makers of alcoholic beverages to sponsor college events, given that many college students are under 21? Is it ethical for cigarette manufacturers to advertise at all (even though it is legal)? Is it ethical for airlines to withhold information about terrorist bomb threats from the public? Is it ethical for manufacturers to produce and sell products they know have faulty parts or defective designs that may not become apparent until after the warranty expires? In submitting bids on a contract, is it unethical to seek access to inside information not available to other bidders? Is it ethical to give some customers special treatment?

A company's ethical duty to its suppliers arises out of the market relationship that exists between them—they are both partners and adversaries. They

---

[14]Harry Downs, "Business Ethics: The Stewardship of Power," forthcoming in *Strategic Management Planning*.

[15]Ibid.

are partners in the sense that the quality of suppliers' parts affects the quality of a firm's own product. They are adversaries in the sense that the supplier wants the highest price and profit it can while the buyer wants a cheaper price, better quality, and speedier service. A business confronts several ethical issues in its supplier relationships. Is it ethical to threaten to cease doing business with a supplier unless the supplier agrees not to do business with key competitors? Is it ethical to reveal one supplier's price quote to a rival supplier? Is it ethical to accept gifts from suppliers? Is it ethical to pay a supplier in cash?

The ethical duty to the community-at-large stems from the business's status as a citizen of the community and as an institution of society. Communities and society are reasonable in expecting businesses to be good citizens—to pay their fair share of taxes for fire and police protection, waste removal, streets and highways, and so on and to exercise care in the impact their activities have on the environment and on the communities in which they operate. The community should be accorded the same recognition and attention as the other four constituencies. Whether a company is a good community citizen is ultimately demonstrated by the way it supports community activities, encourages employees to participate in community activities, handles the health and safety aspects of its operations, accepts responsibility for overcoming environmental pollution, relates to regulatory bodies and employee unions, and exhibits high ethical standards.

NCR Corporation, a $6 billion computer and office equipment company, recently cast its entire mission statement in terms of its duty to stockholders, customers, employees, suppliers, and the community at large. See Illustration Capsule 8.

Carrying Out Ethical Responsibilities It is management, not constituent groups, who is responsible for managing the enterprise. Thus, it is management's perceptions of its ethical duties and of constituents' claims that determine whether and how strategy is linked to ethical behavior. Ideally, managers weigh strategic decisions from each constituent's viewpoint and, where conflicts arise, strike a rational, objective, and equitable balance among the interests of all five. If any of the five constituencies conclude that management is not doing its duty, they have their own avenues for recourse. Concerned investors can complain at the annual shareholders' meeting, appeal to the board of directors, or sell their stock. Concerned employees can unionize and bargain collectively, or they can seek employment elsewhere. Customers can buy from competitors. Suppliers can find other buyers or pursue other market alternatives. The community and society can do anything from staging protest marches to stimulating political and governmental action.[16]

A company that truly cares about business ethics and corporate social responsibility is proactive rather than reactive in linking strategy and ethics. It steers away from ethically or morally questionable business opportunities. It won't do business with suppliers that engage in activities the company does not condone. Its products are safe for its customers to use. Its workplace environment is safe for employees. It recruits and hires employees whose values and behavior are consistent with the company's principles and

---

[16]Ibid.

ILLUSTRATION CAPSULE
8

ETHICS AND VALUES AT NCR CORPORATION

NCR's corporate mission statement formally recognizes the company's duty to serve the interests of all stakeholders, not just those of stockholders, and represents a blend of ethical principles and values. As management stated in a recent annual report:

NCR is a successful, growing company dedicated to achieving superior results by assuring that its actions are aligned with stakeholder expectations. Stakeholders are all constituencies with a stake in the fortunes of the company. NCR's primary mission is to create value for our stakeholders.

We believe in conducting our business activities with integrity and respect while building mutually beneficial and enduring relationships with all of our stakeholders.

We take customer satisfaction personally: we are committed to providing superior value in our products and services on a continuing basis.

We respect the individuality of each employee and foster an environment in which employees' creativity and productivity are encouraged, recognized, valued and rewarded.

We think of our suppliers as partners who share our goal of achieving the highest quality standards and the most consistent level of service.

We are committed to being caring and supportive corporate citizens within the worldwide communities in which we operate.

We are dedicated to creating value for our shareholders and financial communities by performing in a manner that will enhance returns on investments.

Source: 1987 Annual Report.

---

ethical standards. It acts to reduce any environmental pollution it causes. It cares about *how* it does business and whether its actions reflect integrity and high ethical standards. Illustration Capsule 9 describes Harris Corporation's ethical commitments to its stakeholders.

Tests of a Winning Strategy

Strategic Management Principle

A strategy is not a true winner unless it exhibits good fit with the enterprise's situation, builds sustainable competitive advantage, and boosts company performance.

How can a manager judge which strategic option is best for the company? What are the standards for determining whether a strategy is successful or not? Three tests can be used to evaluate the merits of one strategy over another and to gauge how good a strategy is:

The Goodness of Fit Test—A good strategy is well matched to the company's situation—both internal and external factors and its own capabilities and aspirations.

The Competitive Advantage Test—A good strategy leads to sustainable competitive advantage. The bigger the competitive edge that a strategy helps build, the more powerful and effective it is.

The Performance Test—A good strategy boosts company performance. Two kinds of performance improvements are the most telling: gains in profitability and gains in the company's long-term business strength and competitive position.

Strategic options with low potential on one or more of these criteria do not merit strong consideration. The strategic option with the highest potential on all three counts can be regarded as the best or most attractive strategic alternative. Once a strategic commitment has been made and enough time has

ILLUSTRATION CAPSULE
9

HARRIS CORPORATION'S COMMITMENTS TO ITS STAKEHOLDERS

Harris Corp. is a major supplier of information, communication, and semiconductor products, systems, and services to commercial and governmental customers throughout the world. The company utilizes advanced technologies to provide innovative and cost-effective solutions for processing and communicating data, voice, text, and video information. The company's sales exceed $2 billion, and it employs nearly 23,000 people. In a recent annual report, the company set forth its commitment to satisfying the expectations of its stakeholders:

Customers—For customers, our objective is to achieve ever-increasing levels of satisfaction by providing quality products and services with distinctive benefits on a timely and continuing basis worldwide. Our relationships with customers will be forthright and ethical, and will be conducted in a manner to build trust and confidence.

Shareholders—For shareholders, the owners of our company, our objective is to achieve sustained growth in earnings-per-share. The resulting stock-price appreciation combined with dividends should provide our shareholders with a total return on investment that is competitive with similar investment opportunities.

Employees—The people of Harris are our company's most valuable asset, and our objective is for every employee to be personally involved in and share the success of the business. The company is committed to providing an environment which encourages all employees to make full use of their creativity and unique talents; to providing equitable compensation, good working conditions, and the opportunity for personal development and growth which is limited only by individual ability and desire.

Suppliers—Suppliers are a vital part of our resources. Our objective is to develop and maintain mutually beneficial partnerships with suppliers who share our commitment to achieving increasing levels of customer satisfaction through continuing improvements in quality, service, timeliness, and cost. Our relationships with suppliers will be sincere, ethical, and will embrace the highest principles of purchasing practice.

Communities—Our objective is to be a responsible corporate citizen. This includes support of appropriate civic, educational, and business activities, respect for the environment, and the encouragement of Harris employees to practice good citizenship and support community programs. Our greatest contribution to our communities is to be successful so that we can maintain stable employment and create new jobs.

Source: 1988 Annual Report.

elapsed to see results, these same tests can be used to determine how well a company's current strategy is performing. The bigger the margins by which a strategy satisfies all three criteria when put to test in the marketplace, the more it qualifies as a winning strategy.

There are, of course, some additional criteria for judging the merits of a particular strategy: clarity, internal consistency among all the pieces of strategy, timeliness, match to the personal values and ambitions of key executives, the degree of risk involved, and flexibility. These can be used to supplement the three tests posed above whenever it seems appropriate.

APPROACHES TO PERFORMING THE STRATEGY-MAKING TASK

Companies and managers perform the strategy-making task differently. In small, owner-managed companies, strategy-making is developed informally. Often the strategy is never written but exists mainly in the entrepreneur's own mind and in oral understandings with key subordinates. The largest firms, however, tend to develop their plans via an annual strategic planning cycle (complete with prescribed procedures, forms, and timetables) that includes broad management participation, lots of studies, and multiple meetings to probe and question. The larger and more diverse an enterprise, the more managers feel it is better to have a structured annual process with written plans, management scrutiny, and official approval at each level.

Along with variations in the organizational process of formulating strategy are variations in how managers personally participate in analyzing the company's situation and deliberating what strategy to pursue. The four basic strategy-making styles managers use include:[17]

The Master Strategist Approach—Here the manager personally functions as chief strategist and chief entrepreneur, exercising *strong* influence over assessments of the situation, over the strategy alternatives that are explored, and over the details of strategy. This does not mean that the manager personally does all the work; it means the manager personally becomes the chief architect of strategy and wields a proactive hand in shaping some or all of the major pieces of strategy. The manager acts as strategy commander and has a big ownership stake in the chosen strategy.

The Delegate-It-to-Others Approach—Here the manager in charge delegates the exercise of strategy-making to others, perhaps a strategic planning staff or a task force of trusted subordinates. The manager then stays off to the side, keeps in touch via reports and conversations, offers guidance if needed, reacts to informal "trial balloon" recommendations, then puts a stamp of approval on the "strategic plan" after it has been formally presented and discussed and a consensus emerges. But the manager rarely has much ownership in the recommendations and, privately, may not see much urgency in pushing *truly hard* to implement some or much of what has been written down in the company's "official strategic plan." Also, it is generally understood that "of course, we may have to proceed a bit differently if conditions change"—which gives the manager flexibility to go slow or ignore those approaches/moves that "on further reflection may not be the thing to do at this time." This strategy-making style has the advantage of letting the manager pick and choose from the smorgasbord of strategic ideas that bubble up from below, and it allows room for broad participation and input from many managers and areas. The weakness is that a manager can end up so detached from the process of formal strategy-making that he or she exercises no real strategic leadership—indeed, subordinates are likely to conclude that strategic planning isn't important enough to warrant a claim on the boss's personal time and attention. The stage is then set for rudderless direction-setting. Often the strategy-making that does occur is short-run-oriented and reactive; it deals more with today's problems than with positioning the enterprise to capture tomorrow's opportunities.

The Collaborative Approach—This is a middle approach whereby the manager enlists the help of key subordinates in hammering out a

---

[17]This discussion is based on David R. Brodwin and L. J. Bourgeois, "Five Steps to Strategic Action," in Glenn Carroll and David Vogel, *Strategy and Organization: A West Coast Perspective* (Marshfield, Mass.: Pitman Publishing, 1984), pp. 168–78.

consensus strategy that all the key players will back and do their best to implement successfully. The biggest strength of this strategy-making style is that those who are charged with crafting the strategy also have to implement it. Giving subordinate managers such a clear-cut ownership stake in the strategy they subsequently must implement enhances commitment to successful execution. When subordinates have a hand in proposing their part of the overall strategy, they can be held accountable for making it work—the "I told you it was a bad idea" alibi won't fly.

The Champion Approach—In this style, the manager is interested neither in personally crafting the details of strategy nor in the time-consuming task of leading a group to brainstorm a consensus strategy. Rather, the manager encourages subordinate managers to develop, champion, and implement sound strategies. Here strategy moves upward from the "doers" and the "fast-trackers." Executives serve as judges, evaluating the strategy proposals that reach their desks. This approach works best in large diversified corporations where the CEO cannot personally orchestrate strategy-making in each business division. Headquarters executives depend on ambitious and talented entrepreneurs at the business-unit level who can see strategic opportunities that the executives cannot. Corporate executives may articulate general strategic themes as organizationwide guidelines. But the key to strategy-making is stimulating and rewarding new strategic initiatives conceived by champions who believe in the opportunity and badly want the blessing to go after it. With this approach, total "strategy" is shaped by the sum of the championed initiatives that get approved.

These four basic managerial approaches illuminate several aspects about how strategy emerges. In situations where the manager in charge personally functions as the chief architect of strategy, the strategy is a product of his/her own vision, ambitions, values, business philosophies, and sense of what moves to make next. Highly centralized strategy-making works fine when the manager in charge has a powerful, insightful vision of what needs to be done and how to do it. The primary weakness of the master strategist approach is that the caliber of the strategy depends so heavily on one person's strategy-making skills. It also breaks down in large enterprises, where many strategic initiatives are needed and the strategy-making task is too complex for one person to handle.

The group approach to strategy-making has its risks too. Sometimes, the strategy that emerges is a middle-of-the-road compromise that lacks bold, creative initiative. Other times, it represents political consensus, with the outcome shaped by influential subordinates, powerful functional departments, or majority coalitions that have a common interest in promoting their own version of what the strategy ought to be. "Politics" and power plays are most likely in situations where there is no strong consensus on what strategy to adopt. The collaborative approach is especially conducive to political strategy formation, since powerful departments and individuals have ample opportunity to try to build a consensus for their favored strategic approach. However, the big danger of a delegate-it-to-others approach is a serious lack of top-down direction and strategic leadership.

The strength of the champion approach is also its weakness. The value of championing is that it encourages people at lower organizational levels to

Of the four basic approaches managers can use in crafting strategy, none stands out as inherently superior— each has strengths and weaknesses.

propose new strategic initiatives and stay on the lookout for good opportunities to pursue. Individuals with attractive strategic proposals are given the latitude and resources to try them out, thus helping keep strategy fresh and renewing an organization's capacity for innovation. On the other hand, the championed actions, because they come from many parts of the organization, are not likely to form a coherent pattern or promote clear strategic direction. With championing, the chief executive has to work at ensuring that what is championed adds power to the overall organization strategy; otherwise, strategic initiatives may be launched in directions that have no integrating links or overarching rationale.

KEY POINTS

Management's direction-setting task involves developing a mission, setting objectives, and forming a strategy. Early on in the direction-setting process, managers need to form a vision of where to lead the organization and to answer the question, "What is our business and what will it be?" A well-conceived mission statement helps channel organizational efforts along the course management has charted and builds a strong sense of organizational identity. Effective visions are clear, challenging, and inspiring; they prepare a firm for the future, and they make sense in the marketplace. A well-conceived, well-said mission statement serves as a beacon of long-term direction and creates employee "buy-in."

The second direction-setting step is to establish strategic and financial objectives for the organization to achieve. Objectives convert the mission statement into specific performance targets. The agreed-on objectives need to be challenging but achievable, and they need to spell out precisely how much by when. In other words, objectives should be measurable and should involve deadlines for achievement. Objectives are needed at all organizational levels.

The third direction-setting step entails forming strategies to achieve the objectives set in each area of the organization. A corporate strategy is needed to achieve corporate-level objectives; business strategies are needed to achieve business-unit performance objectives; functional strategies are needed to achieve the performance targets set for each functional department; and operating-level strategies are needed to achieve the objectives set in each operating and geographic unit. In effect, an organization's strategic plan is a collection of unified and interlocking strategies. As shown in Table 2–1, different strategic issues are addressed at each level of managerial strategy-making. Typically, the strategy-making task is more top-down than bottom-up. Lower-level strategy supports and complements higher-level strategy and contributes to the achievement of higher-level, companywide objectives.

Strategy is shaped by both outside and inside considerations. The major external considerations are societal, political, regulatory, and community factors; industry attractiveness; and the company's market opportunities and threats. The primary internal considerations are company strengths, weaknesses, and competitive capabilities; managers' personal ambitions, philosophies, and ethics; and the company's culture and shared values. A good strategy must be well matched to all these situational considerations.

There are essentially four basic ways to manage the strategy formation process in an organization: the master strategist approach where the manager in charge personally functions as the chief architect of strategy, the delegate-it-to-others approach, the collaborative approach, and the champion approach. All four have strengths and weaknesses. All four can succeed or fail depending on how well the approach is managed and depending on the strategy-making skills and judgments of the individuals involved.

Andrews, Kenneth R. *The Concept of Corporate Strategy*, 3rd ed. Homewood, Ill.: Dow Jones-Irwin, 1987, chaps. 2, 3, 4, and 5.

Foster, Lawrence W. "From Darwin to Now: The Evolution of Organizational Strategies," *Journal of Business Strategy* 5, no. 4 (Spring 1985), pp. 94–98.

Hamel, Gary, and C. K. Prahalad. "Strategic Intent." *Harvard Business Review* 89, no. 3 (May–June, 1989), pp. 63–76.

McLellan, R., and G. Kelly. "Business Policy Formulation: Understanding the Process." *Journal of General Management* 6, no. 1 (Autumn 1980), pp. 38–47.

Morris, Elinor. "Vision and Strategy: A Focus for the Future." *Journal of Business Strategy* 8, no. 2 (Fall 1987), pp. 51–58.

Mintzberg, Henry. "Crafting Strategy." *Harvard Business Review* 65, no. 4 (July–August 1987), pp. 66–77.

Quinn, James Brian. *Strategies for Change: Logical Incrementalism*. Homewood, Ill.: Richard D. Irwin, 1980, chaps. 2 and 4.

SUGGESTED
READINGS

Industry and Competitive Analysis

—

Analysis is the critical starting point of strategic thinking.
Kenichi Ohmae

—

*Awareness of the environment is not a special project to be undertaken
only when warning of change becomes deafening . . .*
Kenneth R. Andrews

—

Crafting strategy is an analysis-driven exercise, not an activity where managers can succeed by sheer effort and creativity. Judgments about what strategy
to pursue should ideally be grounded in a probing assessment of a company's
external environment and internal situation. Unless a company's strategy is
well-matched to the full range of external and internal situational considerations, its suitability is suspect.

THE ROLE OF SITUATION
ANALYSIS IN STRATEGY-MAKING

While the phrase *situation analysis* tends to conjure up images of collecting
reams of data and developing all sorts of facts and figures, such impressions
don't apply here. From a strategy-making standpoint, *the purpose of situation
analysis is to determine the features in a company's internal/external environment
that will most directly affect its strategic options and opportunities.* The effort concentrates on generating solid answers to a well-defined set of strategic questions, then using these answers first to form an understandable picture of the
company's strategic situation and second to identify what its realistic strategic
options are.

In studying the methods of strategic situation analysis, it is customary to
begin with single-business companies instead of diversified enterprises. This
is because strategic analysis of diversified companies draws on many of the

concepts and techniques used in evaluating the strategic situations of single-business companies. In single-business strategic analysis, the two biggest situational considerations are (1) industry and competitive conditions (the heart of a single-business company's "external environment") and (2) the company's own internal situation and competitive position. This chapter examines the techniques of _industry and competitive analysis, the terms used to refer to external situation analysis of a single-business company._ Chapter 4 covers the tools of _company situation analysis._ Industry and competitive analysis looks broadly at a company's _macroenvironment_; company situation analysis examines the narrower field of its _microenvironment._

Figure 3–1 presents the external-internal framework of strategic situation analysis for a single-business company. It indicates both the analytical steps involved and the connection to developing business strategy. Note the logical flow from analysis of the company's external and internal situation to evaluation of alternatives to choice of strategy. Also note that situation analysis is the starting point in the process. Indeed, as we shall see in the rest of this chapter and in Chapter 4, managers must understand a company's macro- and microenvironments to do a good job of establishing a mission, setting objectives, and crafting business strategy. The three criteria for deciding whether a strategy is "good" are whether it fits the situation, whether it helps build competitive advantage, and whether it is likely to boost company performance.

Analysis of industry and competitive conditions is the starting point in evaluating a company's strategic situation and market position.

THE METHODS OF INDUSTRY AND COMPETITIVE ANALYSIS

Industries differ widely in their economic characteristics, competitive situations, and future outlooks. The pace of technological change can range from fast to slow. Capital requirements can be big or small. The market can be worldwide or local. Sellers' products can be standardized or highly differentiated. Competitive forces can be strong or weak and can center on price, quality, service, or other variables. Buyer demand can be rising briskly or declining. Industry conditions differ so much that leading companies in unattractive industries can find it hard to earn respectable profits, while even weak companies in attractive industries can turn in good performances.

Industry and competitive analysis utilizes a toolkit of concepts and techniques to get a clear fix on changing industry conditions and on the nature and strength of competitive forces. It is a way of thinking strategically about an industry's overall situation and drawing conclusions about whether the industry is an attractive investment for company funds. The framework for industry and competitive analysis hangs on developing probing answers to seven questions:

1. What are the chief economic characteristics of the industry?
2. What factors are driving change in the industry, and what impact will they have?
3. What competitive forces are at work in the industry, and how strong are they?
4. Which companies are in the strongest/weakest competitive positions?
5. Who will likely make what competitive moves next?

There are seven questions to ask in thinking strategically about market conditions in a given industry.

FIGURE 3–1   From Situation Analysis to Strategic Choices

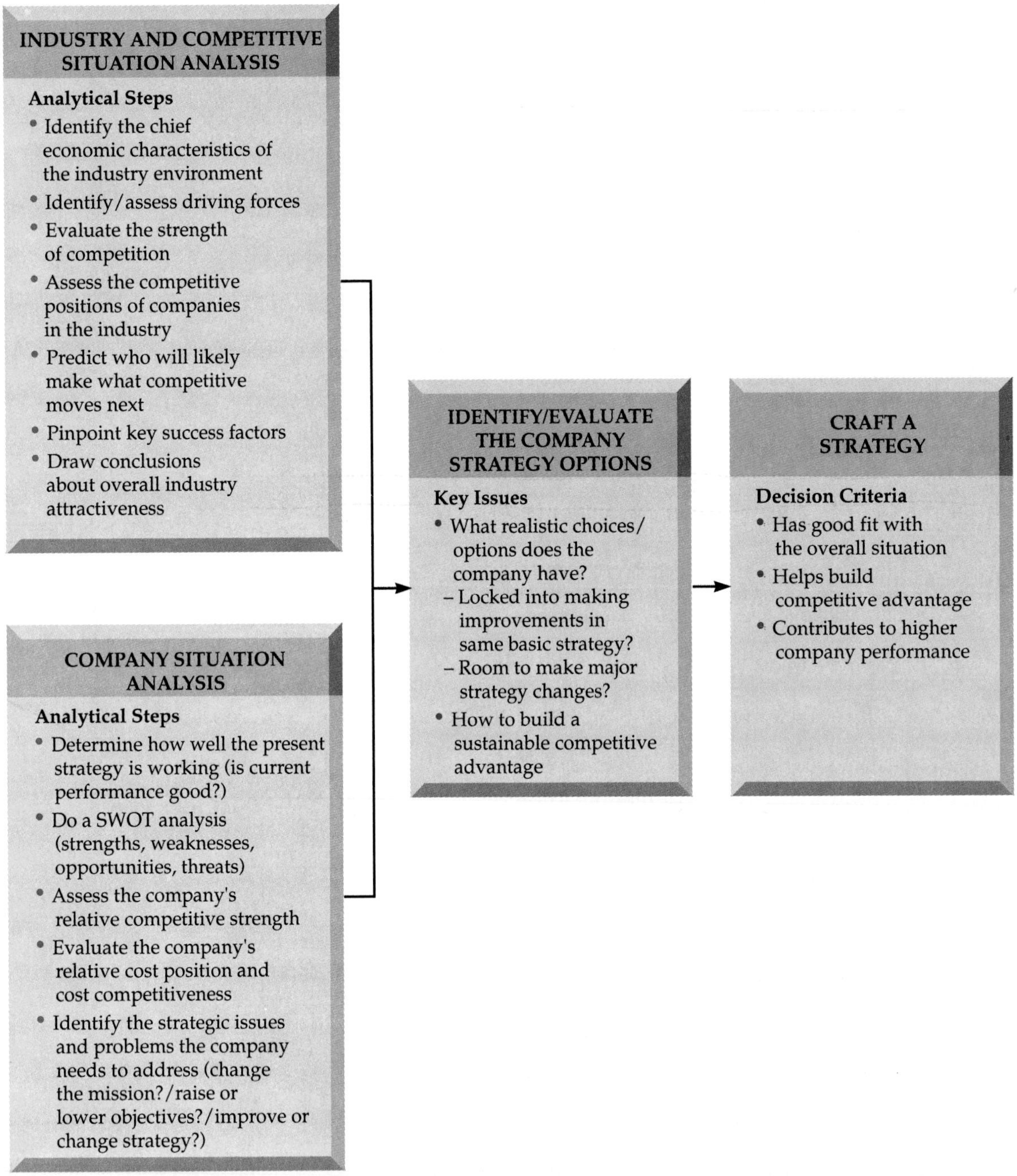

INDUSTRY AND COMPETITIVE SITUATION ANALYSIS

Analytical Steps
- Identify the chief economic characteristics of the industry environment
- Identify/assess driving forces
- Evaluate the strength of competition
- Assess the competitive positions of companies in the industry
- Predict who will likely make what competitive moves next
- Pinpoint key success factors
- Draw conclusions about overall industry attractiveness

COMPANY SITUATION ANALYSIS

Analytical Steps
- Determine how well the present strategy is working (is current performance good?)
- Do a SWOT analysis (strengths, weaknesses, opportunities, threats)
- Assess the company's relative competitive strength
- Evaluate the company's relative cost position and cost competitiveness
- Identify the strategic issues and problems the company needs to address (change the mission?/raise or lower objectives?/improve or change strategy?)

IDENTIFY/EVALUATE THE COMPANY STRATEGY OPTIONS

Key Issues
- What realistic choices/ options does the company have?
  - Locked into making improvements in same basic strategy?
  - Room to make major strategy changes?
- How to build a sustainable competitive advantage

CRAFT A STRATEGY

Decision Criteria
- Has good fit with the overall situation
- Helps build competitive advantage
- Contributes to higher company performance

6. What key factors will determine competitive success or failure?
7. How attractive is the industry in terms of its prospects for above-average profitability?

The collective answers to these questions build understanding of a firm's surrounding environment and form the basis for matching strategy to changing industry conditions and to competitive forces. Let's see what each question involves and consider some concepts and techniques that help managers answer them.

Identifying the Industry's Dominant Economic Characteristics

Because industries differ significantly in their basic character and structure, industry and competitive analysis begins with an overview of the industry's dominant economic traits. As a working definition, we use the word _industry_ to mean a group of firms whose products have so many of the same attributes that they compete for the same buyers. The factors to consider in profiling an industry's economic features are fairly standard:

- Market size.
- Scope of competitive rivalry (local, regional, national, or global).
- Market growth rate and where the industry is in the growth cycle (early development, rapid growth and takeoff, early maturity, late maturity and saturation, stagnant and aging, decline and decay).
- Number of rivals and their relative sizes—is the industry fragmented with many small companies or concentrated and dominated by a few large companies?
- The number of buyers and their relative sizes.
- The prevalence of backward and forward integration.
- Ease of entry and exit.
- The pace of technological change in both production processes and new product introductions.
- Whether the product(s)/service(s) of rival firms are highly differentiated, weakly differentiated, or essentially identical.
- Whether there are economies of scale in manufacturing, transportation, or mass marketing.
- Whether high rates of capacity utilization are crucial to achieving low-cost production efficiency.
- Whether the industry has a strong learning and experience curve such that average unit cost declines as _cumulative_ output (and thus the experience of "learning by doing") builds up.
- Capital requirements.
- Whether industry profitability is above/below par.

Table 3–1 illustrates a profile of an industry's chief economic characteristics.

An industry's economic characteristics are important because of the implications they have for strategy. For example, in capital-intensive industries, where investment in a single plant can run several hundred million dollars, a firm can ease the resulting burden of high fixed costs by pursuing a strategy

An industry's economic characteristics have important implications for crafting an effective strategy.

TABLE 3–1   **A Sample Profile of an Industry's Dominant Economic Characteristics**

Market Size: $400–$500 million annual revenues; 4 million tons, total volume.

Scope of Competitive Rivalry: Primarily regional; producers rarely sell outside a 250-mile radius of plant due to high cost of shipping long distances.

Market Growth Rate: 2–3 percent annually.

Stage in Life Cycle: Mature.

Number of Companies in Industry: About 30 companies with 110 plant locations and capacity of 4.5 million tons. Market shares range from a low of 3 percent to a high of 21 percent.

Customers: About 2,000 buyers; most are industrial chemical firms.

Degree of Vertical Integration: Mixed; 5 of the 10 largest companies are integrated backward into mining operations and also forward in that sister industrial chemical divisions buy over 50 percent of the output of their plants; all other companies are engaged solely in manufacturing.

Ease of Entry/Exit: Moderate entry barriers exist in the form of capital requirements to construct a new plant of minimum efficient size (cost equals $10 million) and ability to build a customer base inside a 250-mile radius of plant.

Technology/Innovation: Production technology is standard and changes have been slow; biggest changes are occurring in products—about 1–2 newly formulated specialty chemicals products are being introduced annually, accounting for nearly all of industry growth.

Product Characteristics: Highly standardized; the brands of different producers are essentially identical (buyers perceive little real difference from seller to seller).

Scale Economies: Moderate; all companies have virtually equal manufacturing costs but scale economies exist in shipping in multiple carloads to same customer and in purchasing large quantities of raw materials.

Experience Curve Effects: Not a factor in this industry.

Capacity Utilization: Manufacturing efficiency is highest between 90–100 percent of rated capacity; below 90 percent utilization, unit costs run significantly higher.

Industry Profitability: Subpar to average; the commodity nature of the industry's product results in intense price-cutting when demand slackens, but prices firm up during periods of strong demand. Profits track the strength of demand for the industry's products.

that promotes high utilization of fixed assets and generates more revenue per dollar of fixed-asset investment. Thus commercial airlines employ strategies to boost the revenue productivity of their expensive jet aircraft fleets by cutting ground time at airport gates (to get in more flights per day with the same plane) and by discounting fares to fill up otherwise empty seats on each flight. In industries characterized by one product advance after another, companies are driven to invest enough time and money in R&D to keep their technical skills and innovative capability abreast of competitors—a strategy of continuous product innovation becomes a condition of survival.

In industries like semiconductors, the presence of a *learning/experience* curve effect in manufacturing causes unit costs to decline about 20 percent each time *cumulative* production volume doubles. With a 20 percent experience curve effect, if the first 1 million chips cost $1 each, by a production volume of 2 million the unit cost would be $.80 (80 percent of $1); by a production volume of 4 million the unit cost would be $.64 (80 percent of $0.80); and so on. When an industry is characterized by a strong experience curve effect in its manufacturing operations, a company that moves first to initiate production of a new-style product and develops a strategy to capture the largest market share can

Basic Concept
When a strong learning/ experience curve effect causes unit costs to decline as production volume builds, a high-volume manufacturer can have the competitive advantage of being the industry's lowest-cost producer.

F I G U R E 3–2　　**Comparison of Experience Curve Effects for 10 Percent, 20 Percent, and 30 Percent Cost Reductions for Each Doubling of Cumulative Production Volume**

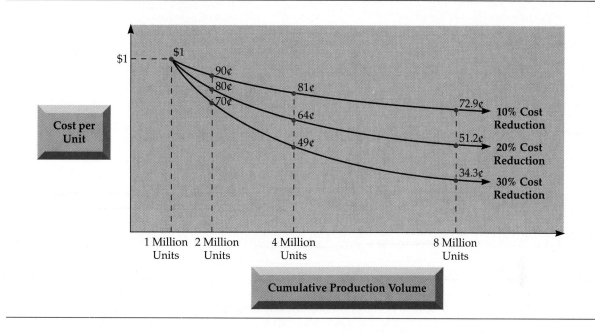

win the competitive advantage of being the low-cost producer. The bigger the experience curve effect, the bigger the cost advantage of the company with the largest *cumulative* production volume, as shown in Figure 3–2.

Table 3–2 presents some additional examples of how an industry's economic characteristics can be relevant to managerial strategy-making.

The Concept of Driving Forces: Why Industries Change

An industry's economic features say a lot about the basic nature of the industry environment but very little about the ways in which the environment may be changing. All industries are characterized by trends and new developments that, either gradually or speedily, produce changes important enough to require a strategic response from participating firms. The popular hypothesis about industries going through evolutionary growth phases or life-cycle stages helps explain why industry conditions change but is still incomplete.[1] The life-cycle stages are strongly keyed to the overall industry growth rate (which is why stages are described with such terms as rapid growth, early maturity, saturation, and decline). Yet there are more causes of industry and competitive change than moving to a new position on the growth curve.

Basic Concept
Industry conditions change because important forces are driving industry participants (competitors, customers, suppliers) to alter their actions; the driving forces in an industry are the major underlying causes of changing industry and competitive conditions.

---

[1]For a more extended discussion of the problems with the life-cycle hypothesis, see Michael E. Porter, *Competitive Strategy: Techniques for Analyzing Industries and Competitors* (New York: Free Press, 1980), pp. 157–62.

T A B L E 3–2   **Examples of the Strategic Importance of an Industry's Key Economic Characteristics**

Factor/Characteristic	Strategic Importance
• Market size	• Small markets don't tend to attract big/new competitors; large markets often draw the interest of corporations looking to acquire companies with established competitive positions in attractive industries.
• Market growth rate	• Fast growth breeds new entry; growth slowdowns spawn increased rivalry and a shakeout of weak competitors.
• Capacity surpluses or shortages	• Surpluses push prices and profit margins down; shortages pull them up.
• Industry profitability	• High-profit industries attract new entrants; depressed conditions encourage exit.
• Entry/exit barriers	• High barriers protect positions and profits of existing firms; low barriers make existing firms vulnerable to entry.
• Product is a big-ticket item for buyers	• More buyers will shop for lowest price.
• Standardized products	• Buyers have more power because it is easier to switch from seller to seller.
• Rapid technological change	• Raises risk factor; investments in technology facilities/equipment may become obsolete before they wear out.
• Capital requirements	• Big requirements make investment decisions critical; timing becomes important; creates a barrier to entry and exit.
• Vertical integration	• Raises capital requirements; often creates competitive differences and cost differences among fully versus partially versus nonintegrated firms.
• Economies of scale	• Increases volume and market share needed to be cost competitive.
• Rapid product innovation	• Shortens product life cycle; increases risk because of opportunities for leapfrogging.

While it is important to judge what growth stage an industry is in, there's more analytical value in identifying the specific factors causing industry change. Industry conditions change *because forces are in motion that create incentives or pressures for change*.[2] The most dominant forces are called *driving forces* because they have the biggest influences on what kinds of changes will take place in the industry's structure and environment. Driving forces analysis has two steps: (1) identifying what the driving forces are and (2) assessing the impact they will have on the industry.

Several different factors can affect an industry powerfully enough to act as driving forces.

The Most Common Driving Forces   Many events affect an industry powerfully enough to qualify as driving forces. Some are one-of-a-kind, but most fall into one of several basic categories. The most common driving forces are shown here.[3]

- **Changes in the Long-Term Industry Growth Rate.** Shifts in industry growth up or down are a force for industry change because they affect the balance between industry supply and buyer demand, entry and exit, and how hard it will be for a firm to capture additional sales. A strong upsurge in long-term demand frequently attracts new firms and encourages

---

[2]Ibid., p. 162.
[3]What follows draws on the discussion in Porter, *Competitive Strategy*, pp. 164–83.

established ones to invest in additional capacity. In a shrinking market, some firms will exit the industry, and the remaining ones may postpone further capacity investments.

- **Changes in Who Buys the Product and How They Use It.** Shifts in buyer demographics and the emergences of new ways to use the product can force adjustments in customer service offerings (credit, technical assistance, maintenance and repair), open the way to market the industry's product through a different mix of dealers and retail outlets, prompt producers to broaden/narrow their product lines, increase/decrease capital requirements, and change sales and promotion approaches. The computer industry has been transformed by the surge of interest in personal and mid-size computers. Consumer interest in cordless telephones and mobile telephones has opened a major new buyer segment for telephone equipment manufacturers.

- **Product Innovation.** Product innovation can broaden an industry's customer base, rejuvenate industry growth, and widen the degree of product differentiation among rival sellers. Successful new product introductions strengthen a company's position, usually at the expense of companies who stick with their old products or are slow to follow with their own versions of the new product. Industries where product innovation has been a key driving force include copying equipment, cameras and photographic equipment, computers, electronic video games, toys, prescription drugs, frozen foods, and personal computer software.

- **Technological Change.** Advances in technology can dramatically alter an industry's landscape, making it possible to produce new and/or better products at a lower cost and opening up whole new industry frontiers. Technological change can also change in capital requirements, minimum efficient plant sizes, and desirability of vertical integration, and learning or experience curve effects.

- **Marketing Innovation.** When firms are successful in introducing new ways to market their products, they can spark a burst of buyer interest, widen industry demand, increase product differentiation, and/or lower unit costs—any or all of which can alter the competitive positions of rival firms and force strategy revisions.

- **Entry or Exit of Major Firms.** The entry of one or more foreign companies into a market once dominated by domestic firms nearly always produces a big shakeup in industry conditions. Likewise, when an established domestic firm in another industry attempts entry either by acquisition or by launching its own startup venture, it usually intends to apply its skills and resources in some innovative fashion. Entry by a major firm often produces a "new ballgame" not only with new key players but also with new rules for competing. Similarly, exit of a major firm changes industry structure by reducing the number of market leaders (perhaps increasing the dominance of the leaders who remain) and causing a rush to capture the exiting firm's customers.

- **Diffusion of Technical Know-How.** As knowledge about how to perform a particular activity or to execute a particular manufacturing technology spreads, any technically-based competitive advantage held by firms possessing this know-how erodes. Diffusion of technical know-how occurs through scientific journals, trade publications, on-site plant tours, word-of-mouth among suppliers and customers, and the hiring away of knowledgeable employees. It can also occur when the possessors of technological know-how license others to use it for a fee or team up with a company interested in turning the technology into a new business venture. Often companies acquire technical know-how by buying a company with the desired skills, patents, or manufacturing capabilities. In recent years technology transfer across national boundaries has emerged as one of the most important driving forces in globalizing markets and competition. As companies in more countries gain access to technical know-how, they upgrade their manufacturing capabilities to compete with established companies. Technology transfer has turned many domestic industries into global ones (e.g., automobiles, tires, consumer electronics, telecommunications, and computers).

- **Increasing Globalization of the Industry.** Global competition usually changes patterns of competitive advantage among key players. Industries move toward globalization for several reasons. Certain firms may launch aggressive long-term strategies to win a globally dominant market position. Demand for the industry's product may emerge in more countries. Trade barriers may drop. Technology-transfer may open the door for more companies in more countries to enter the industry on a major scale. Significant labor cost differences among countries may create a strong reason to locate plants for labor-intensive products in low-wage countries (wages in South Korea, Taiwan, and Singapore, for example, are about one-fourth those in the United States). Significant cost economies may accrue to firms with world-scale volumes as opposed to national-scale volumes. The growing ability of multinational companies to transfer their production, marketing, and management know-how from country to country at significantly lower cost than companies with a one-country production base may give multinational competitors a significant competitive advantage over domestic-only competitors. Globalization is most likely to be a driving force in industries (a) based on natural resources (supplies of crude oil, copper, and cotton, for example, are geographically scattered all over the globe), (b) where low-cost production is a critical consideration (making it imperative to locate plant facilities in countries where the lowest costs can be achieved), and (c) where one or more growth-oriented, market-seeking companies are pushing hard to gain a significant competitive position in as many attractive country markets as they can.

- **Changes in Cost and Efficiency.** In industries where significant economies of scale are emerging or strong learning curve effects are allowing firms with the most production experience to undercut rivals' prices, large market share becomes such a distinct advantage that all firms are pressured to adopt volume-building strategies—a "race for growth" dominates the industry. Likewise, sharply rising costs for a key input (either raw materials or labor) can cause a scramble to either (a) line up reliable supplies at affordable prices or (b) search out lower-cost substitutes. Any time important changes in cost or efficiency take place, firms' positions can change radically concerning who has how big a cost advantage.

- **Emerging Buyer Preferences for a Differentiated Instead of a Commodity Product (or for a more standardized product instead of strongly differentiated products).** Sometimes growing numbers of buyers decide that a standard product at a bargain price meets their needs as effectively as premium priced brands offering more features and options. These swings in buyer demand can drive industry change by shifting patronage to sellers of cheaper commodity products and creating a price-competitive market environment. Such a development may so dominate the market that industry producers can't do much more than compete hard on price. On the other hand, a shift away from standardized products occurs when sellers are able to win a bigger and more loyal buyer following by introducing new features, making style changes, offering options and accessories, and creating image differences via advertising and packaging. Then the driver of change is the struggle among rivals to out-differentiate one another. Industries evolve differently depending on whether the forces in motion are acting to increase or decrease the emphasis on product differentiation.

- **Regulatory Influences and Government Policy Changes.** Regulatory and governmental actions can often force significant changes in industry practices and strategic approaches. Deregulation has been a major driving force in the airline, banking, natural gas, and telecommunications industries. Drunk driving laws and drinking age legislation recently became driving forces in the alcoholic beverage industry. In international markets, newly-enacted regulations of host governments to open up their domestic markets to foreign participation or to close off foreign participation to protect domestic companies are a major factor in shaping whether the competitive struggle between foreign and domestic companies occurs on a level playing field or whether it is one-sided (owing to government favoritism).

- **Changing Societal Concerns, Attitudes, and Lifestyles.** Emerging social issues and changing attitudes and lifestyles can be powerful instigators of industry change. Consumer concerns about salt, sugar, chemical additives, cholesterol, and nutrition are forcing the food industry to reexamine food processing techniques, redirect R&D efforts, and introduce healthier products. Safety concerns are driving change in the automobile, toy, and outdoor power equipment industries. Increased interest in physical fitness is producing whole new industries to supply exercise equipment, jogging clothes and shoes, and medically supervised diet programs. Social concerns about air and water pollution are affecting industries that discharge waste products. Growing antismoking sentiment is posing a major long-term threat to the cigarette industry.

- **Reductions in Uncertainty and Business Risk.** A young, emerging industry is typically characterized by an unproven cost structure and much uncertainty over potential market size, R&D costs, and distribution channels. Emerging industries tend to attract only the most entrepreneurial companies. Over time, however, if pioneering firms succeed and uncertainty about the industry's viability fades, more conservative firms are usually enticed to enter the industry. Often, the entrants are larger, financially-strong firms hunting for attractive growth industries. In international markets, conservatism is prevalent in the early stages of globalization. Firms tend to minimize their risk by relying initially on exporting, licensing, and joint ventures. Then, as their experience accumulates and as perceived risk levels decline, companies move more quickly and aggressively to form wholly owned subsidiaries and to pursue full-scale, multicountry competitive strategies.

The foregoing list of *potential* driving forces in an industry indicates why it is too simplistic to view industry change only in terms of moving from one growth stage to another and why it is essential to probe for the *causes* underlying the emergence of new industry conditions.

The task of driving forces analysis is to separate the major causes of changing industry conditions from minor ones; usually no more than three or four factors qualify as driving forces.

However, while *many* forces of change may be at work in an industry, no more than three or four are likely to be *driving* forces in the sense that they act as *the major determinants* of how the industry evolves and operates. Strategic analysts must resist the temptation to label everything they see changing as driving forces; the analytical task is to evaluate the forces of industry change carefully enough to separate major factors from minor ones.

Analyzing driving forces has practical strategy-making value. First, the driving forces in an industry indicate to managers what external factors will have the greatest effect on the company's business over the next one to three years. Second, to position the company to deal with these forces, managers must assess the implications and consequences of each driving force—that is, they must project what impact the driving forces will have on the industry. Third, strategy-makers need to craft a strategy that is responsive to the driving forces and their effects on the industry.

Basic Concept
Strategists use environmental scanning to spot budding trends and developments that could emerge as new driving forces.

Environmental Scanning Techniques   One way to predict future driving forces is to utilize environmental scanning techniques. *Environmental scanning* involves studying and interpreting social, political, economic, ecological, and technological events in an effort to spot budding trends and conditions that could eventually affect the industry. It attempts to look broadly at "first of its kind" happenings, what kinds of new ideas and approaches are catching on, and extrapolate their possible implications 5 to 20 years into the future. For example, environmental scanning could involve judgments about the demand for energy in the year 2000, uses for computers 20 years from now, or the condition of forests in the 21st century given the growing demand for paper. Environmental scanning raises managers' awareness of potential developments that could have an important impact on industry conditions and pose new opportunities and threats.

Environmental scanning can be accomplished by systematically monitoring and studying current events, constructing scenarios, and employing the Delphi method (a technique for finding consensus among a group of "knowledgeable experts"). Although highly qualitative and subjective, environmental scanning helps managers lengthen their planning horizon, translate vague inklings into clearer strategic issues (for which they can begin to develop a strategic answer), and think strategically about future developments in the surrounding environment.[4] Companies that undertake formal environmental

---

[4]For further discussion of the nature and use of environmental scanning, see Roy Amara and Andrew J. Lipinski, *Business Planning for an Uncertain Future: Scenarios and Strategies* (New York: Pergamon Press, 1983); Harold E. Klein and Robert U. Linneman, "Environmental Assessment: An International Study of Corporate Practice," *Journal of Business Strategy* 5, no. 1 (Summer 1984), pp. 55–75; and Arnoldo C. Hax and Nicolas S. Majluf, *The Strategy Concept and Process* (Englewood Cliffs, N.J.: Prentice Hall, 1991), chaps. 5 and 8.

scanning include General Electric, AT&T, Coca-Cola, Ford, General Motors, Du Pont, and Shell Oil.

Analyzing the Strength of Competitive Forces

One of the big cornerstones of industry and competitive analysis involves carefully studying the industry's competitive process to discover the main sources of competitive pressure and how strong they are. This analytical step is essential because managers cannot devise a successful strategy without understanding the industry's special competitive character.

Even though competitive pressures differ in different industries, competition itself works similarly enough to use a common framework in gauging its nature and intensity. As a rule, *competition in an industry is a composite of five competitive forces*:

1. The rivalry among competing sellers in the industry.
2. The market attempts of companies in other industries to win customers to their own *substitute* products.
3. The potential entry of new competitors.
4. The bargaining power and leverage exercisable by suppliers of key raw materials and components.
5. The bargaining power and leverage exercisable by buyers of the product.

The *five-forces model*, as diagrammed in Figure 3–3, is extremely helpful in systematically diagnosing the principal competitive pressures in a market and assessing how strong and important each one is.[5] Not only is it the most widely used technique of competition analysis, but it is also straightforward to use.

The Rivalry among Competing Sellers   The most powerful of the five competitive forces is *usually* the competitive battle among rival firms.[6] How vigorously sellers use the competitive weapons at their disposal to jockey for a stronger market position and win a competitive edge over rivals shows the strength of this competitive force. *Competitive strategy is the narrower portion of business strategy dealing with a company's competitive approaches for achieving market success, its offensive moves to secure a competitive edge over rival firms, and its defensive moves to protect its competitive position.*[7]

The challenge in crafting a winning competitive strategy, of course, is *how to gain an edge over rivals*. The big complication is that the success of any one firm's strategy hinges on what strategies its rivals employ and the resources rivals

> **Basic Concept**
> *Competitive strategy is the part of business strategy that deals with management's plan for competing successfully— how to build sustainable competitive advantage, how to outmaneuver rivals, how to defend against competitive pressures, and how to strengthen the firm's market position.*

---

[5]For a thorough treatment of the five-forces model by its originator, see Porter, *Competitive Strategy*, chap. 1.

[6]Parts of this section are based on the discussion in Arthur A. Thompson, "Competition as a Strategic Process," *Antitrust Bulletin* 25, no. 4 (Winter 1980), pp. 777–803.

[7]The distinction between *competitive strategy* and *business strategy* is useful here. As we defined it in Chapter 2, business strategy not only addresses the issue of how to compete, it also embraces all of the functional area support strategies, how management plans to respond to changing industry conditions of all kinds (not just those that are competition-related), and how management intends to address the full range of strategic issues. Competitive strategy, however, is narrower in scope. It focuses on the firm's competitive approach, the competitive edge strived for, and specific moves to outmaneuver rival companies.

F I G U R E 3–3   The "Five-Forces" Model of Competition: A Key Analytical Tool

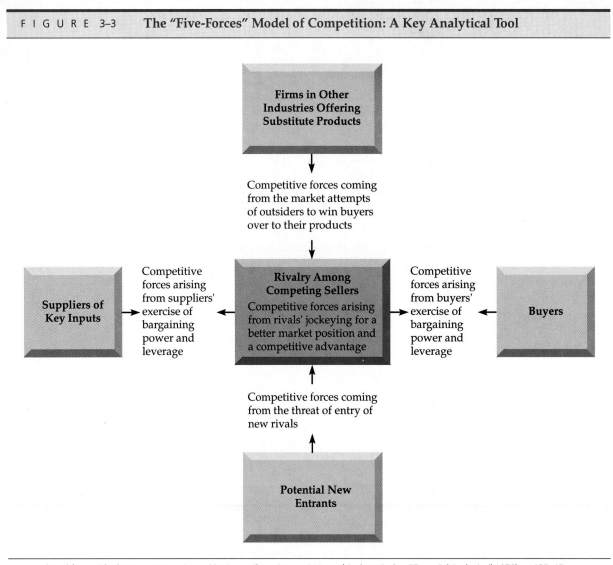

Source: Adapted from Michael E. Porter, "How Competitive Forces Shape Strategy," *Harvard Business Review* 57, no. 2 (March–April 1979), pp. 137–45.

Principle of Competitive Markets

Competitive jockeying among rivals is ever-changing as firms initiate new offensive and defensive moves and as emphasis swings from one mix of competitive weapons to another.

are willing and able to put behind their strategies. The "best" strategy for one firm in maneuvering for competitive advantage depends on the competitive strength and strategies of its rivals. Whenever one firm makes a strategic move, rivals often retaliate with offensive or defensive countermoves. Thus, competitive rivalry turns into a game of strategy, of move and countermove, played under "warlike" conditions according to the rules of business competition—in effect, *competitive markets are economic battlefields.*

Competitive battles among rival sellers can assume many forms and degrees of intensity. The weapons used for competing include price, quality, features, services, warranties and guarantees, advertising, better networks of wholesale distributors and retail dealers, innovation, and so on. The relative dependence that competitors place on each of these weapons can change over time, as first one then another is used more extensively to catch buyers' attention and as competitors initiate fresh offensive and defensive moves. Rivalry is thus dynamic; current conditions are always being modified as companies initiate new moves and countermoves and as the competitive emphasis swings from one weapons mix to another. Two principles of competitive rivalry are particularly important: (1) a powerful competitive strategy used by one company intensifies competitive pressures on the other companies, and (2) the manner in which rivals employ various competitive weapons to try to outmaneuver one another shapes "the rules of competition" in the industry and determines the requirements for competitive success.

Once an industry's rules of competition are understood, then judgments can be made regarding whether competitive rivalry is cutthroat, intense, normal to moderate, or attractively weak. There are several factors that, industry after industry, influence the *strength* of rivalry among competing sellers:[8]

There are many reasons why the rivalry among competing sellers can grow stronger or weaker.

1. *Rivalry tends to intensify as the number of competitors increases and as they become more equal in size and capability.* Up to a point, the greater the number of competitors the greater the probability of fresh, creative strategic initiatives. In addition, when rivals are more equal in size and capability, they compete on a fairly even footing, making it harder for one or two firms to "win" the competitive battle and dominate the market.

2. *Rivalry is usually stronger when demand for the product is growing slowly.* In a rapidly expanding market, there tends to be enough business for everybody to grow. Indeed, it may take all of a firm's financial and managerial resources just to keep pace with buyer demand, much less steal rivals' customers. But when growth slows or when market demand drops unexpectedly, expansion-minded firms and/or firms with excess capacity often cut prices and use other sales-increasing tactics. The ensuing battle for market share can result in a shake out of the weak and less-efficient firms. The industry then "consolidates" into a smaller, but individually stronger, group of sellers.

3. *Rivalry is more intense when industry conditions tempt competitors to use price cuts or other competitive weapons to boost unit volume.* Whenever fixed costs account for a large fraction of total cost, unit costs tend to be lowest at or near full capacity since fixed costs can be spread over more units of production. Unused capacity thus imposes a significant cost-increasing penalty because there are fewer units to carry the fixed cost burden. In such cases, if market demand weakens and capacity utilization begins to fall off, the pressure of rising unit costs pushes firms into secret price concessions, special discounts, rebates, and other sales-increasing tactics, thus heightening competition. Likewise, when a product is perishable, seasonal, or costly to inventory, competitive pressures build quickly anytime one or more competitors decides to dump its excess supplies on the market.

4. *Rivalry is stronger when the costs incurred by customers to switch their purchases from one brand to another are low.* The lower the costs of switching, the easier it is for rival sellers to raid one another's

---

[8]These indicators of what to look for in evaluating the intensity of interfirm rivalry are based on Porter, *Competitive Strategy*, pp. 17–21.

customers. On the other hand, high switching costs give a seller some protection against the efforts of rivals to raid its customers.

5. *Rivalry is stronger when one or more competitors is dissatisfied with its market position and launches moves to bolster its standing at the expense of rivals.* Firms that are losing ground or find themselves in financial trouble often take such aggressive actions as acquiring smaller rivals, introducing new products, increasing advertising, promoting special prices, and so on. Such actions can trigger a new round of competitive maneuvering and a heightened battle for market share.

6. *Rivalry increases in proportion to the size of the payoff from a successful strategic move.* The greater the potential reward, the more likely some firm will aggressively pursue a strategy to capture it. The size of the strategic payoff depends partly on how fast rivals retaliate. When competitors respond slowly (or not at all), the initiator of a fresh competitive strategy can reap benefits in the intervening period and perhaps gain a first-mover advantage that is not easily surmounted. The greater the benefits of moving first, the more likely some firm will accept the risk and try it.

7. *Rivalry tends to be more vigorous when it costs more to get out of a business than to stay in and compete.* The higher the exit barriers (thus the more costly it is to abandon a market), the stronger the incentive for firms to remain and compete as best they can, even though they may be earning low profits or even incurring a loss.

8. *Rivalry becomes more volatile and unpredictable the more diverse competitors are in terms of their strategies, personalities, corporate priorities, resources, and countries of origin.* A diverse group of sellers is more likely to spawn one or more mavericks willing to rock the boat with unconventional moves and approaches, thus generating a more lively and uncertain competitive environment. The added presence of new, lower-cost foreign-based competitors intent on gaining market share is a surefire factor in boosting the intensity of rivalry.

9. *Rivalry increases when strong companies outside the industry acquire weak firms in the industry and launch aggressive, well-funded moves to transform their newly-acquired firms into major market contenders.* For example, Philip Morris, a leading cigarette firm with excellent marketing know-how, shook up the whole beer industry's marketing approach when it acquired stodgy Miller Brewing Company in the late 1960s. In short order, Philip Morris revamped the marketing plan for Miller High Life and pushed it to the number two best-selling brand. PM also pioneered low-calorie beers with the introduction of Miller Lite—a move that made light beer the fastest-growing segment in the beer industry.

Such jockeying for position among competitors unfolds in round after round of moves and countermoves. The strategist has to identify the current competitive weapons, stay on top of how the game is being played, and judge how much pressure competitive rivalry is going to put on profitability. Competitive rivalry is "intense" when competitors' actions are driving down industry profits; rivalry is "moderate" when most companies can earn acceptable profits; and rivalry is "weak" when most companies in the industry can earn above-average returns on investment. Chronic outbreaks of cutthroat competition make an industry brutally competitive.

The Competitive Force of Potential Entry   New entrants to a market bring new production capacity, the desire to establish a secure place in the market, and sometimes substantial resources with which to compete.[9] How serious the threat of entry is in a particular market depends on two factors: *barriers to entry* and the *expected reaction of incumbent firms to new entry*. A barrier to entry exists whenever it is hard for a newcomer to break into a market and/or economic factors put a potential entrant at a disadvantage relative to its competitors. There are several types of entry barriers:[10]

- **Economies of scale.** Scale economies deter entry because they force potential entrants either to enter on a large-scale basis (a costly and perhaps risky move) or to accept a cost disadvantage (and consequently lower profitability). Firms that do attempt large-scale entry can cause overcapacity problems in the industry and so threaten the market shares of existing firms that they retaliate aggressively (with price cuts, increased advertising and sales promotion, and similar steps) to maintain their position. Either way, a new entrant can expect to earn lower profits. Entrants may encounter scale-related barriers not just in production, but in advertising, marketing and distribution, financing, after-sale customer service, raw materials purchasing, and R&D as well.

- **Inability to gain access to technology and specialized know-how.** Many industries require technological capability and skills not readily available to a new entrant. Key patents can bar entry as can lack of technically skilled personnel and an inability to execute complicated manufacturing techniques. Existing firms often carefully guard know-how that gives them an edge in technology and manufacturing capability. Unless new entrants can gain access to such knowledge, they will lack the technical capability to compete on an equal footing.

- **Learning and experience curve effects.** When lower unit costs are partly or mostly a result of experience and other learning curve benefits, a new entrant is faced with a cost disadvantage in competing against existing firms with more accumulated know-how.

- **Brand preferences and customer loyalty.** Buyers are often attached to existing brands. European consumers, for example, are fiercely loyal to European brands of major household appliances. High brand loyalty means that a potential entrant must be prepared to spend enough money on advertising and sales promotion to overcome customer loyalties and build its own clientele. Substantial time and money can be involved. In addition, if it is difficult or costly for a customer to switch to a new brand, a new entrant must persuade buyers that its brand is worth the switching costs. To overcome the switching cost barrier, new entrants may have to offer buyers a bigger price cut or extra quality or service. All this can

[9]Michael E. Porter, "How Competitive Forces Shape Strategy," *Harvard Business Review* 57, no. 2 (March–April 1979), p. 138.

[10]Porter, *Competitive Strategy*, pp. 7–17.

mean lower profit margins for new entrants—something that increases the risk to startup companies dependent on sizable, early profits to support their new investment.

- **Capital requirements.** The larger the total dollar investment needed to enter the market successfully, the more limited the pool of potential entrants. The most obvious capital requirements are associated with manufacturing plant and equipment, working capital to finance inventories and customer credit, introductory advertising and sales promotion to establish a clientele, and covering startup losses.

- **Cost disadvantages independent of size.** Existing firms may have cost advantages not available to potential entrants regardless of the entrant's size. These advantages can include access to the best and cheapest raw materials, possession of patents and proprietary technological know-how, the benefits of learning and experience curve effects, having built and equipped plants years earlier at lower costs, favorable locations, and lower borrowing costs.

- **Access to distribution channels.** In the case of consumer goods, a potential entrant may face the barrier of gaining adequate access to distribution channels. Wholesale distributors may be reluctant to take on a product that lacks buyer recognition. A network of retail dealers may have to be set up from scratch. Retailers may have to be convinced to give a new brand ample display space and an adequate trial period. The more existing producers have tied up present distribution channels, the tougher entry will be. To overcome this barrier, entrants may have to "buy" distribution access by offering better margins to dealers and distributors or by giving advertising allowances and other promotional incentives. As a consequence, a potential entrant's profits may be squeezed until its product gains such acceptance that distributors and retailers want to carry it.

- **Regulatory policies.** Government agencies can limit or even bar entry by requiring licenses and permits. Regulated industries like banking, insurance, radio and television stations, liquor retailing, and railroads feature government-controlled entry. In international markets, host governments commonly limit foreign entry and must approve all foreign investment applications. Stringent government-mandated safety regulations and environmental pollution standards are entry barriers because they raise entry costs.

- **Tariffs and international trade restrictions.** National governments commonly use tariffs and trade restrictions (antidumping rules, local content requirements, and quotas) to raise entry barriers for foreign firms. In 1988, due to tariffs imposed by the South Korean government, a Ford Taurus cost South Korean car buyers over $40,000. European governments require that certain Asian products, from electronic typewriters to copying machines, contain European-made parts and labor equal to 40 percent of the selling price. And to protect European chipmakers from low-cost Asian competition, European governments instituted a rigid formula to calculate floor prices for computer memory chips.

Even if a potential entrant is willing to tackle the problems of entry barriers, it still faces the issue of how existing firms will react.[11] Will incumbent firms react passively, or will they aggressively defend their market positions with price cuts, increased advertising, product improvements, and whatever else will give a new entrant (as well as other rivals) a hard time? A potential entrant often has second thoughts when incumbents send strong signals that they will stoutly defend their market positions against entry and when they have the financial resources to do so. A potential entrant may also turn away when incumbent firms can use leverage with distributors and customers to keep their business.

The best test of whether potential entry is a strong or weak competitive force is to ask if the industry's growth and profit prospects are attractive enough to induce additional entry. When the answer is no, potential entry is not a source of competitive pressure. When the answer is yes (as in industries where lower-cost foreign competitors are seeking new markets), then potential entry is a strong force. The stronger the threat of entry, the greater the motivation of incumbent firms to fortify their positions against newcomers to make entry more costly or difficult.

One additional point: the threat of entry changes as industry prospects grow brighter or dimmer and as entry barriers rise or fall. For example, the expiration of a key patent can greatly increase the threat of entry. A technological discovery can create an economy of scale and advantage where none existed before. New actions by incumbent firms to increase advertising, strengthen distributor-dealer relations, step up R&D, or improve product quality can erect higher roadblocks to entry. In international markets, entry barriers for foreign-based firms ease when tariffs are lowered; domestic wholesalers and dealers seek out lower-cost foreign-made goods, and domestic buyers become more willing to purchase foreign brands.

The Competitive Force of Substitute Products Firms in one industry are, quite often, in close competition with firms in another industry because their respective products are good substitutes. The producers of eyeglasses compete with the makers of contact lenses. The sugar industry competes with companies that produce artificial sweeteners. The producers of plastic containers confront strong competition from makers of glass bottles and jars, paperboard cartons, and tin and aluminum cans.

The competitive force of substitute products comes into play in several ways. First, the presence of readily available and competitively priced substitutes places a ceiling on the prices companies in an industry can afford to charge without giving customers an incentive to switch to substitutes and thus eroding their own market position.[12] This price ceiling, at the same time, puts a lid on the profits that industry members can earn unless they find ways to cut costs. When substitutes are cheaper than an industry's product, industry members come under heavy competitive pressure to reduce prices and find ways to absorb the price cuts with cost reductions. Second, the availability of substitutes invites customers to compare quality and performance as well as

Principle of Competitive Markets
The competitive threat posed by substitute products is strong when prices of substitutes are attractive, buyers' switching costs are low, and buyers believe substitutes have equal or better features.

---

[11]Porter, "How Competitive Forces Shape Strategy," p. 140; and Porter, *Competitive Strategy*, pp. 14–15.
[12]Ibid., p. 142; and pp. 23–24.

price. For example, firms that buy glass bottles and jars from glassware manufacturers monitor whether they can just as effectively package their products in plastic containers, paper cartons, or tin cans. Because of competitive pressure from substitute products, industry rivals have to convince customers their product is more advantageous than substitutes. Usually this requires devising a competitive strategy to differentiate the industry's product from substitute products via some combination of lower cost, better quality, better service, and more desirable performance features.

Another determinant of whether substitutes are a strong or weak competitive force is whether it is difficult or costly for customers to switch to substitutes.[13] Typical switching costs include employee retraining costs, the costs of purchasing additional equipment, costs for technical help needed to make the changeover, the time and cost to test the quality and reliability of the substitute, and the psychic costs of severing old supplier relationships and establishing new ones. If switching costs are high, sellers of substitutes must offer a major cost or performance benefit to steal the industry's customers. When switching costs are low, it's much easier for the sellers of substitutes to convince buyers to change over to their product.

As a rule, then, the lower the price of substitutes, the higher their quality and performance, and the lower the user's switching costs, the more intense are the competitive pressures posed by substitute products. The best indicators of the competitive strength of substitute products are the rate at which their sales are growing, the market inroads they are making, the plans the sellers of substitutes have for expanding production capacity, and the size of their profits.

Principle of Competitive Markets
The suppliers to an industry are a strong competitive force whenever they have sufficient bargaining power to command a price premium for their materials or components and whenever they can affect the competitive well-being of industry rivals by the reliability of their deliveries or by the quality and performance of the items they supply.

The Power of Suppliers   Whether the suppliers to an industry are a weak or strong competitive force depends on market conditions in the supplier industry and the significance of the item they supply.[14] The competitive force of suppliers is greatly diminished whenever the item they provide is a standard commodity available on the open market from a large number of suppliers with ample ability to fill orders. Then it is relatively simple to multiple-source whatever is needed, choosing to buy from whichever suppliers offer the best deal. In such cases, suppliers can win concessions only when supplies become tight and users are so anxious to secure what they need that they agree to terms more favorable to suppliers. Suppliers are also in a weak bargaining position whenever there are good substitute inputs and switching is neither costly nor difficult. For example, soft drink bottlers check the power of aluminum can suppliers by using plastic containers and glass bottles. Suppliers also have less leverage when the industry they are supplying is a *major* customer. In this case, the well-being of suppliers becomes closely tied to the well-being of their major customers. Suppliers then have a big incentive to protect the customer industry via reasonable prices, improved quality, and new products and services that might enhance their customers' positions, sales, and profits. When industry members form a close working relationship with major suppliers, they may gain substantial benefit in the form of better-quality components, just-in-time deliveries, and reduced inventory costs.

---

[13]Porter, *Competitive Strategy*, p. 10.
[14]Ibid., pp. 27–28.

On the other hand, powerful suppliers can put an industry in a profit squeeze with price increases that can't be fully passed on to the industry's own customers. Suppliers become a strong competitive force when their product makes up a sizable fraction of the costs of an industry's product, is crucial to the industry's production process, and/or significantly affects the quality of the industry's product. Likewise, a supplier (or group of suppliers) gains bargaining leverage the more difficult or costly it is for users to switch suppliers. Big suppliers with good reputations and growing demand for their output are harder to wring concessions from than struggling suppliers striving to broaden their customer base.

Suppliers are also more powerful when they can supply a component cheaper than industry members can make it themselves. For instance, the producers of outdoor power equipment (lawnmowers, rotary tillers, snowblowers, and so on) find it cheaper to buy small engines from outside manufacturers rather than make their own because the quantity they need is too small to justify the investment and master the process. Small-engine manufacturers, by supplying many kinds of engines to the whole power equipment industry, sell enough to capture scale economies, become proficient in the manufacturing techniques, and keep costs well below what power equipment firms would incur on their own. Small engine suppliers can price the item below what it would cost the user to self-manufacture but far enough above their own costs to generate an attractive profit margin. In such situations, suppliers' bargaining position is strong *until* a customer needs enough parts to justify backward integration. Then the balance of power shifts away from the supplier. The more credible the threat of backward integration, the more leverage companies have in negotiating favorable terms with suppliers.

A final instance in which an industry's suppliers play an important competitive role is when suppliers, for one reason or another, do not have the manufacturing capability or a strong enough incentive to provide items of adequate quality. Suppliers who lack the ability or incentive to provide quality parts can seriously damage their customers' business. For example, if auto parts suppliers provide lower-quality components to U.S. automobile manufacturers, they can so increase the warranty and defective goods costs that they seriously impair U.S. auto firms' profits, reputation, and competitive position in world markets.

The Power of Buyers　Just as with suppliers, the competitive strength of buyers can range from strong to weak. Buyers have substantial bargaining leverage in a number of situations.[15] The most obvious is when buyers are large and purchase a sizable percentage of the industry's output. The bigger buyers are and the larger the quantities they purchase, the more clout they have in negotiating with sellers. Often, large buyers successfully leverage their size and volume purchases to obtain price concessions and other favorable terms. Buyers also gain power when the cost of switching to competing brands or substitutes is relatively low. Any time buyers can meet their needs by sourcing from several sellers, they have added room to negotiate. When sellers' products are virtually identical, buyers can switch with little or no cost. However, if sellers'

> **Principle of Competitive Markets**
> *Buyers become a stronger competitive force the more they are able to exercise bargaining leverage over price, quality, service, or other terms of conditions of sale.*

---

[15]Ibid., pp. 24–27.

products are strongly differentiated, buyers are less able to switch without incurring sizable switching costs.

One last point: all buyers don't have equal bargaining power with sellers; some may be less sensitive than others to price, quality, or service. For example, in the apparel industry, major manufacturers confront significant customer power when they sell to retail chains like Sears or Kmart. But they can get much better prices selling to small owner-managed boutiques.

Competitive Strategy Principle

A company's competitive strategy is increasingly effective the more it provides good defenses against the five competitive forces, influences the industry's competitive rules in the company's favor, and helps create sustainable competitive advantage.

Strategic Implications of the Five Competitive Forces   The contribution of Figure 3–3 is the assist it provides in exposing the makeup of competitive forces. *To analyze the competitive environment, the strength of each one of the five competitive forces must be assessed.* The collective impact of these forces determines what competition is like in a given market. As a rule, the stronger competitive forces are, the lower the collective profitability of participating firms. The most brutally competitive situation occurs when the five forces are tough enough to cause prolonged subpar profitability or even losses for most or all firms. The competitive structure of an industry is clearly "unattractive" from a profit-making standpoint if rivalry among sellers is very strong, entry barriers are low, competition from substitutes is strong, and both suppliers and customers have considerable bargaining leverage. On the other hand, when an industry offers superior long-term profit prospects, competitive forces are not unduly strong and the competitive structure of the industry is "favorable" and "attractive." The "ideal" competitive environment from a profit-making perspective is one in which both suppliers and customers are in a weak bargaining position, there are no good substitutes, entry barriers are relatively high, and rivalry among present sellers is only moderate. However, even where some of the five competitive forces are strong, an industry can be competitively attractive to those firms whose market position and strategy provide a good enough defense against competitive pressures to preserve their competitive advantage and retain an ability to earn above-average profits.

In coping with competitive forces, successful strategists craft competitive approaches that will (1) insulate the firm as much as possible from the five competitive forces, (2) influence the industry's competitive rules in the company's favor, and (3) provide a strong, secure position of advantage from which to "play the game" of competition as it unfolds in the industry. Strategists cannot do this task well without first perceptively analyzing the whole competitive picture of the industry via the five forces model.

Assessing the Competitive Positions of Rival Companies

Strategic group mapping is a technique for displaying the different competitive positions that rival firms occupy in an industry.

The next step in examining the industry's competitive structure is studying the market positions of rival companies. One technique for comparing the competitive positions of industry participants is *strategic group mapping*.[16] This analytical tool bridges the gap between looking at the industry as a whole and considering the standing of each firm separately. It is most useful when an industry has too many competitors to examine each one in depth.

---

[16]Ibid., chap. 7.

A strategic group consists of those rival firms with similar competitive approaches and positions in the market.[17] Companies in the same strategic group can resemble one another in several ways: they may have comparable product lines, be vertically integrated to the same degree, offer buyers similar services and technical assistance, appeal to similar types of buyers with the same product attributes, emphasize the same distribution channels, depend on identical technology, and/or sell in the same price/quality range. An industry has only one strategic group if all sellers use essentially identical strategies. At the other extreme, there are as many strategic groups as there are competitors if each one pursues a distinctively different competitive approach and occupies a substantially different position in the marketplace.

To construct a strategic group map, analysts need to:

1. Identify the competitive characteristics that differentiate firms in the industry—typical variables are price/quality range (high, medium, low), geographic coverage (local, regional, national, global), degree of vertical integration (none, partial, full), product-line breadth (wide, narrow), use of distribution channels (one, some, all), and degree of service offered (no frills, limited, full service).

2. Plot the firms on a two-variable map using pairs of these differentiating characteristics.

3. Assign firms that fall in about the same strategy space to the same strategic group.

4. Draw circles around each strategic group, making the circles proportional to the size of the group's respective share of total industry sales revenues.

This produces a two-dimensional *strategic group map* such as the one for the beer industry shown in Illustration Capsule 10.

To map the positions of strategic groups accurately in the industry's overall "strategy space," several guidelines must be observed.[18] First, the two variables selected as axes for the map should *not* be highly correlated; if they are, the circles on the map will fall along a diagonal and analysts will learn nothing more than they would by considering only one variable. For instance, if companies with broad product lines use multiple distribution channels while companies with narrow lines use a single distribution channel, one of the variables is redundant. Second, the variables chosen as axes for the map should expose big differences in how rivals have positioned themselves to compete in the marketplace. This means that analysts must identify the characteristics that differentiate rival firms and use these differences as variables for the axes and as the basis for deciding which firm belongs in which group. Third, the variables used for the axes don't have to be either quantitative or continuous; they can be discrete variables or defined in terms of distinct classes and combinations. Fourth, the circles on the map should be drawn proportional to the combined sales of the firms in each group so that the map will reflect the relative size of each strategic group. Fifth, if more than two good competitive variables can be used for axes, several maps can be drawn to give different exposures to

---

[17]Ibid., pp. 129–30.
[18]Ibid., pp. 152–54.

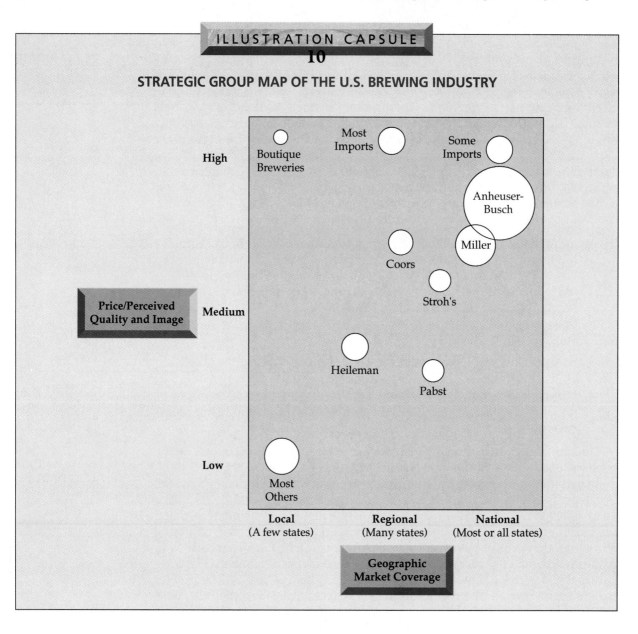

ILLUSTRATION CAPSULE
10

STRATEGIC GROUP MAP OF THE U.S. BREWING INDUSTRY

Principle of Competitive Markets

Some strategic groups are usually more favorably positioned than others because driving forces and competitive pressures do not affect each group evenly and profit prospects vary among groups based on the relative attractiveness of their market positions.

the competitive relationships. Because there is not necessarily one best map, it is advisable to experiment with different pairs of competitive variables.

Strategic group analysis helps deepen understanding of competitive rivalry.[19] To begin with, *driving forces and competitive pressures often favor some strategic groups and hurt others.* Firms in adversely affected strategic groups may try to shift to a more favorably situated group; how hard such a move proves to be depends on whether the entry barriers in the target group are high or low. Attempts by rival firms to enter a new strategic group nearly always increase competitive pressures. If certain firms are known to be changing their

---

[19]Ibid., pp. 130, 132–38, and 154–55.

competitive positions, arrows can be added to the map to show the targeted direction and help clarify the picture of competitive jockeying among rivals.

Second, *the profit potential of different strategic groups may vary due to the strengths and weaknesses in each group's market position*. Differences in profitability can occur because of different bargaining leverage with suppliers or customers and different exposure to competition from substitute products.

Generally speaking, *the closer strategic groups are on the map, the stronger competitive rivalry among member firms tends to be*. Although firms in the same strategic group are the closest rivals, the next closest rivals are in the immediately adjacent groups. Often, firms in strategic groups that are *far apart* on the map hardly compete at all. For instance, Heineken Brewing Co. in Amsterdam and Dixie Brewing Co. in New Orleans both sell beer, but the prices and perceived qualities of their products are much too different to generate any real competition between them. For the same reason, Timex is not a meaningful competitor of Rolex, and Subaru is not a close competitor of Lincoln or Mercedes-Benz.

Competitor Analysis: Predicting What Moves Which Rivals Are Likely to Make Next

Studying the actions and behavior of close competitors is essential. Unless a company pays attention to what competitors are doing, it ends up "flying blind" into battle. A firm can't outmaneuver its rivals without monitoring their actions and anticipating what moves they are likely to make next. The strategies rivals are using and the actions they are likely to take next have direct bearing on what a company's own best strategic moves are—whether it will need to defend against rivals' actions or whether rivals' moves provide an opening for a new offensive thrust.

Competitive Strategy Principle
Successful strategists take great pains in scouting competitors—understanding their strategies, watching their actions, sizing up their strengths and weaknesses, and trying to anticipate what moves they will make next.

Identifying Competitors' Strategies   Strategists can get a quick profile of key competitors by studying where they are in the industry, their strategic objectives (as revealed by their recent actions), and their basic competitive approaches. Table 3–3 provides an easy-to-use scheme for categorizing rivals' objectives and strategies. Such a summary, along with a strategic group map, usually suffices to diagnose the competitive intent of rivals.

Evaluating Who the Industry's Major Players Are Going to Be   It's usually obvious who the *current* major contenders are, but these same firms are not necessarily positioned strongly for the future. Some may be losing ground or be ill-equipped to compete on the industry's future battleground. Smaller companies may be poised for an offensive against larger but vulnerable rivals. In fast-moving, high-technology industries and in globally competitive industries, companies can and do fall from leadership; others end up being acquired. Today's industry leaders don't automatically become tomorrow's.

In deciding whether a competitor is favorably positioned to gain market ground, attention needs to center on *why* there is potential for it to do better or worse than other rivals. Usually, how securely a company holds its present market share is a function of its vulnerability to driving forces and competitive pressures, whether it has a competitive advantage or disadvantage, and whether it is the likely target of offensive attacks from other industry

T A B L E 3–3   Categorizing the Objectives and Strategies of Competitors

Competitive Scope	Strategic Intent	Market Share Objective	Competitive Position/Situation	Strategic Posture	Competitive Strategy

• Local
• Regional
• National
• Multicountry
• Global
	• Be the dominant leader
	• Overtake the present industry leader
	• Be among the industry leaders (top 5)
	• Move into the top 10
	• Move up a notch or two in the industry rankings
	• Overtake a particular rival (not necessarily the leader)
	• Maintain position
	• Just survive
		• Aggressive expansion via both acquisition and internal growth
		• Expansion via internal growth (boost market share at the expense of rival firms)
		• Expansion via acquisition
		• Hold onto present share (by growing at a rate equal to the industry average)
		• Give up share if necessary to achieve short-term profit objectives (stress profitability, not volume)
			• Getting stronger; on the move
			• Well-entrenched; able to maintain its present position
			• Stuck in the middle of the pack
			• Going after a different market position (trying to move from a weaker to a stronger position)
			• Struggling; losing ground
			• Retrenching to a position that can be defended
				• Mostly offensive
				• Mostly defensive
				• A combination of offense and defense
				• Aggressive risk-taker
				• Conservative follower
					• Striving for low cost leadership
					• Mostly focusing on a market niche
					  –High end
					  –Low end
					  –Geographic
					  –Buyers with special needs
					  –Other
					• Pursuing differentiation based on
					  –Quality
					  –Service
					  –Technological superiority
					  –Breadth of product line
					  –Image and reputation
					  –Other attributes

Note: Since a focus strategy can be aimed at any of several market niches and a differentiation strategy can be keyed to any of several attributes, it is best to be explicit about what kind of focus strategy or differentiation strategy a given firm is pursuing. All focusers do not pursue the same market niche, and all differentiators do not pursue the same differentiating attributes.

participants. Trying to identify which rivals are poised to gain or lose market position helps a strategist figure out what kinds of moves key rivals are likely to make next.

Predicting Competitors' Next Moves   Predicting rivals' moves is the hardest yet most useful part of competitor analysis. Good clues about what moves a specific competitor may make next come from finding out how much pressure the rival is under to improve its financial performance. Aggressive rivals usually undertake some type of new strategic initiative. Content rivals are likely to continue their present strategy with only minor fine-tuning. Ailing rivals can be performing so poorly that fresh strategic moves, either offensive or defensive, are virtually certain. Since managers generally operate from assumptions about the industry's future and beliefs about their own firm's situation, strategists can gain insights into the strategic thinking of rival managers by examining their public pronouncements about where the industry is headed and what it will take to be successful, listening to what they are saying about their firm's situation, gathering information about what they are doing, and studying their past actions and leadership styles. Strategists also need to consider whether a rival is flexible enough to make major strategic changes.

To predict a competitor's next moves, an analyst must get a good "feel" for the rival's situation, how its managers think, and what its options are. The detective work can be tedious and time-consuming since the information comes in bits and pieces from many sources. But it is a task worth doing well because the information gives managers more time to prepare countermoves and a chance to beat rivals to the punch by moving first.

Pinpointing the Key Factors for Competitive Success

Key success factors (KSFs) are the major determinants of financial and competitive success in a particular industry. Key success factors highlight the specific outcomes crucial to success in the marketplace and the competences and capabilities with the most bearing on profitability. In the beer industry, the KSFs are full utilization of brewing capacity (to keep manufacturing costs low), a strong network of wholesale distributors (to gain access to as many retail outlets as possible), and clever advertising (to induce beer drinkers to buy a particular brand and thereby pull beer sales through the established wholesale/retail channels). In apparel manufacturing, the KSFs are appealing designs and color combinations (to create buyer interest) and low-cost manufacturing efficiency (to permit attractive retail pricing and ample profit margins). In tin and aluminum cans, where the cost of shipping empty cans is substantial, the KSFs are having plants located close to end-use customers and the ability to market plant output within economical shipping distances (regional market share is far more crucial than national share).

Identifying key success factors is a top-priority strategic consideration. At the very least, management needs to know the industry well enough to conclude what is more important to competitive success and what is less important. At most, KSFs can serve as *the cornerstones* for building a company's strategy. Companies frequently win competitive advantage by concentrating on being distinctively better than rivals in one or more of the industry's key success factors.

Basic Concept
Key success factors spell the difference between profit and loss and, ultimately, between competitive success and failure. A key success factor can be a skill or talent, a competitive capability, or a condition a company must achieve; it can relate to technology, manufacturing, distribution, marketing, or organizational resources.

Key success factors vary from industry to industry, and even over time in the same industry, as driving forces and competitive conditions change. Table 3–4 lists the most common types of key success factors. Only rarely does an industry have more than three or four key success factors at any one time. And even among these three or four, one or two usually outrank the others in importance. Strategic analysts, therefore, have to resist the temptation to include factors that have only minor importance—the purpose of identifying KSFs is to make judgments about what things are more important to competitive success and what things are less important. To compile a list of every factor that matters even a little bit defeats the purpose of training management's eyes on the factors truly crucial to long-term competitive success.

Drawing Conclusions about Overall Industry Attractiveness

The final step of industry and competitive analysis is to review the overall industry situation and develop reasoned conclusions about the relative attractiveness or unattractiveness of the industry, both near-term and long-term. An assessment that the industry is attractive typically calls for some kind of aggressive, expansion-oriented strategic approach. If the industry and competitive situation is judged relatively unattractive, companies are drawn to consider strategies aimed at protecting their profitability. Weaker companies may consider leaving the industry or merging with a rival.

Whether an industry is relatively attractive or unattractive depends on several situational considerations.

Important factors to consider in drawing conclusions about industry attractiveness are:

- The industry's growth potential.
- Whether the industry will be favorably or unfavorably impacted by the prevailing driving forces.
- The potential for the entry/exit of major firms (probable entry reduces attractiveness to existing firms; the exit of a major firm or several weak firms opens up market share growth opportunities for the remaining firms).
- The stability/dependability of demand (as affected by seasonality, the business cycle, the volatility of consumer preferences, inroads by substitutes, and the like).
- Whether competitive forces will become stronger or weaker.
- The severity of problems/issues confronting the industry as a whole.
- The degrees of risk and uncertainty in the industry's future.
- Whether the industry's overall profit prospects are above or below average.

Strategic Management Principle
A company well situated in an unattractive industry can still earn good profits.

However, even if an industry is relatively unattractive overall, it can still be attractive to a company already favorably situated in the industry or to an outsider with the resources and skills to acquire an existing company and turn it into a major contender. Appraising industry attractiveness from the standpoint of a particular company in the industry means looking at the following *additional aspects*:

- The company's competitive position in the industry and whether its position is likely to grow stronger or weaker (a well-entrenched leader in a lackluster industry can still generate good profits).

Technology-Related KSFs
- Scientific research expertise (important in such fields as pharmaceuticals, medicine, space exploration, other "high-tech" industries)
- Production process innovation capability
- Product innovation capability
- Expertise in a given technology

Manufacturing-Related KSFs
- Low-cost production efficiency (achieve scale economies, capture experience curve effects)
- Quality of manufacture (fewer defects, less need for repairs)
- High utilization of fixed assets (important in capital intensive/high fixed-cost industries)
- Low-cost plant locations
- Access to adequate supplies of skilled labor
- High labor productivity (important for items with high labor content)
- Low-cost product design and engineering (reduces manufacturing costs)
- Flexibility to manufacture a range of models and sizes/take care of custom orders

Distribution-Related KSFs
- A strong network of wholesale distributors/dealers
- Gaining ample space on retailer shelves
- Having company-owned retail outlets
- Low distribution costs
- Fast delivery

Marketing-Related KSFs
- A well-trained, effective sales force
- Available, dependable service and technical assistance
- Accurate filling of buyer orders (few back orders or mistakes)
- Breadth of product line and product selection
- Merchandising skills
- Attractive styling/packaging
- Customer guarantees and warranties (important in mail-order retailing, big ticket purchases, new product introductions)

Skills-Related KSFs
- Superior talent (important in professional services)
- Quality control know-how
- Design expertise (important in fashion and apparel industries)
- Expertise in a particular technology
- Ability to come up with clever, catchy ads
- Ability to get newly developed products out of the R&D phase and into the market very quickly

Organizational Capability
- Superior information systems (important in airline travel, car rental, credit card, and lodging industries)
- Ability to respond quickly to shifting market conditions (streamlined decision-making, short lead times to bring new products to market)
- More experience and managerial know-how

Other Types of KSFs
- Favorable image/reputation with buyers
- Overall low cost (not just in manufacturing)
- Convenient locations (important in many retailing businesses)
- Pleasant, courteous employees
- Access to financial capital (important in newly emerging industries with high degrees of business risk and in capital-intensive industries)
- Patent protection
- Overall low cost (not just in manufacturing)

- The company's potential to capitalize on the vulnerabilities of weaker rivals (thereby converting an unattractive *industry* situation into a potentially rewarding *company* opportunity).
- Whether the company is insulated from, or able to defend against, the factors that make the industry unattractive.
- Whether continued participation in the industry adds significantly to the firm's ability to be successful in other industries in which it has business interests.

Conclusions drawn about an industry's attractiveness and competitive situation have a major bearing on a company's strategic options and ultimate choice of strategy.

KEY POINTS

Thinking strategically about a company's external situation involves probing for answers to the following seven questions:

1. What are the chief economic characteristics of the industry?
2. What are the drivers of change in the industry, and what impact will they have?
3. What competitive forces are at work in the industry, and how strong are they?
4. Which companies are in the strongest/weakest competitive positions?
5. Who will likely make what competitive moves next?
6. What key factors will determine competitive success or failure?
7. How attractive is the industry in terms of its prospects for above-average profitability?

To answer these questions, several concepts and techniques are useful—driving forces, the five forces model of competition, strategic groups and strategic group mapping, competitor analysis, key success factors, and industry attractiveness.

Table 3–5 provides a *format* for conducting industry and competitive analysis. It pulls together the relevant concepts and considerations and makes it easier to do a concise, understandable analysis of the industry and competitive environment.

Two final points are worth keeping in mind. First, the task of analyzing a company's external situation is not a mechanical exercise in which analysts plug in data and definitive conclusions come out. There can be several appealing scenarios about how an industry will evolve and what future competitive conditions will be like. For this reason, strategic analysis always leaves room for differences of opinion about how all the factors add up and how industry and competitive conditions will change. However, while no strategic analysis methodology can guarantee a single conclusive diagnosis, it doesn't make sense to shortcut strategic analysis and rely on opinion and casual observation. Managers become better strategists when they know what analytical questions to pose, can use situation analysis techniques to find answers, and have the skills to read clues about industry and competitive change.

Second, in practice, industry and competitive analysis is an incremental and ongoing process, the result of gradually accumulated knowledge and continu-

TABLE 3–5   **Industry and Competitive Analysis Summary Profile**

1. **DOMINANT ECONOMIC CHARACTERISTICS OF THE INDUSTRY ENVIRONMENT** (market growth, geographic scope, industry structure, scale economies, experience curve effects, capital requirements, and so on)

2. **DRIVING FORCES**

3. **COMPETITION ANALYSIS**
   - Rivalry among competing sellers (a strong, moderate, or weak force/weapons of competition)

   - Threat of potential entry (a strong, moderate, or weak force/assessment of entry barriers)

   - Competition from subsitutes (a strong, moderate, or weak force/why)

   - Power of suppliers (a strong, moderate, or weak force/why)

   - Power of customers (a strong, moderate, or weak force/why)

4. **COMPETITIVE POSITION OF MAJOR COMPANIES/ STRATEGIC GROUPS**
   - Favorably positioned/why

   - Unfavorably positioned/why

5. **COMPETITOR ANALYSIS**
   - Strategic approaches/predicted moves of key competitors

   - Who to watch and why

6. **KEY SUCCESS FACTORS**

7. **INDUSTRY PROSPECTS AND OVERALL ATTRACTIVENESS**
   - Factors making the industry attractive

   - Factors making the industry unattractive

   - Special industry issues/problems

   - Profit outlook (favorable/unfavorable)

ous rethinking and retesting. Sweeping industry and competitive analyses need to be done periodically; in the interim, managers must update and reexamine the picture as events unfold. Important strategic actions usually result from a *gradual* build-up of clues and documentation that important changes in the external environment are occurring, a *gradual* understanding of the implications of these changes, and *gradually* reached conclusions about upcoming conditions in the industry.

SUGGESTED READINGS

Ghemawat, Pankaj. "Building Strategy on the Experience Curve." *Harvard Business Review* 64, no. 2 (March–April 1985), pp. 143–49.

Linneman, Robert E., and Harold E. Klein. "Using Scenarios in Strategic Decision Making." *Business Horizons* 28, no. 1 (January–February 1985), pp. 64–74.

Ohmae, Kenichi. *The Mind of the Strategist.* New York: Penguin Books, 1983, chaps. 3, 6, 7, and 13.

Porter, Michael E. "How Competitive Forces Shape Strategy." *Harvard Business Review* 57, no. 2 (March–April 1979), pp. 137–45.

_____. *Competitive Strategy: Techniques for Analyzing Industries and Competitors.* New York: Free Press, 1980, chap. 1.

_____. *Competitive Advantage.* New York: Free Press, 1985, chap. 2.

Company Situation Analysis

Understand what really makes a company "tick."
Charles R. Scott
CEO, Intermark Corp.

---

*If you think what exists today is permanent and forever true,
you inevitably get your head handed to you.*
John Reed
Chairman, Citicorp

The secret of success is to be ready for opportunity when it comes.
Disraeli

In the last chapter, we saw how to use industry and competitive analysis to assess the attractiveness of a company's external environment. In this chapter, we discuss how to evaluate a particular company's strategic situation in that environment. Company situation analysis centers on five questions:

1. How well is the present strategy working?
2. What are the company's strengths, weaknesses, opportunities, and threats?
3. Is the company competitive on cost?
4. How strong is the company's competitive position?
5. What strategic issues does the company face?

There are five questions to answer in analyzing a company's strategic situation.

To explore these questions, strategists use three analytical techniques: SWOT analysis, strategic cost analysis, and competitive strength assessment. These tools are widely used in strategic analysis because they indicate how strongly a company holds its industry position and whether the present strategy is capable of boosting long-term performance.

HOW WELL IS THE PRESENT STRATEGY WORKING?

To evaluate how well a company's present strategy is working, one needs to start with what the strategy is (see Figure 2–2 in Chapter 2 to refresh your recollection of the key components of business strategy). The first thing to understand is the company's competitive approach—whether it is striving for low-cost leadership, trying to differentiate itself from rivals, or focusing narrowly on specific customer groups and market niches. Another important consideration is the firm's competitive scope within the industry—its degree of vertical integration and geographic market coverage. The company's functional area support strategies in production, marketing, finance, human resources, and so on need to be identified and understood as well. In addition, the company may have initiated some recent strategic moves (for instance, a price cut, stepped-up advertising, entry into a new geographic area, or merger with a competitor) that are integral to its strategy and that aim at securing a particular competitive advantage and/or improved competitive position. Examining the rationale for each piece of the strategy—for each competitive move and each functional approach—should clarify what the present strategy is.

While there's merit in evaluating a strategy from a qualitative standpoint (i.e., its completeness, internal consistency, rationale, and suitability), the best evidence of how well a strategy is working comes from the company's recent strategic and financial performance. The most obvious indicators of a firm's strategic and financial performance include: (1) whether the firm's market share is rising or falling, (2) whether the firm's profit margins are increasing or decreasing and how large they are relative to rival firms, (3) trends in the firm's net profits and return on investment, (4) whether the firm's sales are growing faster or slower than the market as a whole, (5) whether the firm enjoys a competitive advantage or is at a disadvantage, and (6) whether its long-term competitive position is becoming stronger or weaker. The better a company's current overall performance, the less likely the need for radical changes in strategy. The weaker a company's strategic and financial performance, the more its current strategy should be questioned.

> *The stronger a company's strategic and financial performance, the more likely it has a well-conceived, well-executed strategy.*

SWOT ANALYSIS

SWOT is an acronym for a company's strengths, weaknesses, opportunities, and threats. A SWOT analysis consists of evaluating a firm's internal strengths and weaknesses and its external opportunities and threats. It is an easy-to-use tool for getting a quick *overview* of a firm's strategic situation. SWOT analysis underscores the basic point that strategy must produce a good fit between a company's internal capability (its strengths and weaknesses) and its external situation (reflected in part by its opportunities and threats).

> **Basic Concept**
> *A company's internal strengths usually represent competitive assets; its internal weaknesses usually represent competitive liabilities. A company's strengths/assets should outweigh its weaknesses/liabilities by a hefty margin.*

Identifying Strengths and Weaknesses

Table 4–1 lists the considerations used to identify a company's internal strengths and weaknesses. A *strength* is something a company is good at doing or a characteristic that gives it an important capability. A strength can be a skill, a competence, a valuable organizational resource or competitive

T A B L E 4–1   **SWOT Analysis—What to Look for in Sizing up a Company's Strengths, Weaknesses, Opportunities, and Threats**

Potential Internal Strengths

- Core competences in key areas
- Adequate financial resources
- Well thought of by buyers
- An acknowledged market leader
- Well-conceived functional area strategies
- Access to economies of scale
- Insulated (at least somewhat) from strong competitive pressures
- Proprietary technology
- Cost advantages
- Better advertising campaigns
- Product innovation skills
- Proven management
- Ahead on experience curve
- Better manufacturing capability
- Superior technological skills
- Other?

Potential Internal Weaknesses

- No clear strategic direction
- Obsolete facilities
- Subpar profitability because . . .
- Lack of managerial depth and talent
- Missing some key skills or competences
- Poor track record in implementing strategy
- Plagued with internal operating problems
- Falling behind in R & D
- Too narrow a product line
- Weak market image
- Weak distribution network
- Below-average marketing skills
- Unable to finance needed changes in strategy
- Higher overall unit costs relative to key competitors
- Other?

Potential External Opportunities

- Serve additional customer groups
- Enter new markets or segments
- Expand product line to meet broader range of customer needs
- Diversify into related products
- Vertical integration (forward or backward)
- Falling trade barriers in attractive foreign markets
- Complacency among rival firms
- Faster market growth
- Other?

Potential External Threats

- Entry of lower-cost foreign competitors
- Rising sales of substitute products
- Slower market growth
- Adverse shifts in foreign exchange rates and trade policies of foreign governments
- Costly regulatory requirements
- Vulnerability to recession and business cycle
- Growing bargaining power of customers or suppliers
- Changing buyer needs and tastes
- Adverse demographic changes
- Other?

capability, or an achievement that gives the company a market advantage (like having a better product, stronger name recognition, superior technology, or better customer service). A *weakness* is something a company lacks or does poorly (in comparison to others) or a condition that puts it at a disadvantage. A weakness may or may not make a company competitively vulnerable, depending on how much it matters in the competitive battle.

Once a company's internal strengths and weaknesses are identified, the two lists have to be carefully evaluated. Some strengths are more important than others because they count for more in determining performance, in competing successfully, and in forming a powerful strategy. Likewise, some internal weaknesses can prove fatal, while others don't matter much or can be easily remedied. A SWOT analysis is like constructing a *strategic balance sheet*—

strengths are *competitive assets* and weaknesses are *competitive liabilities*. The issue is whether the strengths/assets adequately overcome the weaknesses/liabilities (a 50–50 balance is definitely not desirable!), how to meld strengths into an effective strategy, and whether strategic actions are needed to tilt the strategic balance more toward the asset side and away from the liability side.

From a strategy-making perspective, a company's strengths are significant because they can be used as the cornerstones of strategy and the basis on which to build competitive advantage. If a company doesn't have strong competences and competitive assets around which to craft an attractive strategy, management must move quickly to build capabilities on which a strategy can be grounded. At the same time, a good strategy needs to aim at correcting competitive weaknesses that make the company vulnerable, hurt its performance, or disqualify it from pursuing an attractive opportunity. The point here is simple: *an organization's strategy should be well-suited to company strengths, weaknesses, and competitive capabilities.* As a rule, management should build its strategy around what the company does best and should avoid strategies whose success depends heavily on areas where the company is weak or has unproven ability.

Core Competences   One of the "trade secrets" of first-rate strategic management is consolidating a company's technological, production, and marketing know-how into competences that enhance its competitiveness. *A core competence is something a company does especially well in comparison to its competitors.*[1] In practice, there are many possible types of core competences: manufacturing excellence, exceptional quality control, the ability to provide better service, more know-how in low-cost manufacturing, superior design capability, unique ability to pick out good retail locations, innovativeness in developing new products, better skill in merchandising and product display, mastery of an important technology, a strong understanding of customer needs and tastes, an unusually effective sales force, outstanding skill in working with customers on new applications and uses of the product, and expertise in integrating multiple technologies to create families of new products. *The importance of a core competence to strategy-making rests with (1) the added capability it gives an organization in going after a particular market opportunity, (2) the competitive edge it can yield in the marketplace, and (3) its potential for being a cornerstone of strategy.* It is easier to build competitive advantage when a firm has a core competence in an area important to market success, when rivals do not have offsetting competences, and when it is costly and time-consuming for rivals to match the competence. Core competences are thus valuable competitive assets.

Identifying Opportunities and Threats

Table 4–1 also lists factors that help identify a company's external opportunities and threats. Market opportunity is a big factor in shaping a company's strategy. However, there is an important distinction between *industry opportunities* and *company opportunities.* Not every company in an industry is well

> **Strategic Management Principle**
> *Successful strategists seek to exploit what a company does best—its expertise, strengths, core competences, and strongest competitive capabilities.*

> **Strategic Management Principle**
> *Core competences empower a company to build competitive advantage.*

---

[1]For a fuller discussion of the core competence concept, see C. K. Prahalad and Gary Hamel, "The Core Competence of the Corporation," *Harvard Business Review* 90, no. 3 (May–June 1990), pp. 79–93.

positioned to pursue each opportunity that exists in the industry—some companies are always better situated than others and several may be hopelessly out of contention. A company's strengths and weaknesses make it better suited to pursuing some opportunities than others. *The industry opportunities most relevant to a particular company are those that offer important avenues for growth and those where a company has the most potential for competitive advantage.*

Often certain factors in a company's external environment pose *threats* to its well-being. Threats can stem from the emergence of cheaper technologies, rivals' introduction of new or better products, the entry of low-cost foreign competitors into a company's market stronghold, new regulations that are more burdensome to a company than to its competitors, vulnerability to a rise in interest rates, the potential for a hostile takeover, unfavorable demographic shifts, adverse changes in foreign exchange rates, political upheaval at a company's foreign facilities, and the like.

Opportunities and threats not only affect the attractiveness of a company's situation but point to the need for strategic action. To be adequately matched to a company's situation, strategy must (1) be aimed at pursuing opportunities well suited to the company's capabilities and (2) provide a defense against external threats. SWOT analysis is therefore more than an exercise in making four lists. The important part of SWOT analysis involves *evaluating* the strengths, weaknesses, opportunities, and threats and *drawing conclusions* about the attractiveness of the company's situation and the need for strategic action. Some of the pertinent strategy-making questions to consider, once the SWOT listings have been compiled, are:

- Does the company have any internal strengths or core competences an attractive strategy can be built around?
- Do the company's weaknesses make it competitively vulnerable and/or do they disqualify the company from pursuing certain opportunities? Which weaknesses does strategy need to correct?
- Which opportunities does the company have the skills and resources to pursue with a real chance of success? (*Remember*: Opportunity without the means to capture it is an illusion.)
- What threats should managers be worried about most, and what strategic moves should they consider in crafting a good defense?

STRATEGIC COST ANALYSIS AND ACTIVITY-COST CHAINS

One of the most telling signs of the strength of a company's strategic position is its cost position relative to competitors. Cost comparisons are especially critical in a commodity-product industry where price competition typically dominates and lower-cost companies have the upper hand. But even in industries where products are differentiated and competition is based on factors other than price, companies have to keep costs *in line with* rivals or risk jeopardizing their competitive position.

Competitors do not necessarily, or even usually, incur the same costs in supplying their products to end-users. Disparities in costs among rival producers can stem from:

- Differences in the prices paid for raw materials, component parts, energy, and other items purchased from suppliers.

Strategic Management Principle

Successful strategists aim at capturing a company's best growth opportunities and creating defenses against threats to its competitive position and future performance.

Assessing whether a company's costs are competitive with those of its close rivals is a necessary and crucial part of company situation analysis.

- Differences in basic technology and the age of plants and equipment. (Because rivals usually invest in plants and key pieces of equipment at different times, their facilities usually have different technological efficiencies and different fixed costs. Older facilities are typically less efficient, but if they were less expensive to construct or cheaply acquired, they *may* still be reasonably cost competitive with modern facilities.)

- Differences in internal operating costs due to the economies of scale associated with different size plants, learning and experience curve effects, different wage rates, different productivity levels, different administrative overhead expenses, different tax rates, and the like.

- Differences in rivals' exposure to inflation and changes in foreign exchange rates (as can occur in global industries where competitors have plants located in different nations).

- Differences in marketing costs, sales and promotion expenditures, and advertising expenses.

- Differences in inbound transportation costs and outbound shipping costs.

- Differences in forward channel distribution costs (the costs and markups of distributors, wholesalers, and retailers who get the product from the manufacturer to the end-user).

Cost differences among close rivals can stem from many factors.

For a company to be competitively successful, its costs must be in line with those of rival producers. However, some cost disparity is justified when the products of competing companies are *differentiated*. The need to be cost competitive is not so stringent as to *require* the costs of every firm in the industry to be *equal*, but, as a rule, the higher a firm's costs above low-cost producers, the more vulnerable its market position becomes. Given the numerous opportunities for cost disparities, a company must be aware of how its costs compare with rivals'. This is where *strategic cost analysis* comes in.

Strategic Management Principle
The higher a company's costs are above those of rivals, the more competitively vulnerable it becomes.

Strategic cost analysis focuses on a firm's cost position relative to its rivals'. The primary analytical tool of strategic cost analysis is an *activity-cost chain* showing the buildup of value from raw materials supply to the price paid by ultimate customers.[2] The activity-cost chain goes beyond a company's own internal cost structure to cover all the stages in the industry chain: raw materials supply, manufacturing, wholesale distribution, and retailing, as shown in Figure 4–1. An activity-cost chain is especially revealing for a manufacturing firm because its ability to supply its product to end-users at a competitive price can easily depend on costs that originate either *backward* in suppliers' portion of the activity-cost chain, or *forward* in the wholesale and retail stages of the chain.

Basic Concept
Strategic cost analysis involves comparing a company's cost position relative to key competitors, activity by activity, from raw materials purchase to the price paid by ultimate customers.

The data requirements for activity-cost chain analysis are formidable. It requires breaking a firm's own historical cost accounting data out into several principal cost categories and also developing cost estimates for the backward and forward channel portions. To see how the firm's cost position compares with rivals, the same cost elements for each rival must likewise be estimated—an advanced art in competitive intelligence in itself. But despite

---

[2]Strategic cost analysis is described at greater length in Michael E. Porter, *Competitive Advantage* (New York: Free Press, 1985), chap. 2. What follows is a distilled adaptation of the analytical method pioneered by Porter.

Generic Activity-Cost Chain for a Representative Industry Situation

TOTAL INDUSTRY ACTIVITY-COST CHAIN

SUPPLIER-RELATED ACTIVITIES	MANUFACTURING-RELATED ACTIVITIES						FORWARD CHANNEL ACTIVITIES	
Purchased Materials, Components, Inputs, and Inbound Logistics	Production Activities and Operations	Marketing and Sales Activities	Customer Service and Outbound Logistics Activities	In-House Staff Support Activities	General and Administrative Activities	Profit Margin	Wholesale Distributor and Dealer Network Activities	Retailer Activities
Specific activities/costs	Specific activities/costs	Specific activities/costs	Specific activities/costs	Specific activities/costs	Specific activities/costs			
─ Ingredient raw materials and component parts supplied by outsiders	─ Facilities and equipment	─ Salesforce operations	─ Service reps	─ Payroll and benefits	─ Finance and accounting services			
─ Energy	─ Processing	─ Advertising and promotion	─ Order processing	─ Recruiting and training	─ Legal services			
─ Inbound shipping	─ Assembly and packaging	─ Market research	─ Spare parts	─ Internal communications	─ Public relations			
─ Inbound materials handling	─ Labor and supervision	─ Technical literature	─ Other outbound logistics costs	─ Computer services	─ Executive salaries			
─ Warehousing	─ Maintenance	─ Travel and entertainment		─ Procurement functions	─ Interest on borrowed funds			
	─ Product design and testing	─ Dealer/ distributor relations		─ R&D	─ Tax-related costs			
	─ Quality and inspection			─ Safety and security	─ Regulatory compliance			
	─ Inventory management			─ Union relations				

Includes all of the activities, associated costs, and markups of distributors, wholesale dealers, retailers, and any other forward channel allies whose efforts are utilized to get the product into the hands of end-users/customers

ILLUSTRATION CAPSULE
11

ACTIVITY-COST CHAINS FOR ANHEUSER-BUSCH AND ADOLPH COORS BEERS

In the table below are average cost estimates for the combined brands of beer produced by Anheuser-Busch and Coors. The example shows raw material costs, other manufacturing costs, and forward channel distribution costs. The data are for 1982.

Activity-Cost Elements	Estimated Average Cost Breakdown for Combined Anheuser-Busch Brands		Estimated Average Cost Breakdown for Combined Adolph Coors Brands	
	Per 6-Pack of 12-oz. Cans	Per Barrel Equivalent	Per 6-Pack of 12-oz. Cans	Per Barrel Equivalent
1. Manufacturing costs:				
Direct production costs:				
Raw material ingredients	$0.1384	$ 7.63	$0.1082	$ 5.96
Direct labor	0.1557	8.58	0.1257	6.93
Salaries for nonunionized personnel	0.0800	4.41	0.0568	3.13
Packaging	0.5055	27.86	0.4663	25.70
Depreciation on plant and equipment	0.0410	2.26	0.0826	4.55
Subtotal	0.9206	50.74	0.8396	46.27
Other expenses:				
Advertising	0.0477	2.63	0.0338	1.86
Other marketing costs and general administrative expenses	0.1096	6.04	0.1989	10.96
Interest	0.0147	0.81	0.0033	0.18
Research and development	0.0277	1.53	0.0195	1.07
Total manufacturing costs	$1.1203	$ 61.75	$1.0951	$ 60.34
2. Manufacturer's operating profit	0.1424	7.85	0.0709	3.91
3. Net selling price	1.2627	69.60	1.1660	64.25
4. Plus federal and state excise taxes paid by brewer	0.1873	10.32	0.1782	9.82
5. Gross manufacturer's selling price to distributor/wholesaler	1.4500	79.92	1.3442	74.07
6. Average margin over manufacturer's cost	0.5500	30.31	0.5158	28.43
7. Average wholesale price charged to retailer (inclusive of taxes in item 4 above but exclusive of other taxes)	$2.00	$110.23	$1.86	$102.50
8. Plus other assorted state and local taxes levied on wholesale and retail sales (this varies from locality to locality)	0.60		0.60	
9. Average 20% retail markup over wholesale cost . .	0.40		0.38	
10. Average price to consumer at retail	$3.00		$2.84	

Note: The difference in the average cost structures for Anheuser-Busch and Adolph Coors is, to a substantial extent, due to A-B's higher proportion of super-premium beer sales. A-B's super-premium brand, Michelob, was the bestseller in its category and somewhat more costly to brew than premium and popular-priced beers.

Source: Compiled by Tom McLean, Elsa Wischkaemper, and Arthur A. Thompson, Jr., from a wide variety of documents and field interviews.

the tediousness of the task and the imprecision of some of the estimates, the payoff in exposing the cost competitiveness of one's position makes it a valuable analytical tool. Illustration Capsule 11 on page 93 shows a simplified activity-cost chain comparison for various brands of beer produced by Anheuser-Busch (the industry leader) and Adolph Coors (the third ranking brewer).

The most important application of the activity-cost technique is to expose how a particular firm's cost position compares with those of its rivals. What is needed is competitor versus competitor cost estimates for a given product. The size of a company's cost advantage/disadvantage can vary from item to item in the product line, from customer group to customer group (if different distribution channels are used), and from geographic market to geographic market (if cost factors vary across geographic regions).

Strategic actions to eliminate a cost disadvantage need to be linked to the location in the activity-cost chain where the cost differences originate.

Looking again at Figure 4–1, observe that there are three main areas in the cost chain where important differences in competitors' *relative* costs can occur: in suppliers' part of the cost chain, in each company's activity segments, or in the forward channel portion. If a firm's lack of cost competitiveness lies either in the backward or forward sections of the chain, the task of re-establishing cost competitiveness may have to extend beyond its own operations. When a firm's cost disadvantage is principally associated with items purchased from suppliers (the backward end of the activity-cost chain), it can pursue any of several strategic actions to correct the problem:

- Negotiate more favorable prices with suppliers.
- Work with suppliers to help them achieve lower costs.
- Integrate backward to gain control over the costs of purchased items.
- Try to use lower-priced substitute inputs.
- Try to save on inbound shipping costs.
- Try to make up the difference by cutting costs elsewhere in the chain.

A company's strategic options for eliminating cost disadvantages in the forward end of the chain include:

- Pushing distributors and other forward channel allies to reduce their costs and markups.
- Changing to a more economical distribution strategy, including forward integration.
- Trying to make up the difference by cutting costs earlier in the chain.

When the source of a firm's cost disadvantage is internal, it can use any of nine strategic approaches to restore cost parity:

- Initiate internal budget-tightening measures.
- Improve production methods and work procedures (to boost the productivity of workers and increase utilization of high-cost equipment).
- Try to eliminate some cost-producing activities altogether.
- Relocate high-cost activities to geographical areas where they can be performed cheaper.
- See if certain activities can be farmed out to contractors cheaper than they can be done internally.

T A B L E 4–2   **The Signs of Strength and Weakness in a Company's Competitive Position**

Signs of Competitive Strength	Signs of Competitive Weakness
• Important core competences	• Confronted with competitive disadvantages
• Strong market share (or a leading market share)	• Losing ground to rival firms
• A pacesetting or distinctive strategy	• Below average growth in revenues
• Growing customer base and customer loyalty	• Short on financial resources
• Above-average market visibility	• A slipping reputation with customers
• In a favorably situated strategic group	• Trailing in product development
• Concentrating on fastest-growing market segments	• In a strategic group destined to lose ground
• Strongly differentiated products	• Weak in areas where there is the most market potential
• Cost advantages	• A higher-cost producer
• Above-average profit margins	• Too small to be a major factor in the marketplace
• Above-average technological and innovational capability	• Not in good position to deal with emerging threats
• A creative, entrepreneurially alert management	• Weak product quality
• In position to capitalize on opportunities	• Lacking skills and capabilities in key areas

- Invest in cost-saving technological improvements (automation, robotics, flexible manufacturing techniques, computerized controls).
- Innovate around the troublesome cost components as new investments are made in plant and equipment.
- Simplify the product design and make it easier to manufacture.
- Try to make up the internal cost disadvantage by cutting costs in the backward and forward portions of the chain.

Activity-cost chains reveal a great deal about a firm's cost competitiveness. Examining the makeup of a company's own activity-cost chain and comparing it to rivals' indicate who has how much of a cost advantage/disadvantage and which cost components are responsible. Such information is vital in crafting strategies to eliminate a cost disadvantage or create a cost advantage.

COMPETITIVE STRENGTH ASSESSMENT

In addition to the cost competitiveness diagnosis that activity-cost chain analysis provides, a more broad-based assessment needs to be made of a company's competitive position and competitive strength. Particular elements to single out for evaluation are: (1) how strongly the firm holds its present competitive position, (2) whether the firm's position can be expected to improve or deteriorate if the present strategy is continued (allowing for fine-tuning), (3) how the firm ranks *relative to key rivals* on each important measure of competitive strength and industry key success factor, (4) whether the firm has a net competitive advantage or disadvantage, and (5) the firm's ability to defend its position in light of industry driving forces, competitive pressures, and the anticipated moves of rivals.

Table 4–2 lists some indicators of whether a firm's competitive position is improving or slipping. But more is needed than just a listing of the signs of improvement or slippage. The important thing is to develop some judgments

Systematic assessment of whether a company's competitive position is strong or weak relative to close rivals is an essential step in company situation analysis.

T A B L E 4–3   **Illustrations of Unweighted and Weighted Competitive Strength Assessments**

A. Sample of an Unweighted Competitive Strength Assessment
Rating scale: 1 = Very weak; 10 = Very strong

Key Success Factor/Strength Measure	ABC Co.	Rival 1	Rival 2	Rival 3	Rival 4
Quality/product performance	8	5	10	1	6
Reputation/image	8	7	10	1	6
Raw material access/cost	2	10	4	5	1
Technological skills	10	1	7	3	8
Advertising effectiveness	9	4	10	5	1
Marketing/distribution	9	4	10	5	1
Financial resource	5	10	7	3	1
Relative cost position	5	10	3	1	4
Ability to compete on price	5	7	10	1	4
Unweighted overall strength rating	61	58	71	25	32

B. Sample of a Weighted Competitive Strength Assessment
Rating scale: 1 = Very weak; 10 = Very strong

Key Success Factor/Strength Measure	Weight	ABC Co.	Rival 1	Rival 2	Rival 3	Rival 4
Quality/product performance	0.10	8/0.80	5/0.50	10/1.00	1/0.10	6/0.60
Reputation/image	0.10	8/0.80	7/0.70	10/1.00	1/0.10	6/0.60
Raw material access/cost	0.10	2/0.20	10/1.00	4/0.40	5/0.50	1/0.10
Technological skills	0.05	10/0.50	1/0.05	7/0.35	3/0.15	8/0.40
Manufacturing capability	0.05	9/0.45	4/0.20	10/0.50	5/0.25	1/0.05
Marketing/distribution	0.05	9/0.45	4/0.20	10/0.50	5/0.25	1/0.05
Financial strength	0.10	5/0.50	10/1.00	7/0.70	3/0.30	1/0.10
Relative cost position	0.35	5/1.75	10/3.50	3/1.05	1/0.35	4/1.40
Ability to compete on price	0.15	5/0.75	7/1.05	10/1.50	1/0.15	4/1.60
Sum of weights	1.00					
Weighted overall strength rating		6.20	8.20	7.00	2.10	2.90

about whether the company's position will improve or deteriorate under the current strategy and to consider what strategic actions are needed to improve the company's market position.

The really telling part of competitive position assessment, however, is the formal appraisal of whether the company is stronger or weaker than close rivals on each key success factor and indicator of competitive strength. Much of the information for competitive position assessment comes from previous analyses. Industry and competitive analysis reveals the key success factors and competitive strength measures that will separate industry winners and losers. Competitor analysis provides a basis for judging the strengths and capabilities of key rivals. Step one is to make a list of the industry's key success factors and measures of competitive strength or weaknesses (6 to 10 measures usually suffice). Step two is to rate the firm and its key rivals on each factor. Rating scales from 1 to 5 or 1 to 10 are straightforward and simple to use although ratings of stronger (+), weaker (−), and about equal (=) may be appropriate when numerical scores are too subjective. Step three is to sum the individual strength ratings to get an overall measure of competitive strength for each competitor. Step four is to draw conclusions about the size and extent of the company's net competitive advantage or disadvantage, noting areas where the company's competitive position is strongest and weakest.

Table 4–3 gives two examples of competitive strength assessments. The first one employs an *unweighted rating scale*; with unweighted ratings each key success factor/competitive strength measure is assumed to be equally important. Whichever company has the highest strength rating on a given measure has implied competitive edge on that factor. The size of its edge is reflected in the margin of difference between its rating and the ratings assigned to rivals. Summing a company's strength ratings on all the measures produces an overall strength rating. The higher a company's overall strength rating, the stronger its competitive position. The bigger the difference between a company's overall rating and a rival's rating, the greater its implied net competitive advantage. Thus, ABC's score of 61 (see the top half of Table 4–3) signals a greater net competitive advantage over Rival 4 (with a score of 32) than Rival 1 (with a score of 58).

High competitive strength ratings signal a strong competitive position and possession of competitive advantage; low ratings signal a weak position and competitive disadvantage.

However, it is conceptually stronger to use a weighted rating system because the different measures of competitive strength are unlikely to be *equally* important. In a commodity-product industry, for instance, low unit costs relative to rivals are the biggest determinant of competitive strength. In an industry with strong product differentiation, the most significant measures of competitive strength may be brand awareness, amount of advertising, reputation for quality, and distribution capability. In a *weighted rating system*, each measure of competitive strength is assigned a weight based on its perceived importance in shaping competitive success. The largest weight could be as high as .75 (or higher) if a variable is overwhelmingly decisive, or as low as .20 when two or three measures are more important than the rest. Lesser indicators can carry weights of .05 or .10. However, *the sum of the weights must add up to 1.0*.

A weighted competitive strength analysis is conceptually stronger than an unweighted analysis because of the inherent weakness in assuming that all the strength measures are equally important.

Weighted strength ratings are calculated by deciding how a company stacks up on each strength measure (using the 1 to 5 or 1 to 10 rating scale) and multiplying the rating by the assigned weight (a rating score of 4 times a weight of .20 gives a weighted rating of .80). Again, the company with the highest rating on a given measure has an implied competitive edge on that measure, with the size of its edge reflected in the difference between its rating and rivals' ratings. Summing a company's weighted strength ratings for all measures yields an overall strength rating. Comparisons of the weighted overall strength scores indicate which competitors are in the strongest and weakest competitive positions and who has how big a net competitive advantage over who.

The bottom half of Table 4–3 shows a sample competitive strength assessment for ABC Company using a weighted rating system. Note that the unweighted and weighted rating schemes produce a different ordering of the companies. In the weighted system, ABC Company dropped from second to third in strength, and Rival 1 jumped from third into first because of its high ratings on the two most important factors. Weighting the importance of the strength measures can thus make a significant difference in the outcome of the assessment.

The foregoing competitive strength assessment procedure yields useful conclusions about a company's competitive situation. The ratings show how a company compares against rivals, factor by factor or measure by measure, thus revealing where it is strongest and weakest. Moreover, the overall competitive strength scores indicate whether the company is at a net competitive advantage or disadvantage against each rival. The firm with the largest overall competitive strength rating has a net competitive advantage over each rival.

Knowing where a company is competitively strong and where it is weak is essential in crafting a strategy to strengthen its long-term competitive position. Generally, a company should try to convert its competitive strengths into sustainable competitive advantage and take strategic actions to protect against its competitive weaknesses. At the same time, competitive strength ratings clearly indicate which rivals may be vulnerable to competitive attack and the areas where they are weakest. When a company has important strengths in areas where one or more rivals are weak, it should consider offensive moves to exploit rivals' weaknesses.

DETERMINING WHAT STRATEGIC ISSUES NEED TO BE ADDRESSED

The final analytical task is to hone in on the strategic issues management needs to address in forming an effective strategic action plan. This step should be taken very seriously because it entails putting the company's overall situation into perspective and getting a lock on exactly where management needs to focus its strategic attention. Without a clear fix on the issues, strategists are ill-prepared for strategy-making.

To pinpoint issues for the company's strategic action agenda, strategists should consider the following:

- Whether the present strategy is adequate in light of driving forces at work in the industry.
- How closely the present strategy matches the industry's *future* key success factors.
- How good a defense the present strategy offers against the five competitive forces—future ones, not necessarily past or present ones.
- In what ways the present strategy may not adequately protect the company against external threats and internal weaknesses.
- Where and how the company may be vulnerable to competitive attack from one or more rivals.
- Whether the company has competitive advantage or must work to offset competitive disadvantage.
- Where the strong spots and weak spots are in the present strategy.
- Whether additional actions are needed to improve the company's cost position, capitalize on emerging opportunities, and strengthen the company's competitive position.

These considerations should indicate whether the company can continue the same basic strategy with minor adjustments or whether it should undertake a major overhaul.

The better matched a company's strategy is to its external environment and internal situation, the less need there is for big shifts in strategy. On the other hand, when the present strategy is not well suited for the future, crafting a new strategy has to take top priority.

There are five steps to conducting a company situation analysis:

1. *Evaluating how well the current strategy is working.* This involves looking at the company's recent strategic performance and determining whether the various pieces of strategy are logically consistent.

2. *Doing a SWOT analysis.* A company's strengths are important because they can serve as major building blocks for strategy; company weaknesses are important because they may represent vulnerabilities that need correction. External opportunities and threats come into play because a good strategy aims at capturing attractive opportunities and defending against threats to the company's well-being.

3. *Evaluating the company's cost position relative to competitors* (using the concepts of strategic cost analysis and activity-cost chains if appropriate). Strategy must always aim at keeping costs sufficiently in line with rivals to preserve the company's ability to compete.

4. *Assessing the company's competitive position and competitive strength.* This step looks at how a company matches rivals on the chief determinants of competitive success. The competitive strength rankings indicate where a company is strong and weak; as a rule, a company's competitive strategy should be built on its competitive strengths and attempt to shore up areas where it is competitively vulnerable. A company has the best potential for offensive attack in areas where it is strong and rivals are weak.

5. *Determining the strategic issues and problems the company needs to address.* The purpose of this analytical step is to develop a complete strategy-making agenda using the results of both company situation analysis and industry and competitive analysis. This step helps management draw conclusions about the strengths and weaknesses of its strategy and pinpoint the issues strategy-makers need to consider.

Table 4–4, on page 100, provides a format for company situation analysis. It incorporates the concepts and analytical techniques discussed in this chapter and makes it easier to perform the analysis in a systematic, concise manner.

Andrews, Kenneth R. *The Concept of Corporate Strategy*, 3rd ed. Homewood, Ill.: Richard D. Irwin, 1987, chap. 3.

Fahey, Liam, and H. Kurt Christensen. "Building Distinctive Competences into Competitive Advantages." Reprinted in Liam Fahey, *The Strategic Planning Management Reader.* Englewood Cliffs, N.J.: Prentice Hall, 1989, pp. 113–18.

Hax, Arnoldo C., and Nicolas S. Majluf. *Strategic Management: An Integrative Perspective.* Englewood Cliffs, N.J.: Prentice Hall, 1984, chap. 15.

Henry, Harold W. "Appraising a Company's Strengths and Weaknesses." *Managerial Planning,* July–August 1980, pp. 31–36.

1. STRATEGIC PERFORMANCE INDICATORS

Performance Indicator	19__	19__	19__	19__	19__
Market share	____	____	____	____	____
Sales growth	____	____	____	____	____
Net profit margin	____	____	____	____	____
Return on equity investment	____	____	____	____	____
Other?	____	____	____	____	____

2. INTERNAL STRENGTHS

INTERNAL WEAKNESSES

EXTERNAL OPPORTUNITIES

EXTERNAL THREATS

3. COMPETITIVE STRENGTH ASSESSMENT
Rating scale: 1 = Very weak; 10 = Very strong.

Key Success Factor/ Competitive Variable	Weight	Firm A	Firm B	Firm C	Firm D	Firm E
Quality/product performance	____	____	____	____	____	____
Reputation/image	____	____	____	____	____	____
Raw material access/cost	____	____	____	____	____	____
Technological skills	____	____	____	____	____	____
Manufacturing capability	____	____	____	____	____	____
Marketing/distribution	____	____	____	____	____	____
Financial strength	____	____	____	____	____	____
Relative cost position	____	____	____	____	____	____
Other?	====	====	====	====	====	====
Overall strength rating	____	____	____	____	____	____

4. CONCLUSIONS CONCERNING COMPETITIVE POSITION
(Improving/slipping? Competitive advantages/disadvantages?)

5. MAJOR STRATEGIC ISSUES/PROBLEMS THE COMPANY MUST ADDRESS

Paine, Frank T., and Leonard J. Tischler. "Evaluating Your Costs Strategically." Reprinted in Laim Fahey, *The Strategic Planning Management Reader.* Englewood Cliffs, N.J.: Prentice Hall, 1989, pp. 118–23.

Prahalad, C. K., and Gary Hamel. "The Core Competence of the Corporation." *Harvard Business Review* 90, no. 3 (May–June 1990), pp. 79–93.

Stevenson, Howard H. "Defining Corporate Strengths and Weaknesses." *Sloan Management Review* 17, no. 2 (Winter 1976), pp. 1–18.

CHAPTER

5

Strategy and Competitive Advantage

—

Competing in the marketplace is like war. You have injuries and casualties, and the best strategy wins.
John Collins

—

Competitive advantage is at the heart of a firm's performance in competitive markets.
Michael E. Porter

—

Winning business strategies are grounded in sustainable competitive advantage. A company has *competitive advantage* whenever it has an edge over rivals in securing customers and defending against competitive forces. There are many sources of competitive advantage: making the highest-quality product, providing superior customer service, achieving lower costs than rivals, having a more convenient geographic location, designing a product that performs better than competing brands, making a more reliable and longer-lasting product, and providing buyers more value for the money (a combination of good quality, good service, and acceptable price). To succeed in building a competitive advantage, a firm must try to provide what buyers will perceive as "superior value"—either a good product at a low price or a "better" product that is worth paying more for.

This chapter focuses on how a company can achieve or defend a competitive advantage.[1] We begin by describing the basic types of competitive strategies and then examine how these approaches rely on offensive moves to build competitive advantage and defensive moves to protect competitive advantage.

---

[1]The definitive work on this subject is Michael E. Porter, *Competitive Advantage* (New York: Free Press, 1985). The treatment in this chapter draws heavily on Porter's pioneering effort.

In the concluding two sections, we survey the pros and cons of a vertical integration strategy and look at the competitive importance of timing strategic moves—when it is advantageous to be a first-mover or a late-mover.

THE THREE GENERIC TYPES OF COMPETITIVE STRATEGY

Competitive strategy consists of all the moves and approaches a firm has taken and is taking to attract buyers, withstand competitive pressures, and improve its market position. In plainer terms, competitive strategy concerns what a firm is doing to try to knock the socks off rival companies and gain competitive advantage. A firm's strategy can be mostly offensive or mostly defensive, shifting from one to the other as market conditions warrant.

Companies the world over have tried every conceivable approach to outcompeting rivals and winning an edge in the marketplace. And because managers tailor strategy to fit the specifics of their own company's situation and market environment, there are countless variations. In this sense, there are as many competitive strategies as there are companies trying to compete. However, beneath all the nuances, the approaches to competitive strategy fall into three categories:

1. Striving to be the overall low-cost producer in the industry (a *low-cost leadership strategy*).
2. Seeking to differentiate one's product offering from rivals' products (a *differentiation strategy*).
3. Focusing on a narrow portion of the market rather than the whole market (a *focus* or *niche strategy*).[2]

Table 5–1 highlights the distinctive features of these three generic competitive strategy approaches.

Striving to Be the Low-Cost Producer

Striving to be the low-cost producer is a powerful competitive approach in markets where many buyers are price-sensitive. The aim is to open up a sustainable cost advantage over competitors and then use lower cost as a basis for either underpricing competitors and gaining market share at their expense or earning a higher profit margin selling at the going price. A cost advantage will generate superior profitability unless it is used up in aggressive price-cutting efforts to win sales from rivals. Firms that achieve low-cost leadership typically make low cost *relative to competitors* the theme of their entire business strategy—though they must be careful not to pursue low cost so zealously that their products end up being too stripped down and cheaply made to generate buyer appeal.

A low-cost leader's basis for competitive advantage is lower overall costs than competitors.

---

[2]The classification scheme follows that presented in Michael E. Porter, *Competitive Strategy: Techniques for Analyzing Industries and Competitors* (New York: Free Press, 1980), chap. 2, especially pp. 35–39 and 44–46.

T A B L E 5-1   **Distinctive Features of the Generic Competitive Strategies**

Type of Feature	Low-Cost Leadership	Differentiation	Focus
Strategic target	• A broad cross-section of the market.	• A broad cross-section of the market.	• A narrow market niche where buyer needs and preferences are distinctively different from the rest of the market.
Basis of competitive advantage	• Lower costs than competitors.	• An ability to offer buyers something different from competitors.	• Lower cost in serving the niche or an ability to offer niche buyers something customized to their requirements and tastes.
Product line	• A good basic product with few frills (acceptable quality and limited selection).	• Many product variations, wide selection, strong emphasis on the chosen differentiating features.	• Customized to fit the specialized needs of the target segment.
Production emphasis	• A continuous search for cost reduction without sacrificing acceptable quality and essential features.	• Invent ways to create value for buyers.	• Tailor-made for the niche.
Marketing emphasis	• Try to make a virtue out of product features that lead to low cost.	• Build in whatever features buyers are willing to pay for. • Charge a premium price to cover the extra costs of differentiating features.	• Communicate the focuser's unique ability to satisfy the buyer's specialized requirements.
Sustaining the strategy	• Economical prices/good value. • All elements of strategy aim at contributing to a sustainable cost advantage—the key is to manage costs down, year after year, in every area of the business.	• Communicate the points of difference in credible ways. • Stress constant improvement and use innovation to stay ahead of imitative competitors. • Concentrate on a few key differentiating features; use them to create a reputation and brand image.	• Remain totally dedicated to serving the niche better than other competitors; don't blunt the firm's image and efforts by entering other segments and adding other product categories to widen market appeal.

> ## ILLUSTRATION CAPSULE
> ### 12
>
> ### WINNING A COST ADVANTAGE:
> ### IOWA BEEF PACKERS AND FEDERAL EXPRESS
>
> Iowa Beef Packers and Federal Express have been able to win strong competitive positions by restructuring the traditional activity-cost chains in their industries. In beef packing, the traditional cost chain involved raising cattle on scattered farms and ranches, shipping them live to labor-intensive, unionized slaughtering plants, and then transporting whole sides of beef to grocery retailers whose butcher departments cut them into smaller pieces and package them for sale to grocery shoppers.
>
> Iowa Beef Packers revamped the traditional chain with a radically different strategy—large automated plants employing nonunion labor were built near economically transportable supplies of cattle, and the meat was partially butchered at the processing plant into smaller high-yield cuts (sometimes sealed in plastic casing ready for purchase), boxed, and shipped to retailers. IBP's inbound cattle transportation expenses, traditionally a major cost item, were cut significantly by avoiding the weight losses that occurred when live animals were shipped long distances; major outbound shipping cost savings were achieved by not having to ship whole sides of beef with their high waste factor. Iowa Beef's strategy was so successful that it was, in 1985, the largest U.S. meatpacker, surpassing the former
>
> industry leaders, Swift, Wilson, and Armour.
>
> Federal Express innovatively redefined the activity-cost chain for rapid delivery of small parcels. Traditional firms like Emery and Airborne Express operated by collecting freight packages of varying sizes, shipping them to their destination points via air freight and commercial airlines, and then delivering them to the addressee. Federal Express opted to focus only on the market for overnight delivery of small packages and documents. These were collected at local drop points during the late afternoon hours, flown on company-owned planes during early evening hours to a central hub in Memphis where from 11 P.M. to 3 A.M. each night, all parcels were sorted, then reloaded on company planes, and flown during the early morning hours to their destination points, where they were delivered the next morning by company personnel using company trucks. The cost structure so achieved by Federal Express was low enough to permit it to guarantee overnight delivery of a small parcel anywhere in the United States for a price as low as $11. In 1986, Federal Express had a 58 percent market share of the air-express package delivery market versus a 15 percent share for UPS, 11 percent for Airborne Express, and 10 percent for Emery/Purolator.

Source: Based on information in Michael E. Porter, *Competitive Advantage* (New York: Free Press, 1985), p. 109.

Opening up a Cost Advantage   To achieve a cost advantage, a firm's cumulative costs across its activity-cost chain must be lower than competitors' cumulative costs. There are two ways to accomplish this:

- Do a better job of improving efficiency and controlling costs along the existing activity-cost chain.
- Revamp the firm's activity-cost chain to bypass some cost-producing activities altogether.

Achieving a cost advantage entails (a) outmanaging rivals on efficiency and cost control and/or (b) finding creative ways to cut cost-producing activities out of the activity-cost chain.

Both approaches can be used simultaneously. Successful low-cost producers usually achieve their cost advantages by exhaustively pursuing cost savings throughout the activity-cost chain. No area is overlooked. Normally, low-cost producers have a very cost-conscious organizational culture symbolically reinforced by spartan facilities, limited perks for executives, intolerance of waste, intensive screening of budget requests, and broad employee participation in cost control efforts. But while low-cost producers are champions of frugality, they tend to commit funds aggressively to cost-saving improvements.

A firm intent on being a low-cost producer has to scrutinize each cost-creating activity and identify what drives the cost of the activity. Then it has to use its knowledge about the cost drivers to manage the costs of each activity down further year after year. Where possible, whole activities are eliminated from the activity-cost chain entirely. Companies can achieve dramatic cost advantages from restructuring the cost-chain and eliminating unnecessary cost-producing activities. Illustration Capsule 12 describes how two companies won strong competitive positions by revamping the makeup of their industry's traditional activity-cost chain.

Firms well known for their low-cost leadership strategies include: Lincoln Electric in arc welding equipment, Briggs and Stratton in small horsepower gasoline engines, BIC in ballpoint pens, Black and Decker in tools, Design and Manufacturing in dishwashers (marketed under Sears' Kenmore brand), Beaird-Poulan in chain saws, Ford in heavy-duty trucks, General Electric in major home appliances, Wal-Mart in discount retailing, and Southwest Airlines in commercial airline travel.

The Appeal of Being a Low-Cost Producer   Being the low-cost producer in an industry provides some attractive defenses against the five competitive forces:

> **Competitive Strategy Principle**
>
> *A low-cost leader is in the strongest position to set the floor on market price.*

- As concerns *rival competitors*, the low-cost company is in the best position to compete offensively on the basis of price, to defend against price war conditions, to use the appeal of a lower price to win sales (and market share) from rivals, and to earn above-average profits (based on bigger profit margins or greater sales volume) in markets where price competition thrives.
- As concerns *buyers*, the low-cost company has partial profit margin protection from powerful customers, since such customers are rarely able to bargain price down past the survival level of the next most cost-efficient seller.
- As concerns *suppliers*, the low-cost producer is more insulated than competitors from powerful suppliers *if* greater internal efficiency is the primary source of its cost advantage.

> **Competitive Strategy Principle**
>
> *The competitive power of low-cost leadership is greatest when rivals' products are essentially identical, price competition dominates, most buyers use the product similarly and want similar features, buyer switching costs are low, and large customers shop aggressively for the best price.*

- As concerns *potential entrants*, the low-cost producer can use price-cutting to make it harder for a new rival to win customers; the pricing power of the low-cost producer acts as a barrier for a new entrant.
- As concerns *substitutes*, a low-cost producer is better positioned than higher-cost rivals to use low price as a defense against substitutes trying to gain market inroads.

A low-cost producer's ability to set the industry's price floor and still earn a profit erects barriers around its market position. Anytime price competition becomes a major market force, less efficient rivals get squeezed the most. Firms in a low-cost position relative to rivals have a significant edge in appealing to buyers who base their purchase decision on low price.

A competitive strategy based on low-cost leadership is particularly powerful when:

1.   Price competition among rival sellers is a dominant competitive force.

2. The industry's product is an essentially standardized, commodity-type item readily available from a variety of sellers (a condition that allows buyers to shop for price).

3. There are few ways to achieve product differentiation that have value to buyers (put another way, the differences from brand to brand don't matter much to buyers).

4. Most buyers use the product in the same ways—with common user requirements, a standardized product can fully satisfy the needs of all buyers, in which case price, not features or quality, becomes the dominant competitive force.

5. Buyers incur low switching costs in changing from one seller to another, thus giving them flexibility to shop for the best price.

6. Buyers are large and have significant power to bargain down prices.

The Risks of a Low-Cost Producer Strategy A low-cost competitive approach has its drawbacks. Technological breakthroughs can open up cost reductions for rivals that nullify a low-cost producer's past investments and hard-won gains in efficiency. Rival firms may find it easy and/or inexpensive to imitate the leader's low-cost methods, thus making any advantage short-lived. A company driving hard to push its costs down can become so fixated on cost reduction that it fails to pick up on such significant market changes as growing buyer preference for added quality or service, subtle shifts in how buyers use the product, or declining buyer sensitivity to price and thus gets left behind as buyer interest swings to quality, performance, service, and other differentiating features. In sum, heavy investments in cost reduction can lock a firm into both its present technology and its present strategy, leaving it vulnerable to new technologies and to growing customer interest in something other than a cheaper price.

Differentiation Strategies

Differentiation strategies come into play whenever buyers' needs and preferences are too diverse to be satisfied by a standardized product. A successful differentiator studies buyers' needs and behavior carefully to learn what they consider important and valuable. Then the differentiator incorporates one or several of those features into its product offering to encourage buyer preferences for its brand over the brands of rivals. Competitive advantage results when enough buyers become strongly attached to the attributes of a differentiator's product offering. Successful differentiation allows a firm to

With a differentiation strategy, the basis for competitive advantage is a product whose attributes differ significantly from the products of rivals.

- command a premium price for its product, and/or
- sell more units (because additional buyers are won over by the differentiating features), and/or
- gain greater buyer loyalty to its brand (because some buyers are strongly attracted to the differentiating features).

Differentiation enhances profitability whenever the extra price the product commands outweighs the added costs of achieving differentiation. Differentiation is unsuccessful when buyers don't value the additional features highly enough to buy the product in profitable quantities. And differentiation is unprofitable when the price premium buyers are willing to pay won't cover the extra costs of achieving brand distinctiveness.

The approaches to differentiating a product take many forms: a different taste (Dr Pepper and Listerine), special features (Jenn Air's indoor cooking tops with a vented built-in grill for barbecuing), superior service (Federal Express in overnight package delivery), spare parts availability (Caterpillar guarantees 48-hour spare parts delivery to any customer anywhere in the world or else the part is furnished free), overall value to the customer (McDonald's), engineering design and performance (Mercedes), prestige and distinctiveness (Rolex), product reliability (Johnson & Johnson baby products), quality manufacture (Honda), technological leadership (3M in bonding and coating products), a full range of services (Merrill Lynch), a complete line of products (Campbell soups), and top-of-the-line image and reputation (Brooks Brothers and Ralph Lauren in menswear, Kitchen Aid in dishwashers, and Cross in writing instruments).

Achieving Differentiation   *Anything a firm can do to create buyer value represents a potential basis for differentiation.* Once a firm finds good sources of buyer value, it must build the value-creating attributes into its product at an acceptable cost. A differentiator can incorporate attributes that raise the product's performance or make it more economical to use. Or a firm can incorporate features that enhance buyer satisfaction in tangible or intangible ways during use. Differentiation possibilities can grow out of activities performed anywhere in the activity-cost chain. McDonald's gets high ratings on its french fries partly because it has very strict specifications on the potatoes it purchases from its supplier. The quality of Japanese cars stems primarily from Japanese automakers' skills in manufacturing and quality control. IBM boosts buyer value by providing its customers with an extensive array of services and technical support. L. L. Bean makes its mail-order customers feel secure by providing an unconditional guarantee with no time limit: "All of our products are guaranteed to give 100 percent satisfaction in every way. Return anything purchased from us at anytime if it proves otherwise. We will replace it, refund your purchase price, or credit your credit card, as you wish." Commercial airlines use their empty seats during off-peak travel periods (i.e., their excess capacity) as the basis for awarding free travel to frequent flyers.

What Makes Differentiation Attractive   Differentiation provides some buffer against rivals' strategies because buyers become loyal to the brand or model they like best and often are willing to pay a little (perhaps a lot!) more for it. In addition, successful differentiation (1) erects entry barriers in the form of customer loyalty and uniqueness that newcomers find hard to overcome, (2) mitigates the bargaining power of large buyers since rivals' products are less attractive to them, and (3) helps a firm fend off threats from substitutes. If differentiation allows a firm to charge a higher price and boost profit margins, it will be in a stronger position to withstand powerful suppliers' efforts to raise their prices. Thus, as with cost leadership, successful differentiation creates lines of defense for dealing with the five competitive forces.

As a rule, differentiation strategies work best in situations where (1) there are many ways to differentiate the product or service and many buyers perceive these differences as valuable, (2) buyer needs and uses of the item

*Competitive Strategy
Principle*

The competitive power of a differentiation strategy is greatest when buyer needs are diverse, there are many ways to differentiate that have value to buyers, few rivals choose the same approach, and the firm's product can't be quickly or cheaply imitated.

are diverse, and (3) few rival firms are following a similar differentiation approach.

The most appealing types of differentiation strategies are those least subject to quick or inexpensive imitation. Here is where having core competences becomes a major competitive asset. When a firm has skills and expertise that competitors cannot match easily, it can use them as a basis for successful differentiation. Differentiation is most likely to produce an attractive, longer-lasting competitive edge if it is based on:

- Technical superiority.
- Quality.
- More customer support services.
- More value for the money.

Such differentiating attributes tend to be harder for rivals to copy quickly and profitably.

Real Value, Perceived Value, and Signals of Value   Buyers seldom pay for value they don't perceive, no matter how real the unique features may be.[3] Thus the price premium a differentiation strategy commands reflects *the value actually delivered* to the buyer and *the value the buyer perceives* (even if it is not actually delivered). Actual and perceived value can differ whenever buyers have trouble assessing in advance what their experience with the product will be. Buyers with incomplete knowledge of the product often judge value based on such *signals* as seller's word-of-mouth reputation, attractive packaging, extensive ad campaigns (i.e., how "well known" the product is), ad content and image, brochures and sales presentations, the seller's facilities, the seller's list of customers, the firm's market share, length of time the firm has been in business, price (where price connotes "quality"), and the professionalism, appearance, and personality of the seller's employees. Such signals of value may be as important as actual value (1) when the nature of differentiation is subjective or hard to quantify, (2) when buyers are making a first-time purchase, (3) when repurchase is infrequent, and (4) when buyers are unsophisticated.

Keeping the Cost of Differentiation in Line   Attempts to achieve differentiation usually raise costs. The trick to profitable differentiation is either to keep the costs of achieving differentiation below the price premium the differentiating attributes can command in the marketplace (thus increasing the profit margin per unit sold) or to offset thinner profit margins with enough added volume to increase total profits (larger volume can make up for smaller margins provided differentiation adds enough extra sales). In pursuing differentiation, a firm must be careful not to get its overall unit costs so far out of line with competitors that it has to charge a higher price than buyers are willing to pay. There may also be good reason to add extra differentiating features that are not costly but add to buyer satisfaction—fine restaurants typically provide such extras as a slice of lemon in the water glass, valet parking, and complimentary after-dinner mints.

> ───
> ***Competitive Strategy Principle***
> *A firm whose differentiation strategy delivers only modest extra value but signals that value effectively may command a higher price than a firm that actually delivers higher value but signals it poorly.*
> ───

---

[3]This discussion draws from Porter, *Competitive Advantage* pp. 138–42. Porter's insights here are particularly important to formulating differentiating strategies because they highlight the relevance of "intangibles" and "signals."

Competitive Strategy Principle

A low-cost producer strategy can defeat a differentiation strategy when buyers are satisfied with a standard product and don't think "extra" attributes are worth a higher price.

The Risks of a Differentiation Strategy   There are, of course, no guarantees that differentiation will produce a meaningful competitive advantage. If buyers see little value in uniqueness (i.e., a standard item meets their needs), a low-cost strategy can easily defeat a differentiation strategy. In addition, differentiation can be defeated from the outset if competitors can quickly copy the attempt at differentiating. Rapid imitation means that firms never achieve real differentiation because competing brands keep changing in like ways despite continued efforts to create uniqueness. Thus, to be successful at differentiation, a firm must search out durable sources of uniqueness that cannot be quickly or cheaply imitated. Aside from these considerations, other common pitfalls include:[4]

- Trying to differentiate on the basis of something that does not lower a buyer's cost or enhance a buyer's well-being (as perceived by the buyer).
- Overdifferentiating so that price is too high relative to competitors or product quality or service levels exceed buyers' needs.
- Trying to charge too high a price premium (the bigger the premium, the more buyers can be lured away by lower-priced competitors).
- Ignoring the need to signal value and depending only on tangible product attributes to achieve differentiation.
- Not understanding or identifying what buyers consider as value.

The Strategy of Being a Best-Cost Producer   A differentiation strategy aimed at giving customers *more value for the money* usually means combining an emphasis on low-cost with an emphasis on *more than minimally acceptable* quality, service, features, and performance. The idea is to create superior value by meeting or exceeding buyer expectations on quality-service-features-performance attributes and beating their expectations on price. Strategy-wise, the aim is to be the low-cost producer of a product with *good-to-excellent* product attributes, then use the cost advantage to underprice brands with comparable attributes. Such a competitive approach is termed a *best-cost producer strategy* because the producer has the best (lowest) cost relative to producers whose brands are comparably positioned on the quality-service-features-performance scale. The competitive advantage of a best-cost producer comes from matching close rivals on key attributes and beating them on cost. To become a best-cost producer, a company must match quality at a lower cost than rivals, match features at a lower cost than rivals, match product performance at a lower cost than rivals, and so on. What distinguishes a successful best-cost producer is expertise in incorporating upscale product attributes at a low cost; or, to put it a bit differently, an ability to contain the costs of providing customers with a better product. The most successful best-cost producers have the skills to simultaneously manage unit costs down and product caliber up.

Competitive Strategy Principle

The most powerful competitive approach a company can pursue is relentlessly striving to become a lower and lower cost producer of a higher and higher caliber product, with the intent of eventually becoming the industry's absolute lowest cost producer and, simultaneously, the producer of the industry's overall best product.

A best-cost producer strategy has great appeal from the standpoint of competitive positioning. It produces superior customer value by balancing strategic emphasis on low cost against strategic emphasis on differentiation. In effect, such a *hybrid* strategy allows a company to combine the competitive advantage appeals of both low-cost and differentiation. In markets where

---

[4]Ibid., pp. 160–62.

buyer diversity makes product differentiation the norm and buyers are price and value sensitive, a best-cost producer strategy can be more advantageous than either a pure low-cost producer strategy or a pure differentiation strategy keyed to product superiority. This is because a best-cost producer can position itself near the middle of the market with either a medium-quality product at a below-average price or a very good product at a medium price. Many buyers prefer a mid-range product rather than the cheap, basic product of a low-cost producer or the expensive product of a top-of-the-line differentiator.

Focus and Specialization Strategies

Focusing starts by choosing a market niche where buyers have distinctive preferences or requirements. The niche can be defined by geographic uniqueness, by specialized requirements in using the product, or by special product attributes that appeal only to niche members. *A focuser's basis for competitive advantage is either lower costs than competitors in serving the market niche or an ability to offer niche members something different from other competitors.* A focus strategy based on low cost depends on there being a buyer segment whose needs are less costly to satisfy compared to the rest of the market. A focus strategy based on differentiation depends on there being a buyer segment that demands unique product attributes.

What sets a focus strategy apart is concentrated attention on a narrow piece of the total market.

Examples of firms employing a focus strategy include Tandem Computers (a specialist in "nonstop" computers for customers who need a "fail-safe" system), Rolls Royce (in super luxury automobiles), Apple Computer in desktop publishing (Apple computers produce typeset-quality reports and graphics), Fort Howard Paper (specializing in paper products for industrial and commercial enterprises only), commuter airlines like Skywest and Atlantic Southeast (specializing in low-traffic, short-haul flights linking major airports with smaller cities 50 to 250 miles away), and Bandag (a specialist in truck tire recapping that promotes its recaps aggressively at over 1,000 truck stops).

Using a focus strategy to achieve a cost breakthrough is a fairly common technique. Budget-priced motel chains like Days Inn, Motel 6, and LaQuinta have lowered their investment and operating cost per room by using a no-frills approach and catering to price-conscious travelers. Discount stock brokerage houses have lowered costs by focusing on customers mainly interested in buy-sell transactions who are willing to forgo the investment research, investment advice, and financial services offered by full-service firms like Merrill Lynch. Pursuing a cost advantage via focusing works well when a firm can find ways to lower costs by limiting its customer base to a well-defined buyer segment.

Competitive Strategy Principle
The competitive power of a focus strategy is greatest when: (a) fast-growing segments are big enough to be profitable but small enough not to interest large competitors, (b) no other rivals are concentrating on the segment, and (c) segment buyers require special expertise or custom products.

When Focusing Is Attractive A focus strategy becomes increasingly attractive as more of the following conditions are met:

- The segment is big enough to be profitable.
- The segment has good growth potential.
- The segment is not crucial to the success of major competitors.
- The focusing firm has the skills and resources to serve the segment effectively.

- The focuser can defend itself against challengers based on the customer goodwill it has built up and its superior ability to serve buyers in the segment.

A focuser's specialized skills in serving the target market niche provide a basis for defending against the five competitive forces. Multisegment rivals do not have the same competitive capability to serve the target clientele. The focused firm's competence in serving the market niche raises entry barriers, thus making it harder for companies outside the niche to enter. A focuser's unique capabilities in serving the niche also present a hurdle that makers of substitute products must overcome. The bargaining leverage of powerful customers is blunted somewhat by their own unwillingness to shift their business to rival firms less capable of serving their needs.

Focusing works best (1) when it is costly or difficult for multisegment competitors to meet the specialized needs of the niche, (2) when no other rival is attempting to *specialize* in the same target segment; (3) when a firm doesn't have enough resources to pursue a wider part of the total market; and (4) when the industry has many different segments, thereby allowing a focuser to pick an attractive segment suited to its strengths and capabilities.

The Risks of a Focus Strategy   Focusing carries several risks. One is the chance that competitors will find ways to match the focused firm in serving the narrow target market. Second is the potential for the niche buyer's preferences and needs to shift toward the product attributes desired by the market as a whole; such erosion opens the way for rivals with broad market appeal. Third is the chance that the segment will become so attractive that it becomes inundated with competitors, causing profits to be splintered.

USING OFFENSIVE STRATEGIES TO SECURE COMPETITIVE ADVANTAGE

Competitive Strategy Principle

Competitive advantage is usually acquired by employing a creative offensive strategy that can't be easily counteracted by rivals.

An offensive strategy, if successful, can open up a competitive advantage over rivals.[5] How long this process takes depends on the industry's competitive characteristics. The *buildup period*, shown in Figure 5–1, can be short as in service businesses which need little in the way of equipment and distribution support to implement a new offensive move. Or the buildup can take much longer, as in capital intensive and technologically sophisticated industries where firms may need several years to debug a new technology, bring new capacity on line, and win consumer acceptance of a new product. Ideally, an offensive move builds competitive advantage quickly; the longer it takes the more likely rivals will spot the move, see its potential, and begin responding. The size of the advantage (indicated on the vertical scale in Figure 5–1) can be large (as in pharmaceuticals where patents on new drugs produce a substantial advantage) or small (as in apparel where popular new designs can be imitated quickly).

Following a successful competitive offensive, there is a *benefit period* during which the fruits of competitive advantage can be enjoyed. The length of the

[5]Ian C. MacMillan, "How Long Can You Sustain a Competitive Advantage," reprinted in Liam Fahey, *The Strategic Planning Management Reader* (Englewood Cliffs, N.J.: Prentice Hall, 1989), pp. 23–24.

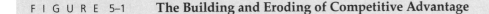

F I G U R E 5–1   **The Building and Eroding of Competitive Advantage**

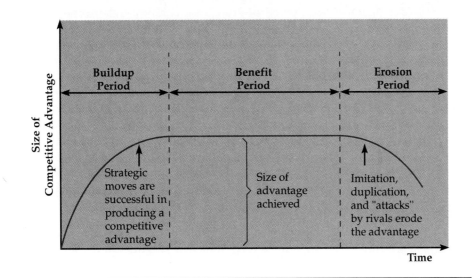

benefit period depends on how much time it takes rivals to launch counter-offensives and begin closing the competitive gap. A lengthy benefit period gives a firm valuable time to earn above-average profits and recoup the investment made in creating the advantage. The best strategic offensives produce big competitive advantages and long benefit periods.

As competitors respond with counteroffensives, the *erosion period* begins. Any competitive advantage a firm currently holds will eventually be eroded by the actions of competent, resourceful competitors.[6] Thus, to sustain its initial advantage, a firm must devise a second strategic offensive. The groundwork for the second offensive needs to be laid during the benefit period so that the firm is ready for launch when competitors respond to the earlier offensive. To successfully sustain a competitive advantage, a firm must stay a step ahead of rivals by mounting one creative strategic offensive after another.

There are six basic ways to mount strategic offensives:[7]

- Attacks on competitor strengths.
- Attacks on competitor weaknesses.
- Simultaneous attack on many fronts.
- End-run offensives.
- Guerrilla offensives.
- Preemptive strikes.

---

[6]Ian C. MacMillan, "Controlling Competitive Dynamics by Taking Strategic Initiative," *The Academy of Management Executive* 2, no. 2 (May 1988), p. 111.

[7]Philip Kotler and Ravi Singh, "Marketing Warfare in the 1980's," *The Journal of Business Strategy* 1, no. 3 (Winter 1981), pp. 30–41; Philip Kotler, *Marketing Management*, 5th ed. (Englewood Cliffs, N.J.: Prentice Hall, 1984), pp. 401–6; and Ian MacMillan, "Preemptive Strategies," *Journal of Business Strategy* 14, no. 2 (Fall 1983), pp. 16–26.

Attacking Competitor Strengths

There are two good reasons to go head-to-head against rivals, pitting one's own strengths against theirs, price for price, model for model, promotion tactic for promotion tactic, and geographic area by geographic area. The first is to try to gain market share by overpowering weaker rivals; challenging weaker rivals where they are strongest is attractive whenever a firm can win a decisive market victory and a commanding edge over struggling competitors. The other reason is to whittle away at a strong rival's competitive advantage; here success is measured by how much the competitive gap is narrowed. The merits of a strength-against-strength offensive challenge, of course, depend on how much the offensive costs compared to its benefits. To succeed, the initiator needs enough competitive strength and resources to take at least some market share from the targeted rivals.

One of the most powerful offensive strategies is to challenge rivals with an equally good or better product and a lower price.

All-out attacks on competitor strengths can involve initiatives on any of several fronts—price-cutting, comparison ads, new features that appeal to a rival's customers, new plant capacity in a rival's backyard, or new models that match rivals'. One of the best ploys is for the aggressor to attack with an equally good product offering and a lower price.[8] This can produce market share gains if the targeted rival has strong reasons for not cutting its prices and if the challenger convinces buyers that its product is just as good. However, such a strategy will increase profits only if volume gains offset the impact of thinner margins per unit sold.

In another type of price-aggressive attack, firms first achieve a cost advantage and then attack competitors with a lower price.[9] Price-cutting supported by a cost advantage is the strongest basis for launching and sustaining a price-aggressive offensive. Without a cost advantage, price-cutting works only if the aggressor has more financial resources and can outlast its rivals in a war of attrition.

Competitive Strategy Principle

Challenging larger, entrenched competitors with aggressive price-cutting is foolhardy unless the aggressor has either a cost advantage or greater financial strength.

Attacking Competitor Weaknesses

In this offensive approach, firms concentrate their competitive attention directly on the weaknesses of rivals. There are a number of weaknesses which can prove fruitful to challenge:

Competitive Strategy Principle

Challenging rivals where they are most vulnerable is more likely to succeed than challenging them where they are strongest, especially if the challenger has advantages in the areas where rivals are weak.

- Attack geographic regions where a rival has a weak market share or is exerting less competitive effort.
- Attack buyer segments that a rival is neglecting or is weakly equipped to serve.
- Attack rivals that lag on quality, features, or product performance; in such cases, a challenger with a better product can often convince the most performance-conscious customers of lagging rivals to switch to its brand.
- Attack rivals that have done a poor job of servicing customers; in such cases, a service-oriented challenger can win a rival's disenchanted customers.

---

[8]Kotler, *Marketing Management*, p. 402.
[9]Ibid., p. 403.

- Attack rivals with weak advertising and brand recognition; a challenger with strong marketing skills and a good image can often move in on lesser-known rivals.
- Attack market leaders that have gaps in their product line; challengers can exploit opportunities to develop these gaps into strong, new market segments.
- Attack market leaders who are ignoring certain buyer needs by introducing product versions that satisfy these needs.

As a rule, attacks on competitor weaknesses have a better chance of succeeding than attacks on competitor strengths, provided the weaknesses represent important vulnerabilities and the rival is caught by surprise with no ready defense.[10]

Simultaneous Attack on Many Fronts

Sometimes aggressors launch a grand competitive offensive involving several major initiatives in an effort to throw a rival off-balance, scatter its attention, and force it into channeling resources to protect all its sides simultaneously. Hunt's tried such an offensive several years ago in an attempt to wrest market share from Heinz ketchup. The attack began when Hunt's introduced two new ketchup flavors to disrupt consumers' taste preferences, try to create new product segments, and capture more shelf space in retail stores. Simultaneously, Hunt's lowered its price to 70 percent of Heinz's; it offered sizable trade allowances to retailers; and it raised its advertising budget to over twice that of Heinz's.[11] The offensive failed because not enough Heinz users tried the Hunt's brands, and many of those who did soon switched back to Heinz. Grand offensives have their best chance of success when a challenger, because of superior resources, can overpower its rivals by outspending them across-the-board long enough to buy its way into a position of market leadership and competitive advantage.

End-Run Offensives

End-run offensives seek to avoid head-on challenges tied to aggressive price-cutting, escalated advertising, or costly efforts to outdifferentiate rivals. Instead the idea is to maneuver *around* competitors and lead the way into unoccupied market territory. Examples of end-run offensives include moving aggressively into geographic areas where close rivals have no market presence, trying to create new segments by introducing products with different attributes and performance features to better meet the needs of selected buyers, and leapfrogging into next-generation technologies to supplant existing products and/or production processes. With an end-run offensive, a firm can gain a significant first-mover advantage in a new arena and force competitors to play catch-up. The most successful end-runs change the rules of the competitive game in the aggressor's favor.

End-run offensives dodge head-to-head confrontations, concentrating instead on innovative product attributes, technological advances, and early entry into less contested geographic markets.

---

[10]For a discussion of the use of surprise, see William E. Rothschild, "Surprise and the Competitive Advantage," *Journal of Business Strategy* 4, no. 3 (Winter 1984), pp. 10–18.

[11]As cited in Kotler, *Marketing Management*, p. 404.

Guerrilla Offensives

Guerrilla offensives are particularly well-suited to small challengers who have neither the resources nor the market visibility to mount a full-fledged attack on industry leaders. A guerrilla offensive uses the hit-and-run principle, selectively attacking where and when an underdog can temporarily exploit the situation to its own advantage. There are several ways to wage a guerrilla offensive:[12]

1. Attack a narrow, well-defined segment that is weakly defended by competitors.
2. Attack areas where rivals are overextended and have spread their resources most thinly (possibilities include going after their customers in less-populated geographic areas, enhancing delivery schedules at times when competitors' deliveries are running behind, adding to quality when rivals have quality control problems, and boosting technical services when buyers are confused by the number of competitors' models and features).
3. Make small, scattered, random raids on leaders with such tactics as occasional lowballing on price (to win a big order or steal a key account), intense bursts of promotional activity, and legal actions charging antitrust violations, patent infringement, and unfair advertising.

Preemptive Strategies

Preemptive strategies create competitive advantage by catapulting the aggressor into a prime competitive position which rivals are prevented or discouraged from matching.

Preemptive strategies involve moving first to secure an advantageous position that rivals are foreclosed or discouraged from duplicating. There are several ways to win a prime strategic position with preemptive moves:[13]

- Expand production capacity ahead of market demand in hopes of discouraging rivals from following suit. When rivals are "bluffed" out of adding capacity by a fear of creating long-term excess supply and underutilized plants, the preemptor can win a bigger market share if market demand grows and its own plant capacity fills.
- Tie up the best (or the most) raw material sources and/or the most reliable, high-quality suppliers via long-term contracts or backward vertical integration. This move can relegate rivals to struggling for second-best supply positions.
- Secure the best geographic locations. An attractive first-mover advantage can often be locked up by moving to obtain the most favorable site along a heavily traveled thoroughfare, at a new interchange or intersection, in a new shopping mall, in a natural beauty spot, close to cheap transportation or raw material supplies or market outlets, and so on.
- Obtain the business of prestigious customers.

[12]For more details, see MacMillan, "How Business Strategists Can Use Guerrilla Warfare Tactics," *Journal of Business Statistics* 1, no. 2 (Fall 1980), pp. 63–65; Kathryn R. Harrigan, *Strategic Flexibility* (Lexington, Mass.: Lexington Books, 1985), pp. 30–45; and Liam Fahey, "Guerrilla Strategy: The Hit-and-Run Attack," in Fahey, *The Strategic Planning Management Reader*, pp. 194–97.
[13]The use of preemptive moves is treated comprehensively in Ian C. MacMillan, "Preemptive Strategies," *Journal of Business Strategy*, pp. 16–26. What follows in this section is based on MacMillan's article.

- Build a "psychological" image in the minds of consumers that is unique and hard to copy and that establishes a compelling appeal and rallying cry. Examples include Avis's well-known "We try harder" theme, Frito-Lay's guarantee to retailers of "99.5% service," Holiday Inn's assurance of "no surprises," and Prudential's "piece of the rock" image of safety and permanence.
- Secure exclusive or dominant access to the best distributors in an area.

Preemption has been used successfully by a number of companies. General Mills' Red Lobster restaurant chain has gained a prime position in the restaurant business by establishing strong relationships with very dependable seafood suppliers. DeBeers became the dominant world distributor of diamonds by buying the production of most of the important diamond mines. Du Pont's aggressive capacity expansions in titanium dioxide, while not blocking all competitors from expanding, did discourage enough to give it a leadership position in the titanium dioxide industry.

To be successful, a preemptive move doesn't have to totally block rivals from following or copying; it merely needs to give a firm a "prime" position. A prime position is one that puts rivals at a competitive disadvantage and is not easily circumvented.

Choosing Who to Attack

Aggressor firms need to analyze which of their rivals to attack as well as how to attack them. There are basically three types of firms that can be attacked offensively:[14]

1. *Market leader*(s). Waging an offensive against strong leader(s) risks squandering valuable resources in a futile effort and even precipitating a fierce and profitless industrywide battle for market share. Offensive attacks on a major competitor make the best sense when the leader in terms of size and market share is not the "true leader" in terms of serving the market well. Signs of leader vulnerability include unhappy buyers, sliding profits, strong emotional commitment to a technology the leader has pioneered, outdated plants and equipment, a preoccupation with diversification into other industries, a product line that is clearly not superior to rivals', and a competitive strategy that lacks real strength based on low-cost leadership or differentiation. Attacks on leaders can also succeed when the challenger is able to revamp its activity-cost chain or innovate to gain a fresh cost-based or differentiation-based competitive advantage.[15] Attacks on leaders need not have the objective of making the aggressor the new leader; a challenger may "win" by simply wresting enough sales from the leader to make the aggressor a stronger runner-up.

2. *Runner-up firms*. Offensives against weaker, vulnerable runner-up firms entail relatively low risk. Attacking a runner-up is an especially attractive option when a challenger's competitive strengths match the runner-up's weaknesses.

---

[14]Kotler, *Marketing Management*, p. 400.
[15]Porter, *Competitive Advantage*, p. 518.

3. *Struggling enterprises that are on the verge of going under.* Challenging a hard-pressed rival in ways that further sap its financial strength and competitive position can weaken its resolve enough to prompt its exit from the market.

4. *Small local and regional firms.* Because these firms typically have limited expertise, a challenger with broader capabilities is well-positioned to raid their biggest and best customers—particularly those who are growing rapidly, have increasingly sophisticated needs, and may already be thinking about switching to a supplier with more full-service capability.

As we have said, successful strategies are grounded in competitive advantage. This goes for offensive strategies too. The competitive advantage potentials that offer the strongest basis for a strategic offensive include:[16]

- Developing a lower-cost product design.
- Making changes in production operations that lower costs or enhance differentiation.
- Developing product features that deliver superior performance or lower user costs.
- Giving buyers more responsive after-sale support.
- Escalating the marketing effort in an undermarketed industry.
- Pioneering a new distribution channel.
- Bypassing wholesale distributors and selling direct to the end-user.

A strategic offensive *must* be tied to what a firm does best—its competitive strengths and capabilities. As a rule, these strengths take the form of a *key skill* (cost reduction capabilities, customer service skills, technical expertise) or a uniquely *strong functional competence* (engineering and product design, manufacturing expertise, advertising and promotion, marketing know-how).[17]

USING DEFENSIVE STRATEGIES TO PROTECT COMPETITIVE ADVANTAGE

The foremost purpose of defensive strategy is to protect competitive advantage and fortify the firm's competitive position.

In a competitive market, all firms are subject to attacks from rivals. Offensive attacks can come both from new entrants and from established firms seeking to improve their market positions. The purpose of defensive strategy is to lower the risk of being attacked, weaken the impact of any attack that occurs, and influence challengers to aim their efforts at other rivals. While defensive strategy usually doesn't enhance a firm's competitive advantage, it should help fortify a firm's competitive position and sustain whatever competitive advantage it has.

There are several basic ways for a firm to protect its competitive position. One approach involves trying to block challengers' avenues for mounting an offensive; the options include:[18]

---

[16]Ibid., pp. 520–22.

[17]For more details, see Macmillan, "Controlling Competitive Dynamics," pp. 112–16.

[18]Porter, *Competitive Advantage*, pp. 489–94.

- Broadening the firm's product line to close off vacant niches and gaps to would-be challengers.
- Introducing models or brands that match the characteristics challengers' models already have or might have.
- Keeping prices low on models that most closely match competitors' offerings.
- Signing exclusive agreements with dealers and distributors to keep competitors from using the same ones.
- Granting dealers and distributors sizable volume discounts to discourage them from experimenting with other suppliers.
- Offering free or low-cost training to buyers' personnel in the use of the firm's product.
- Making it harder for competitors to get buyers to try their brands by (1) giving special price discounts to buyers who are considering trial use of rival brands, (2) resorting to high levels of couponing and sample giveaways to buyers most prone to experiment, and (3) making early announcements about impending new products or price changes so buyers postpone switching.
- Raising the amount of financing provided to dealers and/or buyers.
- Reducing delivery times for spare parts.
- Increasing warranty coverages.
- Patenting alternative technologies.
- Protecting proprietary know-how in products, production technologies, and other parts of the activity-cost chain.
- Signing exclusive contracts with the best suppliers to block access of aggressive rivals.
- Purchasing natural resource reserves ahead of present needs to keep them from competitors.
- Avoiding suppliers that also serve competitors.
- Challenging rivals' products or practices in regulatory proceedings.

There are many ways to blunt offensive challenges from rival firms.

Moves such as these not only buttress a firm's present position, they also present competitors with a moving target. It is not enough just to try to protect the status quo. A good defense entails adjusting quickly to changing industry conditions and, on occasion, being a first-mover to block or preempt moves by would-be aggressors. A mobile defense is always preferable to a stationary defense.

A second approach to defensive strategy entails signaling strong retaliation if a challenger attacks. The goal is to dissuade challengers from attacking at all (by raising their expectations that the resulting battle will be more costly than it is worth) or divert challengers to options less threatening to the defender. Would-be challengers can be signaled by:[19]

One of the best defensive strategies is to signal challengers that aggressive actions will be met with strong retaliatory countermeasures.

- Publicly announcing management's commitment to maintain the firm's present market share.

---

[19]Porter, *Competitive Advantage*, pp. 495–97. The listing here is selective; Porter offers a greater number of options.

- Publicly announcing plans to construct adequate production capacity to meet forecast demand growth, and sometimes building ahead of demand.
- Giving out advance information about a new product, technological breakthrough, or the planned introduction of important new brands or models, in hopes that challengers will be induced to delay moves of their own until they see if the signaled actions are true.
- Publicly committing the firm to a policy of matching the prices or terms offered by competitors.
- Maintaining a war chest of cash and marketable securities.
- Making an occasional strong counterresponse to the moves of weak competitors to enhance the firm's image as a tough defender.

Another way to dissuade rivals involves trying to lower the profit inducement for challengers to launch an offensive. When a firm's or industry's profitability is enticingly high, challengers are more willing to tackle high defensive barriers and combat strong retaliation. A defender can deflect attacks, especially from new entrants, by deliberately forgoing some short-run profits and by using accounting methods that obscure profitability.

VERTICAL INTEGRATION STRATEGIES

Vertical integration strategies aim at extending a firm's competitive scope within the same industry. Firms can expand their range of activities backward into sources of supply and/or forward toward end-users. A manufacturer that builds a new plant to make component parts rather than purchase them from suppliers remains in essentially the same industry as before. The only change is that it has business units in two stages of production in the industry's total activity-chain. Similarly, if a personal computer manufacturer elects to integrate forward by opening retail stores to market its brands, it remains in the personal computer business even though its competitive scope extends further forward in the industry chain.

Moves to vertically integrate can aim at *full integration* (participating in all stages of the process of getting products in the hands of final-users) or *partial integration* (building positions in just some stages of the industry's total production-distribution chain). A firm can accomplish vertical integration by starting its own company in other stages of the industry's activity chain or by acquiring a company already positioned in the stage it wishes to integrate.

Competitive Strategy Principle

A vertical integration strategy has appeal only if it significantly strengthens a firm's competitive position.

The Appeal of Vertical Integration

The only good reason for investing company resources in vertical integration is to strengthen the firm's competitive position.[20] Unless vertical integration produces sufficient cost-savings to justify the extra investment or yields a competitive advantage, it has no real profit or strategic payoff.

---

[20]See Kathryn R. Harrigan, "Matching Vertical Integration Strategies to Competitive Conditions," *Strategic Management Journal* 7, no. 6 (November–December 1986), pp. 535–56; for a fuller discussion of the advantages and disadvantages of vertical integration, see Kathryn R. Harrigan, *Strategic Flexibility* (Lexington, Mass.: Lexington Books, 1985), p. 162.

Integrating backward generates cost-savings only when the volume needed is big enough to capture the same scale economies suppliers have and when it can match or exceed suppliers' production efficiency. Backward integration usually generates the largest cost advantage when suppliers have sizable profit margins, when the item being supplied is a major cost component, and when the needed technological skills are easily mastered. Backward vertical integration can produce a differentiation-based competitive advantage when a company, by supplying its own parts, ends up with a better-quality part and thereby significantly enhances the performance of its final product.

Backward integration can also spare a firm the uncertainty of being dependent on suppliers of crucial raw materials or support services, and it can lessen the firm's vulnerability to powerful suppliers intent on raising prices at every opportunity. Stockpiling, fixed-price contracts, or the use of substitute inputs may not be attractive ways for dealing with uncertain supply conditions or economically powerful suppliers. When this is the case, backward integration can be an organization's most profitable and competitively secure option for accessing reliable supplies of essential materials and support services at favorable prices.

The strategic impetus for forward integration has much the same roots. Undependable sales and distribution channels can give rise to costly inventory pileups and frequent underutilization of capacity, thereby undermining the economies of a steady, near-capacity production operation. In such cases, it is often advantageous for a firm to set up its own wholesale-retail distribution network in order to gain dependable channels through which to push its products to end-users. Sometimes even a small percentage increase in the average rate of capacity utilization can boost manufacturing margins enough to make forward integration economical. On other occasions, forward integration into distribution and retailing is cheaper than dealing with independent distributors and retailers, thus providing a source of cost advantage.

Integrating forward into manufacturing may help a raw materials producer achieve greater product differentiation and escape the price-oriented competition of a commodity business. Often, in the early phases of vertical product flow, intermediate goods are "commodities" in the sense that they have essentially identical technical specifications irrespective of producer (as is the case with crude oil, poultry, sheet steel, cement, and textile fibers). Competition in commodity or commodity-like markets is usually fiercely price-competitive, with shifting supply and demand conditions causing volatile profits. However, the closer the production stage to the ultimate consumer, the greater the opportunities for a firm to break out of a commodity-like competitive environment and differentiate its end-product via design, service, quality features, packaging, promotion, and so on. Product differentiation often reduces the importance of price in comparison with other product attributes and allows for improved profit margins.

For a manufacturer, integrating forward may mean building a chain of closely supervised dealer franchises or establishing company-owned and -operated retail outlets. Or it may entail simply establishing a sales force instead of selling through manufacturer's agents or independent distributors.

The Strategic Disadvantages of Vertical Integration

The big disadvantage of vertical integration is that it locks a firm deeper into an industry; unless it builds competitive advantage, it is a questionable strategic move.

Vertical integration has some potential weaknesses, however. First, it boosts a firm's capital investment in the industry, perhaps denying financial resources to more worthwhile pursuits. Second, integration introduces additional risks, since it extends the enterprise's scope of activity across the industry chain. Third, vertical integration increases a firm's interest in protecting its present technology and production facilities even though they are becoming obsolete. Because of the high cost of abandoning such investments before they are worn out, fully integrated firms are more vulnerable to new technologies and new products than partially integrated or nonintegrated firms.

Fourth, vertical integration can pose problems of balancing capacity at each stage in the activity-chain. The most efficient scale of operation at each step in the chain can vary substantially. Exact self-sufficiency at each interface is the exception not the rule. Where internal capacity is deficient to supply the next stage, the difference has to be bought externally. Where internal capacity is excessive, customers need to be found for the surplus. And if by-products are generated, they must be disposed of.

All in all, a strategy of vertical integration can have both strengths and weaknesses. Which direction the scales tip depends on (1) how compatible vertical integration is with the organization's long-term strategic interests and performance objectives, (2) how much it strengthens an organization's position in the overall industry, and (3) the extent to which it creates competitive advantage. Unless these considerations yield solid benefits, vertical integration is unlikely to be an attractive business strategy option.[21]

FIRST-MOVER ADVANTAGES AND DISADVANTAGES

Competitive Strategy Principle

Because of first-mover advantages and disadvantages, when to make a move is often as crucial as what move to make.

When to make a strategic move is often as crucial as *what* move to make. Timing is especially important when *first-mover advantages* or *disadvantages* exist.[22] Being first to initiate a strategic move can have a high payoff when (1) pioneering helps build a firm's image and reputation with buyers, (2) early commitments to supplies of raw materials, new technologies, distribution channels, and so on can produce an absolute cost advantage over rivals, (3) first-time customers remain strongly loyal to pioneering firms in making repeat purchases, and (4) moving first constitutes a preemptive strike, making imitation extra hard or unlikely. The bigger the first-mover advantages, the more attractive that making the first move becomes.

However, a "wait and see" approach doesn't always carry a competitive penalty. Making the first move may carry greater risks than a late move. First-mover disadvantages (or late-mover advantages) arise when: (1) pioneering leadership is much more costly and only negligible experience curve effects accrue to the leader, (2) technological change is so rapid that early investments are soon obsolete (thus allowing following firms to gain the advantages of next-generation newest products and more efficient processes), (3) it is easy for late-

---

[21]For an extensive, well-researched look at the whole family of approaches to vertical integration, see Kathryn R. Harrigan, "Formulating Vertical Integration Strategies," *Academy of Management Review* 9, no. 4 (October 1984), pp. 638–52.

[22]Porter, *Competitive Strategy*, pp. 232–33.

comers to crack the market because customer loyalty to pioneering firms is weak, and (4) skills and know-how developed by the market leaders can be easily copied or even surpassed by late movers. Good timing, therefore, is an important ingredient in deciding whether to be aggressive or cautious.

KEY POINTS

The challenge of competitive strategy—low-cost, differentiation, or focus—is to create a competitive advantage for the firm. Competitive advantage comes from positioning a firm in the marketplace so it has an edge in coping with competitive forces and in attracting buyers.

A strategy of trying to be the low-cost producer works well in situations where

- The industry's product is pretty much the same from seller to seller.
- The marketplace is dominated by price competition (buyers are prone to shop for the lowest price).
- There are only a few ways to achieve product differentiation that have much value to buyers.
- Most buyers use the product in the same ways and thus have common user requirements.
- Buyers' costs in switching from one seller or brand to another are low (or even zero).
- Buyers are large and have significant bargaining power.

To achieve a low-cost advantage, a company must become more skilled than rivals in controlling cost drivers and/or it must find innovative cost-saving ways to revamp the activity-cost chain.

Differentiation strategies can produce a competitive edge based on technical superiority, quality, service, or more value for the money. Differentiation strategies work *best* when:

- There are many ways to differentiate the product/service that buyers think have value.
- Buyer needs or uses of the product/service are diverse.
- Not many rivals are following a similar differentiation strategy.

Anything a firm can do to create buyer value represents a potential basis for differentiation. Successful differentiation is usually keyed to lowering the buyer's cost of using the item, raising the performance the buyer gets, giving the buyer more value for the money, or boosting a buyer's psychological satisfaction. A best-cost producer strategy works especially well in market situations where product differentiation is the rule and buyers are price sensitive.

The competitive advantage of focusing comes from achieving lower costs in serving the target market niche or from offering niche buyers something different from rivals—in other words, the advantage a firm gains with a focus strategy is either *cost-based* or *differentiation-based*. Focusing works best when:

- Buyer needs or uses of the item are diverse.
- No other rival is attempting to *specialize* in the same target segment.

- A firm lacks the ability to go after a wider part of the total market.
- Buyer segments differ widely in size, growth rate, profitability, and intensity in the five competitive forces, making some segments more attractive than others.

A variety of offensive strategic moves can be used to secure a competitive advantage. Strategic offensives can be aimed at competitors' strengths or weaknesses; they can involve end-runs or grand offensives; they can be designed as guerrilla actions or as preemptive strikes; and the target of the offensive can be a market leader, a runner-up firm, or the smallest and/or weakest firms in the industry.

To defend its current position, a company can: (1) make moves that fortify its current position, (2) present competitors with a moving target to avoid "out-of-date" vulnerability, and (3) dissuade rivals from even trying to attack.

Vertical integration forward or backward makes strategic sense if it strengthens a company's position via either cost reduction or enhanced product differentiation.

The timing of strategic moves is important. First-movers sometimes gain strategic advantage; at other times, it is cheaper and easier to be a follower than a leader.

SUGGESTED READINGS

Aaker, David A. "Managing Assets and Skills: The Key to a Sustainable Competitive Advantage." *California Management Review* 31, no. 2 (Winter 1989), pp. 91–106.

Cohen, William A. "War in the Marketplace." *Business Horizons* 29, no. 2 (March–April 1986), pp. 10–20.

Coyne, Kevin P. "Sustainable Competitive Advantage—What It Is, What It Isn't." *Business Horizons* 29, no. 1 (January–February 1986), pp. 54–61.

Harrigan, Kathryn R. "Guerrilla Strategies of Underdog Competitors." *Planning Review* 14, no. 16 (November 1986), pp. 4–11.

———. "Formulating Vertical Integration Strategies." *Academy of Management Review* 9, no. 4 (October 1984), pp. 638–52.

Hout, Thomas, Michael E. Porter, and Eileen Rudden. "How Global Companies Win Out." *Harvard Business Review* 60, no. 5 (September–October 1982), pp. 98–108.

MacMillan, Ian C. "Preemptive Strategies." *Journal of Business Strategy* 4, no. 2 (Fall 1983), pp. 16–26.

———. "Controlling Competitive Dynamics by Taking Strategic Initiative." *The Academy of Management Executive* 2, no. 2 (May 1988), pp. 111–18.

Porter, Michael E. *Competitive Advantage* (New York: Free Press, 1985), chaps. 3, 4, 5, 7, 14, and 15.

Rothschild, William E. "Surprise and the Competitive Advantage." *Journal of Business Strategy* 4, no. 3 (Winter 1984), pp. 10–18.

Thompson, Arthur A. "Strategies for Staying Cost Competitive." *Harvard Business Review* 62, no. 1 (January–February 1984) pp. 110–17.

Matching Strategy to the Situation

*Strategy isn't something you can nail together in slap-dash fashion
by sitting around a conference table . . .*
Terry Haller

*The essence of formulating competitive strategy is relating a company to its
environment . . . the best strategy for a given firm is ultimately a unique
construction reflecting its particular circumstances.*
Michael E. Porter

You do not choose to become global. The market chooses for you; it forces your hand.
Alain Gomez
CEO, Thomson, S.A.

What kind of strategy best suits a company's business is conditioned partly by
the industry environment in which it competes and partly by the company's
situation. To demonstrate the kinds of considerations involved in matching
strategy to the situation, this chapter examines strategy-making in eight classic
types of industry environments and company situations:

1. Competing in a young, emerging industry.
2. Competing during the transition to industry maturity.
3. Competing in mature or declining industries.
4. Competing in fragmented industries.
5. Competing in international markets.
6. Strategies for industry leaders.
7. Strategies for runner-up firms.
8. Strategies for weak and crisis-ridden firms.

STRATEGIES FOR COMPETING IN EMERGING INDUSTRIES

An emerging industry is one in the early formative stage. Most companies are in a start-up mode, adding people, acquiring or constructing facilities, gearing up production, trying to broaden distribution and gain buyer acceptance. Often, such firms have to work out important product design and technological problems as well. Emerging industries present strategy-makers with some unique challenges:[1]

- Because the market is new and unproven, there are many uncertainties about how it will function, how fast it will grow, and how big it will get; the little historical data available is virtually useless in projecting future trends.

- Much of the technological know-how tends to be proprietary and closely guarded, having been developed in-house by pioneering firms; patent protection is sought for competitive advantage.

- Often, there is no consensus on which production technologies will be most efficient and which product attributes buyers will prefer. The result is industrywide absence of product and technological standardization, wide differences in product quality and performance, and a situation where each firm has to pioneer its own approach to technology, product design, marketing, and distribution.

- Entry barriers tend to be relatively low; additional start-up companies and large outsiders will enter if it becomes more evident that the industry's future is promising.

- Experience curve effects often permit significant cost reductions as volume builds.

- Firms have little hard information about competitors, how fast products are gaining buyer acceptance, and users' experiences with the product; there are no trade associations gathering and distributing information.

- Since all buyers are first-time users, the marketing task is to induce initial purchase and overcome customer concerns about product features, performance reliability, and conflicting claims of rival firms.

- Many buyers expect first-generation products to be rapidly improved, so they wait to buy until technology and product design mature.

- Firms may have trouble securing ample supplies of raw materials and components (until suppliers gear up to meet the industry's needs).

- Many companies find themselves short of funds to support needed R&D and to get through several lean years until the product catches on.

The two critical strategic issues confronting firms in an emerging industry are (1) how to finance the start-up phase and (2) what market segments and competitive advantage to go after to secure a leading industry position.[2] Competitive strategies keyed either to low-cost or differentiation are usually viable. Focusing should be considered when finances are limited and the industry has

---

[1]Michael E. Porter, *Competitive Strategy* (New York: Free Press, 1980), pp. 216–23.
[2]Charles W. Hofer and Dan Schendel, *Strategy Formulation: Analytical Concepts* (St. Paul, Minn.: West Publishing, 1978), pp. 164–65.

too many technological frontiers to pursue at once; one option for financially constrained enterprises is to form a strategic alliance or joint venture with another company to gain access to needed skills and resources. Dealing with all the risks and opportunities of an emerging industry is one of the most challenging business strategy problems. To be successful in an emerging industry, companies need to observe the following guidelines:[3]

1. Try to win the early race for industry leadership by employing a bold, creative entrepreneurial strategy. Because an emerging industry has no established rules of the game and industry participants often try a variety of strategic approaches, a pioneering firm with a powerful strategy can shape the rules and become the industry leader.

2. Push hard to perfect the technology, improve product quality, and develop attractive performance features.

3. Try to capture any first-mover advantages associated with more models, better styling, early commitments to technologies and raw materials suppliers, experience curve effects, and new distribution channels.

4. Search out new customer groups, new geographical areas to enter, and new user applications. Make it easier and cheaper for first-time buyers to try the industry's new product.

5. Gradually shift the advertising emphasis from building product awareness to increasing frequency of use and creating brand loyalty.

6. Move quickly when technological uncertainty clears and a "dominant" technology emerges; try to pioneer the "dominant design" (but be cautious when technology is evolving so rapidly that early investments are likely to become obsolete).

7. Use price cuts to attract price-sensitive buyers into the market.

8. Expect large, established firms looking for growth opportunities to enter the industry as their perceived risk of investing in the industry lessens. Try to prepare for the entry of powerful competitors by forecasting (*a*) who will enter (based on present and future entry barriers) and (*b*) the types of strategies they will employ.

Strategic success in an emerging industry calls for bold entrepreneurship, a willingness to pioneer and take risks, an intuitive feel for what buyers will like and how they will use the product, quick response to new developments, and opportunistic strategy-making.

The short-term value of winning the early race for growth and market share has to be balanced against the longer-range need to build a durable competitive edge and a defendable market position.[4] New entrants, attracted by the growth and profit potential, may crowd the market. Aggressive newcomers, aspiring for industry leadership, can quickly become major players by acquiring and merging the operations of weaker competitors. A young, single-business enterprise in a fast-developing industry can help its cause by selecting knowledgeable members for its board of directors, hiring entrepreneurial managers with experience in guiding young businesses through the development and takeoff, or merging with another firm to gain added expertise and a stronger resource base.

---

[3]Phillip Kotler, *Marketing Management*, 5th ed. (Englewood Cliffs, N.J.: Prentice Hall, 1984), p. 366; and Porter, *Competitive Strategy*, chap. 10.

[4]Hofer and Schendel, *Strategy Formulation*, pp. 164–65.

STRATEGIES FOR COMPETING DURING THE TRANSITION TO INDUSTRY MATURITY

Rapid industry growth doesn't last forever. However, the transition to a slower-growth, maturing environment does not begin on any easily predicted schedule and it can be forestalled by a steady stream of technological advances, product innovations, or other driving forces that keep rejuvenating market demand. Nonetheless, as growth rates slack off, the transition usually produces fundamental changes in the industry's competitive environment:[5]

1. *Slowing growth in buyer demand generates more head-to-head competition for market share.* Firms that want to continue on a rapid-growth track start looking for ways to take customers from competitors. Outbreaks of price-cutting, increased advertising, and other aggressive tactics are common.

2. *Buyers become more sophisticated, often driving a harder bargain on repeat purchases.* Since buyers have experience with the product and are familiar with competing brands, they are better able to evaluate different brands, and will negotiate with sellers to get a better deal.

3. *Competition often produces a greater emphasis on cost and service.* As all sellers begin to offer the product attributes buyers prefer, buyer choices increasingly depend on which seller offers the best combination of price and service.

4. *Firms have a "topping out" problem in adding production capacity.* Slower rates of industry growth mean slowdowns in capacity expansion. Each firm has to monitor rivals' expansion plans and time its own carefully to minimize oversupply conditions in the industry. Adding too much capacity too soon can adversely affect company profits well into the future.

5. *Product innovation and new end-use applications are harder to come by.* Producers find it increasingly difficult to develop new product features, find further uses for the product, and sustain buyer excitement.

6. *International competition increases.* Growth-minded domestic firms start to seek out sales opportunities in foreign markets. Some companies, looking for ways to cut costs, relocate plants to countries with lower wage rates. Greater product standardization and diffusion of technological know-how reduce entry barriers and make it possible for enterprising foreign companies to become serious market contenders in more countries. Industry leadership passes to companies with the biggest global market shares and strong competitive positions in most of the world's major geographic markets.

7. *Industry profitability falls temporarily or permanently.* Slower growth, increased competition, more sophisticated buyers, and occasional periods of overcapacity put pressure on industry profit margins. Weaker, less-efficient firms are usually the hardest hit.

8. *The resulting competitive shakeout induces a number of mergers and acquisitions among former competitors, drives some firms out of the industry, and,*

---

[5]Porter, *Competitive Strategy*, pp. 238–40.

in general, produces industry consolidation. Inefficient firms and firms with weak competitive strategies can survive in a rapid-growth industry. But the much stiffer competition in the industry maturity stage exposes competitive weakness and results in a survival-of-the-fittest market contest.

As market growth slows and competitive pressures build, firms can make several strategic moves to strengthen their competitive positions.[6]

Pruning the Product Line   A wide selection of models, features, and options has competitive value during the growth stage when buyers' needs are still evolving. But such variety can become too costly as price competition stiffens and profit margins are squeezed. Too many product versions prevent firms from achieving the economies of long production runs. In addition, the prices of slow-selling versions may not cover their true costs. Pruning product lines and concentrating sales efforts on items whose margins are highest and/or where the firm has a competitive advantage reduces costs and helps keep strategy matched to company strengths.

More Emphasis on Process Innovation   Efforts to "re-invent" the manufacturing process can have a twofold payoff: lower costs and better quality control. Process innovation can involve mechanizing high-cost activities, revamping production lines to improve labor efficiency, and increased use of advanced technology (robotics, computerized controls, and automatic guided vehicles). Japanese firms have successfully used manufacturing process innovation to become lower-cost producers of higher-quality products.

A Stronger Focus on Cost Reduction   Stiffening price competition gives firms extra incentive to reduce unit costs. Such efforts can cover a broad front: firms can negotiate with suppliers for better prices, switch to lower-priced components, develop more economical product designs, cut unnecessary tasks out of the activity-cost chain, increase manufacturing and distribution efficiency, and trim administrative overhead.

Increasing Sales to Present Customers   In a mature market, growing by taking customers from rivals may not be as appealing as expanding sales to existing customers. Strategies to increase purchases to existing customers can involve broadening the lines offered to include complementary products and ancillary services, finding more ways for customers to use the product, and performing more functions for the buyers (assembling components prior to shipment). Convenience food stores, for example, have boosted average sales per customer by adding video rentals, automatic bank tellers, and deli counters.

Purchasing Rival Firms at Bargain Prices   Sometimes distressed rivals can be acquired cheaply. Bargain-priced acquisitions can help create a low-cost position if they present opportunities for greater operating efficiency. In addition,

As industry growth slows, strategic emphasis shifts to efficiency-increasing, profit-preserving measures: pruning the product line, improving production methods, reducing costs, expanding internationally, and acquiring distressed rivals.

---

[6]The following discussion draws on Porter, *Competitive Strategy*, pp. 241–46.

an acquired firm's customer base can provide expanded market coverage. The most desirable acquisitions are those that will significantly enhance the acquiring firm's competitive strength.

Expanding Internationally   As its domestic market matures, a firm may seek to enter foreign markets where attractive growth potential still exists and competitive pressures are not so strong. Foreign expansion is particularly attractive if equipment no longer suitable for domestic operations is usable for export production or for plants in less developed foreign markets (a condition that lowers entry costs). Such possibilities arise when (1) foreign buyers have less sophisticated needs, (2) end-use applications are much simpler, and (3) foreign competitors are smaller, less formidable, and do not employ the latest production technology. Strategies to expand internationally make particular sense when a domestic firm's skills and reputation are readily transferable to foreign markets.

Strategic Pitfalls

Perhaps the biggest mistake a firm can make during the transition to industry maturity is steering a middle course between low cost, differentiation, and focusing. Such a compromise guarantees that the firm will end up with a fuzzy strategy, no clearly staked out market position, an "average" image with buyers, and no competitive advantage. Other pitfalls include sacrificing long-term competitive position for short-term profit, waiting too long to respond to price-cutting, getting caught with too much capacity as growth slows, overspending on marketing efforts to boost sales growth, and failing to pursue cost reduction soon enough and aggressively enough.

STRATEGIES FOR FIRMS IN MATURE OR DECLINING INDUSTRIES

Many firms operate in industries where demand is growing slower than the economy average—or even declining. Although cash-flow maximization, selling out, and closing down are obvious strategies for uncommitted competitors with dim long-term prospects, strong competitors can still achieve good performance in a stagnant market environment.[7] Stagnant demand by itself is not enough to make an industry unattractive. Selling out may or may not be practical, and closing down operations is always a last resort.

Businesses competing in slow-growth/declining industries have to accept the difficult realities of continuing stagnancy and they must set performance goals consistent with available market opportunities. Although cash flow and return on investment are more appropriate criteria than growth-oriented performance measures, firms don't have to rule out sales and market share growth. Strong competitors may be able to take sales from weaker rivals, and

---

[7]R. G. Hamermesh and S. B. Silk, "How to Compete in Stagnant Industries," *Harvard Business Review* 57, no. 5 (September–October 1979), p. 161.

the acquisition or exit of weaker firms may help remaining companies capture greater market share.

In general, companies that have succeeded in stagnant industries have relied heavily on one of the following strategic themes:[8]

1. *Pursue a focus strategy by identifying, creating, and exploiting the growth segments within the industry.* Slow-growth or declining markets, like other markets, are composed of numerous segments and subsegments. Frequently, one or more of these segments is growing rapidly, despite a lack of growth in the industry as a whole. An astute competitor who is first to concentrate on the most attractive segments can escape stagnating sales and profits and achieve competitive advantage in the target segments.

2. *Stress differentiation based on quality improvement and product innovation.* Either enhanced quality or innovation can rejuvenate demand by creating important new growth segments or inducing buyers to trade up. Successful product innovation opens up an avenue for competing besides meeting or beating rivals' prices. Differentiation based on innovation has the additional advantage of being difficult and expensive for rivals to imitate.

3. *Work diligently and persistently to drive costs down.* When increases in sales cannot be counted on to generate increased earnings, firms can improve profit margins and return on investment by continuously reducing operating costs and increasing efficiency. They can achieve a lower-cost position by: (1) improving the manufacturing process via automation and increased specialization, (2) consolidating underutilized production facilities, (3) adding more distribution channels to ensure the unit volume needed for low-cost production, (4) closing low-volume, high-cost distribution outlets, and (5) revamping the activity-cost chain to eliminate some cost-producing tasks.

These three themes are not mutually exclusive.[9] Attempts to introduce innovative versions of a product can *create* a fast-growing market segment. Similarly, increased operating efficiencies permit price reductions that create price-conscious growth segments. Note that all three themes are spin-offs of the three generic competitive strategies, adjusted to fit the circumstances of a tough industry environment.

The most attractive declining industries are those in which decline is reasonably slow, there is big built-in demand, and some profitable niches remain. Dangers in a stagnating market include: (1) getting trapped in a profitless war of attrition, (2) diverting too much cash out of a business too quickly (thus accelerating a company's demise), and (3) being overly optimistic about the industry's future and waiting complacently for things to get better.

Illustration Capsule 13 describes the creative approach taken by Yamaha to reverse declining market demand for pianos.

Competitive advantage in industries with stagnant or declining market demand usually involves focusing on growth segments, differentiating on the basis of quality improvement and product innovation, or becoming a lower-cost producer.

---

[8]Ibid., p. 162.
[9]Ibid., p. 165.

ILLUSTRATION CAPSULE
13

YAMAHA'S STRATEGY IN THE PIANO INDUSTRY

For some years now, worldwide demand for pianos has been declining—in the mid-1980s the decline was 10 percent annually. Modern-day parents have not put the same stress on music lessons for their children as prior generations of parents did. In an effort to see if it could revitalize its piano business, Yamaha conducted a market research survey to learn what use was being made of pianos in households that owned one. The survey revealed that the overwhelming majority of the 40 million pianos in American, European, and Japanese households were seldom used. In most cases, the reasons the piano had been purchased no longer applied. Children had either stopped taking piano lessons or were grown and had left the household; adult household members played their pianos sparingly, if at all—only a small percentage were accomplished piano players. Most pianos were serving as a piece of fine furniture and were in good condition despite not being tuned regularly. The survey also confirmed that

the income levels of piano owners were well above average.

Yamaha's piano strategists saw the idle pianos in these upscale households as a potential market opportunity. The strategy that emerged entailed marketing an attachment that would convert the piano into an old-fashioned automatic player piano capable of playing a wide number of selections recorded on $3\frac{1}{2}$-inch floppy disks (the same kind used to store computer data). The player piano conversion attachment carried a $2,500 price tag. Concurrently, Yamaha introduced Disklavier, an upright acoustic player piano model that could play *and record* performances up to 90 minutes long; the Disklavier retailed for $8,000. At year-end 1988 Yamaha offered 30 prerecorded disks for $29.95 each. Another 30 selections were scheduled for release in 1989. Yamaha believed that these new high-tech products held potential to reverse the downtrend in piano sales.

STRATEGIES FOR COMPETING IN FRAGMENTED INDUSTRIES

A number of industries are populated with hundreds, even thousands, of small and medium-sized companies, many privately held and none with a substantial share of total industry sales.[10] The outstanding feature of a fragmented industry is the absence of market leaders with king-sized market shares who have the clout and visibility to set the tone of competition. Examples of fragmented industries include book publishing, landscaping and plant nurseries, kitchen cabinets, oil tanker shipping, auto repair, restaurants and fast-food, public accounting, women's dresses, metal foundries, meat packing, paperboard boxes, log homes, hotels and motels, and furniture.

Any of several factors can account for why the supply side of an industry is fragmented.

Many reasons account for why an industry has hundreds or even thousands of small competitors rather than a few large competitors.

- Low entry barriers allow small firms to enter quickly and cheaply.
- An absence of large-scale production economies permit small companies to compete on an equal cost footing with larger firms.
- Buyers require relatively small quantities of customized products (as in business forms, interior design, and advertising); because demand for any particular product version is small, sales volumes can't support producing, distributing, or marketing on a scale that favors a large firm.

---

[10] This section is summarized from Porter, *Competitive Strategy*, chap. 9.

- The market for the industry's product/service is local (dry cleaning, residential construction, medical services, automotive repair), giving competitive advantage to local businesses familiar with local buyers and market conditions.
- Market demand is so large and diverse that it takes large numbers of firms to accommodate buyer requirements (health care, energy, apparel).
- High transportation costs limit the radius a plant can economically service—as in concrete blocks, mobile homes, milk, and gravel.
- Local regulatory requirements make each geographic area unique.
- The industry is so new that no firms have yet developed the skills and resources to command a significant market share.

Some fragmented industries consolidate naturally as they mature. The stiffer competition that accompanies slower growth produces a shake-out of weak, inefficient firms and a greater concentration of larger, more visible sellers. Other industries remain fragmented because it is inherent to the nature of their business. And still others remain "stuck" in a fragmented state because existing firms lack the resources or ingenuity to employ a strategy that might promote industry consolidation.

Firms in fragmented industries usually are in a weak bargaining position with buyers and suppliers. New entrants are an ongoing threat. Competition from substitutes may or may not be a major factor. Rivalry among competitors can vary from moderately strong to fierce. In such an environment, the best a firm can expect is to cultivate a loyal customer base and grow a bit faster than the industry average. Competitive strategies based on low cost, some kind of differentiation theme, or focusing are all viable except when the industry's product is highly standardized; then competitors must rely on low cost or focused specialization. Suitable competitive strategy options in a fragmented industry include:

- **Constructing and operating "formula" facilities**—This is an attractive approach to achieving low cost when firms must operate facilities at multiple locations. Such firms design a standard facility, construct outlets in favorable locations at minimum cost, and then operate them in a super-efficient manner. McDonald's and 7-Eleven have pursued this strategy to perfection, earning excellent profits in their respective industries.

Competitive advantage in a fragmented industry usually comes from low cost, successful differentiation on well-chosen product attributes, or focusing on a particular market segment.

- **Becoming a low-cost operator**—When price competition is intense and profit margins are under constant pressure, firms can pursue no-frills operation featuring low overhead, use of high-productivity/low-cost labor, tight budget control, and total operating efficiency. Successful low-cost producers can play the price-cutting game and still earn profits above the industry average.
- **Increasing customer value through integration**—Backward or forward integration may contain opportunities to lower costs or enhance the value given to customers (like cutting to size, assembling components before shipment to customers, or providing technical advice).
- **Specializing by product type**—When products come in many models and styles, a focus strategy based on specialization in one area of the line can be very effective. Some firms in the furniture industry specialize in only one furniture type such as brass beds, rattan and wicker, lawn and

garden, and early American. In auto repair, firms specialize in transmission repair; body work; and mufflers, brakes, and shocks.

- **Specializing by customer type**—A firm can cope with the intense competition of a fragmented industry by catering to those customers (1) who have the least bargaining leverage (because they are small in size or purchase small amounts), (2) who are the least price sensitive, (3) who are interested in additional services, unique product attributes, or other "extras," (4) who place custom orders, or (5) who have special needs or tastes.

- **Focusing on a limited geographic area**—Even though a firm in a fragmented industry is blocked from winning a big industrywide market share, it can still gain significant internal operating economies by blanketing a local/regional geographic area. Concentrating facilities and marketing activities on a limited territory can produce greater sales force efficiency, speed delivery and customer services, and permit saturation advertising—while avoiding the diseconomies of trying to employ the strategy on a national scale. Convenience food stores, banks, and department store retailers have been successful in operating multiple locations within a limited geographic area.

In fragmented industries, firms have a wide degree of strategic freedom—many different strategic approaches can exist side-by-side.

STRATEGIES FOR COMPETING IN INTERNATIONAL MARKETS

Competing in international markets poses a bigger strategy-making challenge than competing in only the company's home market.

Firms "go international" for any of three basic reasons: a desire to seek out new markets, a competitive need to achieve lower costs, or a desire to access natural resource deposits in other countries. Whatever the reason, an international strategy has to be situation-driven and requires careful analysis of the industry's international aspects. Special attention has to be paid to how national markets differ in buyer needs and habits, distribution channels, long-run growth potential, driving forces, and competitive pressures. In addition to basic market differences from country to country, four other situational considerations are unique to international operations: cost variations among countries, fluctuating exchange rates, host government trade policies, and the pattern of international competition.

Manufacturing Cost Variations   Differences in wage rates, worker productivity, inflation rates, energy costs, tax rates, and the like create sizable variations in manufacturing costs from country to country. Plants in some countries often have major manufacturing cost advantages because of their lower input costs (especially labor) or their unique natural resources. In such cases, the low-cost countries become principal production sites, and most of the output is exported to markets in other parts of the world. Companies with facilities in these locations (or which source their products from contract manufacturers in these countries) typically have a competitive advantage over those that do not. The importance of this consideration is most evident in low-wage countries like Taiwan, South Korea, Mexico, and Brazil, which have become production havens for goods with high labor content.

Another important manufacturing cost consideration in international competition is the concept of *manufacturing share* as distinct from brand share or market share. For example, although less than 40 percent of all the video recorders sold in the United States carry a Japanese brand, Japanese companies do 100 percent of the manufacturing—all sellers source their video recorders from Japanese manufacturers.[11] In microwave ovens, Japanese brands have less than a 50 percent share of the U.S. market, but Japanese companies have a manufacturing share of over 85 percent. *Manufacturing share is significant because it is a better indicator than market share of which competitor is the industry's low-cost producer.* In a globally competitive industry where some competitors are intent on global dominance, being the worldwide low-cost producer is a powerful competitive advantage. Achieving low-cost producer status often requires a company to have the largest worldwide manufacturing share, with production centralized in one or a few super-efficient plants. However, important marketing and distribution economies associated with multinational operations can also yield low-cost leadership.

Fluctuating Exchange Rates   The volatility of exchange rates greatly complicates the issue of locational cost advantages. Exchange rates can fluctuate as much as 20 to 40 percent annually. Changes of this magnitude can totally wipe out a country's low-cost advantage or transform a former high-cost location into a competitive-cost location. A strong U.S. dollar makes it more attractive for U.S. companies to manufacture in foreign countries. A declining dollar can eliminate much of the cost advantage foreign manufacturers have over U.S. manufacturers and can even prompt foreign companies to establish production plants in the United States.

Host Government Trade Policies   National governments have enacted all kinds of measures affecting international trade and the operation of foreign companies in their markets. Host governments may impose import tariffs and quotas, set local content requirements on goods made inside their borders by foreign-based companies, and regulate the prices of imported goods. In addition, firms may face a web of regulations regarding technical standards, product certification, prior approval of capital spending projects, withdrawal of funds from the country, and minority (sometimes majority) ownership by local citizens. Some governments also provide subsidies and low-interest loans to domestic companies to help them compete against foreign-based companies. Other governments, anxious to obtain new plants and jobs, offer foreign companies subsidies, privileged market access, and technical assistance.

Multicountry Competition versus Global Competition

There are important differences in the patterns of international competition from industry to industry.[12] At one extreme, competition can be termed *multicountry* or *multidomestic* because it takes place country-by-country;

> **Basic Concept**
> *Multicountry (or multidomestic) competition exists when competition in one national market is independent of competition in another national market—there is no "international market," just a collection of self-contained country markets.*

---

[11]C. K. Prahalad and Yves L. Doz, *The Multinational Mission* (New York: Free Press, 1987), p. 60.
[12]Michael E. Porter, *The Competitive Advantage of Nations* (New York: Free Press, 1990), pp. 53–54.

competition in each national market is essentially independent of competition in other national markets. For example, there is a banking industry in France, one in Brazil, and one in Japan, but competitive conditions in banking differ markedly in all three countries. Moreover, a bank's reputation, customer base, and competitive position in one nation have little or no bearing on its ability to compete successfully in another. While a company may compete internationally, the power of its strategy in any one nation and any competitive advantage it yields are largely confined to that nation and do not spill over to other countries where it operates. With multicountry competition there is no "international market," just a collection of self-contained country markets. Industries characterized by multicountry competition include many types of food products (coffee, cereals, canned goods, frozen foods), many types of retailing, beer, life insurance, apparel, and metals fabrication.

At the other extreme is *global competition* where prices and competitive conditions across country markets are strongly linked and the term *international* or *global market* has true meaning. In a globally competitive industry, a company's competitive position in one country both affects and is affected by its position in other countries. Rival companies compete against each other in many different countries, but especially so in countries where sales volumes are large and where having a competitive presence is strategically important to building a strong global position in the industry. In global competition, a firm's overall competitive advantage grows out of its entire worldwide operations. The competitive advantage it has created at its home base is supplemented by advantages growing out of its foreign operations (plants in low-wage countries, an ability to serve customers with multinational operations of their own, and brand reputation that is transferable from country to country). *A global competitor's strength is directly proportional to its portfolio of country-based competitive advantages.* Global competition exists in automobiles, television sets, tires, telecommunications equipment, copiers, watches, and commercial aircraft.

An industry can have segments that are globally competitive and segments where competition takes place country-by-country.[13] In the hotel-motel industry, for example, the low- and medium-priced segments are characterized by multicountry competition because competitors mainly serve travelers within the same country. In the business and luxury segments, however, competition is more global; companies like Marriott, Sheraton, and Hilton have hotels in many countries and use worldwide reservation systems and common quality and service standards to service international travelers. In lubricants, the marine engine segment is globally competitive because ships move from port to port and require the same oil everywhere they stop. Brand reputations have a global scope, and successful marine engine lubricant producers (Exxon, British Petroleum, and Shell) operate globally. In automotive motor oil, however, multicountry competition dominates. Countries have different weather conditions and driving patterns, production is subject to limited scale economies and shipping costs are high, and retail distribution channels differ markedly from country to country. Thus domestic firms, like Quaker State and Pennzoil in the United States and Castrol in Great Britain, can be market leaders.

Basic Concept
Global competition exists when competitive conditions across national markets are linked strongly enough to form a true international market and when leading competitors compete head-to-head in many different countries.

In multicountry competition, rival firms vie for national market leadership. In globally competitive industries, rival firms vie for worldwide leadership.

---

[13]Ibid., p. 61.

All these situational considerations, along with the obvious cultural and political differences among countries, shape a company's strategic approach in international markets.

Types of International Strategies

There are six distinct strategic options for a firm participating in international markets. It can:

1. *License foreign firms to use the company's technology or produce and distribute the company's products* (in which case international revenues will equal the royalty income from the licensing agreement).

2. *Maintain a national (one-country) production base and export goods to foreign markets,* using either company-owned or foreign-controlled forward distribution channels.

3. *Follow a multicountry strategy* whereby a company's international strategy is crafted country-by-country to be responsive to buyer needs and competitive conditions in each country where it operates. Strategic moves in one country are made independent of actions taken in another country; strategy coordination across countries is secondary to the need to match company strategy to national conditions.

4. *Follow a global low-cost strategy* where strategy is based on the company being a low-cost supplier to buyers in most or all strategically important markets of the world. The company's strategic efforts are coordinated worldwide to achieve a low-cost position relative to competitors.

5. *Follow a global differentiation strategy* where a firm differentiates its product on the same attributes in all countries to create a consistent image and a consistent competitive theme. The firm's strategic moves are coordinated across countries to achieve consistent worldwide differentiation.

6. *Follow a global focus strategy* where company strategy is aimed at serving the same identifiable niche in each of many strategically important country markets. Strategic actions are coordinated globally to achieve a consistently focused approach in each country market.

Licensing makes sense when a firm with valuable technical know-how or a unique patented product has neither the internal organizational capability nor the resources to compete in foreign markets. By licensing the technology or the production rights to foreign-based firms, it at least realizes income from royalties.

Using domestic plants as a production base for exporting goods to foreign markets is an excellent initial strategy for achieving international sales growth. It minimizes both risk and capital requirements, and it is a conservative way to test the international waters. With an export strategy, a manufacturer can limit its involvement in foreign markets by letting foreign wholesalers experienced in importing assume the entire distribution and marketing function in their countries or regions of the world. If it is more advantageous to maintain control over these functions, a firm can establish its own distribution and sales organizations in some or all of its foreign markets. Either way, a firm minimizes its direct investment in foreign countries because of its home-base production and export strategy. Such strategies are commonly favored by Korean and Italian companies—products are designed and manufactured at home and only marketing activities are performed abroad. Whether such a strategy can be successful over the long run hinges on the relative cost competitiveness of a home-country production base. In some industries, firms gain additional scale economies and experience curve benefits from centralizing production in one or several giant-scale plants whose output capability exceeds demand in any one national market; to capture such economies a company must export to markets in other countries. However, this strategy is competitively vulnerable when manufacturing costs in the home country are substantially higher than in countries where rivals have plants.

The pros and cons of a multicountry versus global strategy are a bit more complex.

A Multicountry Strategy or a Global Strategy?

The logic and appeal of a multicountry strategy derives from the sometimes vast differences in cultural, economic, political, and competitive conditions in different countries. The more diverse national market conditions are, the stronger the case for a *multicountry strategy* where the company tailors its strategic approach to fit each host country's market situation. In such cases, the company's overall international strategy is a collection of its country strategies.

While multicountry strategies are best suited for industries where multicountry competition dominates, global strategies are best suited for globally competitive industries. A *global strategy* is one that is mostly the same in all countries. Although *minor* county-to-country differences do exist to accommodate specific competitive conditions in host countries, the company's fundamental competitive approach (low-cost, differentiation, or focus) remains the same worldwide. Moreover, a global strategy involves (1) integrating and coordinating the company's strategic moves worldwide and (2) selling in many or all nations where there is significant buyer demand. Table 6–1 provides a point-by-point comparison of multicountry versus global strategies. The question of which to pursue is the foremost strategic issue firms face when they compete in international markets.

The strength of a multicountry strategy is that it matches strategy to host-country circumstances. Such a strategy is essential when there are significant national differences in customers' needs and buying habits, when buyers in a country insist on special-order or highly customized products, when buyer demand for the product exists in comparatively few national markets, when host governments enact regulations requiring that products sold locally meet strict manufacturing specifications or performance standards, and when the trade restrictions of host governments are so diverse and complicated they preclude a uniform, coordinated worldwide market approach. However, a multicountry strategy has pitfalls; it entails very little strategic coordination across countries and it is not tightly tied to competitive advantage. Because the primary orientation of a multicountry strategy is responsiveness to local country conditions, it does not help a firm build a multinational-based competitive advantage over other international competitors and the domestic companies of host countries. A global strategy, because it is more uniform from country to country, helps a firm concentrate on securing a sustainable competitive advantage over both international and domestic rivals. Whenever country-to-

T A B L E 6–1   **Differences between Multicountry and Global Strategies**

	Multicountry Strategy	**Global Strategy**
Strategic arena	Selected target countries and trading areas	Most countries which constitute critical markets for the product (at least North America, the European Community, and the Pacific Rim [Australia, Japan, South Korea, and Southeast Asia])
Business strategy	Custom strategies to fit the circumstances of each host country situation; little or no strategy coordination across countries	Same basic strategy worldwide; minor country-by-country variations where essential
Product-line strategy	Adapted to local needs	Mostly standardized products sold worldwide
Production strategy	Plants scattered across many host countries	Plants located on the basis of maximum competitive advantage (in low-cost countries, close to major markets, geographically scattered to minimize shipping costs, or use of a few world-scale plants to maximize economies of scale—as most appropriate)
Source of supply for raw materials and components	Suppliers in host country preferred (local facilities meeting local buyer needs; some local sourcing may be required by host government)	Attractive suppliers from anywhere in the world
Marketing and distribution	Adapted to practices and culture of each host country	Much more worldwide coordination; minor adaption to host country situations if required
Company organization	Form subsidiary companies to handle operations in each host country; each subsidiary operates more or less autonomously to fit host country conditions	All major strategic decisions are closely coordinated at global headquarters; a global organizational structure is used to unify the operations in each country

country differences are small enough to be accommodated within the framework of a global strategy, a global strategy is preferable because of its broader-based competitive advantage potential.

Global Strategy and Competitive Advantage

There are two ways a firm can gain competitive advantage (or offset domestic disadvantages) with a global strategy approach.[14] One involves a global competitor's ability to locate its activities (R&D, parts manufacture, assembly, distribution centers, sales and marketing, customer service centers) among nations in a manner that lowers costs or achieves greater product differentiation. The other concerns a global competitor's ability to coordinate its activities in ways that a domestic-only competitor cannot.

With global strategy a firm can pursue sustainable competitive advantage by locating activities in the most advantageous nations and coordinating strategic actions worldwide; a domestic-only competitor forfeits such opportunities.

Locating Activities   To use location to build competitive advantage, a global firm must consider two issues: (1) whether to concentrate each activity it performs in one or two countries or disperse performance of the activity to many

14Ibid., p. 54.

nations and (2) in which countries to locate particular activities. Activities tend to be concentrated in one or two locations when there are significant economies of scale in performing an activity, when there are advantages in locating related activities in the same area to achieve better coordination, and when there is a steep learning or experience curve associated with concentrating performance of an activity in a single location. In some industries, scale economies in parts manufacture or assembly are so great that a company establishes one large plant from which it serves the world market. Where just-in-time inventory practices yield big cost-savings, parts manufacturing plants may be clustered around final assembly plants.

Dispersing activities is more advantageous than concentrating activities in several instances. Buyer-related activities—such as distribution to dealers, sales and advertising, and after-sale service—usually must take place close to buyers. This means physically locating the capability to perform such activities in every country where a global firm has major customers (unless buyers in several adjoining countries can be served quickly from a nearby central location). For example, firms that make mining and oil drilling equipment maintain operations in many international locations to support customers' needs for speedy equipment repair and technical assistance. Large public accounting firms have numerous international offices to service the foreign operations of their multinational corporate clients. A global competitor that effectively disperses its buyer-related activities can gain a service-based competitive edge in world markets over rivals whose buyer-related activities are more concentrated. Dispersing activities to many locations is also competitively advantageous when high transportation costs, diseconomies of large size, and trade barriers make it too expensive to operate from a central location. In addition, firms often disperse activities to hedge against fluctuating exchange rates, supply interruptions (due to strikes, mechanical failures, and transportation delays), and adverse political developments. Such risks are greater when activities are concentrated in a single location.

The classic reason for locating an activity in a particular country is lower costs.[15] Even though a global firm has strong reason to disperse buyer-related activities to many international locations, such activities as materials procurement, parts manufacture, finished goods assembly, technology research, and new product development can frequently be decoupled from buyer locations and performed wherever the best cost advantage lies. Components can be made in Mexico, technology research done in Frankfurt, new products developed and tested in Phoenix, and assembly plants located in Spain, Brazil, Taiwan, and Illinois. Capital can be raised wherever it is available on the best terms. Low cost is not the only locational consideration, however. A research unit may be located in a particular nation because of its pool of technically trained personnel. A customer service center or sales office may be located in a particular country to help develop strong relationships with pivotal customers. An assembly plant may be located in a country in return for the host government allowing freer import of components from centralized parts plants located elsewhere.

---

[15]Ibid., p. 57.

Coordinating Activities and Strategic Moves   By aligning and coordinating company activities in different countries, a firm can build sustainable competitive advantage in several different ways. If a firm learns how to assemble its product more efficiently at its Brazilian plant, the accumulated knowledge and expertise can be transferred to its assembly plant in Spain. Knowledge gained in marketing a company's product in Great Britain can be used to introduce the product in New Zealand and Australia. A company can shift production from one country to another to take advantage of exchange rate fluctuations, to enhance its leverage with host country governments, and to respond to changing wage rates, energy costs, or trade restrictions. A company can enhance its brand reputation by consistently positioning its products with the same differentiating attributes on a worldwide basis. Honda's worldwide reputation for quality, first in motorcycles and then in automobiles, gave it competitive advantage in positioning its lawnmowers at the upper end of the market—the Honda name gave the company instant credibility with buyers. A global competitor can choose where and how to challenge rivals. It may decide to retaliate against aggressive rivals in the country market where the rival has its biggest sales volume or its best profit margins in order to reduce the rival's financial resources for competing in other countries. It may decide to wage a price-cutting offensive against weak rivals in their home markets, capturing greater market share and subsidizing any short-term losses with profits earned in other country markets.

A company that competes only in its home country has access to none of the competitive advantage opportunities associated with multinational location or coordination. By shifting from a domestic to a global strategy, a domestic company that finds itself at a competitive disadvantage to global companies can begin to restore its competitiveness.

Strategic Alliances

Strategic alliances are cooperative agreements between firms that go beyond normal company-to-company dealings but fall short of merger or full partnership.[16] An alliance can involve joint research efforts, technology-sharing, joint use of production facilities, marketing one another's products, or joining forces to manufacture components or assemble finished products. Strategic alliances are a means for firms in the same industry that are based in different countries to compete on a more global scale while still preserving their independence. Historically, export-minded firms in industrialized nations sought alliances with firms in less-developed countries to import and market their products locally—such arrangements were often necessary to gain access to the less-developed country's market. More recently, leading companies from different parts of the world have formed strategic alliances to strengthen their ability to serve whole continental areas and move toward more global market participation. Both Japanese and American companies have formed alliances with European companies in preparation for Europe 1992 and the opening of Eastern European markets.

Strategic alliances are a means for companies in globally competitive industries to strengthen their competitive positions while still preserving their independence.

---

[16]Ibid., p. 65. See, also, Kenichi Ohmae, "The Global Logic of Strategic Alliances," *Harvard Business Review* 89, no. 2 (March–April 1989), pp. 143–54.

Companies enter into alliances for several strategically beneficial reasons.[17] The three most important are to gain economies of scale in production and/ or marketing, to fill gaps in their technical and manufacturing expertise, and to acquire market access. By joining forces in producing components, assembling models, and marketing their products, companies can realize cost savings not achievable with their own small volumes. Allies learn much from one another in performing joint research, sharing technological know-how, and studying one another's manufacturing methods. Alliances are often used by outsiders to meet governmental requirements for local ownership, and allies can share distribution facilities and dealer networks, thus mutually strengthening their access to buyers. In addition, alliances affect competition; not only can alliances offset competitive disadvantages but they also can result in the allied companies directing their competitive energies more toward mutual rivals and less toward one another. Many runner-up companies, wanting to preserve their independence, have resorted to alliances rather than merger to try to close the competitive gap on leading companies.

Alliances have their pitfalls, however. Effective coordination between independent companies, each with different motives and perhaps conflicting objectives, is a challenging task requiring numerous meetings of numerous people over a period of time to iron out what is to be shared, what is to remain proprietary, and how the cooperative arrangements will work. Allies may have to overcome language and cultural barriers as well as suspicion and mistrust. After a promising start, relationships may cool, and the hoped-for benefits may never materialize. Most important, though, is the danger of depending on another company for essential expertise and capabilities over the long term. To be a serious contender, a company must ultimately develop its own capabilities in all areas important to strengthening its competitive position and building a sustainable competitive advantage. Where this is not feasible, merger is a better solution than strategic alliance. Strategic alliances are best used as a transitional way to combat competitive disadvantage in international markets; rarely if ever can they be relied on to create competitive advantage.

Strategic Intent, Profit Sanctuaries, and Cross-Subsidization

Competitors in international markets can be distinguished not only by their strategies but also by their long-term strategic objectives or strategic intent. Four types of competitors stand out:[18]

- Firms whose strategic intent is *global dominance* or, at least, high rank among the global market leaders; such firms pursue some form of global strategy.
- Firms whose primary strategic objective is *defending domestic dominance* in their home market, even though they derive some of their sales internationally (usually under 20 percent) and have operations in several or many foreign markets.

---

[17]Porter, *The Competitive Advantage of Nations*, p. 66.

[18]Prahalad and Doz, *The Multinational Mission*, p. 52.

- Firms who aspire to a growing share of worldwide sales and whose primary strategic orientation is *host-country responsiveness*; such firms have a multicountry strategy and may already derive a large portion of their revenues from foreign operations.
- *Domestic-only firms* whose strategic intent does not extend beyond building a strong competitive position in their home country market; such firms base their competitive strategies on domestic market conditions and watch events in the international market only for their impact on domestic conditions.

The four types of firms are *not* equally well positioned to succeed in markets where they compete head-on. Consider the case of a purely domestic U.S. company in competition with a Japanese company operating in many country markets and aspiring to global dominance. The Japanese company can cut its prices in the U.S. market to gain market share at the expense of the U.S. company, subsidizing any losses with profits earned in its home sanctuary and in other foreign markets. The U.S. company has no effective way to retaliate. It is vulnerable even if it is the dominant domestic company. However, if the U.S. company is a multinational competitor and operates in Japan as well as elsewhere, it can counter Japanese pricing in the United States with retaliatory price cuts in its competitor's main profit sanctuary, Japan, and in other countries where it competes against the same Japanese company.

Profit Sanctuaries and Critical Markets   *Profit sanctuaries* are country markets where a company has a strong or protected market position and derives substantial profits. Japan, for example, is a profit sanctuary for most Japanese companies because trade barriers erected by the Japanese government effectively block foreign companies from competing for a large share of Japanese sales. Protected from the threat of foreign competition in their home market, Japanese companies can safely charge somewhat higher prices to their Japanese customers and thus earn attractively large profits at home. In most cases, a company's biggest and most strategically crucial profit sanctuary is its home market, but multinational companies also have profit sanctuaries in those country markets where they have strong competitive positions, big sales volumes, and attractive profit margins.

Profit sanctuaries are valuable competitive assets in global industries. Companies with large, protected profit sanctuaries have a competitive advantage over companies that don't have a dependable sanctuary. Companies with multiple profit sanctuaries are more favorably positioned than companies with a single sanctuary. Normally, a global competitor with multiple profit sanctuaries can successfully attack and beat a domestic competitor whose only profit sanctuary is its home market.

To defend against global competitors, firms don't have to compete in all or even most foreign markets, but they do have to compete in all critical markets; *critical markets* are markets in countries

- That are the profit sanctuaries of key competitors.
- That have big sales volumes.
- That contain prestigious customers whose business it is strategically important to have.

Basic Concept
A nation becomes a company's profit sanctuary when a company, because of its strong competitive position or protective governmental trade policies, derives a substantial portion of its total profits from sales in that nation.

Competitive Strategy Principle
A global competitor with multiple profit sanctuaries can wage and generally win a competitive offensive against a domestic competitor whose only profit sanctuary is its home market.

ILLUSTRATION CAPSULE
14

GLOBAL STRATEGIC ALLIANCES
Successes and Failures

As the chairman of British Aerospace recently observed, a strategic alliance with a foreign company is "one of the quickest and cheapest ways to develop a global strategy." AT&T has formed joint ventures with many of the world's largest telephone and electronics companies. Boeing, the world's premier manufacturer of commercial aircraft, has partnered with Kawasaki, Mitsubishi, and Fuji to produce a long-range, wide-body jet for delivery in 1995. General Electric and Snecma, a French maker of jet engines, have a 50-50 partnership to make jet engines to power aircraft made by Boeing, McDonnell-Douglas, and Airbus Industrie (the leading European maker of commercial aircraft and a company that was formed through an alliance among aerospace companies from Britain, Spain, Germany and France); the GE–Snecma alliance was regarded as a model because not only had it been in existence for 17 years but because it had also produced orders totaling $38 billion for 10,300 engines.

During the past 10 years, hundreds of strategic alliances have been formed in the motor vehicle industry as car and truck manufacturers and automotive parts suppliers moved aggressively to get in stronger position to compete globally. Not only have there been alliances between manufacturers strong in one region of the world and manufacturers strong in another region but there have also been strategic alliances between vehicle-makers and key parts suppliers (especially those with high quality parts and strong technological capabilities).

General Motors and Toyota in 1984 formed a 50-50 partnership called New United Motor Manufacturing, Inc. (NUMMI) to produce cars for both companies at an old GM plant in Fremont, California. The strategic value of the GM–Toyota alliance was that Toyota would learn how to deal with suppliers and workers in the U.S. (as a prelude to building its own plants in the U.S.) while GM would learn about Toyota's approaches to manufacturing and management. Each company sent managers to the NUMMI plant to work for two to three years to learn and absorb all they could, then transferred their NUMMI "graduates" to jobs where they could be instrumental in helping their company apply what had been learned.

Gary Hamel, a professor at the London Business School, regards strategic alliances as a "race to learn" and gain the benefits of the partner's know-how and competitive capabilities. The partner that learns the fastest gains the most and, later, may turn such learning into a competitive edge. From this perspective, alliances become a new form of competition as well as a vehicle for globalizing company strategy. According to Hamel, Japanese managers and companies excel at learning from their allies and then exploiting the benefits. Toyota, for example, had moved quickly to capitalize on its experiences at NUMMI; by 1991 Toyota had opened two plants on its own in North America, was constructing a third plant, and was producing about 50 percent of the vehicles it sold

(continued)

- That offer exceptionally good profit margins due to weak competitive pressures.[19]

The more critical markets a company participates in, the greater its ability to use cross-subsidization as a defense against competitors intent on global dominance.

The Competitive Power of Cross-Subsidization   Cross-subsidization is a powerful competitive weapon. It involves using profits earned in one or more country markets to support a competitive offensive against key rivals or to gain

[19]Ibid., p. 61.

ILLUSTRATION CAPSULE
14

(concluded)

in North America in its North American plants. While General Motors had incorporated much of its NUMMI learning into the management practices and manufacturing methods it was using at its newly opened Saturn plant in Tennessee, GM had moved more slowly than Toyota. American and European companies were generally regarded as less skilled than the Japanese in transferring the learning from strategic alliances into their own operations.

Consultants and business school professors who have studied company experiences with strategic alliances see four keys to making a strategic alliance work to good advantage:

- Picking a compatible partner, taking the time to build strong bridges of communication and trust, and not expecting immediate payoffs.
- Choosing an ally whose products and market strongholds *complement* rather than compete directly with the company's own products and customer base.
- Learning thoroughly and rapidly about a partner's technology and management.
- Being careful not to divulge competitively sensitive information to a partner.

Many alliances either fail or are terminated when one partner decides to acquire the other. A 1990 survey of 150 companies involved in terminated alliances found that three-fourths of the alliances had been taken over by Japanese partners. A nine-year alliance between Fujitsu and International Computers, Ltd., a British manufacturer, ended when Fujitsu acquired 80 percent of ICL. According to one observer, Fujitsu deliberately maneuvered ICL into a position of having no better choice than to sell out to its partner; Fujitsu began as a supplier of components for ICL's mainframe computers, then expanded its role over the next nine years to the point where it was ICL's only source of new technology. When ICL's parent, a large British electronics firm, saw the mainframe computer business starting to decline and decided to sell, Fujitsu was the only buyer it could find.

There are several reasons why strategic alliances fail. Often, once the bloom is off the initial getting-together period, partners discover they have deep differences of opinion about how to proceed and conflicting objectives and strategies, such that tensions soon build up and cooperative working relationships never emerge. Another is the difficulty of collaborating effectively in competitively sensitive areas, thus raising questions about mutual trust and forthright exchanges of information and expertise. Perhaps the biggest reason is a clash of egos and company cultures—the key people upon whom success or failure depend turn out to be incompatible and incapable of working closely together on a partnership basis. On occasions, partners become suspicious about each other's motives and sometimes they are unwilling to share control and do things on the basis of consensus.

Source: Jeremy Main, "Making Global Alliances Work," *Fortune*, December 17, 1990, pp. 121–26.

increased penetration of a critical market. Typically, a firm may match (or nearly match) rivals on product quality and service, then charge a low enough price to draw customers away from rivals. While price-cutting may entail lower profits (or even losses), the challenger still realizes acceptable overall profits when the above-average earnings from its profit sanctuaries are added in.

Cross-subsidization is most powerful when a global firm with multiple profit sanctuaries is aggressively intent on achieving global market dominance over the long term. A domestic-only competitor and a multicountry competitor with no strategic coordination between its locally responsive country strategies are both vulnerable to competition from rivals intent on global dominance. A global strategy can defeat a domestic-only strategy because a one-country competitor cannot effectively defend its market share over the long term against a global competitor with cross-subsidization capability. The global company can use lower prices to siphon the domestic company's customers, all the while gaining market share, building market strength, and covering losses with profits earned in its other critical markets. When attacked in this manner, a domestic company's best short-term hope is to seek government protection in the form of tariff barriers, import quotas, and antidumping penalties. In the long term, the domestic company must find ways to compete on a more equal footing—a difficult task when it must charge a price to cover average costs while the global competitor can charge a price only high enough to cover the incremental costs of selling in the domestic company's profit sanctuary. The best long-term strategic defenses for a domestic company are to enter into strategic alliances with foreign firms or adopt a global strategy and compete on an international scale. Competing only domestically is a perilous strategy in an industry populated with global competitors.

While a firm with a multicountry strategy has some cross-subsidy defense against a firm with a global strategy, it lacks competitive advantage and usually faces cost disadvantages. A global competitor with a big manufacturing share and state-of-the-art plants is typically a lower-cost producer than a multicountry strategist with many small plants and short production runs turning out specialized products country-by-country. Companies pursuing a multicountry strategy thus have to develop focusing and differentiation advantages keyed to local responsiveness to defend against a global competitor. Such a defense is adequate in industries with significant enough national differences to impede use of a global strategy. But if an international rival can accommodate necessary local needs within a global strategy and still retain a cost edge, then a global strategy can defeat a multicountry strategy. Illustration Capsule 15, which discusses how Nestlé became the world's number one food company, shows the power of a global strategy in today's markets.

STRATEGIES FOR INDUSTRY LEADERS

The competitive positions of industry leaders normally range from stronger than average to powerful. Leaders typically enjoy a well-known reputation, and strongly entrenched leaders have proven strategies (keyed either to low-cost leadership or differentiation). Some of the best-known industry leaders are Anheuser-Busch (beer), IBM (computers), McDonald's (fast food), Gillette (razor blades), Campbell Soup (canned soups), Gerber (baby food), AT&T (long-distance telephone service), and Levi Strauss (jeans). The main strategic concern for a leader revolves around how to sustain a leadership position, perhaps becoming the dominant leader as opposed to a leader. However, pursuit of industry leadership and large market share per se is primarily important because of the competitive advantage and profitability that accrues to leadership.

Three contrasting strategic postures are open to industry leaders and dominant firms:[20]

---

[20]Kotler, *Marketing Management*, chap. 23; Porter, *Competitive Advantage*, chap. 14; and Ian C. MacMillan, "Seizing Competitive Initiative," *The Journal of Business Strategy* 2, no. 4 (Spring 1982), pp. 43–57.

1. **Stay-on-the-offensive strategy**—This strategy rests on the principle that the best defense is a good offense. Offensive-minded leaders try to be "first-movers" to build a sustainable competitive advantage and a solid reputation as *the* leader. The key to staying on the offensive is relentless pursuit of continuous improvement and innovation. Striving to become *the* source of new products, better performance features, quality enhancements, improved customer services, and ways to cut production costs not only helps a leader avoid complacency but it also keeps rivals on the defensive and scrambling to keep up. The array of offensive options also includes initiatives to expand overall industry demand—discovering new uses for the product, attracting new users, and promoting more frequent use. In addition, a clever offensive leader stays alert for ways to make it easier and less costly for potential customers to switch their purchases from runner-up firms over to its own products. Unless a leader's market share is already so dominant that it presents a threat of antitrust action (a market share under 60 percent is usually "safe"), then a stay-on-the-offensive strategy involves trying to grow *faster* than the industry as a whole and wrest market share from rivals. A leader whose growth does not equal or outpace the industry average is losing ground to competitors.

2. **Fortify and defend strategy**—The essence of "fortify and defend" is to make it harder for new firms to enter and for challengers to gain ground. The goals of a strong defense are to hold onto present market share, strengthen current market position, and protect whatever competitive advantage the firm has. Specific defensive actions can include:

   - Attempting to raise the competitive ante for challengers and new entrants via increased spending for advertising, customer service, and R&D.
   - Introducing more of the company's own brands to match the product attributes challenger brands have or could employ.
   - Figuring out ways to make it harder or more costly for customers to switch to rival products.
   - Broadening the product line to close off possible vacant niches for competitors to slip into.
   - Keeping prices reasonable and quality attractive.
   - Building new capacity ahead of market demand to try to block the market expansion potential of smaller competitors.
   - Investing enough to remain cost competitive and technologically progressive.
   - Patenting alternative technologies.
   - Signing exclusive contracts with the best suppliers and dealer/distributors.

   A fortify-and-defend strategy best suits firms that have already achieved industry dominance and don't wish to risk antitrust action. It is also well-suited to situations where a firm wishes to milk its present position for profits and cash flow because the industry's prospects for growth are low or because further gains in market share do not appear profitable enough to go after. But the fortify-and-defend theme always

Industry leaders can strengthen their long-term competitive positions with strategies keyed to aggressive offense, aggressive defense, or muscling smaller rivals into a follow-the-leader role.

ILLUSTRATION CAPSULE
15

NESTLÉ'S GLOBAL STRATEGY IN FOODS

Once a stodgy Swiss manufacturer of chocolate, Nestlé became one of the first multinational companies and then embarked on a global strategy during the 1980s. The themes of the Nestlé strategy were: acquire a wider lineup of name brands, achieve the economies of worldwide distribution and marketing, accept short-term losses to build a more profitable market share over the long term, and adapt products to local cultures when needed. In 1991 Nestlé ranked as the world's largest food company with over $33 billion in revenues, market penetration on all major continents, and plants in over 60 countries (see table below).

The Nestlé strategy was a response to two driving forces affecting the food industry in more and more nations around the globe: (1) changing consumer demographics, tastes, and cooking habits; and (2) the new cost-volume economics of increasingly "high-tech" food products like gourmet dinners, refrigerated foods, packaged mixes, and even coffee. In both industrialized and developing nations, the 1980s were characterized by growing numbers of relatively affluent single professionals and two-income couples with more cosmopolitan food tastes and less price-sensitive grocery budgets. Moreover, microwave ovens were fast becoming a standard household item, a development that not only affected weeknight and weekend food preparation methods but also changed the kinds of at-home food products people were buying. Products that appealed to this segment had tremendous growth potential. However, bringing such items to market was quickly turned into a high-risk, capital-intensive, R&D-oriented business that required millions of dollars of up-front capital for new product development and market testing, and millions more for advertising and promotional support to win shelf space in grocery chains. To get maximum mileage out of such investments, make up for the cost of product failures, and keep retail prices affordable began to take a larger and larger volume of sales, often more than could be generated from a single national market.

Nestlé management grasped early on that these driving forces would act to globalize the food industry and that companies with worldwide distribution capability, strong brand names, and the flexibility to adapt versions of the basic product to local tastes would gain significant competitive ad-

Continent	1990 Sales	Major Products
Europe	$16.3 billion	Nescafé instant coffee, Vittel mineral water, Chambourcy yogurt, Findus and Lean Cuisine frozen foods, Herta cold cuts, Sundy cereal bars, chocolate candy, Buitoni pasta
North America	$ 8.3 billion	Nescafé instant coffee, Carnation CoffeeMate, Friskies pet foods, Stouffer frozen foods, Nestlé Crunch chocolate bars, Hills Bros. coffee
Asia	$ 3.6 billion	Nescafé instant coffee, Nido powdered milk, Maggi chili powder, infant cereals, and formulas
Latin America	$ 3.6 billion	Nescafé instant coffee, Nido powdered milk, infant cereal, Milo malt-flavored beverages
Africa	$ 1.0 billion	Nescafé instant coffee, Maggi bouillon cubes, Nespray powdered milk, Nestlé chocolates, Milo malt-flavored beverages
Oceania (Australia, New Zealand)	$ 0.9 billion	Nescafé instant coffee, Findus frozen foods, Lean Cuisine frozen foods

(continued)

ILLUSTRATION CAPSULE
15

(concluded)

product to local tastes would gain significant competitive advantages. A series of acquisitions gave Nestlé a strong lineup of brands, some important new food products to push through its distribution channels, and a bigger presence in some key country markets. In 1985 Nestlé bought Carnation (Pet evaporated milk, Friskies pet foods, and CoffeeMate nondairy creamer) and Hills Bros. coffee (the number three coffee brand in the United States) to strengthen its North American presence. In 1988, Nestlé acquired Rountree, a British chocolate company whose leading candy bar is Kit Kat, and Buitoni, an Italian pastamaker. Shortly after the Rountree acquisition, Nestlé management shifted worldwide responsibility for mapping chocolate strategy and developing new candy products from Nestlé headquarters in Vevey, Switzerland, to Rountree's headquarters in York, England. Nestlé management believed this decentralization put the company's candy business in the hands of people "who think about chocolate 24 hours a day." As of 1989, almost everything Nestlé sold involved food products, and the company was the world's largest producer of coffee, powdered milk, candy, and frozen dinners.

The star performer in Nestlé's lineup was coffee, with 1990 sales of $5.2 billion and operating profits of $600 million. Nestlé's Nescafé brand was the leader in virtually every national market except the United States (Philip Morris's Maxwell House brand was the U.S. leader, but Nescafé was number two and Hills Bros., purchased by Nestlé in 1985, was number three). Nestlé produced 200 types of instant coffee, from lighter blends for the U.S. market to dark espressos for Latin America. Four coffee research labs spent a combined $50 million annually to experiment with new blends in aroma, flavor, and color. Although instant coffee sales were declining worldwide due to the comeback of new-style automatic coffeemakers, they were rising in two tea-drinking countries, Britain and Japan. As the cultural shift from tea to coffee took hold during the

1970s in Britain, Nestlé pushed its Nescafé brand hard, coming out with a market share of about 50 percent. In Japan, Nescafé was considered a luxury item; the company made it available in fancy containers suitable for gift-giving.

Another star performer has been the company's Lean Cuisine line of low-calorie frozen dinners produced by Stouffer, a company Nestlé acquired in the 1970s. Introduced in 1981 in the United States, the Lean Cuisine line has boosted Stouffer's U.S. market share in frozen dinners to 38 percent. To follow up on its U.S. success, Nestlé introduced Lean Cuisine into the British market. At the time, Nestlé products in British supermarkets were mostly low-margin items, from fish sticks to frozen hamburger patties. British managers proposed a bold upgrading to a line of more expensive, high-margin items led by Lean Cuisine. Nestlé headquarters endorsed the plan and indicated a willingness to absorb four years of losses to build market share and make Lean Cuisine a transatlantic hit. The Lean Cuisine line was introduced in Britain in 1985. By 1988 the Lean Cuisine line in Britain included 12 entrées tailored to British tastes, from cod with wine sauce to Kashmiri chicken curry. By 1989 Nestlé had a 33 percent share of the British market for frozen dinners. Sales exceeded $100 million in 1990, putting the Lean Cuisine brand into the black in Britain for the first time since its introduction to the British market. Lean Cuisine has recently been introduced in France.

Western Europe is Nestlé's top target for the early 1990s. The 1992 shift to free trade among the 12 member countries in the European Community will sweep away trade barriers which, according to a recent study, cost food companies over $1 billion in added distribution and marketing costs. With market unification in the 12-country EC, Nestlé sees major opportunities to gain wider distribution of its products, achieve economies, and exploit its skills in transferring products and marketing methods from one country and culture to another.

Source: The information in this capsule was drawn from Shawn Tully, "Nestlé Shows How to Gobble Markets," *Fortune*, January 16, 1989, pp. 74–78 and Nestlé's 1990 annual report.

entails trying to grow as fast as the market as a whole (to stave off market share slippage) and reinvesting enough capital in the business to protect the leader's ability to compete.

3. **Follow-the-leader strategy**—The objective of this strategy is to enforce an unwritten tradition that smaller firms follow the industry leader in adjusting prices up or down and otherwise don't try to rock the boat. Assuming the role of industry policeman gives a leader added strategic flexibility and makes it risky for runner-up firms to mount an offensive attack on the leader's position. In effect, the leader uses its competitive muscle to thwart and discourage would-be challengers. The leader signals smaller rivals that any moves to cut into the leader's business will meet with strong retaliation. Specific "hardball" policing actions include quickly meeting all price cuts (with even larger cuts if necessary), countering with large-scale promotional campaigns when challengers make threatening moves to gain market share, and offering better deals to the major customers of next-in-line or "maverick" firms. Other measures that a leader can use to bully aggressive small rivals into playing follow-the-leader include pressuring distributors not to carry rivals' products, having salespeople bad-mouth the aggressor's products, and trying to hire away the better executives of firms that "get out of line."

STRATEGIES FOR RUNNER-UP FIRMS

Runner-up firms occupy weaker market positions than the industry leader(s). Some runner-ups play the role of *market challengers*, favoring offensive strategies to gain market share and a stronger market position. Others behave as *content followers*, willing to coast along in their current positions because profits are still adequate. Follower firms have no urgent strategic issue to confront beyond that of "What kinds of strategic changes are the leaders initiating and what do we need to do to follow?"

A challenger firm interested in improving its market standing needs a strategy aimed at building a competitive advantage of its own. *Rarely can a runner-up improve its competitive position by imitating the leading firm. A cardinal rule in offensive strategy is to avoid attacking a leader head-on with an imitative strategy, regardless of the resources and staying power an underdog may have.*[21] Moreover, if a challenger has a 5 percent market share and needs a 20 percent share to earn attractive returns, it needs a more creative approach to competing than just "try harder."

In cases where large size yields significantly lower unit costs and gives large-share firms an important cost advantage, small-share firms have only two viable strategic options: increase their market share or withdraw from the business (gradually or quickly). The competitive strategies most used to build market share are based on (1) becoming a lower-cost producer and using lower price to win customers from weak, higher-cost rivals and (2) using differentiation strategies based on quality, technological superiority, better customer service, best-cost, or innovation. Achieving low-cost leadership is usually

---

[21]Porter, *Competitive Advantage*, p. 514.

open to an underdog only when one of the market leaders is not already solidly positioned as the industry's low-cost producer. But a small-share firm may still be able to reduce its cost disadvantage by merging with or acquiring smaller firms; the combined market shares may provide the needed access to size-related economies. Other options include revamping the activity-cost chain to produce cost savings and finding ways to better control cost drivers.

In situations where scale economies or experience curve effects are small and a large market share produces no cost advantage, runner-up companies have more strategic flexibility and can consider any of the following six approaches:[22]

1. **Vacant niche strategy**—This version of a focus strategy involves concentrating on customer or end-use applications that major firms have bypassed or neglected. An "ideal" vacant niche is of sufficient size and scope to be profitable, has some growth potential, is well-suited to a firm's own capabilities and skills, and is outside the interest of leading firms. For example, regional commuter airlines serve cities with too few passengers to attract the interest of major airlines, and health food producers (like Health Valley, Hain, and Tree of Life) supply the growing number of local health food stores—a market segment traditionally ignored by Pillsbury, Kraft General Foods, Heinz, Nabisco, Campbell Soup, and other leading food products firms.

2. **Specialist strategy**—A specialist firm trains its competitive effort on one market segment: a single product, a particular end-use, or a special customer group. The aim is to build competitive advantage through product uniqueness, expertise in special-purpose products, or specialized customer services. Smaller companies that have successfully used a specialist type of focus strategy include Formby's (a specialist in stains and finishes for wood furniture, especially refinishing), Liquid Paper Co. (a leader in correction fluid for typists), Canada Dry (known for its ginger ale, tonic water, and carbonated soda water), and American Tobacco (a leader in chewing tobacco and snuff).

3. **"Ours-is-better-than-theirs strategy"**—This approach uses a combination focus-differentiation strategy keyed to product quality. Sales and marketing efforts focus on quality-conscious and performance-oriented buyers. Fine craftsmanship, prestige quality, frequent product innovations, and/or close contact with customers to develop a better product usually undergird this "superior product" type of approach. Some examples include Beefeater and Tanqueray in gin, Tiffany in diamonds and jewelry, Baccarat in fine crystal, Mazola in cooking oil and margarine, Bally in shoes, and Pennzoil in motor oil.

4. **Content follower strategy**—Follower firms deliberately refrain from initiating trend-setting strategic moves and from aggressive attempts to steal customers away from leaders. Followers prefer approaches that will not provoke competitive retaliation, often opting for focus and

---

[22]For more details, see Kotler, *Marketing Management*, pp. 397-412; R. G. Hamermesh, M. J. Anderson, Jr., and J. E. Harris, "Strategies for Low Market Share Businesses," *Harvard Business Review* 56, no. 3 (May–June 1978), pp. 95–102; and Porter, *Competitive Advantage*, chap. 15.

differentiation strategies that keep them out of the leaders' paths. They react and respond rather than initiate and attack. They prefer defense to offense. And they rarely get out of line with the leaders on price. Burroughs (in computers) and Union Camp (in paper products) have been successful market followers by consciously concentrating on selected product uses and applications for specific customer groups, focused R&D, profits rather than market share, and cautious but efficient management.

5. **Growth via acquisition strategy**—One way to strengthen a company's position is to merge with or acquire weaker rivals to form an enterprise that has more competitive strength and a larger share of the market. Commercial airline companies such as Northwest, US Air, and Delta owe their market share growth during the past decade to acquisition of smaller regional airlines. Likewise, public accounting firms have enhanced their national and international coverage by merging or forming alliances with smaller CPA firms at home and abroad.

6. **Distinctive image strategy**—Some runner-up companies try to stand out from competitors. They use a variety of strategic approaches: creating a reputation for the lowest prices, providing prestige quality at a good price, giving superior customer service, designing unique product attributes, being a leader in new product introduction, or devising unusually creative advertising. Examples include Dr Pepper's strategy of calling attention to its distinctive taste, Apple Computer's approach to making it easier and interesting for people to use a personal computer, and Honda's emphasis on the quality and dependability of its cars.

In industries where big size is definitely a key success factor, firms with low market shares have some obstacles to overcome: (1) less access to economies of scale in manufacturing, distribution, or sales promotion; (2) difficulty in gaining customer recognition; (3) an inability to afford mass media advertising on a grand scale; and (4) difficulty in funding capital requirements.[23] But *it is erroneous to view runner-up firms as inherently less profitable or unable to hold their own against the biggest firms.* Many firms with small market shares earn healthy profits and enjoy good reputations with customers. Often, the handicaps of smaller size can be surmounted and a profitable competitive position established by: (1) focusing on a few market segments where the company's strengths can yield a competitive edge; (2) developing technical expertise that will be highly valued by customers; (3) aggressively pursuing the development of new products for customers in the target market segments; and (4) using innovative, "dare-to-be different," "beat-the-odds" entrepreneurial approaches to outmanage stodgy, slow-to-change market leaders. Runner-up companies have a golden opportunity to gain market share if they make a leapfrog technological breakthrough, if the leaders stumble or become complacent, or if they have patience to nibble away at the leaders and build up their customer base over a long period of time.

---

[23]Hamermesh, Anderson, and Harris, "Strategies for Low Market Share Businesses," p. 102.

STRATEGIES FOR WEAK BUSINESSES

A firm in an also-ran or declining competitive position has four basic strategic options. If it has the financial resources, it can launch a modest *strategic offensive* keyed either to low-cost production or "new" differentiation themes, pouring enough money and talent into the effort to move up a notch or two in the industry rankings. It can pursue *aggressive defense*, using variations of the present strategy and fighting hard to keep sales, market share, profitability, and competitive position at current levels. It can opt for an *immediate abandonment* strategy and get out of the business, either by selling out to another firm or by closing down operations if a buyer cannot be found. Or it can employ a *harvest strategy*, keeping reinvestment to a bare-bones minimum and maximizing short-term cash flows in preparation for an orderly exit. The gist of the first three options is self-explanatory. The fourth merits more discussion.

A *harvest strategy* steers a middle course between preserving the status quo and exiting as soon as possible. Harvesting is a phasing down or endgame strategy where the game plan is to sacrifice market position any time short-term financial benefits can be realized. The overriding financial objective is to reap the greatest possible cash harvest to deploy to other business endeavors.

Harvesting actions are fairly standard. Firms cut their operating budgets to rock-bottom and pursue stringent internal cost control. Capital investment in new equipment is minimal or nonexistent depending on the current condition of fixed assets and whether the harvest is to be fast or slow. Firms may gradually raise prices and cut promotional expenses, reduce quality in not so visible ways, curtail nonessential customer services, decrease equipment maintenance, and the like. They understand that sales will shrink, but if they cut costs proportionately, profits will erode slowly.

Professor Kotler has suggested seven indicators of when a business should be harvested:[24]

1. When the industry's long-term prospects are unattractive.
2. When building up the business would be too costly or not profitable enough.
3. When the firm's market share is becoming increasingly costly to maintain or defend.
4. When reduced levels of competitive effort will not trigger an immediate falloff in sales.
5. When the enterprise can redeploy the freed resources in higher opportunity areas.
6. When the business is *not* a major component in a diversified corporation's portfolio of existing businesses.
7. When the business does not contribute other desired features (sales stability, prestige, a well-rounded product line) to a company's overall business portfolio.

The more of these seven conditions present, the more ideal the business is for harvesting.

> *A competitively weak company can wage a modest offensive to improve its position, defend its present position, be acquired by another company, or employ a harvest strategy.*

---

[24]Phillip Kotler, "Harvesting Strategies for Weak Products," *Business Horizons* 21, no. 5 (August 1978), pp. 17–18.

Harvesting strategies make the most sense for diversified companies that have business units with respectable market shares in unattractive industries. In such situations, cash flows from harvesting unattractive business units can be reallocated to business units with greater profit potential in more attractive industries.

Crisis Turnarounds

Turnaround strategies are used when a business worth rescuing goes into crisis; the objective is to arrest and reverse the sources of competitive and financial weakness as quickly as possible. The first task is to diagnose the problem: What is causing the poor performance? Is it bad competitive strategy or poor implementation and execution of an otherwise workable strategy? Are the causes of distress beyond management control? Can the business be saved? To formulate a turnaround strategy, managers must find the problem and determine how serious it is.

Successful turnaround strategies depend on accurate diagnosis of a distressed company's situation and decisive action to resolve its problems.

Some of the most common causes of business trouble are: overly aggressive efforts to "buy" market share with profit-depressing price-cuts, heavy fixed costs due to underutilized plant capacity, ineffective R&D efforts, reliance on technological long-shots, inability to penetrate new markets, frequent changes in strategy (because the previous strategy didn't work out), and being overpowered by the competitive advantages of more successful rivals. There are five ways to pursue business turnaround:[25]

- Revise the existing strategy.
- Launch efforts to boost revenues.
- Pursue cost reduction.
- Sell off assets to raise cash to save the remaining part of the business.
- Use a combination of these efforts.

Strategy Revision   When weak performance is caused by "bad" strategy, the task of strategy overhaul can proceed along any of several paths: (1) shifting to a new competitive approach to rebuild the firm's market position, (2) overhauling internal operations and functional area strategies to better support the same overall business strategy, (3) merging with another firm in the industry and forging a new strategy keyed to the newly merged firm's strengths, and (4) retrenching into a reduced core of products and customers more closely matched to the firm's strengths. The most appealing path depends on prevailing industry conditions, the firm's particular strengths and weaknesses, and the severity of the crisis. "Situation analysis" of the industry, major competitors, the firm's own competitive position, and its skills and resources are prerequisites to action. As a rule, successful strategy revision must be tied directly to the ailing firm's strengths and near-term competitive capabilities and must focus narrowly on its best market opportunities.

---

[25]For excellent discussions of the ins and outs of rescuing distressed firms, see Charles W. Hofer, "Turnaround Strategies," *Journal of Business Strategy* 1, no. 1 (Summer 1980), pp. 19–31; Donald F. Heany, " Businesses in Profit Trouble," *Journal of Business Strategy* 5, no. 4 (Spring 1985), pp. 4–13; and Eugene F. Finkin, "Company Turnaround," *Journal of Business Strategy* 5, no. 4 (Spring 1985), pp. 14–25.

Boosting Revenues   Revenue-increasing turnaround efforts aim at generating increased sales volume. There are a number of revenue-building options: price-cuts, increased promotion, a bigger sales force, added customer services, and quickly achieved product improvements. Attempts to increase revenues and sales volumes are necessary (1) when there is little or no room in the operating budget to cut expenses and still break even and (2) when the key to restoring profitability is increased utilization of existing capacity. In rare situations where buyer demand is not price sensitive, the quickest way to boost short-term revenues may be to raise prices rather than opt for volume-building price cuts.

Cutting Costs   Cost-reducing turnaround strategies work best when an ailing firm's cost structure is flexible enough to permit radical surgery, when operating inefficiencies are identifiable and readily correctable, and when the firm is relatively close to its break-even point. To complement a general belt-tightening, firms need to emphasize budgeting and cost control, eliminate jobs and stop hiring, modernize existing plant and equipment to gain greater productivity, and delay nonessential capital expenditures.

Selling Off Assets   Asset reduction/retrenchment strategies are essential when cash flow is a critical consideration and when the most practical way to generate cash is (1) through sale of some of the firm's assets (plant and equipment, land, patents, inventories, or profitable subsidiaries) and (2) through retrenchment (pruning marginal products from the product line, closing or selling older plants, reducing the work force, withdrawing from outlying markets, cutting back customer service, and the like). Sometimes firms sell their assets not so much to unload losing operations and stem cash drains as to raise funds to save and strengthen their remaining activities.

Combination Efforts   Combination turnaround strategies are usually essential in grim situations that require fast action on a broad front. Likewise, combination actions frequently come into play when a firm brings in new managers and gives them a free hand to make changes. The tougher the problems, the more likely the solutions will involve multiple strategic initiatives.

Turnaround efforts tend to be high-risk undertakings and often fail. A landmark study of 64 companies found no successful turnarounds among the most troubled companies in eight basic industries.[26] Many waited too long to begin a turnaround. Others found themselves short of both cash and entrepreneurial talent to compete in a slow-growth industry characterized by fierce battles for market share; better positioned rivals simply proved too strong to defeat.

THIRTEEN COMMANDMENTS FOR CRAFTING SUCCESSFUL BUSINESS STRATEGIES

Business experiences over the years prove over and over that disastrous courses of action can be avoided by adhering to certain strategy-making principles. The wisdom of these past experiences can be distilled into 13

---

[26]William K. Hall, "Survival Strategies in a Hostile Environment," *Harvard Business Review* 58, no. 5 (September–October 1980), pp. 75–85.

commandments which, if faithfully observed, help strategists craft better strategic action plans.

1. *Always put top priority on crafting and executing strategic moves that enhance the company's competitive position for the long term and that serve to establish it as an industry leader.* In competitive markets, a strongly entrenched leadership position pays off year after year, but the glory of meeting one year's financial targets quickly passes. Shareholders are never well-served by managers who let short-term financial considerations override strategic initiatives that will bolster the company's long-term competitive position and strength.

2. *Understand that a clear, consistent competitive strategy, when well-crafted and well-executed, builds reputation and recognizable industry position; a strategy aimed solely at capturing momentary market opportunities yields fleeting benefits.* The pursuit of short-run financial opportunism without long-term strategic guidance tends to produce the worst kind of profits: one-shot rewards that are unrepeatable. Over the long haul, a company that has a well-conceived competitive strategy aimed at securing a strong market position will outperform and defeat a rival whose strategic decisions are driven by short-term financial expectations. In an ongoing enterprise, the game of competition ought to be played for the long term, not the short term.

3. *Try not to get "stuck back in the pack" with no coherent long-term strategy or distinctive competitive position, an "average" image, and little prospect of climbing into the ranks of the industry leaders.*

4. *Invest in creating a sustainable competitive advantage—it is the single most dependable contributor to above-average profitability.*

5. *Play aggressive offense to build competitive advantage and aggressive defense to protect it.*

6. *Avoid strategies capable of succeeding only in the best of circumstances—* competitors will react with countermeasures and market conditions are not always favorable.

7. *Be cautious in pursuing a rigidly prescribed or inflexible strategy—changing market conditions may render it quickly obsolete.* Any strategy, to perform satisfactorily, must be adaptable to fresh market circumstances. Strategic themes involving "top" quality or "lowest" cost should be interpreted as *relative to competitors* and/or *customer needs* rather than based on arbitrary management standards.

8. *Don't underestimate the reactions and the commitment of rivals—especially* when they are pushed into a corner and their well-being is threatened.

9. *Be wary of attacking strong, resourceful rivals without solid competitive advantage and ample financial strength.*

10. *Consider that attacking competitive weakness is usually more profitable than attacking competitive strength.*

11. *Take care not to cut prices without an established cost advantage—only a low-cost producer can win at price-cutting over the long term.*

12. *Be aware that aggressive moves to wrest market share away from rivals often provoke aggressive retaliation in the form of a marketing "arms race" and/or*

price wars—to the detriment of everyone's profits. Aggressive moves to capture a bigger market share invite cutthroat competition particularly when the market is plagued with high inventories and excess production capacity.

13. *Employ bold strategic moves in pursuing differentiation strategies to open up meaningful gaps in quality, service, or performance features.* Tiny differences between rivals' competitive strategies and product offerings may not be visible or important to buyers.

KEY POINTS

Successful strategies fit a firm's *external* situation (industry and competitive conditions) and *internal* situation (strengths, weaknesses, opportunities, and threats). Table 6–2 provides a summary checklist of the most important situational considerations and strategic options. To match strategy to the situation, analysts must start with an overview of the industry environment and the firm's competitive standing in the industry (columns 1 and 2 in Table 6–2):

1. What type of industry environment does the company operate in (emerging, rapid growth, mature, fragmented, global, commodity product)? What strategic options and strategic postures are best suited for this environment?
2. What position does the firm have in the industry (strong vs. weak vs. crisis-ridden; leader vs. runner-up vs. also-ran)? How does the firm's standing influence its strategic options given the stage of the industry's development—in particular, which options have to be ruled out?

Next, strategists need to factor in the primary external and internal situational consideratons (column 3) and decide how all the factors add up. This should narrow the firm's basic market share and investment options (column 4) and strategic options (column 5).

The final step is to custom-tailor the chosen generic strategic approaches (columns 4 and 5) to fit *both* the industry environment and the firm's standing vis-à-vis competitors. Here it is important to be sure that (1) the customized aspects of the proposed strategy are well-matched to the firm's skills and capabilities and (2) the strategy addresses all strategic issues the firm confronts.

In screening out weak strategies and weighing the pros and cons of the most attractive ones, the answers to the following questions often indicate the way to go:

- What kind of competitive edge can the company realistically hope to have, and what strategic moves/approaches will it take to secure this edge?
- Does the company have the skills and resources to succeed in these moves and approaches—if not, can they be acquired?
- Once built, how can the competitive advantage be protected? What defensive strategies need to be employed? Will rivals counterattack? What will it take to blunt their efforts?
- Are any rivals particularly vulnerable? Should the firm mount an offensive to capitalize on these vulnerabilities? What offensive moves need to be employed?

T A B L E 6-2   **Matching Strategy to the Situation**   (*A checklist of optional strategies and generic situations*)

Industry Environments	Company Positions/Situations	Situational Considerations	Market Share and Investment Options	Strategy Options
• Young, emerging industry	• Dominant leader	• External	• Growth and build	• Competitive approach
• Rapid growth	– Global	– Driving forces	– Capture a bigger market share by growing faster than industry as a whole	– Overall low-cost leadership
• Consolidating to a smaller group of competitors	– National	– Competitive pressures	– Invest heavily to capture growth potential	– Differentiation
• Mature/slow growth	– Regional	– Anticipated moves of key rivals	• Fortify and defend	– Focus/specialization
• Aging/declining	– Local	– Key success factors	– Protect market share; grow at least as fast as whole industry	• Offensive initiatives
• Fragmented	• Leader	– Industry attractiveness	– Invest enough resources to maintain competitive strength and market position	– Attack
• International/global	• Aggressive challenger	• Internal	• Retrench and retreat	– End run
• Commodity product orientation	• Content follower	– Current company performance	– Surrender weakly held positions when forced to, but fight hard to defend core markets/customer base	– Guerrilla warfare
• High technology/rapid changes	• Weak/distressed candidate for turn-around or exit	– Strengths and weaknesses	– Maximize short-term cash flow	– Preemptive strikes
	• "Stuck in the middle"/no clear strategy or market image	– Opportunities and threats	– Minimize reinvestment of capital in the business	• Defensive initiatives
		– Cost position	• Overhaul and reposition	– Fortify/protect
		– Competitive strength	– Try to turn around	– Retaliatory
		– Strategic issues and problems	• Abandon/liquidate	– Harvest
			– Sell out	• International initiatives
			– Close down	– Licensing
				– Export
				– Multicountry
				– Global
				• Vertical integration initiatives
				– Forward
				– Backward

TABLE 6–3   **Sample Format for a Strategic Action Plan**

1. Basic long-term direction and mission

2. Key strategic and financial objectives

3. Overall business strategy

4. Specific functional strategies
   • Production

   • Marketing/sales

   • Finance

   • Personnel/human resources

   • Other

5. Recommended actions

- What additional strategic moves are needed to deal with driving forces into the industry, specific threats and weaknesses, and any other issues/problems unique to the firm?

As the choice of strategic initiatives is developed, there are several pitfalls to watch for:

- Designing an overly ambitious strategic plan—one that calls for a lot of different strategic moves and/or that overtaxes the company's resources and capabilities.
- Selecting a strategy that represents a radical departure from or abandonment of the cornerstones of the company's prior success—a radical strategy change need not be rejected automatically, but it should be pursued only after careful risk assessment.
- Choosing a strategy that goes against the grain of the organization's culture or that conflicts with the values and philosophies of senior executives.

Table 6–3 provides a format for presenting a strategic action plan for a single-business enterprise.

SUGGESTED READINGS

Bleeke, Joel A. "Strategic Choices for Newly Opened Markets." *Harvard Business Review* 68, no. 5 (September–October 1990), pp. 158–65.

Bolt, James F. "Global Competitors: Some Criteria for Success." *Business Horizons* 31, no. 1 (January–February 1988), pp. 34–41.

Carroll, Glenn R. "The Specialist Strategy." In *Strategy and Organization: A West Coast Perspective*, ed. Glenn Carroll and David Vogel. Boston: Pitman Publishing, 1984, pp. 117–28.

Feldman, Lawrence P., and Albert L. Page. "Harvesting: The Misunderstood Market Exit Strategy." *Journal of Business Strategy* 5, no. 4 (Spring 1985), pp. 79–85.

Finkin, Eugene F. "Company Turnaround." *Journal of Business Strategy* 5, no. 4 (Spring 1985), pp. 14–25.

Hall, William K. "Survival Strategies in a Hostile Environment." *Harvard Business Review* 58, no. 5 (September–October 1980), pp. 75–85.

Hamermesh, R. G., and S. B. Silk. "How to Compete in Stagnant Industries." *Harvard Business Review* 57, no. 5 (September–October 1979), pp. 161–68.

Harrigan, Kathryn R. *Strategic Flexibility*. Lexington, Mass.: Lexington Books, 1985, chaps. 6 and 8.

Heany, Donald F. "Businesses in Profit Trouble." *Journal of Business Strategy* 5, no. 4 (Spring 1985), pp. 4–13.

Hofer, Charles W. "Turnaround Strategies." *Journal of Business Strategy* 1, no. 1 (Summer 1980), pp. 19–31.

Hout, Thomas, Michael E. Porter, and Eileen Rudden. "How Global Companies Win Out." *Harvard Business Review* 60, no. 5 (September–October 1982), pp. 98–108.

Kotler, Philip. *Marketing Management: Analysis, Planning, Control,* 5th ed. Englewood Cliffs, N.J.: Prentice Hall, 1984, chap. 11.

Lei, David. "Strategies for Global Competition." *Long Range Planning* 22, no. 1 (February 1989), pp. 102–9.

Mayer, Robert J. "Winning Strategies for Manufacturers in Mature Industries." *Journal of Business Strategy* 8, no. 2 (Fall 1987), pp. 23–31.

Ohmae, Kenichi. "The Global Logic of Strategic Alliances." *Harvard Business Review* 67, no. 2 (March–April 1989), pp. 143–54.

Porter, Michael E. *Competitive Strategy: Techniques for Analyzing Industries and Competitors.* New York: Free Press, 1980, chaps. 9–13.

Porter, Michael E. *The Competitive Advantage of Nations.* New York: Free Press, 1990, chap. 2.

Sugiura, Hideo, "How Honda Localizes Its Global Strategy." *Sloan Management Review* 33 (Fall 1990), pp. 77–82.

Thompson, Arthur A. "Strategies for Staying Cost Competitive." *Harvard Business Review* 62, no. 1 (January–February 1984), pp. 110–17.

Corporate Diversification Strategies

. . . to acquire or not to acquire: that is the question.
Robert J. Terry

*Strategy is a deliberate search for a plan of action that will develop a business's
competitive advantage and compound it.*
Bruce D. Henderson

In this chapter and the next, we move up one level in the strategy-making hierarchy. Attention shifts from formulating strategy for a single-business enterprise to formulating strategy for a diversified enterprise. Because a diversified company is a collection of individual businesses, corporate strategy-making is a bigger-picture exercise than crafting strategy for a single-business company. In a single-business enterprise, management only has to contend with one industry environment and how to compete successfully in it. But in a diversified company, corporate managers have to craft a multibusiness, multi-industry strategic action plan for a number of different business divisions competing in diverse industry environments. Managing a group of diverse businesses is usually so time-consuming and complex that corporate-level managers delegate lead responsibility for business-level strategy-making to the head of each business unit.

As explained in Chapter 2, a corporate strategy in a diversified company concentrates on:

1. Making moves to position the company in the industries chosen for diversification (the basic strategy options here are to acquire a company in the target industry, form a joint venture with another company to enter the target industry, or start a new company internally and try to grow it from the ground up).

2. Taking actions to improve the long-term performance of the corporation's portfolio of businesses once diversification has been achieved (helping to strengthen the competitive positions of existing businesses, divesting businesses that no longer fit into management's long-range plans, and adding new businesses to the portfolio).
3. Trying to capture whatever strategic fit benefits exist within the portfolio of businesses and turn them into competitive advantage.
4. Evaluating the profit prospects of each business unit and steering corporate resources into the most attractive strategic opportunities.

In this chapter we survey the generic type of corporate diversification strategies and how competitive advantage can result from a company's diversification approach. In Chapter 8 we will examine how to assess the strategic attractiveness of a diversified company's business portfolio.

FROM SINGLE-BUSINESS CONCENTRATION TO DIVERSIFICATION

Most companies begin as small single-business enterprises serving a local or regional market. During a company's early years, its product line tends to be limited, its capital base thin, and its competitive position vulnerable. Usually, a young company's strategic emphasis is on increasing sales volume, boosting market share, and cultivating a loyal clientele. Profits are reinvested and new debt is taken on to grow the business as fast as conditions permit. Price, quality, service, and promotion are tailored more precisely to customer needs. As soon as practical, the product line is broadened to meet variations in customer wants and end-use applications.

Opportunities for geographical market expansion are normally pursued next. The natural sequence of geographic expansion proceeds from local to regional to national to international markets, though the degree of penetration may be uneven from area to area because of varying profit potentials. Geographic expansion may, of course, stop well short of global or even national proportions because of intense competition, lack of resources, or the unattractiveness of further market coverage.

Somewhere along the way the potential for vertical integration, either backward to sources of supply or forward to the ultimate consumer, may become a strategic consideration. Generally, vertical integration makes strategic sense only if it significantly enhances a company's profitability and competitive strength.

So long as the company has its hands full trying to capitalize on profitable growth opportunities in its present industry, there is no urgency to pursue diversification. But when company growth potential starts to wane, the strategic options are either to become more aggressive in taking market share away from rivals or diversify into other lines of businesses. A decision to diversify raises the question of "what kind and how much diversification?" The strategic possibilities are wide open. A company can diversify into closely related or totally unrelated businesses. It can diversify to a small extent (less than 10 percent of total revenues and profits) or to a large extent (up to 50 percent). It can move into one or two large new businesses or a greater number of small ones. And once it achieves diversification, the time may come when management has to consider divesting or liquidating businesses that are no longer attractive.

Why a Single-Business Strategy Is Attractive

Companies that concentrate on a single business can achieve enviable success over many decades without relying on diversification to sustain their growth. McDonald's, Delta Airlines, Coca-Cola, Domino's Pizza, Apple Computer, Wal-Mart, Federal Express, Timex, Campbell Soup, Anheuser-Busch, Xerox, Gerber, and Polaroid all won their reputations in a single business. In the nonprofit sector, continued emphasis on a single activity has proved beneficial for the Red Cross, Salvation Army, Christian Children's Fund, Girl Scouts, Phi Beta Kappa, and American Civil Liberties Union.

Concentrating on a single line of business (totally or with a small amount of diversification) has some useful organizational and managerial advantages. First, single-business concentration entails less ambiguity about "who we are and what we do." The energies of the *total* organization are directed down *one* business path. There is less chance that senior management's time or organizational resources will be stretched thinly over too many activities. Entrepreneurial efforts can focus exclusively on keeping the firm's business strategy and competitive approach responsive to industry change and fine-tuned to customer needs. All the firm's managers, especially top executives, can have hands-on contact with the core business and in-depth knowledge of operations. (Senior officers usually have risen through the ranks and possess first-hand experience in field operations—something hard to expect of corporate managers in broadly diversified enterprises.) Furthermore, concentrating on a single business carries a heftier built-in incentive for managers to come up with ways to strengthen the firm's long-term competitive position in the industry rather than pursuing the fleeting benefits of higher short-term profits. The company can use all its organizational resources to become better at what it does. Important competencies and competitive skills are more likely to emerge. With management's attention focused exclusively on just one business, the probability is higher that ideas will emerge on how to improve production technology, better meet customer needs with innovative new product features, or enhance efficiencies anywhere in the activity-cost chain. The more successful a single-business enterprise is, the more able it is to parlay its accumulated experience and distinctive expertise into a sustainable competitive advantage and a prominent leadership position in its industry.

There are important organizational and managerial advantages to concentrating on just one business.

The Risk of a Single-Business Strategy

The big risk of single-business concentration is putting all a firm's eggs in one industry basket. If the industry stagnates, declines, or otherwise becomes unattractive, a company's future outlook dims, its growth rate becomes tougher to sustain, and superior profit performance is much harder to achieve. At times, changing customer needs, technological innovation, or new substitute products can undermine or wipe out a single-business firm. Consider, for example, what word processing has done to the electric typewriter business and what compact disc players are doing to the market for cassette tapes and

FIGURE 7–1   **Matching Corporate Strategy Alternatives to Fit an Undiversifed Firm's Situation**

Competitive Position

	Weak	Strong
Rapid	**Strategy Options** (in probable order of attractiveness) • Reformulate single-business concentration strategy (to achieve turnaround). • Acquire another firm in the same business (to strengthen competitive position). • Vertical integration (forward or backward if it strengthens competitive position). • Diversification. • Be acquired by/sell out to a stronger rival. • Abandonment (a last resort in the event all else fails).	**Strategy Options** (in probable order of attractiveness) • Continue single-business concentration – International expansion (if market opportunities exist). • Vertical integration (if it strengthens the firm's competitive position). • Related diversification (to transfer skills and expertise built up in the company's core business to adjacent businesses).
Slow	**Strategy Options** (in probable order of attractiveness) • Reformulate single-business concentration strategy (to achieve turnaround). • Merger with a rival firm (to strengthen competitive position). • Vertical integration (only if it strengthens competitive position substantially). • Diversification. • Harvest/divest. • Liquidation (a last resort in the event all else fails).	**Strategy Options** (in probable order of attractiveness) • International expansion (if market opportunities exist). • Related diversification. • Unrelated diversification. • Joint ventures into new areas. • Vertical integration (if it strengthens competitive position). • Continue single-business concentration (achieve growth by taking market share from weaker rivals).

Market Growth Rate

records. For this reason most single-business companies turn their strategic attention to diversification when their business starts to show signs of peaking.

When Diversification Starts to Make Sense

To better understand *when* a single-business company needs to consider diversification, consider Figure 7–1 where the variable of competitive position is plotted against various rates of market growth to create four distinct strategic situations that might be occupied by an undiversified company.[1] Firms that fall into the rapid market growth/strong competitive position box have several logical strategy options, the strongest of which in the near term may be continuing to pursue single-business concentration. Given the industry's high growth rate (and implicit long-term attractiveness), it makes sense for firms in this position to push hard to maintain or increase their market shares, further develop core competences, and make whatever capital investments are necessary to continue in a strong industry position. At some juncture, a company in this box may find it desirable to consider a vertical integration strategy to undergird its competitive strength. Later, when market growth starts to slow, prudence dictates looking into diversification as a means of spreading business risks and transferring the skills or expertise the company has built up into closely *related* businesses.

When to diversify depends partly on the remaining opportunities for further industry growth and partly on the competitive position a company occupies.

Firms in the rapid growth/weak position category should first consider their options for reformulating their present competitive strategy (given the high rate of market growth). Second they need to address the questions of (1) why their current approach has resulted in a weak competitive position and (2) what it will take to become an effective competitor. In a rapidly expanding market, even weak firms should be able to improve their performance and make headway in building a stronger market position. If a firm is young and struggling to develop, it usually has a better chance for survival in a growing market where plenty of new business is up for grabs than in a stable or declining industry. However, if a weakly positioned company in a rapid-growth market lacks the resources and skills to hold its own, its best option is to either merge with another company in the industry or merge with an outsider with the cash and resources to support the firm's development. Vertical integration—either forward, backward, or both—is an option for weakly positioned firms whenever it can materially strengthen the firm's competitive position. A third option is diversification into related or unrelated areas (if adequate financing can be found). If all else fails, abandonment—divestiture for a multibusiness firm or liquidation for a single-business firm—has to become an active strategic option. While abandonment may seem extreme because of the high growth potential, a company unable to make a profit in a booming market probably does not have the ability to make a profit at all—particularly if competition stiffens or industry conditions sour.

Companies with a weak competitive position in a relatively slow-growth market should look at (1) reformulating their present competitive strategy to turn their situation around and create a more attractive competitive position, (2) integrating forward or backward provided good profit improvement and competitive positioning opportunities exist, (3) diversifying into related or unrelated areas, (4) merger with another firm, (5) employing a harvest, then divest strategy, and (6) liquidating their position in the business by either selling out to another firm or closing down operations.

Companies that are strongly positioned in a slow-growth industry should consider using their excess cash to begin diversifying. Diversification into businesses where a firm can leverage its core competences and competitive strengths is usually the best strategy. But diversification into totally unrelated

Companies that have strong competitive positions in slow-growth industries are prime candidates for diversifying into new businesses.

---

[1]Roland Christensen, Norman A. Berg, and Malcolm S. Salter, *Policy Formulation and Administration*, 7th ed. (Homewood, Ill: Richard D. Irwin, 1976), pp. 16–18.

businesses has to be considered if none of the related business opportunities offer attractive profit prospects. Joint ventures with other organizations into new fields are another logical possibility. Vertical integration should be a last resort (since it provides no escape from the industry's slow-growth condition) and makes strategic sense only if a firm can expect sizable profit gains. A strong company in a slow-growth industry usually needs to curtail new investment in its present facilities (unless it sees important growth *segments* within the industry) to free cash for new endeavors.

The decision on *when to diversify* is therefore partly a function of a firm's competitive position and partly a function of the remaining opportunities in its home-base industry. There really is no well-defined point at which companies in the same industry should diversify. Indeed, companies in the same industry can rationally choose different diversification approaches and launch them at different times.

BUILDING SHAREHOLDER VALUE: THE ULTIMATE JUSTIFICATION FOR DIVERSIFYING

Strategic Management Principle

To create value for shareholders, a diversifying company must get into businesses that can perform better under common management than they could perform operating as independent enterprises.

The underlying purpose of corporate diversification is to build shareholder value. For diversification to enhance shareholder value, corporate strategy must do more than simply diversify the company's business risk by investing in more than one industry. Shareholders can achieve the same risk diversification on their own by purchasing stock in companies in different industries. Strictly speaking, *diversification does not create shareholder value unless a group of businesses performs better under a single corporate umbrella than they would perform operating as independent, stand-alone businesses.* For example, if company A diversifies by purchasing company B and if A and B's consolidated profits in the years to come prove no greater than what each would have earned on its own, then A's diversification into business B has failed to provide shareholders with added value. Company A's shareholders could have achieved the same $2 + 2 = 4$ result on their own by purchasing stock in company B. Shareholder value is not *created* by diversification unless it produces a $2 + 2 = 5$ effect where sister businesses perform better together as part of the same firm than they could perform as independent companies.

Three Tests for Judging a Diversification Move

The problem with such a strict benchmark of whether diversification has enhanced shareholder value is that it requires speculative judgments about how well a diversified company's business would have performed on its own. Comparisons of actual performance against the hypothetical of what performance might have been under other circumstances are never very satisfactory and, besides, they represent after-the-fact assessments. Strategists have to base diversification decisions on future expectations. Attempts to gauge the impact of particular diversification moves on shareholder value do not have to be abandoned, however. Corporate strategists can make before-the-fact assessments of whether a particular diversification move is capable of increasing shareholder value by using three tests:[2]

---

[2]Michael E. Porter, "From Competitive Advantage to Corporate Strategy," *Harvard Business Review* 45, no. 3 (May–June 1987), pp. 46–49.

1. *The Attractiveness Test:* The industry chosen for diversification must be attractive enough to produce consistently good returns on investment. True industry attractiveness is defined by the presence of favorable competitive conditions and a market environment conducive to long-term profitability. Such simple indicators as rapid growth or a sexy product are unreliable proxies of attractiveness.

2. *The Cost of Entry Test:* The cost to enter the target industry must not be so high as to erode the potential for good profitability. A catch-22 situation can prevail here, however. The more attractive the industry, the more expensive it is to get into. Entry barriers for new start-up companies are nearly always high—were barriers low, a rush of new entrants would soon erode the potential for high profitability. And buying a company already in the business typically entails a high acquisition cost because of the industry's strong appeal. Costly entry undermines the potential for enhancing shareholder value.

3. *The Better-Off Test:* The diversifying company must bring some potential for competitive advantage to the new business it enters, or the new business must offer some potential for added competitive advantage to the company's other businesses. The opportunity to *create* sustainable competitive advantage where none existed before means there is also opportunity for added profitability/and shareholder value.

To build shareholder value via diversification, the industries and businesses a company targets must be capable of passing the attractiveness, cost-of-entry, and better-off tests.

Diversification moves that satisfy all three tests have the greatest potential to build shareholder value over the long term. Diversification moves that can pass only one or two tests are highly suspect.

DIVERSIFICATION STRATEGIES

Once the decision is made to pursue diversification, any of several different paths can be taken. There is plenty of room for varied strategic approaches. We can get a better understanding of the strategic issues corporate managers face in creating and managing a diversified group of businesses by looking at six types of diversification strategies:

1. Strategies for entering new industries—acquisition, start-up, and joint ventures.
2. Related diversification strategies.
3. Unrelated diversification strategies.
4. Divestiture and liquidation strategies.
5. Corporate turnaround, retrenchment, and restructuring strategies.
6. Multinational diversification.

The first three involve ways to diversify; the last three involve strategies to strengthen the positions and performance of companies that have already diversified.

Strategies for Entering New Businesses

Entry into new businesses can take any of three forms: acquisition, internal start-up, and joint ventures. *Acquisition of an existing business* is probably the most popular means of diversifying into another industry and has the advantage of much quicker entry into the target market.[3] At the same time, it helps a diversifier overcome such entry barriers as technological inexperience, establishing supplier relationships, being big enough to match rivals' efficiency and unit costs, having to spend large sums on introductory advertising and promotion to gain market visibility and brand recognition, and getting adequate distribution. In many industries, going the internal start-up route and trying to develop the knowledge, resources, scale of operation, and market reputation necessary to become an effective competitor can take years and entails all the problems of getting a brand new company off the ground and operating. However, finding the right kind of company to acquire sometimes presents a challenge.[4] The big dilemma an acquisition-minded firm faces is whether to buy a successful company at a high price or a struggling company at a "bargain" price. If the buying firm has little knowledge of the industry but ample capital, it is often better off purchasing a capable, strongly positioned firm—unless the acquisition price is unreasonably high. On the other hand, when the acquirer sees promising ways to transform a weak firm into a strong one and has the money, know-how, and patience to do it, a struggling company can be the better long-term investment.

One of the big stumbling blocks to entering attractive industries by acquisition is the difficulty of finding a well-positioned company at a price that satisfies the cost-of-entry test.

The cost-of-entry test requires that the expected profit stream of the acquired business provide an attractive return on the total acquisition cost and on any new capital investment needed to sustain or expand its operations. A high acquisition price can make earning an attractive return improbable or difficult. For instance, suppose that the price to purchase a company is $3 million and that the business is earning after-tax profits of $200,000 on an equity investment of $1 million (a 20 percent annual return). Simple arithmetic requires that the acquired busness's profits be tripled for the purchaser to earn the same 20 percent return on its $3 million acquisition price that the previous owners got on their $1 million equity investment. Building the acquired firm's earnings from $200,000 to $600,000 annually could take several years—and require additional investment on which the purchaser would also have to earn a 20 percent return. Since the owners of a successful and growing company usually demand a price that reflects their business's future profit prospects, it's easy for such an acquisition to flunk the cost-of-entry test. It's difficult to find a successful company in an appealing industry at a price that still permits attractive returns on investment.

The big drawbacks to entering an industry by forming a start-up company internally are the costs of overcoming entry barriers and the extra time it takes to build a strong and profitable competitive position.

Diversification through *internal start-up* involves creating a new company under the corporate umbrella to compete in the desired industry. A newly formed organization not only has to overcome entry barriers, it also has to invest in new production capacity, develop sources of supply, hire and train employees, build distribution channels, grow a customer base, and so on. Generally, forming a start-up company to enter a new industry is more attractive when (1) there is ample time to launch the business from the ground up, (2) incumbent firms are likely to be slow or ineffective in responding to a

---

[3]In recent years, takeovers have become an increasingly used approach to acquisition. The term *takeover* refers to the attempt (often sprung as a surprise) of one firm to acquire ownership or control over another firm against the wishes of the latter's management (and perhaps some of its stockholders).

[4]Michael E. Porter, *Competitive Strategy: Techniques for Analyzing Industries and Competitors* (New York: Free Press, 1980), pp. 354–55.

new entrant's efforts to crack the market, (3) internal entry has lower costs than entry via acquisition, (4) the company already has most or all of the skills it needs to compete effectively, (5) adding new production capacity will not adversely impact the supply-demand balance in the industry, and (6) the targeted industry is populated with many relatively small firms so the new start-up does not have to compete head-to-head against larger, more powerful rivals.[5]

Joint ventures are a useful way to gain access to a new business in at least three types of situations.[6] First, a joint venture is a good device for doing something that is uneconomical or risky for an organization to do alone. Second, joint ventures make sense when pooling the resources and competences of two or more independent organizations produces an organization with more of the skills needed to be a strong competitor. In such cases, each partner brings special talents or resources that the other doesn't have and that are important for success. Third, joint ventures with foreign partners are sometimes the only or best way to surmount import quotas, tariffs, nationalistic political interests, and cultural roadblocks. The economic, competitive, and political realities of nationalism often require a foreign company to team up with a domestic partner in order to gain access to the national market in which the domestic partner is located. Domestic partners offer outside companies the benefits of local knowledge, managerial and marketing personnel, and access to distribution channels. However, such joint ventures often pose complicated questions about how to divide efforts among the partners and who has effective control.[7] Conflicts between foreign and domestic partners can arise over local sourcing of components, how much production to export, whether operating procedures should conform to the foreign company's standards or local preferences, and who should control cash flows and the disposition of profits.

RELATED DIVERSIFICATION STRATEGIES

In choosing which industries to diversify into, companies can pick industries either *related* or *unrelated* to the organization's core business. A related diversification strategy involves diversifying into businesses that possess some kind of "strategic fit." *Strategic fit* exists when different businesses have sufficiently related activity-cost chains that there are important opportunities for activity sharing in one business or another.[8] *A diversified firm that exploits these activity-cost chain interrelationships and captures the benefits of strategic fit achieves a consolidated performance greater than the sum of what the businesses can earn pursuing independent strategies.* The presence of strategic fit within a diversified firm's business portfolio, together with corporate management's skill in capturing the benefits of the interrelationships, makes related diversification a 2 + 2 = 5 phenomenon and becomes a basis for competitive advantage. The bigger the strategic fit benefits, the bigger the competitive advantage of related

Basic Concept
Related diversification involves diversifying into businesses whose activity-cost chains are related in ways that satisfy the better-off test.

---

[5]Ibid., pp. 344–45.

[6]Peter Drucker, *Management, Tasks, Responsibilities, Practices* (New York: Harper & Row, 1974), pp. 720–24.

[7]Porter, *Competitive Strategy*, p. 340.

[8]Michael E. Porter, *Competitive Advantage*, pp. 318–19 and 337–53; Kenichi Ohmae, *The Mind of the Strategist* (New York: Penguin Books, 1983), pp. 121–24; and Porter, "From Competitive Advantage to Corporate Strategy," pp. 53–57.

diversification and the more that related diversification satisfies the better-off test for building shareholder value.

Strategic fit relationships can arise out of technology sharing, common labor skills and requirements, common suppliers and raw material sources, the potential for joint manufacture of parts and components, similar operating methods, similar kinds of managerial know-how, reliance on the same types of marketing and merchandising skills, ability to share a common sales force, ability to use the same wholesale distributors or retail dealers, or potential for combining after-sale service activities. The fit or relatedness can occur anywhere along the businesses' respective activity-cost chains. Strategic fit relationships are important because they represent opportunities for cost-saving efficiencies, technology or skills transfers, or other benefits of activity-sharing, all of which are avenues for gaining competitive advantages over rivals that have not diversified or that have not diversified in ways that give them access to such strategic fit benefits.

Some of the most commonly used approaches to related diversification are:

- Entering businesses where sales force, advertising, and distribution activities can be shared (a bread bakery buying a maker of crackers and salty snack foods).

- Exploiting closely related technologies (a maker of agricultural seeds and fertilizers diversifying into chemicals for insect and plant disease control).

- Transferring know-how and expertise from one business to another (a successful operator of hamburger outlets acquire a chain specializing in Mexican fast foods).

- Transferring the organization's brand name and reputation with consumers to a new product/service (a tire manufacturer diversifying into automotive repair centers).

- Acquiring new businesses that will uniquely help the firm's position in its existing businesses (a cable TV broadcaster purchasing a sports team and a movie production company to provide original programming).

Examples of related diversification abound. BIC Pen, which pioneered inexpensive disposable ballpoint pens, used its core competences in low-cost manufacturing and mass merchandising as its basis for diversifying into disposable cigarette lighters, disposable razors, and pantyhose—all three businesses required low-cost production know-how and skilled consumer marketing for competitive success. Tandy Corp. practiced related diversification when its chain of Radio Shack outlets, which originally handled mostly radio and stereo equipment, added telephones, intercoms, calculators, clocks, electronic and scientific toys, personal computers, and peripheral computer equipment. The Tandy strategy was to use the marketing access provided by its thousands of Radio Shack locations to become one of the world's leading retailers of electronic technology. Philip Morris, a leading cigarette manufacturer, employed a marketing-related diversification strategy when it purchased Miller Brewing, General Foods, and Kraft and transferred its skills in cigarette marketing to the marketing of beer and food products. Lockheed pursued a customer needs-based diversification strategy in creating business units to supply the Department of Defense with missiles, rocket engines, aircraft, electronic equipment, and ships, and contract R&D for weapons. Procter & Gamble's

ILLUSTRATION CAPSULE
16

EXAMPLES OF COMPANIES WITH RELATED BUSINESS PORTFOLIOS

Presented below are the business portfolios of four companies that have pursued some form of related diversification:

Gillette

- Blades and razors
- Toiletries (Right Guard, Silkience, Foamy, Dry Idea, Soft & Dry, Oral-B toothbrushes, White Rain, Toni)
- Writing instruments and stationery products (Paper Mate pens, Liquid Paper correction fluids, Waterman pens)
- Braun shavers, cordless curlers, coffeemakers, alarm clocks, and electric toothbrushes

PepsiCo

- Soft drinks (Pepsi, Mountain Dew, Slice)
- Kentucky Fried Chicken
- Pizza Hut
- Taco Bell
- Frito Lay
- 7 Up International (non-U.S. sales of 7 Up)

Philip Morris Companies

- Cigarettes (Marlboro, Virginia Slims, Benson & Hedges, and Merit)
- Miller Brewing Company
- Kraft General Foods (Maxwell House, Sanka, Oscar Mayer, Kool-Aid, Jell-O, Post cereals, Birds-Eye frozen foods, Kraft cheeses, Sealtest dairy products, Breyer's ice cream)
- Mission Viejo Realty

Johnson & Johnson

- Baby products (powder, shampoo, oil, lotion)
- Disposable diapers
- Bandaids and wound care products
- Stayfree, Carefree, Sure & Natural, and Modess feminine hygiene products
- Tylenol
- Prescription drugs
- Surgical and hospital products
- Dental products
- Oral contraceptives
- Veterinary and animal health products

Source: Company annual reports.

lineup of products includes Jif peanut butter, Duncan Hines cake mixes, Folger's coffee, Tide laundry detergent, Crisco vegetable oil, Crest toothpaste, Ivory soap, Charmin toilet tissue, and Head and Shoulders shampoo—all different businesses with different competitors and different production requirements. But P&G's products still represent related diversification because they all move through the same wholesale distribution systems, are sold in common retail settings to the same shoppers, are advertised and promoted in the same ways, and utilize the same marketing and merchandising skills. Illustration Capsule 16 shows the business portfolios of several companies that have pursued a strategy of related diversification.

Strategic Fit, Economies of Scope, and Competitive Advantage

A related diversification strategy has considerable appeal. It allows a firm to preserve a degree of unity in its business activities, reap the competitive advantages of skills transfer or lower costs, and still spread business risks over

Strategic fits among related businesses offer the competitive advantage potential of (a) lower costs or (b) efficient transfer of key skills, technological expertise, or managerial know-how.

a broader base. A company that has developed valuable skills and competences in its original business can employ a related diversification strategy to exploit what it does best and *transfer* its competences and competitive skills to another business. Successful skills or technology transfers can lead to competitive advantage in the new business.

Diversifying into businesses where technology, facilities, functional activities, or distribution channels can also be shared can lead to lower costs because of economies of scope. *Economies of scope* exist whenever it is less costly for two or more businesses to be operated under centralized management than to function as independent businesses. The economies of operating over a wider range of businesses or product lines can arise from cost-saving opportunities anywhere along the respective activity-cost chains of the businesses. The greater the economies of scope associated with the particular businesses a company has diversified into, the greater the potential for creating a competitive advantage based on lower costs.

Both skills transfer and cost-sharing enable the diversifier to earn greater profits from its businesses than the businesses could earn operating independently. The key to cost-sharing and skills transfer opportunities is diversification into businesses with strategic fit. While strategic fit relationships can occur throughout the activity-cost chain, most fall into one of three broad categories.

Basic Concept
Economies of scope arise from the ability to reduce costs by operating two or more businesses under the same corporate umbrella; cost savings can stem from interrelationships anywhere along the businesses' activity-cost chains.

Market-Related Fits When the activity-cost chains of different businesses overlap such that the products are used by the same customers, distributed through common dealers and retailers, or marketed and promoted in similar ways, then the businesses exhibit market-related strategic fit. A variety of cost-saving opportunities (or economies of scope) can arise from market-related strategic fit: using a single sales force for all related products rather than separate sales forces for each business, advertising related products in the same ads and brochures, using the same brand names, coordinating delivery and shipping, combining after-sale service and repair organizations, coordinating order processing and billing, using common promotional tie-ins (cents-off couponing, free samples and trial offers, seasonal specials, and the like), and combining dealer networks. Such market-related strategic fits usually allow a firm to economize on its marketing, selling, and distribution costs.

In addition to economies of scope, market-related fit can generate opportunities to transfer selling skills, promotional skills, advertising skills, and product differentiation skills from one business to another. Moreover, a company's brand name and reputation in one product can often be transferred to other products. Honda's name in motorcycles and automobiles gave it instant credibility and recognition in the lawnmower business without spending large sums on advertising. Canon's reputation in photographic equipment was a competitive asset that facilitated the company's diversification into copying equipment. Panasonic's name in consumer electronics (radios, TVs) was readily transferred to microwave ovens, making it easier and cheaper for Panasonic to diversify into the microwave oven market.

Operating Fit Different businesses have *operating fit* when there is potential for cost-sharing or skills transfer in procuring materials, conducting R&D, developing technology, manufacturing components, assembling finished goods, or performing administrative support functions. Sharing-related operating fits usually present cost-saving opportunities; some derive from the economies of combining activities into a larger-scale operation (*economies of scale*) and some derive from the ability to eliminate costs by doing things together rather than independently (*economies of scope*). The bigger the proportion of cost a shared activity represents, the more significant the shared cost savings become and the bigger the cost advantage that can result. The most important skills-transfer opportunities usually occur in situations where technological or manufacturing expertise in one business has beneficial applications in another.

Management Fit   This type of fit emerges when different business units have comparable types of entrepreneurial, administrative, or operating problems, thereby allowing managerial know-how in one line of business to be transferable to another business. Transfers of managerial expertise can occur anywhere in the activity-cost chain. Ford Motor Co. transferred its automobile financing and credit management know-how to the savings and loan industry when it acquired some failing S&Ls during the bailout of the crisis-ridden S&L industry. Emerson Electric transferred its skills in low-cost manufacture to its newly acquired Beaird-Poulan chain saw business division. The transfer of management know-how drove Beaird-Poulan's new strategy, changed the way its chain saws were designed and manufactured, and paved the way for new pricing and distribution emphasis.

Capturing Strategic Fit Benefits   It is one thing to diversify into industries with strategic fit and another to actually realize the benefits. To capture the benefits of sharing, related activities must be merged into a single functional unit and coordinated; then the cost-savings (or differentiation advantages) must be squeezed out. Merged functions and coordination can entail reorganization costs, and management must determine that the benefit of *some* centralized strategic control is great enough to warrant sacrifice of business-unit autonomy. Likewise, where skills transfer is the cornerstone of strategic fit, management must find a way to make the transfer effective without stripping too many skilled personnel from the business with the expertise. The more a company's diversification strategy is tied to skills transfer, the more it has to build and maintain a sufficient pool of specialized personnel. And it must not only supply new businesses with the skill but also see that they master the skill sufficiently to create competitive advantage.

> **Strategic Management Principle**
> *Competitive advantage achieved through strategic fits among related businesses adds to the performance potential of the firm's individual businesses; it is this extra source of competitive advantage that allows related diversification to have a 2 + 2 = 5 effect on shareholder value.*

UNRELATED DIVERSIFICATION STRATEGIES

Despite the strategic fit benefits associated with related diversification, a number of companies opt for unrelated diversification strategies. In unrelated diversification, the corporate strategy is to diversify into *any* industry where top management spots a good profit opportunity. There is no deliberate effort to seek out businesses where strategic fit exists. While firms pursuing unrelated diversification may try to ensure that their strategies meet the industry attractiveness and cost-of-entry tests, the conditions needed for the better-off

> **Basic Concept**
> *A strategy of unrelated diversification involves diversifying into whatever industries and businesses hold promise for attractive financial gain; pursuing strategic fit relationships assumes a backseat role.*

test are either disregarded or relegated to secondary status. Decisions to diversify into one industry versus another are based on an opportunistic search for "good" companies to acquire—*the basic premise of unrelated diversification is that any company that can be acquired on good financial terms represents a good business to diversify into.* Much time and effort goes into finding and screening acquisition candidates. Typically, corporate strategists screen candidate companies using such criteria as:

- Whether the business can meet corporate targets for profitability and return on investment.
- Whether the new business will require substantial infusions of capital to replace fixed assets, fund expansion, and provide working capital.
- Whether the business is in an industry with significant growth potential.
- Whether the business is big enough to contribute significantly to the parent firm's bottom line.
- The potential for union difficulties or adverse government regulations concerning product safety or the environment.
- Industry vulnerability to recession, inflation, high interest rates, or shifts in government policy.

Unrelated diversification is usually accomplished through acquisition; corporate strategists use a variety of criteria to identify suitable companies to acquire.

Sometimes, corporate strategy is directed at identifying companies that offer opportunities for financial gain because of their "special situation"; three types of companies make particularly attractive acquisition targets:

- *Companies whose assets are "undervalued"*—opportunities may exist to acquire such companies for less than full market value and make substantial capital gains by reselling their assets and businesses for more than their acquired costs.
- *Companies that are financially distressed*—such businesses can often be purchased at a bargain price, their operations turned around with the aid of the parent companies' financial resources and managerial know-how, and then either held as a long-term investment (because of their strong earnings potential) or sold at a profit, whichever is more attractive.
- *Companies that have bright growth prospects but are short on investment capital*—capital-poor, opportunity-rich companies are usually coveted diversification candidates for a financially strong firm.

Firms that pursue unrelated diversification nearly always enter new businesses by acquiring an established company rather than by forming a start-up subsidiary within its own corporate structure. Their premise is that growth by acquisition translates into enhanced shareholder value. Suspending application of the better-off test is seen as justifiable so long as unrelated diversification results in sustained growth in corporate revenues and earnings and none of the acquired businesses end up performing badly.

Illustration Capsule 17 shows the business portfolios of several companies that have pursued unrelated diversification. Such companies are frequently described as *conglomerates* because they follow no strategic theme in their diversification and because their business interests range broadly across diverse industries.

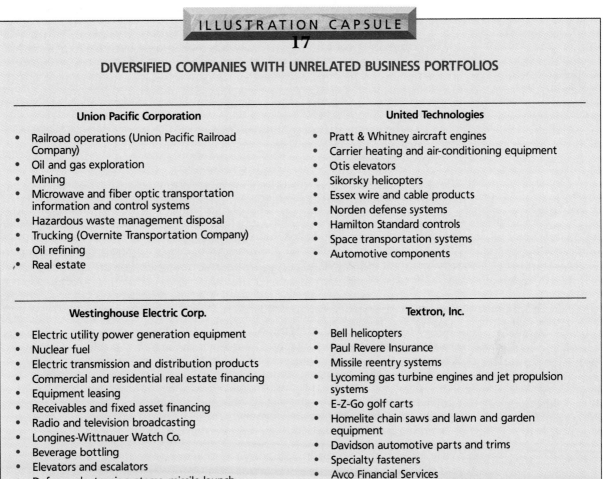

ILLUSTRATION CAPSULE
17

DIVERSIFIED COMPANIES WITH UNRELATED BUSINESS PORTFOLIOS

Union Pacific Corporation

- Railroad operations (Union Pacific Railroad Company)
- Oil and gas exploration
- Mining
- Microwave and fiber optic transportation information and control systems
- Hazardous waste management disposal
- Trucking (Overnite Transportation Company)
- Oil refining
- Real estate

United Technologies

- Pratt & Whitney aircraft engines
- Carrier heating and air-conditioning equipment
- Otis elevators
- Sikorsky helicopters
- Essex wire and cable products
- Norden defense systems
- Hamilton Standard controls
- Space transportation systems
- Automotive components

Westinghouse Electric Corp.

- Electric utility power generation equipment
- Nuclear fuel
- Electric transmission and distribution products
- Commercial and residential real estate financing
- Equipment leasing
- Receivables and fixed asset financing
- Radio and television broadcasting
- Longines-Wittnauer Watch Co.
- Beverage bottling
- Elevators and escalators
- Defense electronic systems, missile launch equipment, marine propulsion)
- Commercial furniture
- Community land development

Textron, Inc.

- Bell helicopters
- Paul Revere Insurance
- Missile reentry systems
- Lycoming gas turbine engines and jet propulsion systems
- E-Z-Go golf carts
- Homelite chain saws and lawn and garden equipment
- Davidson automotive parts and trims
- Specialty fasteners
- Avco Financial Services
- Jacobsen turf care equipment
- Tanks and armored vehicles

The Pros and Cons of Unrelated Diversification

Unrelated or conglomerate diversification has appeal from several financial angles:

1. Business risk is scattered over a variety of industries, making the company less dependent on any one business. While the same can be said for related diversification, unrelated diversification places no restraint on how risk is spread. An argument can be made that unrelated diversification is a superior way to diversify financial risk as compared to related diversification.

2. Capital resources can be invested in whatever industries offer the best profit prospects; cash from businesses with lower profit prospects can be diverted to acquiring and expanding businesses with higher growth

With unrelated diversification, a company can spread financial risks broadly, invest in whatever businesses promise financial gain, and try to stabilize earnings by diversifying into businesses with offsetting up-and-down cycles.

and profit potentials. Corporate financial resources are thus employed to maximum advantage.

3. Company profitability is somewhat more stable because hard times in one industry may be partially offset by good times in another—ideally, cyclical downswings in some of the company's businesses are counterbalanced by cyclical upswings in other businesses the company has diversified into.

4. To the extent that corporate managers are astute at spotting bargain-priced companies with big upside profit potential, shareholder wealth can be enhanced.

While entry into an unrelated business can often pass the attractiveness and cost-of-entry tests (and sometimes even the better-off test), unrelated diversification has drawbacks. The real Achilles' heel of conglomerate diversification is the big demand it places on corporate-level management to make sound decisions about fundamentally different businesses operating in fundamentally different industry and competitive environments. The greater the number of businesses a company is in and the more diverse they are, the harder it is for corporate managers to oversee each subsidiary and spot problems early, to become expert at evaluating the attractiveness of each business's industry and competitive environment, and to judge the caliber of strategic actions and plans proposed by business-level managers. As one president of a diversified firm expressed it:

> we've got to make sure that our core businesses are properly managed for solid, long-term earnings. We can't just sit back and watch the numbers. We've got to know what the real issues are out there in the profit centers. Otherwise, we're not even in a position to check out our managers on the big decisions.[9]

The two biggest drawbacks to unrelated diversification are the difficulties of managing broad diversification and the absence of strategic opportunities to turn diversification into competitive advantage.

With broad diversification, corporate managers have to be shrewd and talented enough to: (1) tell a good acquisition from a bad one, (2) select capable managers to run each business, (3) discern sound strategic proposals, and (4) know what to do if a business unit stumbles. Because every business encounters rough sledding, a good way to gauge the risk of diversifying is to ask, "If the new business got into trouble, would we know how to bail it out?" When the answer is no, unrelated diversification can pose significant financial risk, and the business's profit prospects are more chancy.[10] As the former chairman of a Fortune 500 company advised, "Never acquire a business you don't know how to run." It only takes one or two big strategic mistakes (misjudging industry attractiveness, encountering unexpected problems in a newly acquired business, or being too optimistic about the difficulty of turning a struggling subsidiary around) to cause a precipitous drop in corporate earnings and crash the company's stock price.

Second, without some kind of strategic fit and the added measure of competitive advantage it offers, the consolidated performance of a multibusiness portfolio tends to be no better than the sum of what the individual business

---

[9]Carter F. Bales, "Strategic Control: The President's Paradox," *Business Horizons* 20, no. 4 (August 1977), p. 17.

[10]Of course, some firms may be willing to risk that trouble won't strike before management has time to learn the business well enough to bail it out of almost any difficulty. See Peter Drucker, *Management: Tasks, Responsibilities, Practices* (New York: Harper & Row, 1974), p. 709.

units could achieve independently. And, to the extent that corporate managers meddle unwisely in business-unit operations or hamstring them with corporate policies, overall performance can even be worse. Except for the added financial backing from a cash-rich corporate parent, a strategy of unrelated diversification does nothing to enhance the competitive strength of individual business units. Each business is on its own in trying to build a competitive edge—the unrelated nature of sister businesses offers no basis for cost reduction, skills transfer, or technology sharing. In a widely diversified firm, the value added by corporate managers depends primarily on how good they are at deciding what new businesses to add, which ones to get rid of, how to use financial resources to build a higher-performing collection of businesses, and the quality of the decision-making guidance they give to general managers of their business subsidiaries.

Third, although in theory unrelated diversification offers the potential for greater sales-profit stability over the business cycle, in practice attempts at countercyclical diversification fall short of the mark. Few attractive businesses have opposite up-and-down cycles; most are similarly affected by cyclical economic conditions. There's no convincing evidence that the consolidated profits of broadly diversified firms are more stable or less subject to reversal in periods of recession and economic stress than the profits of less diversified firms.[11]

Despite these drawbacks, unrelated diversification can be a desirable corporate strategy. It certainly makes sense when a firm needs to diversify away from an unattractive industry and has no distinctive skills it can transfer to related businesses. Also, some owners prefer to invest in several unrelated businesses instead of a family of related ones. Otherwise, the advantages of unrelated diversification depend on the prospects for financial gain.

A key issue in unrelated diversification is how broad a net to cast in building the business portfolio. In other words, should the corporate portfolio contain few or many unrelated businesses? How much business diversity can corporate executives successfully manage? A reasonable way to resolve the problem is to answer two questions: What is the least diversification the firm needs to achieve acceptable growth and profitability? What is the most diversification the firm can manage given the complexity it adds?[12] The optimal answer usually lies between these two extremes.

Unrelated Diversification and Shareholder Value

Unrelated diversification is fundamentally a finance-driven approach to creating shareholder value whereas related diversification is fundamentally strategy-driven. *Related diversification represents a strategic approach to value creation* because it is predicated on exploiting the links between the activity-cost chains of different businesses to lower costs, transfer skills and technological expertise, and gain benefit of other kinds of strategic fit. The objective is to convert the strategic fits among the firm's businesses into an extra measure of competitive advantage that goes beyond what business subsidiaries are able to

Unrelated diversification represents a financial approach to creating shareholder value; related diversification in contrast, represents a strategic approach.

---

[11]Ibid., p. 767. Research studies in the interval since 1974, when Drucker made his observation, uphold his conclusion—on the whole, broadly diversified firms do not outperform less diversified firms over the course of the business cycle.

[12]Ibid., pp. 692–93.

achieve on their own. The competitive advantage a firm achieves through related diversification is the driver for building greater shareholder value.

In contrast, *unrelated diversification is principally a financial approach to diversification* where shareholder value accrues from astute deployment of corporate financial resources and from executive skill in spotting financially attractive business opportunities. For unrelated diversification to result in enhanced shareholder value (above the $2 + 2 = 4$ effect of what the subsidiary businesses could produce through independent operations and what shareholders could obtain by purchasing ownership interests in a variety of businesses to spread investment risk on their own behalf), corporate strategists must exhibit superior skills in creating and managing a portfolio of diversified business interests. This specifically means:

- Doing a superior job of diversifying into new businesses that can produce consistently good returns on investment (satisfying the attractiveness test).

- Doing an excellent job of negotiating favorable acquisition prices (satisfying the cost-of-entry test).

- Making astute moves to sell previously acquired business subsidiaries at their peak and getting premium prices (this requires skills in discerning when a business subsidiary is on the verge of confronting adverse industry and competitive conditions and probable declines in long-term profitability).

- Being shrewd in shifting corporate financial resources out of businesses where profit opportunities are dim and into businesses where rapid earnings growth and high returns on investment are occurring.

- Doing such a good job overseeing the firm's business subsidiaries and contributing to how they are managed (by providing expert problem-solving skills, creative strategy suggestions, and decision-making guidance to business-level managers) that the businesses perform at a higher level than they would otherwise be able to do (a possible way to satisfy the better-off test).

To the extent that corporate executives can craft and execute a strategy of unrelated diversification that produces enough of the above outcomes for the enterprise to consistently outperform other firms in generating dividends and capital gains for stockholders, then a case can be made that shareholder value has truly been enhanced.

DIVESTITURE AND LIQUIDATION STRATEGIES

Even a shrewd corporate diversification strategy can result in the acquisition of business units that, down the road, just do not work out. Misfits or partial fits cannot be completely avoided because it is impossible to predict precisely how getting into a new line of business will actually work out. In addition, long-term industry attractiveness changes with the times; what was once a good diversification move into an attractive industry may later turn sour. Subpar performance by some business units is bound to occur, thereby raising questions of whether to keep them or divest them. Other business units, despite adequate financial performance, may not mesh as well with the rest of the firm as was originally thought.

Sometimes, a business that seems sensible from a strategic fit standpoint turns out to lack the compatibility of values essential to a *cultural fit*.[13] Several pharmaceutical companies had just this experience. When they diversified into cosmetics and perfume, they discovered their personnel had little respect for the "frivolous" nature of such products compared to the far nobler task of developing miracle drugs to cure the ill. The absence of shared values and cultural compatibility between the medical research expertise of the pharmaceutical companies and the fashion-marketing orientation of the cosmetics business was the undoing of what otherwise was diversification into businesses with related chemical compounding expertise and distribution channels.

When a particular line of business loses its appeal, the most attractive solution usually is to sell it. Normally such businesses should be divested as fast as is practical, unless time is needed to get them in better shape to sell. The more business units in a diversified firm's portfolio, the more likely it will have to divest poor performers, "dogs," and misfits. A useful guide to determine if and when to divest a subsidiary is to ask the question, "If we were not in this business today, would we want to get into it now?"[14] When the answer is no or probably not, divestiture must be considered.

Divestiture can take either of two forms. The parent can spin off a business as a financially and managerially independent company in which the parent may or may not retain partial ownership. Or the parent may sell the unit outright, in which case a buyer needs to be found. As a rule, divestiture should not be approached from the angle of "Who can we pawn this business off on and what is the most we can get for it?"[15] Instead, it is wiser to ask "For what sort of organization would this business be a good fit, and under what conditions would it be viewed as a good deal?" Organizations for which the business is a good fit are likely to pay the highest price.

Of all the strategic alternatives, liquidation is the most unpleasant and painful, especially for a single-business enterprise where it means the organization ceases to exist. For a multi-industry, multibusiness firm to liquidate one of its lines of business is less traumatic. The hardships of layoffs, plant closings, and so on, while not to be minimized, still leave an ongoing organization that may be healthier after its pruning. In hopeless situations, an early liquidation usually serves owner-stockholder interests better than bankruptcy. Pursuing a lost cause exhausts an organization's resources and leaves less to liquidate; it can also mar reputations and ruin management careers. Unfortunately, it is seldom simple for management to differentiate between a lost cause and a potential for turnaround. This is particularly true when emotions and pride get mixed with sound managerial judgment—as often they do.

CORPORATE TURNAROUND, RETRENCHMENT, AND PORTFOLIO RESTRUCTURING STRATEGIES

Turnaround, retrenchment, and portfolio restructuring strategies come into play when corporate management has to restore an ailing business portfolio to

---

[13]Ibid., p. 709.

[14]Ibid., p. 94.

[15]Ibid., p. 719.

good health. Poor performance can be caused by large losses in one or more business units that pull the corporation's overall financial performance down, a disproportionate number of businesses in unattractive industries, a bad economy adversely impacting many of the firm's business units, an excessive debt burden, or ill-chosen acquisitions that haven't lived up to expectations.

Corporate turnaround strategies focus on restoring money-losing businesses to profitability rather than divesting them. The intent is to get the whole company back in the black by curing the problems of the subsidiaries most responsible for pulling overall performance down. Turnaround strategies are most appropriate in situations where the reasons for poor performance are short-term, the ailing businesses are in attractive industries, and divesting the money-losers does not make long-term strategic sense.

Corporate retrenchment strategies focus on reducing the scope of diversification to a smaller number of businesses. Retrenchment is usually undertaken when corporate management concludes that the company is in too many businesses and needs to concentrate its efforts on a few core businesses. Sometimes diversified firms retrench because they can't make certain businesses profitable after several years of trying or because they lack funds to support the investment needs of all the businesses in their portfolios. Retrenchment is usually accomplished by divesting businesses that are too small to make a sizable contribution to earnings or that have little or no strategic fit with the company's core businesses. Divesting such businesses frees resources that can be used to reduce debt or support expansion of the corporation's core businesses.

Portfolio restructuring strategies involve radical surgery on the mix and percentage makeup of the types of businesses in the portfolio. For instance, one company over a two-year period divested four business units, closed down four others, and added 25 new lines of business to its portfolio—16 through acquisition and 9 through internal start-up. Restructuring can be prompted by any of several conditions: (1) when a strategy review reveals that the firm's long-term performance prospects have become unattractive because the portfolio contains too many slow-growth, declining, or competitively weak businesses, (2) when one or more of the firm's core businesses fall prey to hard times, (3) when a new CEO takes over and decides to redirect where the company is headed, (4) when new technologies or products emerge and the portfolio needs changing to build a position in a potentially big new industry, (5) when the firm has a "unique opportunity" to make an acquisition so big that it has to sell several existing businesses to finance it, or (6) when major businesses in the portfolio have become more and more unattractive, forcing a shakeup in the portfolio in order to produce satisfactory long-term corporate performance.

Portfolio restructuring involves bold strategic action to revamp the diversified company's business makeup through divestitures and acquisitions.

Portfolio restructuring typically involves both divestitures and new acquisitions. Candidates for divestiture include not only weak or up- and-down performers or those in unattractive industries, but also those that no longer "fit" (even though they may be profitable and in attractive enough industries). Many broadly diversified corporations, disenchanted with how some of their acquisitions perform and unable to make successes out of so many unrelated business units, eventually restructure their portfolios. Business units incompatible with newly established related diversification criteria have been divested and the remaining units regrouped and aligned to capture more strategic fit benefits. Illustration Capsule 18 provides an example of corporate restructuring at Times Mirror Company.

The trend to demerge and deconglomerate has been driven by a growing preference to gear diversification toward creating strong competitive positions in a few, well-selected industries. Indeed, in response to investor disenchantment with the conglomerate approach to diversification (conglomerates often have *lower* price-earnings ratios than companies with related diversification strategies), some conglomerates have undertaken portfolio restructuring and retrenchment in a deliberate effort to escape being regarded as a conglomerate.

MULTINATIONAL DIVERSIFICATION STRATEGIES

The distinguishing characteristic of a multinational diversification strategy is a *diversity of businesses* and a *diversity of national markets*.[16] Here, corporate strategists must conceive and execute a substantial number of strategies—at least one for each industry, with as many multinational variations as is appropriate for the situation. At the same time, managers of diversified multinational corporations (DMNCs) need to be alert for beneficial ways to coordinate the firm's strategic actions across industries and countries. The goal of strategic coordination at the headquarter's level is to bring the full force of corporate resources and capabilities to the task of securing sustainable competitive advantages in each business and national market.[17]

The Emergence of Multinational Diversification

Until the 1960s, multinational companies (MNCs) operated fairly autonomous subsidiaries in each host country, each catering to the special requirements of its own national market.[18] Management tasks at company headquarters primarily involved finance functions, technology transfer, and export coordination. In pursuing a national responsiveness strategy, the primary competitive advantage of an MNC was grounded in its ability to transfer technology, manufacturing know-how, brand name identification, and marketing and management skills from country to country at costs lower than could be achieved by host-country competitors. Standardized administrative procedures helped minimize overhead costs, and once an initial organization for managing foreign subsidiaries was put in place, entry into additional national markets could be accomplished at low incremental costs. Frequently, an MNC's presence and market position in a country was negotiated with the host government rather than driven by international competition.

During the 1970s, however, multicountry strategies based on national responsiveness began to lose their effectiveness. Competition broke out on a global scale in more and more industries as Japanese, European, and U.S. companies expanded internationally in the wake of trade liberalization and the opening of market opportunities in both industrialized and less-developed countries.[19] The relevant market arena in many industries shifted from national to global principally because the strategies of global competitors, most

---

[16]C. K. Prahalad and Yves L. Doz, *The Multinational Mission* (New York: Free Press, 1987), p. 2.

[17]Ibid., p. 15.

[18]Yves L. Doz, *Strategic Management in Multinational Companies* (New York: Pergamon Press, 1985), p. 1.

[19]Ibid., pp. 2–3.

ILLUSTRATION CAPSULE
18

CORPORATE RESTRUCTURING AT TIMES MIRROR COMPANY

Times Mirror is a $3.6 billion media and information company principally engaged in newspaper publishing, broadcast and cable television, and book and magazine publishing. During the 1983–90 period, the company engaged in corporate restructuring activities to revamp the content of its business portfolio. The table below summarizes the company's acquisition and divestiture moves:

		Dispositions	Acquisitions
1983	Dec.	New American Library	
1984	Feb.	Spotlight satellite programming	
	Dec.	Commerce Clearing House stock	*The Morning Call*
1985	June	Art and graphic products companies (3)	Learning International, Inc.
	August		Wolfe Publishing Limited
	Sept.	Hartford, Connecticut, Cable Television	
	Oct.	Long Beach, California, Cable Television	
1986	Feb.	80 percent of Publishers Paper Co.	
	May		*National Journal*
	June	Times Mirror Microwave Communications Co.	
		Television stations in Syracuse and Elmira, New York, and Harrisburg, Pennsylvania	
		Las Vegas, Nevada, Cable Television	
	July		*Bottlang Airfield Manual*
	Sept.	*Dallas Times Herald*	
	Oct.		The *Baltimore Sun* newspapers
	Dec.	Times Mirror Magazines book clubs	*Broadcasting* magazine
		Graphic Controls Corporation	60 percent of Rhode Island CATV (cable)
		The H.M. Goushã Company	CRC Press, Inc.
1987	Feb.		*Government Executive*
	Dec.	*The Denver Post*	*Field & Stream, Home Mechanix, Skiing, Yachting* magazines
	Throughout	Continuing timberland sales	
1988	Jan.	Times Mirror Press	
	Feb.		Richard D. Irwin, Inc.
	Throughout	Continuing timberland sales	

(continued)

notably the Japanese companies, involved gaining a foothold in host-country markets by matching or beating the product quality of local companies and undercutting their prices. To fend off global competitors, traditional MNCs were driven to integrate their operations across national borders in a quest for better efficiencies and lower manufacturing costs. Instead of separately manufacturing a complete product range in each country, the plants of MNCs became more specialized in their production operations to gain the economies

ILLUSTRATION CAPSULE
18

(concluded)

		Dispositions	Acquisitions
1989	May		Zenger-Miller
	June		Kaset International
1990	Jan.		Sun City Cable TV (California)
			Lewis Publishers
	May		B. C. Decker
	Oct.		Austen Cornish
	Dec.		The Achieve Group
	Total	Approximately $1 billion	Approximately $1 billion

This series of moves left Times Mirror with the following business portfolio as of 1991:

Newspaper publishing:

Los Angeles Times, Newsday, the *Baltimore Sun* newspapers, *The Hartford Courant, The Morning Call, The (Stamford) Advocate,* and *Greenwich Time.*

Book publishing:

Abrams art books; Matthew Bender law books; Mosby–Year Book medical books; CRC Press scientific books; Wolfe medical color atlases; Lewis Publishers; B. C. Decker; Austin Cornish nursing texts; and college texts by Richard D. Irwin, Inc.

Broadcast and cable television:

CBS network affiliates KDFW-TV, Dallas, Texas, and KTBC-TV, Austin, Texas; ABC affiliate KTVI, St. Louis, Missouri; NBC affiliate WVTM-TV, Birmingham, Alabama; and cable TV operations in 13 states (Dimension Cable Services).

Magazine publishing:

Popular Science, Outdoor Life, Golf Magazine, Ski Magazine, The Sporting News, The Sporting Goods DEALER, National Journal, Government Executive, Broadcasting, Sports inc., The Sports Business Weekly, Field & Stream, Home Mechanix, Skiing, and Yachting.

Other business/properties:

Timberland; Jepperson Sanderson (producer of aeronautical charts and pilot training material); and Learning International, Zenger-Miller, and Kaset International (providers of professional training services).

Source: Company annual reports.

of longer production runs, permit use of faster automated equipment, and capture experience curve effects. Country subsidiaries obtained the rest of the product range they needed from sister plants in other countries. Gains in manufacturing efficiencies from converting to state-of-the-art, world-scale manufacturing plants more than offset increased international shipping costs, especially in light of the other advantages global strategies offered. With a global strategy, an MNC could locate plants in countries with low labor costs—

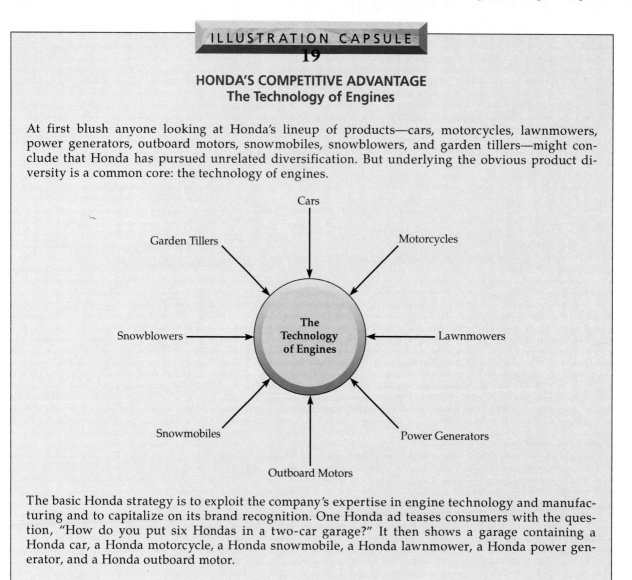

ILLUSTRATION CAPSULE
19

HONDA'S COMPETITIVE ADVANTAGE
The Technology of Engines

At first blush anyone looking at Honda's lineup of products—cars, motorcycles, lawnmowers, power generators, outboard motors, snowmobiles, snowblowers, and garden tillers—might conclude that Honda has pursued unrelated diversification. But underlying the obvious product diversity is a common core: the technology of engines.

The basic Honda strategy is to exploit the company's expertise in engine technology and manufacturing and to capitalize on its brand recognition. One Honda ad teases consumers with the question, "How do you put six Hondas in a two-car garage?" It then shows a garage containing a Honda car, a Honda motorcycle, a Honda snowmobile, a Honda lawnmower, a Honda power generator, and a Honda outboard motor.

Source: Adapted from C. K. Prahalad and Yves L. Doz, *The Multinational Mission* (New York: Free Press, 1987), p. 62.

A multinational corporation can gain competitive advantage by diversifying into global industries with related technologies.

a key consideration in industries whose products have high labor content. With a global strategy, an MNC could also exploit differences in tax rates, setting transfer prices in its integrated operations to produce higher profits in low-tax countries and lower profits in high-tax countries. Global strategic coordination also gave MNCs increased ability to take advantage of country-to-country differences in interest rates, exchange rates, credit terms, government subsidies, and export guarantees. As a consequence of these advantages, it became increasingly difficult for a company that produced and sold its product in only one country to succeed in an industry populated with aggressive competitors intent on achieving global dominance.

During the 1980s another source of competitive advantage began to emerge: using the strategic fit advantages of related diversification to build stronger competitive positions in several related global industries simultaneously.

Being a diversified MNC (DMNC) became competitively superior to being a single-business MNC in cases where strategic fits existed across global industries. Related diversification is most capable of producing competitive advantage for a multinational company where expertise in a core technology can be applied to different industries (at least one of which is global) and where there are important economies of scope and brand name advantages to being in a family of related businesses.[20] Illustration Capsule 19 explains Honda's ability to exploit the technology of engines and its well-known name via its diversification into a variety of products with engines.

Sources of Competitive Advantage for a DMNC

When a multinational company has expertise in a core technology and has diversified into related products and businesses to exploit that core, a centralized R&D effort coordinated at the headquarters level holds real potential for competitive advantage. By channeling corporate resources into a strategically coordinated R&D/technology effort, as opposed to letting each business unit perform its own R&D function, the DMNC can launch a world-class, global-scale assault to advance the core technology, generate technology-based manufacturing economies within and across product/business lines, make across-the-board product improvements, and develop complementary products—all significant advantages in a globally competitive marketplace. In the absence of centralized coordination, R&D/technology investments are likely to be scaled down to match each business's product-market perspective, setting the stage for the strategic fit benefits of coordinated technology management to slip through the cracks and go uncaptured.[21]

A multinational corporation can also gain competitive advantage by diversifying into related global industries where strategic fits produce economies of scope and the benefits of brand name transfer.

The second source of competitive advantage for a DMNC concerns the distribution and brand name advantages that can accrue from diversifying into related global industries. Consider, for instance, the competitive strength of such Japanese DMNCs as Sanyo and Matsushita. Both have diversified into a range of globally competitive consumer goods industries—TVs, stereo equipment, radios, VCRs, small domestic appliances (microwave ovens, for example), and personal computers. By widening their scope of operations in products marketed through similar distribution channels, Sanyo and Matsushita have not only exploited related technologies but also built stronger distribution capabilities, captured logistical and distribution-related economies, and established greater brand awareness for their products.[22] Such competitive advantages are not available to a domestic-only company pursuing a single business. Moreover, with a well-diversified product line and a multinational market base, a DMNC can enter new country or product markets and gain market share with below-market pricing (and below-average cost pricing if need be), subsidizing the entry with earnings from one or more of its country market profit sanctuaries and/or earnings in other businesses.

Both a one-business multinational company and a one-business domestic company are weakly positioned to defend their market positions against a determined DMNC willing to accept lower short-term profits in order to win a stronger long-term competitive position in a desirable new market. A one-

Principle of Global Competition
A multinational corporation diversified into related global industries is well positioned to out-compete both a one-business domestic company and a one-business multinational company.

[20]Prahalad and Doz, *The Multinational Mission*, pp. 62–63.
[21]Ibid.
[22]Ibid., p. 64.

business domestic company has only one profit sanctuary—its home market. A one-business multinational company may have profit sanctuaries in several country markets, but all are in the same business. Both are vulnerable to a DMNC that launches a major strategic offensive in their profit sanctuaries and low-balls its prices to win market share at their expense. A DMNC's ability to keep hammering away at competitors with low-ball prices year after year may reflect either a cost advantage growing out of its related diversification strategy or a willingness to cross-subsidize low profits or even losses with earnings from its profit sanctuaries in other country markets and/or its earnings from other businesses. Sanyo, for example, by pursuing related diversification keyed to product-distribution-technology types of strategic fit and managing its product families on a global scale, can eventually encircle domestic companies like Zenith (TVs and small computer systems) and Maytag (home appliances) and put them under serious competitive pressure. Sanyo can peck away at Zenith's market share in TVs and in the process weaken retailers' loyalty to the Zenith brand. Sanyo can diversify into large home appliances (by acquiring an established appliance maker or manufacturing on its own) and cross-subsidize a low-priced market entry against Maytag and other less-diversified home appliance firms with earnings from its many other business and product lines. If Sanyo chooses, it can keep its prices low for several years to gain market share at the expense of domestic rivals, turning its attention to profits after the battle for market share and competitive position is won.[23]

A DMNC's most potent advantages usually derive from technology-sharing, economies of scope, shared brand names, and its potential to employ cross-subsidization tactics.

The competitive principle is clear: A DMNC has a strategic arsenal capable of defeating both a single-business MNC and a single-business domestic company over the long term. The competitive advantages of a DMNC, however, depend on employing a related diversification strategy in industries that are already globally competitive or are on the verge of becoming so. Then the related businesses have to be managed so as to capture strategic fit benefits. DMNCs have the biggest potential for competitive advantage in industries with technology-sharing and technology-transfer opportunities and in those where there are important economies of scope and brand name benefits associated with competing in related product families.

A DMNC also has important cross-subsidization potential for winning its way into attractive new markets. However, a DMNC's cross-subsidization powers cannot be deployed in the extreme. It is one thing to use a *portion* of the profits and cash flows from existing businesses to cover "reasonable" short-term losses when entering a new business or country market; it is quite another to drain corporate profits indiscriminately (and thus impair overall company performance) to support either deep price discounting and quick market penetration in the short term or continuing losses over the longer term. At some juncture, every business and market entered has to make a profit contribution or become a candidate for abandonment. Moreover, the company has to wrest consistently acceptable performance from the whole business portfolio. So there are limits to cross-subsidization. As a general rule, cross-subsidization is justified only if there is a good chance short-term losses can be amply recouped in some way over the long term.

Illustration Capsule 20 provides examples of the business portfolios and global scope of several DMNCs.

---

[23]Ibid.

THE GLOBAL SCOPE OF PROMINENT DIVERSIFIED
MULTINATIONAL CORPORATIONS

Company (headquarters base)	Major Lines of Business	Number of Employees	1990 Global Sales	Global Plant Locations
Unilever (Netherlands, Britain)	Vaseline products, Cutex, Prince Matchabelli products, Ragu sauces, Lipton teas and soups, laundry detergents, soaps, toothpaste and other personal care products, margarine, frozen foods, agribusiness, and chemicals	304,000	$40 billion in 75 different countries • Europe, 61% • North America, 18% • Rest of world, 21%	340 subsidiary companies in 30 different countries
Siemens (West Germany)	Electrical equipment, lighting, power plants, security systems, medical engineering, communications and information systems, telecommunications networks	373,000	$39 billion • Europe, 73% • North America, 10% • Asia and Australia, 9% • Latin America, 4% • Africa, 4%	28 countries
Philips (Netherlands)	Lighting, consumer electronics, domestic appliances, and telecommunications and data systems	273,000	$31 billion • Europe, 53% • North America, 29% • Asia and Australia, 10% • Latin America, 6% • Africa, 2%	60 countries
Nissan Motor Co. (Japan)	Automobiles, trucks, rockets, forklifts, boats, and textile machinery	130,000	$40.2 billion in 150 countries	15 countries
Toyota Motor Corp. (Japan)	Automobiles, trucks, buses, forklifts, power shovels, residential and commercial construction	97,000	$64.5 billion in 150 countries	11 plants in Japan 30 plants in 21 other countries
Hitachi (Japan)	Power plants, turbines, boilers, TV sets, VCRs, kitchen appliances, lighting fixtures, computers, word processors, fax machines, cranes, locomotives, machinery, wire and cable, chemicals, and steel products	291,000	$51 billion in 30 countries	7 countries
Dow Chemical Co. (United States)	Chemicals, plastics, hydrocarbons, pharmaceuticals, consumer products (1,800 different products in all)	62,000	$20 billion • Europe, 31% • U.S., 45% • Rest of world, 24%	120-plus plant locations in 32 countries
CPC International (United States)	Consumer foods (Hellman's, Mazola, Skippy, Knorr soups and sauces, margarine, English muffins, pasta) and corn refining products (corn starches, corn syrups, dextrose, animal feed ingredients)	35,300	$5.8 billion in 50 countries • North America, 46% • Europe, 36% • Latin America, 13% • Asia and Africa, 5%	28 countries

COMBINATION DIVERSIFICATION STRATEGIES

The six corporate diversification approaches described above are not mutually exclusive. They can be pursued in combination and in varying sequences, allowing ample room for companies to customize their diversification strategies to fit their own circumstances. The most common business portfolios created by corporate diversification strategies are:

- A "dominant-business" enterprise with sales concentrated in one major core business but with a modestly diversified portfolio of either related or unrelated businesses (amounting to one third or less of total corporatewide sales).
- A narrowly diversified enterprise having a *few* (two to five) *related core* business units.
- A broadly diversified enterprise made up of *many* mostly *related* business units.
- A narrowly diversified enterprise comprised of a *few* (two to five) *core* business units in *unrelated* industries.
- A broadly diversified enterprise having *many* business units in mostly *unrelated* industries.
- A multibusiness enterprise diversified into unrelated areas but with a portfolio of related businesses within each area—thus giving it *several unrelated groups of related businesses.*

In each case, the geographic markets of individual businesses within the portfolio can be local, regional, national, multinational, or global. Thus, a company can be competing locally in some businesses, nationally in others, and globally in others.

KEY POINTS

Diversification becomes an attractive strategy when a company runs out of profitable growth opportunities in its present business. There are two fundamental approaches to diversification—into related businesses and into unrelated businesses. The rationale for related diversification is *strategic*: diversify into businesses with strategic fit, capitalize on strategic fit relationships to gain competitive advantage, then use competitive advantage to achieve the desired $2 + 2 = 5$ impact on shareholder value. The reasons for diversifying into unrelated businesses hinge almost exclusively on opportunities for attractive financial gain—there is nothing *strategic* about unrelated diversification.

Figure 7–2 shows the paths an undiversified company can take on the road to managing a diversified business portfolio. Most companies have their strategic roots in single-business concentration. Vertical integration strategies may or may not be involved depending on the extent to which forward or backward integration strengthens a firm's competitive position or helps it secure a competitive advantage. When diversification becomes a serious strategic option, a company must choose to pursue related diversification, unrelated diversification, or some mix of both. There are advantages and disadvantages to all three options. Once diversification has been accomplished, management's task is to figure out how to manage the existing business portfolio. The six primary post-diversification alternatives are (1) make new acquisitions,

FIGURE 7–2   **Checklist of Major Corporate Strategy Alternatives**

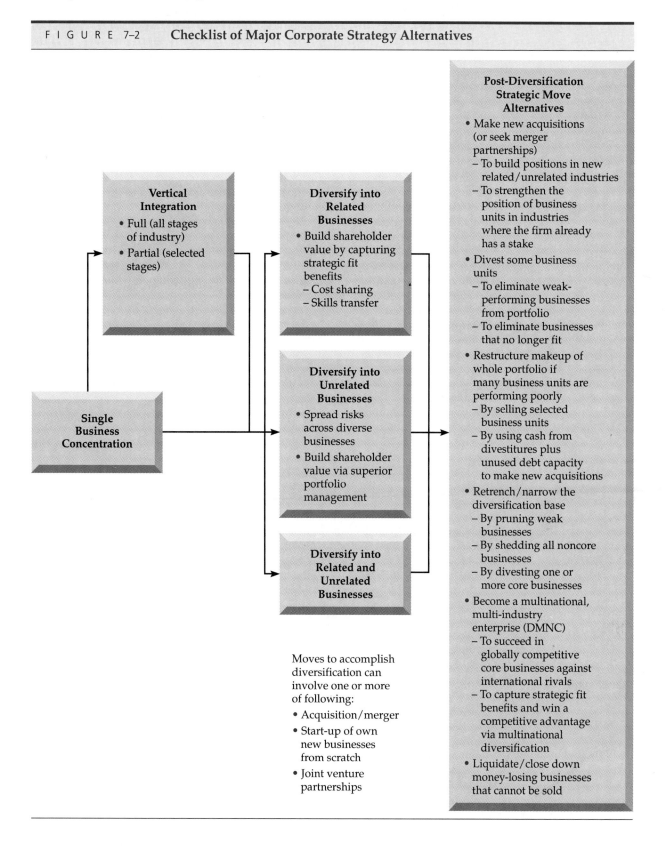

Vertical Integration
- Full (all stages of industry)
- Partial (selected stages)

Diversify into Related Businesses
- Build shareholder value by capturing strategic fit benefits
  – Cost sharing
  – Skills transfer

Diversify into Unrelated Businesses
- Spread risks across diverse businesses
- Build shareholder value via superior portfolio management

Single Business Concentration

Diversify into Related and Unrelated Businesses

Moves to accomplish diversification can involve one or more of following:
- Acquisition/merger
- Start-up of own new businesses from scratch
- Joint venture partnerships

Post-Diversification Strategic Move Alternatives
- Make new acquisitions (or seek merger partnerships)
  – To build positions in new related/unrelated industries
  – To strengthen the position of business units in industries where the firm already has a stake
- Divest some business units
  – To eliminate weak-performing businesses from portfolio
  – To eliminate businesses that no longer fit
- Restructure makeup of whole portfolio if many business units are performing poorly
  – By selling selected business units
  – By using cash from divestitures plus unused debt capacity to make new acquisitions
- Retrench/narrow the diversification base
  – By pruning weak businesses
  – By shedding all noncore businesses
  – By divesting one or more core businesses
- Become a multinational, multi-industry enterprise (DMNC)
  – To succeed in globally competitive core businesses against international rivals
  – To capture strategic fit benefits and win a competitive advantage via multinational diversification
- Liquidate/close down money-losing businesses that cannot be sold

(2) divest weak-performing business units or those that no longer fit, (3) restructure the makeup of the portfolio if overall performance is poor, (4) retrench to a narrower diversification base, (5) pursue multinational diversification, and (6) close down/liquidate money-losing business units that cannot be sold.

SUGGESTED READINGS

Ansoff, H. Igor. *Corporate Strategy.* New York: McGraw-Hill, 1965, chap. 7.

Bright, William M. "Alternative Strategies for Diversification." *Research Management* 12, no. 4 (July 1969), pp. 247–53.

Buzzell, Robert D. "Is Vertical Integration Profitable?" *Harvard Business Review* 61, no. 1 (January–February 1983), pp. 92–102.

Drucker, Peter. *Management: Tasks, Responsibilities, Practices.* New York: Harper & Row, 1974, chaps. 55, 56, 57, 58, 60, and 61.

Guth, William D. "Corporate Growth Strategies." *Journal of Business Strategy* 1, no. 2 (Fall 1980), pp. 56–62.

Hall, William K. "Survival Strategies in a Hostile Environment." *Harvard Business Review* 58, no. 5 (September–October 1980), pp. 75–85.

Harrigan, Kathryn R. "Matching Vertical Integration Strategies to Competitive Conditions." *Strategic Management Journal* 7, no. 6 (November–December 1986), pp. 535–56.

_____. "Formulating Vertical Integration Strategies." *Academy of Management Review* 9, no. 4 (October 1984), pp. 638–52.

_____. *Strategic Flexibility.* Lexington, Mass.: Lexington Books, 1985, chap. 4 and Table A-8, p. 162.

Hax, Arnoldo, and Nicolas S. Majluf. *The Strategy Concept and Process.* Englewood Cliffs, N.J.: Prentice Hall, 1991, chaps. 9, 11, and 15.

Hofer, Charles W. "Turnaround Strategies." *Journal of Business Strategy* 1, no. 1 (Summer 1980), pp. 19–31.

Hoffman, Richard C. "Strategies for Corporate Turnarounds: What Do We Know About Them?" *Journal of General Management* 14, no. 3 (Spring 1989), pp. 46–66.

Kumpe, Ted, and Piet T. Bolwijn. "Manufacturing: The New Case for Vertical Integration." *Harvard Business Review* 88, no. 2 (March–April 1988), pp. 75–82.

Lauenstein, Milton, and Wickham Skinner. "Formulating a Strategy of Superior Resources." *Journal of Business Strategy* 1, no. 1 (Summer 1980), pp. 4–10.

Ohmae, Kenichi. *The Mind of the Strategist.* New York: Penguin Books, 1983, chaps. 10 and 12.

Prahalad, C. K., and Yves L. Doz. *The Multinational Mission.* New York: Free Press, 1987, chaps. 1 and 2.

Techniques for Analyzing Diversified Companies

If we can know where we are and something about how we got there, we might see where we are trending—and if the outcomes which lie naturally in our course are unacceptable, to make timely change.
Abraham Lincoln

No company can afford everything it would like to do. Resources have to be allocated. The essence of strategic planning is to allocate resources to those areas that have the greatest future potential.
Reginald Jones

Once a company has diversified, three strategic issues continuously challenge corporate strategy-makers:

- How attractive is the group of businesses the company is in?
- Assuming the company sticks with its present lineup of businesses, how good is its performance outlook in the years ahead?
- If the previous two answers are not satisfactory, what should the company do in the way of getting out of some existing businesses, strengthening the positions of remaining businesses, and getting into new businesses to boost the performance prospects of its business portfolio?

The task of crafting and implementing action plans to improve the attractiveness and competitive strength of a company's business-unit portfolio is the heart of what corporate-level strategic management is all about.

Strategic analysis of diversified companies builds on the concepts and methods used for single-business companies. But there are also new factors to consider and additional analytical approaches to master. The procedure we will use to systematically evaluate the strategy of a diversified company, assess the caliber and potential of its businesses, and decide what strategic actions to take next consists of an eight-step process:

Strategic analysis in a diversified company is an eight-step process.

1. Identifying the present corporate strategy.
2. Constructing one or more business portfolio matrixes to reveal the character of the company's business portfolio.
3. Comparing the long-term attractiveness of each industry the company is in.
4. Comparing the competitive strength of the company's business units to see which ones are strong contenders in their respective industries.
5. Rating the business units on the basis of their historical performance and their prospects for the future.
6. Assessing each business unit's compatibility with corporate strategy and determining the value of any strategic fit relationships among existing business units.
7. Ranking the business units in terms of priority for new capital investment and deciding whether the general strategy and direction for each business unit should be aggressive expansion, fortify and defend, overhaul and reposition, or harvest/divest. (The task of initiating *specific* business-unit strategies to improve a subsidiary's competitive position is usually delegated to business-level managers, with corporate-level managers offering suggestions and having authority for final approval.)
8. Crafting new strategic moves to improve overall corporate performance—changing the makeup of the portfolio via acquisitions and divestitures, coordinating the activities of related business units to achieve cost-sharing and skills transfer benefits, and steering corporate resources into the areas of greatest opportunity.

The rest of this chapter describes this eight-step process and introduces the new analytical techniques needed to arrive at sound corporate strategy appraisals.

IDENTIFYING THE PRESENT CORPORATE STRATEGY

Evaluating a diversified firm's business portfolio needs to begin with clear identification of the firm's diversification strategy.

Strategic analysis of a diversified company starts by probing the organization's present strategy and business makeup. Recall from Figure 2–2 in Chapter 2 that a good overall perspective of a diversified company's corporate strategy comes from looking at:

- The extent to which the firm is diversified (as measured by the proportion of total sales and operating profits contributed by each business unit and by whether the diversification base is broad or narrow).
- Whether the firm's portfolio is keyed to related or unrelated diversification, or a mixture of both.
- Whether the scope of company operations is mostly domestic, increasingly multinational, or global.
- The nature of recent moves to boost performance of key business units and/or strengthen existing business positions.

- Any moves to add new businesses to the portfolio and build positions in new industries.
- Any moves to divest weak or unattractive business units.
- Corporate management efforts to pursue strategic fit relationships and use diversification to create competitive advantage.
- The proportion of capital expenditures going to each business unit.

Identifying the current corporate strategy lays the foundation for a thorough strategy analysis and, subsequently, for reformulating the strategy as it "should be."

MATRIX TECHNIQUES FOR EVALUATING DIVERSIFIED PORTFOLIOS

The most popular technique for assessing the quality of the businesses a company has diversified into is portfolio matrix analysis. *A business portfolio matrix is a two-dimensional display comparing the strategic positions of every business a diversified company is in.* Matrixes can be constructed using any pair of strategic position indicators. The most revealing indicators are industry growth rate, market share, long-term industry attractiveness, competitive strength, and stage of product/market evolution. Usually one dimension of the matrix relates to the attractiveness of the industry environment and the other to the strength of a business within its industry. Three types of business portfolio matrixes are used most frequently—the growth-share matrix developed by the Boston Consulting Group, the industry attractiveness-business strength matrix pioneered at General Electric, and the Hofer–A. D. Little industry life-cycle matrix.

Basic Concept
A business portfolio matrix is a two-dimensional display comparing the strategic positions of every business a diversified company is in.

The Growth-Share Matrix

The first business portfolio matrix to be widely used was a four-square grid devised by the Boston Consulting Group (BCG), a leading management consulting firm.[1] Figure 8–1 illustrates a BCG-type matrix. The matrix is formed using *industry growth rate* and *relative market share* as the axes. Each business unit appears as a "bubble" on the four-cell matrix, with the size of each bubble or circle scaled to the percent of revenues it represents in the overall corporate portfolio.

Early BCG methodology arbitrarily placed the dividing line between "high" and "low" industry growth rates at around twice the real GNP growth rate plus inflation, but the boundary percentage can be raised or lowered to suit individual preferences. A strong case can be made for placing the line so business units in industries growing faster than the economy as a whole end up in the "high-growth" cells and those in industries growing slower end up in "low-growth" cells ("low-growth" industries are those that can be described as mature, aging, stagnant, or declining).

The BCG portfolio matrix compares a diversified company's businesses on the basis of industry growth rate and relative market share.

---

[1]The original presentation is Bruce D. Henderson, "The Experience Curve—Reviewed. IV. The Growth Share Matrix of the Product Portfolio" (Boston: The Boston Consulting Group, 1973), Perspectives No. 135. For an excellent chapter-length treatment of the use of the BCG growth-share matrix in strategic portfolio analysis, see Arnoldo C. Hax and Nicolas S. Majluf, *Strategic Management: An Integrative Perspective* (Englewood Cliffs, N. J.: Prentice Hall, 1984), chap. 7.

FIGURE 8–1   The BCG Growth-Share Business Portfolio Matrix

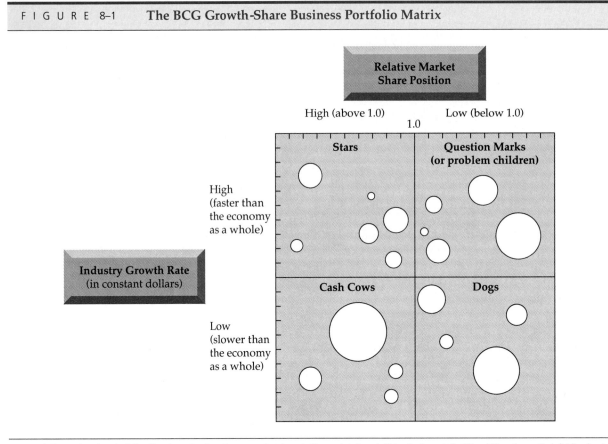

Note: *Relative* market share is defined by the ratio of one's own market share to the market share held by the largest *rival* firm. When the vertical dividing line is set at 1.0, the only way a firm can achieve a star or cash cow position in the growth-share matrix is to have the largest market share in the industry. Since this is a very stringent criterion, it may be "fairer" and more revealing to locate the vertical dividing line in the matrix at about 0.75 or 0.80.

Basic Concept
Relative market share is calculated by dividing a business's percentage share of total industry sales volume by the percentage share held by its largest rival.

Relative market share is the ratio of a business's market share to the market share held by the largest rival firm in the industry, with market share measured in unit volume not dollars. For instance, if business A has a 15 percent share of the industry's total volume and A's largest rival has a 30 percent share, A's relative market share is 0.5. If business B has a market-leading share of 40 percent and its largest rival has 30 percent, B's relative market share is 1.33. Given this definition, only business units that are market-share leaders in their respective industries will have relative market share values greater than 1.0; business units that trail one or more rivals in market share will have ratios below 1.0.

BCG's original standard put the border between "high" and "low" relative market share at 1.0, as shown in Figure 8–1. When the boundary is set at 1.0, circles in the two left-side cells of the matrix represent businesses that are market-share leaders in their industry. Circles in the two right-side cells identify portfolio members that are in runner-up positions in their industry. The degree to which they trail is indicated by the size of the relative market share ratio. A ratio of .10 indicates the business has a market share only $\frac{1}{10}$ that of the largest firm in the market; a ratio of .80 indicates a market share $\frac{4}{5}$ or 80 percent as big as the leading firm's. Many portfolio analysts think that putting the boundary between high and low relative market share at 1.0 is unreasonably stringent because only businesses with the largest market share in their industry qualify for the two left-side cells of the matrix. They advocate putting the boundary at 0.75 or 0.80 so businesses to the left have *strong* or above-average market positions (even though they are not *the* leader) and businesses to the right are clearly in underdog or below-average positions.

Using *relative* market share instead of *actual* market share to construct the growth-share matrix is analytically superior because the former measure is a better indicator of comparative market strength and competitive position. A 10 percent market share is much stronger if the leader's share is 12 percent than if it is 50 percent; the use of relative market share captures this difference. Equally important, relative market share is likely to reflect relative cost based on experience and economies of large-scale production. Large businesses may be able to operate at lower unit costs than smaller ones because of technological and efficiency gains that attach to larger size. But the Boston Consulting Group accumulated evidence that the phenomenon of lower unit costs went beyond just the effects of scale economies; they found that, as the cumulative volume of production increased, the knowledge gained from the firm's growing production experience often led to the discovery of additional efficiencies and ways to reduce costs even further. BCG labeled the relationship between *cumulative production volume* and lower unit costs *the experience curve effect* (for more details, see Figure 3–1 in Chapter 3). A sizable experience curve effect in the industry's activity-cost chain places a strategic premium on market share: the competitor that gains the largest market share tends to realize important cost advantages which, in turn, can be used to lower prices and gain still additional customers, sales, market share, and profit. The stronger the experience curve in a business, the more dominant role in its strategy-making.[2]

With these features of the BCG growth-share matrix in mind, we are ready to explore the portfolio implications for businesses in each cell of the matrix in Figure 8–1.

Question Marks and Problem Children   Business units falling in the upper-right quadrant of the growth-share matrix were labeled by BCG as "question marks" or "problem children." Rapid market growth makes such businesses attractive from an industry standpoint. But their low relative market share (and thus reduced access to experience curve effects) raises a question about whether they can compete successfully against larger, more cost-efficient rivals—hence, the "question mark" or "problem child" designation. Question mark businesses, moreover, are typically "cash hogs"—so labeled because their cash needs are high (owing to the investment requirements of rapid growth and product development) and their internal cash generation is low (owing to low market share, less access to experience curve effects and scale economies, and consequently thinner profit margins). A question mark/cash hog business in a fast-growing industry may require large infusions of cash just to keep up with rapid market growth; it may need even bigger infusions to outgrow the market and become an industry leader. The corporate parent of a cash hog business has to decide if it is worthwhile to fund the perhaps considerable investment requirements of a question mark division.

Relative market share is a better indicator of a business's competitive strength and market position than a simple percentage measure of market share.

Basic Concept
A cash hog business is one whose internal cash flows are inadequate to fully fund its needs for working capital and new capital investment.

---

[2]For two recent discussions of the strategic importance of the experience curve, see Pankoy Ghemawat, "Building Strategy on the Experience Curve," *Harvard Business Review* 64, no. 2 (March–April 1985), pp. 143–49 and Bruce D. Henderson, "The Application and Misapplication of the Experience Curve," *Journal of Business Strategy* 4, no. 3 (Winter 1984), pp. 3–9.

BCG has argued that the two best strategic options for a question mark business are: (1) an aggressive invest-and-expand strategy to capitalize on the industry's rapid-growth opportunities or (2) divestiture if the costs of expanding capacity and building market share outweigh the potential payoff and financial risk. Pursuit of a fast-growth strategy is imperative any time an attractive question mark business is in an industry with strong experience curve effects. In such cases, it takes major gains in market share to begin to match the lower costs of firms with greater cumulative production experience and bigger market shares. The stronger the experience curve effect, the more potent the cost advantages of rivals with larger relative market shares. Consequently, so the BCG thesis goes, unless a question mark/problem child business can successfully pursue a fast-growth strategy and win major market-share gains, it cannot hope to ever become cost competitive with large-volume firms that are further down the experience curve. Divestiture then becomes the only other viable long-run alternative. The corporate strategy prescriptions for managing question mark/problem child businesses are straightforward: divest those that are weaker and have less chance to catch the leaders on the experience curve; invest heavily in high-potential question marks and groom them to become tomorrow's "stars."

Stars   Businesses with high relative market share positions in high-growth markets rank as "stars" in the BCG grid because they offer excellent profit and growth opportunities. They are the business units an enterprise depends on to boost overall performance of the total portfolio.

Given their dominant market-share position and rapid growth environment, stars typically require large cash investments to expand production facilities and meet working capital needs. But they also tend to generate their own large internal cash flows due to the low-cost advantage of scale economies and cumulative production experience. Star businesses vary as to their cash hog status. Some can cover their investment needs with their own cash flows; others need funds from their corporate parents to stay abreast of rapid industry growth. Normally, strongly-positioned star businesses in industries where growth is beginning to slow tend to be self-sustaining in terms of cash flow and make little claim on the corporate parent's treasury. Young stars, however, typically require substantial investment capital *beyond what they can generate on their own* and are thus cash hogs.

Cash Cows   Businesses with a high relative market share in a low-growth market are designated "cash cows" in the BCG scheme. A *cash cow business* generates substantial cash surpluses over what it needs for reinvestment and growth. The reasons why a business in this cell of the matrix tends to be a cash cow are straightforward. Because of the business's high relative market share and industry leadership position, it has the sales volumes and reputation to earn attractive profits. Because it is in a slow-growth industry, it typically generates more cash from current operations than it needs to sustain its market position.

Many of today's cash cows are yesterday's stars, having dropped into the bottom cell as industry demand matured. Cash cows, though less attractive from a growth standpoint, are valuable businesses. Their cash flows can be used to cover dividend payments, finance acquisitions, and provide funds for investing in emerging stars and problem children being groomed as future stars.

Every effort should be made to keep cash cow businesses in healthy condition to preserve their cash-generating capability over the long term. The goal should be to fortify and defend a cash cow's market position while efficiently generating dollars to reallocate to other business investments. Weakening cash cows, however, may become candidates for harvesting and eventual divestiture if industry maturity results in unattractive competitive conditions and dries up the cash flow surpluses.

Dogs   Businesses with a low relative market share in a slow-growth industry are called "dogs" because of their dim growth prospects, their trailing market position, and the squeeze that being behind the leaders on the experience curve puts on their profit margins. Weak dog businesses (those positioned in the lower right corner of the dog cell) are often unable to generate attractive cash flows on a long-term basis. Sometimes they cannot produce enough cash to support a rear-guard fortify- and-defend strategy—especially if competition is brutal and profit margins are chronically thin. Consequently, except in unusual cases, BCG prescribes that weaker-performing dog businesses be harvested, divested, or liquidated, depending on which alternative yields the most cash.

Weaker dog businesses should be harvested, divested, or liquidated; stronger dogs can be retained as long as their profits and cash flows remain acceptable.

Implications for Corporate Strategy   The chief contribution of the BCG growth-share matrix is the attention it draws to the cash flow and investment characteristics of various types of businesses and how corporate financial resources can be shifted between businesses to optimize the performance of the whole corporate portfolio. According to BCG analysis, a sound, long-term corporate strategy should utilize the excess cash generated by cash cow business units to finance market-share increases for cash hog businesses—the young stars unable to finance their own growth and problem children with the best potential to grow into stars. If successful, cash hogs eventually become self-supporting stars. Then, when stars' markets begin to mature and their growth slows, they become cash cows. The "success sequence" is thus problem child/question mark to young star (but perhaps still a cash hog) to self-supporting star to cash cow.

The BCG growth-share matrix highlights the cash flow, investment, and profitability characteristics of various businesses and the benefits of shifting financial resources between them to optimize the whole portfolio's performance.

Weaker, less-attractive question mark businesses unworthy of a long-term invest-and-expand strategy are often a liability to a diversified company because of the high-cost economics associated with their low relative market share and because they do not generate enough cash to keep pace with market growth. According to BCG prescriptions, these question marks should be prime divestiture candidates *unless* they can be kept profitable and viable with their own internally generated funds. Not every question mark business is a cash hog or a disadvantaged competitor, however. Those in industries with small capital requirements, few scale economies, and weak experience curve effects can often compete satisfactorily against larger industry leaders and contribute enough to corporate earnings to justify retention. Clearly, though, weaker question marks still have a low-priority claim on corporate resources and a dim future in the portfolio. Question mark businesses unable to become stars are destined to drift vertically downward in the matrix, becoming dogs, as their industry growth slows and market demand matures.

Dogs should be retained only as long as they contribute adequately to overall company performance. Strong dogs may produce a positive cash flow and show average profitability. But the further right and down a dog business is positioned in the BCG matrix, the more likely it is tying up assets that could be redeployed more profitably. BCG recommends a harvesting strategy for a weakening or already weak dog business. If a harvesting strategy is no longer attractive, a weak dog should be eliminated from the portfolio.

There are two "disaster sequences" in the BCG scheme of things: (1) when a star's position in the matrix erodes over time to that of a problem child and then is dragged by slowing industry growth down into the dog cell of the matrix and (2) when a cash cow loses market leadership to the point where it becomes a dog on the decline. Other strategic mistakes include overinvesting in a safe cash cow; underinvesting in a question mark so instead of becoming a star it tumbles into the dog category; and shotgunning resources over many question marks rather than concentrating on the best ones to boost their chances of becoming stars.

Strengths and Weaknesses in the Growth-Share Matrix Approach   The BCG business portfolio matrix makes a definite contribution to the strategist's tool kit when it comes to evaluating the portfolio's overall attractiveness and reaching broad prescriptions concerning the strategy and direction for each business unit. Viewing a diversified corporation as a collection of cash flows and cash requirements (present and future) is a major step forward in understanding the financial aspects of corporate strategy. The BCG matrix highlights the financial "interaction" within a corporate portfolio, shows the kinds of financial considerations that must be dealt with, and explains why priorities for corporate resource allocation can differ from business to business. It also provides good rationalizations for both invest-and-expand strategies and divestiture. Yet it has several legitimate shortcomings:

Despite the analytical insights it yields, the growth-share matrix has significant shortcomings.

1. A four-cell matrix based on high-low classifications hides the fact that many businesses (the majority?) are in markets with an "average" growth rate and have relative market shares that are neither high nor low but in-between or intermediate. In which cells do these average businesses belong?

2. While labeling businesses as stars, cash cows, dogs, or question marks does have communicative appeal, it is a misleading simplification to pigeonhole all businesses into one of four categories. Some market-share leaders have never really been stars in terms of profitability. All businesses with low relative market shares are not dogs or question marks—in many cases, runner-up firms have proven track records in terms of growth, profitability, and competitive ability, even gaining on the so-called leaders. Hence, a key characteristic to assess is the *trend* in a firm's relative market share. Is it gaining ground or losing ground and why? This weakness can be overcome by placing directional arrows on each of the circles in the matrix—see Figure 8–2.

3. The BCG matrix is not a reliable indicator of relative investment opportunities across business units.[3] For example, investing in a star is not necessarily more attractive than investing in a lucrative cash cow. The matrix doesn't indicate if a question mark is a potential winner or

---

[3]Derek F. Abell and John S. Hammond, *Strategic Market Planning* (Englewood Cliffs, N.J.: Prentice Hall, 1979), p. 212.

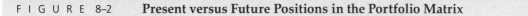

FIGURE 8-2   **Present versus Future Positions in the Portfolio Matrix**

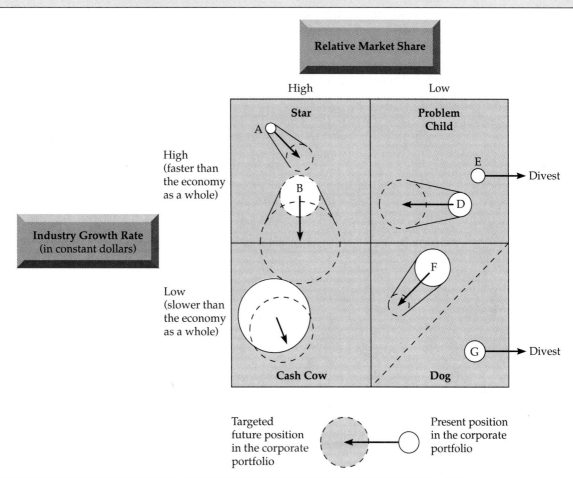

a likely loser. It says nothing about whether shrewd investment can turn a strong dog into a cash cow.

4. Being a market leader in a slow-growth industry does not guarantee cash cow status because (*a*) the investment requirements of a fortify-and-defend strategy, given the impact of inflation on the costs of replacing worn-out facilities and equipment, can soak up much or all of the available internal cash flows and (*b*) as markets mature, competitive forces often stiffen, and the ensuing battle for volume and market share can shrink profit margins and wipe out any surplus cash flows.

5. To thoroughly assess the long-term attractiveness of the portfolio's business units, strategists need to examine more than just industry growth and relative market share variables—as we discussed in Chapter 3.

6. The connection between relative market share and profitability is not as tight as the experience curve effect implies. The importance of cumulative production experience in lowering unit costs varies from

industry to industry. Sometimes a larger market share translates into a unit-cost advantage; sometimes it doesn't. Hence, it is wise to be cautious when prescribing strategy based on the assumption that experience curve effects are strong enough and cost differences among competitors big enough to totally drive competitive advantage (there are more sources of competitive advantage than just experience curve economics).

The Industry Attractiveness/Business Strength Matrix

In the attractiveness-strength matrix, each business is plotted using quantitative measures of long-term industry attractiveness and business strength/competitive position.

An alternative approach avoids some of the shortcomings of the BCG growth-share matrix. Pioneered by General Electric as a way to analyze its own diversified portfolio (with help from the consulting firm of McKinsey and Company), this nine-cell matrix is based on the two dimensions of long-term industry attractiveness and business strength/competitive position (see Figure 8–3).[4] Both dimensions of the matrix are a composite of *several* considerations as opposed to a single factor. The criteria for determining long-term industry attractiveness include market size and growth rate; technological requirements; the intensity of competition; entry and exit barriers; seasonality and cyclical influences; capital requirements; emerging industry threats and opportunities; historical and projected industry profitability; and social, environmental, and regulatory influences. To arrive at a formal, quantitative measure of long-term industry attractiveness, the chosen measures are assigned weights based on their importance to corporate management and their role in the diversification strategy. The sum of the weights must add up to 1.0. Weighted attractiveness ratings are calculated by multiplying the industry's rating on each factor (using a 1 to 5 or 1 to 10 rating scale) by the factor's weight. For example, a rating score of 8 times a weight of .25 gives a weighted rating of 2.0. The sum of weighted ratings for all the attractiveness factors yields the industry's long-term attractiveness. The procedure is shown below:

Industry/Attractiveness Factor	Weight	Rating	Weighted Industry Rating
Market size and projected growth	.15	5	0.75
Seasonality and cyclical influences	.10	8	0.80
Technological considerations	.10	1	0.10
Intensity of competition	.25	4	1.00
Emerging opportunities and threats	.15	1	0.15
Capital requirements	.05	2	0.10
Industry profitability	.10	3	0.30
Social, political, regulatory, and environmental factors	.10	7	0.70
	1.00		
Industry attractiveness rating			3.90

---

[4]For an expanded treatment, see Michael G. Allen, "Diagramming G.E.'s Planning for What's WATT," in *Corporate Planning: Techniques and Applications*, ed. Robert J. Allio and Malcolm W. Pennington (New York: AMACOM, 1979); and Hax and Majluf, *Strategic Management: An Integrative Perspective*, chap. 8.

| FIGURE 8–3 | General Electric's Industry Attractiveness/Business Strength Matrix |

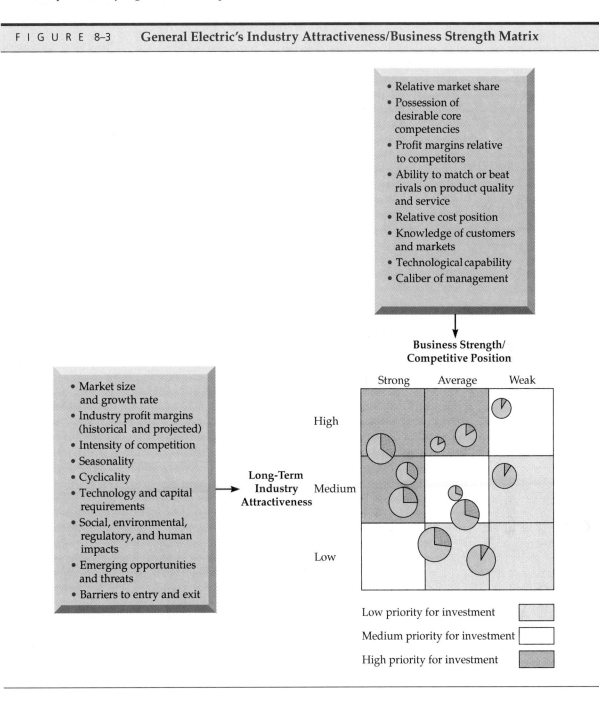

Attractiveness ratings are calculated for each industry represented in the corporate portfolio. Each industry's attractiveness score determines its position on the vertical scale in Figure 8–3.

To arrive at a quantitative measure of business strength/competitive position, each business in the corporate portfolio is rated using the same kind of approach as for industry attractiveness. The factors used to assess business strength/competitive position include such criteria as market share, relative cost position, ability to match rival firms on product quality and service, knowledge of customers and markets, possession of desirable core competences, adequacy of technological know-how, caliber of management, and profitability relative to competitors (as specified in the box in Figure 8–3). The analytical issue is whether to rate each business unit on the same generic factors (which strengthens the basis for interindustry comparisons) or on each unit's strength on the factors most pertinent to its own industry (which gives a sharper measure of competitive position). Each business's strength/position rating determines its position along the horizontal axis of the matrix—that is, whether it merits a strong, average, or weak designation.[5]

The industry attractiveness and business strength scores provide the basis for placing a business in one of the nine cells of the matrix. In the GE attractiveness-strength matrix, the area of the circles is proportional to the size of the industry, and the pie slices within the circle reflect the business's market share.

Corporate Strategy Implications   The most important strategic implications from the attractiveness-strength matrix concern the assignment of investment priorities to each of the company's business units. Businesses in the three cells at the upper left, where long-term industry attractiveness and business strength/competitive position are favorable, are accorded top investment priority. The strategic prescription for businesses falling in these three cells is "grow and build," with businesses in the high-strong cell having the highest claim on investment funds. Next in priority come businesses positioned in the three diagonal cells stretching from the lower left to the upper right. These businesses are usually given medium priority. They merit steady reinvestment to maintain and protect their industry positions; however, if a business in one of these three cells has an unusually attractive opportunity, it can win a higher investment priority and be given the go- ahead to employ a more aggressive strategic approach. The strategy prescription for businesses in the three cells in the lower right corner is typically harvest or divest (in exceptional cases where good turnaround potential exists, it can be "overhaul and reposition" using some type of turnaround approach).[6]

The nine-cell attractiveness-strength matrix has a stronger conceptual basis than the four-cell growth-share matrix.

The nine-cell attractiveness-strength approach has three desirable attributes. One, it allows for intermediate rankings between high and low and between strong and weak. Two, it incorporates a much wider variety of strategically relevant variables. The BCG matrix is based totally on two considerations—industry growth rate and relative market share; the nine-cell GE

---

[5]Essentially the same procedure is used in company situation analysis to do a competitive strength assessment (see Table 4–3 in Chapter 4). The only difference is that in the GE method the same set of competitive strength factors is used for every industry to provide a common benchmark for making comparisons across industries. In strategic analysis at the business level, the strength measures are *always* industry specific, never generic generalizations.

[6]At General Electric, each business actually ended up in one of five categories: (1) *high-growth potential* businesses deserving top investment priority; (2) *stable base* businesses that merit steady reinvestment to maintain position; (3) *support* businesses deserving periodic investment funding; (4) *selective pruning or rejuvenation* businesses deserving reduced investment; and (5) *venture* businesses meriting heavy R&D investment.

matrix takes many factors into account to determine long-term industry attractiveness and business strength/competitive position. Three, and most important, it stresses the channeling of corporate resources to businesses with the greatest probability of achieving competitive advantage and superior performance. It is hard to argue against the logic of concentrating resources in those businesses that enjoy a higher degree of attractiveness and competitive strength, being very selective in making investments in businesses with "intermediate" positions, and withdrawing resources from businesses that are lower in attractiveness and strength unless they offer exceptional turnaround potential.

However, the nine-cell GE matrix, like the four-cell growth-share matrix, provides no real guidance on the *specifics* of business strategy; the most that can be concluded from the GE matrix analysis is what *general* strategic posture to take—aggressive expansion, fortify-and-defend, or harvest-divest. Such prescriptions, though valuable for overall portfolio management, don't address the issue of strategic coordination across related businesses and the specific competitive approaches and strategic actions to take at the business-unit level. Another weakness has been pointed out by Professors Hofer and Schendel: the GE method tends to obscure businesses that are about to become winners because their industries are entering the takeoff stage.[7]

The Life-Cycle Matrix

To better identify a *developing-winner* type of business, Hofer developed a 15-cell matrix. In this matrix businesses are plotted in terms of stage of industry evolution and competitive position, as shown in Figure 8–4.[8] Again, the circles represent the sizes of the industries involved, and pie wedges denote the business's market share. In Figure 8–4, business A could be labeled a *developing winner*; business C a *potential loser*, business E an *established winner*, business F a cash cow, and business G a loser or dog. The power of the life-cycle matrix is the story it tells about the distribution of the firm's businesses across the stages of industry evolution.

The life-cycle matrix highlights whether a firm's businesses are evenly distributed across the stages of the industry life-cycle.

Deciding Which Matrix to Construct

Restricting the analysis to just one type of portfolio matrix is unwise. Each matrix has its pros and cons, and each tells a different story about the portfolio's strengths and weaknesses. Provided adequate data is available, all three matrixes should be constructed since it's best to assess the company's portfolio from different perspectives. The analytical objective is to understand the portfolio's mix of industries, the strategic position each business has in its industry, the portfolio's performance potential, and the kinds of financial and resource allocation considerations that have to be dealt with.

---

[7]Charles W. Hofer and Dan Schendel, *Strategy Formulation: Analytical Concepts* (St. Paul, Minn.: West Publishing, 1978), p. 33.

[8]Ibid., p. 34. This approach to business portfolio analysis was reportedly first used in practice by consultants at Arthur D. Little, Inc. For a full-scale review of this portfolio matrix approach, see Hax and Majluf, *Strategic Management: An Integrative Perspective*, chap. 9.

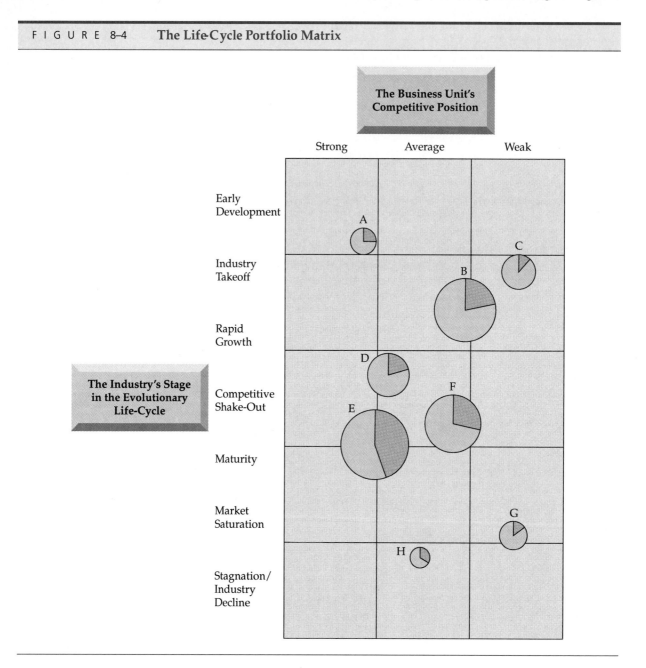

COMPARING INDUSTRY ATTRACTIVENESS

The attractiveness of the industries that a firm has diversified into needs to be evaluated from several angles.

A central issue in evaluating a diversified company's strategy is judging the attractiveness of the industries it is in. Industry attractiveness has to be judged from three perspectives:

1. *The attractiveness of each industry represented in the portfolio.* The relevant question is "Is this a good *industry* for the company to be in?" Ideally, each industry the firm has diversified into can pass the attractiveness test.

2. *Each industry's attractiveness relative to the others.* The question to answer here is "Which industries in the portfolio are the most attractive, and which are the least attractive?" Ranking the industries from most attractive to least attractive is a prerequisite to deciding how to allocate corporate resources.

3. *The attractiveness of all the industries as a group.* The question here is "How appealing is the *mix* of industries?" A company whose revenues and profits come chiefly from businesses in unattractive industries probably needs to consider restructuring its business portfolio.

All the industry attractiveness considerations discussed in Chapter 3 have application in this analytical phase.

An industry attractiveness/business strength portfolio matrix gives a strong, systematic basis for judging which business units are in the most attractive industries. If such a matrix has not been constructed, quantitative rankings of industry attractiveness can be developed using the same procedure described earlier for the nine-cell GE matrix. As a rule, all the industries represented in the business portfolio should, at minimum, be judged on the following attractiveness factors:

- *Market size and projected growth rate*—faster-growing industries tend to be more attractive than slow-growing industries, other things being equal.

- *The intensity of competition*—industries where competitive pressures are relatively weak are more attractive than industries with strong competitive pressures.

- *Technological and production skills required*—industries where the skill requirements are closely matched to company capabilities are more attractive than industries where the company's technical and/or manufacturing know-how is limited.

- *Capital requirements*—industries with low or attainable capital requirements are relatively more attractive than industries where investment requirements could strain corporate resources.

- *Seasonal and cyclical factors*—industries where demand is relatively stable and dependable are more attractive than industries where there are wide swings in buyer demand.

- *Industry profitability*—industries with healthy profit margins and high rates of return on investment are generally more attractive than industries where profits have historically been low or where the business risks are high.

- *Social, political, regulatory, and environmental factors*—industries with significant problems in these areas are less attractive than industries where such problems are no worse than most businesses encounter.

- *Strategic fits with other industries the firm has diversified into*—an industry can be attractive simply because it has valuable strategic fit relationships with other industries in the portfolio.

Strategic Management Principle
The more attractive the industries that a firm has diversified into, the better its performance prospects are likely to be.

Calculation of industry attractiveness ratings for all industries in the corporate portfolio provides a basis for ranking the industries from most to least attractive. If formal industry attractiveness ratings seem too cumbersome or tedious to calculate, analysts can rely on their knowledge of conditions in each industry to classify individual industries as having "high," "medium," or "low" attractiveness. However, the validity of such subjective assessments depends on whether analysts have studied industry conditions enough to make dependable judgments.

For a diversified company to be a strong performer, a substantial portion of its revenues and profits must come from business units in attractive industries. It is particularly important that core businesses be in industries with a good outlook for growth and above-average profitability. Businesses in the least attractive industries may be divestiture candidates, unless they are positioned strongly enough to overcome the adverse industry environment or they are a critical component of the portfolio.

COMPARING BUSINESS-UNIT STRENGTH

Assessments of how a firm's subsidiaries compare in competitive strength should be based on several factors.

Doing an appraisal of each business unit's strength and competitive position in its industry helps corporate managers judge a business unit's chances for success in its industry. The task here is to evaluate whether the business is well-positioned in its industry and the extent to which it already is or can become a strong market contender. The two most revealing techniques for evaluating a business's position in its industry are SWOT analysis and competitive strength assessment. Quantitative rankings of the strength/position of the portfolio's businesses can be calculated using either the attractiveness-strength matrix or the procedure presented in Chapter 4. Assessments of how a diversified company's subsidiaries compare in competitive strength should be based on such factors as:

- *Relative market share*—business units with higher relative market shares have greater competitive strength than business units with lower shares.
- *Ability to compete on price and/or quality*—business units that are cost competitive and/or that have established brand names and a reputation for quality tend to be more strongly positioned than those struggling to establish a name or achieve cost parity with major rivals.
- *Technology and innovation capabilities*—business units recognized for their technological leadership and track record in innovation are usually strong competitors in their industry.
- *How well the business unit's skills and competences match industry key success factors*—the more a business unit's strengths match the industry's key success factors, the stronger its competitive position tends to be.
- *Profitability relative to competitors*—business units that consistently earn above-average returns on investment and have bigger profit margins than their rivals usually have stronger competitive positions than businesses with below-average profitability for their industry. Moreover, above-average profitability signals competitive advantage while below-average profitability usually denotes competitive disadvantage.

Other competitive strength indicators that can be employed include knowledge of customers and markets, production capabilities, marketing skills, reputation and brand name awareness, and the caliber of management.

Calculation of competitive strength ratings for each business unit provides a basis for judging which ones are in strong positions in their industries and which are in weak positions. If calculating competitive strength ratings is complicated by lack of sufficient data, analysts can rely on their knowledge of each business unit's competitive situation to classify each business unit as being in a "strong," "average," or "weak" competitive position. If trustworthy, such subjective judgments can substitute for quantitative measures.

Evaluating which businesses in the portfolio enjoy the strongest competitive positions adds further rationale for corporate resource allocation. A company may earn larger profits over the long term by investing in a business with a strong position in a moderately attractive industry than a weak business in a glamour industry. This is why a diversified company needs to consider *both* industry attractiveness and business strength in deciding where to steer resources.

Many diversified companies concentrate their resources on industries where they can be strong market contenders and divest businesses that are not good candidates for becoming leaders. At General Electric, the whole thrust of corporate strategy and resource allocation is aimed at putting GE's businesses into a number one or two position both in the United States and globally—see Illustration Capsule 21.

> *Strategic Management Principle*
>
> *Shareholder interests are generally best served by concentrating corporate resources on businesses that can contend for market leadership in their industry.*

COMPARING BUSINESS-UNIT PERFORMANCE

Once each subsidiary has been rated on the basis of industry attractiveness and competitive strength, the next step is to evaluate which businesses have the best performance prospects and which ones have the worst. The most important considerations in judging business-unit performance are sales growth, profit growth, contribution to company earnings, and the return on capital invested in the business; sometimes, cash flow generation is a big consideration, especially for cash cows or businesses with potential for harvesting. Information on a business's past performance can be gleaned from financial records. While past performance doesn't necessarily predict future performance, it does signal which businesses have been strong performers and which have not. Industry attractiveness/business strength evaluations should provide a solid basis for judging future prospects. Normally, strong business units in attractive industries have significantly better prospects than weak businesses in unattractive industries.

> *Judgments about the expected future performance of each subsidiary indicate whether a firm's outlook for profitable growth with its current business lineup is bright or dim.*

The growth and profit outlook for the company's core businesses generally determine whether the portfolio as a whole will turn in a strong or weak performance. Noncore businesses with subpar track records and little expectation for improvement are logical candidates for divestiture. Business subsidiaries with the brightest profit and growth prospects should have priority for having their capital investment requests funded.

STRATEGIC FIT ANALYSIS

The next analytical step is to determine how well each business unit fits into the company's overall business picture. Fit needs to be looked at from two angles: (1) whether a business unit has valuable strategic fit with other

---

ILLUSTRATION CAPSULE
21

PORTFOLIO MANAGEMENT AT GENERAL ELECTRIC

When Jack Welch became CEO of General Electric in 1981, he launched a corporate strategy effort to reshape the company's diversified business portfolio. Early on he issued a challenge to GE's business-unit managers to become number one or number two in their industry; failing that, the business units either had to capture a decided technological advantage translatable into a competitive edge or face possible divestiture.

By 1989, GE was a different company. Under Welch's prodding, GE divested operations worth $9 billion—TV operations, small appliances, a mining business, and computer chips. It spent a

total of $24 billion acquiring new businesses, most notably RCA, Roper (a maker of major appliances whose biggest customer was Sears), and Kidder Peabody (a Wall Street investment banking firm). Internally, many of the company's smaller business operations were put under the direction of larger "strategic business units." But, most significantly, in 1989, 12 of GE's 14 strategic business units were market leaders in the United States and globally (the company's financial services and communications units served markets too fragmented to rank):

	Market Standing in the United States	Market Standing in the World
Aircraft engines	First	First
Broadcasting (NBC)	First	Not applicable
Circuit breakers	Tied for first with 2 others	Tied for first with 3 others
Defense electronics	Second	Second
Electric motors	First	First
Engineering plastics	First	First
Factory automation	Second	Third
Industrial and power systems	First	First
Lighting	First	Second
Locomotives	First	Tied for first
Major home appliances	First	Tied for second
Medical diagnostic imaging	First	First

In 1989, having divested most of the weak businesses and having built existing businesses into leading contenders, Welch launched a new initiative within GE to dramatically boost productivity and reduce the size of GE's bureaucracy. Welch argued that for GE to continue to be successful in a

global marketplace, the company had to press hard for continuous cost reduction in each of its businesses and cut through bureaucratic procedures to shorten response times to changing market conditions.

Source: Developed from information in Stratford P. Sherman, "Inside the Mind of Jack Welch," *Fortune,* March 27, 1989, pp. 39–50.

Strategic Management Principle

Business subsidiaries that don't fit strategically should be considered for divestiture unless their financial performance is outstanding.

businesses the firm has diversified into (or has an opportunity to diversify into) and (2) whether the business unit meshes well with corporate strategy or adds a beneficial dimension to the corporate portfolio. A business is more attractive *strategically* when it has cost-sharing or skills transfer opportunities that can be translated into stronger competitive advantage and when it fits in with the firm's strategic direction. A business is more valuable *financially* when it can contribute heavily to corporate performance objectives (sales growth, profit growth, above-average return on investment, and so on) and materially enhance the company's overall worth. Just as businesses with poor profit prospects ought to become divestiture candidates so should businesses that don't fit strategically into the company's overall business picture. Firms that emphasize related diversification probably should divest businesses with little or no strategic fit unless such businesses are unusually good financial performers.

RANKING THE BUSINESS UNITS ON INVESTMENT PRIORITY

Using the information and results of the preceding evaluation steps, corporate strategists can rank business units in terms of priority for new capital investment and develop a general strategic direction for each business unit. The task is to decide where the corporation should be investing its financial resources. Which business units should have top priority for new capital investment and financial support? Which business units should carry the lowest priority for new investment? Out of this ranking comes a clearer idea of what the basic strategic approach for each business unit should be—grow and build (aggressive expansion), fortify and defend (protect current position with new investments as needed), overhaul and reposition (try to move the business into a more desirable industry position and a better spot in the business portfolio matrix), or harvest/divest. In deciding whether to divest a business unit, strategists need to use a number of evaluating criteria: industry attractiveness, competitive strength, strategic fit with other businesses, performance potential (profit, return on capital employed, contribution to cash flow), compatibility with corporate priorities, capital requirements, and value to the overall portfolio.

Improving the long-term financial performance of a diversified company entails giving priority to investments in businesses with good to excellent prospects and investing minimally, if at all, in businesses with subpar prospects.

As part of this evaluation step, consideration should be given to whether and how corporate resources and skills can be used to enhance the competitive standing of particular business units.[9] The potential for skills transfer and infusion of new capital become especially important when the firm has business units in less-than-desirable competitive positions and/or where improvement in some key success area could make a big difference to the unit's performance. It is also important when corporate strategy is predicated on strategic fit and the managerial game plan calls for transferring corporate skills and strengths to recently acquired business units in an effort to give them a competitive edge and bolster their market positions.[10]

CRAFTING A CORPORATE STRATEGY

The preceding analysis sets the stage for crafting strategic moves to improve a diversified company's overall performance. The basic issue of "what to do" hinges on the conclusions drawn about the overall *mix* of businesses in the portfolio.[11] Key considerations here are: Does the portfolio contain enough

---

[9]Hofer and Schendel, *Strategy Formulation: Analytical Concepts*, p. 80.

[10]Michael E. Porter, *Competitive Advantage* (New York: Free Press, 1985), chap. 9.

[11]Barry Hedley, "Strategy and the Business Portfolio," *Long Range Planning* 10, no. 1 (February 1977), p. 13; and Hofer and Schendel, *Strategy Formulation*, pp. 82–86.

businesses in very attractive industries? Does the portfolio contain too many marginal businesses or question marks? Is the proportion of mature or declining businesses so great that corporate growth will be sluggish? Does the firm have enough cash cows to finance the stars and emerging winners? Do the company's core businesses generate dependable profits and/or cash flow? Is the portfolio overly vulnerable to seasonal or recessionary influences? Does the portfolio contain businesses that the company really doesn't need to be in? Is the firm burdened with too many businesses in average-to-weak competitive positions? Does the makeup of the business portfolio put the corporation in good position for the future? Answers to these questions indicate whether corporate strategists should consider divesting certain business, acquiring new ones, or restructuring the portfolio.

The Performance Test

Corporate strategists can pursue any of five basic options to avoid a probable shortfall in financial performance.

A good test of the strategic and financial attractiveness of a firm's portfolio is whether the company can attain its performance objectives with its current lineup of businesses. If so, no major corporate strategy changes are indicated. However, if a performance shortfall is probable, corporate strategists can take any of several actions to close the gap:[12]

1. *Alter the strategic plans for some (or all) of the businesses.* This option involves renewed corporate efforts to get better performance out of its present business units. Corporate managers can push business-level managers for better business-unit performance. However, pursuing better short-term performance, if done too zealously, can impair a business's potential to perform better over the long term. Cancelling expenditures that will bolster a business's long-term competitive position in order to squeeze out better short-term financial performance is a perilous strategy. In any case, there are limits as to how much extra performance can be squeezed out.

2. *Add new business units.* Boosting overall performance by making new acquisitions and/or starting new businesses internally raises some new strategy issues. Corporate managers must decide: (*a*) whether to acquire related or unrelated businesses, (*b*) what size acquisition(s) to make, (*c*) how the new units will fit into the present corporate structure, (*d*) what specific features to look for in an acquisition candidate, and (*e*) if acquisitions can be financed without shortchanging present business units in funding their investment requirements. Nonetheless, adding new businesses is a major strategic option, one frequently used by diversified companies to escape sluggish earnings performance.

3. *Divest weak-performing or money-losing businesses.* The most likely candidates for divestiture are businesses in a weak competitive position, in a relatively unattractive industry, or in an industry that does not "fit." Funds from divestitures can, of course, be used to finance new acquisitions, pay down corporate debt, or fund new strategic thrusts in the remaining businesses.

---

[12]Hofer and Schendel, *Strategy Formulation*, pp. 93–100.

4. *Form alliances to try to alter conditions responsible for subpar performance potentials.* In some situations, alliances with domestic or foreign firms, trade associations, suppliers, customers, or special interest groups may help ameliorate adverse performance prospects.[13] Forming or supporting a political action group may be an effective way to lobby for solutions to import-export problems, tax disincentives, and onerous regulatory requirements.

5. *Lower corporate performance objectives.* Adverse market circumstances or declining fortunes in one or more core business units can render companywide performance targets unreachable. So can overly ambitious objective-setting. Closing the gap between actual and desired performance may then require revision of corporate objectives to bring them more in line with reality. Lowering performance objectives is usually a "last-resort" option, used only after other options have come up short.

Finding Additional Diversification Opportunities

One of the major corporate strategy-making concerns in a diversified company is whether to pursue further diversification and, if so, how to identify the "right" kinds of industries and businesses to get into. For firms pursuing unrelated diversification, the issue of where to diversify next is wide open— the search for acquisition candidates is based more on financial criteria than on industry or strategic criteria. Decisions to add unrelated businesses to the firm's portfolio are usually based on such considerations as whether the firm has the financial ability to make another acquisition, whether new acquisitions are needed to boost overall corporate performance, whether one or more acquisition opportunities have to be acted on before they are purchased by other firms, and whether the timing is right for another acquisition (corporate management may have its hands full dealing with the current portfolio of businesses).

In firms with unrelated diversification strategies, the problem of where to diversify next is addressed by hunting for businesses that offer attractive financial returns irrespective of what industry they're in.

With a related diversification strategy, however, the search for new industries needs to be aimed at identifying those that have strategic fits with one or more of the firm's present businesses.[14] This means looking for industries whose activity-cost chains relate to the activity-cost chains of businesses already in the company's portfolio. The interrelationships can concern (1) product or process R&D, (2) opportunities for joint manufacturing and assembly, (3) marketing and distribution channel interrelationships, (4) customer overlaps, (5) opportunities for joint after-sale service, or (6) common managerial know-how requirements—essentially any area where market-related, operating, or management fits can occur.

In firms with related diversification strategies, the problem of where to diversify next is addressed by locating an attractive industry having good strategic fit with one or more of the firm's present businesses.

Once strategic fit opportunities in other industries are identified, corporate strategists have to distinguish between opportunities where important competitive advantage potential exists (through cost-savings, skill transfers, and so on) and those where the strategic fit benefits are really very minor. The size

---

[13]For an excellent discussion of the benefits of alliances among competitors in global industries, see Kenichi Ohmae, "The Global Logic of Strategic Alliances," *Harvard Business Review* 67, no. 2 (March–April 1989), pp. 143–54.

[14]Porter, *Competitive Advantage*, pp. 370–71.

of the competitive advantage potential depends on whether the strategic fit benefits are competitively significant, how much it will cost to capture the benefits, and how difficult it will be to merge and coordinate the business-unit interrelationships.[15] Analysis usually reveals that while there are many actual and potential interrelationships and linkages, only a few have enough strategic importance to generate meaningful competitive advantage.

Deploying Corporate Resources

To get ever-higher levels of performance out of a diversified company's business portfolio, corporate managers must also do an effective job of allocating corporate resources. Their strategy-making task is to steer resources out of low-opportunity areas into high-opportunity areas. Divesting marginal businesses serves this purpose by freeing unproductive assets for redeployment. Surplus funds from cash cows and harvested businesses also add to the corporate treasury. Options for allocating these funds include: (1) investing in the maintenance and expansion of existing businesses, (2) making acquisitions if needed, (3) funding long-range R&D ventures, (4) paying off existing long-term debt, (5) increasing dividends, and (6) repurchasing the company's stock. The first three are *strategic* actions; the last three, *financial* moves. Ideally, funds are available to serve both strategic and financial purposes. If not, strategic uses should take precedence over financial uses except in unusual and compelling circumstances.

GUIDELINES FOR MANAGING THE CORPORATE STRATEGY FORMATION PROCESS

Although formal analysis and entrepreneurial brainstorming are important factors in the corporate strategy-making process, there is more to where corporate strategy comes from and how it evolves. Rarely is there an all-inclusive formulation of the total corporate strategy. Instead, corporate strategy in major enterprises emerges incrementally from the unfolding of many different internal and external events, the result of probing the future, experimenting, gathering more information, sensing problems, building awareness of the various options, developing ad hoc responses to unexpected "crises," communicating partial consensus as it emerges, and acquiring a "feel" for all the strategically relevant factors, their importance, and their interrelationships.[16]

Strategic analysis is not something the executives of diversified companies do all at once in comprehensive fashion. Such big reviews are sometimes scheduled, but studies indicate that major strategic decisions emerge gradually rather than from periodic, full-scale analysis followed by prompt decision. Typically, top executives approach major strategic decisions a step at a time, often starting from broad, intuitive conceptions and then embellishing, fine-tuning, and modifying their original thinking as more information is gathered, as formal analysis confirms or modifies emerging judgments, and as confidence and consensus build for what strategic moves need to be made. Often attention and resources are concentrated on a few critical strategic thrusts that illuminate and integrate corporate direction, objectives, and strategies.

---

[15]Ibid., pp. 371–72.
[16]Ibid., pp. 58 and 196.

Strategic analysis in diversified companies is an eight-step process. Step one is to identify the present corporate strategy. Step two is to construct business portfolio matrixes as needed to examine the overall composition of the present portfolio. Step three is to profile the industry and competitive environment of each business unit and draw conclusions about how attractive each industry in the portfolio is. Step four is to probe the competitive strength of the individual businesses and how well situated each is in its respective industry. Step five is to rank the different business units on the basis of their past performance record and future performance prospects. Step six is to determine how well each business unit fits in with corporate direction and strategy and whether it has important strategic fit relationships with other businesses in the portfolio. Step seven is to rank the business units from highest to lowest in investment priority, drawing conclusions about where the firm should be putting its money and what the general strategic direction of each business unit should be (invest-and-expand, fortify-and-defend, overhaul and reposition, harvest, or divest). Step eight is to use the preceding analysis to craft a series of moves to improve overall corporate performance. The primary corporate strategy moves involve:

- Making acquisitions, starting new businesses from within, and divesting marginal businesses or businesses that no longer match the corporate direction and strategy.
- Devising moves to strengthen the long-term competitive positions of the company's core businesses.
- Acting to create strategic fit opportunities and turn them into long-term competitive advantage.
- Steering corporate resources out of low-opportunity areas into high-opportunity areas.

SUGGESTED READINGS

Bettis, Richard A., and William K. Hall. "Strategic Portfolio Management in the Multi-business Firm." *California Management Review* 24 (Fall 1981), pp. 23–38.

_____. "The Business Portfolio Approach—Where It Falls Down in Practice." *Long Range Planning* 16, no. 2 (April 1983), pp. 95–104.

Christensen, H. Kurt, Arnold C. Cooper, and Cornelius A. Dekluyuer. "The Dog Business: A Reexamination." *Business Horizons* 25, no. 6 (November–December 1982), pp. 12–18.

Hamermesh, Richard G. *Making Strategy Work* (New York: John Wiley & Sons, 1986), chaps. 1, 4, and 7.

Haspeslagh, Phillippe. "Portfolio Planning: Uses and Limits." *Harvard Business Review* 60, no. 1 (January–February 1982), pp. 58–73.

Hax, Arnoldo, and Nicolas S. Majluf. *Strategic Management: An Integrative Perspective.* Englewood Cliffs, N.J.: Prentice Hall, 1984, chaps. 7–9.

_____. *The Strategy Concept and Process.* Englewood Cliffs, N.J.: Prentice Hall, 1991, chaps. 8–11 and 15.

Henderson, Bruce D. "The Application and Misapplication of the Experience Curve." *Journal of Business Strategy* 4, no. 3 (Winter 1984), pp. 3–9.

Naugle, David G., and Garret A. Davies. "Strategic-Skill Pools and Competitive Advantage." *Business Horizons* 30, no. 6 (November–December 1987), pp. 35–42.

Porter, Michael E. *Competitive Advantage.* New York: Free Press, 1985, chaps. 9–11.

_____. "From Competitive Advantage to Corporate Strategy." *Harvard Business Review* 65, no. 3 (May–June 1987), pp. 43–59.

CHAPTER

9

Implementing Strategy
Organization-Building, Budgets, and Support Systems

We strategize beautifully, we implement pathetically.
An auto-parts firm executive

Just being able to conceive bold new strategies is not enough. The general manager must also be able to translate his or her strategic vision into concrete steps that "get things done."
Richard G. Hamermesh

Organizing is what you do before you do something, so that when you do it, it is not all mixed up.
A. A. Milne

Once the course of strategy has been charted, the manager's priorities swing to converting the strategic plan into actions and good results. Putting the strategy into effect and getting the organization moving in the chosen direction call for a different set of managerial tasks and skills. Whereas crafting strategy is largely an *entrepreneurial* activity, implementing strategy is largely an internal *administrative* activity. Whereas successful strategy formulation depends on business vision, market analysis, and entrepreneurial judgment, successful implementation depends on working through others, organizing, motivating, culture-building, and creating strong fits between strategy and how the organization does things. Ingrained behavior does not change just because a new strategy has been announced.

Implementing strategy is a tougher, more time-consuming challenge than crafting strategy. Practitioners emphatically agree that is is a whole lot easier to develop a sound strategic plan than it is to "make it happen."

THE STRATEGY IMPLEMENTATION FRAMEWORK

Strategy implementation entails *converting the strategic plan into action and then into results.* Implementation is successful if the company achieves its strategic objectives and targeted levels of financial performance. What makes the process so demanding is the wide sweep of managerial activities that have to be attended to, the many ways managers can tackle each activity, the skill it takes to get a variety of initiatives launched and moving, and the resistance to change that has to be overcome. Moreover, each strategy implementation situation is unique enough to require its own specific *action agenda.* Strategy should be implemented in a manner that fits that organization's situation. Managers have to take into account the nature of the strategy (implementing a strategy to become the low-cost producer is different from implementing a differentiation strategy keyed to superior quality and premium prices). And they must consider the amount of strategic change involved (shifting to a bold new strategy poses different implementation problems than making minor changes in an already existing strategy).

The strategy-implementer's task is to convert the strategic plan into action and get on with what needs to be done to achieve the targeted strategic and financial objectives.

The Principal Tasks

While the details of strategy implementation are specific to every situation, certain administrative bases have to be covered no matter what the organization's situation. Figure 9–1 shows the principal administrative tasks that crop up repeatedly in the strategy implementation process. Depending on the organization's circumstances, some of these tasks will prove more significant and time-consuming than others. To devise an action agenda, managers have to determine what internal conditions are necessary to execute the strategy successfully and then create these conditions as rapidly as practical.

The keys to successful implementation are to unite the total organization behind the strategy and to see that every relevant activity and administrative task is done in a manner that tightly matches the requirements for first-rate strategy execution. The motivational and inspirational challenge is to build such determined commitment up and down the ranks that an enthusiastic organizationwide crusade emerges to carry out the strategy and meet performance targets. Along with enthusiasm and strategic commitment, however, must come a concerted managerial effort to create a series of strategy-supportive "fits." The internal organization structure must be matched to the strategy. The necessary organizational skills and capabilities must be developed. Resource and budget allocations must support the strategy, and departments must be given the people and budgets needed to carry out their assigned strategic roles. The company's reward structure, policies, information system, and operating practices all need to reinforce the push for effective strategy execution, as opposed to having a passive role or, even worse, acting as obstacles. Equally important, managers must do things in a manner and style that creates and nurtures a strategy-supportive work environment and corporate culture. The stronger

Successful strategy-implementers generate strong organizationwide commitment to carrying out the strategy.

They also build tight fits between how things are managed internally and what is required for first-rate strategy execution.

FIGURE 9–1   **Implementing Strategy**   (*The principal tasks*)

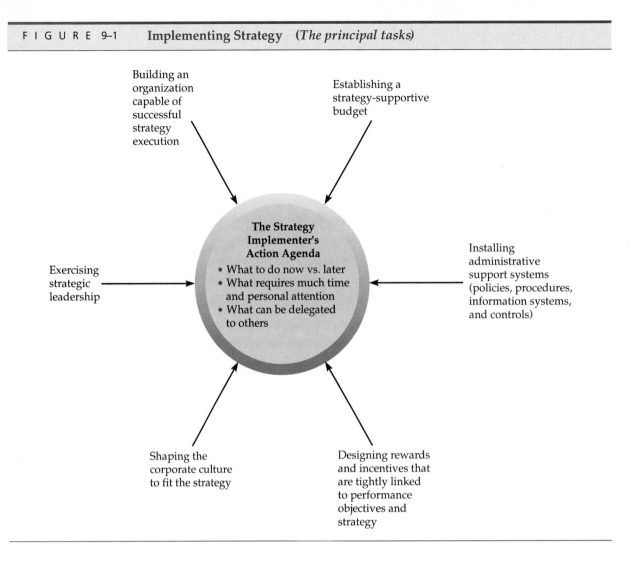

the strategy-supportive fits created internally, the greater the chances of successful implementation.

Who Are the Strategy Implementers?

Every manager has an active role in the process of implementing and executing the firm's strategic plan.

An organization's chief executive officer and the heads of major organizational units are the persons most responsible for seeing that strategy is implemented successfully. However, implementing strategy is not a job just for senior managers; it is a job for the whole management team. Strategy implementation involves every organization unit, from the head office down to each operating department, asking "What do we have to do to implement our part of the strategic plan, and how can we best get it done?" In this sense, all managers become strategy implementers in their areas of authority and responsibility. Although major implementation initiatives have to be orchestrated by the CEO and other senior officers, top-level managers still have to rely on the active support and cooperation of lower-level managers to get things done. Lower-level managers are always active participants in the strategy implementation process. They not only initiate and supervise the implementation process in their areas of responsibility, they also are instrumental in seeing that the desired results and performance targets continue to be met day after day once the strategy is in place.

Leading the Implementation Process

One of the make-or-break determinants of successful strategy implementation is how well management leads the process. Implementers can exercise leadership in many ways. They can play an active, visible role or a low-key, behind-the-scenes one. They can make decisions authoritatively or on the basis of consensus, delegate much or little, be personally involved in the details or stand on the sidelines and coach others, proceed swiftly (launching implementation initiatives on many fronts) or deliberately (working for gradual progress over a long time frame). How managers lead the implementation task tends to be a function of: (1) their experience and accumulated knowledge about the business; (2) whether they are new to the job or seasoned incumbents; (3) their network of personal relationships with others in the organization; (4) their own diagnostic, administrative, interpersonal, and problem-solving skills; (5) the authority they've been given; (6) the leadership style they're comfortable with; and (7) their view of the role they need to play to get things done.

There is no one right way to manage the implementation process; each firm's situation is unique enough to require custom actions and managerial approaches.

Another factor that affects a manager's approach to strategy implementation is the context of the organization's situation: the seriousness of the firm's strategic difficulties, the nature and extent of the strategic change involved, the type of strategy being implemented, the strength of any ingrained behavior that has to be changed, the financial and organizational resources available to work with, the configuration of personal and organization relationships in the firm's history, the pressures for quick results and improvements in near-term financial performance, and other such factors that make up the firm's "culture" and overall work climate. Each company's internal situation is unique enough that managers usually have to custom-tailor their action agenda to fit it. Successful strategy implementers carefully consider all the internal ramifications of implementing a new strategy and carefully diagnose the action priorities and the sequence in which things need to be done; then they get their organization moving and keep pushing it along.

In the remainder of this chapter and in Chapter 10, we survey the ins and outs of the manager's role as chief strategy implementer. For convenience, the discussion will be organized around the six administrative components of the strategy implementation process and the recurring administrative issues associated with each (see Figure 9–2). This chapter explores the management tasks of building an organization, establishing strategy-supportive budgets, and installing administrative support systems. Chapter 10 deals with linking rewards and incentives to performance objectives and strategy, building a strategy-supportive corporate culture, and exercising strategic leadership.

BUILDING A CAPABLE ORGANIZATION

Successful strategy execution depends greatly on good internal organization and competent personnel. Building a capable organization is always a top priority. Three types of organizational actions are paramount:

FIGURE 9–2   The Administrative Components of Strategy Implementation

Building an Organization Capable of Executing the Strategy

Specific Tasks

- Creating a strategy-supportive organization structure.
- Developing the skills and core competencies needed to execute the strategy successfully.
- Selecting people for key positions.

Establishing a Strategy-Supportive Budget

Specific Tasks

- Seeing that each organizational unit has a big enough budget to carry out its part of the strategic plan.
- Ensuring that resources are used efficiently to get "the biggest bang for the buck."

Installing Internal Administrative Support Systems

Specific Tasks

- Establishing and administering strategy-facilitating policies and procedures.
- Developing administrative and operating systems to give the organization strategy-critical capabilities.
- Generating the right strategic information on a timely basis.

Devising Rewards and Incentives That Are Tightly Linked to Objectives and Strategy

Specific Tasks

- Motivating organizational units and individuals to do their best to make the strategy work.
- Designing rewards and incentives that induce employees to do the very things needed for successful strategy execution.
- Promoting a results orientation.

Shaping the Corporate Culture to Fit the Strategy

Specific Tasks

- Establishing shared values.
- Setting ethical standards.
- Creating a strategy-supportive work environment.
- Building a spirit of high performance into the culture.

Exercising Strategic Leadership

Specific Tasks

- Leading the process of shaping values, molding culture, and energizing strategy accomplishment.
- Keeping the organization innovative, responsive, and opportunistic.
- Dealing with the politics of strategy, coping with power struggles, and building consensus.
- Enforcing ethical standards and behavior.
- Initiating corrective actions to improve strategy execution.

1. Developing an organizational structure that is conducive to successful strategy execution.
2. Seeing that the organization has the skills, core competencies, managerial talents, technical know-how, and competitive capabilities it needs.
3. Selecting the right people for key positions.

Matching Organization Structure to Strategy

There are very few hard and fast rules for designing a strategy-supportive organization structure. Every firm's internal organization is somewhat idiosyncratic, the result of many organizational decisions and historical circumstances. Moreover, every strategy is grounded in its own set of key success factors and critical tasks. The only real imperative is to design the internal organization structure around the key success factors and critical tasks inherent in the firm's strategy. The following five-sequence procedure is a useful guide for fitting structure to strategy:[1]

Matching structure to strategy requires making strategy-critical activities and organizational units the main building blocks in the organization structure.

1. Pinpoint the key functions and tasks necessary for successful strategy execution.
2. Reflect on how strategy-critical functions and organizational units relate to those that are routine and to those that provide staff support.
3. Make strategy-critical business units and functions the main organizational building blocks.
4. Determine the degrees of authority needed to manage each organizational unit bearing in mind both the benefits and costs of decentralized decision making.
5. Provide for coordination among the various organizational units.

Pinpointing the Strategy-Critical Activities   In any organization, some activities and skills are always more critical to strategic success than others. From a strategy perspective, much of an organization's total work is routine; it involves such administrative housekeeping as handling payrolls, managing cash flows, controlling inventories, processing grievances, warehousing and shipping, processing customer orders, and complying with regulations. Other activities are primarily support functions (data processing, accounting, training, public relations, market research, and purchasing). Yet there are usually certain crucial tasks and functions that have to be done exceedingly well for the strategy to be successful. For instance, tight cost control is essential for a firm trying to be the low-cost producer in a commodity business characterized by low margins and price cutting. For a luxury goods manufacturer, critical skills may be quality craftsmanship, distinctive design, and sophisticated promotional appeal. In high-tech industries, the critical activities tend to be R&D, product innovation, and getting newly-developed products out of the lab and onto the market quickly. Strategy-critical activities vary according to the particulars of a firm's strategy and competitive requirements.

---

[1]LaRue T. Hosmer, *Strategic Management: Text and Cases on Business Policy* (Englewood Cliffs, N.J.: Prentice Hall, 1982), chap. 10; and J. Thomas Cannon, *Business Strategy and Policy* (New York: Harcourt Brace Jovanovich, 1968), p. 316.

Two questions help identify what an organization's strategy-critical activities are: "What functions have to be performed extra well and in timely fashion for the strategy to succeed?" and "In what areas of the organization would malperformance seriously endanger strategic success?"[2] The answers generally show what activities and areas are crucial and where to concentrate organization-building efforts.

Understanding the Relationships among Activities   Before critical, supportive, and routine activities are grouped into organizational units, the strategic relationships among them need to be scrutinized thoughtfully. Activities can be related by the flow of material through the production process, the type of customer served, the distribution channels used, the technical skills and know-how needed to perform them, a strong need for coordination, the sequence in which tasks must be performed, and by geographic location, to mention a few. Such relationships are important because one (or more) of the interrelationships usually become the basis for grouping activities into organizational units. If strategic needs are to drive organization design, then the relationships to look for are those that link one piece of the strategy to another.

Grouping Activities into Organization Units   The chief guideline here is to make strategy-critical activities the main building blocks in the organization structure. The rationale is compelling: if activities crucial to strategic success are to get the attention and visibility they merit, they have to be a prominent part of the organizational scheme. When key business units and strategy-critical functions take a backseat to less important activities, they usually get fewer resources and end up with less clout in the organization's power structure than they deserve. On the other hand, when key units form the core of the whole organization structure, their role and power is highlighted and institutionalized. Senior executives seldom send a stronger signal about what is strategically important than by making key business units and critical functions the most prominent organizational building blocks and, further, giving the managers of these units a visible, influential position in the organization.

Determining the Degree of Authority and Independence to Give Each Unit   Companies must decide how much authority and decision-making latitude to give managers of each organization unit, especially the heads of business subsidiaries. Companies that are extremely centralized retain authority for big strategy and policy decisions at the corporate level and delegate only operating decisions to business-level managers. Those that are extremely decentralized give business units enough autonomy to function independently, with little direct authority exerted by corporate staff.

As a rule, authority to make strategic decisions for an organizational unit should be delegated to the unit's manager.

There are several guidelines for delegating authority to various units. Activities and organizational units with a key role in strategy execution should not be subordinate to routine and nonkey activities. Revenue-producing and results-producing activities should not be subordinate to internal support or staff functions. Decision-making authority should be decentralized (i.e.,

---

[2]Peter F. Drucker, *Management: Tasks, Responsibilities, Practices* (New York: Harper & Row, 1974), pp. 530, 535.

pushed down to managers closest to the scene of the action) whenever lower-level managers are in a position to make better, more informed, and more timely decisions than higher-level managers. However, decision-making authority should be centralized if higher-level managers are in the best decision-making position. With few exceptions, the authority to choose a strategy for an organizational unit and to decide how to implement it should be delegated to the manager in charge of the unit. Corporate-level authority over strategic and operating decisions at the business-unit level and below should be held to a minimum. The best approach is to select strong managers to head each organizational unit and give them enough authority to craft and execute an appropriate strategy; managers that consistently produce unsatisfactory results and have a poor track record in strategy-making and strategy-implementing should be weeded out.

One of the biggest exceptions to decentralizing strategy-related decisions arises in diversified companies with related businesses in their portfolios; in such cases, capturing strategic fit benefits is sometimes best done by centralizing decision-making authority. Suppose, for instance, that businesses with related process and product technologies are performing their own R&D. Merging each business's R&D activities into a single unit under the authority of a corporate officer may be both more cost efficient and more strategically effective.

Centralizing strategic decisions at the corporate level has merit when the related activities of related business units need to be tightly coordinated.

Providing for Coordination among the Units   Coordinating the activities of organizational units is accomplished mainly through positioning them in the hierarchy of authority. Managers higher up in the pecking order generally have authority over more organizational units and thus the clout to coordinate, integrate, and arrange for the cooperation of units under their supervision. The chief executive officer, chief operating officer, and business-level managers are central points of coordination because of their positions of authority over the whole unit. Besides positioning organizational units according to managerial authority, strategic efforts can also be coordinated through project teams, special task forces, standing committees, formal strategy reviews, and annual strategic planning and budgeting cycles. Additionally, the formulation of the strategic plan itself serves a coordinating role. The process of setting objectives and strategies for each organizational unit and making sure related activities mesh helps coordinate operations across units.

On the other hand, when a firm is pursuing a related diversification strategy, coordination may be best accomplished by centralizing authority for a related activity under a corporate-level officer. Also, diversified companies with either related or unrelated diversification strategies commonly centralize such staff support functions as public relations, finance and accounting, employee benefits, and data processing at the corporate level.

The Structure-Follows-Strategy Thesis

The practice of *consciously* matching organization design and structure to the particular needs of strategy is a fairly recent—and research-based—management development. A landmark study by Alfred Chandler found that changes in an organization's strategy bring about new administrative problems which, in turn, require a new or refashioned structure for the new strategy to be

Strategic Management Principle

Attempting to carry out a new strategy with an old organizational structure is usually unwise.

successfully implemented.[3] His study of 70 large corporations revealed that structure tends to follow the growth strategy of the firm—but often not until inefficiency and internal operating problems provoke a structural adjustment. The experiences of these firms followed a consistent sequential pattern: new strategy creation, emergence of new administrative problems, decline in profitability and performance, a shift to a more appropriate organizational structure, and recovery to more profitable levels and improved strategy execution. Chandler found this sequence to be oft-repeated as firms grew and modified their corporate strategies. Chandler's research shows that the choice of organization structure *does make a difference* in how an organization performs. A company's internal organization should be reassessed whenever strategy changes.[4] A new strategy is likely to entail new or different skills and key activities; if these go unrecognized, the resulting mismatch between strategy and structure can open the door for implementation and performance problems.

The *structure-follows-strategy* thesis is undergirded with powerful logic: how organizational activities are structured is a means to an end—not an end in itself. Structure is a managerial device for facilitating execution of the organization's strategy and helping to achieve performance targets. An organization's structural design is a tool for "harnessing" individual efforts and coordinating the performance of diverse tasks; a good design helps people do things efficiently and effectively. If activities and responsibilities are *deliberately* organized to link structure and strategy, it is easier to coordinate strategic moves across functional areas. Moreover, efforts to execute strategy on a day-to-day basis are less likely to result in frustration, finger-pointing when foul-ups occur, interdepartmental frictions, and inefficiency.[5]

How Structure Evolves as Strategy Evolves   As firms expand from small, single-business enterprises to more complex strategic phases of vertical integration, geographic expansion, and line-of-business diversification, their organizational structures tend to evolve from one-person management to functional departments to divisions to decentralized business units. Single-business companies almost always have a centralized functional structure. Vertically integrated firms and companies with broad geographic coverage typically are organized into operating divisions. The basic building blocks of a diversified company are its individual businesses; the authority for most decisions is decentralized, and each business operates as an independent, stand-alone unit with corporate headquarters performing only minimal functions for the business.

---

[3]Alfred Chandler, *Strategy and Structure* (Cambridge, Mass.: MIT Press, 1962). Although the stress here is on matching structure to strategy, structure can and does influence the choice of strategy. A "good" strategy must be doable. When an organization's present structure is so far out of line with the requirements of a particular strategy that the organization would have to be turned upside down to implement it, the strategy may not be doable and should not be given further consideration. In such cases, structure shapes the choice of strategy. The point here, however, is that once a strategy is chosen, structure must be modified to fit the strategy if an approximate fit does not already exist. Any influences of structures on strategy should come before the point of strategy selection rather than after it.

[4]For an excellent study documenting how companies have revised their internal organization to accommodate strategic change, see Raymond Corey and Steven H. Star, *Organizational Strategy: A Marketing Approach* (Boston: Harvard Business School, 1971), chap. 3.

[5]Drucker, *Management*, p. 523.

The Strategic Advantages and Disadvantages of Different Organizational Structures

There are five strategy-driven approaches to organization: (1) functional specialization, (2) geographic organization, (3) decentralized business divisions, (4) strategic business units, and (5) matrix structures featuring dual lines of authority and strategic priority. Each form has its own strategic advantages and disadvantages.

The Functional Organization Structure A functional organization structure tends to be effective in single-business firms where key activities revolve around well-defined skills and areas of specialization. In such cases, in-depth specialization and focused concentration on performing functional tasks and activities can enhance both operating efficiency and the development of core competencies. Generally, organizing by functional specialties promotes full utilization of the most up-to-date technical skills and helps a business capitalize on efficiency gains from using specialized manpower, facilities, and equipment. These are strategically important considerations for single-business companies, dominant-product companies, and vertically integrated firms and account for why they usually have some kind of centralized, functionally specialized structure.

However, just what form the functional specialization takes varies according to customer-product-technology considerations. For instance, a technical instruments manufacturer may be departmentalized into research and development, engineering, production, technical services, quality control, marketing, personnel, and finance and accounting. A municipal government, on the other hand, may be departmentalized according to purposeful function—fire, public safety, health services, water and sewer, streets, parks and recreation, and education. A university may divide its organizational units into academic affairs, student services, alumni relations, athletics, buildings and grounds, institutional services, and budget control. Two types of functional organizational approaches are diagrammed in Figure 9–3.

The Achilles heel of a functional structure is the difficulty of getting and keeping tight strategic coordination across functional departments that don't "talk the same language" and that often don't adequately appreciate one another's strategic role and problems. Members of functional departments tend to have strong departmental loyalties and be protective of departmental interests, thus making it hard to achieve strategic and operating coordination across departmental lines. There's a natural tendency for each functional department to push for solutions and decisions that advance its own cause and give it more influence (despite the lip service given to cooperation and "what's best for the company").

Interdepartmental politics, attempts at functional empire-building, and conflicting functional viewpoints can impose a time-consuming administrative burden on the general manager, who is the only person with authority to resolve cross-functional differences and enforce cooperation. In a functional structure, much of a GM's time is spent opening lines of communication across departments, tempering departmental rivalries, and securing cooperation. In addition, a functionally dominated organization, because of strong

Functional departments develop strong functional mindsets and are prone to approach strategic issues more from a functional than a business perspective.

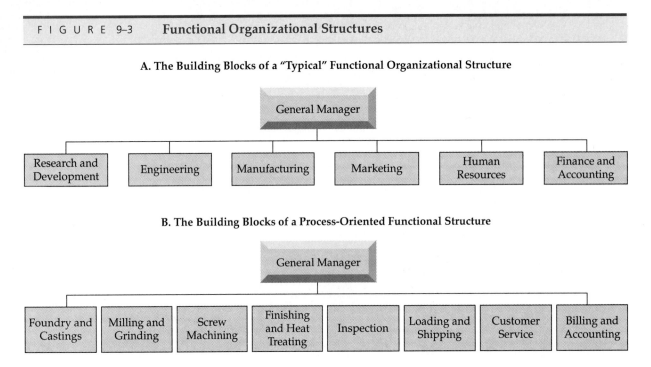

FIGURE 9–3   **Functional Organizational Structures**

A. The Building Blocks of a "Typical" Functional Organizational Structure

B. The Building Blocks of a Process-Oriented Functional Structure

Strategic Advantages	Strategic Disadvantages
• Permits centralized control of strategic results.	• Poses problems of functional coordination.
• Very well suited for structuring a single business.	• Can lead to interfunctional rivalry and conflict, rather than cooperation—GM must referee functional politics.
• Structure is linked tightly to strategy by designating key activities as functional departments.	• May promote overspecialization and narrow management viewpoints.
• Promotes in-depth functional expertise.	• Hinders development of managers with cross-functional experience because the ladder of advancement is up the ranks within the same functional area.
• Well suited to developing a functional-based distinctive competence.	• Forces profit responsibility to the top.
• Conducive to exploiting learning/experience curve effects associated with functional specialization.	• Functional specialists often attach more importance to what's best for the functional area than to what's best for the whole business—can lead to functional empire-building.
• Enhances operating efficiency where tasks are routine and repetitive.	• Functional myopia often works against creative entrepreneurship, adapting to change, and attempts to restructure the activity-cost chain.

preoccupation with developing functional expertise and improving functional performance, tends to have tunnel vision when it comes to promoting entrepreneurial venturesomeness, developing creative responses to major customer-market-technological changes, and pursuing opportunities beyond the industry's conventional boundaries.

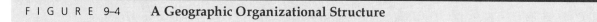

FIGURE 9–4   **A Geographic Organizational Structure**

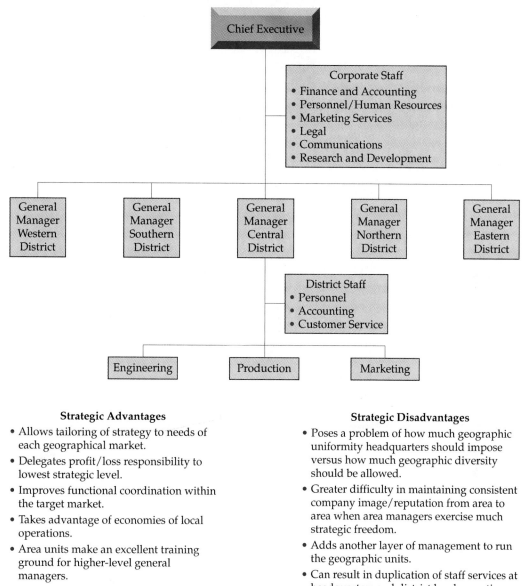

Strategic Advantages	Strategic Disadvantages
• Allows tailoring of strategy to needs of each geographical market.	• Poses a problem of how much geographic uniformity headquarters should impose versus how much geographic diversity should be allowed.
• Delegates profit/loss responsibility to lowest strategic level.	
• Improves functional coordination within the target market.	• Greater difficulty in maintaining consistent company image/reputation from area to area when area managers exercise much strategic freedom.
• Takes advantage of economies of local operations.	
• Area units make an excellent training ground for higher-level general managers.	• Adds another layer of management to run the geographic units.
	• Can result in duplication of staff services at headquarters and district levels, creating a relative-cost disadvantage.

Geographic Forms of Organization   Organizing on the basis of geographic areas or territories is a common structural form for enterprises operating in diverse geographic markets or serving an expansive geographic area. As indicated in Figure 9–4, geographic organization has its advantages and disadvantages, but the chief reason for its popularity is that it promotes improved performance.

A geographic organization structure is well suited for firms pursuing different strategies in different geographic regions.

In the private sector, a territorial structure is typically used by chain stores, power companies, cement firms, restaurant chains, and dairy products enterprises. In the public sector, such organizations as the Internal Revenue Service, the Social Security Administration, the federal courts, the U.S. Postal Service, state troopers, and the Red Cross have adopted territorial structures to be directly accessible to geographically dispersed clienteles. Multinational enterprises use geographic structures to manage the diversity they encounter by operating across national boundaries.

Corey and Star cite Pfizer International as a good example of a company whose strategic requirements made geographic decentralization propitious:

> Pfizer International operated plants in 27 countries and marketed in more than 100 countries. Its product lines included pharmaceuticals (antibiotics and other ethical prescription drugs), agriculture and veterinary products (such as animal feed supplements and vaccines and pesticides), chemicals (fine chemicals, bulk pharmaceuticals, petrochemicals, and plastics), and consumer products (cosmetics and toiletries).
>
> Ten geographic Area Managers reported directly to the President of Pfizer International and exercised line supervision over Country Managers. According to a company position description, it was "the responsibility of each Area Manager to plan, develop, and carry out Pfizer International's business in the assigned foreign area in keeping with company policies and goals."
>
> Country Managers had profit responsibility. In most cases a single Country Manager managed all Pfizer activities in his country. In some of the larger, well-developed countries of Europe there were separate Country Managers for pharmaceutical and agricultural products and for consumer lines.
>
> Except for the fact that New York headquarters exercised control over the to-the-market prices of certain products, especially prices of widely used pharmaceuticals, Area and Country Managers had considerable autonomy in planning and managing the Pfizer International business in their respective geographic areas. This was appropriate because each area, and some countries within areas, provided unique market and regulatory environments. In the case of pharmaceuticals and agriculture and veterinary products (Pfizer International's most important lines), national laws affected formulations, dosages, labeling, distribution, and often price. Trade restrictions affected the flow of bulk pharmaceuticals and chemicals and packaged products, and sometimes required the establishment of manufacturing plants to supply local markets. Competition, too, varied significantly from area to area.[6]

In a diversified firm, the basic organizational building blocks are its business units; each business is operated as a stand-alone profit center.

Decentralized Business Units　Grouping activities along business and product lines has been a trend among diversified enterprises for the past half century, beginning with the pioneering efforts of DuPont and General Motors in the 1920s. Separate business/product divisions emerged because diversification made a functionally specialized manager's job incredibly complex. Imagine the problems a manufacturing executive and his/her staff would have if put in charge of, say, 50 different plants using 20 different technologies to produce 30 different products in eight different businesses/industries. In a multibusiness enterprise, the needs of strategy virtually dictate that the organizational sequence be corporate to business to functional area within a business rather than corporate to functional area (aggregated for all businesses).

---

[6]Corey and Star, *Organization Strategy*, pp. 23–24.

Thus while functional departments and geographic divisions are the standard organizational building blocks in a single-business enterprise, in a multibusiness corporation the basic building blocks are the businesses the firm has diversified into. Diversification is generally managed by decentralizing decision-making and delegating authority over each business unit to a business-level manager. The approach, very simply, is to put entrepreneurially oriented general managers in charge of each business unit, give them authority to formulate and implement a business strategy, motivate them with incentives, and hold them accountable for the results they produce. Each business unit then operates as a stand-alone profit center and is organized around whatever functional departments and geographic units suit the business's strategy, key activities, and operating requirements.

Fully independent business units, however, pose a big problem to companies pursuing related diversification: *there is no mechanism for coordinating related activities across business units.* It can be tough to get autonomy-conscious business-unit managers to coordinate and share related activities; they are prone to argue about "turf" and about being held accountable for activities outside their control. To capture strategic fit benefits in a diversified company, corporate headquarters must devise some internal organizational means for achieving strategic coordination across related business-unit activities. One option is to centralize related functions at the corporate level. Examples include having a corporate R&D department if there are technology and product development fits to be managed, creating a corporate sales force to call on customers who purchase from several of the company's businesses, combining dealer networks and sales forces of closely related businesses, merging the order processing and shipping functions of businesses with common customers, and consolidating the production of related components and products into fewer, more efficient plants. Alternatively, corporate officers can develop bonus arrangements that give business-units managers strong incentives to cooperate to achieve the full benefits of strategic fit. If the strategic fit relationships involve skills or technology transfers across businesses, corporate headquarters can set up interbusiness task forces, standing committees, or project teams to work out the specifics of transferring proprietary technology, managerial know-how, and related skills from one business to another.

A typical line-of-business organizational structure is shown in Figure 9–5, along with the strategy-related pros and cons of this type of organizational form.

Strategic Business Units   In broadly diversified companies, the number of decentralized business units can be so great that the span of control is too much for a single chief executive. Then it may be useful to group related businesses and to delegate authority over them to a senior executive who reports directly to the chief executive officer. While this imposes a layer of management between business-level managers and the chief executive, it may nonetheless improve strategic planning and top-management coordination of diverse business interests. This explains both the popularity of the group vice president concept among multi-business companies and the recent trend toward the formation of strategic business units.

A *strategic business unit* (SBU) is a grouping of business subsidiaries based on some important strategic elements common to each. The related elements could be an overlapping set of competitors, a closely related strategic mission,

F I G U R E   9–5   **A Decentralized Line-of-Business Type of Organization Structure**

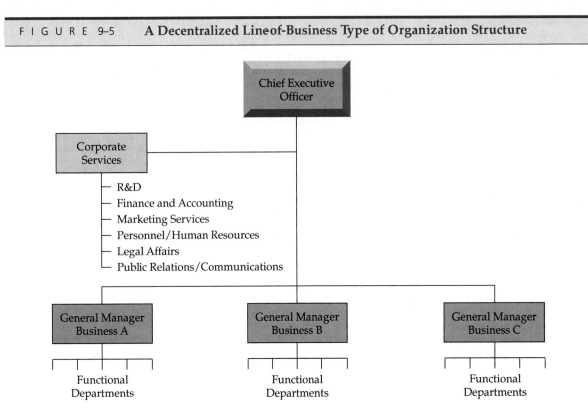

Strategic Advantages

- Offers a logical and workable means of decentralizing responsibility and delegating authority in diversified organizations.
- Puts responsibility for business strategy in closer proximity to each business's unique environment.
- Allows each business unit to organize around its own set of key activities and functional requirements.
- Frees CEO to handle corporate strategy issues.
- Puts clear profit/loss accountability on shoulders of business-unit managers.

Strategic Disadvantages

- May lead to costly duplication of staff functions at corporate and business-unit levels, thus raising administrative overhead costs.
- Poses a problem of what decisions to centralize and what decisions to decentralize (business managers need enough authority to get the job done, but not so much that corporate management loses control of key business-level decisions).
- May lead to excessive division rivalry for corporate resources and attention.
- Business/division autonomy works against achieving coordination of related activities in different business units, thus blocking to some extent the capture of strategic fit benefits.
- Corporate management becomes heavily dependent on business-unit managers.
- Corporate managers can lose touch with business-unit situations, end up surprised when problems arise, and not know much about how to fix such problems.

a common need to compete globally, an ability to accomplish integrated strategic planning, common key success factors, and technologically related growth opportunities. General Electric, a pioneer in the concept of SBUs, grouped 190 units into 43 SBUs and then aggregated them further into six "sectors."[7] At Union Carbide, 15 groups and divisions were decomposed into 150 "strategic planning units" and then regrouped and combined into 9 new "aggregate planning units." General Foods (now a division of Philip Morris) originally defined SBUs on a product-line basis but later redefined them according to menu segments (breakfast foods, beverages, main meal products, desserts, and pet foods).

The SBU concept provides broadly diversified companies with a way to rationalize the organization of many different businesses and a management arrangement for capturing strategic fit benefits and streamlining the strategic planning process. The strategic function of the group vice president is to provide the SBU with some cohesive direction and enforce strategic coordination across related businesses. The group vice president, as strategic coordinator for all businesses in the SBU, is in a position to organize the SBU in ways that facilitate sharing and skills transfers and to centralize "big" strategic decisions at the SBU level. The SBU, in effect, becomes a decision-making unit with broader strategic perspective than a single-business unit. It serves as the organizational mechanism for capturing strategic benefits and helps build competitive advantage for all businesses in the SBU.

SBU structures are a means for managing broad diversification and enforcing strategic coordination across related businesses.

SBUs also help reduce the complexity of dovetailing corporate strategy and business strategy and make it easier to "cross-pollinate" the growth opportunities in different industries. SBUs make headquarters' reviews of the strategies of lower-level units less imposing (there is no practical way for a CEO to review a hundred or more different businesses). A CEO can, however, effectively review the strategic plans of a lesser number of SBUs, leaving strategy reviews and direct supervision of individual businesses to the SBU heads. Figure 9–6 illustrates the SBU form of organization, along with its strategy-related pros and cons.

Matrix Forms of Organization   A matrix organization is a structure with two (or more) channels of command, two lines of budget authority, and two sources of performance and reward. The key feature of the matrix is that business (or product, project, or venture) and functional lines of authority are overlaid (to form a matrix or grid), and managerial authority over the activities in each unit/cell of the matrix is shared between the business/project/venture team manager and the functional manager, as shown in Figure 9–7. In a matrix structure, subordinates have a continuing dual assignment: to the business/product/project and to their home-base function.[8] The outcome is a compromise between functional specialization (engineering, R&D, manufacturing,

Matrix structures, although complex to manage and sometimes unwieldy, allow a firm to be organized in two different strategy-supportive ways at the same time.

---

[7]William K. Hall, "SBUs: Hot, New Topic in the Management of Diversification," *Business Horizons* 21, no. 1 (February 1978), p. 19. For an excellent discussion of the problems of implementing the SBU concept at 13 companies, see Richard A. Bettis and William K. Hall, "The Business Portfolio Approach—Where It Falls Down in Practice," *Long Range Planning* 16, no. 2 (April 1983), pp. 95–104.

[8]A more thorough treatment of matrix organizational forms can be found in Jay R. Galbraith, "Matrix Organizational Designs," *Business Horizons* 15, no. 1 (February 1971), pp. 29–40; and Christopher A. Bartlett and Sumantra Ghoshal, "Matrix Management: Not a Structure, a Frame of Mind," *Harvard Business Review* 68, no. 4 (July–August 1990), pp. 138–45.

F I G U R E 9–6   **An SBU Type of Organization Structure**

FIGURE 9–6   **An SBU Type of Organization Structure**

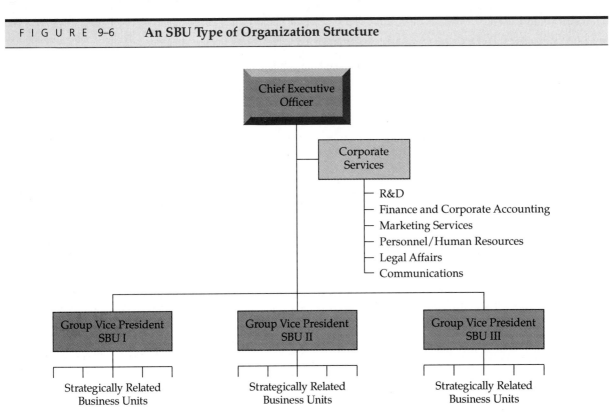

Strategic Advantages

- Provides a strategically relevant way to organize the business-unit portfolio of a broadly diversified company
- Facilitates the coordination of related activities within an SBU, thus helping to capture the benefits of strategic fits in the SBU.
- Promotes more cohesiveness among the new initiatives of separate but related businesses.
- Allows strategic planning to be done at the most relevant level within the total enterprise.
- Makes the task of strategic review by top executives more objective and more effective.
- Helps allocate corporate resources to areas with greatest growth opportunities.

Strategic Disadvantages

- It is easy for the definition and grouping of businesses into SBUs to be so arbitrary that the SBU serves no other purpose than administrative convenience. If the criteria for defining SBUs are rationalizations and have little to do with the nitty-gritty of strategy coordination, then the groupings lose real strategic significance.
- The SBUs can still be myopic in charting their future direction.
- Adds another layer to top management.
- The roles and authority of the CEO, the group vice president, and the business-unit manager have to be carefully worked out or the group vice president gets trapped in the middle with ill-defined authority.
- Unless the SBU head is strong willed, very little strategy coordination is likely to occur across business units in the SBU.
- Performance recognition gets blurred; credit for successful business units tends to go to corporate CEO, then to business-unit head, last to group vice president.

marketing, finance) and specialization by product line, project, line-of-business, or special venture. All of the specialized talent needed for the product line/project/line-of-business/venture are assigned to the same divisional unit.

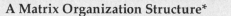

F I G U R E 9–7   **A Matrix Organization Structure***

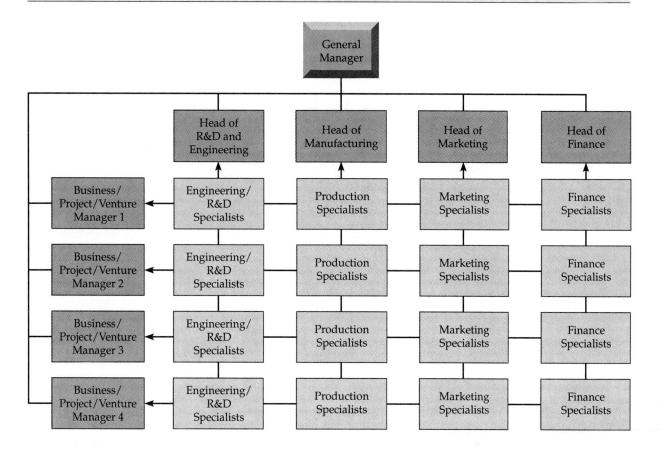

Strategic Advantages

- Gives formal attention to each dimension of strategic priority.
- Creates checks and balances among competing viewpoints.
- Facilitates capture of functionally based strategic fits in diversified companies.
- Promotes making trade-off decisions on the basis of "what's best for the organization as a whole."
- Encourages cooperation, consensus-building, conflict resolution, and coordination of related activities.

Strategic Disadvantages

- Very complex to manage.
- Hard to maintain "balance" between the two lines of authority.
- So much shared authority can result in a transactions logjam and disproportionate amounts of time being spent on communications.
- It is hard to move quickly and decisively without getting clearance from many other people.
- Promotes an organizational bureaucracy and hamstrings creative entrepreneurship.

*Arrows indicate reporting channels

A matrix-type organization is a genuinely different structural form and represents a "new way of life." It breaks the unity-of-command principle; two reporting channels, two bosses, and shared authority create a new kind of organizational climate. In essence, the matrix is a conflict resolution system through which strategic and operating priorities are negotiated, power is shared, and resources are allocated internally on the basis of "strongest case for what is best overall for the unit."[9]

The impetus for matrix organizations stems from growing use of strategies that add new diversity (products, customer groups, technology, lines of business) to a firm's range of activities. Such diversity creates a need for product managers, functional managers, geographic area managers, new venture managers, and business-level managers—all of whom have important strategic responsibilities. When at least two of several variables (product, customer, technology, geography, functional area, and market segment) have roughly equal strategic priorities, a matrix organization can be an effective structural form. A matrix structure promotes internal checks and balances among competing viewpoints and perspectives, with separate managers for different dimensions of strategic initiative. A matrix arrangement thus allows each of several strategic considerations to be managed directly and to be formally represented in the organization structure. In this sense, it helps middle managers make trade-off decisions from an organizationwide perspective.[10] The other big advantage of matrix organization is that it can serve as a mechanism for capturing strategic fit. When the strategic fits in a diversified company are related to a specific functional area (R&D, technology, marketing), matrix organization can be a reasonable structural arrangement for coordinating sharing and skills transfer.

Companies using matrix structures include General Electric, Texas Instruments, Citibank, Shell Oil, TRW, Bechtel, Boeing, and Dow Chemical. Illustration Capsule 22 describes how one broadly diversified corporation with global strategies in each of its businesses has developed a matrix-type structure to manage its operations worldwide. However, most applications of matrix organization are limited to a portion of what the firm does (certain important functions) rather than spanning the whole of a large-scale diversified enterprise.

A number of companies shun matrix organization because of its chief weaknesses.[11] It is a complex structure to manage; people often end up confused over who to report to for what. Moreover, because the matrix signals that everything is important and, further, that everybody needs to communicate with everybody else, a "transactions logjam" can emerge. Action turns into paralysis since, with shared authority, it is hard to move decisively without first considering many points of view and getting clearance from many other people. Sizable transactions costs, communications inefficiency, and delays in responding can result. Even so, in some situations the benefits of conflict resolution and consensus-building outweigh these weaknesses.

Combination and Supplemental Methods of Organization   A single type of structural design is not always sufficient to meet the requirements of strategy. When this occurs, one option is to blend the basic organization forms, match-

---

[9]For two excellent critiques of matrix organizations, see Stanley M. Davis and Paul R. Lawrence, "Problems of Matrix Organizations," *Harvard Business Review* 56, no. 3 (May–June 1978), pp. 131–42; and Erik W. Larson and David H. Gobeli, "Matrix Management: Contradictions and Insights," *California Management Review* 29, no. 4 (Summer 1987), pp. 126–38.

[10]Ibid., p. 132.

[11]Thomas J. Peters and Robert H. Waterman, Jr., *In Search of Excellence* (New York: Harper & Row, 1982), pp. 306–7.

ing structure to strategy requirement by requirement and unit by unit. Another is to supplement a basic organization design with special-situation devices. Three of the most frequently used ones are:

1. The *project team* or *project staff approach*, where a separate, largely self-sufficient work group is created to oversee the completion of a special activity (setting up a new technological process, bringing out a new product, starting up a new venture, consummating a merger with another company, seeing through the completion of a government contract, supervising the construction of a new plant). Project teams are a relatively popular means of handling one-of-a-kind situations with a finite life expectancy when the normal organization is ill-equipped to achieve the same results in addition to regular duties.

2. The *task force approach*, where a number of top-level executives and/or specialists are brought together to work on interdisciplinary assignments requiring specialized expertise from several parts of the organization. Special task forces provide increased opportunity for creativity, open communication across lines of authority, tight integration of specialized talents, expeditious conflict resolution, and common identification for coping with the problem at hand. One study showed that task forces were most effective when they had less than 10 members, membership was voluntary, the seniority of the members was proportional to the importance of the problem, the task force moved swiftly to deal with its assignment, the task force was pulled together only on an as-needed basis, no staff was assigned, and documentation was scant.[12] In these companies, the prevailing philosophy about task forces is to use them to solve real problems, produce some solution efficiently, and then disband them. At the other extreme, Peters and Waterman report one instance where a company had formed 325 task forces, none of which had completed its charge in three years and none of which had been disbanded.

3. The *venture team approach*, whereby a group of individuals is formed for the purpose of bringing a specific product to market or a specific new business into being. Dow, General Mills, Westinghouse, General Electric, and Monsanto have used the venture team approach to regenerate an entrepreneurial spirit. The difficulties with venture teams include deciding who the venture manager should report to; whether funding for ventures should come from corporate, business, or departmental budgets; how to keep the venture clear of bureaucratic and vested interests; and how to coordinate large numbers of different ventures.

Perspectives on the Methods of Organizing

The foregoing discussion brings out two points: (1) there is no perfect or ideal organization design and (2) there are no universally applicable rules for matching strategy and structure. All of the basic organizational forms have their strategy-related strengths and weaknesses. Moreover, two or more can

---

[12]Peters and Waterman, *In Search of Excellence*, pp. 127–32.

ILLUSTRATION CAPSULE
22

MATRIX ORGANIZATION IN A DIVERSIFIED GLOBAL COMPANY
The Case of Asea Brown Boveri

Asea Brown Boveri (ABB) is a diversified multinational corporation headquartered in Zurich, Switzerland. ABB was formed in 1987 through the merger of Asea, one of Sweden's largest industrial enterprises, and Brown Boveri, a major Swiss company. Both companies manufactured electrical products and equipment. Following the merger, ABB acquired or took minority positions in 60 companies, mostly outside Europe. In 1991 ABB had annual revenues of $25 billion and employed 240,000 people around the world, including 150,000 in Western Europe, 40,000 in North America, 10,000 in South America, and 10,000 in India. The company was a world leader in the global markets for electrical products, electrical installations and service, and power-generation equipment and was the dominant European producer. European sales accounted for 60 percent of revenues, while North America accounted for 30 percent and Asia 15 percent.

To manage its global operations, ABB had devised a matrix organization that leveraged its core competencies in electrical-power technologies and its ability to achieve global economies of scale while, at the same time, maximizing its national market visibility and responsiveness. At the top of ABB's corporate organization structure was an executive committee composed of the CEO, Percy Barnevik, and 12 colleagues; the committee con-

sisted of Swedes, Swiss, Germans, and Americans, several of whom were based outside Switzerland. The group, which met every three weeks at various locations around the world, was responsible for ABB's corporate strategy and performance.

Along one dimension of ABB's global matrix were 50 or so business areas (BAs), each representing a closely related set of products and services. The BAs were grouped into eight "business segments"; each segment was supervised by a different member of the executive committee. Each BA had a leader charged with responsibility for (1) devising and championing a global strategy, (2) setting quality and cost standards for the BA's factories worldwide, (3) deciding which factories would export to which country markets, (4) rotating people across borders to share technical expertise, create mixed-nationality teams to solve BA problems, and build a culture of trust and communication, and (5) pooling expertise and research funds for the benefit of the BA worldwide. BA leaders worked out of whatever world location made the most sense for their BA. For example, the BA leader for power transformers, who had responsibility for 25 factories in 16 countries, was a Swede who worked out of Mannheim, Germany; the BA leader for electric

(continued)

be used simultaneously. Many organizations are large enough and diverse enough to have subunits organized by functional specialty, geographical area, market segment, line of business, SBU, and matrix principles. In a very real sense, *the best organizational arrangement is the one that best fits the firm's situation at the moment.* Judging from the frequency with which firms reorganize, every organizational arrangement outlives its usefulness—either an internal rearrangement becomes desirable or changes in the size and scope of customer-product-technology relationships make the firm's structure strategically obsolete. An organization's structure is dynamic, and changes are inevitable.

There is room to quibble over whether organization design should commence with a strategy-structure framework or with a pragmatic consideration of the situation at hand—the corporate culture, the personalities involved, and the way things have been done before. By and large, agonizing over where to begin is unnecessary; both considerations have to be taken into account. However, strategy-structure factors usually take precedence if structure is to be

ILLUSTRATION CAPSULE
22

(concluded)

metering was an American based in North Carolina.

Along the other dimension of the matrix was a group of national enterprises with presidents, boards of directors, financial statements, and career ladders. The presidents of ABB's national enterprises had responsibility for maximizing the performance and effectiveness of all ABB activities within their country's borders. Country presidents worked closely with the BA leaders to evaluate and improve what was happening in ABB's business areas in his/her country.

Inside the matrix were 1,200 "local" ABB companies with an average of 200 employees, each headed by a president. The local company president reported both to the national president in whose country the local company operated and to the leader of the BA to which its products/services were assigned. Each local company was a subsidiary of the ABB national enterprise where it was located. Thus, all of ABB's local companies in Norway were subsidiaries of ABB Norway, the national company for Norway; all ABB operations in Portugal were subsidiaries of ABB Portugal, and so on. The 1,200 presidents of ABB's local companies were expected to be excellent profit center managers, able to answer to two bosses effectively. The local president's global boss was the BA manager who established the local company's role in ABB's

global strategy and, also, the rules a local company had to observe in supporting this strategy. The local president's country boss was the national CEO, with whom it was necessary to cooperate on local issues.

ABB believed that its matrix structure allowed it to optimize its pursuit of global business strategies and, at the same time, maximize its performance in every country market where it operated. The matrix was a way of being global and big strategically, yet small and local operationally. Decision-making was decentralized (to BA leaders, country presidents, and local company presidents), but reporting and control was centralized (through the BA leaders, the country presidents, and the executive committee). ABB saw itself as a federation of national companies with a global coordination center.

Only 100 professionals were located in ABB's corporate headquarters in Zurich. A management information system collected data on all profit centers monthly, comparing actual performance against budgets and forecasts. Data was collected in local currencies but translated into U.S. dollars to allow for cross-border analysis. ABB's corporate financial statements were reported in U.S. dollars, and English was ABB's official language. All high-level meetings were conducted in English.

Source: Compiled from information in William Taylor, "The Logic of Global Business: An Interview with ABB's Percy Barnevik," *Harvard Business Review* 69, no. 2 (March–April 1991), pp. 90–105.

built around the organization's strategy-critical tasks, key success factors, and high-priority business units. Adapting structure to the peculiar circumstances of the organization's internal situation and personalities is usually done to modify the strategy-structure match in "minor" ways.

Drucker sums up the intricacies of organization design thusly:

The simplest organization structure that will do the job is the best one. What makes an organization structure "good" are the problems it does not create. The simpler the structure, the less that can go wrong.

Some design principles are more difficult and problematic than others. But none is without difficulties and problems. None is primarily people-focused rather than task-focused; none is more "creative," "free," or "more democratic." Design principles are tools; and tools are neither good nor bad in themselves. They can be used properly or improperly; and that is all. To obtain both the greatest possible simplicity and the greatest "fit," organization design has to start out

ORGANIZATION LESSONS FROM THE "EXCELLENTLY MANAGED" COMPANIES

Peters and Waterman's study of America's best-managed corporations provides some important lessons in building a strategically capable organization:

- The organizational underpinning of most of the excellently managed companies is a fairly stable, unchanging form—usually a decentralized business/product division—that provides the structural building block which everyone in the enterprise understands and that serves as the base for approaching day-to-day issues and complexities.

- Beyond the crystal-clear primacy of this basic and simple organizational building block, the rest of the organization structure is deliberately kept fluid and flexible to permit response to changing environmental conditions. Much use is made of task forces, project teams, and the creation of new, small divisions to address emerging issues and opportunities.

- New divisions are created to pursue budding business opportunities, as opposed to letting them remain a part of the originating division. Often, there are established guidelines when a new product or product line automatically becomes an independent division.

- People and even products and product lines are frequently shifted from one division to another—to improve efficiency, promote shared costs, enhance competitive strength,

and adapt to changing market conditions.

- Many excellently managed companies have comparatively few people at the corporate level, and many of these are out in the field frequently, rather than in the home office all the time. Emerson Electric with 54,000 employees had a headquarters staff of fewer than 100 people. Dana Corporation employed 35,000 people and had a corporate staff numbering about 100. Schlumberger Ltd., a $56 billion diversified oil service company, ran its worldwide organization with a corporate staff of 90 people. At Intel (sales of over $1 billion), all staff assignments were temporary ones given to line officers. Rolm managed a $200 million business with about 15 people in corporate headquarters. In addition, corporate planners were few and far between. Hewlett-Packard Company, Johnson & Johnson, and 3M had no planners at the corporate level; Fluor Corporation ran a $6 billion operation with three corporate planners. At IBM, management rotated staff assignments every three years. Few IBM staff jobs were manned by "career staffers"; most were manned temporarily by managers with line jobs in the divisions who eventually rotate back to line jobs.

- Functional organization forms are efficient and get the basic activities performed well; yet they are not particularly creative or en-

(continued)

with a clear focus on *key activities* needed to produce *key results*. They have to be structured and positioned in the simplest possible design. Above all, the architect of organization needs to keep in mind the purpose of the structure he is designing.[13]

Peters and Waterman, in their study of excellently managed companies, confirm what Drucker says; their organization prescription is "simple form, lean staff." Illustration Capsule 23 explains some of the organizational principles and approaches being used at these companies.

***

[13]Drucker, *Management*, pp. 601–2.

ILLUSTRATION CAPSULE
23

(concluded)

trepreneurial, they do not adapt quickly, and they are apt to ignore important changes.

- The key to maintaining an entrepreneurial, adaptive organization is *small size*—and the way to keep units small is to spin off new or expanded activities into independent units. Division sizes often run no bigger than $50 to $100 million in sales, with a maximum of 1,000 or so employees. At Emerson Electric, plants rarely employed more than 600 workers, so that management could maintain personal contact with employees. (Emerson, by the way, has a good track record on efficiency; its strategy of being the low-cost producer has worked beautifully in chain saws and several other products.) At Blue Bell, a leading apparel firm, manufacturing units usually employ under 300 people. The lesson seems to be that small units are both more cost-effective and more innovative.

- To prevent "calcification" and stodginess, it helps to rely on such "habitbreaking" techniques as (a) reorganizing regularly; (b) putting top talent on project teams and giving them a "charter" to move quickly to solve a key problem or execute a central strategic thrust (i.e., the creation of the General Motors Project Center to lead the downsizing effort); (c) shifting products or product lines among divisions to take advantage of special management talents or the need for market realignments; (d) break-

ing up big, bureaucratic divisions into several new, smaller divisions; and (e) being flexible enough to try experimental organization approaches and support the pursuit of new opportunities.

- It is useful to adopt a simultaneous "loose-tight" structure that on the one hand fosters autonomy, entrepreneurship, and innovation from rank-and-file managers yet, on the other hand, allows for strong central direction from the top. Such things as regular reorganization, flexible form (the use of teams and task forces), lots of decentralized autonomy for lower-level general managers, and extensive experimentation all focus on the excitement of trying things out in a slightly "loose" fashion. Yet, regular communication, quick feedback, concise paperwork, strong adherence to a few core values, and self-discipline can impose "tight" central control so that nothing gets far out of line.

Application of these "principles" in the best-managed companies tends to produce an environment that fosters entrepreneurial pursuit of new opportunities and adaptation to change. A fluid, flexible structure is the norm—the basic form is stable, but there is frequent reorganization "around the edges." The aim is to keep structure matched to the changing needs of an evolving strategy and to avoid letting the current organization structure become so ingrained and political that it becomes a major obstacle to be hurdled.

Source: Drawn from Thomas J. Peters and Robert H. Waterman, Jr., *In Search of Excellence* (New York: Harper & Row, 1982), especially chaps. 11 and 12.

Building Core Competencies

A good match between structure and strategy is one key facet of organizational capability. But an equally dominant organization-building concern is that of staffing the structure with the requisite managerial talent, specialized skills, and technical expertise—and, most particularly, staffing in a manner calculated to give the firm a clear edge over rivals in performing one or more critical activities. *When it is difficult or impossible to outstrategize rivals (beat them with a superior strategy), the other main avenue to industry leadership is to outexecute them (beat them with superior strategy implementation).* Superior strategy execution is essential in situations where rivals have very similar strategies and can readily imitate one another's strategic maneuvers. Building core competencies and organizational capabilities that rivals can't match is one of the best ways to outexecute them. This is why one of top management's most important strategy-implementing tasks is to guide the building of core competencies in competitively important ways.[14] Core competencies can relate to any strategically relevant factor: greater proficiency in product development, better manufacturing know-how, the capability to provide customers better after-sale services, an ability to respond quickly to changing customer requirements, superior ability to minimize costs, an ability to re-engineer and redesign products more quickly than rivals, superior inventory management capabilities, better marketing and merchandising skills, or greater effectiveness in promoting union-management cooperation.

However, core competencies don't just appear naturally. They have to be deliberately developed and consciously nurtured. For core competencies to emerge from organization-building actions, strategy implementers have to build a critical mass of technical skills and capabilities in those subunits where superior performance of strategically critical tasks can mean greater strategic success. Usually, this means (1) giving above-average operating budgets to strategy-critical tasks and activities, (2) seeing that these areas are staffed with high-caliber managerial and technical talent, (3) insisting on high standards in performing these tasks/activities, backed up with a policy of rewarding people for outstanding results. In effect, strategy implementers must take actions to see that the organization is staffed with enough of the right kinds of people and that these people have the budgets, the administrative support, and the incentive rewards needed to generate the desired competencies and competitive capabilities.

Distinctive internal skills and capabilities are not easily duplicated by rivals; any competitive advantage that results is likely to be sustainable for some time, thus paving the way for above- average performance. Conscious management attention to building strategically relevant internal skills and strengths into the overall organizational scheme is therefore one of the central tasks of organization-building and effective strategy implementation.

Employee Training   Employee training and retraining are important parts of the strategy implementation process when a company shifts to a strategy requiring different skills, managerial approaches, and operating methods. Training is also strategically important in organizational efforts to build skills-based competencies. And it is a key activity in businesses where technical know-how is changing so rapidly that a company loses its ability to compete unless its skilled people are kept updated and maintain their cutting-edge expertise. Successful strategy implementers see that the training function is adequately funded and that effective training programs are in place. Normally, training should be near the top of the action agenda because it needs to be done early in the strategy implementation process.

Strategic Management Principle

Building core competencies and organizational capabilities that rivals can't match is a sound basis for sustainable competitive advantage.

---

[14]C. K. Prahalad and Gary Hamel, "The Core Competence of the Corporation," *Harvard Business Review* 68 (May–June 1990), pp. 79–93.

Selecting People for Key Positions

Assembling a capable management team is also part of the strategy implementation task. Companies must decide what kind of core management team they need to carry out the strategy and find the right people to fill each slot. Sometimes the existing management team is suitable; sometimes it needs to be strengthened and/or expanded by promoting qualified people from within or by bringing in skilled managers from outside to help infuse fresh ideas and approaches. In turnaround and rapid-growth situations, and in instances where a company doesn't have the necessary type of management skills in-house, recruiting outsiders for key management slots is a fairly standard organization-building approach.

The important skill in assembling a core executive group is discerning what mix of backgrounds, experiences, know-how, values, beliefs, styles of managing, and personalities will contribute to successful strategy execution. As with any kind of team-building, it is important to put together a compatible group of skilled managers. The personal "chemistry" needs to be right, and the talent base needs to be appropriate for the chosen strategy. Molding a solid management team is an essential organization-building function—often the first strategy implementation step to take.[15] Until all the key slots are filled with the right people, it is hard for strategy implementation to proceed at full speed.

A strong management team with the right personal chemistry and mix of skills must be put together early in the implementation process.

LINKING BUDGETS WITH STRATEGY

Keeping an organization on the strategy implementation path thrusts a manager squarely into the budgeting process. Not only must a strategy implementer oversee "who gets how much," but the budget must also be put together with an equal concern for "getting the biggest bang for the buck."

Obviously, organizational units need enough resources to carry out their part of the strategic plan. This includes having enough of the right kinds of people and sufficient operating funds for them to do their work successfully. Moreover, organizational units need to: (1) set up detailed, step-by-step action programs for putting each piece of the strategy into place, (2) establish schedules and deadlines for accomplishment, and (3) designate who is responsible for what by when.

How well a strategy implementer links budget allocations to the needs of strategy can either promote or impede the implementation process. With too little funding, organizational units can't execute their part of the strategic plan proficiently. Too much funding wastes organizational resources and reduces financial performance. Both outcomes argue for the strategy implementer to be deeply involved in the budgeting process, closely reviewing the programs and budget proposals of strategy-critical subunits.

Strategic Management Principle
Depriving strategy-critical organizational units of the funds needed to execute their part of the strategic plan can undermine the implementation process.

Implementers must also be willing to shift resources when strategy changes. A change in strategy nearly always calls for budget reallocation. Units important in the old strategy may now be oversized and overfunded. Units that now have a bigger and more critical strategic role may need more people,

---

[15]For a fuller discussion of the top management team's strategic role, see Donald C. Hambrick, "The Top Management Team: Key to Strategic Success," *California Management Review* 30, no. 1 (Fall 1987), pp. 88–108.

new equipment, additional facilities, and above-average increases in their operating budgets. The strategy implementer must engineer reallocations, downsizing some areas, upsizing others, and steering ample resources into particularly critical activities. *Strategy must drive how budget allocations are made.* Underfunding organizational units essential for strategic success can defeat the whole implementation process.

Successful strategy implementers are good resource reallocators. For example, at Harris Corporation, one element of strategy is to diffuse research ideas into areas that are commercially viable. Top management regularly shifts groups of engineers out of government projects and moves them (as a group) into new commercial venture divisions. Boeing has a similar approach to reallocating ideas and talent; according to one Boeing officer, "We can do it [create a big new unit] in two weeks. We couldn't do it in two years at International Harvester."[16] A fluid, flexible approach to reorganization and reallocation of people and budgets is key to successful implementation of strategic change.

Fine-tuning existing strategy usually involves less reallocation and more extrapolation. Big movements of people and money from one area to another are seldom necessary. Fine-tuning can usually be accomplished by incrementally increasing or decreasing the budgets and staffing of existing organization units. The chief exception occurs where a prime strategy ingredient is to generate fresh, new products and business opportunities from within. Then, as attractive ventures "bubble up" from below, major decisions have to be made regarding budgets and staffing. Companies like 3M, GE, Boeing, IBM, and Digital Equipment shift resources and people from area to area on an "as-needed" basis to support budding ideas and ventures. They empower "product champions" and small groups of would-be entrepreneurs by giving them financial and technical support and by setting up organizational units and programs to help new ventures blossom more quickly.

PUTTING INTERNAL ADMINISTRATIVE SUPPORT SYSTEMS IN PLACE

A third key task of strategy implementation is to install internal administrative support systems that fit the needs of strategy. The specific considerations here are:

1. What kinds of strategy-facilitating policies and procedures to establish.
2. How to enhance organizational capabilities via the installation of new or enhanced administrative and operating systems.
3. How to get the right strategy-critical information on a timely basis.

Creating Strategy-Supportive Policies and Procedures

Changes in strategy generally call for some changes in how internal activities are conducted and administered. The process of changing from old ways to new has to be initiated and managed. Asking people to change their actions always "upsets" the internal order of things. It is normal for pockets of resis-

---

[16]Peters and Waterman, *In Search of Excellence*, p. 125.

tance to emerge and questions to be raised about the *hows* as well as the whys of change. The role of new and revised policies is to promulgate "standard operating procedures" that will (1) channel individual and group efforts in the right direction and (2) counteract any tendencies for parts of the organization to resist or reject the actions needed to make the strategy work. Policies and procedures help enforce strategy implementation in several ways:

1. Policy institutionalizes strategy-supportive practices and operating procedures throughout the organization, thus pushing day-to-day activities in the direction of efficient strategy execution.

2. Policy limits independent action and discretionary decisions and behavior. By stating procedures for how things are to be handled, policy communicates what is expected, guides strategy-related activities in particular directions, and restricts unwanted variations.

3. Policy helps align actions and behaviors with strategy, thereby minimizing zigzag decisions and conflicting practices and establishing more regularity, stability, and dependability in how the organization is attempting to make the strategy work.

4. Policy helps to shape the character of the working environment and to translate the corporate philosophy into how things are done, how people are treated, and what corporate beliefs and attitudes mean in terms of everyday activities. Policy operationalizes the corporate philosophy, helping establish a fit between corporate culture and strategy.

Managers need to be inventive in establishing policies to support a strategic plan. McDonald's policy manual, in an attempt to boost quality and service, spells out such detailed procedures as: "Cooks must turn, never flip, hamburgers. If they haven't been purchased, Big Macs must be discarded 10 minutes after being cooked and french fries 7 minutes. Cashiers must make eye contact with and smile at every customer." At Delta Airlines, it is corporate policy to test all applicants for flight attendants' positions for friendliness, cooperativeness, and teamwork. Caterpillar Tractor has a policy of guaranteeing 48-hour parts delivery anywhere in the world; if it fails to fulfill the promise, it supplies the part free. Hewlett-Packard requires R&D people to visit customers to learn about their problems, talk about new-product applications, and, in general, keep the company's R&D programs customer-oriented.

Thus there is a definite role for policies and procedures in the strategy implementation process. Wisely constructed policies and procedures help enforce strategy implementation by channeling actions, behavior, decisions, and practices in directions that promote effective strategy execution. When policies aren't strategy-supportive, they become obstacles and there is risk that people who disagree with the strategy will hide behind outdated policies to thwart the strategic plan. On the other hand, instituting policies that promote strategy-supportive behavior builds organization commitment to the strategic plan and creates a tighter fit between corporate culture and strategy.

None of this is meant to imply, however, that a huge manual full of policies is called for. Too much policy can be as stifling as wrong policy or as chaotic as no policy. Sometimes, the best policy for implementing strategy is a willingness to let subordinates do it any way they want if it makes sense and works. A little "structured chaos" can be a good thing when individual creativity is more essential to strategy than standardization and strict conformity. When Rene McPherson became CEO at Dana Corp., he dramatically threw out 22½ inches of policy manuals and replaced them with a one-page statement of philosophy focusing on "productive people."[17] Creating a strong supportive fit between strategy and policy can mean more policies, fewer policies, or different policies. It can mean policies that require things to be done a certain way or policies that give employees the autonomy to do the job the way they think best.

Installing Support Systems

Strategic Management Principle

An innovative, state-of-the-art support system can be a basis for competitive advantage if it gives the firm capabilities that rivals can't match.

Effective strategy execution typically involves developing a number of support systems. An airline, for example, cannot function without a computerized reservation system, a baggage handling system at every airport it serves, and a strong aircraft maintenance program. A supermarket that stocks 17,000 different items has to have systems for tracking inventories, maintaining shelf freshness, and allocating shelf space among fast-selling and slow-selling items. A company that manufactures many models and sizes of its product must have a sophisticated cost accounting system to price each item intelligently and know which items generate the biggest profit contribution. In businesses where large number of employees need cutting-edge technical know-how, companies have to install systems to train and retrain employees regularly and keep them supplied with up-to-date information. Fast-growing companies have to develop employee recruiting systems to attract and hire qualified employees in large numbers. Well-conceived, state-of-the-art support systems not only facilitate better strategy execution, they also can strengthen organizational capabilities enough to provide a competitive edge over rivals.

Strategy implementers must be alert to what specific support systems their company needs to execute its strategy successfully. A company with a strategy of superior quality, for example, must develop superior methods for quality control. A company whose strategy is to be a low-cost producer must develop systems to enforce tight cost containment. If the present administrative support and operating systems are inadequate, resources must be allocated to improve them. Illustration Capsule 24 describes the administrative support systems put in place at Mrs. Fields Cookies.

Instituting Formal Reporting of Strategic Information

Accurate, timely information allows strategists to monitor progress and take corrective actions promptly.

Accurate information is an essential guide to action. Every organization needs a system for gathering and reporting strategy-critical information. Information is needed *before* actions are completed to steer them to successful conclusion in case the early steps don't produce the intended outcome and need to be modified. Monitoring the outcomes of the first round of implementation actions (1) allows early detection of need to adjust either the strategy or how it is being implemented and (2) provides some assurance that things are moving ahead as planned.[18] Early experiences are sometimes difficult to assess, but

---

[17]Ibid., p. 65.

[18]Boris Yavitz and William H. Newman, *Strategy in Action* (New York: Free Press, 1982), pp. 209–10.

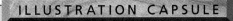

ILLUSTRATION CAPSULE
24

STRATEGY IMPLEMENTATION AT MRS. FIELDS COOKIES, INC.

In 1988 Mrs. Fields Cookies was one of the fastest growing specialty foods companies in the United States. Sales in 1987 were $150 million, up from $87 million in 1986. The company had over 400 Mrs. Fields outlets in operation and over 250 outlets retailing other bakery and cookie products. Debbi Fields, age 31, was the company's founder and CEO. Her business concept for Mrs. Fields Cookies was "to serve absolutely fresh, warm cookies as though you'd stopped by my house and caught me just taking a batch from the oven." Cookies not sold within two hours were removed from the case and given to charity. The company's major form of advertising was sampling; store employees walked around the shopping mall giving away cookie samples. People were hired for store crews on the basis of warmth, friendliness, and the ability to have a good time giving away samples, baking fresh batches, and talking to customers during the course of a sale.

To implement its strategy, the company developed several novel practices and a customized computer support system. One key practice was giving each store an *hourly* sales quota. Another was for Fields to make unannounced visits to her stores, where she masqueraded as a casual shopper to test the enthusiasm and sales techniques of store crews, sample the quality of the cookies they were baking, and observe customer reactions; she visited each outlet once or twice annually.

Debbi's husband Randy developed a software program that kept headquarters and stores in close contact. Via the computer network, each store manager receives a daily sales goal (broken down by the hour) based on the store's recent performance history and on such special factors as special promotions, mall activities, weekdays vs. weekends, holiday shopping patterns, and the weather forecast. With the hourly sales quotas also comes a schedule of the number of cookies to bake and when to bake them. As the day progresses, store managers type in actual hourly sales figures and customer counts. If customer counts are up but sales are lagging, the computer is programmed to recommend more aggressive sampling or more suggestive selling. If it becomes obvious the day is going to be a bust for the store, the computer automatically revises the sales projections for the day, reducing hourly quotas and instructing how much to cut back cookie baking. To facilitate crew scheduling by the store manager, sales projections are also provided for two weeks in advance. All job applicants must sit at the store's terminal and answer a computerized set of questions as part of the interview process.

In addition, the computer software contains a menu giving store staff immediate access to company personnel policies, maintenance schedules for store equipment, and repair instructions. If a store manager has a specific problem, it can be entered on the system and routed to the appropriate person. Messages can be sent directly to Debbi Fields via the computer; even if she is on a store inspection trip, her promise is to respond to all inquiries within 48 hours.

The computerized information support system serves several objectives: (1) it gives store managers more time to work with their crews and achieve sales quotas as opposed to handling administrative chores and (2) it gives headquarters instantaneous information on store performance and a means of controlling store operations. Debbi Fields sees the system as a tool for projecting her influence and enthusiasm into more stores more frequently than she could otherwise reach.

Source: Developed from information in Mike Korologos, "Debbi Fields," *Sky Magazine,* July 1988, pp. 42–50.

they yield the first hard data from the action front and should be closely scrutinized as a basis for corrective action.

Information systems need to be more comprehensive than just monitoring the first signs of progress. All key strategic performance indicators have to be tracked as often as practical. Many retail companies generate daily sales reports for each store and maintain up-to-the-minute inventory and sales records on each item. Manufacturing plants typically generate daily production reports and track labor productivity on every shift. Monthly profit-and-loss statements are common, as are monthly statistical summaries.

In designing formal reports to monitor strategic progress, five guidelines should be observed:[19]

1. Information and reporting systems should involve no more data and reporting than is needed to give a reliable picture of what is going on. The data gathered should emphasize strategically meaningful variables and symptoms of potentially significant developments. Temptations to supplement "what managers need to know" with other "interesting" but marginally useful information should be avoided.

2. Reports and statistical data-gathering have to be timely—not too late to take corrective action or so often as to overburden.

3. The flow of information and statistics should be kept simple. Complicated reports are likely to confound and obscure because of the attention that has to be paid to mechanics, procedures, and interpretive guidelines instead of measuring and reporting the really critical variables.

4. Information and reporting systems should aim at "no surprises" and generating "early-warnings signs" rather than just producing information. Reports don't necessarily need wide distribution, but they should always be provided to managers who are in a position to act when trouble signs appear.

5. Statistical reports should make it easy to flag big or unusual variances from plan, thus directing management attention to significant departures from targeted performance.

Statistical information gives the strategy implementer a feel for the numbers; reports and meetings provide a feel for new developments and problems; and personal contacts add a feel for the people dimension. All are good barometers of overall performance and good indicators of which things are on and off track. Identifying deviations from plan and the problem areas to be addressed are prerequisites for initiating any actions to either improve implementation or fine-tune strategy.

KEY POINTS

The job of strategy implementation is to translate plans into actions and achieve the intended results. The test of successful strategy implementation is whether actual organization performance matches or exceeds the targets spelled out in the strategic plan. Shortfalls in performance signal weak strategy, weak implementation, or both.

In deciding how to implement strategy, managers have to determine what internal conditions are needed to execute the strategic plan successfully. Then

[19]Drucker, *Management*, pp. 498–504; Harold Hoontz, "Management Control: A Suggested Formulation of Principles," *California Management Review* 2, no. 2 (Winter 1959), pp. 50–55; and William H. Sihler, "Toward Better Management Control Systems," *California Management Review* 14, no. 2 (Winter 1971), pp. 33–39.

they must create these conditions as rapidly as practical. The process involves creating a series of tight fits:

- Between strategy and organization structure.
- Between strategy and the organization's skills and competencies.
- Between strategy and budget allocations.
- Between strategy and internal policies, procedures, and support systems.
- Between strategy and the reward structure.
- Between strategy and the corporate culture.

The tighter the fits, the more powerful strategy execution becomes and the more likely targeted performance can actually be achieved.

Implementing strategy is not just a top management function; it is a job for the whole management team. All managers function as strategy implementers in their respective areas of authority and responsibility. All managers have to consider what actions to take in their areas to achieve the intended results—they each need an *action agenda*.

The three major components of organization-building are (1) deciding how to organize and what the organization chart should look like, (2) developing the skills and competencies needed to execute the strategy successfully, and (3) filling key positions with the right people. All organization structures have strategic advantages and disadvantages; there is no one best way to organize. In choosing a structure, the guiding principles are to make strategy-critical activities the major building blocks, keep the design simple, and put decision-making authority in the hands of managers closest to the action. Functional and geographic organization structures are well suited to single-business companies. SBU structures are well suited to companies pursuing related diversification. Decentralized business-unit structures are well suited to companies pursuing unrelated diversification. Project teams, task forces, and new venture teams can also be useful organizational mechanisms to handle temporary or one-time strategic initiatives.

The other two aspects of organization-building—skills development and filling key positions—are just as important as matching structure to strategy. Taking action to develop strategy-supportive skills and create a distinctive competence not only strengthens execution but also helps build competitive advantage. Selecting the right people for key positions tends to be one of the earliest strategy implementation steps because it takes a full complement of capable managers to put the strategy into operation and make it work.

Reworking the budget to make it more strategy-supportive is a crucial part of the implementation process because every organization unit needs to have the people, equipment, facilities, and other resources to carry out its part of the strategic plan (but no *more* than what it really needs!). Strategy implementation often entails shifting resources from one area to another—downsizing units that are overstaffed and overfunded and upsizing those more critical to strategic success.

A third key implementation task is to install some necessary support systems—policies and procedures to establish desired types of behavior, information systems to provide strategy-critical information on a timely basis, and whatever inventory, materials management, customer service, cost accounting, and other administrative systems are needed to give the organization important strategy-executing capability.

In the next chapter, we examine the remaining three key tasks of the strategy implementation process: designing the reward system, creating a strategy-supportive corporate culture, and exercising strategic leadership.

SUGGESTED
READINGS

Aaker, David A. "Managing Assets and Skills: The Key to a Sustainable Competitive Advantage." *California Management Review* 31 (Winter 1989), pp. 91–106.

Bartlett, Christopher A., and Sumantra Ghoshal. "Matrix Management: Not a Structure, a Frame of Mind." *Harvard Business Review* 68, no. 4 (July–August 1990), pp. 138–45.

Bettis, Richard A., and William K. Hall. "The Business Portfolio Approach—Where It Falls Down in Practice." *Long Range Planning* 16, no. 2 (April 1983), pp. 95–104.

Chandler, Alfred D. *Strategy and Structure.* Cambridge, Mass.: MIT Press, 1962.

Hall, William K. "SBUs: Hot, New Topic in the Management of Diversification." *Business Horizons* 21, no. 1 (February 1978), pp. 17–25.

Hambrick, Donald C. "The Top Management Team: Key to Strategic Success." *California Management Review* 30, no. 1 (Fall 1987), pp. 88–108.

Larson, Erik W., and David H. Gobeli. "Matrix Management: Contradictions and Insights." *California Management Review* 29, no. 4 (Summer 1987), pp. 126–27.

Leontiades, Milton. "Choosing the Right Manager to Fit the Strategy." *Journal of Business Strategy* 3, no. 2 (Fall 1981), pp. 58–69.

Mintzberg, Henry. "Organization Design: Fashion or Fit." *Harvard Business Review* 59, no. 1 (January–February 1981), pp. 103–16.

Paulson, Robert D. "Making It Happen: The Real Strategic Challenge." *The McKinsey Quarterly,* Winter 1982, pp. 58–66.

Peters, Thomas J., and Robert H. Waterman, Jr. *In Search of Excellence.* New York: Harper & Row, 1982.

Powell, Walter W. "Hybrid Organizational Arrangements: New Form or Transitional Development?" *California Management Review* 30, no. 1 (Fall 1987), pp. 67–87.

Prahalad, C. K., and Gary Hamel. "The Core Competence of the Corporation." *Harvard Business Review* 68 (May–June 1990), pp. 79–93.

Waterman, Robert H.; Thomas J. Peters; and Julien R. Phillips. "Structure Is Not Organization." *Business Horizons* 23, no. 3 (June 1980), pp. 14–26.

Implementing Strategy
Commitment, Culture, and Leadership

---

*Weak leadership can wreck the soundest strategy; forceful execution of even a poor
plan can often bring victory.*
Sun Zi

Effective leaders do not just reward achievement, they celebrate it.
Shelley A. Kirkpatrick and Edwin A. Locke

---

*Ethics is the moral courage to do what we know is right, and not to do
what we know is wrong.*
C. J. Silas
CEO, Philips Petroleum

. . . a leader lives in the field with his troops.
H. Ross Perot

In the previous chapter, we examined three of the strategy-implementer's
tasks—building a capable organization, steering resources into strategy-
critical programs and activities, and creating a series of internal support
systems to enable better execution. In this chapter, we explore the three
remaining implementation tasks: designing rewards and incentives for carrying out the strategy, creating a strategy-supportive corporate culture, and
exercising strategic leadership.

DEVELOPING AN EFFECTIVE REWARD STRUCTURE

The strategy-implementer's challenge is to design a reward structure that motivates people to do the things it takes to make the strategy work successfully.

It is important for organizational subunits and individuals to be committed to implementing strategy and accomplishing strategic objectives. Companies typically try to solidify organizationwide commitment through motivation, incentives, and rewards for good performance. The range of options includes all the standard reward-punishment techniques—salary raises, bonuses, stock options, fringe benefits, promotions, fear of being "sidelined," praise, recognition, constructive criticism, tension, peer pressure, more (or less) responsibility, increased (or decreased) job control and decision-making autonomy, attractive geographic assignments, group acceptance, and opportunities for personal satisfaction. But rewards have to be used *creatively* and tightly linked to the factors necessary for good strategy execution.

Motivational Practices

Successful strategy-implementers are good at inspiring employees to do their best. They are skilled at getting employees to buy in to the strategy and commit to making it work. They work at devising strategy-supportive motivational approaches and using them effectively. Consider some actual examples:[1]

Part of a strategy-implementer's job is to devise motivational techniques that build wholehearted commitment and winning attitudes among employees.

- At Mars, Inc. (best known for its candy bars), every employee, including the president, gets a weekly 10 percent bonus by coming to work on time each day that week. This on-time incentive is based on minimizing absenteeism and tardiness to boost worker productivity and to produce the greatest number of candy bars during each available minute of machine time.
- In a number of Japanese companies, employees meet regularly to hear inspirational speeches, sing company songs, and chant the corporate litany. In the United States, Tupperware conducts a weekly Monday night rally to honor, applaud, and fire up its salespeople who conduct Tupperware parties. Amway and Mary Kay Cosmetics hold similar inspirational get-togethers for their sales force organizations.
- A San Diego area company assembles its 2,000 employees at its six plants the first thing every workday to listen to a management talk about the state of the company. Then they engage in brisk calisthenics. This company's management believes "that by doing one thing together each day, it reinforces the unity of the company. It's also fun. It gets the blood up." Managers take turns making the presentations. Many of the speeches "are very personal and emotional, not approved beforehand or screened by anybody."
- Texas Instruments and Dana Corp. insist that teams and divisions set their own goals and have regular peer reviews.
- Procter & Gamble's brand managers are asked to compete fiercely against each other; the official policy is "a free-for-all among brands with no holds barred." P&G's system of purposeful internal competition breeds people who love to compete and excel. Those who "win" become corporate "heroes." Around them emerges a folklore of "war stories" of

---

[1]The list that follows is abstracted from Thomas J. Peters and Robert H. Waterman, Jr., *In Search of Excellence* (New York: Harper & Row, 1982), pp. xx, 213–14, 276, and 285.

their valiant uphill struggles against great odds to make a market success out of their assigned brands.

These motivational approaches accentuate the positive; others blend positive and negative features. Consider the way Harold Geneen, former president and chief executive officer of ITT, allegedly combined the use of money, tension, and fear:

> Geneen provides his managers with enough incentives to make them tolerate the system. Salaries all the way through ITT are higher than average—Geneen reckons 10 percent higher—so that few people can leave without taking a drop. As one employee put it: "We're all paid just a bit more than we think we're worth." At the very top, where the demands are greatest, the salaries and stock options are sufficient to compensate for the rigors. As some said, "He's got them by their limousines."
>
> Having bound his men to him with chains of gold, Geneen can induce the tension that drives the machine. "The key to the system," one of his men explains, "is the profit forecast. Once the forecast has been gone over, revised, and agreed on, the managing director has a personal commitment to Geneen to carry it out. That's how he produces the tension on which the success depends." The tension goes through the company, inducing ambition, perhaps exhilaration, but always with some sense of fear: what happens if the target is missed?[2]

If a strategy-implementer's use of rewards and punishments induces too much tension, anxiety, and job insecurity, the results can be counterproductive. Yet implementers should not completely eliminate tension, pressure for performance, and anxiety from the implementation process. There is, for example, no evidence that a no-pressure work environment leads to superior strategy execution. High-performing organizations need a cadre of ambitious people who relish the opportunity to succeed, love a challenge, thrive in a performance-oriented environment, and find some competition and pressure useful to satisfy their own drives for personal recognition, accomplishment, and self-satisfaction. There has to be some meaningful incentive and career consequences associated with implementation or few people will attach much significance to the strategic plan.

Rewards and Incentives

The conventional view is that a manager's plan for strategy implementation should incorporate more positive than negative motivational elements because when cooperation is positively enlisted and rewarded, people tend to respond with more enthusiasm and effort. Nevertheless, how much of which incentives to use depends on how hard the strategy implementation task will be. A manager has to do more than just talk to everyone about how important strategy implementation is to the organization's future well-being. Talk, no matter how inspiring, seldom commands people's best efforts for long. To get employees' sustained, energetic commitment, management almost always has to be resourceful in designing and using incentives. The more a manager understands what motivates subordinates and the more he or she relies on motivational incentives as a tool for implementing strategy, the greater will be employees' commitment to carrying out the strategic plan.

Positive motivational approaches generally work better than negative ones.

[2]Anthony Sampson, *The Sovereign State of ITT* (New York: Stein and Day, 1973), p. 132.

Linking Work Assignments to Performance Targets   The first step in creating a strategy-supportive system of rewards and incentives is to define jobs and assignments in terms of the *results to be accomplished*, not the duties and functions to be performed. Training the job holder's attention and energy on what to *achieve* as opposed to what to do improves the chances of reaching the agreed-on objectives. It is flawed thinking to stress duties and activities in job descriptions in hopes that the by-products will be the desired kinds of accomplishment. In any job, performing activities is not equivalent to achieving objectives. Working hard, staying busy, and diligently attending to assigned duties do not guarantee results. As any student knows, just because an instructor teaches doesn't mean students are learning. Teaching and learning are different things—the first is an activity and the second is a result.

Emphasizing what to accomplish—i.e., performance targets for individual jobs, work groups, departments, businesses, and the entire company—makes the whole work environment results-oriented. Without target objectives, people and organizations can become so engrossed in doing their duties and performing assigned functions on schedule that they lose sight of what the tasks are intended to accomplish. By keeping the spotlight on achievement and targeted performance, strategy-implementers take proactive steps to make the right things happen rather than passively hoping they will happen (this, of course, is what "managing by objectives" is all about).

Creating a tight fit between work assignments and accomplishing the strategic plan thus goes straight to the objectives and performance targets spelled out in the strategic plan. If the details of strategy have been fleshed out thoroughly from the corporate level down to the operating level, performance targets exist for the whole company, for each business unit, for each functional department, and for each operating unit. These become the targets that strategy-implementers aim at achieving and the basis for deciding how many jobs and what skills, expertise, funding, and time frame it will take to achieve them.

Usually a number of performance measures are needed at each level; rarely does a single measure suffice. At the corporate and line-of-business levels, typical performance measures include profitability (measured in terms of total profit, return on equity investment, return on total assets, return on sales, operating profit, and so on), market share, growth rates in sales and profits, and hard evidence that competitive position and future prospects have improved. In the manufacturing area, strategy-relevant performance measures may focus on unit manufacturing costs, productivity increases, production and shipping schedules, quality control, the number and extent of work stoppages due to labor disagreements and equipment breakdowns, and so on. In the marketing area, measures may include unit selling costs, increases in dollar sales and unit volume, sales penetration of each target customer group, increases in market share, the success of newly introduced products, the severity of customer complaints, advertising effectiveness, and the number of new accounts acquired. While most performance measures are quantitative, several have elements of subjectivity—labor-management relations, employee morale, customer satisfaction, advertising success, and how far the firm is ahead or behind rivals on quality, service, and technological capability.

Rewarding Performance   The only dependable way to keep people focused on strategic objectives and to make achieving them "a way of life" throughout the organization is to reward individuals who achieve targets and deny rewards to those who don't. For strategy-implementers, "doing a good job" needs to mean "achieving the agreed-on performance targets." Any other standard undermines implementation of the strategic plan and condones the diversion of time and energy into activities that don't matter much (if such activities are really important, they deserve a place in the strategic plan). The pressure to achieve the targeted strategic performance should be unrelenting. A "no excuses" standard has to prevail.[3]

Strategic Management Principle
The strategy-implementer's standard for judging whether individuals and units have done a good job must be whether they achieved their performance targets.

But with pressure to perform must come ample rewards. Without a payoff, the system breaks down, and the strategy-implementer is left with the unworkable options of barking orders or pleading for compliance. Some of the most successful companies—Wal-Mart Stores, Nucor Steel, Lincoln Electric, Electronic Data Systems, Remington Products, and Mary Kay Cosmetics—owe much of their success to incentive and reward systems that induce people to do the very things needed to hit performance targets and execute strategy. Nucor's strategy was (and is) to be *the* low-cost producer of steel products. Because labor costs are a significant portion of total cost in the steel business, successful implementation of such a strategy required Nucor to achieve lower labor costs per ton of steel than competitors. To drive its labor costs per ton below rivals, Nucor management introduced production incentives that gave workers a bonus roughly equal to their regular wages provided their production teams met or exceeded weekly production targets; the regular wage scale was set at levels comparable to other manufacturing jobs in the local areas where Nucor had plants. Bonuses were paid every two weeks based on the prior weeks' actual production levels measured against the target. The results of Nucor's piece-rate incentive plan were impressive. Nucor's labor productivity (in output per worker) was more than double the average of the unionized work forces of the industry's major producers. Nucor enjoyed about a $100 per ton cost advantage over large, integrated steel producers like U.S. Steel and Bethlehem Steel (a substantial part of which came from its labor cost advantage), and Nucor workers were the highest paid workers in the steel industry. At Remington Products, only 65 percent of factory workers' paychecks is salary; the rest is based on piece-work incentives. The company inspects all products and counts rejected items against incentive pay for the responsible worker. Top-level managers earn more from bonuses than from their salaries. During the first four years of Remington's incentive program, productivity rose 17 percent.

These and other experiences demonstrate some important lessons about designing rewards and incentives:

There are some important guidelines to observe in designing rewards and incentives.

1. *The performance payoff must be a major, not minor, piece of the total compensation package*—incentives that amount to 20 percent or more of total compensation are big attention-getters and are capable of driving individual effort.

2. *The incentive plan should extend to all managers and all workers*, not just be restricted to top management (why should all workers and managers work their tails off and hit performance targets so a few senior executives can get lucrative rewards?).

3. *The system must be administered with scrupulous care and fairness*—if performance standards are set unrealistically high or if individual

---

[3]Tom Peters and Nancy Austin, *A Passion for Excellence* (New York: Random House, 1985), p. xix.

performance evaluations are not accurate and well-documented, dissatisfaction and disgruntlement with the system will overcome any positive benefits.

4. *The incentives must be tightly linked to achieving only those performance targets spelled out in the strategic plan*—performance evaluations based on factors not related to the strategy signal that either the strategic plan is incomplete (because important performance targets were left out) or the real managerial action agenda is something other than what was stated in the strategic plan.

5. *The performance targets each individual is expected to achieve should involve outcomes that the individual can personally affect*—the role of incentives is to enhance individual commitment and channel behavior in beneficial directions. This role is not well-served when the performance measures an individual is judged by are outside his/her arena of influence.

Aside from these general guidelines it is hard to prescribe what kinds of incentives and rewards to develop except to say that the payoff must be directly attached to performance measures that indicate the strategy is working and implementation is on track. If the company's strategy is to be a low-cost producer, the incentive system must reward performance that lowers costs. If the company has a differentiation strategy predicated on superior quality and service, the incentive system must reward such outcomes as zero defects, infrequent need for product repair, low numbers of customer complaints, and speedy order processing and delivery. If a company's growth is predicated on a strategy of new-product introduction, incentives should be based on the percentages of revenues and profits coming from new products.

Why the Performance-Reward Link Is Important

Strategic Management Principle

The reward structure is management's most powerful strategy-implementing tool.

The use of incentives and rewards is the single most powerful tool management has to win strong employee commitment to carrying out the strategic plan. Failure to use this tool wisely and powerfully weakens the entire implementation process. *Decisions on salary increases, incentive compensation, promotions, key assignments, and the ways and means of awarding praise and recognition are the strategy-implementer's foremost attention-getting, commitment-generating devices.* How a manager structures incentives and parcels out rewards signals what sort of behavior and performance management wants and who is doing a good job. Such matters seldom escape the scrutiny of every employee. The system of incentives and rewards thus ends up as the vehicle by which strategy is emotionally ratified in the form of real commitment. Incentives make it in employees' self-interest to do what is needed to achieve the performance targets spelled out in the strategic plan.

Using Performance Contracts

Creating a tight fit between strategy and the reward structure is generally best accomplished by agreeing on performance objectives, fixing responsibility and deadlines for achieving them, and treating their achievement as a *contract*. Next, the contracted-for strategic performance has to be the *real* basis for designing incentives, evaluating individual efforts, and handing out rewards. To prevent undermining the "managing-with-objectives" approach to strategy implementation, a manager must insist that actual performance be judged against the contracted-for target objectives. Any deviations must be fully explored to determine whether the causes are poor performance or circumstances beyond the individual's control. And all managers need to understand how their rewards have been calculated. In short, managers at all levels have to be held accountable for carrying out their part of the strategic plan, and they have to know their rewards are based on their strategic accomplishments (allowing for both the favorable and unfavorable impacts of uncontrollable, unforeseeable, and unknowable circumstances).

BUILDING A STRATEGY-SUPPORTIVE CORPORATE CULTURE

Every organization is a unique culture. It has its own history, its own ways of approaching problems and conducting activities, its own mix of managerial personalities and styles, its own patterns of "how we do things around here," its own set of war stories and heroes, its own experiences of how changes have been instituted—in other words, its own atmosphere, folklore, and personality. A company's culture can be weak and fragmented in the sense that most people have no deepfelt sense of company purpose, view their jobs as simply a way to make money, and have divided loyalties—some to their department, some to their colleagues, some to the union, and some to their boss.[4] On the other hand, a company's culture can be strong and cohesive in the sense that most people understand the company's objectives and strategy, know what their individual roles are, and work conscientiously to do their part. A strong culture is a powerful lever for channeling behavior and helping employees do their jobs in a more strategy-supportive manner; this occurs in two ways:[5]

Basic Concept
Corporate culture refers to a company's inner values, beliefs, rituals, operating style, and political-social atmosphere.

- By knowing exactly what is expected of them, employees in strong-culture firms don't have to waste time figuring out what to do or how to do it—the culture provides a system of informal rules and peer pressures regarding how to behave most of the time. In a weak-culture company, the absence of strong company identity and a purposeful work climate results in substantial employee confusion and wasted effort.

Strategic Management Principle
A strong culture and a tight strategy-culture fit are powerful levers for influencing people to do their jobs better.

- A strong culture turns a job into a way of life; it provides structure, standards, and a value system in which to operate; and it promotes strong company identification among employees. As a result, employees feel better about what they do, and more often than not, they work harder to help the company become more successful.

This says something important about the leadership task of strategy implementation: *to implement and execute a strategic plan, an organization's culture must be closely aligned with its strategy.* The optimal condition is a work environment

---

[4]Terrence E. Deal and Allen A. Kennedy, *Corporate Culture* (Reading, Mass.: Addison-Wesley, 1982), p. 4.
[5]Ibid., pp. 15–16.

so in tune with strategy that strategy-critical activities are performed in superior fashion. As one observer noted:

> It has not been just strategy that led to big Japanese wins in the American auto market. It is a culture that enspirits workers to excel at fits and finishes, to produce moldings that match and doors that don't sag. It is a culture in which Toyota can use that most sophisticated of management tools, the suggestion box, and in two years increase the number of worker suggestions from under 10,000 to over 1 million with resultant savings of $250 million.[6]

What Is Corporate Culture?

The taproot of corporate culture is the organization's beliefs and philosophy about how its affairs ought to be conducted—the reasons why it does things the way it does. A company's philosophy and beliefs can be hard to pin down, even harder to characterize. In a sense they are intangible. They are manifest in the values and business principles that senior managers espouse, in the ethical standards they demand, in the policies they set, in the style with which things are done, in the traditions the organization maintains, in people's attitudes and feelings and in the stories they tell, in the peer pressures that exist, in the organization's politics, and in the "chemistry" that surrounds the work environment and defines the organization's culture. We are beginning to learn that an organization's culture is an important contributor (or obstacle) to successful strategy execution. A close culture-strategy match is crucial to managing a company's people resources with maximum effectiveness. A culture that energizes people all over the firm to do their jobs in a strategy-supportive manner adds significantly to the power and effectiveness of strategy execution. When a company's culture and strategy are out of sync, the culture has to be changed as rapidly as possible; a sizable and prolonged strategy-culture conflict weakens and may even defeat managerial efforts to make the strategy work.

Illustration Capsule 25 looks at some of the traits and characteristics of strong-culture companies to provide more insight into why the culture-strategy fit makes such a big difference. While the examples help demonstrate the contribution culture can make toward "keeping the herd moving roughly West" (as Professor Terry Deal puts it), the strategy-implementer's concern is with what actions to take to create a culture that facilitates strategy execution.

Creating the Fit between Strategy and Culture

It is the *strategy-maker's* responsibility to select a strategy compatible with the "sacred" or unchangeable parts of prevailing corporate culture. It is the *strategy-implementer's* task, once strategy is chosen, to bring corporate culture into close alignment with the strategy and keep it there.

Aligning culture with strategy presents a strong challenge. The first step is to diagnose which facets of the present culture are strategy-supportive and which are not. Then, there must be some innovative thinking about concrete actions management can take to modify the cultural environment and create a stronger fit with the strategy.

[6]Robert H. Waterman, Jr., "The Seven Elements of Strategic Fit," *Journal of Business Strategy* 2, no. 3 (Winter 1982), p. 70.

> ## ILLUSTRATION CAPSULE 25
>
> ## TRAITS AND CHARACTERISTICS OF STRONG-CULTURE COMPANIES
>
> To better understand what corporate culture is and why it plays a role in successful strategy execution, consider the distinctive traits and themes of companies with strong cultures:
>
> - At Frito-Lay, stories abound about potato chip route salesmen slogging through sleet, mud, hail, snow, and rain to uphold the 99.5 percent service level to customers in which the entire organization takes such great pride. At McDonald's the constant message from management is the overriding importance of quality, service, cleanliness, and value; employees are drilled over and over on the need for attention to detail and perfecting every fundamental of the business. At Delta Airlines, the culture is driven by "Delta's family feeling" that builds a team spirit and nurtures each employee's cooperative attitude toward others, cheerful outlook toward life, and pride in a job well done. At Johnson & Johnson, the credo is that customers come first, employees second, the community third, and shareholders fourth and last. At DuPont, there is a fixation on safety—a report of every accident must be on the chairman's desk within 24 hours (DuPont's safety record is 17 times better than the chemical industry average and 68 times better than the all-manufacturing average).
>
> - Companies with strong cultures are unashamed collectors and tellers of stories, anecdotes, and legends in support of basic beliefs. L. L. Bean tells customer service stories. 3M tells innovation stories. P&G, Johnson & Johnson, Perdue Farms, and Maytag tell quality stories. From an organizational standpoint, such tales are very important because people in the organization take pride in identifying strongly with the stories, and they start to share in the traditions and values which the stories relate.
>
> - The most typical values and beliefs that shape culture include (1) a belief in being the best (or at GE "better than the best"), (2) a belief in
>
> superior quality and service, (3) a belief in the importance of people as individuals and a faith in their ability to make a strong, positive contribution, (4) a belief in the importance of the details of execution, the nuts and bolts of doing the job well, (5) a belief that customers should reign supreme, (6) a belief in inspiring people, whatever their ability, (7) a belief in the importance of informality to enhance communication, and (8) a recognition that growth and profits are essential to a company's well-being. While the themes are common, however, every company implements them differently (to fit their particular situations), and every company's values are the articulated handiwork of one or two legendary figures in leadership positions. Accordingly, each company has its own distinct culture which, they believe, no one can copy successfully.
>
> - In companies with strong cultures, managers and workers either "buy in" to the culture and accept its norms or they opt out and leave the company.
>
> - The stronger the corporate culture and the more it is directed toward customers and markets, the less a company uses policy manuals, organization charts, and detailed rules and procedures to enforce discipline and norms. The reason is that the guiding values inherent in the culture convey in crystal-clear fashion what everybody is supposed to do in most situations. Often, poorly performing companies have strong cultures too. The difference is that their cultures are dysfunctional, being focused on internal politics or operating by the numbers as opposed to emphasizing customers and the people who make and sell the product.
>
> Companies with strong cultures are clear on what they stand for, and they are serious about the tasks of establishing company values, winning employees over to these values, and causing employees to observe cultural norms religiously.

Source: Compiled from Thomas J. Peters and Robert H. Waterman, Jr., *In Search of Excellence* (New York: Harper & Row, 1982), pp. xxi, 75–77, and 280–85; and Thomas J. Peters and Nancy Austin, *A Passion for Excellence* (New York: Random House, 1985), pp. 282–83 and 334.

Symbolic Actions and Substantive Actions   Normally, managerial actions to tighten the culture-strategy fit are both symbolic and substantive. Symbolic actions are valuable for the signals they send about the kinds of behavior and performance strategy-implementers wish to encourage. The most common symbolic actions are events held to honor new kinds of heroes—people whose actions and performance serve as role models. Many universities give outstanding teacher awards each year to symbolize their commitment to and esteem for instructors who display exceptional classroom talents. Numerous businesses have employee-of-the-month awards. The military has a long-standing custom of awarding ribbons and medals for exemplary actions. Some football coaches award emblems to players to wear on their helmets as symbols of their exceptional performance.

Successful strategy-implementers are experts in the use of symbols to build and nurture the culture. They personally conduct ceremonial events, and they go out of their way to personally and publicly congratulate individuals who exhibit the desired traits. Individuals and groups that "get with the program" are singled out for special praise and visibly rewarded. Successful implementers use every ceremonial function and every conversation to implant values, send reinforcing signals, and praise good deeds.

In addition to being out front, personally leading the push for new attitudes and communicating the reasons for new approaches, the manager has to convince all those concerned that the effort is more than cosmetic. Talk and symbols have to be complemented by substance and real movement. The actions taken have to be credible, highly visible, and unmistakably indicative of management's commitment to a new culture and new ways of doing business. There are several ways to accomplish this. One is to engineer some quick successes in reorienting the way some things are done to highlight the value of the new order, thus making enthusiasm for the changes contagious. However, instant results are usually not as important as creating a solid, competent team psychologically committed to carrying out the strategy in a superior fashion. The strongest signs that management is committed to creating a new culture come from actions to replace traditional managers with "new breed" managers, changes in long-standing policies and operating practices, major reorganizational moves, big shifts in how raises and promotions are granted, and reallocations in the budget.

At the same time, chief strategy-implementers must be careful to *lead by example*. For instance, if the organization's strategy involves a drive to become the industry's low-cost producer, senior managers must be frugal in their own actions and decisions: spartan decorations in the executive suite, conservative expense accounts and entertainment allowances, a lean staff in the corporate office, and so on.

Implanting the needed culture-building values and behavior depends on a sincere, sustained commitment by the chief executive coupled with extraordinary persistence in reinforcing the culture through both word and deed. Neither charisma nor personal magnetism are essential. However, being highly visible around the organization is essential; culture-building cannot be done from an office. Moreover, creating and sustaining a strategy-supportive culture is a job for the whole management team. Senior officers have to keynote the values and shape the organization's philosophy. But for the effort to be successful, strategy-implementers must enlist the support of subordinate

TABLE 10–1	Topics Generally Covered in Values Statements and Codes of Ethics

Topics Covered in Values Statements	Topics Covered in Codes of Ethics
• Importance of customers and customer service	• Honesty and observance of the law
• Commitment of quality	• Conflicts of interest
• Commitment to innovation	• Fairness in selling and marketing practices
• Respect for the individual employee and the duty the company has to employees	• Using inside information and securities trading
• Importance of honesty, integrity, and ethical standards	• Supplier relationships and purchasing practices
• Duty to stockholders	• Payments to obtain business/Foreign Corrupt Practices Act
• Duty to suppliers	• Acquiring and using information about others
• Corporate citizenship	• Political activities
• Importance of protecting the environment	• Use of company assets, resources, and property
	• Protection of proprietary information
	• Pricing, contracting, and billing

managers, getting them to instill values and establish culture norms at the lowest levels in the organization. Until a big majority of employees have joined the culture and share an emotional commitment to its basic values and beliefs, there's considerably more work to be done in both installing the culture and tightening the culture-strategy fit.

The task of making culture supportive of strategy is not a short-term exercise. It takes time for a new culture to emerge and prevail. The bigger the organization and the greater the cultural shift needed to produce a culture-strategy fit, the longer it takes. In large companies, changing the corporate culture in significant ways can take three to five years at minimum. In fact, it is usually tougher to reshape a deeply ingrained culture that is not strategy-supportive than it is to instill a strategy-supportive culture from scratch in a brand new organization.

Establishing Ethical Standards and Values

A strong corporate culture founded on ethical principles and sound values is a vital driving force behind continued strategic success. Many executives are convinced that a company must care about *how* it does business; otherwise it puts its reputation at risk and ultimately its performance. Corporate ethics and values programs are not window-dressing; they are undertaken to create an environment of strongly held values and convictions and to make ethical conduct a way of life. Strong values and high ethical standards nurture the corporate culture in a very positive way.

An ethical corporate culture has a positive impact on a company's long-term strategic success; an unethical culture can undermine it.

Companies establish values and ethical standards in a number of different ways.[7] Firms steeped in tradition with a rich folklore to draw on rely on word-of-mouth indoctrination and the power of tradition to instill values and enforce ethical conduct. But many companies today set forth their values and code of ethics in written documents. Table 10–1 shows the kinds of

---

[7]The Business Roundtable, *Corporate Ethics: A Prime Asset*, February 1988, pp. 4–10.

ILLUSTRATION CAPSULE
26

THE JOHNSON & JOHNSON CREDO

—We believe our first responsibility is to the doctors, nurses and patients, to mothers and all others who use our products and services.

—In meeting their needs everything we do must be of high quality.

—We must constantly strive to reduce our costs in order to maintain reasonable prices.

—Customers' orders must be serviced promptly and accurately.

—Our suppliers and distributors must have an opportunity to make a fair profit.

—We are responsible to our employees, the men and women who work with us throughout the world.

—Everyone must be considered as an individual.

—We must respect their dignity and recognize their merit.

—They must have a sense of security in their jobs.

—Compensation must be fair and adequate, and working conditions clean, orderly, and safe.

—Employees must feel free to make suggestions and complaints.

—There must be equal opportunity for employment, development and advancement for those qualified.

—We must provide competent management, and their actions must be just and ethical.

—We are responsible to the communities in which we live and work and to the world community as well.

—We must be good citizens—support good works and charities and bear our fair share of taxes.

—We must encourage civic improvements and better health and education.

—We must maintain in good order the property we are privileged to use, protecting the environment and natural resources.

—Our final responsibility is to our stockholders.

—Business must make a sound profit.

—We must experiment with new ideas.

—Research must be carried on, innovative programs developed and mistakes paid for.

—New equipment must be purchased, new facilities provided and new products launched.

—Reserves must be created to provide for adverse times.

—When we operate according to these principles, the stockholders should realize a fair return.

Source: 1982 Annual Report.

topics such statements cover. Written statements have the advantage of explicitly stating what the company intends and expects; and they serve as benchmarks for judging both company policies and actions and individual conduct. They put a stake in the ground and define the company's position. Value statements serve as a cornerstone for culture-building; a code of ethics serves as a cornerstone for creating a corporate conscience. Illustration Capsule 26 presents the Johnson & Johnson Credo, the most publicized and celebrated code of ethics and values among U.S. companies. J & J's CEO calls the credo "the unifying force for our corporation." Illustration Capsule 27 presents the pledge that Bristol-Myers Squibb makes to all of its stakeholders.

Values and ethical standards not only must be explicitly stated but they also must be deeply ingrained into the corporate culture.

Once values and ethical standards have been formally set forth, they must be institutionalized and ingrained in the company's policies, practices, and actual conduct. Implementing the values and code of ethics entails several actions:

- Incorporating the statement of values and the code of ethics into employee training and educational programs.

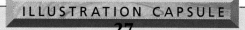

ILLUSTRATION CAPSULE
27

THE BRISTOL-MYERS SQUIBB PLEDGE

To those who use our products ...
We affirm Bristol-Myers Squibb's commitment to the highest standards of excellence, safety and reliability in everything we make. We pledge to offer products of the highest quality and to work diligently to keep improving them.

To our employees and those who may join us ...
We pledge personal respect, fair compensation and equal treatment. We acknowledge our obligation to provide able and humane leadership throughout the organization, within a clean and safe working environment. To all who qualify for advancement, we will make every effort to provide opportunity.

To our suppliers and customers ...
We pledge an open door, courteous, efficient and ethical dealing, and appreciation for their right to a fair profit.

To our shareholders ...
We pledge a companywide dedication to contin-
ued profitable growth, sustained by strong finances, a high level of research and development, and facilities second to none.

To the communities where we have plants and offices ...
We pledge conscientious citizenship, a helping hand for worthwhile causes, and constructive action in support of civic and environmental progress.

To the countries where we do business ...
We pledge ourselves to be a good citizen and to show full consideration for the rights of others while reserving the right to stand up for our own.

Above all, to the world we live in ...
We pledge Bristol-Myers Squibb to policies and practices which fully embody the responsibility, integrity and decency required of free enterprise if it is to merit and maintain the confidence of our society.

Source: 1990 Annual Report.

- Giving explicit attention to values and ethics in recruiting and hiring to screen out applicants who do not exhibit compatible character traits.
- Communicating the values and ethics codes to all employees and explaining compliance procedures.
- Management involvement and oversight, from the CEO to first-line supervisors.
- Strong endorsements by the CEO.
- Word-of-mouth indoctrination.

In the case of codes of ethics, special attention must be given to those sections of the company that are particularly sensitive and vulnerable—purchasing, sales, and political lobbying.[8] Employees who deal with external parties are in ethically sensitive positions and are often drawn into compromising situations. Procedures for enforcing ethical standards and handling potential violations have to be developed.

The implementation effort must permeate the company, extending into every organizational unit. The attitudes, character, and work history of prospective employees must be scrutinized. Every employee must receive adequate training. Line managers at all levels must give serious and continuous attention to the task of explaining how the values and ethical conduct apply

[8]Ibid., p. 7.

in their areas. In addition, they must insist that company values and ethical standards become a way of life. In general, instilling values and insisting on ethical conduct must be viewed as a continuous culture-building, culture-nurturing exercise. Whether the effort succeeds or fails depends largely on how well corporate values and ethical standards are visibly integrated into company policies, managerial practices, and actions at all levels.

Building a Spirit of High Performance into the Culture

A results-oriented culture that inspires people to do their best is conducive to superior strategy execution.

An ability to instill strong individual commitment to strategic success and create constructive pressure to perform is one of the most valuable strategy-implementing skills. When an organization performs consistently at or near peak capability, the outcome is not only improved strategic success but also an organizational culture permeated with a spirit of high performance. This should not be confused with whether employees are "happy" or "satisfied," or "get along well together." An organization with a spirit of performance emphasizes achievement and excellence. Its culture is results-oriented, and its management pursues policies and practices that inspire people to do their best.

High-performance cultures make champions out of people who excel.

Companies with a spirit of high performance typically are intensely people-oriented; and they reinforce this orientation at every conceivable occasion in every conceivable way to every employee. They treat employees with dignity and respect, train each employee thoroughly, encourage employees to use their own initiative and creativity in performing their work, set reasonable and clear performance expectations, utilize the full range of rewards and punishment to enforce high performance standards, hold managers at every level responsible for developing the people who report to them, and grant employees enough autonomy to stand out, excel, and contribute. To create a results-oriented organizational culture, a company must make champions out of the people who turn in winning performances:[9]

- At Boeing, IBM, General Electric, and 3M Corporation, top executives deliberately make "champions" out of individuals who believe so strongly in their ideas that they take it on themselves to hurdle the bureaucracy, maneuver their projects through the system, and turn them into improved services, new products, or even new businesses. In these companies, "product champions" are given high visibility, room to push their ideas, and strong executive support. Champions whose ideas prove out are usually handsomely rewarded; those whose ideas don't pan out still have secure jobs and are given chances to try again.

- The manager of a New York area sales office rented the Meadowlands Stadium (home field of the New York Giants) for an evening. After work, the salesmen were all assembled at the stadium and asked to run one at a time through the player's tunnel onto the field. As each one emerged, the electronic scoreboard flashed his name to those gathered in the stands—executives from corporate headquarters, employees from the office, family, and friends. Their role was to cheer loudly in honor of the individual's sales accomplishments. The company involved was IBM. The occasion for this action was to reaffirm IBM's commitment to

---

[9]Peters and Waterman, *In Search of Excellence*, pp. xviii, 240, and 269; and Peters and Austin, *A Passion for Excellence*, pp. 304–7.

satisfy an individual's need to be part of something great and to reiterate IBM's concern for championing individual accomplishment.

- Some companies upgrade the importance and status of individual employees by referring to them as Cast members (Disney), Crew Members (McDonald's), or Associates (Wal-Mart and J. C. Penney). Companies like IBM, Tupperware, and McDonald's actively seek out reasons and opportunities to give pins, buttons, badges, and medals to good showings by average performers—the idea being to express appreciation and help give a boost to the "middle 60 percent" of the work force.

- McDonald's has a contest to determine the best hamburger cooker in its entire chain. It begins with a competition to determine the best hamburger cooker in each store. Store winners go on to compete in regional championships, and regional winners go on to the "All-American" contest. The winners get trophies and an All-American patch to wear on their shirts.

- Milliken & Co. holds Corporate Sharing Rallies once every three months; teams come from all over the company to swap success stories and ideas. A hundred or more teams make five-minute presentations over a two-day period. Each rally has a major theme—quality, cost reduction, and so on. No criticisms and negatives are allowed, and there is no such thing as a big idea or a small one. Quantitative measures of success are used to gauge improvement. All those present vote on the best presentation, and several ascending grades of awards are handed out. Everyone, however, receives a framed certificate for participating.

What makes a spirit of high performance come alive is a complex network of practices, words, symbols, styles, values, and policies pulling together to produce extraordinary results with ordinary people. The drivers of the system are a belief in the worth of the individual, strong company commitments to job security and promotion from within, managerial practices that encourage employees to exercise individual initiative and creativity, and pride in doing the "itty-bitty, teeny-tiny things" right. A company that treats its employees well benefits from increased teamwork, higher morale, and greater employee loyalty.

While emphasizing a spirit of high performance nearly always accentuates the positive, there are negative aspects too. Managers whose units consistently perform poorly have to be removed. Aside from the organizational benefits, weak performing managers should be reassigned for their own good—people who find themselves in a job they cannot handle are usually frustrated, anxiety ridden, harassed, and unhappy.[10] Moreover, subordinates have a right to be managed with competence, dedication, and achievement; unless their boss performs well, they themselves cannot perform well. Weak-performing workers and people who reject the cultural emphasis on dedication and high performance have to be weeded out. Recruitment practices need to aim at selecting highly motivated, ambitious applicants whose attitudes and work habits mesh well with a results-oriented culture.

Illustration Capsule 28 shows how one major company has linked its values and culture with its performance objectives.

---

[10]Peter Drucker, *Management: Tasks, Responsibilities, Practices* (New York: Harper & Row, 1974), p. 457.

ILLUSTRATION CAPSULE
28

SQUARE D COMPANY: VISION, MISSION, PRINCIPLES, OBJECTIVES, PERFORMANCE

Square D Company is a $1.7 billion producer of electrical equipment and electronic products. Below is the company's presentation of its vision, mission, principles, objectives, and actual performance against its long-term financial goals.

Vision

Dedicated to Growth
Committed to Quality

Mission

We are dedicated to growth for our customers, shareholders and employees through quality, innovation and profitable reinvestment.

Principles

As a company responsible to our customers, shareholders and employees, we will:

- Provide our customers with innovative, functional and reliable products and services at a cost and quality level consistent with their needs.
- Concentrate on enhancing long-term shareholder value.
- Actively pursue equal opportunity for all individuals and provide an environment which encourages open communications, personal growth and creativity.
- Expect integrity and professional conduct from our employees in every aspect of our business.
- Conduct our operations ethically and well within the framework of the law.
- Actively contribute to the communities and in-

dustries in which we participate.

Financial Objectives

We are committed to providing our shareholders with an attractive return on their investment, and our specific goals for doing so are to:

- Achieve a minimum after-tax return on capital of 14%.
- Leverage return on shareholders' equity through a capital structure which includes 25 to 35% debt.
- Achieve a minimum return on equity of 18%.
- Pay dividends equal to approximately 40% of earnings.
- Achieve average annual growth in earnings of at least 10%.

Operating Objectives

Market Leadership
- Have a leading market share position in our major markets.
- Be recognized as a leader in the application of technology to meet customer requirements.
- Be a "best-value" supplier throughout the world.
- Expand our international business to a level equaling 20 to 25% of company sales.
- Invest in research and development at a rate of 4% of sales as a means of achieving our market leadership objectives.

(continued)

Bonding the Fits: The Role of Shared Values

As emphasized earlier, "fits" with strategy need to be created internally as concerns structure, organizational skills and distinctive competence, budgets, support systems, rewards and incentives, policies and procedures, and culture. The better the "goodness of fit" among these administrative activities and characteristics, the more powerful strategy execution is likely to be.

McKinsey & Co., a leading consulting firm with wide-ranging experience in strategic analysis, has developed a framework for examining the fits in seven

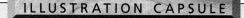

ILLUSTRATION CAPSULE
28

(concluded)

Employee Development

- Encourage initiative, innovation and productivity by appropriately recognizing and rewarding employee performance.
- Invest in employee training and development at a rate of 2% of payroll.
- Honestly and accurately appraise and evaluate the performance of each employee on at least an annual basis.
- Provide for the orderly succession of management.
- Maintain a positive affirmative action program and provide employees with the opportunity for advancement commensurate with their abilities.

Social/Community Responsibility

- Maintain a safe, clean and healthy environment for our employees and the communities in which we operate.
- Invest 1.5% of net income in social, cultural, educational and charitable activities.
- Encourage appropriate employee involvement in community activities.

Performance against Financial Goals

Year Ended December 31	Long-Term Financial Goals	1988	1987	1986	1985	1984
After-tax return from continuing operations on average capital	14.0%	14.8%	13.5%	12.5%	13.9%	16.4%
Average total debt as a percentage of average capital	25.0–35.0	28.2	23.7	29.9	30.5	29.5
Return from continuing operations on average equity	18.0	18.1	15.7	15.5	17.7	20.6
Dividend payout percentage	40.0	45.7	48.6	53.9	60.9	49.7
Annual growth in earnings from continuing operations	10.0	8.1	11.2	(3.4)	(6.7)	65.0

Source: 1988 Annual Report.

broad areas: (1) strategy, (2) structure, (3) shared values, attitudes, and philosophy, (4) approach to staffing the organization and its overall "people orientation," (5) administrative systems, practices, and procedures used to run the organization on a day-to-day basis, including the reward structure, formal and informal policies, budgeting and programs, training, cost accounting, and financial controls, (6) the organization's skills, capabilities, and core competencies, and (7) style of top management (how they allocate their time and attention, symbolic actions, their leadership skills, the way the top

The values widely shared by managers and employees are the core of the corporate culture.

FIGURE 10–1   **Bonding the Administrative Fits**   *(The McKinsey 7-S framework)*

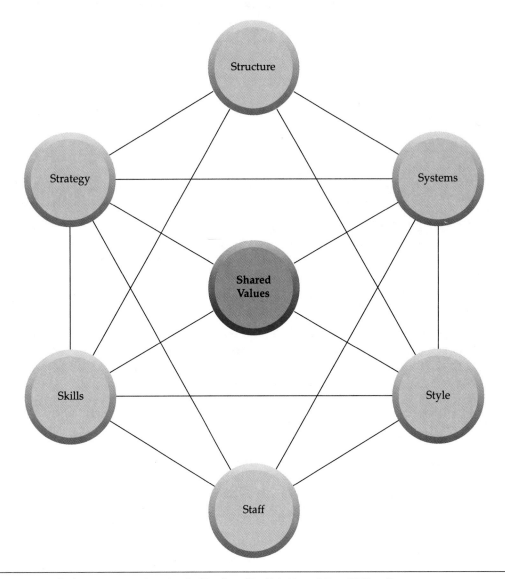

Source: Thomas J. Peters and Robert H. Waterman, Jr., *In Search of Excellence* (New York: Harper & Row, 1982), p. 10.

management team comes across to the rest of the organization).[11] McKinsey has diagrammed these seven elements into what it calls the McKinsey 7-S framework (the seven S's are strategy, structure, shared values, staff, systems, skills, and style—so labeled to promote recall) shown in Figure 10–1.

---

[11]For a more extended discussion, see Robert H. Waterman, Jr., Thomas J. Peters, and Julien R. Phillips, "Structure Is Not Organization," *Business Horizons* 23, no. 3 (June 1980), pp. 14–26; and Robert H. Waterman, Jr., "The Seven Elements of Strategic Fit," *Journal of Business Strategy* 2, no. 3 (Winter 1982), pp. 68–72.

Shared values are the core of the 7-S framework because they are the heart-and-soul themes around which an organization rallies. They define its main beliefs and aspirations, its guiding concepts of "who we are, what we do, where we are headed, and what principles we will stand for in getting there." They bond the corporate culture and give it energy.

The McKinsey 7-S framework draws attention to some important organizational interconnections and why these interconnections are relevant in trying to effect change. In orchestrating a major shift in strategy and gathering momentum for implementation, the pace of change will be governed by all seven S's. The 7-S framework is a simple way to illustrate that the job of implementing strategy is one of creating fits and harmonizing the seven S's.

EXERTING STRATEGIC LEADERSHIP

The formula for good strategic management is simple enough: develop a sound strategic plan, implement it, execute it to the fullest, win! But it's easier said than done. Exerting take-charge leadership, being a "spark plug," ramrodding things through, and getting things done by coaching others are difficult tasks. Moreover, a strategy manager has many different leadership roles to play: chief entrepreneur and strategist, chief administrator and strategy-implementer, crisis solver, taskmaster, figurehead, spokesperson, resource allocator, negotiator, motivator, adviser, inspirationist, consensus builder, policymaker, mentor, and head cheerleader. Sometimes a strategy manager needs to be authoritarian and hardnosed, sometimes a perceptive listener and compromising decision-maker. And sometimes a participative, collegial approach works best. Many occasions call for a highly visible role and extensive time commitments, while others entail a brief ceremonial performance with the details delegated to subordinates.

Strategic Management Principle
Strong leadership is almost always essential for effective strategy execution.

In general, the problem of strategic leadership is one of diagnosing the situation and choosing from any of several ways to handle it. Six leadership roles dominate the strategy-implementer's action agenda:

1. Staying on top of what is happening and how well things are going.
2. Promoting a culture in which the organization is "energized" to accomplish strategy and perform at a high level.
3. Keeping the organization responsive to changing conditions, alert for new opportunities, and bubbling with innovative ideas.
4. Building consensus, dealing with the politics of strategy formulation and implementation, and containing "power struggles."
5. Enforcing ethical standards.
6. Taking corrective actions to improve strategy execution and overall strategic performance.

Managing By Walking Around (MBWA)

To stay on top of how well the implementation process is going, a manager needs to develop a broad network of contacts and information sources, both formal and informal. The regular channels include talking with key subordinates, reading written reports and the latest operating results, getting feedback from customers, watching the competitive reactions of rivals, tapping into the grapevine, listening to rank-and-file employees, and observing the situation firsthand. However, some information is more reliable than the rest. Written reports can cover up or minimize bad news—or not report it at all. Sometimes subordinates delay reporting failures and problems, hoping that extra time will help them turn things around. As information flows up an organization, it tends to get "censored" and "sterilized" to the point that it may block or obscure strategy-critical information. Strategy managers must guard against surprises by making sure that they have accurate information and a "feel" for the situation. One way to do so is to visit "the field" regularly and talk with many different people at many different levels. The technique of *managing by walking around* (MBWA) is practiced in a variety of styles:[12]

MBWA is one of the techniques effective leaders use.

- At Hewlett-Packard, there are weekly beer busts in each division, attended by both executives and employees, to create a regular opportunity to keep in touch. Tidbits of information flow freely between down-the-line employees and executives—facilitated in part because "the H-P Way" is for people at all ranks to be addressed by their first names. Bill Hewlett, one of HP's co-founders, had a companywide reputation for getting out of his office and "wandering around" the plant greeting people, listening to what was on their minds, and asking questions. He found this so valuable that he made MBWA a standard practice for all HP managers. Furthermore, ad hoc meetings of people from different departments spontaneously arise; they gather in rooms with blackboards and work out solutions informally.

- McDonald's founder Ray Kroc regularly visited store units and did his own personal inspection on Q.S.C.& V. (Quality, Service, Cleanliness, and Value)—the themes he preached regularly. There are stories of him pulling into a unit's parking lot, seeing litter lying on the pavement, getting out of his limousine to pick it up himself, and then lecturing the store staff at length on the subject of cleanliness.

- The CEO of a small manufacturing company spends much of his time riding around the factory in a golf cart, waving and joking with workers, listening to them, and calling all 2,000 employees by their first names. In addition, he spends a lot of time with union officials, inviting them to meetings and keeping them well informed about what is going on.

- Sam Walton, Wal-Mart's founder, insists "The key is to get out into the store and listen to what the associates have to say. Our best ideas come from clerks and stockboys." Walton himself has had a longstanding practice of spending two to three days every week visiting Wal-Mart's stores and talking with store managers and employees. On one occasion he flew the company plane to a Texas town, got out, and instructed the copilot to meet him 100 miles down the road. Then he flagged a Wal-Mart truck and rode the rest of the way to "chat with the driver—it seemed like so much fun." Walton makes a practice of greeting store managers and their spouses by name at annual meetings and has been known to go to the company's distribution centers at 2:00 A.M. (carrying boxes of

---

[12]Ibid., pp. xx, 15, 120–23, 191, 242–43, 246–47, 287–90. For an extensive report on the benefits of MBWA, see Thomas J. Peters and Nancy Austin, *A Passion for Excellence*, (New York: Random House, 1985), chaps. 2, 3, and 19.

doughnuts to share with all those on duty) to have a chance to find out what was on their minds.

- When Ed Carlson became CEO at United Airlines, he traveled some 200,000 miles a year talking with United's employees. He observed, "I wanted these people to identify me and to feel sufficiently comfortable to make suggestions or even argue with me if that's what they felt like doing. . . . Whenever I picked up some information, I would call the senior officer of the division and say that I had just gotten back from visiting Oakland, Reno, and Las Vegas, and here is what I found."

- At Marriott Corp., Bill Marriott not only personally inspects all Marriott hotels at least once a year, but he also invites all Marriott guests to send him their evaluations of Marriott's facilities and services. He personally reads every customer complaint and has been known to telephone hotel managers about them.

Managers at many companies attach great importance to informal communication. They report that it is essential to have a "feel" for situations and to gain quick, easy access to information. When executives stay in their offices, they tend to become isolated and often surround themselves with people who are not likely to offer criticism or different perspectives; the information they get is secondhand, screened and filtered, and sometimes dated.

Fostering a Strategy-Supportive Climate and Culture

Strategy-implementers have to be "out front" in promoting a strategy-supportive organizational climate. When major strategic changes are being implemented, a manager's time is best spent personally leading the changes. When only strategic fine-tuning is being implemented, it takes less time and effort to bring values and culture into alignment with strategy, but there is still a lead role for the manager to play in pushing ahead and prodding for continuous improvements. Successful strategy leaders know it is their responsibility to convince people that the chosen strategy is right and that implementing it to the best of the organization's ability is "top priority."

Both words and deeds play a part. Words inspire people, infuse spirit and drive, define strategy-supportive cultural norms and values, articulate the reasons for strategic and organizational change, legitimize new viewpoints and new priorities, urge and reinforce commitment, and arouse confidence in the new strategy. Deeds add credibility to the words, create strategy-supportive symbols, set examples, give meaning and content to the language, and teach the organization what sort of behavior is needed and expected.

Highly visible symbols and imagery are needed to complement substantive actions. One General Motors manager explained the striking difference in performance between two large plants:[13]

> At the poorly performing plant, the plant manager probably ventured out on the floor once a week, always in a suit. His comments were distant and perfunctory. At South Gate, the better plant, the plant manager was on the floor all the time. He wore a baseball cap and a UAW jacket. By the way, whose plant do you think was spotless? Whose looked like a junkyard?

---

[13]As quoted in Peters and Waterman, *In Search of Excellence*, p. 262.

**Strategic Management
Principle**
*The bigger the strategic
change being implemented,
the more necessary it is for
the chief executive to
personally lead the effort.*

As a rule, the greater the degree of strategic change being implemented and/or the greater the shift in cultural norms needed to accommodate a new strategy, the more visible the strategy-implementer's words and deeds need to be. Lessons from well-managed companies show that what the strategy-leader says and does has a significant bearing on down-the-line strategy implementation and execution.[14] According to one view, "It is not so much the articulation . . . about what an [organization] should be doing that creates new practice. It's the imagery that creates the understanding, the compelling moral necessity that the new way is right."[15] Moreover, the actions and images, both substantive and symbolic, have to be repeated regularly, not just at ceremonies and special occasions. This is where a high profile and "managing by walking around" comes into play. As a Hewlett-Packard official expresses it in the company publication *The HP Way*:

> Once a division or department has developed a plan of its own—a set of working objectives—it's important for managers and supervisors to keep it in operating condition. This is where observation, measurement, feedback, and guidance come in. It's our "management by wandering around." That's how you find out whether you're ontrack and heading at the right speed and in the right direction. If you don't constantly monitor how people are operating, not only will they tend to wander off track but also they will begin to believe you weren't serious about the plan in the first place. It has the extra benefit of getting you off your chair and moving around your area. By wandering around, I literally mean moving around and talking to people. It's all done on a very informal and spontaneous basis, but it's important in the course of time to cover the whole territory. You start out by being accessible and approachable, but the main thing is to realize you're there to listen. The second reason for MBWA is that it is vital to keep people informed about what's going on in the company, especially those things that are important to them. The third reason for doing this is because it is just plain fun.

Such contacts give the manager a feel for how things are progressing, and they provide opportunities to encourage employees, lift spirits, shift attention from the old to the new priorities, create some excitement, and project an atmosphere of informality and fun—all of which drive implementation in a positive fashion and intensify the organizational energy behind strategy execution. John Welch of General Electric sums up the hands-on role and motivational approach well: "I'm here every day, or out into a factory, smelling it, feeling it, touching it, challenging the people."[16]

Keeping the Internal Organization Responsive and Innovative

*One of the toughest
strategic leadership tasks
is keeping the
organization innovative
and responsive to
changing conditions.*

While formulating and implementing strategy is a manager's responsibility, the task of generating fresh ideas, identifying new opportunities, and responding to changing conditions cannot be accomplished by a single person. It is an organizationwide task, particularly in large corporations. Strategic leadership must result in a dependable supply of fresh ideas from the rank and file—man-

---

[14]Peters and Waterman, *In Search of Excellence*, chap. 9.
[15]Warren Bennis, *The Unconscious Conspiracy: Why Leaders Can't Lead* (New York: AMACOM, 1987), p. 93.
[16]As quoted in Ann M. Morrison, "Trying to Bring GE to Life," *Fortune*, January 25, 1982, p. 52.

agers and employees alike—and promote an entrepreneurial, opportunistic spirit that permits continuous adaptation to changing conditions. A flexible, responsive, innovative internal environment is critical in fast-moving high-technology industries, in businesses where products have short life cycles and growth depends on new-product innovation, in corporations with widely diversified business portfolios (where opportunities are varied and scattered), in industries where successful product differentiation is key, and in businesses where the strategy of being the low-cost producer hinges on productivity improvement and cost reduction. Managers cannot mandate such an environment by simply exhorting people to be "creative."

One useful leadership approach is to take special pains to foster, nourish, and support people who are willing to champion new ideas, better services, new products and product applications, and who are eager for a chance to turn their ideas into new divisions, new businesses, and even new industries. When Texas Instruments reviewed some 50 or so successful and unsuccessful new-product introductions, one factor marked every failure: "Without exception we found we hadn't had a volunteer champion. There was someone we had cajoled into taking on the task. When we take a look at a product and decide whether to push it or not these days, we've got a new set of criteria. Number one is the presence of a zealous, volunteer champion. After that comes market potential and project economics in a distant second and third."[17] The rule seems to be an idea for something new or something different must either find a champion or die. And the champion needs to be someone who is persistent, competitive, tenacious, committed, and fanatic about the idea and seeing it through to success.

Empowering Champions   In order to promote an organizational climate where champions can blossom and thrive, strategy managers need to do several things. First, individuals and groups have to be encouraged to bring their ideas forward, be creative, and exercise initiative. Second, the champion's maverick style has to be tolerated and given room to operate. People's imaginations need to be encouraged to "fly in all directions." Freedom to experiment and informal brainstorming sessions need to become ingrained. Above all, people with creative ideas must not be looked on as disruptive or troublesome. Third, managers have to induce and promote lots of attempts and be willing to tolerate mistakes and failures. Most ideas don't pan out, but people learn from a good attempt even when it fails. Fourth, strategy managers should use all kinds of ad hoc organizational forms to support ideas and experimentation— venture teams, task forces, internal competition among different groups working on the same project (IBM calls the showdown between the competing approaches a "performance shootout"), informal "bootlegged" projects composed of volunteers, and so on. Fifth, strategy managers have to ensure that rewards for a successful champion are large and visible and that people who champion an unsuccessful idea are encouraged to try again rather than punished or shunted aside. In effect, the leadership task here is to devise internal support systems for entrepreneurial innovation.

---

[17]As quoted in Peters and Waterman, *In Search of Excellence*, pp. 203–4.

Dealing with Company Politics

A manager can't formulate and implement strategy effectively without being perceptive about company politics and adept at political maneuvering.[18] Politics virtually always comes into play in formulating the strategic plan. Inevitably, key individuals and groups form coalitions, and each group presses the benefits and potential of its own ideas and vested interests. Politics can influence which objectives take precedence and which businesses in the portfolio have priority in resource allocation. Internal politics is a factor in building a consensus for one strategic option over another.

As a rule, politics has even more influence in strategy implementation. Typically, internal political considerations affect organization structure (whose areas of responsibility need to be reorganized, who reports to who, who has how much authority over subunits), staffing decisions (what individuals should fill key positions and head strategy-critical activities), and budget allocations (which organizational units will get the biggest increases). As a case in point, Quinn cites a situation where three strong managers who fought each other constantly formed a potent coalition to resist a reorganization scheme that would have coordinated the very things that caused their friction.[19]

In short, political considerations and the forming of individual and group alliances are integral parts of building organizationwide support for the strategic plan and gaining consensus on how to implement it. Political skills are a definite, maybe even necessary, asset for managers in orchestrating the whole strategic process.

Company politics presents strategy leaders with the challenge of building consensus for the strategy and how to implement it.

A strategy manager must understand how an organization's power structure works, who wields influence in the executive ranks, which groups and individuals are "activists" and which are "defenders of the status quo," who can be helpful in a showdown on key decisions, and which direction the political winds are blowing on a given issue. When major decisions have to be made, strategy managers need to be especially sensitive to the politics of managing coalitions and reaching consensus. As the chairman of a major British corporation expressed it:

> I've never taken a major decision without consulting my colleagues. It would be unimaginable to me, unimaginable. First, they help me make a better decision in most cases. Second, if they know about it and agree with it, they'll back it. Otherwise, they might challenge it, not openly, but subconsciously.[20]

The politics of strategy centers chiefly around stimulating options, nurturing support for strong proposals and killing weak ones, guiding the formation of coalitions on particular issues, and achieving consensus and commitment. A recent study of strategy management in nine large corporations showed that successful executives used the following political tactics:[21]

---

[18]For further discussion of this point see Abraham Zaleznik, " Power and Politics in Organizational Life," *Harvard Business Review*, 48, no. 3 (May–June 1970), pp. 47–60; R. M. Cyert, H. A. Simon, and D. B. Trow, "Observation of a Business Decision," *Journal of Business*, October 1956, pp. 237–48; and James Brian Quinn, *Strategies for Change: Logical Incrementalism* (Homewood, Ill.: Richard D. Irwin, 1980).

[19]Quinn, *Strategies for Change*, p. 68.

[20]This statement was made by Sir Alastair Pilkington, Chairman, Pilkington Brothers, Ltd.; the quote appears in Quinn, *Strategies for Change*, p. 65.

[21]Quinn, *Strategies for Change*, pp. 128–45.

- Letting weakly supported ideas and proposals die through inaction.
- Establishing additional hurdles or tests for strongly supported ideas that the manager views as unacceptable but that are best not opposed openly.
- Keeping a low political profile on unacceptable proposals by getting subordinate managers to say no.
- Letting most negative decisions come from a group consensus that the manager merely confirms, thereby reserving personal veto for big issues and crucial moments.
- Leading the strategy but not dictating it—giving few orders, announcing few decisions, depending heavily on informal questioning and seeking to probe and clarify until a consensus emerges.
- Staying alert to the symbolic impact of one's actions and statements lest a false signal stimulate proposals and movements in unwanted directions.
- Ensuring that all major power bases within the organization have representation in or access to top management.
- Injecting new faces and new views into considerations of major changes to preclude those involved from coming to see the world the same way and then acting as systematic screens against other views.
- Minimizing political exposure on issues that are highly controversial and in circumstances where opposition from major power centers can trigger a "shootout."

There are several political tactics managers should be adept in using.

The politics of strategy implementation is especially critical when attempting to introduce a new strategy against the support enjoyed by the old strategy. Except for crisis situations where the old strategy is plainly revealed as out-of-date, it is usually bad politics to push the new strategy through attacks on the old one.[22] Bad-mouthing old strategy can easily be interpreted as an attack on those who formulated it and those who supported it. The former strategy and the judgments behind it may have been well-suited to the organization's earlier circumstances, and the people who made these judgments may still be influential.

In addition, the new strategy and/or the plans for implementing it may not have been others' first choices, and lingering doubts may remain. Good arguments may exist for pursuing other actions. Consequently, in trying to surmount resistance, nothing is gained by "knocking" the arguments for alternative approaches. Such attacks often produce alienation instead of cooperation.

In short, to bring the full force of an organization behind a strategic plan, the strategy manager must assess and deal with the most important centers of potential support and opposition to new strategic thrusts.[23] He or she needs to secure the support of key people, co-opt or neutralize serious opposition and resistance, learn where the zones of indifference are, and build as much consensus as possible.

Enforcing Ethical Behavior

High ethical standards cannot be enforced without the open and unequivocal commitment of the chief executive.

For an organization to display consistently high ethical standards, the CEO and those around the CEO must be openly and unequivocally committed to ethical

---

[22]Ibid., pp. 118–19.
[23]Ibid., p. 205.

conduct.[24] In companies that strive hard to make high ethical standards a reality, top management communicates its commitment in a code of ethics, in speeches and company publications, in policies concerning the consequences of unethical behavior, in the deeds of senior executives, and in the actions taken to ensure compliance. Senior management iterates and reiterates to employees that it is not only their *duty* to observe ethical codes but also to report ethical violations. While such companies have provisions for disciplining violators, the main purpose of enforcement is to encourage compliance rather than administer punishment. Although the CEO leads the enforcement process, all managers are expected to contribute by stressing ethical conduct with their subordinates and by monitoring compliance. "Gray areas" must be identified and openly discussed with employees, and mechanisms provided for guidance and resolution. Managers can't assume activities are being conducted ethically or that employees understand they are expected to act with integrity.

There are several things managers can do to exercise ethics leadership.[25] First and foremost, they must set an excellent ethical example in their own behavior and establish a tradition of integrity. Company decisions have to be seen as ethical—"actions speak louder than words." Second, managers and employees have to be educated about what is ethical and what is not; ethics training programs may have to be established and "gray areas" identified and discussed. Everyone must be encouraged to raise ethical issues and discuss them. Third, top management should explicitly refer to the company's ethical code and take a strong stand on ethical issues. Fourth, top management must be prepared to act as the final arbiter on hard calls; this means removing people from a key position or terminating them when they are guilty of a violation. It also means reprimanding those who have been lax in monitoring and enforcing ethical compliance. Failure to act swiftly and decisively in pursuing ethical misconduct is interpreted as a lack of real commitment.

A well-developed program to ensure compliance with ethical standards typically includes: (1) an oversight committee of the board of directors, usually made up of outside directors; (2) a committee of senior managers to direct ongoing training, implementation, and compliance; (3) an annual audit of each manager's efforts and formal reports on managers' actions to remedy deficient conduct, and (4) periodically requiring people to sign documents certifying compliance with ethical standards.[26]

Leading the Process of Making Corrective Adjustments

Corrective adjustments in the company's approach to strategy implementation should be made on an "as-needed" basis.

No strategic plan and no scheme for strategy implementation can foresee all the events and problems that will arise. Making adjustments and "midcourse" corrections is a normal and necessary part of strategic management.

When responding to new conditions involving either the strategy or its implementation, management must first determine if immediate action needs to be taken. In a crisis, the typical approach is to push key subordinates to gather information and formulate recommendations, personally preside over

---

[24]The Business Roundtable, *Corporate Ethics*, pp. 4–10.

[25]Ibid.

[26]Ibid.

extended discussions of the proposed responses, and try to build a quick consensus among members of the executive "inner circle." If no consensus emerges or if several key subordinates remain divided, the burden falls on the strategy manager to choose the response and urge its support.

When time permits a full-fledged evaluation, strategy managers seem to prefer a process of incrementally solidifying commitment to a response.[27] The approach involves:

1. Staying flexible and keeping a number of options open.
2. Asking a lot of questions.
3. Gaining in-depth information from specialists.
4. Encouraging subordinates to participate in developing alternatives and proposing solutions.
5. Getting the reactions of many different people to proposed solutions to test their potential and political acceptability.
6. Seeking to build commitment to a response by gradually moving toward a consensus solution.

The governing principle seems to be to make a final decision as late as possible to: (1) bring as much information to bear as needed, (2) clarify the situation enough to know what to do, and (3) allow the various political constituencies and power bases to move toward a consensus solution. Executives are often wary of committing themselves to a major change too soon because it discourages others from asking questions that need to be raised.

Corrective adjustments to strategy need not be just reactive, however. Proactive adjustments can improve either the strategy or its implementation. The distinctive feature of a proactive adjustment is that it arises from management initiatives rather than forced reactions. Successful strategy managers employ a variety of proactive tactics.[28]

Strategy leaders should be proactive as well as reactive in reshaping strategy and how it is implemented.

1. Commissioning studies to explore and amplify areas where they have a "gut feeling" or sense a need exists.
2. Shopping ideas among trusted colleagues and putting forth trial concepts.
3. Teaming people with different skills, interests, and experiences and letting them push and tug on interesting ideas to expand the variety of approaches considered.
4. Contacting a variety of people inside and outside the organization to sample viewpoints, probe, and listen, thereby trying to get early warning signals of impending problems/issues and deliberating short-circuiting all the careful screens of information flowing up from below.
5. Stimulating proposals for improvement from lower levels, encouraging the development of competing ideas and approaches, and letting the momentum for change come from below, with final choices postponed until it is apparent which option best matches the organization's situation.

---

[27]Quinn, *Strategies for Change*, pp. 20–22.
[28]Ibid., chap. 4.

6. Seeking options and solutions that go beyond extrapolations from the status quo.

7. Accepting and committing to partial steps forward as a way of building comfort levels before going ahead.

8. Managing the politics of change to promote managerial consensus and solidify management's commitment to whatever course of action is chosen.

The process leaders use to decide on adjusting actions is essentially the same for proactive as for reactive changes; they sense needs, gather information, amplify understanding and awareness, put forth trial concepts, develop options, explore the pros and cons, test proposals, generate partial solutions, empower champions, build a managerial consensus, and formally adopt an agreed-on course of action.[29] The ultimate managerial prescription may have been given by Rene McPherson, former CEO at Dana Corporation. In speaking to a class of students at Stanford, he said, "You just keep pushing. You just keep pushing. I made every mistake that could be made. But I just kept pushing."[30]

This points to a key feature of strategic management: the job of formulating and implementing strategy is not one of steering a clear-cut, linear course (i.e., carrying out an original strategy intact according to some preconceived and highly detailed implementation plan). Rather, it is one of creatively (1) adapting and reshaping strategy to unfolding events and (2) applying whatever managerial techniques are needed to align internal activities and attitudes with strategy. The process is iterative, with much looping and recycling to fine-tune and adjust in a continuously evolving process where the conceptually separate acts of strategy formulation and strategy implementation blur and join together.

KEY POINTS
The managerial tasks of designing rewards and incentives, creating a strategy-supportive corporate culture, and exercising strategic leadership are key facets of successful strategy implementation. The use of incentives is management's single most powerful tool in gaining employee buy-in and energetic commitment to carrying out the strategy. For incentives to work well (1) the monetary payoff should be a major percentage of the compensation package, (2) the incentive plan should extend to all managers and workers, (3) the system should be administered with care and fairness, (4) the incentives should be linked to performance targets spelled out in the strategic plan, and (5) each individual's performance targets should involve outcomes the person is able to affect personally.

Building a strategy-supportive corporate culture is important to successful implementation because it produces a work climate and organizational *esprit de corps* that thrives on meeting performance targets and being part of a winning effort. An organization's culture emerges from why and how it does things the way it does, the values and beliefs that senior managers espouse, the

---

[29]Ibid., p. 146.

[30]As quoted in Peters and Waterman, *In Search of Excellence*, p. 319.

ethical standards expected, the tone and philosophy underlying key policies, and the traditions the organization maintains. Culture, thus, concerns the "atmosphere" and "feeling" a company has and the style in which it gets things done. Companies with strong cultures are clear on what they stand for, and they take the process of getting people to "buy-in" to the cultural norms very seriously. The stronger the fit between culture and strategy, the less managers have to depend on policies, rules, procedures, and supervision to enforce what people should and should not do; rather, cultural norms are so well observed that they automatically guide behavior.

Successful strategy-implementers also exercise an important leadership role. They stay on top of how well things are going by spending considerable time outside their offices, wandering around the organization, listening, coaching, cheerleading, picking up important information, and keeping their fingers on the organization's pulse. They take pains to reinforce the corporate culture through the things they say and do. They encourage people to be creative and innovative in order to keep the organization responsive to changing conditions, alert to new opportunities, and anxious to pursue fresh initiatives. They support "champions" who are willing to stick their necks out and try something new. They work hard at building consensus on how to proceed, on what to change and what not to change. They enforce high ethical standards. And they push corrective action to improve strategy execution and overall strategic performance.

The action agenda for strategy implementation is expansive. It involves virtually every aspect of administrative and managerial work. However, each strategy implementation situation is unique to the organization and to its own circumstances. The strategy-implementer's action agenda, therefore, always depends on the current situation. Diagnosing the situation and devising actions to put strategy into place and achieve the desired results are major managerial challenges.

SUGGESTED READINGS

Bettinger, Cass. "Use Corporate Culture to Trigger High Performance." *Journal of Business Strategy* 10, no. 2 (March–April 1989), pp. 38–42.

Bower, Joseph L., and Martha W. Weinberg. "Statecraft, Strategy, and Corporate Leadership." *California Management Review* 30, no. 2 (Winter 1988), pp. 39–56.

Deal, Terence E., and Allen A. Kennedy. *Corporate Cultures.* Reading, Mass.: Addison-Wesley, 1982, especially chaps. 1 and 2.

Eccles, Robert G. "The Performance Measurement Manifesto." *Harvard Business Review* 69 (January–February 1991), pp. 131–37.

Freeman, R. Edward, and Daniel R. Gilbert, Jr. *Corporate Strategy and the Search for Ethics* (Englewood Cliffs, N.J.: Prentice Hall, 1988).

Gabarro, J. J. "When a New Manager Takes Charge." *Harvard Business Review* 64, no. 3 (May–June 1985), pp. 110–23.

Green, Sebastian. "Strategy, Organizational Culture, and Symbolism." *Long Range Planning* 21, no. 4 (August 1988), pp. 121–29.

Herzberg, Frederick. "One More Time: How Do You Motivate Employees?" *Harvard Business Review* 65, no. 4 (September–October 1987), pp. 109–20.

Kirkpatrick, Shelley A., and Edwin A. Locke. "Leadership: Do Traits Matter?" *Academy of Management Executive* 5, no. 2 (May 1991), pp. 48–60.

Kotter, John P. "What Leaders Really Do." *Harvard Business Review* 68 (May–June 1990), pp. 103–11.

O'Toole, James. "Employee Practices at the Best-Managed Companies." *California Management Review* 28, no. 1 (Fall 1985), pp. 35–66.

Pascale, Richard. "The Paradox of 'Corporate Culture': Reconciling Ourselves to Socialization." *California Management Review* 27, no. 2 (Winter 1985), pp. 26–41.

Peters, Thomas J., and Robert H. Waterman, Jr. *In Search of Excellence.* New York: Harper & Row, 1982, chaps. 4, 5, and 9.

Peters, Thomas J., and Nancy Austin. *A Passion for Excellence.* New York: Random House, 1985, especially chaps. 11, 12, 15–19.

Quinn, James Brian. *Strategies for Change: Logical Incrementalism.* Homewood, Ill.: Richard D. Irwin, 1980, chap. 4.

————. "Managing Innovation: Controlled Chaos." *Harvard Business Review* 64, no. 3 (May–June 1985), pp. 73–84.

Reimann, Bernard C., and Yoash Wiener. "Corporate Culture: Avoiding the Elitest Trap." *Business Horizons* 31, no. 2 (March–April 1988), pp. 36–44.

Scholz, Christian. "Corporate Culture and Strategy—The Problem of Strategic Fit." *Long Range Planning* 20 (August 1987), pp. 78–87.

Vancil, Richard F. *Implementing Strategy: The Role of Top Management.* Boston: Division of Research, Harvard Business School, 1985.

PART

II

READINGS IN STRATEGIC MANAGEMENT

CRAFTING STRATEGY

Henry Mintzberg
Professor of Management, McGill University

Imagine someone planning strategy. What likely springs to mind is an image of orderly thinking: a senior manager, or a group of them, sitting in an office formulating courses of action that everyone else will implement on schedule. The keynote is reason—rational control, the systematic analysis of competitors and markets, of company strengths and weaknesses, the combination of these analyses producing clear, explicit, full-blown strategies.

Now imagine someone *crafting* strategy. A wholly different image likely results, as different from planning as craft is from mechanization. Craft evokes traditional skill, dedication, perfection through the mastery of detail. What springs to mind is not so much thinking and reason as involvement, a feeling of intimacy and harmony with the materials at hand, developed through long experience and commitment. Formulation and implementation merge into a fluid process of learning through which creative strategies evolve.

My thesis is simple: The crafting image better captures the process by which effective strategies come to be. The planning image, long popular in the literature, distorts these processes and thereby misguides organizations that embrace it unreservedly.

In developing this thesis, I shall draw on the experiences of a single craftsperson, a potter, and compare them with the results of a research project that tracked the strategies of a number of corporations across several decades. Because the two contexts are so obviously different, my metaphor, like my assertion, may seem farfetched at first. Yet if we think of a craftsperson as an organization of one, we can see that he or she must also resolve one of the great challenges the corporate strategist faces: knowing the organization's capabilities well enough to think deeply enough about its strategic direction. By considering strategy making from the perspective of one person, free of all the paraphernalia of what has been called the strategy industry, we can learn something about the formation of strategy in the corporation. For much as our potter has to manage her craft, so too managers have to craft their strategy.

At work, the potter sits before a lump of clay on the wheel. Her mind is on the clay, but she is also aware of sitting between her past experiences and her future prospects. She knows exactly what has and has not worked for her in the past. She has an intimate knowledge of her work, her capabilities, and her markets. As a craftsperson, she senses rather than analyzes these things; her knowledge is "tacit." All these things are working in her mind as her hands are working the clay. The product that emerges on the wheel is likely to be in the tradition of her past work, but she may break away and embark on a new direction. Even so, the past is no less present, projecting itself into the future.

In my metaphor, managers are craftspersons and strategy is their clay. Like the potter, they sit between a past of corporate capabilities and a future of

Tracking Strategy

In 1971, I became intrigued by an unusual definition of strategy as a pattern in a stream of decisions (later changed to actions). I initiated a research project at McGill University, and over the next 13 years a team of us tracked the strategies of 11 organizations over several decades of their history. (Students at various levels also carried out about 20 other less comprehensive studies.) The organizations we studied were: Air Canada (1937–1976), Arcop, an architectural firm (1953–1978), Asbestos Corporation (1912–1975), Canadelle, a manufacturer of women's undergarments (1939–1976), McGill University (1829–1980), the National Film Board of Canada (1939–1976), Saturday Night Magazine (1928–1971), The Sherbrooke Record, a small daily newspaper (1946–1976), Steinberg Inc., a large supermarket chain (1917–1974), the U.S. military's strategy in Vietnam (1949–1973), and Volkswagenwerk (1934–1974).

As a first step, we developed chronological lists and graphs of the most important actions taken by each organization—such as store openings and closings, new flight destinations, and new product introductions. Second, we inferred patterns in these actions and labeled them as strategies.

Third, we represented graphically all the strategies we inferred in an organization so that we could line them up to see whether there were distinct periods in their development—for example, periods of stability, flux, or global change. Fourth, we used interviews and in-depth reports to study what appeared to be the key points of change in each organization's strategic history.

Finally, armed with all this strategic history, the research team studied each set of findings to develop conclusions about the process of strategy formation. Three themes guided us: the interplay of environment, leadership, and organization; the pattern of strategic change; and the processes by which strategies form. This article presents those conclusions.

market opportunities. And if they are truly craftspersons, they bring to their work an equally intimate knowledge of the materials at hand. That is the essence of crafting strategy.

In the pages that follow, we will explore this metaphor by looking at how strategies get made as opposed to how they are supposed to get made. Throughout, I will be drawing on the two sets of experiences I've mentioned. One, described in the insert, is a research project on patterns in strategy formation that has been going on at McGill University under my direction since 1971. The second is the stream of work of a successful potter, my wife, who began her craft in 1967.

Ask almost anyone what strategy is, and he will define it as a plan of some sort, an explicit guide to future behavior. Then ask what strategy a competitor or a government or even he himself has actually pursued. Chances are he will describe consistency in *past* behavior—a pattern in action over time. Strategy, it turns out, is one of those words that people define in one way, and often use in another, without realizing the difference.

The reason for this is simple. Strategy's formal definition and its Greek military origins notwithstanding, we need the word as much to explain past actions as to describe intended behavior. After all, if strategies can be planned and intended, they can also be pursued and realized (or not realized, as the case may be). And pattern in action, or what we call realized strategy, explains that pursuit. Moreover, just as a plan need not produce a pattern (some strategies that are intended are simply not realized), so too a pattern need not result from a plan. An organization can have a pattern (or realized strategy) without knowing it, let alone making it explicit.

Patterns, like beauty, are in the mind of the beholder, of course. But anyone reviewing a chronological lineup of our craftsperson's work would have little trouble discerning clear patterns, at least in certain periods. Until 1974, for example, she made small, decorative ceramic animals and objects of various kinds. Then this "knickknack strategy" stopped abruptly, and eventually new patterns formed around waferlike sculptures and ceramic bowls, highly textured and unglazed.

Finding equivalent patterns in action for organizations isn't that much more difficult. Indeed, for such large companies as Volkswagenwerk and Air Canada, in our research, it proved simpler! (As well it should. A craftsperson, after all, can change what she does in a studio a lot more easily that a Volkswagenwerk can retool its assembly lines.) Mapping the product models at Volkswagenwerk from the late 1940s to the late 1970s, for example, uncovers a clear pattern of concentration on the Beetle, followed in the late 1960s by a frantic search for replacements through acquisitions and internally developed new models, to a strategic reorientation around more stylish, water-cooled, front-wheel-drive vehicles in the mid-1970s.

But what about intended strategies, those formal plans and pronouncements we think of when we use the term *strategy*? Ironically, here we run into all kinds of problems. Even with a single craftsperson, how can we know what her intended strategies really were? If we could go back, would we find expressions of intention? And if we could, would we be able to trust them? We often fool ourselves, as well as others, by denying our subconscious motives. And remember that intentions are cheap, at least when compared with realizations.

READING THE ORGANIZATION'S MIND

If you believe all this has more to do with the Freudian recesses of a craftsperson's mind than with the practical realities of producing automobiles, then think again. For who knows what the intended strategies of a Volkswagenwerk really mean, let alone what they are? Can we simply assume in this collective context that the company's intended strategies are represented by its formal plans or by other statements emanating from the executive suite? Might these be just vain hopes or rationalizations or ploys to fool the competition? And even if expressed intentions exist, to what extent do others in the organization share them? How do we read the collective mind? Who is the strategist anyway?

The traditional view of strategic management resolves these problems quite simply, by what organizational theorists call attribution. You see it all the time in the business press. When General Motors acts, it's because Roger Smith has made a strategy. Given realization, there must have been intention, and that is automatically attributed to the chief.

In a short magazine article, this assumption is understandable. Journalists don't have a lot of time to uncover the origins of strategy, and GM is a large, complicated organization. But just consider all the complexity and confusion that gets tucked under this assumption—all the meetings and debates, the many people, the dead ends, the folding and unfolding of ideas. Now imagine trying to build a formal strategy-making system around that assumption. Is it any wonder that formal strategic planning is often such a resounding failure?

To unravel some of the confusion—and move away from the artificial complexity we have piled around the strategy-making process—we need to get back to some basic concepts. The most basic of all is the intimate connection between thought and action. That is the key to craft, and so also to the crafting strategy.

Virtually everything that has been written about strategy making depicts it as a deliberate process. First we think, then we act. We formulate, then we implement. The progression seems so perfectly sensible. Why would anybody want to proceed differently?

Our potter is in the studio, rolling the clay to make a waferlike sculpture. The clay sticks to the rolling pin, and a round form appears. Why not make a cylindrical vase? One idea leads to another, until a new pattern forms. Action has driven thinking; A strategy has emerged.

Out in the field, a salesman visits a customer. The product isn't quite right, and together they work out some modifications. The salesman returns to his company and puts the changes through; after two or three more rounds, they finally get it right. A new product emerges, which eventually opens up a new market. The company has changed strategic course.

In fact, most salespeople are less fortunate than this one or than our craftsperson. In an organization of one, the implementor is the formulator, so innovations can be incorporated into strategy quickly and easily. In a large organization, the innovator may be 10 levels removed from the leader who is supposed to dictate strategy and may also have to sell the idea to dozens of peers doing the same job.

Some salespeople, of course, can proceed on their own, modifying products to suit their customers and convincing skunkworks in the factory to produce them. In effect, they pursue their own strategies. Maybe no one else notices or cares. Sometimes, however, their innovations do get noticed, perhaps years later, when the company's prevalent strategies have broken down and its leaders are groping for something new. Then the salesperson's strategy may be allowed to pervade the system, to become organizational.

Is this story farfetched? Certainly not. We've all heard stories like it. But since we tend to see only what we believe, if we believe that strategies have to be planned, we're unlikely to see the real meaning such stories hold.

Consider how the National Film Board of Canada (NFB) came to adopt a feature-film strategy. The NFB is a federal government agency, famous for its creativity and expert in the production of short documentaries. Some years back, it funded a filmmaker on a project that unexpectedly ran long. To distribute his film, the NFB turned to theaters and so inadvertently gained experience in marketing feature-length films. Other filmmakers caught onto the idea, and eventually the NFB found itself pursuing a feature-film strategy—a pattern of producing such films.

My point is simple, deceptively simple: strategies can *form* as well as be *formulated*. A realized strategy can emerge in response to an evolving situation, or it can be brought about deliberately, through a process of formulation followed by implementation. But when these planned intentions do not produce the desired actions, organizations are left with unrealized strategies.

Today we hear a great deal about unrealized strategies, almost always in concert with the claim that implementation has failed. Excuses abound. At times, indeed, they may be valid. But often these explanations prove too easy. So some people look beyond implementation to formulation. The strategists haven't been smart enough.

While it is certainly true that many intended strategies are ill conceived, I believe that the problem often lies one step beyond, in the distinction we make between formulation and implementation, the common assumption that thought must be independent of (and precede) action. Sure, people could be smarter—but not only by conceiving more clever strategies. Sometimes they can be smarter by allowing their strategies to develop gradually, through the organization's actions and experiences. Smart strategists appreciate that they cannot always be smart enough to think through everything in advance.

HANDS AND MINDS

No craftsperson thinks some days and works others. The craftsperson's mind is going constantly, in tandem with her hands. Yet large organizations try to separate the work of minds and hands. In so doing, they often sever the vital feedback link between the two. The salesperson who finds a customer with an unmet need may possess the most strategic bit of information in the entire organization. But that information is useless if he or she cannot create a strategy in response to it or else convey the information to someone who can—because the channels are blocked or because the formulators have simply finished formulating. The notion that strategy is something that should happen way up there, far removed from the details of running an organization on a daily basis, is one of the great fallacies of conventional strategic management. And it explains a good many of the most dramatic failures in business and public policy today.

We at McGill call strategies like the NFB's that appear without clear intentions—or in spite of them—emergent strategies. Actions simply converge into patterns. They may become deliberate, of course, if the pattern is recognized and then legitimated by senior management. But that's after the fact.

All this may sound rather strange, I know. Strategies that emerge? Managers who acknowledge strategies already formed? Over the years, our research group at McGill has met with a good deal of resistance from people upset by what they perceive to be our passive definition of a word so bound up with proactive behavior and free will. After all, strategy means control—the ancient Greeks used it to describe the art of the army general.

STRATEGIC LEARNING

But we have persisted in this usage for one reason: learning. Purely deliberate strategy precludes learning once the strategy is formulated; emergent strategy fosters it. People take actions one by one and respond to them, so that patterns eventually form.

Our craftsperson tries to make a freestanding sculptural form. It doesn't work, so she rounds it a bit here, flattens it a bit there. The result looks better, but still isn't quite right. She makes another and another and another. Eventually, after days or months or years, she finally has what she wants. She is off on a new strategy.

In practice, of course, all strategy making walks on two feet, one deliberate, the other emergent. For just as purely deliberate strategy making precludes learning, so purely emergent strategy making precludes control. Pushed to the limit, neither approach makes sense. Learning must be coupled with control. That is why the McGill research group uses the word *strategy* for both emergent and deliberate behavior.

Likewise, there is no such thing as a purely deliberate strategy or a purely emergent one. No organization—not even the ones commanded by those ancient Greek generals—knows enough to work everything out in advance, to ignore learning en route. And no one—not even a solitary potter—can be flexible enough to leave everything to happenstance, to give up all control. Craft requires control just as it requires responsiveness to the material at hand. Thus deliberate and emergent strategy form the end points of a continuum along which the strategies that are crafted in the real world may be found. Some strategies may approach either end, but many more fall at intermediate points.

Effective strategies can show up in the strangest places and develop through the most unexpected means. There is no one best way to make strategy.

The form for a cat collapses on the wheel, and our potter sees a bull taking shape. Clay sticks to a rolling pin, and a line of cylinders results. Wafers come into being because of a shortage of clay and limited kiln space in a studio in France. Thus errors become opportunities, and limitations stimulate creativity. The natural propensity to experiment, even boredom, likewise stimulate strategic change.

Organizations that craft their strategies have similar experiences. Recall the National Film Board with its inadvertently long film. Or consider its experiences with experimental films, which made special use of animation and sound. For 20 years, the NFB produced a bare but steady trickle of such films. In fact, every film but one in that trickle was produced by a single person, Norman McLaren, the NFB's most celebrated filmmaker. McLaren pursued a *personal strategy* of experimentation, deliberate for him perhaps (though who can know whether he had the whole stream in mind or simply planned one film at a time?) but not for the organization. Then 20 years later, others followed his lead and the trickle widened, his personal strategy becoming more broadly organizational.

Conversely, in 1952, when television came to Canada, a *consensus strategy* quickly emerged at the NFB. Senior management was not keen on producing films for the new medium. But while the arguments raged, one filmmaker quietly went off and made a single series for TV. That precedent set, one by one his colleagues leapt in, and within months the NFB—and its management—found themselves committed for several years to a new strategy with an intensity unmatched before or since. This consensus strategy arose spontaneously, as a result of many independent decisions made by the filmmakers about the films they wished to make. Can we call this strategy deliberate? For the filmmakers perhaps; for senior management certainly not. But for the organization? It all depends on your perspective, on how you choose to read the organization's mind.

While the NFB may seem like an extreme case, it highlights behavior that can be found, albeit in muted form, in all organizations. Those who doubt this might read Richard Pascale's account of how Honda stumbled into its enormous success in the American motorcycle market. Brilliant as its strategy may have looked after the fact, Honda's managers made almost every conceivable mistake until the market finally hit them over the head with the right formula.

The Honda managers on site in America, driving their products themselves (and thus inadvertently picking up market reaction), did only one thing right: they learned, firsthand.[1]

GRASS-ROOTS STRATEGY MAKING

These strategies all reflect, in whole or part, what we like to call a grass-roots approach to strategic management. Strategies grow like weeds in a garden. They take root in all kinds of places, wherever people have the capacity to learn (because they are in touch with the situation) and the resources to support that capacity. These strategies become organizational when they become collective, that is, when they proliferate to guide the behavior of the organization at large.

Of course, this view is overstated. But it is no less extreme than the conventional view of strategic management, which might be labeled the hothouse approach. Neither is right. Reality falls between the two. Some of the most effective strategies we uncovered in our research combined deliberation and control with flexibility and organizational learning.

Consider first what we call the *umbrella strategy.* Here senior management sets out broad guidelines (say, to produce only high-margin products at the cutting edge of technology or to favor products using bonding technology) and leaves the specifics (such as what these products will be) to others lower down the organization. This strategy is not only deliberate (in its guidelines) and emergent (in its specifics), but it is also deliberately emergent in that the process is consciously managed to allow strategies to emerge en route. IBM used the umbrella strategy in the early 1960s with the impending 360 series, when its senior management approved a set of broad criteria for the design of a family of computers later developed in detail throughout the organization.[2]

Deliberately emergent, too, is what we call the *process strategy.* Here management controls the process of strategy formation—concerning itself with the design of the structure, its staffing, procedures, and so on—while leaving the actual content to others.

Both process and umbrella strategies seem to be especially prevalent in businesses that require great expertise and creativity—a 3M, a Hewlett-Packard, a National Film Board. Such organizations can be effective only if their implementors are allowed to be formulators because it is people way down in the hierarchy who are in touch with the situation at hand and have the requisite technical expertise. In a sense, these are organizations peopled with craftspersons, all of whom must be strategists.

The conventional view of strategic management, especially in the planning literature, claims that change must be continuous: the organization should be adapting all the time. Yet this view proves to be ironic because the very concept of strategy is rooted in stability, not change. As this same literature makes clear, organizations pursue strategies to set direction, to lay out courses of action, and to elicit cooperation from their members around common, established guidelines. By any definition, strategy imposes stability on an

[1]Richard T. Pascale, "Perspective on Strategy: The Real Story Behind Honda's Success," *California Management Review,* May–June 1984, p. 47.

[2]James Brian Quinn, IBM (A) case, in James Brian Quinn, Henry Mintzberg, and Robert M. James. *The Strategy Process: Concepts, Contexts, Cases* (Englewood Cliffs, N.J.: Prentice Hall, 1987).

organization. No stability means no strategy (no course to the future, no pattern from the past). Indeed, the very fact of having a strategy, and especially of making it explicit (as the conventional literature implores managers to do), creates resistance to strategic change!

What the conventional view fails to come to grips with, then, is how and when to promote change. A fundamental dilemma of strategy making is the need to reconcile the forces for stability and for change—to focus efforts and gain operating efficiencies on the one hand, yet adapt and maintain currency with a changing external environment on the other.

QUANTUM LEAPS

Our own research and that of colleagues suggest that organizations resolve these opposing forces by attending first to one and then to the other. Clear periods of stability and change can usually be distinguished in any organization: While it is true that particular strategies may always be changing marginally, it seems equally true that major shifts in strategic orientation occur only rarely.

In our study of Steinberg Inc., a large Quebec supermarket chain headquartered in Montreal, we found only two important reorientations in the 60 years from its founding to the mid-1970s: a shift to self-service in 1933 and the introduction of shopping centers and public financing in 1953. At Volkswagenwerk, we saw only one between the late 1940s and the 1970s, the tumultuous shift from the traditional Beetle to the Audi-type design mentioned earlier. And at Air Canada, we found none over the airline's first four decades, following its initial positioning.

Our colleagues at McGill, Danny Miller and Peter Friesen, found this pattern of change so common in their studies of large numbers of companies (especially the high-performance ones) that they built a theory around it, which they labeled the quantum theory of strategic change.[3] Their basic point is that organizations adopt two distinctly different modes of behavior at different times.

Most of the time they pursue a given strategic orientation. Change may seem continuous, but it occurs in the context of that orientation (perfecting a given retailing formula, for example) and usually amounts to doing more of the same, perhaps better as well. Most organizations favor these periods of stability because they achieve success not by changing strategies but by exploiting the ones they have. They, like craftspersons, seek continuous improvement by using their distinctive competencies in established courses.

While this goes on, however, the world continues to change, sometimes slowly, occasionally in dramatic shifts. Thus gradually or suddenly, the organization's strategic orientation moves out of sync with its environment. Then what Miller and Friesen call a strategic revolution must take place. That long period of evolutionary change is suddenly punctuated by a brief bout of revolutionary turmoil in which the organization quickly alters many of its established patterns. In effect, it tries to leap to a new stability quickly to reestablish an integrated posture among a new set of strategies, structures, and culture.

---

[3]See Danny Miller and Peter H. Friesen, *Organization: A Quantum View* (Englewood Cliffs, N.J.: Prentice Hall, 1984).

But what about all those emergent strategies, growing like weeds around the organization? What the quantum theory suggests is that the really novel ones are generally held in check in some corner of the organization until a strategic revolution becomes necessary. Then as an alternative to having to develop new strategies from scratch or having to import generic strategies from competitors, the organization can turn to its own emerging patterns to find its new orientation. As the old, established strategy disintegrates, the seeds of the new one begin to spread.

This quantum theory of change seems to apply particularly well to large, established, mass-production companies. Because they are especially reliant on standardized procedures, their resistance to strategic reorientation tends to be especially fierce. So we find long periods of stability broken by short disruptive periods of revolutionary change.

Volkswagenwerk is a case in point. Long enamored of the Beetle and armed with a tightly integrated set of strategies, the company ignored fundamental changes in its markets throughout the late 1950s and 1960s. The bureaucratic momentum of its mass-production organization combined with the psychological momentum of its leader, who institutionalized the strategies in the first place. When change finally did come, it was tumultuous: the company groped its way through a hodgepodge of products before it settled on a new set of vehicles championed by a new leader. Strategic reorientations really are cultural revolutions.

CYCLES OF CHANGE

In more creative organizations, we see a somewhat different pattern of change and stability, one that's more balanced. Companies in the business of producing novel outputs apparently need to fly off in all directions from time to time to sustain their creativity. Yet they also need to settle down after such periods to find some order in the resulting chaos.

The National Film Board's tendency to move in and out of focus through remarkably balanced periods of convergence and divergence is a case in point. Concentrated production of films to aid the war effort in the 1940s gave way to great divergence after the war as the organization sought a new raison d'être. Then the advent of television brought back a very sharp focus in the early 1950s, as noted earlier. But in the late 1950s, this dissipated almost as quickly as it began, giving rise to another creative period of exploration. Then the social changes in the early 1960s evoked a new period of convergence around experimental films and social issues.

We use the label "adhocracy" for organizations, like the National Film Board, that produce individual, or custom-made, products (or designs) in an innovative way, on a project basis.[4] Our craftsperson is an adhocracy of sorts too, since each of her ceramic sculptures is unique. And her pattern of strategic change was much like that of the NFB's, with evident cycles of convergence and divergence: a focus on knickknacks from 1967 to 1972; then a period of

---

[4]See my article "Organization Design: Fashion or Fit:" *HBR* January–February 1981, p. 103; also see my book *Structure in Fives: Designing Effective Organizations* (Englewood Cliffs, NJ: Prentice Hall, 1983). The term *adhocracy* was coined by Warren G. Bennis and Philip E. Slater in *The Temporary Society* (New York: Harper & Row, 1964).

exploration to about 1976 which resulted in a refocus on ceramic sculptures; that continued to about 1981, to be followed by a period of searching for new directions. More recently, a focus on ceramic murals seems to be emerging.

Whether through quantum revolutions or cycles of convergence and divergence, however, organizations seem to need to separate in time the basic forces for change and stability, reconciling them by attending to each in turn. Many strategic failures can be attributed either to mixing the two or to an obsession with one of these forces at the expense of the other.

The problems are evident in the work of many craftspersons. On the one hand, there are those who seize on the perfection of a single theme and never change. Eventually the creativity disappears from their work and the world passes them by—much as it did Volkswagenwerk until the company was shocked into its strategic revolution. And then there are those who are always changing, who flit from one idea to another and never settle down. Because no theme or strategy ever emerges in their work, they cannot exploit or even develop any distinctive competence. And because their work lacks definition, identity crises are likely to develop, with neither the craftsperson nor her clientele knowing what to make of it. Miller and Friesen found this behavior in conventional business too; they label it "the impulsive firm running blind."[5] How often have we seen it in companies that go on acquisition sprees?

The popular view sees the strategist as a planner or as a visionary, someone sitting on a pedestal dictating brilliant strategies for everyone else to implement. While recognizing the importance of thinking ahead and especially of the need for creative vision in this pedantic world, I wish to propose an additional view of the strategist—as a pattern recognizer, a learner if you will—who manages a process in which strategies (and visions) can emerge as well as be deliberately conceived. I also wish to redefine that strategist, to extend that someone into the collective entity made up of the many actors whose interplay speaks an organization's mind. This strategist *finds* strategies no less than creates them, often in patterns that form inadvertently in its own behavior.

What, then, does it mean to craft strategy? Let us return to the words associated with craft: dedication, experience, involvement with the material, the personal touch, mastery of detail, a sense of harmony and integration. Managers who craft strategy do not spend much time in executive suites reading MIS reports or industry analyses. They are involved, responsive to their materials, learning about their organizations and industries through personal touch. They are also sensitive to experience, recognizing that, while individual vision may be important, other factors must help determine strategy as well.

Manage Stability Managing strategy is mostly managing stability, not change. Indeed, most of the time senior managers should not be formulating strategy at all; they should be getting on with making their organizations as effective as possible in pursuing the strategies they already have. Like distinguished craftspersons, organizations become distinguished because they master the details.

---

[5]Danny Miller and Peter H. Friesen, "Archetypes of Strategy Formulation," *Management Science*, May 1978, p. 921.

To manage strategy, then, at least in the first instance, is not so much to promote change as to know *when* to do so. Advocates of strategic planning often urge managers to plan for perpetual instability in the environment (for example, by rolling over five-year plans annually). But this obsession with change is dysfunctional. Organizations that reassess their strategies continuously are like individuals who reassess their jobs or their marriages continuously—in both cases, people will drive themselves crazy or else reduce themselves to inaction. The formal planning process repeats itself so often and so mechanically that it desensitizes the organization to real change, programs it more and more deeply into set patterns, and thereby encourages it to make only minor adaptations.

So-called strategic planning must be recognized for what it is: a means, not to create strategy, but to program a strategy already created—to work out its implications formally. It is essentially analytic in nature, based on decomposition, while strategy creation is essentially a process of synthesis. That is why trying to create strategies through formal planning most often leads to extrapolating existing ones or copying those of competitors.

This is not to say that planners have no role to play in strategy formation. In addition to programming strategies created by other means, they can feed ad hoc analyses into the strategy-making process at the front end to be sure that the hard data are taken into consideration. They can also stimulate others to think strategically. And of course people called planners can be strategists too, so long as they are creative thinkers who are in touch with what is relevant. But that has nothing to do with the technology of formal planning.

Detect Discontinuity   Environments do not change on any regular or orderly basis. And they seldom undergo continuous dramatic change, claims about our "age of discontinuity" and environmental "turbulence" notwithstanding. (Go tell people who lived through the Great Depression or survivors of the siege of Leningrad during World War II that ours are turbulent times.) Much of the time, change is minor and even temporary and requires no strategic response. Once in a while there is truly significant discontinuity or, even less often, a gestalt shift in the environment, where everything important seems to change at once. But these events, while critical, are also easy to recognize.

The real challenge in crafting strategy lies in detecting the subtle discontinuities that may undermine a business in the future. And for that, there is no technique, no program, just a sharp mind in touch with the situation. Such discontinuities are unexpected and irregular, essentially unprecedented. They can be dealt with only by minds that are attuned to existing patterns yet able to perceive important breaks in them. Unfortunately, this form of strategic thinking tends to atrophy during the long periods of stability that most organizations experience (just as it did at Volkswagenwerk during the 1950s and 1960s). So the trick is to manage within a given strategic orientation most of the time yet be able to pick out the occasional discontinuity that really matters.

The Steinberg chain was built and run for more than half a century by a man named Sam Steinberg. For 20 years, the company concentrated on perfecting a self-service retailing formula introduced in 1933. Installing fluorescent lighting and figuring out how to package meat in cellophane wrapping were the "strategic" issues of the day. Then in 1952, with the arrival of the first shopping center in Montreal, Steinberg realized he had to redefine his business almost overnight. He knew he needed to control those shopping centers and that control would require public financing and other major changes. So he reoriented his business. The ability to make that kind of switch in thinking is the essence of strategic management. And it has more to do with vision and involvement than it does with analytic technique.

Know the Business   Sam Steinberg was the epitome of the entrepreneur, a man intimately involved with all the details of his business, who spent Saturday mornings visiting his stores. As he told us in discussing his company's competitive advantage:

"Nobody knew the grocery business like we did. Everything has to do with your knowledge. I knew merchandise, I knew cost, I knew selling, I knew customers. I knew everything, and I passed on all my knowledge; I kept teaching my people. That's the advantage we had. Our competitors couldn't touch us."

Note the kind of knowledge involved: not intellectual knowledge, not analytical reports or abstracted facts and figures (though these can certainly help), but personal knowledge, intimate understanding, equivalent to the craftsperson's feel for the clay. Facts are available to anyone; this kind of knowledge is not. Wisdom is the word that captures it best. But wisdom is a word that has been lost in the bureaucracies we have built for ourselves, systems designed to distance leaders from operating details. Show me managers who think they can rely on formal planning to create their strategies, and I'll show you managers who lack intimate knowledge of their businesses or the creativity to do something with it.

Craftspersons have to train themselves to see, to pick up on things other people miss. The same holds true for managers of strategy. It is those with a kind of peripheral vision who are best able to detect and take advantage of events as they unfold.

Manage Patterns   Whether in an executive suite in Manhattan or a pottery studio in Montreal, a key to managing strategy is the ability to detect emerging patterns and help them take shape. The job of the manager is not just to preconceive specific strategies but also to recognize their emergence elsewhere in the organization and intervene when appropriate.

Like weeds that appear unexpectedly in a garden, some emergent strategies may need to be uprooted immediately. But management cannot be too quick to cut off the unexpected, for tomorrow's vision may grow out of today's aberration. (Europeans, after all, enjoy salads made from the leaves of the dandelion, America's most notorious weed.) Thus some patterns are worth watching until their effects have more clearly manifested themselves. Then those that prove useful can be made deliberate and be incorporated into the formal strategy, even if that means shifting the strategic umbrella to cover them.

To manage in this context, then, is to create the climate within which a wide variety of strategies can grow. In more complex organizations, this may mean building flexible structures, hiring creative people, defining broad umbrella strategies, and watching for the patterns that emerge.

Reconcile Change and Continuity   Finally, managers considering radical departures need to keep the quantum theory of change in mind. As Ecclesiastes reminds us, there is a time to sow and a time to reap. Some new patterns must be held in check until the organization is ready for a strategic revolution, or at least a period of divergence. Managers who are obsessed with either change or stability are bound eventually to harm their organizations. As pattern recognizer, the manager has to be able to sense when to exploit an established crop of strategies and when to encourage new strains to displace the old.

While strategy is a word that is usually associated with the future, its link to the past is no less central. As Kierkegaard once observed, life is lived forward but understood backward. Managers may have to live strategy in the future, but they must understand it through the past.

Like potters at the wheel, organizations must make sense of the past if they hope to manage the future. Only by coming to understand the patterns that form in their own behavior do they get to know their capabilities and their potential. Thus crafting strategy, like managing craft, requires a natural synthesis of the future, present, and past.

Author's note: Readers interested in learning more about the results of the tracking strategy project have a wide range of studies to draw from. Works published to date can be found in Robert Lamb and Paul Shivastava, eds., *Advances in Strategic Management* 4 (Greenwich, Conn.: Jai Press, 1986), pp. 3–41; *Management Science*, May 1978, p. 934; *Administrative Science Quarterly,* June 1985, p. 160; J. Grant, ed. *Strategic Management Frontiers* (Greenwich, Conn.: Jai Press, 1988); *Canadian Journal of Administrative Sciences,* June 1984, p. 1; *Academy of Management Journal*, September 1982, p. 465; Robert Lamb, ed., *Competitive Strategic Management* (Englewood Cliffs, NJ: Prentice Hall, 1984).

STRATEGIC INTENT

Gary Hamel, London Business School
C. K. Prahalad, University of Michigan

Today managers in many industries are working hard to match the competitive advantages of their new global rivals. They are moving manufacturing offshore in search of lower labor costs, rationalizing product lines to capture global scale economies, instituting quality circles and just-in-time production, and adopting Japanese human resource practices. When competitiveness still seems out of reach, they form strategic alliances—often with the very companies that upset the competitive balance in the first place.

Important as these initiatives are, few of them go beyond mere imitation. Too many companies are expending enormous energy simply to reproduce the cost and quality advantages their global competitors already enjoy. Imitation may be the sincerest form of flattery, but it will not lead to competitive revitalization. Strategies based on imitation are transparent to competitors who have already mastered them. Moreover, successful competitors rarely stand still. So it is not surprising that many executives feel trapped in a seemingly endless game of catch-up—regularly surprised by the new accomplishments of their rivals.

For these executives and their companies, regaining competitiveness will mean rethinking many of the basic concepts of strategy.[1] As "strategy" has blossomed, the competitiveness of Western companies has withered. This may be coincidence, but we think not. We believe that the application of concepts such as "strategic fit" (between resources and opportunities), "generic strategies" (low cost versus differentiation versus focus), and the "strategy hierarchy" (goals, strategies, and tactics) have often abetted the process of competitive decline. The new global competitors approach strategy from a perspective that is fundamentally different from that which underpins Western management thought. Against such competitors, marginal adjustments to current orthodoxies are no more likely to produce competitive revitalization than are marginal improvements in operating efficiency. (The insert, "Remaking Strategy," describes our research and summarizes the two contrasting approaches to strategy we see in large, multinational companies.)

Few Western companies have an enviable track record anticipating the moves of new global competitors. Why? The explanation begins with the way most companies have approached competitor analysis. Typically, competitor analysis focuses on the existing resources (human, technical, and financial) of present competitors. The only companies seen as a threat are those with the resources to erode margins and market share in the next planning period.

Source: Reprinted by permission of *Harvard Business Review*. "Strategic Intent," by Gary Hamel and C. K. Prahalad, May–June 1989, pp. 63–76.

[1] Among the first to apply the concept of strategy to management were H. Igor Ansoff in *Corporate Strategy: An Analytic Approach to Business Policy for Growth and Expansion* (New York: McGraw-Hill, 1965) and Kenneth R. Andrews in *The Concept of Corporate Strategy* (Homewood, Ill.: Dow Jones–Irwin, 1971).

Resourcefulness, the pace at which new competitive advantages are being built, rarely enters in.

In this respect, traditional competitor analysis is like a snapshot of a moving car. By itself, the photograph yields little information about the car's speed or direction—whether the driver is out for a quiet Sunday drive or warming up for the Grand Prix. Yet many managers have learned through painful experience that a business's initial resource endowment (whether bountiful or meager) is an unreliable predictor of future global success.

Think back. In 1970, few Japanese companies possessed the resource base, manufacturing volume, or technical prowess of U.S. and European industry leaders. Komatsu was less than 35 percent as large as Caterpillar (measured by sales), was scarcely represented outside Japan, and relied on just one product line—small bulldozers—for most of its revenue. Honda was smaller than American Motors and had not yet begun to export cars to the United States. Canon's first halting steps in the reprographics business looked pitifully small compared with the $4 billion Xerox powerhouse.

If Western managers had extended their competitor analysis to include these companies, it would merely have underlined how dramatic the resource discrepancies between them were. Yet by 1985, Komatsu was a $2.8 billion company with a product scope encompassing a broad range of earth-moving equipment, industrial robots, and semiconductors. Honda manufactured almost as many cars worldwide in 1987 as Chrysler. Canon had matched Xerox's global unit market share.

The lesson is clear: assessing the current tactical advantages of known competitors will not help you understand the resolution, stamina, and inventiveness of potential competitors. Sun-tzu, a Chinese military strategist, made the point 3,000 years ago: "All men can see the tactics whereby I conquer," he wrote, "but what none can see is the strategy out of which great victory is evolved."

Companies that have risen to global leadership over the past 20 years invariably began with ambitions that were out of all proportion to their resources and capabilities. But they created an obsession with winning at all levels of the organization and then sustained that obsession over the 10- to 20-year quest for global leadership. We term this obsession "strategic intent."

On the one hand, strategic intent envisions a desired leadership position and establishes the criterion the organization will use to chart its progress. Komatsu set out to "Encircle Caterpillar." Canon sought to "Beat Xerox." Honda strove to become a second Ford—an automotive pioneer. All are expressions of strategic intent.

At the same time, strategic intent is more than simply unfettered ambition. (Many companies possess an ambitious strategic intent yet fall short of their goals.) The concept also encompasses an active management process that includes: focusing the organization's attention on the essence of winning; motivating people by communicating the value of the target; leaving room for individual and team contributions; sustaining enthusiasm by providing new operational definitions as circumstances change; and using intent consistently to guide resource allocations.

Strategic intent captures the essence of winning. The Apollo program—landing a man on the moon ahead of the Soviets—was as competitively focused as

Remaking Strategy

Over the last 10 years, our research on global competition, international alliances, and multi-national management has brought us into close contact with senior managers in America, Europe, and Japan, As we tried to unravel the reasons for success and surrender in global markets, we became more and more suspicious that executives in Western and Far Eastern companies often operated with very different conceptions of competitive strategy. Understanding these differences, we thought, might help explain the conduct and outcome of competitive battles as well as supplement traditional explanations for Japan's ascendance and the West's decline.

We began by mapping the implicit strategy models of managers who had participated in our research. Then we built detailed histories of selected competitive battles. We searched for evidence of divergent views of strategy, competitive advantage, and the role of top management.

Two contrasting models of strategy emerged. One, which most Western managers will recognize, centers on the problem of maintaining strategic fit. The other centers on the problem of leveraging resources. The two are not mutually exclusive, but they represent a significant difference in emphasis—an emphasis that deeply affects how competitive battles get played out over time.

Both models recognize the problem of competing in a hostile environment with limited resources. But while the emphasis in the first is on trimming ambitions to match available resources, the emphasis in the second is on leveraging resources to reach seemingly unattainable goals.

Both models recognize that relative competitive advantage determines relative profitability. The first emphasizes the search for advantages that are inherently sustainable, the second emphasizes the need to accelerate organizational learning to outpace competitors in building new advantages.

Both models recognize the difficulty of competing against larger competitors. But while the first leads to a search for niches (or simply dissuades the company from challenging an entrenched competitor), the second produces a quest for new rules that can devalue the incumbent's advantages.

Both models recognize that balance in the scope of an organization's activities reduces risk. The first seeks to reduce financial risk by building a balanced portfolio of cash-generating and cash-consuming businesses. The second seeks to reduce competitive risk by ensuring a well-balanced and sufficiently broad portfolio of advantages.

Both models recognize the need to disaggregate the organization in a way that allows top management to differentiate among the investment needs of various planning units. In the first model, resources are allocated to product-market units in which relatedness is defined by common products, channels, and customers. Each business is assumed to own all the critical skills it needs to execute its strategy successfully. In the second, investments are made in core competences (microprocessor controls or electronic imaging, for example) as well as in product-market units. By tracking these investments across businesses, top management works to assure that the plans of individual strategic units don't undermine future developments by default.

Both models recognize the need for consistency in action across organizational levels. In the first, consistency between corporate and business levels is largely a matter of conforming to financial objectives. Consistency between business and functional levels comes by tightly restricting the means the business uses to achieve its strategy—establishing standard operating procedures, defining the served market, adhering to accepted industry practices. In the second model, business-corporate consistency comes from allegiance to a particular strategic intent. Business-functional consistency comes from allegiance to intermediate-term goals, or challenges, with lower level employees encouraged to invent how those goals will be achieved.

Komatsu's drive against Caterpillar. The space program became the scorecard for America's technology race with the USSR. In the turbulent information technology industry, it was hard to pick a single competitor as a target, so NEC's strategic intent, set in the early 1970s, was to acquire the technologies that would put it in the best position to exploit the convergence of computing and telecommunications. Other industry observers foresaw this convergence, but only NEC made convergence the guiding theme for subsequent strategic decisions by adopting "computing and communications" as its intent. For Coca-Cola, strategic intent has been to put a Coke within "arm's reach" of every consumer in the world.

Strategic intent is stable over time. In battles for global leadership, one of the most critical tasks is to lengthen the organization's attention span. Strategic intent provides consistency to short-term action, while leaving room for reinterpretation as new opportunities emerge. At Komatsu, encircling Caterpillar encompassed a succession of medium-term programs aimed at exploiting specific weaknesses in Caterpillar or building particular competitive advantages. When Caterpillar threatened Komatsu in Japan, for example, Komatsu responded by first improving quality, then driving down costs, then cultivating export markets, and then underwriting new product development.

Strategic intent sets a target that deserves personal effort and commitment. Ask the chairmen of many American corporations how they measure their contributions to their companies' success and you're likely to get an answer expressed in terms of shareholder wealth. In a company that possesses a strategic intent, top management is more likely to talk in terms of global market leadership. Market share leadership typically yields shareholder wealth, to be sure. But the two goals do not have the same motivational impact. It is hard to imagine middle managers, let alone blue-collar employees, waking up each day with the sole thought of creating more shareholder wealth. But mightn't they feel different given the challenge to "Beat Benz"—the rallying cry at one Japanese auto producer? Strategic intent gives employees the only goal that is worthy of commitment: to unseat the best or remain the best, worldwide.

Many companies are more familiar with strategic planning than they are with strategic intent. The planning process typically acts as a "feasibility sieve." Strategies are accepted or rejected on the basis of whether managers can be precise about the "how" as well as the "what" of their plans. Are the milestones clear? Do we have the necessary skills and resources? How will competitors react? Has the market been thoroughly researched? In one form or another, the admonition "Be realistic!" is given to line managers at almost every turn.

But can you *plan* for global leadership? Did Komatsu, Canon, and Honda have detailed, 20-year "strategies" for attacking Western markets? Are Japanese and Korean managers better planners than their Western counterparts? No. As valuable as strategic planning is, global leadership is an objective that lies outside the range of planning. We know of few companies with highly developed planning systems that have managed to set a strategic intent. As tests of strategic fit become more stringent, goals that cannot be planned for fall by the wayside. Yet companies that are afraid to commit to goals that lie outside the range of planning are unlikely to become global leaders.

Although strategic planning is billed as a way of becoming more future oriented, most managers, when pressed, will admit that their strategic plans reveal more about today's problems than tomorrow's opportunities. With a fresh set of problems confronting managers at the beginning of every planning cycle, focus often shifts dramatically from year to year. And with the pace of change accelerating in most industries, the predictive horizon is becoming shorter and shorter. So plans do little more than project the present forward incrementally. The goal of strategic intent is to fold the future back into the present. The important question is not "How will next year be different from this year?" but "What must we do differently next year to get closer to our strategic intent?" Only with a carefully articulated and adhered to strategic intent will a succession of year-on-year plans sum up to global leadership.

Just as you cannot plan a 10- to 20-year quest for global leadership, the chance of falling into a leadership position by accident is also remote. We don't believe that global leadership comes from an undirected process of intrapreneurship. Nor is it the product of a skunkworks or other techniques for internal venturing. Behind such programs lies a nihilistic assumption: the organization is so hidebound, so orthodox ridden that the only way to innovate is to put a few bright people in a dark room, pour in some money, and hope that something wonderful will happen. In this "Silicon Valley" approach to innovation, the only role for top managers is to retrofit their corporate strategy to the entrepreneurial successes that emerge from below. Here the value added of top management is low indeed.

Sadly, this view of innovation may be consistent with the reality in many large companies.[2] On the one hand, top management lacks any particular point of view about desirable ends beyond satisfying shareholders and keeping raiders at bay. On the other, the planning format, reward criteria, definition of served market, and belief in accepted industry practice all work together to tightly constrain the range of available means. As a result, innovation is necessarily an isolated activity. Growth depends more on the inventive capacity of individuals and small teams than on the ability of top management to aggregate the efforts of multiple teams towards an ambitious strategic intent.

In companies that overcame resource constraints to build leadership positions, we see a different relationship between means and ends. While strategic intent is clear about ends, it is flexible as to means—it leaves room for improvisation. Achieving strategic intent requires enormous creativity with respect to means: witness Fujitsu's use of strategic alliances in Europe to attack IBM. But this creativity comes in the service of a clearly prescribed end. Creativity is unbridled, but not uncorralled, because top management establishes the criterion against which employees can pretest the logic of their initiatives. Middle managers must do more than deliver on promised financial targets; they must also deliver on the broad direction implicit in their organization's strategic intent.

Strategic intent implies a sizable stretch for an organization. Current capabilities and resources will not suffice. This forces the organization to be more inventive, to make the most of limited resources. Whereas the traditional view of strategy focuses on the degree of fit between existing resources and current opportunities, strategic intent creates an extreme misfit between resources and ambitions. Top management then challenges the organization to close the gap by systematically building new advantages. For Canon this meant first understanding Xerox's patents, then licensing technology to create a product that would yield early market experience, then gearing up internal R&D efforts, then licensing its own technology to other manufacturers to fund

---

[2]Robert A. Burgelman, "A Process Model of Internal Corporate Venturing in the Diversified Major Firm," *Administrative Science Quarterly,* June 1983.

further R&D, then entering market segments in Japan and Europe where Xerox was weak, and so on.

In this respect, strategic intent is like a marathon run in 400-meter springs. No one knows what the terrain will look like at mile 26, so the role of top management is to focus the organization's attention on the ground to be covered in the next 400 meters. In several companies, management did this by presenting the organization with a series of corporate challenges, each specifying the next hill in the race to achieve strategic intent. One year the challenge might be quality, the next total customer care, the next entry into new markets, the next a rejuvenated product line. As this example indicates, corporate challenges are a way to stage the acquisition of new competitive advantages, a way to identify the focal point for employees' efforts in the near to medium term. As with strategic intent, top management is specific about the ends (reducing product development times by 75 percent for example) but less prescriptive about the means.

Like strategic intent, challenges stretch the organization. To preempt Xerox in the personal copier business, Canon set its engineers a target price of $1,000 for a home copier. At the time, Canon's least expensive copier sold for several thousand dollars. Trying to reduce the cost of existing models would not have given Canon the radical price-performance improvement it needed to delay or deter Xerox's entry into personal copiers. Instead, Canon engineers were challenged to reinvent the copier—a challenge they met by substituting a disposable cartridge for the complex image-transfer mechanism used in other copiers.

Corporate challenges come from analyzing competitors as well as from the foreseeable pattern of industry evolution. Together these reveal potential competitive openings and identify the new skills the organization will need to take the initiative away from better positioned players. The exhibit, "Building Competitive Advantage at Komatsu," illustrates the way challenges helped that company achieve its intent.

For a challenge to be effective, individuals and teams throughout the organization must understand it and see its implications for their own jobs. Companies that set corporate challenges to create new competitive advantages (as Ford and IBM did with quality improvement) quickly discover that engaging the entire organization requires top management to:

Create a sense of urgency, or quasi crisis, by amplifying weak signals in the environment that point up the need to improve, instead of allowing inaction to precipitate a real crisis. (Komatsu, for example, budgeted on the basis of worst case exchange rates that overvalued the yen.)

Develop a competitor focus at every level through widespread use of competitive intelligence. Every employee should be able to benchmark his or her efforts against best-in-class competitors so that the challenge becomes personal. (For example, Ford showed production-line workers videotapes of operations at Mazda's most efficient plant.)

Provide employees with the skills they need to work effectively—training in statistical tools, problem solving, value engineering, and team building, for example.

Give the organization time to digest one challenge before launching another. When competing initiatives overload the organization, middle managers often try to protect their people from the whipsaw of shifting priorities. But this "wait and

Building Competitive Advantage at Komatsu

Corporate Challenge	Protect Komatsu's home market against Caterpillar		Reduce costs while maintaining quality		Make Komatsu an international enterprise and build export markets		Respond to external shocks that threaten markets		Create new products and markets	
Programs	early 1960s	Licensing deals with Cummins Engine, International Harvester, and Bucyrus-Erie to acquire technology and establish benchmarks	1965	CD (Cost Down) program	early 1960s	Develop Eastern bloc countries	1975	V-10 program to reduce costs by 10% while maintaining quality; reduce parts by 20%; rationalize manufacturing system	late 1970s	Accelerate product development to expand line
	1961	Project A (for Ace) to advance the product quality of Komatsu's small- and medium-sized bulldozers above Caterpillar's	1966	Total CD program	1967	Komatsu Europe marketing subsidiary established			1979	Future and Frontiers program to identify new businesses based on society's needs and company's know-how
					1970	Komatsu America established	1977	¥180 program to budget company-wide for 180 yen to the dollar when exchange rate was 240	1981	EPOCHS program to reconcile greater product variety with improved production efficiencies
	1962	Quality Circles companywide to provide training for all employees			1972	Project B to improve the durability and reliability and to reduce costs of large bulldozers				
					1972	Project C to improve payloaders	1979	Project E to establish teams to redouble cost and quality efforts in response to oil crisis		
					1972	Project D to improve hydraulic excavators				
					1974	Establish presales and service department to assist newly industrializing countries in construction projects				

see if they're serious this time" attitude ultimately destroys the credibility of corporate challenges.

Establish clear milestones and review mechanisms to track progress and ensure that internal recognition and rewards reinforce desired behavior. The goal is to make the challenge inescapable for everyone in the company.

It is important to distinguish between the process of managing corporate challenges and the advantages that the process creates. Whatever the actual challenge may be—quality, cost, value engineering, or something else—there is the same need to engage employees intellectually and emotionally in the development of new skills. In each case, the challenge will take root only if senior executives and lower-level employees feel a reciprocal responsibility for competitiveness.

We believe workers in many companies have been asked to take a disproportionate share of the blame for competitive failure. In one U.S. company, for example, management had sought a 40 percent wage-package concession from hourly employees to bring labor costs into line with Far Eastern competitors. The result was a long strike and, ultimately, a 10 percent wage concession from employees on the line. However, direct labor costs in manufacturing accounted for less than 15 percent of total value added. The company thus succeeded in demoralizing its entire blue-collar work force for the sake of a 1.5 percent reduction in total costs. Ironically, further analysis showed that their competitors' most significant cost savings came not from lower hourly wages but from better work methods invented by employees. You can imagine how eager the U.S. workers were to make similar contributions after the strike and concessions. Contrast this situation with what happened at Nissan when the yen strengthened: top management took a big pay cut and then asked middle managers and line employees to sacrifice relatively less.

Reciprocal responsibility means shared gain and shared pain. In too many companies, the pain of revitalization falls almost exclusively on the employees least responsible for the enterprise's decline. Too often, workers are asked to commit to corporate goals without any matching commitment from top management—be it employment security, gain sharing, or an ability to influence the direction of the business. This one-sided approach to regaining competitiveness keeps many companies from harnessing the intellectual horsepower of their employees.

Creating a sense of reciprocal responsibility is crucial because competitiveness ultimately depends on the pace at which a company embeds new advantages deep within its organization, not on its stock of advantages at any given time. Thus we need to expand the concept of competitive advantage beyond the scorecard many managers now use: Are my costs lower? Will my product command a price premium?

Few competitive advantages are long lasting. Uncovering a new competitive advantage is a bit like getting a hot tip on a stock: The first person to act on the insight makes more money than the last. When the experience curve was young, a company that built capacity ahead of competitors, dropped prices to fill plants, and reduced costs as volume rose went to the bank. The first mover traded on the fact that competitors undervalued market share—they didn't price to capture additional market share because they didn't understand how market share leadership could be translated into lower costs and better margins. But there is no more undervalued market share when each of 20 semiconductor companies builds enough capacity to serve 10 percent of the world market.

Keeping score of existing advantages is not the same as building new advantages. The essence of strategy lies in creating tomorrow's competitive advantages faster than competitors mimic the ones you possess today. In the 1960s, Japanese producers relied on labor and capital cost advantages. As Western manufacturers began to move production offshore, Japanese companies accelerated their investment in process technology and created scale and quality advantages. Then as their U.S. and European competitors rationalized manufacturing, they added another string to their bow by accelerating the rate of product development. Then they built global brands. Then they deskilled competitors through alliances and outsourcing deals. The moral? An organization's capacity to improve existing skills and learn new ones is the most defensible competitive advantage of all.

To achieve a strategic intent, a company must usually take on larger, better financed competitors. That means carefully managing competitive engagements so that scarce resources are conserved. Managers cannot do that simply by playing the same game better—making marginal improvements to competitors' technology and business practices. Instead, they must fundamentally change the game in ways that disadvantage incumbents—devising novel approaches to market entry, advantage building, and competitive warfare. For smart competitors, the goal is not competitive imitation but competitive innovation, the art of containing competitive risks within manageable proportions.

Four approaches to competitive innovation are evident in the global expansion of Japanese companies. These are: building layers of advantage, searching for loose bricks, changing the terms of engagement, and competing through collaboration.

The wider a company's portfolio of advantages, the less risk it faces in competitive battles. New global competitors have built such portfolios by steadily expanding their arsenals of competitive weapons. They have moved inexorably from less defensible advantages such as low wage costs to more defensible advantages like global brands. The Japanese color television industry illustrates this layering process.

By 1967, Japan had become the largest producer of black- and-white television sets. By 1970, it was closing the gap in color televisions. Japanese manufacturers used their competitive advantage—at that time, primarily, low labor costs—to build a base in the private-label business, then moved quickly to establish world-scale plants. This investment gave them additional layers of advantage—quality and reliability—as well as further cost reductions from process improvements. At the same time, they recognized that these cost-based advantages were vulnerable to changes in labor costs, process and product technology, exchange rates, and trade policy. So throughout the 1970s, they also invested heavily in building channels and brands, thus creating another layer of advantage, a global franchise. In the late 1970s, they enlarged the scope of their products and businesses to amortize these grand investments and by 1980 all the major players—Matsushita, Sharp, Toshiba, Hitachi, Sanyo—had established related sets of businesses that could support global marketing investments. More recently, they have been investing in regional manufacturing and design centers to tailor their products more closely to national markets.

These manufacturers thought of the various sources of competitive advantage as mutually desirable layers, not mutually exclusive choices. What some call competitive suicide—pursuing both cost and differentiation—is exactly what many competitors strive for.[3] Using flexible manufacturing technologies and better marketing intelligence, they are moving away from standardized "world products" to products like Mazda's mini-van, developed in California expressly for the U.S. market.

Another approach to competitive innovation—searching for loose bricks—exploits the benefits of surprise, which is just as useful in business battles as it is in war. Particularly in the early stages of a war for global markets, successful new competitors work to stay below the response threshold of their larger, more powerful rivals. Staking out underdefended territory is one way to do this.

To find loose bricks, managers must have few orthodoxies about how to break into a market or challenge a competitor. For example, in one large U.S. multinational, we asked several country managers to describe what a Japanese competitor was doing in the local market. The first executive said, "They're coming at us in the low end. Japanese companies always come in at the bottom." The second speaker found the comment interesting but disagreed:

---

[3]For example, see Michael E. Porter, *Competitive Strategy* (New York: Free Press, 1980).

"They don't offer any low-end products in my market, but they have some exciting stuff at the top end. We really should reverse engineer that thing." Another colleague told still another story. "They haven't taken any business away from me," he said, "but they've just made me a great offer to supply components." In each country, their Japanese competitor had found a different loose brick.

The search for loose bricks begins with a careful analysis of the competitor's conventional wisdom: How does the company define its "served market"? What activities are most profitable? Which geographic markets are too troublesome to enter? The objective is not to find a corner of the industry (or niche) where larger competitors seldom tread but to build a base of attack just outside the market territory that industry leaders currently occupy. The goal is an uncontested profit sanctuary, which could be a particular product segment (the "low end" in motorcycles), a slice of the value chain (components in the computer industry), or a particular geographic market (Eastern Europe).

When Honda took on leaders in the motorcycle industry, for example, it began with products that were just outside the conventional definition of the leaders' product-market domains. As a result, it could build a base of operations in underdefended territory and then use that base to launch an expanded attack. What many competitors failed to see was Honda's strategic intent and its growing competence in engines and power trains. Yet even as Honda was selling 50cc motorcycles in the United States, it was already racing larger bikes in Europe—assembling the design skills and technology it would need for a systematic expansion across the entire spectrum of motor-related businesses.

Honda's progress in creating a core competence in engines should have warned competitors that it might enter a series of seemingly unrelated industries—automobiles, lawn mowers, marine engines, generators. But with each company fixated on its own market, the threat of Honda's horizontal diversification went unnoticed. Today companies like Matsushita and Toshiba are similarly poised to move in unexpected ways across industry boundaries. In protecting loose bricks, companies must extend their peripheral vision by tracking and anticipating the migration of global competitors across product segments, businesses, national markets, value-added stages, and distribution channels.

Changing the terms of engagement—refusing to accept the front runner's definition of industry and segment boundaries—represents still another form of competitive innovation. Canon's entry into the copier business illustrates this approach.

During the 1970s, both Kodak and IBM tried to match Xerox's business system in terms of segmentation, products, distribution, service, and pricing. As a result, Xerox had no trouble decoding the new entrants' intentions and developing countermoves. IBM eventually withdrew from the copier business, while Kodak remains a distant second in the large copier market that Xerox still dominates.

Canon, on the other hand, changed the terms of competitive engagement. While Xerox built a wide range of copiers, Canon standardized machines and components to reduce costs. Canon chose to distribute through office-product dealers rather than try to match Xerox's huge direct sales force. It also avoided the need to create a national service network by designing reliability and serviceability into its product and then delegating service responsibility to the dealers. Canon copiers were sold rather than leased, freeing Canon from the burden of financing the lease base. Finally, instead of selling to the heads of corporate duplicating departments, Canon appealed to secretaries and department managers who wanted distributed copying. At each stage, Canon neatly sidestepped a potential barrier to entry.

Canon's experience suggests that there is an important distinction between barriers to entry and barriers to imitation. Competitors that tried to match Xerox's business system had to pay the same entry costs—the barriers to imitation were high. But Canon dramatically reduced the barriers to entry by changing the rules of the game.

Changing the rules also short-circuited Xerox's ability to retaliate quickly against its new rival. Confronted with the need to rethink its business strategy and organization, Xerox was paralyzed for a time. Xerox managers realized that the faster they downsized the product line, developed new channels, and improved reliability, the faster they would erode the company's traditional profit base. What might have been seen as critical success factors—Xerox's national sales force and service network, its large installed base of leased machines, and its reliance on service revenues—instead became barriers to retaliation. In this sense, competitive innovation is like judo: The goal is to use a larger competitor's weight against it. And that happens not by matching the leader's capabilities but by developing contrasting capabilities of one's own.

Competitive innovation works on the premise that a successful competitor is likely to be wedded to a "recipe" for success. That's why the most effective weapon new competitors possess is probably a clean sheet of paper. And why an incumbent's greatest vulnerability is its belief in accepted practice.

Through licensing, outsourcing agreements, and joint ventures, it is sometimes possible to win without fighting. For example, Fujitsu's alliances in Europe with Siemens and STC (Britain's largest computer maker) and in the United States with Amdahl yield manufacturing volume and access to Western markets. In the early 1980s, Matsushita established a joint venture with Thorn (in the United Kingdom), Telefunken (in Germany), and Thomson (in France), which allowed it to quickly multiply the forces arrayed against Philips in the battle for leadership in the European VCR business. In fighting larger global rivals by proxy, Japanese companies have adopted a maxim as old as human conflict itself: My enemy's enemy is my friend.

Hijacking the development efforts of potential rivals is another goal of competitive collaboration. In the consumer electronics war, Japanese competitors attacked traditional businesses like TVs and hi-fis while volunteering to manufacture "next generation" products like VCRs, camcorders, and compact disc players for Western rivals. They hoped their rivals would ratchet down development spending, and in most cases that is precisely what happened. But companies that abandoned their own development efforts seldom reemerged as serious competitors in subsequent new product battles.

Collaboration can also be used to calibrate competitors' strengths and weaknesses. Toyota's joint venture with GM, and Mazda's with Ford, give these automakers an invaluable vantage point for assessing the progress their U.S. rivals have made in cost reduction, quality, and technology. They can also learn how GM and Ford compete—when they will fight and when they won't. Of course, the reverse is also true: Ford and GM have an equal opportunity to learn from their partner-competitors.

The Process of Surrender

In the battles for global leadership that have taken place during the last two decades, we have seen a pattern of competitive attack and retrenchment that was remarkably similar across industries. We call this the process of surrender.

The process started with unseen intent. Not possessing long-term, competitor-focused goals themselves, Western companies did not ascribe such intentions to their rivals. They also calculated the threat posed by potential competitors in terms of their existing resources rather than their resourcefulness. This led to sytematic underestimation of smaller rivals who were fast gaining technology through licensing arrangements, acquiring market understanding from downstream OEM partners, and improving product quality and manufacturing productivity through companywide employee involvement programs. Oblivious of the strategic intent and intangible advantages of their rivals, American and European businesses were caught off guard.

Adding to the competitive surprise was the fact that the new entrants typically attacked the periphery of a market (Honda in small motorcycles; Yamaha in grand pianos, Toshiba in small black-and-white televisions) before going head-to-head with incumbents. Incumbents often misread these attacks, seeing them as part of a niche strategy and not as a search for "loose bricks." Unconventional market entry strategies (minority holdings in less developed countries, use of nontraditional channels, extensive corporate advertising) were ignored or dismissed as quirky. For example, managers we spoke with said Japanese companies' position in the European computer industry was nonexistent. In terms of brand share that's nearly true, but the Japanese control as much as one-third of the manufacturing value added in the hardware sales of European-based computer businesses. Similarly, German auto producers claimed to feel unconcerned over the proclivity of Japanese producers to move upmarket. But with its low-end models under tremendous pressure from Japanese producers, Porsche has now announced that it will no longer make "entry level" cars.

Western managers often misinterpreted their rivals' tactics. They believed that Japanese and Korean companies were competing solely on the basis of cost and quality. This typically produced a partial response to those competitors' initiatives: moving manufacturing offshore, outsourcing, or instituting a quality program. Seldom was the full extent of the competitive threat appreciated—the multiple layers of advantage, the expansion across related product segments, the development of global brand positions. Imitating the currently visible tactics of rivals put Western businesses into a perpetual catch-up trap. One by one, companies lost battles and came to see surrender as inevitable. Surrender was not inevitable, of course, but the attack was staged in a way that disguised ultimate intentions and sidestepped direct confrontation.

The route to competitive revitalization we have been mapping implies a new view of strategy. Strategic intent assures consistency in resource allocation over the long term. Clearly articulated corporate challenges focus the efforts of individuals in the medium term. Finally, competitive innovation helps reduce competitive risk in the short term. This consistency in the long term, focus in the medium term, and inventiveness and involvement in the short term provide the key to leveraging limited resources in pursuit of ambitious goals. But just as there is a process of winning, so there is a process of surrender. Revitalization requires understanding that process too.

Given their technological leadership and access to large regional markets, how did U.S. and European companies lose their apparent birthright to dominate global industries? There is no simple answer. Few companies recognize the value of documenting failure. Fewer still search their own managerial orthodoxies for the seeds for competitive surrender. But we believe there is a pathology of surrender (summarized in "The Process of Surrender") that gives some important clues.

It is not very comforting to think that the essence of Western strategic thought can be reduced to eight rules for excellence, seven S's, five competitive forces, four product life-cycle stages, three generic strategies, and innumerable two-by-two matrices.[4]

Yet for the past 20 years, "advances" in strategy have taken the form of ever more typologies, heuristics, and laundry lists, often with dubious empirical bases. Moreover, even reasonable concepts like the product life cycle, experience curve, product portfolios, and generic strategies often have toxic side effects: They reduce the number of strategic options management is willing to consider. They create a preference for selling businesses rather than defending them. They yield predictable strategies that rivals easily decode.

Strategy "recipes" limit opportunities for competitive innovation. A company may have 40 businesses and only four strategies—invest, hold, harvest, or divest. Too often strategy is seen as a positioning exercise in which options are tested by how they fit the existing industry structure. But current industry structure reflects the strengths of the industry leader, and playing by the leader's rules is usually competitive suicide.

Armed with concepts like segmentation, the value chain, competitor benchmarking, strategic groups, and mobility barriers, many managers have become better and better at drawing industry maps. But while they have been busy mapmaking, their competitors have been moving entire continents. The strategist's goal is not to find a niche within the existing industry space but to create new space that is uniquely suited to the company's own strengths, space that is off the map.

This is particularly true now that industry boundaries are becoming more and more unstable. In industries such as financial services and communications, rapidly changing technology, deregulation, and globalization have undermined the value of traditional industry analysis. Mapmaking skills are worth little in the epicenter of an earthquake. But an industry in upheaval presents opportunities for ambitious companies to redraw the map in their favor, so long as they can think outside traditional industry boundaries.

Concepts like "mature" and "declining" are largely definitional. What most executives mean when they label a business mature is that sales growth has stagnated in their current geographic markets for existing products sold through existing channels. In such cases, it's not the industry that is mature, but the executives' conception of the industry. Asked if the piano business was mature, a senior executive in Yamaha replied, "Only if we can't take any market share from anybody anywhere in the world and still make money. And anyway, we're not in the 'piano' business, we're in the 'keyboard' business." Year after year, Sony has revitalized its radio and tape recorder businesses, despite the fact that other manufacturers long ago abandoned these businesses as mature.

A narrow concept of maturity can foreclose a company from a broad stream of future opportunities. In the 1970s, several U.S. companies thought that consumer electronics had become a mature industry. What could possibly top the color TV? they asked themselves. RCA and GE, distracted by opportunities in

---

[4]Strategic frameworks for resource allocation in diversified companies are summarized in Charles W. Hofer and Dan E. Schendel, *Strategy Formulation: Analytical Concepts* (St. Paul, Minn.: West Publishing, 1978).

more "attractive" industries like mainframe computers, left Japanese products with a virtual monopoly in VCRs, camcorders, and compact disc players. Ironically, the TV business, once thought mature, is on the verge of a dramatic renaissance. A $20 billion-a-year business will be created when high-definition television is launched in the United States. But the pioneers of television may capture only a small part of this bonanza.

Most of the tools of strategic analysis are focused domestically. Few force managers to consider global opportunities and threats. For example, portfolio planning portrays top management's investment options as an array of businesses rather than as an array of geographic markets. The result is predictable: As businesses come under attack from foreign competitors, the company attempts to abandon them and enter others in which the forces of global competition are not yet so strong. In the short term, this may be an appropriate response to waning competitiveness, but there are fewer and fewer businesses in which a domestic-oriented company can find refuge. We seldom hear such companies asking: Can we move into emerging markets overseas ahead of our global rivals and prolong the profitability of this business? Can we counterattack in our global competitors' home markets and slow the pace of their expansion? A senior executive in one successful global company made a telling comment: "We're glad to find a competitor managing by the portfolio concept—we can almost predict how much share we'll have to take away to put the business on the CEO's 'sell list.'"

Companies can also be overcommitted to organizational recipes, such as strategic business units and the decentralization an SBU structure implies. Decentralization is seductive because it places the responsibility for success or failure squarely on the shoulders of line managers. Each business is assumed to have all the resources it needs to execute its strategies successfully, and in this no-excuses environment, it is hard for top management to fail. But desirable as clear lines of responsibility and accountability are, competitive revitalization requires positive value added from top management.

Few companies with a strong SBU orientation have built successful global distribution and brand positions. Investments in a global brand franchise typically transcend the resources and risk propensity of a single business. While some Western companies have had global brand positions for 30 or 40 years or more (Heinz, Siemens, IBM, Ford, and Kodak, for example), it is hard to identify any American or European company that has created a new global brand franchise in the last 10 to 15 years. Yet Japanese companies have created a score or more—NEC, Fujitsu, Panasonic (Matsushita), Toshiba, Sony, Seiko, Epson, Canon, Minolta, and Honda, among them.

General Electric's situation is typical. In many of its businesses, this American giant has been almost unknown in Europe and Asia. GE made no coordinated effort to build a global corporate franchise. Any GE business with international ambitions had to bear the burden of establishing its credibility and credentials in the new market alone. Not surprisingly, some once-strong GE businesses opted out of the difficult task of building a global brand position. In contrast, smaller Korean companies like Samsung, Daewoo, and Lucky Gold Star are busy building global-brand umbrellas that will ease market entry for a whole range of businesses. The underlying principle is simple: Economies of scope may be as important as economies of scale in entering global markets. But capturing economies of scope demands interbusiness coordination that only top management can provide.

We believe that inflexible SBU-type organizations have also contributed to the deskilling of some companies. For a single SBU, incapable of sustaining investment in a core competence such as semiconductors, optical media, or combustion engines, the only way to remain competitive is to purchase key components from potential (often Japanese or Korean) competitors. For an SBU defined in product-market terms, competitiveness means offering an end product that is competitive in price and performance. But that gives an SBU manager little incentive to distinguish between external sourcing that achieves "product embodied" competitiveness and internal development that yields deeply embedded organizational competences that can be exploited across multiple businesses. Where upstream component manufacturing activities are seen as cost centers with cost-plus transfer pricing, additional investment in the core activity may seem a less profitable use of capital than investment in downstream activities. To make matters worse, internal accounting data may not reflect the competitive value of retaining control over core competence.

Together a shared global corporate brand franchise and shared core competence act as mortar in many Japanese companies. Lacking this mortar, a company's businesses are truly loose bricks—easily knocked out by global competitors that steadily invest in core competences. Such competitors can co-opt domestically oriented companies into long-term sourcing dependence and capture the economies of scope of global brand investment through interbusiness coordination.

Last in decentralization's list of dangers is the standard of managerial performance typically used in SBU organizations. In many companies, business unit managers are rewarded solely on the basis of their performance against return on investment targets. Unfortunately, that often leads to denominator management because executives soon discover that reductions in investment and head count—the denominator—"improve" the financial ratios by which they are measured more easily than growth in the numerator—revenues. It also fosters a hair-trigger sensitivity to industry downturns that can be very costly. Managers who are quick to reduce investment and dismiss workers find it takes much longer to regain lost skills and catch up on investment when the industry turns upward again. As a result, they lose market share in every business cycle. Particularly in industries where there is fierce competition for the best people and where competitors invest relentlessly, denominator management creates a retrenchment ratchet.

The concept of the general manager as a movable peg reinforces the problem of denominator management. Business schools are guilty here because they have perpetuated the notion that a manager with net present value calculations in one hand and portfolio planning in the other can manage any business anywhere.

In many diversified companies, top management evaluates line managers on numbers along because no other basis for dialogue exists. Managers move so many times as part of their "career development" that they often do not understand the nuances of the businesses they are managing. At GE, for example, one fast-track manager heading an important new venture had moved across five businesses in five years. His series of quick successes finally came to an end when he confronted a Japanese competitor whose managers had been plodding along in the same business for more than a decade.

Regardless of ability and effort, fast-track managers are unlikely to develop the deep business knowledge they need to discuss technology options, competitors' strategies, and global opportunities substantively. Invariably, therefore, discussions gravitate to "the numbers," while the value added of managers is limited to the financial and planning savvy they carry from job to job. Knowledge of the company's internal planning and accounting systems substitutes for substantive knowledge of the business, making competitive innovation unlikely.

When managers know that their assignments have a two- to three-year time frame, they feel great pressure to create a good track record fast. This pressure often takes one of two forms. Either the manager does not commit to goals whose time line extends beyond his or her expected tenure. Or ambitious goals are adopted and squeezed into an unrealistically short time frame. Aiming to be number one in a business is the essence of strategic intent; but imposing a three- to four-year horizon on the effort simply invites disaster. Acquisitions are made with little attention to the problems of integration. The organization becomes overloaded with initiatives. Collaborative ventures are formed without adequate attention to competitive consequences.

Almost every strategic management theory and nearly every corporate planning system is premised on a strategy hierarchy in which corporate goals guide business unit strategies and business unit strategies guide functional tactics.[5] In this hierarchy, senior management makes strategy and lower levels execute it. The dichotomy between formulation and implementation is familiar and widely accepted. But the strategy hierarchy undermines competitiveness by fostering an elitist view of management that tends to disenfranchise most of the organization. Employees fail to identify with corporate goals or involve themselves deeply in the work of becoming more competitive.

The strategy hierarchy isn't the only explanation for an elitist view of management, of course. The myths that grow up around successful top managers— "Lee Iacocca saved Chrysler," "De Benedetti rescued Olivetti," "John Sculley turned Apple around"—perpetuate it. So does the turbulent business environment. Middle managers buffeted by circumstances that seem to be beyond their control desperately want to believe that top management has all the answers. And top management, in turn, hesitates to admit it does not for fear of demoralizing lower-level employees.

The result of all this is often a code of silence in which the full extent of a company's competitiveness problem is not widely shared. We interviewed business unit managers in one company, for example, who were extremely anxious because top management wasn't talking openly about the competitive challenges the company faced. They assumed the lack of communication indicated a lack of awareness on their senior managers' part. But when asked whether they were open with their own employees, these same managers replied that while they could face up to the problems, the people below them could not. Indeed, the only time the work force heard about the company's

---

[5]For example, see Peter Lorange and Richard E. Vancil, *Strategic Planning Systems* (Englewood Cliffs, NJ: Prentice Hall, 1977).

competitiveness problems was during wage negotiations when problems were used to extract concessions.

Unfortunately, a threat that everyone perceives but no one talks about creates more anxiety than a threat that has been clearly identified and made the focal point for the problem-solving efforts of the entire company. That is one reason honesty and humility on the part of top management may be the first prerequisite of revitalization. Another reason is the need to make participation more than a buzzword.

Programs such as quality circles and total customer service often fall short of expectations because management does not recognize that successful implementation requires more than administrative structures. Difficulties in embedding new capabilities are typically put down to "communication" problems, with the unstated assumption that if only downward communication were more effective—"if only middle management would get the message straight"—the new program would quickly take root. The need for upward communication is often ignored, or assumed to mean nothing more than feedback. In contrast, Japanese companies win, not because they have smarter managers, but because they have developed ways to harness the "wisdom of the anthill." They realize that top managers are a bit like the astronauts who circle the earth in the space shuttle. It may be the astronauts who get all the glory, but everyone knows that the real intelligence behind the mission is located firmly on the ground.

Where strategy formulation is an elitist activity it is also difficult to produce truly creative strategies. For one thing, there are not enough heads and points of view in divisional or corporate planning departments to challenge conventional wisdom. For another, creative strategies seldom emerge from the annual planning ritual. The starting point for next year's strategy is almost always this year's strategy. Improvements are incremental. The company sticks to the segments and territories it knows, even though the real opportunities may be elsewhere. The impetus for Canon's pioneering entry into the personal copier business came from an overseas sales subsidiary—not from planners in Japan.

The goal of the strategy hierarchy remains valid—to ensure consistency up and down the organization. But this consistency is better derived from a clearly articulated strategic intent than from inflexibly applied top-down plans. In the 1990s, the challenge will be to enfranchise employees to invent the means to accomplish ambitious ends.

We seldom found cautious administrators among the top managements of companies that came from behind to challenge incumbents for global leadership. But in studying organizations that had surrendered, we invariably found senior managers who, for whatever reason, lacked the courage to commit their companies to heroic goals—goals that lay beyond the reach of planning and existing resources. The conservative goals they set failed to generate pressure and enthusiasm for competitive innovation or give the organization much useful guidance. Financial targets and vague mission statements just cannot provide the consistent direction that is a prerequisite for winning a global competitive war.

This kind of conservatism is usually blamed on the financial markets. But we believe that in most cases investors' so-called short-term orientation simply reflects their lack of confidence in the ability of senior managers to conceive and deliver stretch goals. The chairman of one company complained bitterly that even after improving return on capital employed to over 40 percent (by ruthlessly divesting lackluster businesses and downsizing others), the stock market held the company to an 8:1 price/earnings ratio. Of course the market's message was clear: "We don't trust you. You've shown no ability to achieve profitable growth. Just cut out the slack, manage the denominators, and perhaps you'll be taken over by a company that can use your resources more creatively." Very little in the track record of most large Western companies warrants the confidence of the stock market. Investors aren't hopelessly short-term, they're justifiably skeptical.

We believe that top management's caution reflects a lack of confidence in its own ability to involve the entire organization in revitalization—as opposed to simply raising financial targets. Developing faith in the organization's ability to deliver on tough goals, motivating it to do so, focusing its attention long enough to internalize new capabilities—this is the real challenge for top management. Only by rising to this challenge will senior managers gain the courage they need to commit themselves and their companies to global leadership.

MANAGING ASSETS AND SKILLS: THE KEY TO A SUSTAINABLE COMPETITIVE ADVANTAGE

David A. Aaker, University of California at Berkeley

According to one Xerox executive, a key sustainable competitive advantage in addition to the firm's technology has been its sales and service organization. It helped them to penetrate the medium and high end of the copier market during the 1960s.[1] Kodak plans to build its 200,000 store distribution system and the marketing clout of its yellow- and-black logo to penetrate the growing $2 billion battery market.[2] In each case, the firms developed, nurtured, and then exploited key assets and skills.

A business strategy, as suggested by Figure 1, involves the *way you compete*—what you do, the product strategy, positioning strategy, pricing strategy, distribution strategy, global strategy, manufacturing strategy, and so on. It also involves *where you compete*—the selection of the competitive arena, the markets, and the competitors. Competing the right way in the right arena can be extremely profitable, but only for a limited time. The assets and skills of the business, which are the *basis of competition*, provide the foundation of a sustainable competitive advantage (SCA) and long-term performance. Unless there is an advantage over competitors that it not easily duplicated or countered, long-term profitability is likely to be elusive.

For an SCA to be truly sustainable it needs to be based upon assets or skills possessed by the business. An asset is something your firm possesses such as a brand name or retail location that is superior to the competition. A skill is something that your firm does better than competitors such as advertising or efficient manufacturing. Without the support of assets or skills it is unlikely that the SCA will be enduring. What a business does, the way it competes and where it chooses to compete, is usually easily imitated. It is more difficult to respond to what a business is, to acquire or neutralize specialized assets or skills. Anyone can decide to distribute cereal or detergent through supermarkets but few have the clout to do it as effectively as a General Mills or Procter & Gamble. The right assets and skills can provide the needed barriers to competitor thrusts that make the SCA persist over time.

The essence of strategic management is the development and maintenance of meaningful assets and skills and the selection of strategies and competitive arenas such that those assets and skills form SCAs. Indicators of the strength of the assets and skills are thus required to measure performance and guide programs needed to improve assets and skills. The ability to produce high-quality products is a skill that could be monitored by quality goals such as a defect ratio to customer problem index. The asset of brand loyalty might be measured by a customer satisfaction index. Clearly, such measures suggest

---

Source: Copyright 1989 by The Regents of the University of California. Reprinted from *California Management Review* 31, no. 2 (Winter 1989), pp. 91–106. By permission of The Regents.

[1]Gary Jacobson and John Hillkirk, *Xerox, American Samurai* (New York: Macmillan, 1986), p. 275.

[2]"What's Recharging the Battery Business," *Business Week*, June 23, 1986, p. 124.

FIGURE 1   Obtaining a Sustainable Competitive Advantage

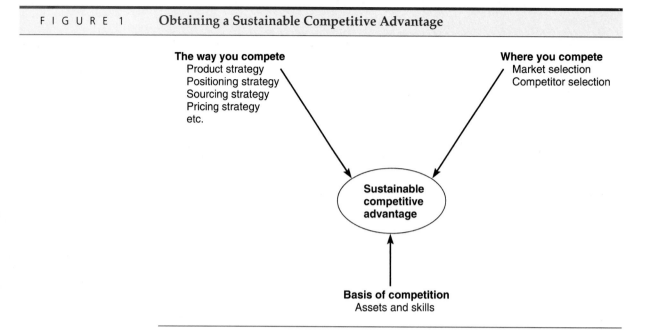

---

that assets and skills go beyond simply stating that a firm is a "high-quality" firm or a "low-cost" business, although such statements of strategic thrusts or culture can be helpful.

Instead of a strategic focus upon assets and skills, U.S. management too often is driven by short-term measures such as sales, market share, ROI, or ROA. As a result, there is a temptation to overinvest in fast-payoff projects such as sales promotions (which have grown dramatically in the last 10 years) and to milk assets instead of creating new ones. For example, brand extensions are frequently used as a way to reduce the risk and investment required in new product introductions. Yet extensions can easily damage the brand by creating harmful associations or by clouding a previously well-defined image. Consider the decline of the Izod's alligator symbol following efforts to put it on just about anything.[3]

The short-term measures also encourage an underinvestment in the future. The reduction in expense items such as image advertising and new product development can provide an immediate impact on the bottom line while sacrificing asset enhancement that will pay off in the future. In contrast, the management of skills and assets provides an alternative to short-term financial measures that will provide the foundation for long-term success.

Four sets of practical questions can guide the implementation of a strategic focus upon the assets and skills of the business:

- What are the relevant skills and assets for your industry? What assets and skills either should be obtained or neutralized if you are to compete successfully?

[3]John L. Graham and Cathy Anterasian, "The Mouse That Roared," *Los Angeles Times*, May 8, 1988, p. IV 3.

- What is or should be the assets and skills that underlie your SCA? Of the set of relevant assets and skills, how do you select the optimal ones to develop, strengthen, or maintain?
- How can you go about creating assets and skills that will support SCAs?
- Finally, how can formidable assets and skills of competitors be neutralized?

WHAT ARE THE RELEVANT ASSETS AND SKILLS?

Most industries will have a set of relevant assets and skills the presence or absence of which can directly affect the performance of a competitor. The first step in the management of assets and skills is to identify this set. Attention can then turn to selecting those assets and skills that should be associated with a business and identifying the assets and skills of competitors that should be neutralized.

WHAT BUSINESS MANAGERS SAY IS THEIR SCA

A sample of 248 managers of Strategic Business Units (SBUs) from the Northern California area were contacted and asked what was the SCA of their business.[4] A total of 113 of these businesses were services such as consulting, financial services, real estate, airlines, hotels, law, insurance, retailing, venture capital, and restaurants. Another 68 were high-technology firms involved in products such as personal computers, software, information systems, lasers, medical instrumentation, and CAD/CAM equipment. The remaining 67 firms were in manufacturing or raw materials and included businesses in clothing, pharmaceuticals, air conditioning, chemicals, metal fabrication, garden supplies, oil, and specialty forging. The responses were recorded and coded into categories of assets and skills. The results, summarized in Table 1, provide some insights into the SCA construct.

For a subset of 95 of the businesses, a second SBU manager was independently interviewed. The result suggests that managers can identify SCAs with a high degree of reliability. Of the 95 businesses, 71 of the manager pairs gave answers that were coded the same and 20 more only had a single difference in the SCA list.

Table 1 shows a list of 31 SCAs, all assets or skills that were mentioned by at least 7 of the 248 respondents. This list provides a point of departure for determining what assets and skills are relevant.

By a significant margin, the most frequently named SCA was "quality reputation," undoubtedly reflecting the importance of the dimension to most markets. Given the incidence of quality in this SCA study, most businesses should probably consider the following questions:

- What are the quality dimensions in this industry?
- How should quality be measured?

---

[4]The interviews were each conducted by a different MBA student who recorded the responses. The responses were coded by two different coders. The between coder reliability was .92. The coding was supervised by Shubra Sen, whose help is gratefully acknowledged.

T A B L E   1   **Sustainable Competitive Advantages of 248 Businesses**

		High-Tech	Service	Other	Total
1.	Reputation for quality	26	50	29	105
2.	Customer service/product support	23	40	15	78
3.	Name recognition/high profile	8	42	21	71
4.	Retain good management and engineering staff	17	43	5	65
5.	Low-cost production	17	15	21	53
6.	Financial resources	11	26	14	51
7.	Customer orientation/feedback/market research	13	26	9	48
8.	Product line breadth	11	25	17	47
9.	Technical superiority	30	7	9	46
10.	Installed base of satisfied customers	19	22	4	45
11.	Segmentation/focus	7	22	16	45
12.	Product characteristics/differentiation	12	15	10	37
13.	Continuing production innovation	15	20	10	35
14.	Market share	12	14	9	35
15.	Size/location of distribution	10	12	13	34
16.	Low-price/high-value offering	6	20	6	32
17.	Knowledge of business	2	25	4	31
18.	Pioneer/early entrant in industry	11	11	6	28
19.	Efficient, flexible production/operations adaptable to customers	4	17	4	26
20.	Effective sales force	10	9	4	23
21.	Overall marketing skills	7	9	7	23
22.	Shared vision/culture	5	13	4	22
23.	Strategic goals	6	7	9	22
24.	Powerful well-known parent	7	7	6	20
25.	Location	0	10	10	20
26.	Effective advertising/image	5	6	6	17
27.	Enterprising/entrepreneurial	4	3	6	11
28.	Good coordination	3	2	5	10
29.	Engineering research development	8	2	0	10
30.	Short-term planning	2	1	5	8
31.	Good distributor relations	2	4	1	7
32.	Other	6	20	5	31
	Total	322	552	283	1,157
	Number of businesses	68	113	67	248
	Average number of SCAs	4.73	4.88	4.22	4.65

- What are customers perceptions of the quality of the competing businesses and how are these perceptions developed?

It is important to realize that quality, like many of the 31 dimensions, is itself complex and multidimensional. One writer, for example, suggested that product quality can include dimensions such as functional performance, "fit and finish," durability, incidence of defects, reliability, serviceability, features, or simply an overall "quality name."[5] A study of service quality found eight quality dimensions: the appearance of the facilities and people, service reliability, competence, trustworthiness, empathy, courtesy and communication. Ultimately, of course, quality is defined by customer expectations.[6]

The second and seventh SCA both suggest customer orientation. A customer focus (perhaps like quality reputation) is something that nearly all organizations profess. The problem is to distinguish between lip service and a meaningful culture, an effective system, and motivated people that together can represent a set of assets and skills driving a customer-oriented business. Again customer orientation is complex and will take different forms in different contexts.[7]

The third-ranked SCA was "name recognition/high profile," which often translated into a significant industry presence, high top-of-mind awareness, and the image of a substantial, committed player. Olivetti, for example, has used a "name" as the key to its strategy.[8] They became the world's third largest maker of personal computers (and the second largest in Europe) by making IBM clones under names such as AT&T in America and several other leading "names" in Europe.

Several of the assets and skills listed clearly represent barriers to competitors. "Product line breadth," for example, reduces the windows of opportunity for competitors. An "installed base of satisfied customers" is uniquely associated with a firm and is usually very costly and difficult to dislodge. A "pioneer or early entrant" is a historical heritage that can usually only be attached to one firm in the market. A "powerful well-known parent" and "location" are not easily duplicated. Over two-thirds of the SCAs are externally oriented and visible to the customer.

Suggestive differences arise when the list is analyzed for the high-tech and service firms. For high-tech firms, "technical superiority," which could include process technology as well as product technology, is listed relatively more frequently than in other industry contexts. For service firms, "the retention of good management" is relatively more frequently mentioned and low-cost production is relatively less frequently mentioned.

One finding of note is that businesses listed an average of 4.65 SCAs each. In reading the popular business press and books, the impression is often given that a successful business can be based upon doing some "one thing well" or having a single key asset. A firm can be a "quality company," an "R&D" company, an efficient manufacturing firm, a new product company, or a firm that excels in promotion and, thus, a single asset or skill could seem to be the basis for success. However, these results suggest that multiple strengths are needed in order to compete successfully and that assets and skills are defined at a more specific and detailed level.

---

[5]David A. Garvin, "Product Quality: An Important Strategic Weapon," *Business Horizons* 27 (May–June 1984), pp. 40–43.

[6]A. Parasuraman, Valarie A. Zeithaml, and Leonard L. Berry, "A Conceptual Model of Service Quality and Its Implications for Future Research," *Journal of Marketing* 49 (Fall 1985), pp. 41–50.

[7]For a profile of a customer-driven organization see David A. Aaker, *Developing Business Strategies: Second Edition* (New York: John Wiley & Sons, 1988), pp. 212–13.

[8]"How Olivetti Clones Its Way to the Top," *Business Week*, June 16, 1986, p. 82.

Four Questions

The list in Table 1 provides a set of assets and skills to consider. To identify the relevant assets and skills for a particular industry, however, it is useful to pose a series of four questions:

1. Who are the successful businesses over time? What assets or skills have contributed to their success? Who are the businesses that have chronically low performance? Why? What assets or skills do they lack?

By definition assets and skills that provide SCAs should affect performance over time. Thus, businesses that differ with respect to performance over time should also differ with respect to their skills and assets. Analyzing the causes of the performance suggests sets of relevant assets and skills. The superior performers will usually have developed and maintained some key assets and skills that have been the basis for their performance. Conversely, weakness in several assets and skills relevant to their industry should visibly contribute to the inferior performance over time of the weak competitors.

For example, General Electric, the best performer in the CT scanner industry, has superior product technology and R&D, has a systems capability due to its related businesses, and has a strong sales and service organization due to its X-Ray product line and an installed base. GE's largest competitor is Johnson & Johnson, which has been a chronic money loser for a decade because it lacks the synergistic combination of businesses, the product technology and R&D, and the sales and service organization.[9]

2. What are the key customer motivations? What is really important to the customer?

Customer motivations usually drive buying decisions and thus can dictate what assets and skills can potentially create meaningful advantages. In the heavy equipment industry, customers value service and parts back-up. Caterpillar's "24-hour parts service anywhere in the world" has been a key asset for them because of its importance to customers.

Sometimes motivations exist that are unmet by current offerings. Unmet motivations represent opportunities for the "outs" and threats for the "ins." For example, the successful Apple MacIntosh computer was developed in response to an unmet motivation for a user-friendly system. The technology surrounding the MacIntosh provides an enormous asset in an industry full of IBM clones.

An analysis of customer motivations can also identify assets and skills that a business will need to deliver. If the prime buying criteria for a snack is freshness, a brand will have to develop the skills to deliver that attribute. A business which lacks competence in an area important to the customer segment can be in trouble even if it has substantial other SCAs.

3. What are the key activities providing customer value? What are the large cost components?

Porter has suggested that the business identify its value-added activities—the distinct activities performed such as operations, marketing and sales, ser-

---

[9]"Changing a Corporate Culture," *Business Week*, May 14, 1984, pp. 130–37.

vice, logistics, procurement, R&D, and human resource management.[10] The activities should then be analyzed as to their potential for having a high impact upon differentiation and whether they represent a significant or growing proportion of cost. In either case, the analysis should lead to an identification of assets and skills that would result in a meaningful advantage. Obtaining a cost advantage in a large value-added stage, for example, can represent a significant SCA, whereas a cost advantage in a lower value-added stage will have less leverage. Thus in the metal can business, transportation costs are relatively high and a competitor that can locate plants near customers will have a cost advantage—plant location then becomes a significant strategic asset.

4. What are the mobility barriers in the industry?

The cost and difficulty of creating assets and skills needed to support SCA represent the mobility barriers in an industry. Mobility represents both entry barriers and barriers to the movement from one strategic group or competitive arena to another. For example, in the oil-well drilling industry of the 1970s and early 1980s, barriers prevented firms from moving from shallow on-shore drilling to deep on-shore drilling to off-shore to foreign drilling.[11] Foreign, off-shore drilling requires specialized assets and skills in establishing and operating offshore equipment, in dealing with foreign governments and firms, and in operating in different countries. The assets and skills that prevent entry into an industry or segment of an industry should be among those that are relevant to that industry.

SELECT ASSETS AND SKILLS TO DEVELOP, STRENGTHEN, OR MAINTAIN

Which assets or skills should be selected to develop or maintain? How much emphasis should be placed upon each? Clearly, a business needs to be selective. Limited resources will need to be focused upon those assets and skills that will support SCAs. Estimates of the costs and benefits will often be difficult. In making strategic judgments about assets and skills the following questions should be helpful. Is the asset or skill:

- defined with respect to the competition? Will a competitive advantage result?
- relevant to the market?
- feasible and cost effective?
- going to result in an SCA that is sustainable?
- appropriate to the future?

The Competitive Strength Grid

A competitive advantage must be both a point of difference and an advantage as defined with respect to the firms regarded as competitors. A skill that all competitors have will not be the basis for an SCA. For example, flight safety is

---

[10]Michael E. Porter, *Competitive Advantage* (New York: The Free Press, 1985), Chapter 2.

[11]Briance Macarenhus and David A. Aaker, "Mobility Barriers and Strategic Groups," *Strategic Management Journal* 10, no. 5 (September–October 1989), pp. 475–85.

F I G U R E 2	Competitor Strength Grid

Assets and Skills	Weakness ←					→ Strength		
Product quality	W	V	B	A	G L M			
Market share/share economies	V B	W		A G		M		L
Parent in related business	B	W				V G	A M	L
Package		V	W B L	G	A M			
Low calorie position	V		G	M	B	A	L	W
Sales force/distribution	V		B		W	G	A M L	
Advertising/promotion	V		B	G	W	A M		L
Ethnic position	W		A	L M			G	V B

L   Stouffer's Lean Cuisine (Nestle's—also makes Stouffer "Red Box" line).
M   Le Menu (Campbell Soup—also makes Swanson's, Mrs. Paul's).
W   Weight Watchers (Heinz).
A   Armour Dinner Classic/Classic Lite (Conagra—also makes Banquet).
V   Van deKamp Mexican Classic and other ethnic lines.
B   Benihana.
G   Green Giant Stir Fry Entrees (Pillsbury).

important among airline passengers but if airlines are perceived to be equal with respect to pilot quality and plane maintenance, it cannot be the basis for an SCA. Of course, if some airlines can convince passengers that they are superior with respect to antiterrorist security, then an SCA could indeed exist.

To help provide the correct point of reference and summarize relevant information, it is usually helpful to scale your own firm and the major competitors or strategic groups of competitors (competitors who have similar strategies and characteristics) on the relevant assets and skills.[12] For each competitor, which are areas of strengths and which are weaknesses?

A competitor strength grid, as illustrated in Figure 2 for the gourmet frozen food industry, provides a compact representation of the results. The relevant assets and skills are listed in order of their importance to the extent that an ordering can be obtained. The principal competitors are then positioned on each dimension according to the relative strengths and weaknesses. The process can generate insight into the nature of the assets and skills, competitor capabilities, and a particular SBU's position relative to competitors.

In Figure 2, eight assets and skills are listed and seven main competitors in the gourmet frozen food industry in the mid-1980s are positioned. The grid suggests that Lean Cuisine is well positioned with the dominant market share, distribution and advertising effort. However, other firms may have developed packaging advantages and there may be an industry gap with respect to quality.

---

[12]The competitive strength grid was first introduced in David A. Aaker, "How to Select a Business Strategy," *California Management Review* 26, no. 3 (Spring 1984), pp. 167–75. The material on the gourmet frozen foods was drawn from work of students Alan Donald, Harvey Scodel, Dave Barnes, Jacquelyn Boykin, Joe Jimenez, Barbara May, and Jill Stewarts.

It is often desirable, or even necessary, to conduct the analysis for submarkets or strategic groups and for different products. A firm may not compete with all the other firms in the industry but only those engaged in similar strategies and markets. For example, a competitor strength grid may look very different for the controlled calorie portion of the gourmet frozen food industry or the ethnic submarket. The relevant assets and skills may differ. The ethnic portion may not involve the asset "low calorie" position, for example. Further, the composition of the competitors and their relative strengths can change as well.

Relevant to the Market

An analysis of customer motivations should help evaluate as well as identify SCAs. On nearly all cases, an SCA should result in either a point of differentiation or a price advantage that is valued by the customer.

A case in point is the P&G Pringle experience. P&G developed a potato chip that was neither burnt nor greasy, was of uniform shape and would "stack," had a package that protected the chips from breakage, and had a shelf life of over one year. P&G was the only firm that could really mount a national distribution and advertising effort for such a product. They had a series of substantial assets and skills to rely on. However, the customer was interested primarily in taste and had little concern with shelf life or breakability. Associating the product with "artificiality," consumers concluded that it had an inferior taste (despite the fact that blind taste tests indicated that it had a taste parity). As a result, the repeat purchase was weak and the product has had disappointing performance relative to expectations.

Feasible and Cost Effective

Sometimes an objective analysis will conclude that the development of a desired asset or skill is so costly that it is simply not economically feasible. A competitor might be so entrenched with respect to a dimension such as quality or service or performance that the market would not find credible a claim that the competitor had been surpassed even if physical superiority had been achieved. Or there could be an implementation issue. The culture of the firm may simply not be compatible with creating a strong innovation strength, for example. The people, culture, systems and rewards may all be geared to production and cost reduction in a way that would be impossible to change without doing substantial harm.

Sustainable

Will the resulting SCA be neutralized by the strategy of a competitor? There is little point to investing resources into assets and skills that can be easily neutralized by a competitor's strategy. A location advantage might be easily neutralized by an innovative logistical system. A distribution advantage that can be bypassed by using promotions or a different channel is not the basis of an SCA.

Another key consideration is whether competitors or potential competitors have the motivation to respond. Honda's reaction to the Yamaha challenge in motorcycles provides a vivid illustration of how a committed competitor can respond to emerging SCAs.[13] Through aggressive product introductions, capacity expansions, and the development of distribution strengths, Yamaha took over the leading position in Japan's motorcycle market at a time when Honda was diverted by its efforts to enter the automobile market. Yamaha publicly boasted that it would become number one worldwide. Honda's pride and historical commitment motivated it to counter with a wide variety of product options and lower price. The result of provoking Honda was nearly disastrous for Yamaha, which subsequently announced that it would be very happy to be number two.

A business should look for strategies that are sustainable when a competitor is inhibited or otherwise unable to respond. For example, a competitor might believe that a response to a low-end entry would result in cannibalizing an existing product line or tarnishing its image. A strategy of product breadth might leave no niche that would support an aggressive response by a competitor. A large competitor might be inhibited by antitrust laws and by a large installed base to respond to a niche strategy. Dominant firms like Anheuser-Busch, General Motors, and IBM are restricted by antitrust laws in the strategic options they can pursue. Further, they have to be sensitive to the impact upon their installed base of any strategic reaction to a competitor's strategy.

Relevant to the Future

Changing conditions can undercut strategies and the assets and skills upon which they are based. In many technical industries, for example, technology is of prime importance at the outset. The successful firms are those that can deliver the most advanced technology. The product then evolves in one of two directions. The product may become a commodity, in which case a key success factor for most firms tends to be achieving low production costs and an effective distribution system. Personal computers and low-cost copiers are examples of this. Or, the product may evolve toward a system in which case it becomes important to participate in related businesses to control the system and to have a strong direct sales and service capability. The CT Scanner and high-end copiers are examples.

It is thus important to anticipate what assets and skills will be needed as conditions evolve. Teece notes that innovator firms such as RC Cola in diet colas, Bowmar in pocket calculators, and DeHavilland in planes all were first with a successful innovative product but lacked the assets and skills to compete when others became established.[14] Pepsi-Cola, Texas Instruments, and Boeing had the complementary assets that were needed to compete after the initial phase of the product life. In these cases, the assets and skills needed were so crucial that the alternative to obtaining them (either internally or through a strategic alliance) was to lose nearly all the benefits of the innovation.

The task of projecting the environment and the needed assets and skills is not at all easy. Trends emerging from analyses of the customers, compet-

---

[13]James C. Abegglen and George Stalk, Jr., *Kaisha: The Japanese Corporation* (New York: Basic Books, 1985), pp. 45–50.

[14]David J. Teece, "Profiting from Technological Innovation: Implications for Integration, Collaboration, Licensing and Public Policy," *Research Policy* 15 (1986) pp. 285–305.

itors, distribution channel, technology, and the industry environment need to be identified, monitored, and analyzed. The development of scenarios can be helpful because the realization of the new assets and skills that will be needed often only emerges from a picture of the future that is both rich and convincing.

HOW TO DEVELOP AND MAINTAIN SCAs

The creation of assets and skills can be difficult and costly. There is no right way or shortcut that will work in every situation, but the following should provide both useful suggestions as to how to proceed and additional insight into the SCA concept.

Link to Business Objectives

One key to the management of assets and skills is to link them to business objectives. An objective could thus be to create the asset of brand name awareness or distribution coverage or the skill of low-cost production or providing high-quality service. Such objectives hopefully would dominate short-term financial objectives and provide a strategic focus to management of the operations.

The objectives need to be supported by measurable indicators of strength of assets and skills. Tom Peters provides examples of indicators of such assets and skills as quality, service, responsiveness, niches, creation, and innovation.[15] He notes that firms such as Ford, Tennant, and Perdue Farms use quality objectives as a basis for compensation. IBM measures customer satisfaction and analyzes complaints in order to help protect the loyalty of its installed base, perhaps its most important asset.

Fit with Strategies

Assets and skills will generate SCAs only in the context of the appropriate strategies and the right competitive environment. A large installed base facing substantial switching costs may be an SCA only if it is exploited. Micropro's Wordstar, the early leader in word processing, developed a new generation product, Wordstar 2000, that was sufficiently different from Wordstar so that its customers could switch to competitors almost as easily as they could learn the new Micropro product. As a result, Micropro's position eroded. Had it upgraded its basic Wordstar product instead, it might have held its position. Belatedly, it did introduce Wordstar Professional, an advanced program compatible with the original product.

The goal should be to develop strategies that exploit assets and skills. One longtime observer of Japanese firms notes that one key to their success is their creation and exploitation of competitive advantage.[16] Historically a SCA of many Japanese firms was based upon low-cost manufacturing in part

---

[15]Tom Peters, *Thriving on Chaos* (New York: Alfred A. Knopf, 1987). See especially sections C-2, C-3, and S-1.
[16]Abegglen and Stalk, pp. 10–11.

driven by low wages. This advantage supported aggressive pricing policies aimed at generating share dominance. More recently, some of these firms, finding the cost advantage eroding, have developed additional skills such as highly flexible factories that permit them to generate wide product lines without a cost premium. Their strategy is to exploit the manufacturing flexibility by creating a broad product line and segmenting the market to continue to pursue share growth. The point is that they have developed new assets and skills and then engaged in strategies that exploit those assets and skills.

An SCA can often be leveraged by making it part of the positioning strategy. The distinction is between an asset or skill that is developed because its absence would create a problem or competitive opportunity and an asset or skill that is created to provide a visible consumer benefit. Thus, Maytag developed a product line and service system geared to delivering reliability and used that to position the firm with respect to the market. If the customers perceive the business with respect to its assets and skills, those assets and skills perform a marketing function as well. Further, the more visibility and commitment that are placed behind the assets and skills, the more likely that there will be supporting commitment and culture inside the business to maintain those assets and skills.

Routes to an SCA

The development of an SCA often requires not only insight and good management but also luck and/or substantial investment. For example, the creation and maintenance of American Express's 15 million cardholder base required an enormous expenditure of advertising and promotion funds. Although there are many routes to an SCA, a few are worth singling out because they illustrate the basic concept and because when they can be applied they can result in the development of assets and skills with a relatively modest investment.

Patent and Trade Secret Protection   In some situations, patents can provide a substantial barrier to competitive response. Howard Head, who in the 50s revolutionized the ski industry with his metal skis, did the same thing to the tennis racket industry in the late 1970s by creating and obtaining a patent on the oversized Prince racket. The Prince market share went from zero in 1975 to 30.7 in 1981, while the total market for rackets collapsed from $183.7 million to $135.9 million.[17] Competitors proliferated products but could not compete with the basic Prince design because of the patent.

A study of 650 R&D executives attempted to determine the relative effectiveness of various means of protecting the returns from innovations such as patents, secrecy, lead time, and superior sales and service.[18] They found that patents tended to be more important in products rather than processes, as products are often patentable and are vulnerable to reverse engineering when patent protection is absent. Further, they found that patents are most useful in

---

[17]Walter McQuade, "Prince Triumphant," *Fortune*, February 22, 1982, pp. 84–90.

[18]Sidney G. Winter, "Knowledge and Competence as Strategic Assets," in David Teece, ed., *The Competitive Challenge: Strategies for Industrial Innovation and Renewal* (Cambridge, MA: Ballinger Publishing Company, 1987), pp. 159–84.

the chemical and drug areas where the product is easily analyzed and copied. Patents were found to be less of a factor in innovative industries such as computers and communications equipment where the environment is so dynamic that patents become obsolete.

When patents are not strong enough to provide an adequate barrier, trade secret protection may protect an asset such as a process development or even an information system.[19] A trade secret can be protected by nondisclosure agreements, avoiding personnel turnover, and by avoiding access by vendor or customer firms.

Preemptive Strategies   A preemptive strategic move is the first implementation of a strategy into a business area that, because it was first, generates an asset or skill that creates a competitive advantage that is sustainable because competitors are inhibited or prevented from duplicating or countering it. A preemptive move can be directed at any element of strategy involving the supply systems, the product, the production system, the customers, or the distribution and service systems.[20] Thus, a key advantage of Red Lobster restaurants was their access to the best seafood sources and seafood distribution. A brand that enters a market first with a strong position upon a key dimension makes it more difficult for future competitors to engage in a similar strategy.

If key customers can be committed, competitors may be shut off from part of the market. For example, a hospital supply firm made substantial inroads against a dominant, established firm by offering to place computer terminals in hospitals to facilitate ordering emergency items. The terminals ultimately were used to order routine as well as emergency orders. Since hospitals had a need for only one such terminal, the established firm found its belated effort to duplicate the service frustrated—it had been preempted.

Exploiting Synergy   Synergy exists when the combination of two or more businesses provides either more customer value, less product cost, or less investment than would be the case if those businesses operated separately.[21] Thus, a firm that makes a printer, modem, and software in addition to a computer can furnish a systems solution which will provide customer value in selecting a system and in obtaining service. It could also provide reduced cost in that the lines could share a sales force and reduced investment if they could share manufacturing and warehousing facilities.

An advantage based upon synergy is likely to be sustainable because the firm itself is unique. No other firm will have the identical set of firm characteristics and profile of businesses. To the extent that the synergistic advantage is linked to the uniqueness of the firm it will be sustainable.

American Express decided that an important asset that they wanted to develop was their synergy among their bank, insurance, brokerage, and card operations.[22] As a result they developed the One Enterprise program to

---

[19]Teece, p. 287.

[20]Ian C. MacMillan, "Preemptive Strategies," *Journal of Business Strategy,* Fall 1983, pp. 16–26.

[21]For a discussion of the synergy concept, see Aaker, *Developing Business Strategies,* p. 242.

[22]Monci Jo Williams, "Synergy Works at American Express," *Fortune,* February 16, 1987, p. 80.

encourage the exploitation of the synergy. Significantly, each manager was evaluated on his or her contribution to the program; tied to the evaluation was compensation in the form of bonuses.

NEUTRALIZING COMPETITORS' ASSETS AND SKILLS

A key to winning is thus to create SCAs involving strategies that are based upon assets and skills. A companion approach to strategy developments is to recognize the assets and skills of competitors and look for strategies that neutralize them by making them irrelevant.

An example of a firm that developed a strategy to neutralize competitor strengths was a small software firm that lacked a retail distribution capability or the resources to engage in retail advertising. It directed its efforts to value-added software systems firms, firms that sell total software and sometimes hardware systems to industries such as investment firms or hospitals. These value-added systems firms could understand and exploit the power of the product, integrate it into their system, and use it in quantity. The absence of a distribution channel or resources to support an advertising effort was thus neutralized.

CONCLUSION

Too often a concentration upon short-term profit measures sacrifices strategic position and long-term performance. The question is how to manage for the long term. One answer is to focus upon the assets and skills that provide the foundation for sustainable competitive advantage. The essence of strategic management then should be the development and maintenance of meaningful assets and skills, the selection of strategies and competitive arenas to exploit such assets and skills, and the neutralizing of competitors' assets and skills.

Managing assets and skills involves three steps. The first is the identification of relevant assets and skills by observing successful and unsuccessful firms, key customer motivations, large value-added items, and mobility barriers. Among those named by managers were product quality reputation, name recognition, and customer service/product support. The second step is to select those assets and skills to support a strategy that will provide an advantage over competitors, be relevant to the market, be feasible, be sustainable, and be appropriate to the future. The third step is to develop and implement programs and procedures to develop, enhance, or protect assets and skills. One key is the use of appropriate objectives and supporting measures. Another is to make sure that what a business does and where it competes supports and exploits its assets and skills and neutralizes the assets and skills of competitors.

KOREA: COMPETING IN THE MICROWAVE INDUSTRY

Ira Magaziner and Mark Patinkin*

The microwave oven, invented in America 40 years ago,[1] just recently became one of the best-selling appliances in the world. It has created a multibillion-dollar industry that's spawned tens of thousands of jobs. Yet today, were you to buy a microwave oven in the United States, the odds are one in three that it was built 10,000 miles away, in South Korea.[2] The odds are one in five that it was designed by a 43-year-old engineer named Yun Soo Chu. His company, Samsung, is now the world's leading microwave oven producer.[3] But it wasn't until 1979, when millions of the new ovens were being manufactured each year in America, that Samsung set up its first crude assembly line. That year, the company made only a few dozen a week. Today, it makes over 80,000 a week. The story of how Samsung succeeded speaks of the growing sophistication of our competition in the developing world.

When Chu joined Samsung in 1973, it had just taken on a manufacturing challenge new to Korea: making home appliances. He started his company career designing washing machines, soon moving to electric skillets. Then, in 1976, he received an unexpected assignment. That year, on a visit to the United States, a Samsung vice-president named J. U. Chung had been intrigued by a new kind of oven, heated not by electricity or gas, but by microwaves.

Chung knew there was no way he could market such an oven at home—few Koreans could afford it—but that wasn't a concern. In Korea, when companies consider a new product, the most common first question is whether they can export it. That same year, for example, Samsung had decided to make color televisions, even though there wasn't a single TV station in the country that could broadcast in color.[4]

---

*Ira C. Magaziner is the founder and president of *Telesis*, an international consulting firm. His books include *Minding America's Business* (Random House, 1983) and *Japanese Industrial Policy* (University of California-Berkeley Press, 1981). Mark Patinkin is a nationally syndicated columnist for the *Providence Journal-Bulletin*.

[1]The idea of cooking with microwaves originated with Raytheon managers involved in the production of magnetron tubes for radar installations during World War II. They worked on the concept beginning in 1942 and received their first microwave cooking patents in 1949. Raytheon introduced the first microwave-cooking oven, the Radar-range, in 1953. The original versions were as big and heavy as refrigerators and cost as much as some automobiles. Raytheon licensed its invention to Tappan and Litton, who in 1955 began selling home models.

[2]This estimate is based on internal production figures from Samsung and from GE internal sources. Publicly reported industry-association data is not accurate in market-share breakdowns, as companies do not necessarily report accurate figures to these associations. Korean-made microwaves are sold under many labels, including GE, J. C. Penney, Montgomery Ward, Whirlpool, Sears, Emerson, Samsung, and Goldstar.

[3]In 1988, Samsung surpassed Matsushita, Sanyo, and Sharp in total number of units produced, though its total sales valued in dollars may still be slightly smaller at the retail level due to mix and high retail prices in Japan.

[4]Korea did not begin to offer color-television transmission until four years after the production of color televisions commenced at Samsung, Goldstar, and Lucky (now part of Goldstar).

Knowing that Americans like convenience, Chung felt the microwave oven was perfect for that market, the world's largest. When he got back to Korea, he asked Chu to form a team to design a Samsung microwave. Chu knew his company was starting well behind Japanese and American producers, but Samsung, he felt, had two advantages: low-wage workers, and a willingness to wait for a payback. The company's first priority, he knew, wasn't high profits; it was high production. Samsung was especially interested in modern products. For Korean industry, that was almost unprecedented.

Traditionally, low-wage countries have been content to let their factories lag a decade behind countries like America, making bicycles in the age of the automobile, black-and-white televisions in the age of color. Samsung was one of the first Third World companies to take a new approach, deciding to compete directly in modern products.

Chu began by ordering a new U.S. microwave model called the Jet 230, made by General Electric, America's leading appliance company. Soon, Chu was looking at his first microwave. He took it apart, but still had no idea how it worked. The plastic cavity seemed simple enough, as did the door assembly and some of the wiring; but there were several complex parts, especially the device that generated the microwaves—the magnetron tube. To build it, he could tell, required expertise Samsung lacked. He began to tinker anyway. His team was given 15 square feet in the corner of an old lab that served the company's entire electronics division, which at the time consisted of three Quonset-hut factories. It seemed absurd that such a place could consider challenging major corporations in America and Japan, and Chu knew it. But he also knew Samsung's executives cared little about marketing at the moment. They'd told him they had only one objective right now—production. They'd worry about selling the oven later.

It was around that time, 1977, that I got my first glimpse of South Korea, at the request of the British government. A few years before, Korean black-and-white televisions had begun arriving in England. At first, British TV producers hadn't been concerned. The Koreans gained only a small market share, and besides, this was exactly what developing countries were expected to do: compete in 20-year-old products. But then something disturbing happened. Korean color televisions began arriving, also cheap. The British government wanted to know whether the assault would get more serious. I was asked to do a study.[5]

My first day in Seoul showed me that South Korea was more a Third World country than I imagined. My rental car, a tinny local brand, had a hole in the floor. The road from the airport was dusty, and much of the housing run-down. The city had only one first-class hotel, which lost power for a few hours shortly after I arrived. Only a decade before, the World Bank had listed South Korea as one of the world's poorest countries.[6] Could a nation like this be a threat?

---

[5]The study was commissioned by the National Economic Development Office in Great Britain, an industry-, labor-, and government-sponsored organization with separate councils for a variety of industries. Britain's television makers were suffering and wanted to understand the new competition they were facing from Japan and Korea. They asked for a strategy on what they could do to become competitive again.

[6]In 1960, Korea's GNP per capita was less than 10 percent of that of the United States.

At first, I didn't think so, except maybe in old technologies. But after a few days, I began to hear that the government was helping companies get into more modern industries. I purchased a copy of its latest official five-year plan,[7] then sat down with one of the country's leading economic officials. He explained that to invest in new factories, Korea needed foreign cash, so it had been encouraging export, mostly of textiles and black- and white TVs. Korea's next goal was to export cars and ships. And recently, the country had finished a steel plant. I decided to visit it.

At the time, developing nations everywhere were breaking into steel. I'd seen several Third World plants, and had been especially impressed by those in Brazil and Mexico. I wondered if Korea's would be as good. It turned out to be better. The equipment was modern and the layout efficient. They'd done it by licensing foreign technology and hiring advisers from Japan.[8]

Next, I decided to visit one of Korea's auto plants. The hole in my rental car had left me skeptical, so I went to see the manufacturer, a company called Hyundai. A first glance left me even more skeptical. The workers were simply assembling old Japanese-designed models, then relabeling them, almost all for local sale. But just before I left, I met a British business-man who'd been brought in by Hyundai as an executive. He had good credentials—he'd worked as a senior manager at British Leyland, England's biggest carmaker. He, too, had at first been unsure about Hyundai, he said, but was now ecstatic. He was convinced that the ingredients were here for a real breakthrough—not just at Hyundai, but throughout the country. The nation, he said, had come to a consensus that manufacturing would be its road to prosperity. The workers were industrious, and South Korea's major corpo-rations—with government help—were now poised to invest big dollars in new factories.

My next stop was Samsung, one of the companies exporting televisions to England. The company's electronics division, in Suweon, an hour's drive from Seoul, wasn't much. The factory floors were bare concrete, and people were hand-wheeling parts to and from the production line. I moved on to Samsung's research lab, which reminded me of a dilapidated high-school science class-room. But the work going on there intrigued me. They'd gathered color televi-sions from every major company in the world—RCA, GE, Hitachi—and were using them to design a model of their own. They were working on refrigera-tors and other appliances, as well. The chief engineer was young, well trained, a recent graduate of an American university. I asked him about Samsung's color-television strategy, telling him I presumed the company planned to buy parts from overseas, only doing assembly in Korea. Not at all, he said. They were going to make everything themselves—even the color picture tube. They'd already picked the best foreign models, he said, and signed agreements for technical assistance. Soon, he predicted, Samsung would be exporting around the globe. I wasn't convinced. Maybe in 10 or 15 years, I thought, but not sooner. To be a world player, you need world-class engineers, and that was something Korea was short on.

---

[7]Every five years, the Korean government publishes a detailed economic plan. As part of that plan, targets for growth by industrial sector are set, and specific proposals are made on how to reach the goals.

[8]The Pohang steelworks in South Korea was, at the time, one of the world's most modern and efficient mills. It was built with technical assistance from Nippon Steel and NKK of Japan.

What I didn't realize was that the company's chairman, Lee Byung Chull, was investing not just in better technology, but better minds. He'd been sending waves of young Koreans to American universities, slowly building what was soon to become the biggest company engineering pool in any developing country.

Had I looked in all corners of the Samsung lab that day in 1977, I might have seen Chu, just beginning work on a microwave-oven prototype. By then, he too had gathered a number of the world's best models—GE, Toshiba, Litton—and was choosing the best parts of each. One thing that drove Chu was his failure at his last assignment at Samsung—designing an electric skillet. He just hadn't been able to make it work right. This time, he told himself, he had to succeed.

Samsung didn't have all the manufacturing machines he needed to make microwave ovens, so Chu began visiting press vendors, plastic vendors, toolmakers. When he couldn't find anyone in the country to do the kind of welding he wanted, he chose to seal his oven prototype with caulking instead. Slowly, it came together—brackets, outer panel, door. But when he got to the magnetron tube, source of the microwaves, he was lost. There was no way Samsung could make it, or even subcontract it locally. At the time, only three manufacturers in the world had that ability—two in Japan and one in Rhode Island. Chu decided to buy the magnetron tube outright, from Japan. As months passed, he drove himself ever harder, often staying in the lab all night. It took him a year of 80-hour weeks to finish the prototype, but finally, he was ready to test it. He pushed the "on" button. In front of his eyes, the plastic in the cavity melted. So much for a year's work.

He spent more 80-hour weeks to rebuild it, readjust it, redesign it. And again he turned it on. This time, the stir shaft melted. Even his wife began to question his obsessiveness. "You must be mad," she'd tell him. At times, he agreed with her. The Japanese and Americans, he knew, were now selling over four million microwave ovens a year, and he couldn't even get a single prototype to work.

Microwave-oven technology was pioneered in the late 1940s by a U.S. defense contractor—Raytheon. While experimenting with radar microwaves, a researcher there noticed that a candy bar in his pocket melted. That led to the idea of an oven. Raytheon and another defense-oriented company, Litton, tried to sell the product in America, without much success.[9] Few U.S. appliance makers saw promise in it. True, it was the first new major appliance in a generation, but in America it seemed unnecessary. Most households already had an oven. Who would want two? Besides, quick defrost for quick meals—a strong point of microwaves—wasn't yet the American way of eating.

The product seemed ideal for Japan, however, a nation with a taste for smallness—small houses, small kitchens, small appliances. And the Japanese cooking style did rely heavily on reheating. Though a few American com-

---

[9]In the years from 1952 to 1967, fewer than 10,000 microwave ovens were sold in the United States, most of them made by hand assembly at Raytheon and sold to restaurants and airlines. Litton tried to introduce them for home sale during this period with little success. Both Raytheon and Litton had over 75 percent of their revenues at the time in defense industries.

panies were aware of the Japanese sales potential, they weren't interested. Exporting to distant markets wasn't worth the trouble.

That's how Japanese companies became the first major manufacturers of microwave ovens. They seized our technology, began perfecting it, and soon went beyond their backyard. They saw export as an opportunity, not a burden. They pushed the product overseas, harvesting a windfall when the world market took off, going from 600,000 units in 1970 to 2.2 million in 1975.[10] Finally, in the late-1970s, American appliance makers like GE began serious investment in microwave ovens.[11] But they paid a price for being late. In 1979, the U.S. market became bigger than Japan's for the first time. But by then, Japanese companies already had over 25 percent of it.[12]

In June of 1978, in the corner of his Suweon lab, Chu finally finished another prototype. He turned it on for a test, ready for the worst, but this time, nothing melted. His bosses were encouraged. They knew Chu's oven was still too crude to compete on the world market, but they told him to make more anyway. Chu himself had few global hopes. At best, he felt, Samsung would find a small, low-priced niche in the United States. But that didn't discourage him. The company's preeminent goal was production; marketing was second priority. Soon Samsung management did send out a few salesmen with the prototypes. They didn't have much success, but headquarters decided to put together a makeshift production line anyway. In case an order came in, they wanted to be ready. It was one of the company's rules: Never, ever, keep a customer waiting.

---

[10]The microwave oven was first demonstrated in Japan by Raytheon in 1960 at a trade show. Japanese consumer-electronics companies led by Toshiba and Sanyo took an interest in the product and began building copies of the restaurant model shown by Raytheon. By that time, the New Japan Radio Company (NJRC) was the only maker of magnetron tubes in Japan left over from World War II. The other companies that had made radar systems ceased doing so when the American occupation authorities prohibited military work by Japanese firms.

NJRC continued funding nonmilitary uses for microwave tubes in medical heat therapy and civilian communications. NJRC and Raytheon linked up and traded technology in the 60s. Spurred on by Sanyo and Toshiba, a scientist at NJRC named Keishi Ogura developed a low-cost magnetron for consumer application in 1964.

By 1968, Japanese companies were exporting consumer microwave ovens to the United States. Raytheon bought Amana to try to sell to U.S. consumers, but the Japanese market took off quicker, spurred by lower-cost product designs and Japanese cooking tastes, which fit the microwaves' capability.

In 1968, 30,000 microwave ovens were sold worldwide. By 1975, 2.2 million were sold, with 1.3 million sold in Japan and 900,00 in the U.S. By then, all the major Japanese consumer-electronics companies had developed products, and a number of them, including Toshiba and Matsushita, were producing their own magnetron tubes. As the ovens' volume and quality grew their costs for the tube decreased. NJRC, the Japanese inventor of the microwave tube for cooking, now partly owned by Raytheon, was surpassed, stopped making tubes in 1980.

[11]In the mid- and late 1970s, Raytheon-Amana and Litton dominated U.S. microwave-oven production. General Electric entered the business in the early 1970s, but had only 7 percent market share in 1973, well under its more than 30 percent share in electric ranges. GE did not invest seriously in the business until the late 1970s. Whirlpool, White/Westinghouse, and Maytag, America's other large appliance companies, did not enter the microwave business at all in the 1970s.

[12]Japanese producers had 30 percent market share in the United States by the mid-1970s. Raytheon and Litton dominated, with over 60 percent of the U.S. market at the time. The Japanese share decreased to 25 percent in the late 1970s due to the rise of the Japanese yen and trade pressure that forced the Japanese companies to begin opening assembly plants in the United States. Characteristically, U.S. producers and the business press hailed the demise of the Japanese threat at this time. By 1982, however, the Japanese share of the U.S. market was back up to over 45 percent, and Raytheon and Litton's combined share was down below 25 percent.

The production team began making one microwave oven a day, then two. Soon, they were up to five. By mid-1979, when over four million ovens were sold around the world, Samsung had finished only 1,460 of them. That's when the company decided to try its first real sales push. They chose to focus on the local market. Unfortunately, their low scale meant they had to charge an exorbitant $600 each—half the yearly income of an average Korean family. Almost no one bought. But management was upbeat. The machines worked. Having no sales was no reason to stop development.

Still, with the domestic push a washout, Samsung's salespeople began to look abroad. They sent out brochures and hired distributors in dozens of countries. They offered to cut price and were ready to fill the smallest order. The first came in from Panama, for 240 ovens. By the time the ovens were all shipped, Samsung had lost money, but there was celebration in Suweon. The company had broken through. And besides, this would be a good way to learn what customers wanted. Samsung felt it best to refine the product in a few small markets before trying big ones.

The Panama sales gave them confidence to apply for underwriter's laboratory approval, necessary for exporting to the United States. Late in 1979, they got it. For Samsung, America wasn't a totally foreign market. Many of the company's managers had gone to school there; they had American knowledge, knew the American language. And Samsung was ready to do something few American manufacturers did at the time: tailor its product to foreign tastes. If that meant retooling production back in Suweon, Samsung would spend the money. Instead of planning on a single line of ovens for the world, its strategy was to make unique models for unique markets.

At the time, microwave ovens sold for $350–$400 each in America. One of the country's biggest retailers, J. C. Penney, had been searching for a $299 model. They hadn't had any luck with the two countries then producing microwaves—Japan and the United States. Then Penney heard about Samsung. The retailer saw an opportunity—a low-wage country capable of building a modern product. In 1980, Penney decided to ask Samsung if it could build a microwave oven to sell in America for $299.

By then, world sales were up to 4.7 million a year.[13] Samsung was being asked for a few thousand only. On top of that, Penney's order would mean designing a whole new oven and taking heavy losses, all in the name of gaining a fraction of 1 percent of the U.S. market. In Suweon, management was ecstatic anyway, promising Penney anything it wanted. To deliver, Samsung promised Chu any investment he needed. The firm put no pressure on him for profits; all it wanted was production.

Penney's technical people would be helping Chu with product quality, but Chu knew the greatest burden would be on Samsung. The challenge now was to turn a still-primitive assembly room into an efficient factory almost overnight. And Samsung would have to get it right the first time. This wasn't another Panama. These machines would be going to Americans, the most sophisticated consumers in the world.

---

[13]Almost all of the world market growth from 1975 to 1980 came in the United States. The U.S. market grew from 900,000 units in 1975 to 3.2 million units in 1980. Meanwhile, the Japanese market declined from 1.3 million units in 1975 to 900,000 units in 1980. The competitive battleground clearly shifted to United States territory.

Chu's boss was a quiet mechanical engineer named Kyung Pal Park. Ask him why he chose manufacturing and he'll tell you of his memory of American soldiers during the Korean War. Everything about them suggested wealth: their clothes, their equipment, their vehicles. How, Park wondered, had America achieved that? In time, he came to see the answer as production. America was wealthy because it made things. Park wanted that for Korea, too: a nation not of rice paddies, but factories. In 1969, he joined Samsung. In 1980, at age 39, he was named head of home appliances. It was his responsibility to deliver the Penney order.

Soon he came up with his plan for organizing a team. In America, such a team typically would be headed by product designers; factory engineers would come second. At Samsung, production is king. So Park merged his product and factory people, stressing that design should be done with manufacturing in mind. He gave the team one unbreakable rule: No matter what, they would deliver on every deadline, not a day later. That responsibility would fall to Park's chief lieutenant, a production engineer just transferred from Samsung's motor division named I. J. Jang.

Before his transfer, Jang was managing the production of millions of motors a year on four separate lines. Now, he found himself in a division making five or six ovens a day. He didn't see it as a demotion. "There is one thing more valued at Samsung than high production," he explains, "the potential of high production." The best engineers aren't placed with boom products, but products that have yet to take off.

Jang immersed himself in learning the product, spending hours talking with designers like Chu, then journeying overseas to Matsushita, Sanyo, and GE. Once he'd learned world standards, he began to make sure Samsung was living up to them. He studied the prototype test results, pausing on the microwave-leakage numbers, which seemed high. That was a problem. He asked if it could be fixed, and was told the seal design made it hard to weld any better. So Jang, one of Samsung's most senior production managers, personally went to the welding vendor to help upgrade his process. Of the 100 outside vendors working on the project, he ended up visiting 30 of them himself.

Then he turned his attention to building the assembly line. He started with an empty factory room and a delivery date only months away. His senior people would begin at dawn, often working until 10:30 P.M., then take a few hours' nap before going back to work for the rest of the night. Even Jang's boss, Kyung Pal Park, one of the highest executives in Suweon, kept the same hours. Samsung's executives rarely ask a sacrifice they're not ready to make themselves. Actually, there was one area of privilege. There were a few cots littered around the factory. The executives got those, the others grabbed naps in chairs.

The line took shape, production began, but inevitably, there were dozens of bugs. The Samsung people decided they couldn't afford to lose production though, so they fell into a pattern of manufacturing by day, then running the line all night to fine-tune it. Production improved, up to 10 a day, then 15. Soon, they got it to 1,500 a month, enough to meet Penney's order of several thousand.

Penney liked the ovens, and soon asked for more. Could Samsung deliver 5,000 in another month? Samsung made that deadline, too, but there wasn't time for celebration. Now Penney wanted 7,000. There was time only to work. "Like a cow," Jang would say later.

The team felt it would be wise to install more assembly lines and asked management for the money. "It was no problem," Jang said. As long as they got production, they would get the investment. By the end of 1981, Samsung had increased microwave production a hundredfold over the previous year, from just over 1,000 to over 100,000. Still, it was only a fraction of the world market. And almost none of the giants in America or Japan noticed. South Korea, they still felt, could never be a serious competitor in such sophisticated technology.

In 1978, while working on a study for the Swedish government, I visited some Korean shipyards. I was surprised to find how modern they were—and more surprised when the managers said they planned to invest in even better technology. Then, in 1979, while in Athens to make a speech, I was given a Hyundai as a rental car. It was only two years after I'd all but written Hyundai off after touring their factory. But this car was much better. And I noticed a number of other Hyundai cars on the roads. A month later, on a trip to Dubai, I saw more Hyundai cars, as well as Samsung color TVs.

I decided to look into what was happening, and returned to Korea. After a number of days meeting with both corporate managers and government economic planners,[14] I learned that Korea's progress was driven by its government. The key player was the Economic Development Board. Its job was to think about where South Korea's economy should head and then give incentives to help business get there. EDB built industrial parks, subsidized utilities, provided tax rebates for export and low-cost loans for investing in selected new products. The incentives were of particular help to big companies like Samsung, whose managers met frequently with government officials, plotting strategy, trading ideas, and discussing projects. Both business and government understood the country couldn't depend on low-wage industries for long, not with even cheaper labor in countries next door. Just as America had lost thousands of clothing jobs to Korea, soon, the Koreans knew, they would be losing such jobs to Malaysia and China. To prepare, the government, in consultation with companies, developed incentives for investing in new industries. By 1980, the country had gone beyond textiles, into steel and ships. Now they were making automobiles. And they'd begun moving toward world-class electronics.[15] South Korea was developing faster than I'd expected.

---

[14]During this trip, I spent two weeks in intensive meetings with government and industry leaders discussing South Korea's economic development. They were avidly interested in the new concepts of economic development we were discussing with Swedish leaders, and anxious for me to comment on their plans. I was impressed with the close cooperation that existed between the government and large industrial leaders, though some industrial leaders were not completely happy with the degree of control exerted by the government. There was a clear common understanding of growth priorities and a sharing of investment.

When I returned to the United States from this trip, I met with a Department of Transportation team studying the world automobile industry. They were mostly interested in Japan, and hopeful that the high yen (190 to the dollar at the time) would make Japanese small cars uncompetitive.

I told them this was unlikely, and then mentioned that Hyundai was likely to be the biggest threat in small cars in a decade. Despite my descriptions of South Korea's plans, the U.S. officials were unimpressed.

[15]Samsung's desire to push ahead and develop a microelectronics industry in the late 1970's was highly controversial within the government of South Korea. Many felt it was necessary if the nation was to become a developed country and build a successful electronics industry. Others felt that South Korea could never compete in this fast-moving, expensive new technology and would waste

In 1982, Samsung's microwave production topped 200,000, double the previous year. But Mr. Park and his team didn't think it was enough. They knew that Samsung was still a global afterthought. American manufacturers were making over 2 million ovens per year, and the Japanese even more—2.3 million at home, and another 820,000 in their U.S. plants. The giant Matsushita company had 17 percent of the world market. Sanyo had 15 percent, while Samsung had less than 3 percent.[16]

One problem was that the big producers were bringing their prices down, narrowing Samsung's key advantage. If Samsung was going to keep growing, it realized it had to lower its own prices even more. The executives looked over their cost structure. The highest item was the magnetron tube, which they were still buying from the Japanese. They began to wonder if they could make it themselves. It would mean millions of dollars of investment for a new, highly complex factory. They approached Japan's magnetron producers for technical assistance, but were turned down. That left only one other company to approach—Amperex, the Rhode Island firm that was America's only manufacturer. But that plant, Samsung found, had been unable to compete with Japan and was going out of business.[17]

About that time, in Louisville, Kentucky, the head marketing manager for GE's Major Appliance Business Group, Bruce Enders, was beginning to see warning signs in his microwave-oven division. Because GE had come into microwave ovens so late, it had yet to make money on them. In 1982, the losses began to get worse. The Japanese were chipping away at GE's U.S. share, pushing it down from over 16 percent in 1980 to 14 percent in 1982.[18] No one at GE thought of conceding ground, though. Japan's wage rates were no lower than America's and GE was just completing a multimillion-dollar modernization at its microwave oven factory in Columbia, Maryland. The company was convinced it would turn things around.

Enders knew that GE understood the American consumer better than any other appliance maker. It had just scored a tremendous success with the Spacemaker, for example, the industry's first under-shelf model. If the Maryland modernization could make GE cost-competitive, he was convinced the company could make the business profitable.

But then, in late 1982, the Japanese began to export a new mid-sized line of ovens at an alarmingly low price—it was even below GE's costs at its modernized plant. GE's manufacturing people insisted that the Japanese

---

billions of dollars trying. Samsung did go ahead, and was followed by others. South Korea is not on the cutting edge of integrated-circuit technology, but is now a low-cost, fast follower whose companies supply ICs to many U.S. companies today, including on an OEM basis to U.S. IC makers.

[16]These figures were derived from a Telesis survey of producers. In addition to Matsushita and Sanyo, Sharp had 14 percent share, Toshiba 7 percent, Hitachi 2 percent, and Mitsubishi 1 percent. Altogether, Japanese companies had about 60 percent of world production.

[17]Amperex is actually a subsidiary of the Dutch electronics giant Philips. Its magnetron facility was relatively new in Rhode Island, but did not have the scale, cost levels, or technology to be competitive.

The prices Amperex needed to be profitable were 30 percent higher than those quoted by their Japanese competitors. GE and other U.S. manufacturers did not want to purchase from their competitors in Japan, but could not suffer the 30 percent price penalty that purchasing from Amperex entailed. They switched to the Japanese, and Amperex had to shut down.

[18]Telesis study for GE. GE's share had risen from 7 percent in 1975 to 16 percent by 1980, and had then declined.

must be dumping. But Enders wanted to know for sure. He asked me to do a study.

The study was supposed to focus on Japan, so I spent three weeks there. But I knew Samsung had begun to make microwaves, so before coming home, I flew to Korea for a two-day visit. It was my first trip to Samsung since 1977. It was soon clear that there had been big changes.

In Suweon, the three Quonset huts had been replaced by a dozen new buildings. Some Samsung executives took me on a tour, beginning in the basement of the microwave building, where the machining was done. That part wasn't very impressive. Most of the equipment was old. Then they took me to the second floor, where the ovens were being assembled. It was a little better, but still backward. Samsung's wage rates, I thought, could perhaps outcompete GE, but not their technology.

Then they invited me to see their TV plant. The old one, I remembered, had long lines of women plugging in parts by hand. But this was different—as automated as any TV plant I'd seen in America. Next, they invited me to see their new television-tube factory. It was much larger, and more modern than I'd expected. The biggest surprise was a highly complex TV glass plant being put up in partnership with America's Corning Glass Works. Clearly, Samsung had been serious about producing every color television part by itself.

Finally, I went to the R&D lab. It had gone from an old high-school science room to a large, modern operation. Instead of a handful of engineers, there were 500. Everything Samsung had said it would do in 1977, it had done. I understood that the Koreans weren't showing me all this out of pride alone. They knew I was doing a study for GE and hoped I'd bring back a message: that they could do in microwaves what they'd done in TVs.

As I was leaving the Suweon campus, I saw a truck pull up, and men begin to unload equipment. I looked at it, then looked closer. Months before, I'd visited Amperex, America's last magnetron plant. Afterward, I'd learned it had shut down. Now, here in Korea, coming off this truck, I was looking at Amperex's equipment. Park and the others had decided to build their own magnetrons after all. In an almost disturbingly symbolic strategy, they were going to transplant an American factory that could no longer compete, and sell its goods—now Korean-made—back to America.

Before finishing the final microwave report, I gave my initial impressions to GE in early 1983. The Japanese, I said, weren't dumping. Their plants and product designs were so efficient they could indeed land microwave ovens in the United States cheaper than those coming off GE's new assembly line.[19] They'd done it by first building volume and then investing the extra profits into brainpower. Matsushita, for example, had 280 engineers and technicians in microwave ovens.[20] That cost the company up front, but was now enabling it to get costs ever lower by continually redesigning both its ovens and plants. As for GE, it had only 30 engineers in its microwave operation.

---

[19]Telesis study for GE.

[20]Interviews with Matsushita for Telesis study for GE.

Then there were the most disturbing numbers of all. GE's share was falling even as the world market grew. Global sales had gone from 4.7 million in 1980 to 7 million in 1983, but GE's U.S. market share had shrunk. It was down to 12 percent. Other U.S. producers had declined even more. The shift had almost all gone to the Japanese.[21]

I put forward two options. One was to invest as the Japanese had, in hundreds of engineers. It would be expensive, but in time, I was convinced, it would pay back well. The key word, however, was time. It might take GE a decade of heavy investment—and losses—to take the lead. It was a common strategy in Japan or Korea, but in America it's harder to tell stockholders to wait 5 or 10 years for a return. Besides, GE was already pouring enormous investment into refrigerators and dishwashers, products where it led the market. Microwaves were a lower priority. They chose my other option—to get product from overseas, either through a joint venture or sourcing from a competitor.

While I was finishing my final report, GE management did decide to explore a joint-venture factory with the Japanese, though they wanted it built in the States. They chose to work with Matsushita, the biggest producer. Enders traveled to Japan to negotiate, and seemed to be getting close. He even got the Japanese to agree that a co-venture would be highly profitable for both. But in the end, the Japanese declined.

When they told him, Enders was surprised. He asked one of Matsushita's key executives why. If the co-venture would make them money, why wouldn't they agree to it? Because, the executive said, it would mean losing some of the American market to GE. In Japan, he explained, foreign market share is a key priority.

"Enders-san," he said, "you have to understand. In Japan, it's our destiny to export. If we don't export, we don't survive."

"That's what this guy said to me," Enders would say later. "Could you imagine a U.S. business manager thinking that way? I've never forgotten it."

Matsushita's decision left GE with one other option: sourcing—buying Japanese products and putting the GE label on them. No one in Louisville was ready to shut down the new Maryland plant, but maybe it made sense to source a few lines.

In April 1983, I finished my full report. In it, I raised a Korean option. If GE sourced only with Matsushita, I said, the Americans would be at the mercy of a direct competitor. Korean costs, however, were potentially low enough to undercut the Japanese. And because the Koreans were anxious for volume, it would be easier to negotiate a good deal with them.

Louisville was skeptical. The Koreans? Perhaps they were making a few ovens for Penney, but they were a Third World country. A high-quality firm like GE—selling a million ovens—couldn't risk depending on South Korea.

I showed them the costs differences. In 1983, it cost GE $218 to make a typical microwave oven. It cost Samsung only $155.[22] I went on to break it down.

---

[21]The share of other U.S. manufacturers had gone from 50 percent in 1976 to 42 percent in 1979 to 30 percent by 1983. Meanwhile, the Japanese share of the U.S. market climbed from 27 percent in 1976 to 38 percent by 1980 to 48 percent by 1983.

[22]Telesis analysis.

Assembly labor cost GE $8 per oven; for Samsung, only 63 cents. The differences in overhead labor—supervision, maintenance, setup—were even more astounding. For GE, overhead labor was $30 per oven; for Samsung, 73 cents. GE was spending $4 on material handling for each oven, Samsung 12 cents. The biggest area of difference was in GE's line and central management—that came to $10 per oven. At Samsung, it was two cents. What did the companies get for their money? That was the most disturbing figure of all. Samsung workers were paid less, but delivered more. GE got four ovens per person each day, Samsung got nine. And once volume increased, Korean costs could go even lower.

The GE managers continued to waver. Japanese costs, though not at Korean levels, were better than those at GE. And Japan's products were clearly high quality. Many felt it was more prudent to source there. Still, to be sure, Enders decided to go to Korea himself. At the end of his first day, he asked Samsung's management for a proposal, including a cost breakdown, a delivery schedule, and a description of how they'd build the GE ovens. In America, it takes companies four to six weeks to develop that kind of plan. The next morning, Enders had a final breakfast meeting with Samsung executives.

"A group of engineers came in," Enders recalls, "and they gave us their proposal. Their hair was messed up—their eyes were bloodshot. Those guys had worked all night. And it met our target. I couldn't believe it."

A few weeks later, Roger Schipke, the head of the GE Major Appliance Business Group, decided to go to South Korea. He was walking down a Samsung corridor with his hosts when a crowd of white coats came bustling the other way. He had to stand against the wall to let them by. There were dozens of them, all very young. When they'd passed, he asked who they were. "Those are our new microwave-oven engineers," his host told him. There were more of them than Schipke had working in his whole microwave division, and these were just Samsung's newest hires. Louisville, he realized, was probably out-engineered 10 to 1. He asked where the new hirees had been trained. The answer came back: Purdue, University of Southern California, University of Washington.

"I'm a simple guy," Schipke would say later. "I just looked around. And I said, 'Wow, I'm not getting into that game.' "

In June 1983, management in Louisville decided to begin sourcing microwave ovens from the Far East, but only small and mid-sized models. GE would continue to make full-sized ovens in America. The company's biggest order was with Japan. But GE did give Samsung a much smaller order, only about 15,000. The Americans wanted to see if the Koreans could deliver.

It was now up to Samsung's appliance director, K. P. Park, to produce high-quality goods at a cost America's biggest appliance maker could no longer match. GE sent technical people to Korea to outline its standards. In GE's thinking, this was simply quality control for a second-rate supplier. In Suweon, Park saw it differently. If he was a good student, he'd learn world-class skills. Once again, he told his people there was one unbreakable rule: Every deadline must be met. He knew he'd have to depend on his foot soldiers as much as his lieutenants. Managers like Park feel that Korea's most important resource is disciplined workers who give 70-hour weeks. Who, exactly, are they?

At the Suweon complex, more than half of those who do basic assembly are women. Most stay with Samsung four or five years, arriving with high-school educations and leaving with husbands to start life as housewives. Jo Yon Hwang and Jang Mee Hur, both in their early 20s, applied to Samsung because of its reputation for being good to its workers. They were among the third of all applicants accepted. Upon arrival, they were given blue uniforms, and after two weeks' training were put to work on the microwave line 11 hours a day, 27 days a month. Everyone, even the senior people, works the same schedule. The two women say it's why they feel so committed to the company—their bosses make the same sacrifices they do. In 1988, their base wage was just over $350 a month—a little over $1.20 an hour. The male assembly workers are paid the same. Medical services are provided free by Samsung, and so is lunch. Dinner and breakfast, both offered in company dining areas, cost 15 cents each. The workers are given gifts several times a year: clothes, shoes, hiking bags, tape recorders. The recorders are made by Samsung.

The two women get five days off in winter and five in summer, during which the majority go to a beach camp on the coast. It's run by Samsung. Like most of the women in the Suweon complex, Miss Hwang lives free in a company dormitory. There are 15 such dormitories, housing 420 women each, 6 to a room. Miss Hur chose to live outside the complex, in an apartment with a girlfriend. Rent is not a problem. Samsung lends her $2,000, which she gives to the landlord, who invests it and gets to keep whatever interest it yields. Miss Hur, meanwhile, pays Samsung 10 percent interest on the loan. When she leaves, the $2,000 is given back to the company.

The two young women usually get up at six and have breakfast at seven. Miss Hwang walks to her factory, Miss Hur comes by company bus. At day's end, Miss Hwang has to be back in the dorm by 9:30 P.M., even on the three Sundays a month she gets off. On those days, she and Miss Hur like to watch television, read books, or go hiking. They also like music, particularly Michael Jackson. They know the Beatles are the most legendary of rock groups, but they don't care for them. "Too old," says Miss Hwang. Occasionally, they go on dates, though rarely to nightclubs; usually, they go for daytime walks in the park.

Though they'd welcome promotions, neither actively seeks them. When they think of their futures, they think of marriage. Most female Samsung employees wed between 24 and 26. Thirty percent marry Samsung men. Most of the others wed men they've met through their families, though there's no obligation. Miss Hwang will tell you she's already rejected one parental choice. "I didn't like him," she explains.

The subject the two women are most enthusiastic about is product quality. Miss Hwang is convinced no workers in the world pay as close attention to products as those at Samsung. She herself checks her own work a final time even after an inspector double-checks it. Her specific function is to attach serial numbers and name-brand labels to microwave ovens. If you own a GE Spacemaker, chances are the label was attached by Miss Hwang, here in Suweon. She does 1,200 GE labels a day. Miss Hur's job is to attach microwave doors—also about 1,200 a day. They admit it's the same simple function, hour after hour, but neither thinks the days are dull. They see their jobs as a challenge to personal discipline, even integrity. Doing their work perfectly each time is a way of teaching themselves excellence. They feel their work should reflect their vision of themselves as people of quality. "I put my spirit, put my soul into this product," explains Miss Hwang.

As she does her work, she thinks of making each product as if she herself were going to buy it. She also thinks of the actual customer, some unseen American family. Such families are paying her livelihood; she feels she owes them a good product. Although neither has ever left Korea, both young women are keenly aware of global economic forces. They understand that a great company can no longer endure if it doesn't see the world as both market and competitor. They also understand that products sold abroad will improve the nation's standard of living more than products sold at home. They will tell you that exports bring in new wealth, while domestic sales only recycle it.

Like everyone, they would love higher salaries, but they're motivated by other considerations as well. They see themselves as planting seeds for both company and country. They feel that's a difference between Korean workers and Americans. Though they are in their early 20s, they still remember a Korea of dirt roads, few cars, and many slums. They've seen that change, and though they can't analyze all the reasons, they know manufacturing has been a big one. As factory workers, they feel they're part of that, part of something historic.

At first, Samsung's ovens were not up to GE standards. But with the help of GE's quality engineers, things soon got better.[23] Enders grew increasingly impressed, and eventually put in another order. Sales steadily improved. It was the GE label customers reached for, but Korean workmanship that satisfied them. On his next trip to Suweon, Enders was surprised at the changes. The assembly line had gone from roller conveyors to automatic-transfer mechanisms. Clearly, Samsung had the capacity to deliver far more than GE had been asking for. Enders put in a still-bigger order. Sales kept improving. It was around that time, mid-1983, that the factory in Suweon made a milestone. Samsung shipped its 500,000th oven. For the first time since the company had begun four years before, Park said it was time to celebrate. The Koreans paused for a brief party. When the party was over, they went back to work.

If Suweon's biggest regiment is the assembly-line foot soldiers, its second biggest is the engineers who work a notch above them. The company has thousands, all working the same 68 hours a week. S. D. Lee is typical—a smart, energetic young man who's committed to staying with Samsung. He knows if he works hard, his managers will promote him when he's ready. Although he's a junior engineer, Samsung has already schooled him with extra knowledge. He'll tell you such training is the company's mainstay. Samsung has given him 20 days of full-time quality-control instruction, and once sent him to Japan for two weeks to learn technology from Toshiba. Before that trip, the firm gave him three months of Japanese-language training. "Three years after college," he explains, "you forget what you learned. Reeducation is needed."

---

[23]GE sent over a number of quality-control and manufacturing engineers who helped Samsung develop its testing and production techniques. It took well over a year of joint work before GE felt that an acceptable quality level had been met. This assistance probably cut years off of the time Samsung would have required to become a high-quality, high-volume microwave-oven producer on its own.

What are Samsung's most lasting lessons? Two things, Lee says. First, management by target. You set a goal, then meet it no matter what, even if it means working through the night for a week. Second, you learn always to think several years ahead. It's not enough to be ahead of your competition today, he says. The question to ask is where things will be next decade. Lee's specific assignment illustrates that. Although Samsung's microwave ovens have the lowest cost in the world, Lee is working on factory automation to make the cost lower still.

Does he know Americans work only eight hours a day, five days a week?

He smiles. He is envious of that.

So why is it worth working so much harder, for less money?

Because you don't measure your success against Americans, he says, you measure it against the last generation of Koreans. And his lifestyle is going up faster than he ever expected. His father, he says, never could afford a car. Soon Lee plans to buy one. He sees even greater promise for his children. "If our generation doesn't work hard," he says, "the next generation will suffer."

By the end of 1983, Samsung's annual microwave production topped 750,000, and by 1984, it passed 1 million. The Suweon factory expanded, as well. In four years, Samsung had gone from a few prototypes to 10 mass-production lines. The product that began with melted plastic in an old lab was now becoming a major performer in America's market. But for Samsung, that wasn't good enough.

The company had grown concerned over some new projections. From 1982 to 1986, U.S. microwave sales were expected to keep growing at a healthy rate, but for the four years after that, the predictions said things would slow. It was time, Samsung decided, to seek out other markets. Europe, which was expected to grow by 20 percent a year, offered the most promise. The U.S. manufacturers were aware of the same trend, but Europe didn't seem a worthwhile market to them. The Americans didn't know those countries. It would take too much money to build a marketing network there, too long to get a profit. Samsung faced the same burdens, but its goal wasn't short-term return on investment, it was long-term growth in volume. Among those assigned to Europe was a young marketing executive named J. K. Kim, soon to be named head of appliance-export sales before he was 40.

Like many Samsung executives, Kim is fluent in foreign languages and graduated from an American university. Although his parents had little money, they still found the means to send him to Berkeley. Education, he will tell you, is a Confucian priority. In South Korea, that and family come before all else. Even the poorer sections of the countryside are over 95 percent literate—a far higher rate than in America. Kim still remembers arriving in California for school. The size of America's cities, the number of cars, the wealth of the people—all of it astounded him. He returned to Korea with an urge to help build his own country. One secret of Korea's success, Kim will tell you, is the drive to escape poverty.

With his prestigious Berkeley degree, he had many career choices. Banking was one, lawyer another. Although it paid far less, he chose manufacturing. "I thought it could help more the totality of Korea," he would explain. "If I work for a lawyer's office, I can get my job, and my secretary's job. In Samsung, I can contribute 10,000 jobs." He knows Americans don't quite think that way. In the United States, young businessmen are more drawn to careers in finance. In

South Korea, the prestige lies in factories. Services? "Britain," he says, "is a leader in services, but has one of the lowest living standards in Western Europe. Obviously, it's not the way to build a nation."

Kim found Samsung an ideal home. The hours were long, but he liked the idea of working for Korea's biggest company. Part of its appeal was the three weeks of training a year, another part of the company's willingness to invest. Samsung seemed to blend the risk-taking mentality of a start-up venture with the resources of a great corporation. Most of all, he liked Samsung's drive to be a world player. Now, with the European strategy, the company was asking him to be part of that.

Curiously, it was America that taught Kim how to succeed abroad. It taught him what not to do. As most Koreans know, American firms rarely customize. "They just send us products made for Americans and say, 'Why don't you Koreans buy them?' " he explains. Sometimes, American exports are almost unusable. Although Korean households have 220-volt electricity, U.S. firms have been known to try selling refrigerators built for 110 volts, with only rudimentary converters. "Even the chocolate," says Kim. "My kids like chocolate very much, but they don't like American chocolate. Too sweet. You want to sell chocolate here, you have to know our taste."

Kim learned from that. Each market has its own tastes. If you're going to sell, you have to tailor. His company embraced the same philosophy. The Samsung people knew that would make things hard—each time they began in a new country, they'd have to design new products, retool lines, invest more dollars. They accepted it. The producer who doesn't tailor, Samsung felt, is the producer who will fail.

Kim began to focus on Europe, studying how it was different from America. Europeans, he found, like colder dishes. That meant the microwave defrost function should be different. Europeans like fish; Americans, meat and chicken. All that was fed back to Suweon's design division, which soon began tailoring new European models. In 1983, Samsung microwaves broke into Germany and Norway. In 1984, Samsung added France, Finland, Australia, and Belgium. And, all along, the Koreans kept pushing for a bigger piece of America.

In most companies, it's the sales force alone that travels to learn buyer habits. Samsung doesn't think that's enough; it sends its engineers abroad, too. A successful production manager, the company feels, has to know more than just his assembly line, he has to know his customer. That's why I. J. Jang, head of production, was sent on regular marketing trips to America. Jang remembers flying in with a dozen other engineers from Suweon for an electronics show in Las Vegas. At one point, Jang took a side trip on his own to stores, visiting Sears, talking to salespeople. He asked what microwave models are most popular, what features attract customers. Once, he spotted a woman customer and went so far as to stop her and ask what she looked for in a microwave oven.

Why couldn't he rely on Samsung's marketing people? He will explain that there are some things an engineer has to see for himself. You can't describe color by phone or fax. Telling the designers to make a model red isn't enough. They want to know just what shade of red. They want to know exactly what size the knobs should be. They seek more than technical knowledge alone. They seek something subtler—a feel for America's tastes, its character, its people.

GE began shifting more of its orders from the Japanese to Samsung. Soon GE's Korean models began to sell as well as those GE itself made in America, and at a much higher profit. Some of the executives in Louisville began to wonder whether it was time to shut down the new factory and source everything. The factory men resisted. How could GE stop production during the peak of the harvest? Microwave ovens, they pointed out, were blossoming into a $2 billion industry. Enders decided to give the plant defenders a final chance to make their case. He asked them for a proposal on streamlining. Soon they delivered it. It was an impressive job. They'd been able to get far lower cost than Enders had expected. But even if the company went through with the plan, its costs would remain far higher than those in Korea. It left management with little choice. In May 1985, GE publicly announced it would stop U.S. production of microwave ovens.

In early 1979, Samsung had produced exactly one crude prototype of a microwave oven. In 1987, it made 3.5 million microwaves[24] in 250 separate models for over 20 countries. Samsung had gambled correctly. Its appetite to produce had proven stronger than America's. From now on, GE would be doing the sales and service side of the product, Samsung the manufacturing. Soon, the people of Suweon would be the biggest makers of microwave ovens in the world.

Some businessmen in America saw the Korean wage protests of 1987 as a hopeful sign. The higher their pay, the less competitive their products. But the fact is, South Korea is bound to remain a low-wage competitor into the next century. Even if Korean paychecks went up 20 percent a year and ours stayed flat—highly unlikely—it would still take a decade and a half for Korean wages to match our own.

And the political turmoil? It's possible that it could flare up from time to time, of course, but go to South Korea and you'll find a subsurface stability. Even at the height of the marches of 1987, many of the protestors were careful to put in their normal workday before going to the streets to demonstrate.

Koreans did not set out to chip away at our standard of living in order to build their own. But today, South Korea is dotted with factories that have replaced many in America. Its economy is growing at three times our rate. In 1987, the Koreans sold America $9 billion more in goods than we sold them. The trade balance has gotten so lopsided that Korea's version of *Business Week* recently ran a cover urging its readers to buy more American goods—to help America.

I recently visited with Suk Chae Lee, the Korean president's secretary for economic affairs. We spoke in a conference room near the Blue House, South Korea's equivalent of our own White House. Behind him, there was a portrait of traditional Korean warlords in full battle dress. They were on horseback, looking confident, poised on the edge of a river, ready to cross it. Lee began to speak of how the developing world has always been envious of America's industrial might. But today, there is surprise at America—a confusion over why we seem to be letting our industry decline. To him, it's a sign that we no

---

[24]Interviews with Samsung management in Suweon in July 1988.

longer care about world economic supremacy. He doesn't understand it. "America," he says, "isn't really tuned toward export." Later, he adds a thought: "In this age, you have to reach beyond yourselves. Nations are no longer islands. It's as important for American companies to sell in Japan as in Chicago."

He is quick to acknowledge that the world still sees America as a prosperous giant. But he wonders whether too much prosperity isn't part of the problem. When you've been the world champion for too long, Mr. Lee says, you have to remind yourself not to let your guard down. America, he continues, should know that nations like South Korea, which are striving for their first taste of prosperity, are now working harder than nations that take prosperity for granted. An aide sitting beside him at our meeting asks if he can quote a joke. Do we know how the two superpowers can destroy their enemies? There's an easier way than weaponry. "All Russia has to do," says the aide, "is send its enemies its economic planners. All America would have to do is send its lawyers."

Lee explains that a different kind of profession is preeminent in Korea. "Scientists and engineers," he says. "Our president treats them like heroes." True, he says, the nation's most revered businessmen are the chairmen of the great companies—but most of them are engineers themselves. It's hard even to start a company in South Korea, he says, unless you're an engineer.

The training of America's first industrialists, of course, was the same. Men like Henry Ford were inventors first, men of finance second. Perfecting the product was their priority. Speaking to Secretary Lee, you have the impression that South Korea is a glimpse of an earlier America, where people felt themselves part of a nation emerging through production. There's a sense of limitless opportunity here, but it's tempered. Even as Lee speaks of South Korea's achievements, he stresses that it has a long way to go. The reward will be there, he says, but only if they fear it won't be.

I recently had another discussion in Seoul, this time with a young Korean studying for an MBA and a career in strategy consulting. Though Koreans have historically been hostile to Japan, he doesn't hesitate when asked which country is his economic model. "Japan is the future," he says. He adds that he admires America more—its freedom, its spirit, its culture. But economically, there is more to learn from the Japanese. You need only look at one statistic to know that, he says. The Japanese have a trade surplus, America, a deficit.

In 1970, Samsung, the largest Korean company, had only $100 million in sales. Its main businesses at the time were insurance, medical services, textiles and trading. That same year, General Electric had sales of $4.4 billion. Today, GE has grown dramatically into a diversified company with almost $40 billion in sales. Samsung has grown, as well. Today, it is one of the biggest industrial corporations on earth. Today, it too has almost $40 billion in sales.

At the gate of the Suweon complex, headquarters for Samsung's electronics and appliance division, a uninformed guard salutes all executive cars. Inside, the central offices are as modern as the most sophisticated in America. But the executives who staff them have not forgotten tradition. If you look under the fine wooden desks, you will often see a pair of slippers. In conversation, the managers sometimes speak of the values of Confucianism. "Less selfish," one explains of its essence. "More for the group."

Visitors to Suweon are first ushered into a screening room to see a video introduction of the company. It's broadcast on a Samsung TV with a Samsung VCR. The video begins with a statistic: Almost two-thirds of all the company manufactures is for export.

Speak with Samsung's managers, and a common theme recurs. What to manufacture next? What's on the world's horizon? Recently, employees at Suweon were wearing a button that said BREAKTHROUGH 87. Its point was to keep everyone thinking like entrepreneurs. "We are always looking for the next product," one manager explains. Samsung, he knows, will almost always be ready to invest in new ideas.

Today, the company designs and makes its own integrated circuits. In 1985, it began a data-systems division. In 1986, it started in aerospace. That year, net profits were only $182 million, among the lowest of the world's large corporations. It is by design. Samsung's priority for money is to plow it back into the company.

Samsung electronics now has over 1,500 engineers. In almost every building, showrooms display what they've done. There are VCRs, personal computers, video cameras, compact-disc players: products of the future, the kind that boost a nation's standard of living. There was a time when only high-wage countries had the vision to invest in such goods. No longer. Sometimes, even the opposite holds true. Although America invented most of these products, and buys more of them than any other country, we make almost none of them. In the case of VCRs and video cameras, we never manufactured them at all. Today, if an American company decided to start making VCRs, it would have to come to South Korea or Japan to get technical assistance. We remain the world's innovator, but others are challenging us as producers. Too often, the dollars we spend buying our own inventions are boosting the living standard of the Far East.

Samsung is not alone in enjoying its microwave-oven success. General Electric is enjoying it, too. With Samsung's manufacturing help, GE's market share has shot up. Microwave ovens have become one of GE's most profitable appliances. In Louisville, management will say, rightly, that sourcing from the Koreans was good for the company. It allowed GE to leap over its Japanese and U.S. competitors to gain share and succeed.

But there is also the question of country. Over 40,000 Koreans make their living producing microwave ovens. In America, the number is a fraction of that. In 1980, almost 100 percent of every hundred dollars Americans spent on GE microwave ovens stayed in America. Today, well over half flows to South Korea.[25] While over 84,000 microwave ovens are made in Suweon each week, GE's Maryland plant stands idle.

A lower dollar—America's key strategy to boost exports—won't change that. Even if South Korea's currency doubled in value, GE wouldn't be able to reopen that plant. The engineers are dispersed, the equipment sold. Nor will a low dollar dampen Samsung's resolve to produce microwave ovens. Currency levels alone won't correct our trade deficit. Only superior production will.

---

[25]The distribution, marketing, and selling elements of the price, as well as part of quality control and engineering and profit, stay with GE in the United States. The exact proportion is confidential, but it is less than half of the selling price.

In the end, GE made a prudent choice in deciding to source from Korea. The company had discovered the potential for microwave ovens too late. By the time GE invested, the Japanese were way ahead. Going to the Koreans was a good way to leap past the Japanese and fight back. But the scenario could have been different. What if GE, or other American appliance companies, had acted earlier, not at the height of market demand, but ahead of it? If it had, it could have built enough scale to afford more product research and factory investment when competition got intense. Dollar-an-hour countries can be beaten. Our technology can often overwhelm low wages—but only if we're among the first in the arena. We can no longer afford to spend years analyzing new products. Too many other nations, like South Korea, are willing to seize them immediately.

Often, those nations do it with our help. Samsung would have had a hard time succeeding so quickly in microwave ovens without J. C. Penney and GE. The Americans helped bring Samsung world-class design, quality, scale, and legitimacy with other global customers—if GE sources from them, Samsung must be good. GE got a good deal in return—a low-cost source of ovens. But how long can an American company thrive by buying from the competition? Put another way, how long will Samsung be content to be a supplier? Its final vision, as with all great corporations, is to emerge as another General Electric, a household name. In some ways, this is already happening. Most luggage carts in West Germany's Frankfurt airport bear an advertisement for Samsung. Drivers in New York's Times Square, Chicago's Loop, London's M1, and even Tokyo's Keio Highway are beginning to see billboards with the same name—Samsung. Someday, Korea will no longer need to market its products through American labels, but will do it directly, as Hyundai is now doing in cars.

Gradually, the South Koreas of the world will move from supplier to competitor. If, by then, we've shut down our own factories, how will we ever fight back? GE made a good business decision for this decade. But what are the implications of this and hundreds of similar decisions for our children's generation?

Each morning in Suweon, at 7:50 A.M., Miss Jang Mee Hur pauses before she begins work. Like all 30,000 Suweon employees, even the division president, she stands silent as the company song is played throughout the complex. "We who gather under the flag of Samsung," goes the final stanza, "let's push ahead the wheel of new history." Then the song will end and all will begin yet another 11-hour day.

Does Miss Hur really think Korean workers are better than American workers?

She is almost timid as she answers, but says she is sure they are.

Why?

Korean workers, she says, are driven not just by money, but by company, by country, by quality. American workers, she thinks, do it mostly for the money. Which product, she asks, would you want to buy?

Miss Jo Yon Hwang stands at a nearby line, continuing to attach company labels. "General Electric," the labels say. "Louisville, Ky. Made in Korea."

Does she feel bad that she has an American's job?

She says she wishes Americans only well, but is proud that by working harder, Koreans are now doing a job Americans had to give up. "Besides," she says, "in a sense, both countries are benefiting." Americans like to buy things, she says, and Koreans to make things—that is good for both sides, isn't it?

It's hard for Mr. Yun Soo Chu, Samsung's microwave oven designer, to sit still for an interview. He'd rather be working. His office is no longer the corner of a primitive lab, it's a vast room filled with dozens of desks, and surrounded by another dozen rooms for research and testing. Behind his own desk are five clocks, each marking Samsung offices: L.A., Chicago/Mexico, London/Madrid, Frankfurt/Paris and New York/Miami. At the moment, Chu has a map of Sweden on his desk. Samsung began exporting there this year. The map is to help him organize trips for his staff; not marketing staff—engineers. He wants them to go to Sweden as often as possible. He wants them to know their customers.

Ask him what he works for, and he will tell you. His goal, he says, is to give his own children a higher standard of living than he knows himself. And so, each morning, he dons his company jacket, stands for the company song, and then goes back to designing the next line of microwave ovens that will fill the modern world's kitchens. On most nights, he is likely to be at the office very late.

GENERAL ELECTRIC: BATTLING FOR COMPETITIVENESS IN REFRIGERATORS

Ira C. Magaziner and Mark Patinkin

Fifty miles south of Nashville, outside the city of Columbia, where the restaurants offer Bar-B-Q and catfish, there is an unlikely piece of smokestack America. There, nestled amid the pine and hardwood of rural Tennessee, is one of the world's most automated factories. Had it not been built, America's households might soon have had yet another product—the refrigerator—stamped MADE IN JAPAN. Instead, here in the heartland, General Electric found a way to build products both better and cheaper than those made by foreign workers paid a tenth our wages. The going has been rough, but GE's struggle shows the challenges we must meet if we are to compete against Korea and Singapore for world manufacturing leadership.

In a sense, Tom Blunt is a figure from an earlier America. He loves factories. He's convinced they are the country's strength. He was disturbed, back in the late 1970s, to see so many shut down. It was around then that Blunt made a career change. He left Ford Motor Corporation, where he'd overseen plant automation, to work in major appliances. His new home was General Electric, Thomas Edison's company. He moved to Louisville, headquarters of GE's Major Appliance Business Group (MABG). He found its manufacturing complex so huge that the parking lot needed dozens of traffic lights.

Blunt liked one thing in particular about this industry: Maybe foreign cars were succeeding in the U.S. market, and foreign steel, but not foreign appliances. The Japanese were strong in microwave ovens, but America still made better washing machines, better ranges, and, most important, better refrigerators. By the mid-1980s, refrigerators alone were to become a $4 billion industry in the United States. In 1979, they were already bringing in $1 billion of GE's $2.5 billion in annual appliance sales.[1]

But that year, shortly after Blunt arrived as chief manufacturing engineer for ranges, he found something disheartening. There didn't seem to be any clear direction at MABG. There were no great projects, just a lot of starts and stops. Most disheartening of all, he found that America's biggest appliance company made little money. No one could figure out why. There were almost no Japanese refrigerators landing at American ports, no German ranges in U.S. stores. Except for microwave ovens, there didn't seem to be any foreign threat. The group's executives told GE headquarters in Fairfield, Connecticut, not to worry.

Ira C. Magaziner is the founder and president of *Telesis*, an international consulting firm. His books include *Minding America's Business* (Random House, 1983) and *Japanese Industrial Policy* (University of California-Berkeley Press, 1981). Mark Patinkin is a nationally syndicated columnist for the *Providence Journal-Bulletin*.

[1]GE also manufactured and sold electric ranges, washers and dryers, dishwashers, disposal units, and microwave ovens in 1979.

A few adjustments in marketing and they were sure profits would improve—probably by the next quarter.

But they'd been saying that now for a number of quarters. Finally, someone in Fairfield decided to act.

In the fall of 1979, Paul Van Orden had just been named GE's head of consumer businesses.[2] He had confidence in his Louisville people, but he feels it's occasionally helpful to get an outside perspective. He searched for a business consultant, and was given my name by his chief planner. Soon I flew to Louisville to begin looking at the profit problem. The group's executives were not happy to see me. Who was this outsider sent to tell them how to fix their own business? They already knew how to fix it: by finding a way to boost price. As a rule, that meant cosmetics—catchy features that could be added for $1 cost while commanding $10 more in price. Bells and whistles, they called them. In appliances, group management felt, you can best compete by catching the consumer's eye. I didn't necessarily disagree, but my job was to look for profit problems everywhere, including the factories. They told me I'd be wasting my time. If GE knew how to do anything, it was manufacturing.

I began my detective work. Where to start? I didn't discount the bells-and-whistles theory. It's a classic marketing strategy that works with plenty of consumer goods: Develop unique features, add a good brand image, and people will be happy to pay a premium. But GE's features, I found, weren't unique. That year, the line's most promising innovation was size—a new model with 17 cubic feet of space. Management was convinced it would be a breakthrough, but the competition had seventeen-cubic-foot refrigerators, too. I compared other innovations—ice makers, electronic controls, special trim. The competition had those, as well. Finally, I talked to store owners. Yes, they said, GE has a prestigious name and catchy features, but that's not enough anymore, not when everyone's selling something similar. Customers like cosmetics, they said, but in appliances, they like a competitive price and reliability even more.

If that was true, if high-priced features weren't sufficient, it left one other strategy for boosting profit: lowering costs. That meant making manufacturing more efficient. I discussed the idea with the managers in Louisville. Was it possible, I asked, that the problem—and solution—was on the inside, not the outside? They told me that if I knew appliances, I'd know the most important area is marketing. It was the accepted wisdom; if anyone was going to save MABG, it would be marketers, not engineers.

Tom Blunt had been hired to upgrade MABG's range factories. His instinct was to do it from the ground up, but he soon found there wasn't as much capital for that as he'd hoped. The money was all on the marketing side, on product features. All Blunt was allowed was an adjustment here, an adjustment there, and he soon began to wonder whether leaving Ford had been the right move after all.

It was about that time that MABG brought in a new chief engineer. John Truscott was an Englishman by birth, but by passion an American—a believer

---

[2]At the time, GE was divided into six sectors. The consumer sector included GE's major-appliance, lighting, small appliance and audio, air-conditioning, and television businesses which at the time had about $6 billion in total sales. The major-appliance business was the sector's largest.

in unbridled free enterprise. Throughout his working life, Truscott's real fulfillment had come from pushing technology forward. At each step of his career, he'd been able to do that, first on an aerospace team involved in breaking the sound barrier, then when he helped perfect medical CAT scanning. Now, GE had transferred him to Louisville, insisting it would be a step up for him; the money was better, and so was the title—head of technology for an entire group. But the atmosphere, Truscott found, was worse. The group was floundering. He felt you could actually see the malaise. "Everyone had a glazed look in their eyes," he would later say.

What made it especially hard for Truscott was the priority: adding gadgets rather than engineering all-new product designs. Worst of all, the gadgets didn't seem to be boosting group profit. First they changed the size of the refrigerator; it made no difference. They put chocolate gaskets on the door; it made no difference. They did similar things with the other products; no difference. Like Blunt, Truscott was beginning to think this was a bad turn in his career. From the sound barrier to CAT scanning to washing machines. Later, he would recall thinking a grim thought: I'd rather be dead than working in washing machines. It didn't look like Louisville would offer him much chance to push technology's edge after all.

After putting in several weeks of work, I'd grown convinced that MABG's profit problem was on the inside—in the factories. But I wasn't sure where. As I walked through first one factory then another, I found plenty of inefficiencies. In some areas, the product flow was complicated, parts were strewn everywhere, and too many tasks were done by hand. The plants making refrigerators, the most important product, seemed the worst. A cost breakdown, I felt, might help me know what specifically to look for in the refrigerator operation, so I put one together. It turned out that the compressor—the pump that creates the cold air—was by far the product's most expensive part. It was also the machine's heart, as important as an engine in a car. If the compressor breaks, there's no refrigerator.

I decided to spend a few hours in the plant where compressors were built—Building 4. It was clearly the most antiquated at MABG. If you took 1,000 old auto-repair garages and patched them together, it wouldn't look much different from Building 4. It seemed this was worth exploring more. I asked management if the compressor could be a problem. They told me it wasn't. The competition, they insisted, all had similar designs, similar factories, similar costs. No one in the business, they said, was producing a cheaper compressor.

Perhaps, then, there was competition management didn't know about. As I went from office to office, doing background interviews, I began to ask, Was it possible there was someone new in the business? Someone overseas, perhaps? Someone making compressors more efficiently? I was told it was out of the question. Appliances were an American bastion, and the world knew it. Whatever foreigners were doing, they were doing it worse. Besides, the executives told me, the Japanese and Europeans make different kinds of refrigerators—smaller ones. It made no sense for them to target the American market. A dozen times, I got the same answer. I asked about it one more time while interviewing an engineer who was about to leave the company. Foreign competition?

No, said the engineer. Nothing obvious.

How about a possible Japanese threat?

No, he said, nothing. Then, almost as an afterthought, the engineer added a brief sentence.

"But I did hear something about Canada."

He was speaking of GE's Canadian refrigerator plant, which did not report to Louisville. I asked what he'd heard.

"That the Japanese had tried to sell them compressors." He quickly added that it didn't seem significant. Compressors, he said, are all the same. You won't find any technological breakthroughs there, even from the Japanese. Perhaps he was right. But to be sure, I decided to go to Canada.

Management might have thought that marketing would save MABG, but Tom Blunt had his own theory. You build a great manufacturing company on one thing—great factories. During his first few months in Louisville, he made a point of walking through all of them. He still remembers the day he stepped into Building 4. It was a loud, dirty operation built around 1950's technology— old grinders, old furnaces and too many people. Finishing a single piston, he learned, took 220 steps. Even the simplest functions had to be done by hand. Workers loaded machines, unloaded machines, carried parts to the next machine. Then there was the scrap rate, which was ten times higher than it should have been. The plant was throwing out 30 percent of everything it made. There was only one thing Blunt liked about this plant. He liked the thought of beating it—changing it, rebuilding it. But it wasn't his place to suggest that. He was too new to start urging on major projects in someone else's department. Besides, he felt management would never pour huge dollars into redoing a whole factory. MABG's preference was cosmetics, not engineering.

I sat down with the head refrigerator executive of GE Canada. I asked if it was true that they'd been approached by the Japanese.

Yes, he said, it was. Matsushita wanted to sell them compressors.

I knew it cost MABG $45 to make each GE compressor. In Louisville, management insisted that the competition was building them for at least as much. If that were true, once Matsushita finished adding on profit and overseas shipping, I figured it had to be selling them for $50 or $60. I asked the Canadian executive what price the Japanese were quoting.

Matsushita, he said, was planning to build compressors in Singapore to cut labor costs. It was planning to land them in Canada for $37 each.

I asked about quality.

The executive had seen some samples of the Matsushitas. He said they appeared to be better than GE compressors.

Did Canada plan to buy them?

Well, said the executive, it would be hard to buy a product competing with one made by his own parent company, but he was about to start. He had to do what was best for his business.

I asked one final question. had any other foreign companies approached them with compressors?

The answer was yes—an Italian firm called Necchi. It, too, had a lower price than GE.

As much as Tom Blunt was bothered by the way MABG neglected its factories, something else bothered him even more: the way it neglected its engineers.

He'd never worked with engineers who had such low self-esteem. It wasn't hard to see why. The money men had turned down their proposals so often that they no longer believed in themselves. It was routine, he said, to see engineers given $2 million for a $10 million automation plan and then scolded for doing half a job. Now, they were becoming timid, which Blunt felt could ruin an engineer. "To do technologically daring things," he says, "you have to get your people to say, 'All right, I'm willing to take a risk.' Instead, you had a climate down there for years that said, 'If you screw something up, you're going to get shot.' "

People, Blunt says, become what their bosses tell them they are. "And they'd been telling these guys," he explains, "that they were just a bunch of dumbheads." What Louisville needed, Blunt thought, wasn't better bells and whistles, it needed better technology. The only way to get it was with engineers willing to knock on management's door with new ideas. But most at MABG had become too timid to risk it. Pretty soon, Blunt feared, GE was going to be passed by, and he had a good idea who might try. During the 1950s, while in the air force, he had lived in both Japan and Korea. What struck him most about that part of the world was the attitude.

"They'd convinced themselves they can do things better than anyone else," he says.

Blunt is convinced that self-confidence is the key to innovation. "We're better than they are," he says, "but the difference is, they're allowed to try."

I returned from Canada expecting Louisville management to be as stunned as I was by what I'd found, and also as relieved. I'd spotted a possible foreign threat while there was still time to respond. That hadn't happened with American steel, or cars—the Japanese had taken both by surprise. With refrigerators, the story could be different. I presented my findings at an executive meeting, then waited for the expressions of concern. There weren't any. The executives told me they didn't see why this was a problem. The Matsushita compressor wasn't a breakthrough; it was the same kind as theirs—a reciprocating model.

But your Canadian subsidiary, I told them, is convinced that it's a better machine.

They said I was being alarmist. Believe us, they told me, it will be a long time before an overseas newcomer outdoes the appliance technology of the General Electric company. They knew their competition, and it wasn't Matsushita; it was Whirlpool, or White. It was in America, not Japan.

But the Matsushita compressor, I told them, is also cheaper.

They told me there was a simple explanation for that. Dumping.

I mentioned the Italians, stressing that others were entering the field, and it was bound to get worse.

Again, they dismissed it. This wasn't an invasion, they said; it was a trickle. They'd seen such trickles before. None had ever amounted to much. This one wouldn't either.

Tom Blunt was not in on that discussion, but if he had been he'd have doubtless been more concerned. Later, he would say that while he had worked for Ford, he had learned the importance of looking overseas. What were foreigners making? What were they likely to make next year? How do we compete? At MABG, no senior managers asked those questions. Blunt knew of no engineer who'd even taken a business trip to the Far East. In Louisville, there was one measure of progress. It didn't matter what the rest of the world was up to, if you were doing 2 percent better than last year, you were making adequate headway.

Perhaps management was right, I thought. Perhaps the Matsushita compressors were just a trickle, not an invasion. Still, it was worth exploring, so I booked a plane for Japan and Singapore. My first task was to break down Matsushita's cost. How much to build a compressor in Japan? How much in Singapore? Matsushita, of course, wasn't about to share that information with a competitor's consultant. So I decided to purchase sample compressors from repair shops, take them apart, and see what the Japanese were putting into them. I broke each down to raw parts—iron castings, powdered metals, silver solder—then called suppliers to get prices. I weighed the steel and copper wire being used, and got quotes on those, as well.

The next question was wage rates. Matsushita wasn't going to share those figures either, so I reviewed public reports the company had to file with the government which gave out that information. Next on my list was transport costs. Shipping companies were able to give me the standard rate. Finally, I wanted to know what Matsushita's version of Building 4 looked like. For that, I talked to Japanese machinery makers, the people who would have supplied Matsushita with motor winders, grinders, and welders. After two weeks of gathering string, I was convinced. It seemed clear that compressor-manufacturing technology in Japan was far beyond Louisville. There was no dumping after all. Matsushita was simply making compressors more efficiently. By cutting labor costs with Singapore wage rates and using low-cost Japanese steel, Matsushita was able to tack on profit, pay shipment and duty, and still undersell GE by at least 15 percent.

Now, the other question: trickle or invasion? How many compressors were they making? This time, I approached Matsushita directly. They agreed to meet, partly as a courtesy to GE, and perhaps more important, because they hoped Louisville could be talked into buying compressors from them. They told me their Japan plant made a million compressors a year. All right, that didn't seem to be much of an export threat—Japan's domestic market took the whole million.[3] But what about the Singapore factory? Was that being geared for large-scale production? At first, my Matsushita hosts were hesitant to speak. Finally, during our last lunch together, one of them mentioned their plans. The plant, he said, was being designed eventually to produce 3 million compressors a year. As I sat there, it was hard to keep from reacting. Three million was more than GE made itself. And it was clear almost all of those would be for export. Where? Not to Europe; trade barriers there wouldn't allow it. Most would be going to North America.

---

[3]Japan's refrigerator and compressor producers had concentrated on their own home market in the 1970's. The only exception was in small six-cubic-foot- and-under models, where the Japanese, Italians, Yugoslavs, and more recently the Koreans dominated world markets. U.S. producers had pulled out of these small-size markets long ago. In 1979, Sanyo set up a plant in California to assemble these small refrigerators.

Matshsuhita's compressor move to Singapore was the first sign of a Japanese company moving into world markets in large refrigerators.

The more MABG's profit slide deepened, the more John Truscott, new head of technology, brooded. A confirmed smoker, he was smoking more and more. There were cigarette ashes everywhere in his office—on his desk, even on his pants. Like Blunt, he loved factories. Now, here in Louisville, GE's factories were struggling. Occasionally, he'd read articles proclaiming that declining factories were okay; the country was supposedly shedding its old, rust-belt skin, turning toward a more modern economy—a service economy. Truscott was of a different school. "How do you have a service economy without a foundation underneath?" he asked. He saw only one way to hold on to that foundation—by investing in factories. He found it disturbing that Japan and South Korea were doing more of that than America. He was convinced that if we didn't fight back, it would cost us. "Just because I have a U.S. passport," he says, "doesn't mean I have a right to a better standard of living."

He had a theory of how that standard came about. "Our fathers' productivity," he would say, "Our grandfathers'." When he looked for that same sense of mission now, he saw it in only one place, the Far East. They learned it from us, he felt; now was the time to relearn it from them. How? "There's no doing it with mirrors," he says. "You have to get right back to fundamentals." But at MABG, management wasn't letting him. Fundamentals—new factories—were considered too expensive, and too risky.

I returned from Japan confident that even the most skeptical among Louisville's management team would be startled by what I found. First, I showed that Matsushita wasn't dumping. Second, I told them about the Singapore plant. But at least it wasn't too late, I said. If MABG responded now, it could fend off the threat. One of the executives spoke. He was sorry, but he just didn't believe those cost numbers. He still thought Matsushita was dumping. Someone else spoke. What about quality? He didn't think the Japanese could ever match GE.

"Your Canada man says they're better," I said.

"But they haven't really fully tested them yet," said the executive. Besides, he asked, what more could MABG do about compressors?

I asked them to think about Building 4. Everyone knew it was an antiquated factory. The executives said they already had plans to upgrade the rough spots, save a few cents on the final product here and there.

Wouldn't it be better to consider revamping the whole thing?

"Look," said one of the executives, "we can't even get $1 million from headquarters to do little things, let alone $100 million for a whole factory."

"Maybe it's because your plans aren't big enough," I said.

Still they hesitated. To make a new factory pay off, they said, you have to have a new product—or at least a more sophisticated one. You don't get lower cost by building the same kind of machine. And the machine they had—a reciprocating compressor—was the only kind that made sense for a refrigerator.

Then look into redesigning the compressor, I said. Maybe you can make a technological leap. I'd seen how Japan had succeeded that way in cars and televisions. New technology's the only way high-wage American industry can fight back against low-wage countries: If you can't undercut them in labor costs, you leap past them in engineering—a better product, better automation, better productivity.

But reciprocating compressors were already mature, they told me. You can't make a technological leap with a product that's been taken as far as it can go.

I asked if there might be another possibility. While exploring Louisville, I had gone to Building 6, where air-conditioners were made. They ran on compressors, as well, but a different kind—rotary compressors. The air-conditioning engineering manager had told me rotaries were cheaper, quieter, and more efficient than the ones refrigerators used. He also felt they could be redesigned to fit a refrigerator. Even more significantly, GE had invented the rotary; that put the company in a good position to tailor it in a new way, which was the key to market leadership—being first in the world with a new, efficient redesign.

No, the executives said, out of the question. No point in even trying. Rotaries could never be durable enough to run refrigerators.

I looked around the room. Most of the executives there, I knew, were nearing retirement. Many of the voices, I noticed, were tired. Give us time, they said. We've got some great new features coming down the line. In a few months, everything will turn around.

In January 1980, having failed to convince Louisville, I took my findings to Paul Van Orden, the sector executive who'd asked me to do the study. Together, we went over the numbers. Van Orden seemed disturbed and persuaded. He said he would discuss it with MABG. I hoped Louisville wouldn't be resentful. It's always best to galvanize an organization from the bottom up. But I believed strongly that I'd found a serious problem, and that it had to be addressed. I was sure it now would be.

A few weeks later, I got a phone call from Van Orden's assistant, whose message wasn't what I'd expected to hear. Van Orden had talked to Louisville's management, and they'd been adamant. They hadn't bought the compressor theory. They were convinced that they were competitive in compressors. They vowed that by July, their numbers would turn. Van Orden's assistant thanked me for all I'd done, and said his boss's decision was to go with his people.

July came, and MABG did not make its numbers. Instead, it had actually lost market share, and was now barely breaking even. That was the first sign that the problem hadn't been solved. Then came a second sign. In December 1980, the manager of GE's Canadian appliance plants told headquarters he wanted to increase his purchase of Matsushita compressors. In June 1981, there came a third sign. John Truscott had told his engineers it was time to take a closer look at the competition, especially the foreigners. The staff bought an assortment of refrigerators and tore them apart. Then they called Truscott to say they'd found something interesting inside a Mitsubishi. They'd found a rotary compressor—the type most in Louisville felt could not be used in a refrigerator. Finally, in July 1981, a fourth warning. It was the most unnerving of all. MABG learned that its chief competitor, Whirlpool, which had been making compressors in Ohio, had invested in a new compressor plant, to be located in Brazil, where wages were a tenth those in America. While Louisville had been focusing on bells and whistles, Whirlpool had looked abroad, glimpsed the future, and acted.

Finally, Van Orden acted, too. He called MABG. You said rotaries couldn't be done, he told them, and now they're being done. You said imports are no threat; Canada now wants more of them. You said your numbers would turn;

they've gotten worse. You've got a compressor problem, he said, and it's time to fix it. Then he called me. Eighteen months had gone by since I had handed in my first report. Now, he asked if a second one could be done, this one of greater scope. It seemed clear that overseas forces were badly undercutting MABG's compressor manufacturing. It was time to explore whether anything could be done about it.

Don Awbrey, a Louisville general manager, was put in charge of the compressor project. His mission was to make GE competitive in compressors. He had nine months to develop a plan. My study was to be the first step. When we met, he made it clear that he wanted me to explore all options—to look at any potential technology, no matter how new, and to travel anywhere in the world, no matter how far, to find the right solution.

It had been a year and a half since I'd been in Louisville. When I was last there, in February 1980, the mood had been one of malaise. Now, in October 1981, it was more like confusion. The old fixation on bells and whistles was gone. There was a new obsession: What do we do about compressors? The confusion deepened when both Matsushita and Necchi approached MABG itself, in Louisville, offering lower-priced compressors that were indeed fine machines. Finally, management acknowledged it: Foreigners were building a better product. Had that happened 10 years before, there would have been one response: Fight back. Even to whisper the word *sourcing* in Louisville would have been sacrilege. MABG manufactured at home—in America. Its factories were unequaled. It was unthinkable that a country like Japan should make anything for the GE label. Now, many in Louisville had begun to wonder if Japan could be MABG's deliverance. Instead of bells and whistles, people began talking of a new strategy—sourcing.

Lately, there'd been rumors that headquarters was so frustrated by Louisville's poor performance they were ready to sell the division, possibly to the Japanese themselves. No one wanted that to happen. Sourcing seemed a good way to stop it from happening. It would involve no investment and bring in fast profit. That was the goal—to turn the business around by next quarter, next year at the latest.

Tom Blunt, who by now had been named head of advanced manufacturing for refrigerators, did not appreciate that kind of talk. Few things put him in a worse mood than a decision to close a plant. "Sourcing makes sense in some circumstances, but you can't source everything," he says. "My instinct is always—always—to make things."

He did not think America was meant to become a service economy. "There are a lot of people who don't particularly want to work at Wendy's," he says. "I'm one of them." Colleagues tried to tell him it was time to face the truth: There are certain areas, certain products, that America can't compete in anymore. "Bull," he would say. "All we have to do is find a way to make it faster, cheaper, better."

John Truscott agreed, especially in this case. "The compressor is the heart of the refrigerator," he says. "The refrigerator is the heart of this group. I didn't want to give away our heart." No one was quite ready to go that far yet. Although sourcing was a compelling idea, it was still a new one. MABG needed more information. My new report was supposed to supply it.

I started the research by looking again at the competition. That now meant more than Whirlpool and White, GE's U.S. rivals. My first destination was Japan. When I got there, I found that Matsushita wasn't the only company making refrigerator compressors. Four more Japanese firms had invested in new plants: Sanyo, Toshiba, Hitachi, and Mitsubishi. Two of them, Toshiba and Mitsubishi, were beginning to make rotaries. Sanyo was also planning to move into rotaries for refrigerators. None of this was a fluke. As obsessive exporters, the Japanese had spent the last few years traveling to America, probing the appliance market in search of a weakness—and had found it. They'd zeroed in on the compressor, the most important part of the most important appliance. This time, companies were anxious to show me their plants. They knew that GE was considering sourcing, and they all wanted to sell.

Next, I went to Italy, where I saw that Necchi was as great a threat as the Japanese. Necchi's new compressor plant was far more automated than Building 4. Finally, I visited the new Whirlpool plant in Brazil—Embraco. Nearby, GE itself had a subsidiary making refrigerators for the regional market, just as it had in Canada. It turned out that this plant, too, wanted to buy a rival's compressors—Embraco's.

An Embraco executive, anxious for GE's business, welcomed a meeting with me. I met him in a small, southeastern Brazilian town called Joinville, where the plant was based. I was surprised to find it a highly industrialized pocket, colonized mainly by Germans over the last few decades. The best hotel in town was called the Tannehof. The area's largest plant built Mercedes trucks. The three Embraco managers who met me, all Brazilians, were named Helmut Sommer, Gilberto Krause, and Johann Richter. The cultural touch went beyond the surface. The plant itself had been shaped by a German work ethic. It was efficient, mechanized, and had good quality control. While parts in Louisville's Building 4 were manually machined, most of the operations here were automated.

It seemed that in every corner of the world, GE was being outmanufactured.[4] In February of 1982 I returned to Louisville to give my interim report.

MABG's executives gathered to hear what I'd found. I began with the numbers. It now cost MABG over $48 dollars to make each compressor. Necchi and Mitsubishi were doing it for between $32 and $38. Sanyo, Hitachi, and Toshiba were designing plants that would be making them for under $30. And Embraco and Matsushita's Singapore plant were planning to be at $25—almost half of GE's cost. One reason was labor. GE was paying over $17 an hour, including benefits. That compared to Matsushita's $1.70 in Singapore and Embraco's $1.40 in Brazil. Even more astounding was the difference in productivity. It took GE 65 minutes of labor to make a compressor, compared to 48 minutes in Singapore, 35 minutes in Brazil, and under 25 minutes in Japan and Italy.[5] A company that's paying higher wages for lower efficiency doesn't have much of a chance.

Then there were the competitors' export plans. Embraco, already shipping 10,000 compressors a month to America, was aiming for 10 times that amount

---

[4]The only exception was the United States, where Whirlpool, Tecumseh, and White, GE's traditional competition, were all as high-cost as GE.

[5]Telesis study.

within four years. Meanwhile, Necchi had just boosted exports to 1 million a year, and Matsushita would soon be in the multimillions. Overnight, foreign companies had gone from a few percent of the U.S. market to a full 20 percent. And the biggest invasion had yet to begin.

MABG's biggest product—the refrigerator—was in jeopardy. If management didn't act soon, I said, it could be disastrous for the whole group. The options? One possibility was to source. A second option: build a factory overseas, in a low-wage country, perhaps in a joint venture. Third, invest in a new, more efficient factory here at home.

I waited for the response. It turned out to be the opposite of what I had heard before. "If they're that far ahead of us," someone said, "how can we possibly catch up?"

"We ought to just go for the source," someone else added.

The report made even John Truscott waver. What most shocked him was the difference in labor costs. For each compressor MABG made, it was paying out $19.73 in factory labor. The others were paying between $1.12 and $3.32 per compressor.[6] How, he asked, can a company—one with average wages and benefits of $17 an hour—compete with dollar-an-hour workers? GE was clearly being outcompeted, which was a shame, and it was a bigger shame to think about closing a factory, but a company's first mission is to survive.

Everyone knew that this was only an initial overview—my final report was still two months away. But for many, this had been enough. The sourcing bandwagon began to roll. It was a measure of how far MABG had come that most executives were now asking why anyone would even think of manufacturing compressors in America. Awbrey, the new project leader, who'd been discussing sourcing for months, sensed it was now the likeliest option. He decided to speed up plans to be ready. I agreed it was a good idea. Even if GE were to build a new plant, which was doubtful at this point, it would still take years. Meanwhile, they'd need a bridge, and sourcing could be it. Soon Awbrey went beyond planning. He had to get away from those $48 models. He began to arrange to source smaller compressors for the low end of the refrigerator line from Necchi, GE's Italian competitor.

Although Tom Blunt had not yet met me, he'd decided he didn't like me. He was convinced I'd been sent down by GE headquarters in Fairfield with a preordained mission: to recommend that the compressor factory be closed. Blunt dislikes people who close factories. He dislikes the idea of sourcing just as much. "All everyone wants to do these days," he says, "is find someone overseas who makes something, someone over here who wants it, and then pat it on the fanny for 30 percent as it goes by." He will tell you that's not how a great nation maintains a high standard of living.

I made an appointment to meet him. As the day approached, Blunt recalled later, his resentment grew. If consultants had their way, he felt, there wouldn't be a plant left in America. They'd turn MABG into one big shipping and receiving station. Its factories would become warehouses, and its engineers retired as obsolete. Why should he meet with someone who thought he and his staff weren't as good as the Japanese? I remember the meeting clearly.

---

[6]Telesis study.

"You're a hard man to get hold of," I said as I was shown into Blunt's office.

"I don't want to see you," said Blunt.

I asked why.

"Your study's just a setup."

The truth, I said, was that I was here to learn what he'd recommend.

That was easy, replied Blunt—a new plant. Give us enough money to build one, and we'll make more in the long run.

I said I'd take that into account; I was there to explore all options.

"No, you're not," said Blunt. "You're here to say what they want you to say, Which is to close down a plant."

"That's not why I'm here."

"Bull," said Blunt. "You guys are all alike."

I told him I intended to do a fair report, and for that, I hoped to interview a number of his engineers.

"They're busy," said Blunt. "I'll tell them to cooperate because I have to, but don't take too much of their time."

As compelling as sourcing seemed, I knew there were still good arguments against it. Once you shut your plants, you're in danger of being hostage to your suppliers.[7] Buying Matsushita's compressors would turn around next year's numbers, but what about next decade's? And what if Matsushita decided to market its own refrigerators in America? They'd no longer be simple suppliers then, they'd be rivals. And a rival wouldn't sell to you cheap. Eventually, they'd hike their compressor price to give themselves the edge on the showroom floor. With its plant closed, how would MABG fight back then? Of course, it could turn to a different supplier, but that would mean retooling its refrigerator for a new machine. And who was to say that new supplier wouldn't become competition, as well? Could MABG afford to stop being a producer of the most important appliance? To source a product when you're a second-level producer to begin with—as GE was with microwave ovens—is one thing. But to source the heart of your biggest product when you are the market leader is a much larger risk. I knew the tide in Louisville was moving toward sourcing. It might be the right tide, but I wanted to explore alternatives.

The ideal alternative would be to build a new American plant that could make compressors cheaply enough to undercut those built by the dollar-an-hour people in Brazil. Could a high-wage country do that? Theoretically, yes—through automation. But not with the standard model, reciprocating compressors. The Germans at Brazil's Embraco had automated those about as far as they could go, and with low-wage workers, GE's only choice was to explore a new kind of compressor. The rotary was the main hope. Because it had fewer parts, there seemed a good chance of making it quicker, boosting productivity. Toshiba had plans for making rotaries much faster than Embraco was making the recips, as they were called. Could MABG do even better than Toshiba with rotaries of its own? I was doubtful. Not by themselves, anyway. It's hard to

---

[7]In my consulting work, I have seen many examples of companies ceasing the manufacture of key components to source from abroad at lower prices, only to find substantial price increases a few years later when their factories are irrevocably closed.

For a product like compressors, which require major investment, the barriers to reentry are prohibitive.

become the leader in a new technology that a competitor has already started to run with. But there was no need to do it alone. If GE could get the leader—Toshiba—to help them with either a joint venture or a technology license, it would have a better chance, and at less of a gamble. At least, I decided, it would be an alternative. But even to propose it, I'd need to come up with a plan.

I went back to Tom Blunt's office.

"I hear you've given away the store," said Blunt. He was talking about my interim presentation. It had accelerated the sourcing bandwagon, and he wanted to let me know he wasn't pleased.

In fact, I told him, I was here to explore an alternative to sourcing. I went over the idea of a rotary plant, adding that proposing it would take more than rhetoric; it would take a plan. That's where Blunt came in. Could he put one together?

He nodded. That's what he did for a living. If we wanted a plan for a factory, it wouldn't be a problem, he said.

I told him he needn't design it from the ground up. GE could possibly work with either Toshiba or another Japanese producer.

Blunt had a standard way of reacting to that kind of suggestion. "You tell a manufacturing engineer someone's better than he is," he'd say, "and he'll want to prove they aren't." If we gave his guys a chance, he added, they could out-perform the Japanese. But he doubted management would allow him to try.

"We can do it alone," he said, "but they won't let us. The decision's already made."

"As far as I know," I told him, "it's not already made."

"They'd never give us the money," he said. "A factory wouldn't be cheap."

I knew that. And I knew that in the last few years it was almost unheard of for a U.S. smokestack company, surprised by foreign competition, to fight back with an expensive new plant. But I told Blunt not to think about money for the moment. Just come up with a plan. If he didn't want to work with the Japanese, I suggested involving some engineers from the air-conditioning business who knew rotaries. I had a feeling that wouldn't be easy; the two divisions had a rivalry going and barely talked. But an outside enemy, I thought, could bring them together.

"All right," said Blunt, "we'll do it. But I don't think anything will come of it."

Before going forward with the factory option, I wanted the support of one other man. I met with John Truscott. He was intrigued. His career, in his words, had always been a search for the technological Holy Grail. Having left the sound barrier and CAT scanning behind, he'd begun to think he'd never find the Grail again. But now, for the first time since coming to Louisville, he saw a possibility. If aeronautics was the frontier of the 1950s and medicine of the 1960s, this could be the challenge for this decade—automating smokestack America. Everywhere, it seemed, the sun was setting on American manufacturing. Now was the time to show the trend could be reversed. High-wage America, Truscott felt, could still be the industrial leader of a low-wage world. But it would take investment. It would take leadership in both product design and factory automation. He wanted to be part of showing it could be done.

He spent some time studying the rotary with an engineer's eye. He found it could indeed be made simpler than the old-fashioned reciprocating compressor. He also found that even the Toshibas were far from perfect. There was room to take this technology to new heights, beyond the competition. He assembled a team to come up with a new design.

Truscott's engineers spent several months designing a GE rotary compressor. The challenge was to make it as simple as possible, with low noise and high efficiency. Then there was the hardest challenge of all—durability. Refrigerator compressors had to work far harder than those in air-conditioners. The design would have to be for a tough machine. At the same time, GE couldn't load it up with too much metal, or it would cost too much.

After a few months of work, the engineers came up with a model that could be made in America even cheaper than the Japanese models being made in Singapore. The design, however, had a problem. It called for the key parts to work together at a friction point of 50 millionths of an inch—about 100th the width of a human hair. No product on earth had ever been mass-produced at such an extreme tolerance. No one had even tried it; most engineers thought technology hadn't advanced that far. Tom Blunt knew there were some machines—like jet engines—that operated at those tolerances, but those things weren't mass-produced. Their parts had to be tooled one at a time, over long hours. Was it possible to get such precision in a plant that made 3,000 pumps a day? Everyone they talked to doubted it could be done. Blunt took the design to Truscott anyway. Truscott looked it over. "It looks possible," he said. He told Blunt to gather the manpower necessary to plan a factory. Blunt knew he'd just bargained himself into an obsessive few months. Designing a new factory, he will tell you, is an enormously complex job, with a hundred new headaches a day. But that is why he likes doing it. "Because it's hard," he says.

Blunt knew this would be a first of a kind—one of the world's most automated factories. To design it, he figured he'd need 40 people. Where could he find ones with the right skills? Many GE colleagues advised him to go outside. To pioneer new technology, they said, you have to find designers already on technology's edge. Blunt decided against that. He would stay with his own people. But where in MABG would he find them? He gathered up many from an unlikely place: Building 4. "We didn't go out and get a bunch of Star Wars guys," he would say later. "Most of these people came from one of the most non-automated places you've ever seen in your life."

Why did he risk that? Blunt is convinced that American industry doesn't have to recruit experts for breakthrough projects. Most seasoned engineers, he thinks, can do it. All they need is the backing—and confidence. At MABG, he knew his people had neither. "Some of the engineers here were the brightest people I had ever seen," he recalls. "They had degrees coming out of their ears. But they'd never been allowed to do anything." For years, they'd been free to innovate on gadgetry, but not basic manufacturing. That cost too much. It left most engineers in a malaise. What made it worse, said Blunt, was that they were treated as the group's second-class citizens. It was the opposite of how things were in the Far East. There, he knew, manufacturing engineers were heroes. Here? "A lot of people thought we couldn't walk and chew gum at the same time."

If they were to come up with a worldwide breakthrough, Blunt felt they first had to believe they could do it. That is where he started—on morale. "I had to spend a long time convincing them that they really were worth a shit," he says. As they began their work, Blunt pep-talked them. The reason he'd plucked them from Building 4, he said, was because he needed people who knew factories—and still believed in them. He knew they could design a better one than anyone in Japan or Korea. As they progressed, he kept up the pep-talking. It was true, he said, that no one had ever built a factory that could mass-produce parts of this precision. It was true that no one had ever achieved interchangeability at 50 millionths of an inch. None of that mattered. Here in America, in Louisville, they'd be the first. One of his favorite approaches was to remind his team that few outsiders would understand why they'd chosen to build factories for a living. You get no credit for it, he'd say, even though it's about the most difficult thing there is to do. But that's why they'd picked it; because of the challenge. And then he'd give his most heartfelt line: "Anyone can source," he'd say. Gradually, his people began to feel more confident than they had in years.

The problem with most manufacturing, Blunt felt, was that factories are designed around products. This time, with the compressor plant, he and Truscott decided to design the two together, adjusting each as they went. They began by moving the product and manufacturing engineers across the hall from each other. With each day, there was more and more movement across the linoleum. Gradually, they fine-tuned the pump down to the most automatable of models—a stationary vane rotary. It was also the simplest; it had fewer than 20 parts. The computer simulation said it would work, but only if the machining went far beyond anything the Japanese were doing. To help find a way to do that, Blunt brought in specialists from GE's jet-engine division. He brought in the head of the Swiss Institute of Technology and consultants from the Structural Research Dynamics Corporation. But they were just for occasional advice—and even many of them doubted Blunt's team could bring this off. He still relied mostly on his own people, the people from Building 4.

His main rule was never to allow them to say it couldn't be done.

"We figured it was the way to drive our people beyond state of the art," says Blunt. "If you say it can't be done, you won't do it. But if you say, 'We don't care that it's never been done, we're going to be the first'—then you have a shot."

Slowly, week by week, the plan came together. "There weren't great Eureka breakthroughs," Blunt recalls. "It doesn't work that way. The whole thing was block- and-tackle grunt work." As he expected, there were 100 headaches a day. There was constant frustration. There were late nights. Blunt hadn't enjoyed work this much since he'd come to Louisville.

The factory began to take shape on paper. Each time the engineering team finished roughing out a new piece of it, they taped it into a matrix unfolding along a corridor wall. The matrix soon took up a quarter-block of space. To keep it going, they had to find empty offices and extend the paper in there. They spent a lot of time just sitting, drinking coffee, and looking at it. How to integrate the grinding and the gauging? The loading and the material handling? They moved around pages, deciding what to automate and what to do with manpower.

And then it was done. "But that still didn't mean anything," says Blunt. "It was just a bunch of sheets of paper. Anybody can do that." Now came the second stage. Could they design machines that would make the parts the paper called for?

Blunt had one other rule. He wanted every piece of equipment in this plant to be made in America. His stated reason was that it's too hard to deal with vendors 12,000 miles distant. But there was another reason. He wanted to show that America could outdo the world with only its own resources.

One of Blunt's chief engineers was Dave Heimedinger. Under his direction, a team of engineers began to negotiate with suppliers of grinding and gauging machines. The vendors would look over the plan to mass-produce parts at jet-engine precision and then shake their heads. Heimedinger and Blunt remember a typical conversation.

"You can't do that," one vendor said.

"We think we can," said Heimedinger.

"Well," said the vendor, "it's our equipment, and we don't think it'll do that."

"We think we can find a way to make it do it."

"Well," said the vendor, "all right. We'll sell it to you. But it won't do that."

One maker of grinders insisted on putting a clause into the sales agreement saying the purchasers had been warned they would not be able to get the tolerances they hoped for. He also added a no-return clause. Heimedinger bought it anyway.

Blunt's theory of how to make machines do something they weren't built to do was simple enough. "We played around with them," he recalled. "We knew that five things determine how good a grinder is. First, there's the way the machine spins the grinding wheel. Then there's the wheel itself. There are the fluids that lubricate the process, the computer that fine-tunes it, and, finally, there's the material that's being cut." Heimedinger and his team began experimenting with combinations that had never been tried before. Blunt describes how they brainstormed: "If I take this machine, and combine it with that wheel and use this fluid on that material, and then tell the computer to have the whole thing act this way, let's see how far we can go."

Often, people would come by and ask Blunt why he was bothering. MABG is in trouble, they told him. Why gamble on a factory? Let's just source and get on with it. You can lose with a factory. With sourcing, it's a guarantee. Blunt smiles at the memory of it. "I just put my head down and said, 'Well, we're working on the son of a bitch.' "

The first prototype machines started to work. They began to deliver parts the manufacturers had warned they could not. Blunt knew it still wasn't final proof. Test machining is a good guide, but when you're building an unprecedented manufacturing process, the only real test, he says, is the plant itself. "A first-of-its-kind factory," says Blunt, "is its own prototype."

In one sense, he considered that a welcome risk, a sign of limitless potential. "If we could have proved this would work," he recalls, "it would have meant we were breaking no new ground." In another sense, it made for sleepless nights. Until it was done, and the switch was thrown on, there was no way of knowing whether the plant would succeed. Blunt did, however, have one test he used to gauge whether each of the new ideas would work. He calls it the eye test, "If you look into an engineer's eyes," he explains, "you can see whether he feels good about something, or whether he's afraid of it." Then there's the "I'll try" test. If an engineer thinks an assignment is impossible, says Blunt, he'll say, "I'll try."

"If you hear someone say, 'I'll try, ' " Blunt says, "you better look real close, because he's afraid." When they'd finally finished their plan, no one was saying, "I'll try."

One thing made Blunt more nervous than the technical question—the financial question. Would this plant, if built in America, make cheaper compressors than anyone else in the world? It was up to me to make those first projections. Both Blunt and I knew that if they didn't add up, it wouldn't matter how brilliant the design was. Headquarters couldn't possibly go ahead with it.

First, there was the estimate of the cost of the plant itself—$120 million. Then it would cost 10s of millions more to redesign the refrigerator so the new compressor would fit it. It would add up to one of the biggest single investments GE had ever made in a factory. It was a lot to gamble on the hope that it would still produce cheaper goods at $17-an-hour labor than rival factories paying less than $2. It was beginning to loom as an almost unacceptable risk. Then GE's engineers came up with a way to make it more attractive. GE had a Columbia, Tennessee, plant that made air-conditioning compressors—rotary models. Instead of going from nothing to the new prototype factory in a single leap, we could begin by adapting the machinery already there. It would allow a quicker move into rotaries and a chance to work out the bugs in advance while the new factory was being completed. The numbers on that proposal looked better. Even at 10 times the wages, it would still be lower cost than any other compressor plant on earth. At least on paper.

Blunt knew that was no guarantee that GE's Connecticut headquarters would back the proposal. Fairfield was wary of huge capital investments, especially since GE had recently lost money on a failed washing-machine plan. How could MABG convince management to invest an even bigger amount on an even higher-risk venture? Especially when they could source for almost nothing?

I finished my calculations and called Blunt. He asked me what I thought. I said I'd weighed the two options carefully—sourcing or building—and had decided to recommend that GE invest the $120 million. I took Blunt's reaction as a compliment. "You really are a crazy son of a bitch," he said.

I went to Don Awbrey, who was overseeing the compressor project. When I finished my presentation, he hesitated. Awbrey had made it no secret he'd been leaning toward sourcing, and now told me it still struck him as the safest route to better profits. Over the next hour, I carefully showed him the numbers proving the factory could do it better. I pointed out the risks of sourcing your core product—long term—from potential competitors. Afterward, Awbrey called together people from marketing, production, quality control, and finance. He told them that he was prepared to go with the factory. But he wanted an airtight proposal.

Jim Lehmann had been a finance man with GE for 30 years. His job was to be skeptical of any big spending plan. Like all good finance men, he treated money requests as if they would be coming from his own pocket. At first, when asked to review the $120 million, he was doubtful. He'd never seen so high a figure before. He forced us to recompute the numbers with every possible risk factored in. But finally, everything seemed to add up. And in truth, after so many years of bells and whistles, he was drawn to the challenge of a major manufacturing project. His support eventually proved crucial. Later, when Don Awbrey suddenly left General Electric, Lehmann was named to replace him as head of the compressor project.

Like Blunt and Truscott, Lehmann had sensed for years that Louisville had been in malaise. Now, from his new helm, he was able to feel the atmosphere from a different angle. He was surprised at how changed things were. Even those who'd been most inclined to source were now excited. "There was electricity in the air," recalls Lehmann. "It was like the early days, when we were proud of being technology pioneers."

The completed plan was finally sent to the head of MABG. A new man now held that post: Roger Schipke. Many in Louisville were surprised when Fairfield took him from head of dishwashers, the smallest of MABG's products, to head of the entire group, one of the premier positions in General Electric. Schipke doesn't fit the profile of a corporate titan. In many ways, he is the opposite of the man who gave him the job—Jack Welch, the chairman. Welch is demanding and constantly energized. Schipke seems more like the kindly owner of a small-town general store. "I'm just a simple guy," he often says, and he isn't being disingenuous. He is low key, and readily jokes that the only thing he knows about engineering is that you don't glue two shiny surfaces together.

The main reason he'd been selected as group head was his success a few years earlier in managing the redesign of a new dishwasher, both product and factory. It was one of the few MABG projects in a decade that went beyond bells and whistles. Its success was still a matter of pride in Louisville; the project did all the things the Japanese were then known for doing—a long-term investment that cut costs, improved quality, and doubled market share.

But this didn't mean that Schipke favored big investments. By nature, he was conservative, another reason Welch had selected him. Though proud of the dishwasher project, Schipke had come up through selling, knew the importance of profit, and like most in Louisville, had gone beyond the early 70s mind-set about having to manufacture everything in America. A manager can't make decisions on patriotism, he'd say. The priority is to keep the company's numbers strong. Schipke's other priority, upon taking over the group, was to get rid of the Louisville malaise. When a division becomes lackluster, he saw, people tend to turn on each other. He worked hard to change that, getting rival managers to work together and stressing cooperation with unions. It worked. Slowly, MABG was settling into more cohesion. It was around then that we brought him the compressor proposal.

Still new at his post, Schipke didn't know much about refrigerators, and knew less about compressors. We began by trying to explain to him the differences between rotary and reciprocating. That kind of discussion tended to bore him. "That wasn't my thing," he would say. "It was a big yawn to me. That was Truscott's job." He did understand that compressors were losing money because foreign competition had a seemingly unbeatable edge—a 10th the labor costs. But the compressor team had numbers proving the new factory would overcome that. It would be more than 10 times as productive as any other factory, they said. A high-wage country can fight back, they argued—with technology. The plan was to apply it on two fronts: Both the plant and the product would be the world's best.

Schipke looked it over. The proposal seemed to make sense to him. Because of the high automation, labor costs weren't nearly as big a factor as he'd expected. He said it was time to take the proposal to Jack Welch, the chairman in Fairfield.

Schipke, Truscott, and Blunt flew to Connecticut to sell the proposal to Welch. I was not part of that final meeting, but did all I could to brief Welch's top staff people in advance by phone. I knew their briefings of Welch before the meeting could make a difference.

Later, Blunt would recall the plane ride from Louisville to Fairfield. The betting was that they would not get approval. They knew there was a new world outlook in GE headquarters. A few years before, management had been almost haughty about the Japanese; they could never touch GE's quality, or technology. That had changed. The Japanese had become manufacturing geniuses. Why try to beat them when you can borrow from them? Or buy? Words no one dared speak before—words like "sourcing"—were now accepted wisdom.

It was Blunt's first time in the Fairfield boardroom. It was nearly empty as he filed in along with the Louisville team. Then a half-dozen executives from headquarters, including Jack Welch, entered the room. The Louisville people made their pitch.

"Then Jack poked at us three or four times," recalled Blunt.

The chairman asked some of his colleagues their opinion. A few said they doubted it could be done. It had never been done before, and seemed too great a risk. Welch looked at Blunt. "Why should I believe you people can do this?" he asked. "Why should I? You've never done anything like this before."

"No one ever asked us to," said Blunt. "And I believe we can do it."

Welch nodded.

"Essentially," Blunt would say later, "it boiled down to, 'You bums have never done anything worthwhile down there—why should we let you try this now?' "

Welch turned to Ed Hood, a vice-chairman of GE and one of his most trusted technical advisers. Blunt watched as he drew out Hood's comfort level. Blunt was counting on three things. Welch, he thought, had faith in Schipke's new management team. He'd seen the numbers showing the plant could do it—if the technology worked. Finally, the chairman wanted to keep major appliances as a core business for GE, and was concerned enough about Louisville's slide to know that only major investments could turn things around.

Welch turned back to Schipke, Truscott, and Blunt.

"Okay," he said. "Go ahead."

It was up to Keith Moore, recently transferred from GE's lighting business in Cleveland, to start up the new factory. First, that meant retrofitting the old Columbia, Tennessee, air-conditioner-compressor factory with the new processes developed by Blunt's engineers.

Moore's people soon found that it's easier to design a new process than to make it work. The warnings of the machinery suppliers proved true. At first, GE couldn't make the equipment do what Blunt's engineers wanted. It took endless hours of debugging, and hundreds of changes to each machine. The required tolerances—100th of a human hair—were so extraordinary that even the tiniest slippage could throw a whole process off. Ultimately, to keep the equipment at absolute precision, GE had to develop new gauging and sensing systems to get the machines to instantaneously readjust as they worked.

Deliveries of machinery were 2 months late at the start, and up to 14 months late at the end. Management found it hard to shepherd the process from Louisville, 200 miles from Columbia, so they rented 22 apartments in Columbia to house engineers. The company even started a daily air shuttle between the two cities. That way, they could instantly fly lab results in from Louisville and test experiences back from Columbia. Finally, by October 1985, they'd begun Phase One. The old factory started producing the new compressor—first 5 per day, then 10, then 100. By month five, they were up to volume production, with the quality holding just fine.

But if they were to succeed at Phase Two—making the new fully automated plant work—GE faced another challenge just as important as improving its hardware: improving its people.

A high-wage country can't compete with better technology alone; its other weapon has to be a better-trained work force. Could MABG create that in a place like Columbia, Tennessee, where the biggest annual celebration is Mule Day? Could blue-collar American workers in the rural heartland run one of the world's most automated plants? GE knew it would have to try. It would be too expensive to hire high-salary technicians from around the country. At $17 an hour—benefits included—the new plant could still beat the competition, but not at $25 or $30 an hour. So GE planned to staff the new factory with the same assembly people already employed next door at its Columbia air-conditioner complex. Most were unskilled, and few had more than a high-school education.

Historically, U.S. companies have put little investment into shop-floor training. With this kind of technology, GE management knew they had to make it a priority. They ended up deciding on yet another major investment: one of the most sophisticated blue-collar training centers ever built in an American factory. The cost would be over $2 million, which would have been difficult had GE not gotten help from a welcome partner: government. The state of Tennessee gave the company a training grant to help build the center.[8] But MABG was still left with a problem. It wouldn't be able to afford the additional expense of paying workers for the hundreds of hours it would take to train them. That left one choice: asking unskilled men and women to sacrifice between 120 and 400 hours in classrooms, labs, and computer stations at no pay and with no guarantee of promotion, either; that would depend on how they performed. All GE would offer was the promise of a skill. Would the workers volunteer? Would they show the same kind of commitment to company most associate not with Americans, but Asians?

Paul Varner, who'd been named by GE to help run the new training center, thought it a bad mistake. Having been an assembly worker in Columbia himself, he knew most on the line were conservative souls, wary of anything new.

---

[8]Tennessee, like many other states, offers training money to firms that expand or modernize plants in their state. In this case, state grants ran over $1 million.

They already had secure jobs; what would be the point of sacrificing up to a year of nights and weekends for no pay? His guess was that almost no one would volunteer. "It took me two weeks to realize I was totally wrong," Varner says today. "I ate crow."

Workers lined up for the training. Partly, it was because of the prestige GE gave it. Those who got through it were offered diplomas and graduation dinners. But there was another draw, as well, the same one that had prompted Varner to apply for a training-center job himself. He was aware of the world. He knew how vulnerable his job was. He saw why plants throughout America were closing: foreign competition. He was convinced it was a question of time before distant forces put him out of work as well. "We knew what the Japanese could do," he said. "A lot of people were aware we were fighting for our lives." As an assembly worker, Varner knew he didn't have the weapons to fight back. Columbia's old machines were antiquated. How, he wondered, could they hope to beat 1980s rivals with a 1960s factory?

Then came the announcement of a new plant. Finally, here was the means to fight back. Varner wanted to be part of it. He didn't mind unpaid nights and weekends in the training center. For him, joining the future was incentive enough. Still, he was at first convinced most others would need more than that. He was wrong. Hundreds of workers flooded into the training center. Clayton Russell was one of the first.

Russell had been hired by GE Columbia in 1974 for an unskilled assembly job. "That's all we had then," he explains. His job was to put four screws into the rear case of an air-conditioner. He did it 712 times each day. Gloria Anthony began the same year, also on the line. "A monotonous job," she says. "Over and over and over." Then construction began on the new plant. To have a chance at being part of it, they were told they'd have to put in hundreds of hours of training, all on their own time. It didn't matter. They began to do so—mornings, nights, weekends. "Whenever we had a chance," says Russell. His reason was similar to Varner's. He'd heard this would be the world's most automated plant; he wanted a piece of the future. He trained almost 300 hours.

Dan Edlin, another line worker, put in 400 hours. Like the others, his motivation was more than the chance of a bigger paycheck. "For me, money wasn't the major factor," he says. "I wanted the opportunity to be in on something totally brand new. This is where business is going—automation."

Was there any resentment that automation would cost jobs?

"Machines aren't taking people's jobs," he says. "Machines are making new jobs. Anyone who wants to get off his duff and train can have them."

Gloria Anthony saw it the same way. "You have to start thinking skilled labor," she says. "If you don't get on that bandwagon, you're lost."

"It's the wave of the future," says Clayton Russell. "And it's already here."

In the first year of the training center, the workers of GE Columbia spent over 50,000 hours, all on their own time, learning new skills. Paul Varner was taught a lesson: Give an American worker an opportunity and he'll sacrifice for it. "From Welch on down, they were saying, 'You can do it,' " says Varner. "We wanted to prove their faith in us."

Soon, Keith Moore, head of compressor production, was facing his next challenge: moving manufacturing from the converted air-conditioner plant into the new factory. Making the just-completed factory perfect, he knew, would mean thousands of adjustments. He also knew that his floor workers would be best able to spot many of those adjustments. So, right from the start, he involved them in developing the final setup. He began holding meetings with workers and engineers sitting shoulder to shoulder to discuss how to get better quality and efficiency. Moore was just as likely to reorganize a part of the plant at the suggestion of an assembly worker as an engineer. When they came across tough trouble spots, Moore would put the two groups together on joint teams to figure out solutions. He soon got an unexpected payback from spreading responsibility down through the ranks. In the past, even if a small thing went wrong, line workers would call a supervisor to deal with it. Now, they fixed it themselves. Part of it, says Moore, is that the training gave them the knowledge to know what to do. But it was more than that. By being involved in the planning, they'd started to feel as though they owned their part of the factory; that making it run right was on them, not their bosses.

"To this day," Moore says, "the facility runs without a manager or supervisor calling the shots on what has to be done." That, he says, can save an enormous amount of time. "If a supervisor has to become involved, you're an hour or two behind before it gets fixed. If you don't need the supervisor, you only lose minutes."

Moore also got workers involved in writing training manuals for the equipment. He figured that if they were compelled to teach the techniques, they'd learn them better themselves.

Finally, he laid down a rule against finger pointing. When things went wrong, Moore noted, the instinct was for workers to blame each other. That didn't solve anything. So he announced that any failed project would be considered the fault of the whole team. That way, Moore hoped, if one worker was having trouble, everyone would rally to back him up. That's exactly what happened.

Looking back, Moore realizes how important it was to keep up camaraderie. Frustrations could have easily gotten out of hand. The late equipment deliveries backed up the timetable. Dozens of times, processes that worked in the lab ended up failing on the factory floor. It meant late nights and occasional 7:00 A.M. Sunday morning meetings. But they made it; the plant opened on schedule, in March 1986. Both production and quality went smoothly, though inevitably there were bugs. It turned out to be a blessing that they had the older plant to occasionally fall back on while they worked the bugs through. GE will also admit it had to pour in more investment than expected. The managers there will tell you that happens when you're pushing technology's edge. But the factory is working. Ask Moore to point to one thing that did it and he won't mention hardware; he mentions the freedom he gave his workers. "We provided people with the tools to run their own businesses on the factory floor."

As the new plant was being built, John Truscott heard rumors that GE was thinking of putting him back in aerospace. A few years earlier, he'd have done anything to leave low-tech appliances for a high-tech division like that. But now he told his wife he wouldn't be interested. He wanted to stay where he was, in appliances. Aerospace, he felt, wasn't the cutting edge anymore. America's most urgent technological challenge, he felt, now lay in something as hard to master as space itself: factories. He explains the challenge: "Revitalizing

American industry. Chrome-plating the rust belt. Turning around smokestack America. That's the best way to reestablish ourselves as a world power."

Ask him how a high-wage country can do that, and he'll give you a ready answer.

"Productivity," he says, "is the only tie-breaker."

When Truscott first arrived in Louisville, colleagues from GE medical and aerospace kidded him about getting factory dirt under his fingernails. The kidding bothered him a little. But now, with the compressor plant nearing completion, he'd grown proud of being a factory man. "You know what's the cutting edge for graduating engineers today?" he says. "This. Doing compressor factories. Automation. Robots. It's another sound barrier. Building missiles was exciting, but that's old hat now. I'd rather do things that've never been done before."

Four years after deciding he'd rather be dead than working in washing machines, the man who worked on the sound barrier and CAT scanning had found his life's greatest challenge in an appliance factory.

Blunt, too, saw how important the plant was. It was especially plain to him when he went to Columbia to visit the site. Other factories outside the city were struggling, mostly because of faraway competition. Foreign companies were modernizing, America wasn't, and this was the price. It bothered him to see those plants in decline—Blunt never likes to see a factory go under—but what bothered him as much was the way newspapers seemed to focus only on that: plant failures, never successes. "A lot of us get really riled up when the popular press beats the hell out of us for not being competitive," Blunt says. "The truth is, we can be. It's just that most companies don't have the balls to spend money on productive capacity. Manufacturing may not seem like a lot of fun to people who don't do it—but it's necessary. And if you're going to do it, you can't short-sheet it."

As he drove past Columbia's older, struggling plants, he was proud that in this case, MABG was doing it right.

But eventually, he was to find the struggle wasn't over yet. Being at the cutting edge of new technology often involves risk.

In January 1988, 22 months after the first compressor rolled out of the new factory, a problem arose. Some of the larger compressors—those in GE's bigger refrigerators—began to fail.[9] It was only a small percentage of the plant's total production, but GE clearly had a problem. For a consumer product like this, reliability is essential. So is customer satisfaction. Immediately, Truscott formed a team of design engineers to find what was going wrong. They worked for weeks, often through the night. What made the job especially difficult was that only a small portion of the compressors had actually failed. But based on those few, they'd gone into a massive program of testing and found that others could fail in the future. Soon, Truscott's people solved the riddle. There was a lubrication problem with one of the compressor's smaller parts, causing it to wear quicker than they'd expected. It was mostly affecting the compressors that had to work hardest—those in the biggest refrigerators in the

---

[9]Refrigerators must work harder in hot climates, so it is not surprising that the problems began to occur there. The problem was serious mainly for larger compressors.

hottest climates, but some others were affected, too. Eventually, Truscott found that GE wasn't alone. The Japanese companies using rotaries were having similar problems.

Now that the cause was isolated, finding a fix became Louisville's obsession. Truscott and some corporate engineers led a new team that worked on it for months. Finally, they came up with a better design and showed it to Roger Schipke. He was confident it would work, and told them to go ahead with it. Meanwhile, he approved a plan to immediately replace any compressor that broke down by dispatching servicemen to customers' homes at GE expense.

But Schipke still faced a serious dilemma. True, the projections showed that only a few percent of the compressors would fail. But the redesign of the lubrication device would take months to implement, and Schipke didn't want to risk GE's reputation by shipping refrigerators that might develop problems. To be as safe as possible, he made a painful choice. In the spring of 1988, he decided that MABG would start to source medium and large reciprocating compressors from abroad while the engineering team put the fix into place. It would mean a temporary layoff at the old plant in the Columbia complex. It would also mean a high-cost burden. GE had to pay top dollar for the sourced recips, and take longer contracts than it needed.

In November 1988, GE decided to go into the field and replace all rotaries that might someday break down. The one-time financial penalty was very large—well over $150 million. The losses will offset several years of savings from the program. But GE will continue to make rotaries with the corrected design for most of its refrigerators at its automated Columbia facility. The failure problem has drawn hard criticism from both the competition and the press. Some at GE are embarrassed at having been forced to source compressors. Others are irritated at how much money the problem has cost. Still others are angry that it was potentially avoidable. Early lab tests showed the compressors would last 20 years, but obviously the truest test is performance in the field. Looking back, many GE executives see a lesson. When using a brand-new technology, it may be wiser to introduce it gradually, working out the bugs over a year or two, rather than converting your entire production immediately.

The irony is that over 80 percent of GE's compressor investment—and risk—was tied up in the factory, by far the most complex technical challenge. And the factory worked well. It was a relatively simple part of the product design that caused the problem.

Still, GE management preferred facing the problem to giving up. Occasional product recalls are part of the price of being willing to gamble on new technologies. It happened with fuel-injected car engines, electric shavers, and microwave ovens when they were first introduced, and now it is happening with rotary refrigerator compressors. The cost to GE is high. Profits are seriously off in 1988 and morale is low. But the achievement still stands: Here in America, GE continues to make compressors that are 20 percent cheaper than any made by dollar-an-hour competition.

Clayton Russell, who used to put four screws into the rear case of an air-conditioner 712 times each day, now runs a $700,000 synchronous machine with 12 different stations. Gloria Anthony is now a skilled controlperson who can operate machines by computer, adjusting them whenever the terminal tells her there's a slight quality problem. "I never thought I'd go this high," she says. "When I began, I was just sweeping." Both are proud to be part of a plant that makes twice as many compressors as the old one, with less than a quarter the people. Productivity, they say, is the only way America can compete. "There's a good feeling to it," says Russell. "We got production. That's a feeling of pride."

Edward Fite, director of the training center, dressed in gray pinstripes gives a tour of the automated Columbia plant with the pride of someone showing off a new home. Overhead, compressor pieces roll down long, winding chutes, into machines that stamp, cut, and refine; computers direct them to the next machine, warning that they're on the way. The machines work and work, never stopping. Grinders, welders, testers, and robots do their drilling, milling, tapping, and gauging. There may be no other mass-production factory in the world that makes goods this precisely. Most of the line people stand before computer terminals: They're symbols of the new American blue-collar worker, equipped with the tools to outcompete the world.

"They knew that if the work had stayed the way it was," Fite says, "it would have been a matter of time before it went overseas." They knew about dollar-an-hour Brazilian workers. They knew they had to outproduce them. They knew if they failed, they'd be lucky to be back in unskilled jobs, stuffing wires into panels, for half the pay. "To be trusted with a plant like this," says Fite, "that made them prideful. They know they've met an extreme challenge that's never been done before. And they know they're bringing the whole community up. They're making it a skilled community."

It sometimes surprises Fite to know that today, at 36, he's come from stuffing wires to teaching workers how to run a high-technology plant. He sees people like himself as the final mission of a factory like this: They give common workers a standard of living beyond what they ever hoped for.

John Truscott, recently retired from GE, will tell you that now, more than ever, he knows the risks of trying to pioneer new technologies. But he'll tell you that if GE—and America—are to compete, we have no choice but to take those risks.

"Our future is not dependent on the bells and whistles," he says, "or even distribution. Those aren't the things that will make or break you in a world-class environment. What's really important is having world-class cost leadership, and world-class quality leadership." He makes one other point. America still has a productivity problem, but it's not because our workers aren't as good as foreigners. It's that they're not used as well. Give them the best of factories, he says, and the best of training, and they can still outproduce the world.

"It's the major need for the nation," he says. "Call it the Third Wave in industrial products—call it what you will. It's our biggest challenge." Three years ago, he recalls, few people felt smokestack America could meet that challenge as well as the world's Japans and West Germanys. "Well," Truscott says today, "at Columbia, Tennessee, we are doing it."

In a sense, Tom Blunt will always be a figure from an earlier America. The noblest kind of business, he will always believe, is manufacturing; the highest form of architecture is a factory. "I like the gritty stuff," he says. His father was a toolmaker, and he proudly traces his ancestry back through 11 generations of factory mechanics. But he knows America can lead the world in factories only by building a new kind. At his desk in Louisville, he leans over a computer terminal and punches a few keys. A moving diagram appears on the screen. He explains that he is now monitoring the Columbia factory. Sitting here in Louisville, 200 miles away, he can peer by computer into the guts of any machine he wants to—judging how it's working, how many parts are made correctly, how many had to be set aside for rework.

"Let me show you something interesting," Blunt says. He punches a few more keys, then leans back, clasping his hands behind his head. "Since seven A.M.," he says, "we've made 3,413 pumps." He pushes an update button. "I'm sorry, he says, "3,415." He pushes the update button again. "3,417." He's a big man, well over six feet. He finds it hard to get through most sentences without at least a mild oath, and few things make him smile. But when he works this computer, if you look close, you can almost see the trace of one.

"So far," he says, "we've only had five defective parts today." He punches another button and nods; the computer is showing him a diagram of the day's tolerances for one of the machined parts. "The problem was with one of the grinders that went down," he says. "It's fixed now." Is there any other plant in the world that has this automated an information system?

"There isn't," says Blunt.

Building 4 still stands a few hundred yards from Tom Blunt's Louisville office. Only now, it's half-empty. Even if Columbia hadn't been built, he points out, Building 4 still would have been dead by now. Its time was up. The choice was simple: Either it was replaced with a foreign plant or an American plant; a foreign payroll or an American one. He's glad GE chose to go with this side of the ocean. Sourcing, he says, is not America's future. He's come out of this with one main lesson.

"I'll tell you something you just think about for a while," says Blunt. "In late seventy-nine, early eighty, this place was the garbage dump of the universe. Could do no good. Bunch of dumbheads. Low tech. Well, I didn't go out and hire a bunch of world-class experts to fix it. I didn't bring anybody in. The people that fixed it were mostly here. You stop and think about that. The only thing that really changed was that we told them they could do it. And we let them. We've starved the manufacturing community for challenge—and that's what we thrive on. Challenge."

As much as mastering technology—that, he feels, should be industry's goal: confidence. If a floundering corporation can start believing in itself, he says, it can beat the world. "I don't think the battle in American industry is mainly a technical battle," he says, "it's an attitude battle. People become what you tell them they are. If you tell them they can't do it, they won't."

There are other lessons, often overlooked. Most wouldn't have thought that compressors—which have been around for decades—could have been turned into a technological breakthrough. It's how most old, smokestack products are seen. Once low-wage countries begin making them, it's supposedly over; the only choice is to source—or put a factory overseas yourself. In truth, we need only lose a minority of products. Most can still be kept ahead of world competition with new technology. But only if we invest in time. Had Louisville slept another few years, it could have been too late. By then, foreign refrigerator compressors would have flooded America, forcing a decision to source forever. That's what happened with microwave ovens. The only defense is to track the competition and know when to act. But you can't win with technology alone. Eventually, the world will match it. To stay ahead, you also need the most skilled workers. That's far harder for the competition to match.

Finally, there must be a willingness to take risks. That means being ready for failures. Some might argue that if GE had sourced compressors to begin with, it never would have had the product-failure problem in 1988. But there are ways to minimize risk. GE probably moved into the marketplace too fast with its new compressors. A year or two of limited field testing would have exposed the minor design flaw, allowing a fix with limited financial losses.

GE's basic decision to manufacture was the right one. Sourcing so essential a product would have left GE's appliance group vulnerable, and America without a vital piece of its production base. Because GE risked, and persevered, in the long run it will be ahead of the world in both technology and cost. As long as the company maintains that lead, it's guaranteed to win. Had it sourced instead of invested, it would have no guarantee at all.

Tom Blunt, Dave Heimedinger, Don Awbrey, Jim Lehmann, and the hundreds of others who made the compressor factory happen have never made the cover of *Business Week*. We're more prone to celebrate CEOs or even brokers and speculators. Many Wall Streeters, of course, do contribute to a vibrant economy, but there's something more important. Drive 50 miles south of Nashville, outside the city of Columbia, into the rolling hills of tobacco country, where the restaurants offer Bar-B-Q and catfish, and you'll find a symbol. It's a symbol of how, with the right vision, and investments, and risks, we can still keep our trade balance, our jobs, and our quality of life, from going overseas.

How Honda Localizes Its Global Strategy

Hideo Sugiura, Honda Motor Company

Advances in information technology and increased exchanges of information in all fields are making nations more dependent on each other than ever before. This interdependence is creating a solid foundation for global economic development.

However, interdependence is also increasing the impact nations are having on each other, weakening their economies and making the global economy less predictable. As trade frictions between industrially advanced nations intensify and the economic gap between developed and developing nations widens, governments are leaning heavily toward economic nationalism, seeking quick, unilateral, political solutions to economic problems.

But economic problems must be discussed at the global level, not at the level of individual countries or even regions. It is extremely important to build interdependent relationships among nations, and in doing so to restore mutual trust. This will open the way to stable development of the world economy. Such development will require international efforts of various kinds at the government level. At the same time, industrial activities at the corporate level, including investment, assume great significance. Yet the uncertainty of the world economy makes international corporate activity very risky.

The Pacific Basin must be a key focal point in any discussion of the evolving world economy. The countries in the Pacific Basin have grown increasingly important, both politically and economically. Their economic growth rates have far surpassed those of North America and the European Community. Their share of global trade has also risen every year. More important, industrial products account for a fast-growing portion of their exports—proof that they are making dramatic progress in industrialization. A mutually trusting relationship must be established between the region's relatively advanced countries and its rising nations to ensure further growth and prosperity in the Pacific Basin, which I think is indispensable for revitalization of the world economy.

There are many ways in which the advanced countries can support the region's development. The most important is the creation of new business and employment opportunities by private enterprises. Specifically, the two key means by which corporations from the advanced nations can contribute are *investment* and the *transfer of technology*. Such corporate activities should, of course, be different from government assistance programs.

The cultural diversity of the Pacific Rim countries presents major obstacles that must be overcome before the economic sphere can be solidified through investment and technology transfer. (In my view, such solidification has already occurred in the Mediterranean and Atlantic spheres—and indeed, the cultural diversity was less remarkable there to begin with.) Two factors are prerequisite to overcoming such cultural differences. First, the countries involved must clearly understand the goals to be attained through mutual

Source: Reprinted from *Sloan Management Review*, Fall 1990, pp. 77–82, by permission of the publisher.

cooperation. Second, each country's role must be recognized and agreed upon. Unless these two conditions are met, one cannot expect any cooperation program to succeed.

These beliefs are based on Honda's experience during its many years of international activities. It may be useful, then, to look at specific examples of Honda's overseas strategy.

THE FOUR LOCALIZATIONS

Since its modest beginning in 1948, Honda has grown into a corporation with $25 billion in sales, largely because of its successful international activities. More than 60 percent of our total sales take place outside of Japan; our products are marketed in well over 100 countries. Moreover, we manufacture products at 77 plants in 40 countries outside Japan, and our cumulative total investments abroad have surpassed $1 billion, not counting over $2 billion reinvested locally by our overseas subsidiaries, which I will describe in detail later.

Honda is often described as an international enterprise. But in promoting internationalization, we place the utmost important on *localization*—adapting our activities to those practiced in the countries where we operate. This overseas strategy consists of four target concepts: localization of *products, profit, production*, and *management*.

Localization of Products   This means developing, manufacturing, and marketing the products best suited to the actual and potential needs of the customers *and* to the social and economic conditions of the marketplace. While it is true that a good product knows no national boundaries, there are subtle differences, from country to country and from region to region, in ways a product is used and what customers expect of it. If a corporation believes that simply because a product has succeeded in a certain market, it will sell well throughout the world, it is most likely destined for large and expensive errors or even total failure.

Take our motorcycles as an example. North Americans use motorcycles primarily for leisure and sports; a racer looks for high horsepower output and speed. Southeast Asians, on the other hand, use motorcycles as a basic means of transportation, so they want ease of maintenance, at low cost. In Australia, shepherds use motorcycles to drive sheep; they look for low-speed torque, rather than high speed or ease of maintenance. So, while we do use a common basic technology, we develop different types of motorcycles for different regions. Such differences apply not only to cars and motorcycles, but to most industrial products as well. Corporations must be capable of accurately grasping such differences and producing appropriately targeted products.

To localize products, corporations must invest in research and development of both products and constantly increasing production efficiency. Honda earmarks 5 percent of the parent company's unconsolidated gross annual sales for R&D of products and production techniques regardless of fluctuation in profits. In addition, we have established R&D centers in North and South America, Western Europe, and Southeast Asia. Japanese and local engineers work together to understand local market conditions and to develop the products best suited to each market.

Localization of Profits This means reinvesting as much of the profits as possible in the local market. A company investing abroad must regard itself as a local company and endeavor to prosper together with the host country. Reinvestment effectively addresses the concern that multinational enterprises are interested only in sending profits home and not in benefiting the host country.

In 1959, for example, Honda established a wholly owned marketing subsidiary, American Honda, in Los Angeles with a capital investment of $250,000. This sum has now grown 800 times to $200 million, a dramatic increase achieved through the reinvestment of American Honda's profits. More than $1.7 billion in reinvested American Honda profits has gone into the construction and expansion of motorcycle, automobile, and engine manufacturing plants in Ohio. Meanwhile, automobile production began at our new plant in Allison, near Toronto, in November 1986. Most of the $200 million Canadian investment represents reinvestment of profits earned by Honda Canada, our marketing subsidiary.

Localization of Production A corporation does not merely make profits by exporting completed products; it carries out production activities where major markets exist, thereby contributing to the development of the host nation and achieving mutual prosperity. Normally, a corporation explores a new market by establishing a marketing base and importing completed goods. Yet, whenever the host country needs the product manufactured locally, the corporation should as soon as practicable set up a manufacturing base; this is the best way to assure acceptance of both the product and the corporation, and achieve long-term prosperity. There are two ways to make local production activity most effective. One is to increase the ratio of local content, which gives added impetus to related industries. The other is to increase the value added in local production, which not only expands employment opportunities, but also gives employees a greater sense of responsibility for and pride in manufacturing their own products.

Establishing local production can mean entering into a technical collaboration agreement with a local partner for technological transfer, setting up a joint venture with local capital, or establishing a wholly owned manufacturing subsidiary. A corporation must choose the method best suited to the requirements and conditions of the host country. In so doing, it should consider such factors as level of industrialization, market size, restraints arising from local economic and social needs, and the needs and capabilities of the local partner. Honda, for example, has chosen to establish wholly owned manufacturing subsidiaries in the United States and Canada, while in Europe, we are collaborating with the Rover Group of Britain. In Thailand, we produce motorcycles in a joint venture with local capital, and cars through a technical collaboration. In Indonesia, we produce motorcycles and cars, their engines, and other components through joint ventures and technological tie-ins.

Localization of Management This goes beyond transferring knowledge about management systems operations. Local managers and employees must understand the corporate philosophy. Managers dispatched from the head office should be encouraged to become part of the community by understanding local culture and ways of thinking; to delegate authority to local personnel;

and to create a sense of unity between management and labor so that everyone is working toward a common goal. In implementing these measures, managers should avoid forcing local people to accept management know-how or corporate philosophy in its original form, which may be foreign to them. Every effort must be made to modify it, where feasible, to suit local conditions. These efforts create a sense of unity that is essential for the achievement of common goals.

Through years of experience in many parts of the world, we have become convinced that good communication between management and labor, as well as delegation of authority, elevate the employees' sense of participation in decision making. This, in turn, gives the employees a stronger sense of responsibility and motivation, which leads to improved productivity and maintenance of high quality standards.

I would like to emphasize that management initiatives are essential to achieving these ideals. Success or failure depends on management. Good management and good labor-management relations go hand in hand.

The four kinds of localization represent our fundamental international philosophy. We developed this philosophy by way of repeated successes and failures. We fully realize that pursuing this philosophy is not the easy way, and that it sometimes requires sacrificing short-term profits. Yet we are convinced that it is the best way to conduct business on a long-term basis.

HOW THIS CORPORATE PHILOSOPHY WORKS

Our activities in North America are perhaps the best examples of localization of production. In 1974 we started studying the feasibility of production in the United States. At that time, there was very little auto trade friction between Japan and the United States, and nobody was talking about restricting Japanese car imports, let alone local content. I wish to emphasize that our decision to produce in the United States was not meant to circumvent trade restrictions. We started producing motorcycles in Ohio in 1979 and automobiles in 1982. Automobile production there has now reached 360,000 units per year, more than double the original capacity. We also produce motorcycle and car engines in Ohio and began manufacturing lawn mowers in North Carolina in 1984. Our dealers and customers tell us that the quality of our American-made products is equal to or better than that of our cars produced in Japan, and we have found that our North American employees are as diligent and hard working as any in the world.

In September 1987, we announced our "Five-Part Strategy," which was intended to make the automobile manufacturing operation in Ohio a fully integrated, self-reliant entity. The strategy consists of the following:

- By 1991, 70,000 Ohio-built cars will be exported to various world markets, including Japan.
- The number of engineers engaged in research and development activities in North America will be increased to 500 by 1991, compared with 200 in 1989. Another 200 engineers will design and develop new production equipment and machinery.
- A new automobile production plant will soon start operating adjacent to the existing factory. It will ultimately produce 150,000 cars a year,

bringing Honda's total car production capacity in Ohio to 510,000 units annually.

- The engine plant located in Anna, Ohio, will be expanded to produce half a million engines per year.
- The domestic content of the Ohio-built cars will reach 75 percent in the near future.

The Five-Part Strategy will bring the total investments made in Ohio to more than $2 billion and create more than 11,000 jobs.

In administering the plants in Ohio, Honda attaches particular importance to three policies. The first is to establish good human relations between the management and the work force. Any production activity requires a good deal of coordination and cooperation among various departments. This is possible only through teamwork that encompasses the entire company. One cannot expect to develop that capacity without close labor-management communications, initiated by management. Management encourages employees to communicate problems directly and then promptly seeks solutions through discussions with them. The management staff wears the same white work clothing and eats at the same cafeteria as the other employees. Much effort has gone into creating a safe, clean, pleasant, friendly work environment. These and other measures have contributed to intracompany unity and to an employee sense of responsibility for and pride in their own work.

The second policy is to maintain and promote harmony with the local community. An important factor in producing high-quality goods is securing high-quality labor. For this reason, Honda has gone beyond just educating and training its employees. It has worked at creating a good understanding with the local community, which is the source of its labor. We now release information through newspapers and other mass media and invite local families to factory tours, test rides, Honda festivals, and field days.

The third policy is to give top priority to maintaining high quality standards in our products. I believe that quality level is determined primarily by the actual design of the product itself, not by quality control in the production processes. Still, assuring high quality standards requires good production equipment and technology. This is why our plants in Ohio are equipped with sophisticated machinery, some of which does not even exist at our Japanese factories. Even with such good equipment and technology, however, assuring high quality standards is not possible without quality consciousness on the part of all individuals concerned. Such consciousness can be generated only where there are good human relations. For this reason, our Ohio plants promote dialogues between the management and the work force, as well as providing employees with an extensive training program, including classroom training on product design and engineering and intensive on-the-job training in production techniques. The employees now have a broad understanding of how to perform their jobs and meet quality expectations, and they are committed to the corporate policy of winning customer satisfaction by supplying quality products.

One episode at our Ohio plant is a good example of quality consciousness on the part of employees. Shortly after our motorcycle production started, I visited the plant. After landing in Columbus sometime after 6:00 P.M., which was already after the plant's working hours, I was driven directly to the plant.

When I walked through it, I was surprised to see six or seven American employees polishing motorcycle fuel tanks with compound wax so late in the evening. When I asked them why they were doing that, they told me that earlier in the day, following a change in the fuel tank paint material, minor defects had appeared on the surface finish of some tanks. Although these defects were of the kind that could easily be rectified in the final inspection area after the vehicles were completed, the employees in the painting section decided that they could not send substandard fuel tanks to the assembly line. They voluntarily worked overtime so that the motorcycles to be assembled the following day would be fitted with tanks free of defects.

Up until that time, I had been given to understand that such voluntary overtime would never be practiced at U.S. plants. Generally speaking, that is probably still true. What I witnessed at our Ohio plant, however, clearly shows that individual employees understand and accept the management policy of achieving top quality standards, that both management and the work force share the goal of winning maximum customer satisfaction, and that employees are fully aware of their roles and are prepared to fulfill their responsibilities completely. You may think this a minor incident. But I think it is of great importance because it could not have happened without a well-formulated management policy. I have rarely been more impressed by employee enthusiasm and motivation.

A well-formulated management policy serves to unify the members of the corporation, which, in turn, adds to corporate vitality. Such a policy requires that management establish goals that the employees can fully understand, appreciate, and commit themselves to. It also requires that management take the lead in motivating the work force.

These three policies—establishing good human relations, maintaining harmony with the local community, and placing highest priority on quality standards—represent the embodiment of Honda's philosophy of localization.

A less successful attempt at localization occurred in Belgium, where, in 1962, Honda began the production of mopeds. This is said to be the first instance of direct Japanese investment in a manufacturing venture in an industrially advanced country. Japan's economy in those days was not what it is today, and there was apparently considerable opposition in the Japanese government to Honda's investment in Belgium.

But Europe was a big market; it accounted for 85 percent of the world's non-Japanese motorcycle ownership. The motorcycle was firmly established and widely used by Europeans as a means of transportation. Honda decided to manufacture mopeds in Belgium because it had confidence in its technical process and believed that a good product knows no national boundaries.

In spite of this confidence, our manufacturing venture turned into a series of mistakes and miscalculations. The plant in Belgium was in the red for more than 10 years.

Our early failure was caused by several problems: the model we developed with so much confidence did not match European users' needs; we had put too much of Honda's distinctive technology and design into the model and were thus unable to find local manufacturers who could supply us with parts that met our specifications; and our inadequate comprehension of local labor practices led to misunderstandings between management and local employees, resulting in unexpected disruptions of routine production activities.

In other words, the difficulties we encountered in Belgium were caused by our failure to understand and respond to the differences in history, culture, and values.

The lesson we learned was that to invest and do business overseas, it is not enough to have abstract knowledge about the host country. It is essential to develop a deeper understanding. This can be achieved only by immersion in local society and by working with the people of the country.

We learned the importance of adopting a locally oriented approach and building up a new way of doing work in the host country. It took us a long time to make our factory in Belgium pay, but we do not think that the cost of the lesson was too high. From that experience, we learned how difficult it is and how much time and patience it takes to establish mutual understanding between different cultures. Our Belgian experience gave us the valuable know-how essential for launching Honda's subsequent overseas activities, and this know-how has become a valuable asset.

CONCLUSIONS

Two points are particularly critical when discussing Honda's localization policy. First, as the degree of localization rises, the amount of investment naturally increases in proportion. As I mentioned at the outset, this is an inevitable result of the growing interdependence between countries and regions. Increased investment is a manifestation of commitment. This must be clearly recognized by the host country.

Second, localization of production through investment is not confined to the transfer of technology. It involves the transfer of a philosophy, that is, the corporate culture that constitutes the basis of technology and management, developed within a corporation since its founding.

In this connection, I believe it important that both the investing party and the host party should make efforts to overcome, intelligently and flexibly, the difficulties that might eventually arise, so that the cultural background of the host country and the investor's transplanted corporate culture will blend in a proper way. It is essential to solve problems arising out of differences in culture, ways of thinking, and values. A corporation seeking to be globally active must be capable of creating a new corporate culture that results from the blending of two different cultures.

I am convinced that the success or failure of investment depends on whether the enterprise can build mutual understanding and trust. International investment at the corporate level will contribute greatly to expanding interdependence, revitalizing the world economy, and bringing about stable development. To invigorate corporate investment, every effort must be made, on private, national, and international levels, to create an environment that will convince the potential investor that investment will result in mutual prosperity.

I think it is fair to say that today Honda's activities in many corners of the world are accepted and appreciated. I attribute this to the policy of localization. Through this policy, we have been able to generate new corporate cultures in different parts of the world by directing the minds of all concerned to common goals, while respecting the traditional cultures of Japan and of the host countries. In so doing, we have paid maximum attention to taking good care of our human resources in order to consolidate the labor-management partnership.

Let me close by noting that Honda's strategies and policies are aimed at achieving maximum customer satisfaction. In a narrow sense, this means satisfying individual customers by providing high-quality products that meet their needs at reasonable prices. But it is also essential for a corporation to interpret the word "customer" in a broader sense—to cover the whole society in which it operates. Corporate behaviors must be such that the corporation itself and all of its activities are satisfactory to the community, society, and country. In other words, the corporation must be a good citizen. The four types of localization represent Honda's strategy for achieving this broader sense of customer satisfaction.

FROM COMPETITIVE ADVANTAGE TO CORPORATE STRATEGY

Michael E. Porter, Harvard Business School

Corporate strategy, the overall plan for a diversified company, is both the darling and the stepchild of contemporary management practice—the darling because CEOs have been obsessed with diversification since the early 1960s, the stepchild because almost no consensus exists about what corporate strategy is, much less about how a company should formulate it.

A diversified company has two levels of strategy: business unit (or competitive) strategy and corporate (or companywide) strategy. Competitive strategy concerns how to create competitive advantage in each of the businesses in which a company competes. Corporate strategy concerns two different questions: what businesses the corporation should be in and how the corporate office should manage the array of business units.

Corporate strategy is what makes the corporate whole add up to more than the sum of its business unit parts.

The track record of corporate strategies has been dismal. I studied the diversification records of 33 large, prestigious U.S. companies over the 1950–1986 period and found that most of them had divested many more acquisitions than they had kept. The corporate strategies of most companies have dissipated instead of created shareholder value.

The need to rethink corporate strategy could hardly be more urgent. By taking over companies and breaking them up, corporate raiders thrive on failed corporate strategy. Fueled by junk bond financing and growing acceptability, raiders can expose any company to takeover, no matter how large or blue chip.

Recognizing past diversification mistakes, some companies have initiated large-scale restructuring programs. Others have done nothing at all. Whatever the response, the strategic questions persist. Those who have restructured must decide what to do next to avoid repeating the past; those who have done nothing must awake to their vulnerability. To survive, companies must understand what good corporate strategy is.

A SOBER PICTURE

While there is disquiet about the success of corporate strategies, none of the available evidence satisfactorily indicates the success or failure of corporate strategy. Most studies have approached the question by measuring the stock market valuation of mergers, captured in the movement of the stock prices of acquiring companies immediately before and after mergers are announced.

These studies show that the market values mergers as neutral or slightly negative, hardly cause for serious concern.[1] Yet the short-term market reaction is a highly imperfect measure of the long-term success of diversification, and no self-respecting executive would judge a corporate strategy this way.

Studying the diversification programs of a company over a long period of time is a much more telling way to determine whether a corporate strategy has succeeded or failed. My study of 33 companies, many of which have reputations for good management, is a unique look at the track record of major corporations. (For an explanation of the research, see the insert "Where the Data Come From.") Each company entered an average of 80 new industries and 27 new fields. Just over 70 percent of the new entries were acquisitions, 22 percent were start-ups, and 8 percent were joint ventures. IBM, Exxon, Du Pont, and 3M, for example, focused on start-ups, while ALCO Standard, Beatrice, and Sara Lee diversified almost solely through acquisitions (Exhibit 1 has a complete rundown).

My data paint a sobering picture of the success ratio of these moves (see Exhibit 2). I found that on average corporations divested more than half their acquisitions in new industries and more than 60 percent of their acquisitions in entirely new fields. Fourteen companies left more than 70 percent of all the acquisitions they had made in new fields. The track record in unrelated acquisitions is even worse—the average divestment rate is a startling 74 percent (see Exhibit 3). Even a highly respected company like General Electric divested a very high percentage of its acquisitions, particularly those in new fields. Companies near the top of the list in Exhibit 2 achieved a remarkably low rate of divestment. Some bear witness to the success of well-thought-out corporate strategies. Others, however, enjoy a lower rate simply because they have not faced up to their problem units and divested them.

I calculated total shareholder returns (stock price appreciation plus dividends) over the period of the study for each company so that I could compare them with its divestment rate. While companies near the top of the list have above-average shareholder returns, returns are not a reliable measure of diversification success. Shareholder return often depends heavily on the inherent attractiveness of companies' base industries. Companies like CBS and General Mills had extremely profitable base businesses that subsidized poor diversification track records.

I would like to make one comment on the use of shareholder value to judge performance. Linking shareholder value quantitatively to diversification performance only works if you compare the shareholder value that is with the shareholder value that might have been without diversification. Because such a comparison is virtually impossible to make, my own measure of diversification success—the number of units retained by the company—seems to be as good an indicator as any of the contribution of diversification to corporate performance.

---

[1] The studies also show that sellers of companies capture a large fraction of the gains from merger. See Michael C. Jensen and Richard S. Rubeck, "The Market for Corporate Control: The Scientific Evidence," *Journal of Financial Economics*, April 1983, p. 5, and Michael C. Jensen, "Takeovers: Folklore and Science," *Harvard Business Review*, November–December 1984, p. 109.

EXHIBIT 1   Diversification Profiles of 33 Leading U.S. Companies

Company	Number Total Entries	All Entries into New Industries	Percent Acquisitions	Percent Joint Ventures	Percent Start-Ups	Entries into New Industries that Represented Entirely New Fields	Percent Acquisitions	Percent Joint Ventures	Percent Start-Ups
ALCO Standard	221	165	99%	0%	1%	56	100%	0%	0%
Allied Corp.	77	49	67	10	22	17	65	8	29
Beatrice	382	204	97	1	2	61	97	0	3
Borden	170	96	77	4	19	32	75	3	22
CBS	148	81	67	16	17	28	65	21	14
Continental Group	75	47	77	6	17	19	79	11	11
Cummins Engine	30	24	54	17	29	13	46	23	31
Du Pont	80	39	33	16	51	19	37	0	63
Exxon	79	56	34	5	61	17	29	6	65
General Electric	160	108	47	20	33	29	48	14	38
General Foods	92	53	91	4	6	22	86	5	9
General Mills	110	102	84	7	9	27	74	7	19
W. R. Grace	275	202	83	7	10	66	74	5	21
Gulf & Western	178	140	91	4	6	48	88	2	10
IBM	46	38	18	18	63	16	19	0	81
IC Industries	67	41	85	3	12	17	88	8	6
ITT	246	178	89	2	9	50	92	0	8
Johnson & Johnson	88	77	77	0	23	18	56	0	44
Mobil	41	32	53	16	31	15	60	7	33
Procter & Gamble	28	23	61	0	39	14	79	0	21
Raytheon	70	58	66	9	5	16	81	19	6
RCA	53	46	35	15	50	19	37	21	42
Rockwell	101	75	73	24	3	27	74	22	4
Sara Lee	197	141	96	1	4	41	95	2	2
Scovill	52	36	97	0	3	12	92	0	8
Signal	53	45	67	4	29	20	75	0	25
Tenneco	85	62	81	6	13	26	73	8	19
3M	144	125	54	2	45	34	71	3	56
TRW	119	82	77	10	13	28	64	11	25
United Technologies	82	49	57	18	24	17	23	17	39
Westinghouse	129	73	63	11	26	36	61	3	36
Wickes	71	47	83	0	17	22	68	0	32
Xerox	59	50	66	6	28	18	50	11	39
Total	3,788	2,644				906			
Average	114.8	80.1	70.3%	7.9%	21.8%	27.4	67.9%	7.0%	25.9%

Note: Beatrice, Continental Group, General Foods, RCA, Scovill, and Signal were taken over as the study was being completed. Their data cover the period up through takeover but not subsequent divestments.

EXHIBIT 2   **Acquisition Track Records of Leading U.S. Diversifiers Ranked by Percent Divested**

Company	All Acquisitions in New Industries	Percent Made by 1980 and Then Divested	Percent Made by 1975 and Then Divested	Acquisitions in New Industries that Represented Entirely New Fields	Percent Made by 1980 and Then Divested	Percent Made by 1975 and Then Divested
Johnson & Johnson	59	17%	12%	10	33%	14%
Procter & Gamble	14	17	17	11	17	17
Raytheon	50	17	25	13	25	33
United Technologies	28	25	13	10	17	0
3M	67	26	27	24	42	45
TRW	63	27	31	18	40	38
IBM	7	33	0*	3	33	0*
Du Pont	13	38	43	7	60	75
Mobil	17	38	57	9	50	50
Borden	74	39	40	24	45	50
IC Industries	35	42	50	15	46	44
Tenneco	50	43	47	19	27	33
Beatrice	198	46	45	59	62	51
ITT	159	52	52	46	61	61
Rockwell	65	56	67	20	71	71
Allied Corp.	33	57	45	11	40	80
Exxon	19	62	20*	5	80	50*
Sara Lee	135	62	65	39	80	76
General Foods	48	63	62	19	93	83
Scovill	85	64	77	11	64	70
Signal	30	65	63	15	70	67
ALCO Standard	164	85	70	56	72	76
W. R. Grace	167	65	70	49	71	70
General Electric	51	65	78	14	100	100
Wickes	38	67	72	15	73	70
Westinghouse	46	68	69	22	61	59
Xerox	33	71	79	9	100	100
Continental Group	36	71	72	15	60	60
General Mills	86	75	73	20	65	60
Gulf & Western	127	79	78	42	75	72
Cummins Engine	13	80	80	6	83	83
RCA	16	80	92	7	86	100
CBS	54	87	89	18	88	88
Total	2,021			661		
Average per company†	61.2	53.4%	56.5%	20.0	60.0%	61.5%

*Companies with three or fewer acquisitions by the cutoff year.

†Companies with three or fewer acquisitions by the cutoff year are excluded from the average to minimize statistical distortions.

Note: Beatrice, Continental Group, General Foods, RCA, Scovill, and Signal were taken over as the study was being completed. Their data cover the period up through takeover but not subsequent divestments.

EXHIBIT 3   **Diversification Performance in Joint Ventures, Start-Ups, and Unrelated Acquisitions**   *(Companies in same order as in Exhibit 2)*

Company	Joint Ventures as a Percent of New Entries	Percent Made by 1980 and Then Divested	Percent Made by 1975 and Then Divested	Start-Ups as a Percent of New Entries	Percent Made by 1980 and Then Divested	Percent Made by 1975 and Then Divested	Unrelated Acquisitions as a Percent of Total Acquisitions	Percent Made by 1980 and Then Divested	Percent Made by 1975 and Then Divested
Johnson & Johnson	0%	†	†	23%	14%	20%	0%	†	†
Procter & Gamble	0	†	†	39	0	0	9	†	†
Raytheon	9	60%	60%	5	50	50	46	40%	40%
United Technologies	18	50	50	24	11	20	40	0*	0*
3M	2	100*	100*	45	2	3	33	75	86
TRW	10	20	25	13	63	71	39	71	71
IBM	18	100*	†	63	20	22	33	100*	100*
Du Pont	16	100*	†	51	61	61	43	0*	0*
Mobil	16	33	33	31	50	56	67	60	100
Borden	4	33	33	19	17	13	21	80	80
IC Industries	3	100*	100*	13	80	30	33	50	50
Tenneco	6	67	67	13	67	80	42	33	40
Beatrice	1	†	†	2	0	0	63	59	53
ITT	2	0	†	8	38	57	61	67	64
Rockwell	24	38	42	3	0	0	35	100	100
Allied Corp.	10	100	75	22	38	29	45	50	0
Exxon	5	0	0	61	27	19	100	80	50*
Sara Lee	1	†	†	4	75	100*	41	73	73
General Foods	4	†	†	6	67	50	42	86	83
Scovill	0	†	†	3	100	100*	45	80	100
Signal	4	†	†	29	20	11	67	50	50
ALCO Standard	0	†	†	1	†	†	63	79	81
W. R. Grace	7	33	38	10	71	71	39	65	65
General Electric	20	20	33	33	33	44	36	100	100
Wickes	0	†	†	17	63	57	60	80	75
Westinghouse	11	0*	0*	26	44	44	36	57	67
Xerox	6	100*	100*	28	50	56	22	100	100
Continental Group	6	67	67	17	14	0	40	83	100
General Mills	7	71	71	9	89	80	65	77	67
Gulf & Western	4	75	50	6	100	100	74	77	74
Cummins Engine	17	50	50	29	0	0	67	100	100
RCA	15	67	67	50	99	55	36	100	100
CBS	16	71	71	17	86	80	39	100	100
Average per company‡	7.9%	50.3%	48.9%	21.8%	44.0%	40.9%	46.1%	74.0%	74.4%

*Companies with two or fewer entries.

†No entries in this category.

‡Average excludes companies with two or fewer entries to minimize statistical distortions.

Note: Beatrice, Continental Group, General Foods, RCA, Scovill, and Signal were taken over as the study was being completed. Their data cover the period up through takeover but not subsequent divestments.

My data give a stark indication of the failure of corporate strategies.[2] Of the 33 companies, 6 had been taken over as my study was being completed (see the note on Exhibit 2). Only the lawyers, investment bankers, and original sellers have prospered in most of these acquisitions, not the shareholders.

PREMISES OF CORPORATE STRATEGY

Any successful corporate strategy builds on a number of premises. These are facts of life about diversification. They cannot be altered, and when ignored, they explain in part why so many corporate strategies fail.

Competition occurs at the business unit level. Diversified companies do not compete; only their business units do. Unless a corporate strategy places primary attention on nurturing the success of each unit, the strategy will fail, no matter how elegantly constructed. Successful corporate strategy must grow out of and reinforce competitive strategy.

Diversification inevitably adds costs and constraints to business units. Obvious costs such as the corporate overhead allocated to a unit may not be as important or subtle as the hidden costs and constraints. A business unit must explain its decisions to top management, spend time complying with planning and other corporate systems, live with parent company guidelines and personnel policies, and forgo the opportunity to motivate employees with direct equity ownership. These costs and constraints can be reduced but not entirely eliminated.

Shareholders can readily diversify themselves. Shareholders can diversify their own portfolios of stocks by selecting those that best match their preferences and risk profiles.[3] Shareholders can often diversify more cheaply than a corporation because they can buy shares at the market price and avoid hefty acquisition premiums.

These premises mean that corporate strategy cannot succeed unless it truly adds value—to business units by providing tangible benefits that offset the inherent costs of lost independence and to shareholders by diversifying in a way they could not replicate.

PASSING THE ESSENTIAL TESTS

To understand how to formulate corporate strategy, it is necessary to specify the conditions under which diversification will truly create shareholder value. These conditions can be summarized in three essential tests:

1. **The attractiveness test.** The industries chosen for diversification must be structurally attractive or capable of being made attractive.

---

[2]Some recent evidence also supports the conclusion that acquired companies often suffer eroding performance after acquisition. See Frederick M. Scherer, "Mergers, Sell-Offs and Managerial Behavior," in *The Economics of Strategic Planning*, ed. Lacy Glenn Thomas (Lexington, MA: Lexington Books, 1986), p. 143, and David A. Ravenscraft and Frederick M. Scherer, "Mergers and Managerial Performance," paper presented at the Conference on Takeovers and Contests for Corporate Control, Columbia Law School, 1985.

[3]This observation has been made by a number of authors. See, for example, Malcolm S. Salter and Wolf A. Weinhold, *Diversification Through Acquisition* (New York: Free Press, 1979).

Where the Data Come From

We studied the 1950–1988 diversification histories of 33 large diversified U.S. companies. They were chosen at random from many broad sectors of the economy.

To eliminate distortions caused by World War II, we chose 1950 as the base year and then identified each business the company was in. We tracked every acquisition, joint venture, and start-up made over this period—3,788 in all. We classified each as an entry into an entirely new sector or field (financial services, for example), a new industry within a field the company was already in (insurance, for example), or a geographic extension of an existing product or service. We also classified each new field as related or unrelated to existing units. Then we tracked whether and when each entry was divested or shut down and the number of years each remained part of the corporation.

Our sources included annual reports, 10K forms, the F&S Index, and Moody's, supplemented by our judgment and general knowledge of the industries involved. In a few cases, we asked the companies specific questions.

It is difficult to determine the success of an entry without knowing the full purchase or start-up price, the profit history, the amount and timing of ongoing investments made in the unit, whether any write-offs or write-downs were taken, and the selling price and terms of sale. Instead, we employed a relatively simple way to gauge success: *whether the entry was divested or shut down.* The underlying assumption is that a company will generally not divest or close down a successful business except in a comparatively few special cases. Companies divested many of the entries in our sample within five years, a reflection of disappointment with performance. Of the comparatively few divestments where the company disclosed a loss or a gain, the divestment resulted in a reported loss in more than half the cases.

The data in Exhibit 1 cover the entire 1950–1988 period. However, the divestment ratios in Exhibit 2 and Exhibit 3 do not compare entries and divestments over the entire period because doing so would overstate the success of diversification. Companies usually do not shut down or divest new entries immediately but hold them for some time to give them an opportunity to succeed. Our data show that the average holding period is 5 to slightly more than 10 years, though many divestments occur within 5 years. To accurately gauge the success of diversification, we calculated the percentage of entries made by 1975 and by 1980 that were divested or closed down as of January 1987. If we had included more recent entries, we would have biased upward our assessment of how successful these entries had been.

As compiled, these data probably understate the rate of failure. Companies tend to announce acquisitions and other forms of new entry with a flourish but divestments and shutdowns with a whimper, if at all. We have done our best to root out every such transaction, but we have undoubtedly missed some. There may also be new entries that we did not uncover, but our best impression is that the number is not large.

2. **The cost-of-entry test.** The cost of entry must not capitalize all the future profits.
3. **The better-off test.** Either the new unit must gain competitive advantage from its link with the corporation or vice versa.

Of course, most companies will make certain that their proposed strategies pass some of these tests. But my study clearly shows that when companies ignored one or two of them, the strategic results were disastrous.

How Attractive Is the Industry?

In the long run, the rate of return available from competing in an industry is a function of its underlying structure, which I have described in another HBR article.[4] An attractive industry with a high average return on

---

[4]See Michael E. Porter, "How Competitive Forces Shape Strategy," *Harvard Business Review* (March–April 1979), p. 86.

investment will be difficult to enter because entry barriers are high, suppliers and buyers have only modest bargaining power, substitute products or services are few, and the rivalry among competitors is stable. An unattractive industry like steel will have structural flaws, including a plethora of substitute materials, powerful and price-sensitive buyers, and excessive rivalry caused by high fixed costs and a large group of competitors, many of whom are state supported.

Diversification cannot create shareholder value unless new industries have favorable structures that support returns exceeding the cost of capital. If the industry doesn't have such returns, the company must be able to restructure the industry or gain a sustainable competitive advantage that leads to returns well above the industry average. An industry need not be attractive before diversification. In fact, a company might benefit from entering before the industry shows its full potential. The diversification can then transform the industry's structure.

In my research, I often found companies had suspended the attractiveness test because they had a vague belief that the industry "fit" very closely with their own businesses. In the hope that the corporate "comfort" they felt would lead to a happy outcome, the companies ignored fundamentally poor industry structures. Unless the close fit allows substantial competitive advantage, however, such comfort will turn into pain when diversification results in poor returns. Royal Dutch Shell and other leading oil companies have had this unhappy experience in a number of chemicals businesses, where poor industry structures overcame the benefits of vertical integration and skills in process technology.

Another common reason for ignoring the attractiveness test is a low entry cost. Sometimes the buyer has an inside track or the owner is anxious to sell. Even if the price is actually low, however, a one-shot gain will not offset a perpetually poor business. Almost always, the company finds it must reinvest in the newly acquired unit, if only to replace fixed assets and fund working capital.

Diversifying companies are also prone to use rapid growth or other simple indicators as a proxy for a target industry's attractiveness. Many that rushed into fast-growing industries (personal computers, video games, and robotics, for example) were burned because they mistook early growth for long-term profit potential. Industries are profitable not because they are sexy or high tech; they are profitable only if their structures are attractive.

What Is the Cost of Entry?

Diversification cannot build shareholder value if the cost of entry into a new business eats up its expected returns. Strong market forces, however, are working to do just that. A company can enter new industries by acquisition or start-up. Acquisitions expose it to an increasingly efficient merger market. An acquirer beats the market if it pays a price not fully reflecting the prospects of the new unit. Yet multiple bidders are commonplace, information flows rapidly, and investment bankers and other intermediaries work aggressively to make the market as efficient as possible. In recent years, new financial instruments such as junk bonds have brought new buyers into the market and made even large companies vulnerable to takeover. Acquisition premiums are high and reflect the acquired company's future prospects—sometimes too well. Philip Morris paid more than four times book value for The Seven-Up Company, for example. Simple arithmetic meant that profits had to more than quadruple to sustain the preacquisition ROI. Since there proved to be little Philip Morris could add in marketing prowess to the sophisticated marketing wars in the soft-drink industry, the result was the unsatisfactory financial performance of Seven-Up and ultimately the decision to divest.

In a start-up, the company must overcome entry barriers. It's a real catch-22 situation, however, since attractive industries are attractive because their entry barriers are high. Bearing the full cost of the entry barriers might well dissipate any potential profits. Otherwise, other entrants to the industry would have already eroded its profitability.

In the excitement of finding an appealing new business, companies sometimes forget to apply the cost-of-entry test. The more attractive a new industry, the more expensive it is to get into.

Will the Business Be Better Off?

A corporation must bring some significant competitive advantage to the new unit, or the new unit must offer potential for significant advantage to the corporation. Sometimes, the benefits to the new unit accrue only once, near the time of entry, when the parent instigates a major overhaul of its strategy or installs a first-rate management team. Other diversification yields ongoing competitive advantage if the new unit can market its product, through the well-developed distribution system of its sister units, for instance. This is one of the important underpinnings of the merger of Baxter Travenol and American Hospital Supply.

When the benefit to the new unit comes only once, the parent company has no rationale for holding the new unit in its portfolio over the long term. Once the results of the one-time improvement are clear, the diversified company no longer adds value to offset the inevitable costs imposed on the unit. It is best to sell the unit and free up corporate resources.

The better-off test does not imply that diversifying corporate risk creates shareholder value in and of itself. Doing something for shareholders that they can do themselves is not a basis for corporate strategy. (Only in the case of a privately held company, in which the company's and the shareholder's risk are the same, is diversification to reduce risk valuable for its own sake.) Diversification of risk should only be a by-product of corporate strategy, not a prime motivator.

Executives ignore the better-off test most of all or deal with it through arm waving or trumped-up logic rather than hard strategic analysis. One reason is that they confuse company size with shareholder value. In the drive to run a bigger company, they lose sight of their real job. They may justify the suspension of the better-off test by pointing to the way they manage diversity. By cutting corporate staff to the bone and giving business units nearly complete autonomy, they believe they avoid the pitfalls. Such thinking misses the whole point of diversification, which is to create shareholder value rather than to avoid destroying it.

CONCEPTS OF CORPORATE STRATEGY

The three tests for successful diversification set the standards that any corporate strategy must meet; meeting them is so difficult that most diversification fails. Many companies lack a clear concept of corporate strategy to guide their diversification or pursue a concept that does not address the tests. Others fail because they implement a strategy poorly.

My study has helped me identify four concepts of corporate strategy that have been put into practice—portfolio management, restructuring, transferring skills, and sharing activities. While the concepts are not always mutually exclusive, each rests on a different mechanism by which the corporation creates shareholder value and each requires the diversified company to manage and organize itself in a different way. The first two require no connections among business units; the second two depend on them. (See Exhibit 4.) While all four concepts of strategy have succeeded under the right circumstances, today some make more sense than others. Ignoring any of the concepts is perhaps the quickest road to failure.

Portfolio Management

The concept of corporate strategy most in use is portfolio management, which is based primarily on diversification through acquisition. The corporation acquires sound, attractive companies with competent managers who agree to stay on. While acquired units do not have to be in the same industries as existing units, the best portfolio managers generally limit their range of business in some way, in part to limit the specific expertise needed by top management.

The acquired units are autonomous, and the teams that run them are compensated according to unit results. The corporation supplies capital and works with each to infuse it with professional management techniques. At the same time, top management provides objective and dispassionate review of business unit results. Portfolio managers categorize units by potential and regularly transfer resources from units that generate cash to those with high potential and cash needs.

In a portfolio strategy, the corporation seeks to create shareholder value in a number of ways. It uses its expertise and analytical resources to spot attractive acquisition candidates that the individual shareholder could not. The company provides capital on favorable terms that reflect corporatewide fundraising ability. It introduces professional management skills and discipline. Finally, it provides high-quality review and coaching, unencumbered by conventional wisdom or emotional attachments to the business.

The logic of the portfolio management concept rests on a number of vital assumptions. If a company's diversification plan is to meet the attractiveness and cost-of-entry tests, it must find good but undervalued companies. Acquired companies must be truly undervalued because the parent does little for the new unit once it is acquired. To meet the better-off test, the benefits the corporation provides must yield a significant competitive advantage to acquired units. The style of operating through highly autonomous business units must both develop sound business strategies and motivate managers.

In most countries, the days when portfolio management was a valid concept of corporate strategy are past. In the face of increasingly well-developed

EXHIBIT 4   Concepts of Corporate Strategy

	Portfolio Management	Restructuring	Transferring Skills	Sharing Activities
Strategic prerequisites	Superior insight into identifying and acquiring undervalued companies Willingness to sell off losers quickly or to opportunistically divest good performers when buyers are willing to pay large premiums Broad guidelines for and constraints on the types of units in the portfolio so that senior management can play the review role effectively A private company or undeveloped capital markets Ability to shift away from portfolio management as the capital markets get more efficient or the company gets unwieldy	Superior insight into identifying restructuring opportunities Willingness and capability to intervene to transform acquired units Broad similarities among the units in the portfolio Willingness to cut losses by selling off units where restructuring proves unfeasible Willingness to sell units when restructuring is complete, the results are clear, and market conditions are favorable	Proprietary skills in activities important to competitive advantage in target industries Ability to accomplish the transfer of skills among units on an ongoing basis Acquisitions of beachhead positions in new industries as a base	Activities in existing units that can be shared with new business units to gain competitive advantage Benefits of sharing that outweigh the costs Both start-ups and acquisitions as entry vehicles Ability to overcome organizational resistance to business unit collaboration
Organizational prerequisites	Autonomous business units A very small, low-cost, corporate staff Incentives based largely on business unit results	Autonomous business units A corporate organization with the talent and resources to oversee the turnarounds and strategic repositionings of acquired units Incentives based largely on acquired units' results	Largely autonomous but collaborative business units High-level corporate staff members who see their role primarily as integrators Cross-business-unit committees, task forces, and other forums to serve as focal points for capturing and transferring skills Objectives of line managers that include skills transfer Incentives based in part on corporate results	Strategic business units that are encouraged to share activities An active strategic planning role at group, sector, and corporate levels High-level corporate staff members who see their roles primarily as integrators Incentives based heavily on group and corporate results
Common pitfalls	Pursuing portfolio management in countries with efficient capital marketing and a developed pool of professional management talent Ignoring the fact that industry structure is not attractive	Mistaking rapid growth of a "hot" industry as sufficient evidence of a restructuring opportunity Lacking the resolve or resources to take on troubled situations and to intervene in management Ignoring the fact that industry structure is not attractive Paying lip service to restructuring but actually practicing passive portfolio management	Mistaking similarity of comfort with new businesses as sufficient basis for diversification Providing no practical ways for skills transfer to occur Ignoring the fact that industry structure is not attractive	Sharing for its own sake rather than because it leads to competitive advantage Assuming sharing will occur naturally without senior management playing an active role Ignoring the fact that industry structure is not attractive

capital markets, attractive companies with good managements show up on everyone's computer screen and attract top dollar in terms of acquisition premium. Simply contributing capital isn't contributing much. A sound strategy can easily be funded; small to medium-size companies don't need a munificent parent.

Other benefits have also eroded. Large companies no longer corner the market for professional management skills; in fact, more and more observers believe managers cannot necessarily run anything in the absence of industry-specific knowledge and experience. Another supposed advantage of the portfolio management concept—dispassionate review—rests on similarly shaky ground since the added value of review alone is questionable in a portfolio of sound companies.

The benefit of giving business units complete autonomy is also questionable. Increasingly, a company's business units are interrelated, drawn together by new technology, broadening distribution channels, and changing regulations. Setting strategies of units independently may well undermine unit performance. The companies in my sample that have succeeded in diversification have recognized the value of interrelationships and understood that a strong sense of corporate identify is as important as slavish adherence to parochial business unit financial results.

But it is the sheer complexity of the management task that has ultimately defeated even the best portfolio managers. As the size of the company grows, portfolio managers need to find more and more deals just to maintain growth. Supervising dozens or even hundreds of disparate units and under chain-letter pressures to add more, management begins to make mistakes. At the same time, the inevitable costs of being part of a diversified company take their toll and unit performance slides while the whole company's ROI turns downward. Eventually, a new management team is installed that initiates wholesale divestments and pares down the company to its core businesses. The experiences of Gulf & Western, Consolidated Foods (now Sara Lee), and ITT are just a few comparatively recent examples. Reflecting these realities, the U.S. capital markets today reward companies that follow the portfolio management model with a "conglomerate discount"; they value the whole less than the sum of the parts.

In developing countries, where large companies are few, capital markets are undeveloped, and professional management is scarce, portfolio management still works. But it is no longer a valid model for corporate strategy in advanced economies. Nevertheless, the technique is in the limelight today in the United Kingdom, where it is supported so far by a newly energized stock market eager for excitement. But this enthusiasm will wane—as well it should. Portfolio management is no way to conduct corporate strategy.

Restructuring

Unlike its passive role as a portfolio manager, when it serves as banker and reviewer, a company that bases its strategy on restructuring becomes an active restructurer of business units. The new businesses are not necessarily related to existing units. All that is necessary is unrealized potential.

The restructuring strategy seeks out undeveloped, sick, or threatened organizations or industries on the threshold of significant change. The parent intervenes, frequently changing the unit management team, shifting strategy, or infusing the company with new technology. Then it may make follow-up acquisitions to build a critical mass and sell off unneeded or unconnected parts and thereby reduce the effective acquisition cost. The result is a strengthened company or a transformed industry. As a coda, the parent sells off the stronger unit once results are clear because the parent is no longer adding value and top management decides that its attention should be directed elsewhere. (See the insert "An Uncanny British Restructurer" for an example of restructuring.)

When well implemented, the restructuring concept is sound, for it passes the three tests of successful diversification. The restructurer meets the cost-of-entry test through the types of company it acquires. It limits acquisition premiums by buying companies with problems and lackluster images or by buying into industries with as yet unforeseen potential. Intervention by the corporation clearly meets the better-off test. Provided that the target industries are structurally attractive, the restructuring model can create enormous shareholder value. Some restructuring companies are Loew's, BTR, and General Cinema. Ironically, many of today's restructurers are profiting from yesterday's portfolio management strategies.

To work, the restructuring strategy requires a corporate management team with the insight to spot undervalued companies or positions in industries ripe for transformation. The same insight is necessary to actually turn the units around even though they are in new and unfamiliar businesses.

These requirements expose the restructurer to considerable risk and usually limit the time in which the company can succeed at the strategy. The most skillful proponents understand this problem, recognize their mistakes, and move decisively to dispose of them. The best companies realize they are not just acquiring companies but restructuring an industry. Unless they can integrate the acquisitions to create a whole new strategic position, they are just portfolio managers in disguise. Another important difficulty surfaces if so many other companies join the action that they deplete the pool of suitable candidates and bid their prices up.

Perhaps the greatest pitfall, however, is that companies find it very hard to dispose of business units once they are restructured and performing well. Human nature fights economic rationale. Size supplants shareholder value as the corporate goal. The company does not sell a unit even though the company no longer adds value to the unit. While the transformed units would be better off in another company that had related business, the restructuring company instead retains them. Gradually, it becomes a portfolio manager. The parent company's ROI declines as the need for reinvestment in the units and normal business risks eventually offset restructuring's one-shot gain. The perceived need to keep growing intensifies the pace of acquisition; errors result and standards fall. The restructuring company turns into a conglomerate with returns that only equal the average of all industries at best.

Transferring Skills

The purpose of the first two concepts of corporate strategy is to create value through a company's relationship with each autonomous unit. The corporation's role is to be a selector, banker, and an intervenor.

The last two concepts exploit the interrelationships between businesses. In articulating them, however, one comes face-to-face with the often ill-defined concept of synergy. If you believe the text of the countless corporate annual reports, just about anything is related to just about anything else! But imagined synergy is much more common than real synergy. GM's purchase of Hughes Aircraft simply because cars were going electronic and Hughes was an electronics concern demonstrates the folly of paper synergy. Such corporate relatedness is an ex post facto rationalization of a diversification undertaken for other reasons.

Even synergy that is clearly defined often fails to materialize. Instead of cooperating, business units often compete. A company that can define the synergies it is pursuing still faces significant organizational impediments in achieving them.

But the need to capture the benefits of relationships between businesses has never been more important. Technological and competitive developments already link many businesses and are creating new possibilities for competitive advantage. In such sectors as financial services, computing, office equipment, entertainment, and health care, interrelationships among previously distinct businesses are perhaps the central concern of strategy.

To understand the role of relatedness in corporate strategy, we must give new meaning to this often ill-defined idea. I have identified a good way to start—the value chain.[5] Every business unit is a collection of discrete activities ranging from sales to accounting that allow it to compete. I call them value activities. It is at this level, not in the company as a whole, that the unit achieves competitive advantage.

I group these activities in nine categories. *Primary* activities create the product or service, deliver and market it, and provide after-sale support. The categories of primary activities are inbound logistics, operations, outbound logistics, marketing and sales, and service. *Support* activities provide the input and infrastructure that allow the primary activities to take place. The categories are company infrastructure, human resource management, technology development, and procurement.

The value chain defines the two types of interrelationships that may create synergy. The first is a company's ability to transfer skills or expertise among similar value chains. The second is the ability to share activities. Two business units, for example, can share the same sales force or logistics network.

The value chain helps expose the last two (and most important) concepts of corporate strategy. The transfer of skills among business units in the diversified company is the basis for one concept. While each business unit has a separate value chain, knowledge about how to perform activities is transferred among the units. For example, a toiletries business unit, expert in the marketing of convenience products, transmits ideas on new positioning concepts, promotional techniques, and packaging possibilities to a newly acquired unit that sells cough syrup. Newly entered industries can benefit from the expertise of existing units and vice versa.

These opportunities arise when business units have similar buyers or channels, similar value activities like government relations or procurement, similarities in the broad configuration of the value chain (for example, managing a

---

[5]Michael E. Porter, *Competitive Advantage* (New York: Free Press, 1985).

multisite service organization), or the same strategic concept (for example, low cost). Even though the units operate separately, such similarities allow the sharing of knowledge.

Of course, some similarities are common; one can imagine them at some level between almost any pair of businesses. Countless companies have fallen into the trap of diversifying too readily because of similarities; mere similarity is not enough.

Transferring skills leads to competitive advantage only if the similarities among businesses meet three conditions:

1. The activities involved in the businesses are similar enough that sharing expertise is meaningful. Broad similarities (marketing intensiveness, for example, or a common core process technology such as bending metal) are not a sufficient basis for diversification. The resulting ability to transfer skills is likely to have little impact on competitive advantage.

2. The transfer of skills involves activities important to competitive advantage. Transferring skills in peripheral activities such as government relations or real estate in consumer goods units may be beneficial but is not a basis for diversification.

3. The skills transferred represent a significant source of competitive advantage for the receiving unit. The expertise or skills to be transferred are both advanced and proprietary enough to be beyond the capabilities of competitors.

The transfer of skills is an active process that significantly changes the strategy or operations of the receiving unit. The prospect or change must be specific and identifiable. Almost guaranteeing that no shareholder value will be created, too many companies are satisfied with vague prospects or faint hopes that skills will transfer. The transfer of skills does not happen by accident or by osmosis. The company will have to reassign critical personnel, even on a permanent basis, and the participation and support of high-level management in skills transfer is essential. Many companies have been defeated at skills transfer because they have not provided their business units with any incentives to participate.

Transferring skills meets the tests of diversification if the company truly mobilizes proprietary expertise across units. This makes certain the company can offset the acquisition premium or lower the cost of overcoming entry barriers.

The industries the company chooses for diversification must pass the attractiveness test. Even a close fit that reflects opportunities to transfer skills may not overcome poor industry structure. Opportunities to transfer skills, however, may help the company transform the structures of newly entered industries and send them in favorable directions.

The transfer of skills can be one-time or ongoing. If the company exhausts opportunities to infuse new expertise into a unit after the initial post-acquisition period, the unit should ultimately be sold. The corporation is no longer creating shareholder value. Few companies have grasped this point, however, and many gradually suffer mediocre returns. Yet a company diversified into well-chosen businesses can transfer skills eventually in many directions. If corporate management conceives of its role in this way and creates appropriate organizational mechanisms to facilitate cross-unit interchange, the opportunities to share expertise will be meaningful.

An Uncanny British Restructurer

Hanson Trust, on its way to becoming Britain's largest company, is one of several skillful followers of the restructuring concept. A conglomerate with units in many industries, Hanson might seem on the surface a portfolio manager. In fact, Hanson and one or two other conglomerates have a much more effective corporate strategy. Hanson has acquired companies such as London Brick, Eveready Batteries, and SCM, which the city of London rather disdainfully calls "low tech."

Although a mature company suffering from low growth, the typical Hanson target is not just in any industry; it has an attractive structure. Its customer and supplier power is low and rivalry with competitors moderate. The target is a market leader, rich in assets but formerly poor in management. Hanson pays little of the present value of future cash flow out in an acquisition premium and reduces purchase price even further by aggressively selling off businesses that it cannot improve. In this way, it recoups just over a third of the cost of a typical acquisition during the first six months of ownership. Imperial Group's plush properties in London lasted barely two months under Hanson ownership, while Hanson's recent sale of Courage Breweries to Elders recouped £1.4 billion of the original £2.1 billion acquisition price of Imperial Group.

Like the best restructurers, Hanson approached each unit with a modus operandi that it has perfected through repetition.

Hanson emphasizes low costs and tight financial controls. It has cut an average of 25% of labor costs out of acquired companies, slashed fixed overheads, and tightened capital expenditures. To reinforce its strategy of keeping costs low, Hanson carves out detailed one-year financial budgets with divisional managers and (through generous use of performance-related bonuses and share option schemes) gives them incentive to deliver the goods.

It's too early to tell whether Hanson will adhere to the last tenet of restructuring—selling turned-around units once the results are clear. If it succumbs to the allure of bigness, Hanson may take the course of the failed U.S. conglomerates.

By using both acquisitions and internal development, companies can build a transfer-of-skills strategy. The presence of a strong base of skills sometimes creates the possibility for internal entry instead of the acquisition of a going concern. Successful diversifiers that employ the concept of skills transfer may, however, often acquire a company in the target industry as a beachhead and then build on it with their internal expertise. By doing so, they can reduce some of the risks of internal entry and speed up the process. Two companies that have diversified using the transfer-of-skills concept are 3M and Pepsico.

Sharing Activities

The fourth concept of corporate strategy is based on sharing activities in the value chains among business units. Procter & Gamble, for example, employs a common physical distribution system and sales force in both paper towels and disposable diapers. McKesson, a leading distribution company, will handle such diverse lines as pharmaceuticals and liquor through superwarehouses.

The ability to share activities is a potent basis for corporate strategy because sharing often enhances competitive advantage by lowering cost or raising differentiation. But not all sharing leads to competitive advantage, and companies can encounter deep organizational resistance to even beneficial sharing possibilities. These hard truths have led many companies to reject synergy prematurely and retreat to the false simplicity of portfolio management.

A cost-benefit analysis of prospective sharing opportunities can determine whether synergy is possible. Sharing can lower costs if it achieves economies

---

Adding Value with Hospitality

Marriott began in the restaurant business in Washington, D.C. Because its customers often ordered takeouts on the way to the national airport, Marriott eventually entered airline catering. From there, it jumped into food service management for institutions. Marriott then began broadening its base of family restaurants and entered the hotel industry. More recently, it has moved into restaurants, snack bars, and merchandise shops in airport terminals and into gourmet restaurants. In addition, Marriott has branched out from its hotel business into cruise ships, theme parks, wholesale travel agencies, budget motels, and retirement centers.

Marriott's diversification has exploited well-developed skills in food service and hospitality. Marriott's kitchens prepare food according to more than 6,000 standardized recipe cards; hotel procedures are also standardized and painstakingly documented in elaborate manuals. Marriott shares a number of important activities across units. A shared procurement and distribution system for food serves all Marriott units through nine regional procurement centers. As a result, Marriott earns 50 percent higher margins on food service than any other hotel company. Marriott also has a fully integrated real estate unit that brings corporatewide power to bear on site acquisitions as well as on the designing and building of all Marriott locations.

Marriott's diversification strategy balances acquisitions and start-ups. Start-ups or small acquisitions are used for initial entry, depending on how close the opportunities for sharing are. To expand its geographic base, Marriott acquires companies and then disposes of the parts that do not fit.

Apart from this success, it is important to note that Marriott has divested 36 percent of both its acquisitions and its start-ups. While this is an above-average record, Marriott's mistakes are quite illuminating. Marriott has largely failed in diversifying into gourmet restaurants, theme parks, cruise ships, and wholesale travel agencies. In the first three businesses, Marriott discovered it could not transfer skills despite apparent similarities. Standardized menus did not work well in gourmet restaurants. Running cruise ships and theme parks was based more on entertainment and pizzazz than the carefully disciplined management of hotels and mid-price restaurants. The wholesale travel agencies were ill fated from the start because Marriott had to compete with an important customer for its hotels and had no proprietary skills or opportunities to share with which to add value.

---

of scale, boosts the efficiency of utilization, or helps a company move more rapidly down the learning curve. The costs of General Electric's advertising, sales, and after-sales service activities in major appliances are low because they are spread over a wide range of appliance products. Sharing can also enhance the potential for differentiation. A shared order-processing system, for instance, may allow new features and services that a buyer will value. Sharing can also reduce the cost of differentiation. A shared service network, for example, may make more advanced, remote servicing technology economically feasible. Often, sharing will allow an activity to be wholly reconfigured in ways that can dramatically raise competitive advantage.

Sharing must involve activities that are significant to competitive advantage, not just any activity. P&G's distribution system is such an instance in the diaper and paper towel business, where products are bulky and costly to ship. Conversely, diversification based on the opportunities to share only corporate overhead is rarely, if ever, appropriate.

Sharing activities inevitably involves costs that the benefits must outweigh. One cost is the greater coordination required to manage a shared activity. More important is the need to compromise the design or performance of an activity so that it can be shared. A salesperson handling the products of two business units, for example, must operate in a way that is usually not what either unit would choose were it independent. And if compromise greatly erodes the unit's effectiveness, then sharing may reduce rather than enhance competitive advantage.

Many companies have only superficially identified their potential for sharing. Companies also merge activities without consideration of whether they are sensitive to economies of scale. When they are not, the coordination costs kill the benefits. Companies compound such errors by not identifying costs of sharing in advance, when steps can be taken to minimize them. Costs of compromise can frequently be mitigated by redesigning the activity for sharing. The shared salesperson, for example, can be provided with a remote computer terminal to boost productivity and provide more customer information. Jamming business units together without such thinking exacerbates the costs of sharing.

Despite such pitfalls, opportunities to gain advantage from sharing activities have proliferated because of momentous developments in technology, deregulation, and competition. The infusion of electronics and information systems into many industries creates new opportunities to link businesses. The corporate strategy of sharing can involve both acquisition and internal development. Internal development is often possible because the corporation can bring to bear clear resources in launching a new unit. Start-ups are less difficult to integrate than acquisitions. Companies using the shared-activities concept can also make acquisitions as beachhead landings into a new industry and then integrate the units through sharing with other units. Prime examples that have diversified via using shared activities include P&G, Du Pont, and IBM. The fields into which each has diversified are a cluster of tightly related units. Marriott illustrates both successes and failures in sharing activities over time. (See the insert "Adding Value with Hospitality.")

Following the shared-activities model requires an organizational context in which business unit collaboration is encouraged and reinforced. Highly autonomous business units are inimical to such collaboration. The company must put into place a variety of what I call horizontal mechanisms—a strong sense of corporate identity, a clear corporate mission statement that emphasizes the importance of integrating business unit strategies, an incentive system that rewards more than just business unit results, cross-business-unit task forces, and other methods of integrating.

A corporate strategy based on shared activities clearly meets the better-off test because business units gain ongoing tangible advantages from others within the corporation. It also meets the cost-of-entry test by reducing the expense of surmounting the barriers to internal entry. Other bids for acquisitions that do not share opportunities will have lower reservation prices. Even widespread opportunities for sharing activities do not allow a company to suspend the attractiveness test, however. Many diversifiers have made the critical mistake of equating the close fit of a target industry with attractiveness diversification. Target industries must pass the strict requirement test of having an attractive structure as well as a close fit in opportunities if diversification is to ultimately succeed.

CHOOSING A CORPORATE STRATEGY

Each concept of corporate strategy allows the diversified company to create shareholder value in a different way. Companies can succeed with any of the concepts if they clearly define the corporation's role and objectives, have the skills necessary for meeting the concept's prerequisites, organize themselves to manage diversity in a way that fits the strategy, and find themselves in an appropriate capital market environment. The caveat is that portfolio management is only sensible in limited circumstances.

A company's choice of corporate strategy is partly a legacy of its past. If its business units are in unattractive industries, the company must start from scratch. If the company has few truly proprietary skills or activities it can share in related diversification, then its initial diversification must rely on other concepts. Yet corporate strategy should not be a once-and-for-all choice but a vision that can evolve. A company should choose its long-term preferred concept and then proceed pragmatically toward it from its initial starting point.

Both the strategic logic and the experience of the companies I studied over the last decade suggest that a company will create shareholder value through diversification to a greater and greater extent as its strategy moves from portfolio management toward sharing activities. Because they do not rely on superior insight or other questionable assumptions about the company's capabilities, sharing activities and transferring skills offer the best avenues for value creation.

Each concept of corporate strategy is not mutually exclusive of those that come before, a potent advantage of the third and fourth concepts. A company can employ a restructuring strategy at the same time it transfers skills or shares activities. A strategy based on shared activities becomes more powerful if business units can also exchange skills. As the Marriott case illustrates, a company can often pursue the two strategies together and even incorporate some of the principles of restructuring with them. When it chooses industries in which to transfer skills or share activities, the company can also investigate the possibility of transforming the industry structure. When a company bases its strategy on interrelationships, it has a broader basis on which to create shareholder value than if it rests its entire strategy on transforming companies in unfamiliar industries.

My study supports the soundness of basing a corporate strategy on the transfer of skills or shared activities. The data on the sample companies' diversification programs illustrate some important characteristics of successful diversifiers. They have made a disproportionately low percentage of unrelated acquisitions, *unrelated* being defined as having no clear opportunity to transfer skills or share important activities (see Exhibit 3). Even successful diversifiers such as 3M, IBM, and TRW have terrible records when they have strayed into unrelated acquisitions. Successful acquirers diversify into fields, each of which is related to many others. Procter & Gamble and IBM, for example, operate in 18 or 19 interrelated fields respectively and so enjoy numerous opportunities to transfer skills and share activities.

Companies with the best acquisition records tend to make heavier-than-average use of start-ups and joint ventures. Most companies shy away from modes of entry besides acquisition. My results cast doubt on the conventional wisdom regarding start-ups. Exhibit 3 demonstrates that while joint ventures are about as risky as acquisitions, start-ups are not. Moreover, successful companies often have very good records with start-up units, as 3M, P&G, Johnson & Johnson, IBM, and United Technologies illustrate. When a company has the internal strength to start up a unit, it can be safer and less costly to launch a company than to rely solely on an acquisition and then have to deal with the problem of integration. Japanese diversification histories support the soundness of start-up as an entry alternative.

My data also illustrate that none of the concepts of corporate strategy works when industry structure is poor or implementation is bad, no matter how related the industries are. Xerox acquired companies in related industries, but the businesses had poor structures and its skills were insufficient to provide enough competitive advantage to offset implementation problems.

An Action Program

To translate the principles of corporate strategy into successful diversification, a company must first take an objective look at its existing businesses and the value added by the corporation. Only through such an assessment can an understanding of good corporate strategy grow. That understanding should guide future diversification as well as the development of skills and activities with which to select further new businesses. The following action program provides a concrete approach to conducting such a review. A company can choose a corporate strategy by:

   1. **Identifying the interrelationships among already existing business units.**

A company should begin to develop a corporate strategy by identifying all the opportunities it has to share activities or transfer skills in its existing portfolio of business units. The company will not only find ways to enhance the competitive advantage of existing units but also come upon several possible diversification avenues. The lack of meaningful interrelationships in the portfolio is an equally important finding, suggesting the need to justify the value added by the corporation or, alternately, a fundamental restructuring.

   2. **Selecting the core business that will be the foundation of the corporate strategy.**

Successful diversification starts with an understanding of the core businesses that will serve as the basis for corporate strategy. Core businesses are those that are in an attractive industry, have the potential to achieve sustainable competitive advantage, have important interrelationships with other business units, and provide skills or activities that represent a base from which to diversify.

The company must first make certain its core businesses are on sound footing by upgrading management, internationalizing strategy, or improving technology. My study shows that geographic extensions of existing units, whether by acquisition, joint venture, or start-up, had a substantially lower divestment rate than diversification.

The company must then patiently dispose of the units that are not core businesses. Selling them will free resources that could be better deployed elsewhere. In some cases disposal implies immediate liquidation, while in others the company should dress up the units and wait for a propitious market or a particularly eager buyer.

   3. **Creating horizontal organizational mechanisms to facilitate interrelationships among the core businesses and lay the groundwork for future related diversification.**

Top management can facilitate interrelationships by emphasizing cross-unit collaboration, grouping units organizationally and modifying incentives, and taking steps to build a strong sense of corporate identity.

4. Pursuing diversification opportunities that allow shared activities.

This concept of corporate strategy is the most compelling, provided a company's strategy passes all three tests. A company should inventory activities in existing business units that represent the strongest foundation for sharing, such as strong distribution channels or world-class technical facilities. These will in turn lead to potential new business areas. A company can use acquisitions as a beachhead or employ start-ups to exploit internal capabilities and minimize integrating problems.

5. Pursuing diversification through the transfer of skills if opportunities for sharing activities are limited or exhausted.

Companies can pursue this strategy through acquisition, although they may be able to use start-ups if their existing units have important skills they can readily transfer.

Such diversification is often riskier because of the tough conditions necessary for it to work. Given the uncertainties, a company should avoid diversifying on the basis of skills transfer alone. Rather it should be viewed as a stepping-stone to subsequent diversification using shared activities. New industries should be chosen that will lead naturally to other businesses. The goal is to build a cluster of related and mutually reinforcing business units. The strategy's logic implies that the company should not set the rate of return standards for the initial foray into a new sector too high.

6. Pursuing a strategy of restructuring if this fits the skills of management or no good opportunities exist for forging corporate interrelationships.

When a company uncovers undermanaged companies and can deploy adequate management talent and resources to the acquired units, then it can use a restructuring strategy. The more developed the capital markets and the more active the market for companies, the more restructuring will require a patient search for that special opportunity rather than headlong race to acquire as many bad apples as possible. Restructuring can be a permanent strategy, as it is with Loew's, or a way to build a group of businesses that supports a shift to another corporate strategy.

7. Paying dividends so that the shareholders can be the portfolio managers.

Paying dividends is better than destroying shareholder value through diversification based on shaky underpinnings. Tax considerations, which some companies cite to avoid dividends, are hardly legitimate reason to diversify if a company cannot demonstrate the capacity to do it profitably.

Creating a Corporate Theme

Defining a corporate theme is a good way to ensure that the corporation will create shareholder value. Having the right theme helps unite the efforts of business units and reinforces the ways they interrelate as well as guides the choice of new businesses to enter. NEC Corporation, with its "C&C" theme, provides a good example. NEC integrates its computer, semiconductor, telecommunications, and consumer electronics businesses by merging computers and communication.

It is all too easy to create a shallow corporate theme. CBS wanted to be an "entertainment company," for example, and built a group of businesses related to leisure time. It entered such industries as toys, crafts, musical instruments, sports teams, and hi-fi retailing. While this corporate theme sounded good, close listening revealed its hollow ring. None of these businesses had any significant opportunity to share activities or transfer skills among themselves or with CBS's traditional broadcasting and record businesses. They were all sold, often at significant losses, except for a few of CBS's publishing-related units. Saddled with the worst acquisition record in my study, CBS has eroded the shareholder value created through its strong performance in broadcasting and records.

Moving from competitive strategy to corporate strategy is the business equivalent of passing through the Bermuda Triangle. The failure of corporate strategy reflects the fact that most diversified companies have failed to think in terms of how they really add value. A corporate strategy that truly enhances the competitive advantage of each business unit is the best defense against the corporate raider. With a sharper focus on the tests of diversification and the explicit choice of a clear concept of corporate strategy, companies' diversification track records from now on can look a lot different.

Author's note: The research for this article was done with the able assistance of my research associate Cheng G. Ong. Malcolm S. Salter, Andrall E. Pearson, A. Michael Kechner, and the Monitor Company also provided helpful comments.

ATTILAISMS: SELECTED THOUGHTS OF ATTILA THE HUN

Wess Roberts, Ph.D.

Note: This reading is excerpted from a witty book entitled *Leadership Secrets of Attila the Hun*; what follows consists of a series of proverbs and "truths" about the traits and behavior of leaders, as well as common sense advice about what to do and not do in managing people..

ADVICE AND COUNSEL

- Written reports have purpose only if read by the king.
- A king with chieftains who always agree with him reaps the counsel of mediocrity.
- A wise chieftain never kills the Hun bearing bad news. Rather, the wise chieftain kills the Hun who fails to deliver bad news.
- A chieftain who asks the wrong questions always hears the wrong answers.
- A wise chieftain never asks a question for which he doesn't want to hear the answer.

CHARACTER

- The greatness of a Hun is measured by the sacrifices he is willing to make for the good of the nation.
- A chieftain should always rise above pettiness and cause his Huns to do the same.
- A chieftain cannot win if he loses his nerve. He should be self-confident and self-reliant and even if he does not win, he will know he has done his best.
- A chieftain does not have to be brilliant to be successful, but he must have an insatiable hunger for victory, absolute belief in his cause, and an invincible courage that enables him to resist those who would otherwise discourage him.
- Seldom are self-centered, conceited, and self-admiring chieftains great leaders, but they are great idolizers of themselves.
- Great chieftains never take themselves too seriously.
- A wise chieftain adapts—he doesn't compromise.
- Chieftains who drink with their Huns become one with them and are no longer their chieftain.
- Weak chieftains surround themselves with weak Huns.
- Strong chieftains surround themselves with strong Huns.
- As a chieftain achieves greater success, the jealousy others feel for him intensifies.

Source: Reprinted from *Leadership Secrets of Attila the Hun* (New York: Warner Books, 1987), pp. 101–10. Used with permission.

COURAGE

- Huns must learn early that working through a hardship is an experience that influences them all the days of their lives.
- Successful Huns learn to deal with adversity and to overcome mistakes.
- A Hun can achieve anything for which he is willing to pay the price. Competition thins out at the top of the ranks.

DECISION MAKING

- Every decision involves some risk.
- Time does not always improve a situation for a king or his Huns.
- Fundamental errors are inescapable when the unqualified are allowed to exercise judgment and make decisions.
- Quick decisions are not always the best decisions. On the other hand, unhurried decisions are not always the best decisions.
- Chieftains should never rush into confrontations.
- A chieftain's confidence in his decision making preempts name-dropping to his Huns.
- It is unfortunate when final decisions are made by chieftains headquartered miles away from the front, where they can only guess at conditions and potentialities known only to the captain on the battlefield.
- When victory will not be sweet, the chieftain must keep his Huns from war.
- The ability to make difficult decisions separates chieftains from Huns.

DELEGATION

- Wise chieftains never place their Huns in situations where their weaknesses will prevail over their strengths.
- Good Huns normally achieve what their chieftain expects from them.
- A wise chieftain never expects his Huns to act beyond their wisdom and understanding.
- A wise chieftain always gives tough assignments to Huns who can rise to the occasion.
- Abdication is not delegation. Abdication is a sign of weakness. Delegation is a sign of strength.

DEVELOPING CHIEFTAINS

- Strong chieftains always have strong weaknesses. A king's duty is to make a chieftain's strengths prevail.
- Huns learn less from success than they do from failure.
- Huns learn much faster when faced with adversity.
- A good chieftain takes risks by delegating to an inexperienced Hun in order to strengthen his leadership abilities.

- The experience of Huns must be structured to allow them to broaden and deepen themselves to develop the character they will need when appointed a chieftain.
- Huns are best prepared to become chieftains when given appropriate challenges at successively higher levels of responsibility.
- If it were easy to be a chieftain, everyone would be one.
- Without challenge, a Hun's potential is never realized.
- Appropriate stress is essential in developing chieftains.

DIPLOMACY AND POLITICS

- When in a political war, a Hun must always keep an eye to the rear.
- The essence of Hunnish victory lies in the answers to the questions Where? and When?
- Huns should engage only in wars they can win.
- Huns may enter war as the result of failed diplomacy; however, war may be necessary for diplomacy to begin.
- For Huns, conflict is a natural state.
- Huns only make enemies on purpose.
- Huns never take by force what can be gained by diplomacy.
- Chieftains should remember that hospitality, warmth and courtesy will captivate even the most oppressive foe.
- Chieftains are often betrayed by those they trust most.

GOALS

- Superficial goals lead to superficial results.
- As a nation, we would accomplish more if Huns behaved as though national goals were as important to them as personal goals.
- Critical to a Hun's success is a clear understanding of what the king wants.
- A Hun's goals should always be worthy of his efforts.
- A Hun without a purpose will never know when he has achieved it.
- A Hun's conformance does not always result in desired performance.
- Chieftains should always aim high, going after things that will make a difference rather than seeking the safe path of mediocrity.

LEADERS AND LEADERSHIP

- Kings should always appoint their best Huns as chieftains, no matter how much they are needed in their current position.
- Never appoint acting chieftains. Put the most capable Hun in charge, give him both the responsibility and authority, then hold him accountable.
- A wise chieftain never depends on luck. Rather, he always trusts his future to hard work, stamina, tenacity, and a positive attitude.
- A wise chieftain knows he is responsible for the welfare of his Huns and acts accordingly.

- Being a leader of the Huns is often a lonely job.
- Once committed to action, chieftains must press for victory, not for stalemate—and surely not for compromise.
- Shared risk-taking will weld the relationship of a chieftain and his Huns.
- Strong chieftains stimulate and inspire the performance of their Huns.
- The best chieftains develop the ability to ask the right questions at the right time.
- A chieftain can never be in charge if he rides in the rear.

PERCEPTIONS AND PUBLICITY

- In tough times, the nation will always call the meanest chieftain to lead.
- A Hun who takes himself too seriously has lost his perspective.
- A Hun's perception is reality for him.
- Huns who appear to be busy are not always working.
- It is best if your friends and foes speak well of you; however, it is better for them to speak poorly of you than not at all. When nothing can be said of a Hun, he has probably accomplished nothing very well.
- Contrary to what most chieftains think, you're not remembered by what you did in the past, but by what most Huns think you did.

PERSONAL ACHIEVEMENT

- There is more nobility in being a good Hun than in being a poor chieftain.
- Even the Romans have the strength to endure the misfortunes they bring on others.
- If all Huns were blind, a one-eyed warrior would be king.
- Great chieftains accept failure at some things in order to excel in more important ones.
- Every Hun is responsible for shaping his life's circumstances and experiences into success—no other Hun, and certainly no Roman, can do for a Hun what he neglects to do for himself.

PROBLEMS AND SOLUTIONS

- Huns should be taught to focus on opportunities rather than on problems.
- Some Huns have solutions for which there are no problems.

REWARD AND PUNISHMENT

- If an incompetent chieftain is removed, seldom do we appoint his highest-ranking subordinate to his place. For when a chieftain has failed, so likewise have his subordinate leaders.
- If you tell a Hun he is doing a good job when he isn't, he will not listen long and, worse, will not believe praise when it is justified.

TOLERANCE

- Every Hun has value—even if only to serve as a bad example.
- The error in appointing an incompetent chieftain is in leaving him in a position of authority over other Huns.
- To experience the strength of chieftains we must tolerate some of their weaknesses.
- Suffer long for mediocre but loyal Huns. Suffer not for competent but disloyal Huns.

TRAINING

- Adequate training of Huns is essential to war and cannot be disregarded by chieftains in more peaceful times.
- Teachable skills are for developing Huns. Learnable skills are reserved for chieftains.
- The consequence for not adequately training your Huns is their failure to accomplish that which is expected of them.

CORPORATIONS, CULTURE, AND COMMITMENT: MOTIVATION AND SOCIAL CONTROL IN ORGANIZATIONS

Charles O'Reilly, University of California at Berkeley

Corporate culture is receiving much attention in the business press. A recent article in *Fortune* describes how the CEO at Black & Decker "transformed an entire corporate *culture*, replacing a complacent manufacturing mentality with an almost manic, market-driven way of doing things."[1] Similarly, the success of Food Lion (a $3 billion food-market chain that has grown at an annual rate of 37 percent over the past 20 years with annual returns on equity of 24 percent) is attributed to a culture which emphasizes "hard work, simplicity, and frugality."[2] Other well-known firms such as 3M, Johnson & Johnson, Apple, and Kimberly-Clark have been routinely praised for their innovative cultures.[3] Even the success of Japanese firms in the U.S. has been partly attributed to their ability to change the traditional culture developed under American managers. Peters and Waterman report how a U.S. television manufacturing plant, under Japanese management, reduced its defect rate from 140 to 6, its complaint rate from 70 percent to 7 percent, and the turnover rate among employees from 30 percent to 1 percent, all due to a changed management philosophy and culture.[4]

Even more dramatic is the turnaround at the New United Motors Manufacturing Incorporated (NUMMI) plant in Fremont, California. When General Motors closed this facility in 1982, it was one of the worst plants in the GM assembly division with an 18 percent daily absenteeism rate and a long history of conflict in its labor relations. The plant reopened as a joint venture between Toyota and GM in 1983. Over 85 percent of the original labor force was rehired, and workers are still represented by the UAW. Although the technology used is vintage 1970s and the plant is not as automated as many others within GM and Toyota, productivity is almost double what GM gets in other facilities. In 1987, it took an estimated 20.8 hours to produce a car at NUMMI versus 40.7 in other GM plants and 18.0 at Toyota. Quality of the NUMMI automobiles is the highest in the GM system, based on both internal audits and owner surveys, and absenteeism is at 2 percent compared to 8 percent at other GM facilities. What accounts for this remarkable success? According to one account, "At the system's core is a *culture* in which the assembly line workers maintain their machines, ensure the quality of their work, and improve the production process."[5]

Source: Copyright 1989 by The Regents of the University of California. Reprinted from *California Management Review* 31, no. 4 (Summer 1989), pp. 9–25. By permission of The Regents.

[1]*Fortune*, January 2, 1989.

[2]*Fortune*, August 15, 1988.

[3]*Fortune*, June 6, 1988.

[4]T. Peters and R. H. Waterman, *In Search of Excellence: Lessons From American's Best-Run Companies* (New York: Harper & Row, 1982), p. 32.

[5]*Fortune*, January 30, 1989.

But a culture is not always a positive force. It has also been implicated when firms run into difficulties. The CEO of financially troubled Computerland, William Tauscher, has attempted to restructure the firm, noting that "a low-cost culture is a must."[6] Henry Wendt, CEO of SmithKline Beckman, has attributed his firm's current difficulties to complacency. "We've been victims of our own success. . . . I want to create a new culture."[7] Corporate culture has also been implicated in problems faced by Sears, Caterpillar, Bank of America, Polaroid, General Motors, and others. Even difficulties in mergers and acquisitions are sometimes attributed to cultural conflicts which make integration of separate units difficult. Failure to merge two cultures can lead to debilitating conflict, a loss of talent, and an inability to reap the benefits of synergy.

But what is really meant when one refers to a firm's "culture"? Do all organizations have them? Are they always important? Even if we can identify cultures, do we know enough about how they work to manage them? Four major questions need to be answered:

- What is culture?
- From a manager's perspective, when is culture important?
- What is the process through which cultures are developed and maintained?
- How can cultures be managed?

WHAT IS CULTURE?

If culture is to be analyzed and managed, it is important that we be clear about what is meant by the term. Failure to clearly specify what "culture" is can result in confusion, misunderstanding, and conflict about its basic function and importance.

Culture as Control

Clearly, little would get done by or in organizations if some control systems were not in place to direct and coordinate activities. In fact, organizations are often seen to be efficient and effective solely because control systems operate.[8]

But what is a "control system"? A generic definition might be that a control system is "the knowledge that someone who knows and cares is paying close attention to what we do and can tell us when deviations are occurring." Although broad, this definition encompasses traditional formal control systems ranging from planning and budgeting systems to performance appraisals. According to this definition, control systems work when those who are monitored are aware that someone who matters, such as a boss or staff department, is paying attention and is likely to care when things aren't going according to plan.

---

[6]*Business Week*, October 10, 1988.

[7]*Business Week*, October 10, 1988.

[8]A. Wilkins and W. Ouchi, "Efficient Cultures: Exploring the Relationship between Culture and Organizational Performance," *Administrative Science Quarterly* 28 (1983), pp. 468–81; O. Williamson, *Markets and Hierarchies* (New York: The Free Press, 1975).

Several years ago a large toy manufacturer installed, at considerable expense, a management-by-objectives (MBO) performance appraisal system. After a year or so, top management became aware that the system was working well in one part of the organization but not another. They conducted an investigation and discovered the reason for the failure. In the part of the organization where MBO was working well, senior management was enthusiastic and committed. They saw real benefits and conveyed their belief up and down the chain of command. In the part of the organization where the system had failed, senior management saw MBO as another bureaucratic exercise to be endured. Subordinate managers quickly learned to complete the paperwork but ignore the purpose. The lesson here was that a control system, no matter how carefully designed, works only when those being monitored believe that people who matter care about the results and are paying close attention. When Jan Carlzon became head of SAS Airline, he was concerned about the poor on-time record. To correct this, he personally requested a daily accounting of the on-time status of all flights. In the space of two years, SAS on-time record went from 83 percent to 97 percent.[9]

In designing formal control systems, we typically attempt to measure either outcomes or behaviors. For example, in hospitals it makes no sense to evaluate the nursing staff on whether patients get well. Instead, control systems rely on assessing behaviors. Are specified medical procedures followed? Are checks made at appropriate times? In other settings, behavior may not be observable. Sales people, for instance, are usually measured on their productivity, since the nature of their job often precludes any effective monitoring of their behavior. In other situations, control systems can be designed that monitor both behaviors and outcomes. For example, for some retail sales jobs both behaviors (how the customer is addressed, how quickly the order is taken, whether the sales floor is kept stocked) and outcomes (sales volume) can be measured.

However, it is often the case that neither behavior nor outcomes can be adequately monitored.[10] These are the activities that are nonroutine and unpredictable, situations that require initiative, flexibility, and innovation. These can be dealt with only by developing social control systems in which common agreements exist among people about what constitutes appropriate attitudes and behavior.

Culture may be thought of as a potential social control system. Unlike formal control systems that typically assess outcomes or behaviors only intermittently, social control systems can be much more finely tuned. When we care about those with whom we work and have a common set of expectations, we are "under control" whenever we are in their presence. If we want to be accepted, we try to live up to their expectations. In this sense, social control systems can operate more extensively than most formal systems. Interestingly, our response to being monitored by formal and social control systems may also differ. With formal systems people often have a sense of external constraint which is binding and unsatisfying. With social controls, we often feel as though we have great autonomy, even though paradoxically we are conforming much more.

---

[9] J. Carlzon, *Moments of Truth* (Cambridge, MA: Ballinger, 1987).

[10] S. Dornbusch and W. R. Scott, *Evaluation and the Exercise of Authority* (San Francisco: Jossey-Bass, 1975).

Thus, from a management perspective, culture in the form of shared expectations may be thought of as a social control system. Howard Schwartz and Stan Davis offer a practical definition of culture as "a pattern of beliefs and expectations shared by the organization's members. These beliefs and expectations produce norms that powerfully shape the behavior of individuals and groups."[11]

Culture as Normative Order

What Schwartz and Davis are referring to as culture are the central norms that may characterize an organization. Norms are expectations about what are appropriate or inappropriate attitudes and behaviors. They are socially created standards that help us interpret and evaluate events. Although their content may vary, they exist in all societies and, while often unnoticed, they are pervasive. For instance, in our society we have rather explicit norms about eye-contact. We may get uncomfortable when these are violated. Consider what happens when someone doesn't look at you while speaking or who continues to look without pause. In organizations we often find peripheral or unimportant norms around issues such as dress or forms of address. In the old railroads, for example, hats were a must for all managers, while everyone addressed each other with a formal "mister."

More important norms often exist around issues such as quality, performance, flexibility, or how to deal with conflict. In many organizations, it is impolite to disagree publicly with others. Instead, much behind-the-scenes interaction takes place to anticipate or resolve disputes. In other organizations, there may be norms that legitimate and encourage the public airing of disputes. Intel Corporation has an explicit policy of "constructive confrontation" that encourages employees to deal with disagreements in an immediate and direct manner.

In this view, the central values and styles that characterize a firm, perhaps not even written down, can form the basis for the development of norms that attach approval or disapproval to holding certain attitudes or beliefs and to acting in certain ways. For instance, the fundamental value of aggressiveness or competition may, if widely held and supported, be expressed as a norm that encourages organizational participants to stress winning competition. Pepsico encourages competition and punishes failure to compete.[12] Service is a pivotal norm at IBM; innovation is recognized as central at 3M. It is through norms—the expectations shared by group members and the approval or disapproval attached to these expectations—that culture is developed and maintained.

However, there is an important difference between the guiding beliefs or vision held by top management and the daily beliefs or norms held by those at lower levels in the unit or organization. The former reflect top management's beliefs about how things ought to be. The latter define how things actually are. Simply because top management is in agreement about how they would like the organization to function is no guarantee that these beliefs will be held by others. One CEO spoke at some length about the glowing corporate philoso-

---

[11]H. Schwartz and S. Davis, "Matching Corporate Culture and Business Strategy," *Organizational Dynamics,* 1981, pp. 30–48.
[12]*Fortune,* April 10, 1989.

phy that he believed in and felt characterized his firm's culture. After spending some time talking to mid-level managers in the organization, a very different picture emerged. A central norm shared by many of these managers was "Good people don't stay here." It is a common occurrence to find a noble sounding statement of corporate values framed on the wall and a very different and cynical interpretation of this creed held by people who have been around long enough to realize what is really important.

Moreover, norms can vary on two dimensions: the intensity or amount of approval/disapproval attached to an expectation; and the crystallization or degree of consensus or consistency with which a norm is shared. For instance, when analyzing an organization's culture it may be that for certain values there can be wide consensus but no intensity. Everyone understands what top management values, but there is no strong approval or disapproval attached to these beliefs or behaviors. Or, a given norm, such as innovation, can be positively valued in one group (e.g., marketing or R&D) and negatively valued in another (manufacturing or personnel). There is intensity but no crystallization.

It is only when there exist both intensity and consensus that strong cultures exist. This is why it is difficult to develop or change culture. Organizational members must come to know and share a common set of expectations. These must, in turn, be consistently valued and reinforced across divisions and management levels.[13] Only when this is done will there be both intensity and consensus. Similarly, a failure to share the central norms or to consistently reinforce them may lead to vacuous norms, conflicting interpretations, or to micro-cultures that exist only within subunits.

To have a strong culture, an organization does not have to have very many strongly held values. Only a few core values characterize strong culture firms such as Mars, Marriott, Hewlett-Packard, and Wal-Mart. What is critical is that these beliefs be widely shared and strongly held; that is, people throughout the organization must be willing to tell one another when a core belief is not being lived up to.

The Role of Culture in Promoting Innovation

How is it that firms such as Intel, Hewlett-Packard, Cray Research, 3M, and Johnson & Johnson successfully develop both new products and new ways of doing things? How can culture help or hinder this process? The answer lies in those norms that if they were widely shared and strongly held by members of the organization, they would actively promote the generation of new ideas and would help in the implementation of new approaches.

What are these norms? This question was put to over 500 managers in firms as diverse as pharmaceuticals, consumer products, computers and semiconductors, and manufacturing. Table 1 contains a list of the norms that were most frequently cited. Several things are notable about this list. First, regardless of the industry or technology, managers identified virtually the same set of norms as important. While the process of innovation varies widely across efforts to discover new drugs, improve oil exploration, build new electronic

---

[13]D. Feldman, "The Development and Enforcement of Group Norms," *Academy of Management Review* 9 (1984), pp. 47–53.

TABLE 1   **Norms That Promote Innovation**

A. Norms to Promote Creativity

1. Risk Taking
- Freedom to try things and fail
- Acceptance of mistakes
- Allow discussion of "dumb" ideas
- No punishments for failure
- Challenge the status quo
- Forget the past
- Willingness *not* to focus on the short term
- Expectation that innovation is part of your job
- Positive attitudes about change
- Drive to improve

2. Rewards for Change
- Ideas are valued
- Respect for beginning ideas
- Build into the structure:
  - budget   - opportunities
  - resources   - tools
  - time   - promotions
- Top management attention and support
- Celebration of accomplishments
- Suggestions are implemented
- Encouragement

3. Openness
- Open communication and share information
- Listen better
- Open access
- Bright people, strong egos
- Scanning, broad thinking
- Force exposure outside the company
- Move people around
- Encourage lateral thinking
- Adopt the customer's perspective
- Accept criticism
- Don't be too sensitive
- Continuous training
- Intellectual honesty
- Expect and accept conflict
- Willingness to consult others

B. Norms to Promote Implementation

1. Common Goals
- Sense of pride in the organization
- Teamwork
- Willingness to share the credit
- Flexibility in jobs, budgets, functional areas
- Sense of ownership
- Eliminate mixed messages
- Manage interdependencies
- Shared visions and a common direction
- Build consensus
- Mutual respect and trust
- Concern for the whole organization

2. Autonomy
- Decision-making responsibility at lower levels
- Decentralized procedures
- Freedom to act
- Expectation of action
- Belief that *you* can have an impact
- Delegation
- Quick, flexible decision making
- Minimize the bureaucracy

3. Belief in Action
- Don't be obsessed with precision
- Emphasis on results
- Meet your commitments
- Anxiety about timeliness
- Value getting things done
- Hard work is expected and appreciated
- Empower people
- Emphasis on quality
- Eagerness to get things done
- Cut through the bureaucracy

devices, or develop a new toilet bowl cleaner, the norms that facilitate these efforts are remarkably consistent. Second, these norms all function to facilitate the process of introducing new ways of doing things and to help people implement them. For example, when people share the expectation that it is not only permissible but also desirable to challenge the status quo, the likelihood of innovation is increased.

At Cray Research, a prime example of a firm whose success depends on its ability to innovate, creativity and diversity are seen as virtues. Similarly, at Intel Corporation, a company whose strategy has long been to be a first-mover and innovator, all employees are told to expect conflict and to deal with it directly. To resolve conflicts, employees are trained in a process called "constructive confrontation," which helps them deal with the conflict in productive rather than destructive ways. At Johnson & Johnson a similar belief is referred to as "creative conflict."

To appreciate how critical the norms shown in Table 1 can be to innovation, envision an organization that is characterized by norms the opposite of those listed. Imagine an organization where failure is punished severely, where no recognition or rewards are provided for those doing things differently, where the past is venerated and only ideas generated internally are considered worthwhile, where "dumb" ideas are ridiculed and people are never encouraged to take risks, and where there is no drive to change or improve things. In this environment, one would be amazed to see any change. Contrast this with an organization such as 3M in which a basic financial goal is to have 25 percent of annual sales come from products developed over the last five years. Allen Jacobsen, 3M's CEO, says, "People ask me how do you get people to be innovative. It's simple. You give them responsibility for their own destinies and encourage them to take risks."[14] The secret to 3M's success isn't in Mr. Jacobsen's words but in the norms that form 3M's culture. These norms are widely shared and strongly held because management up and down the line provides the resources and encouragement to sustain them. It is the expectations held by people throughout the company, not just in R&D, that makes 3M and similar firms so innovative.

There is nothing magical or elusive about corporate culture. One has only to be clear about the specific attitudes and behaviors that are desired, and then to identify the norms or expectations that promote or impede them.

WHY CULTURE IS IMPORTANT

There are two reasons why a strong culture is valuable:

- The fit of culture and strategy, and
- The increased commitment by employees to the firm.

Both these factors provide a competitive edge, giving a strong culture firm an advantage over its competitors.[15]

Strategy and Corporate Culture

Every firm has, implicitly or explicitly, a competitive strategy which dictates how it attempts to position itself with respect to its competitors. Once established, a firm's strategy dictates a set of critical tasks or objectives that

---

[14]*Fortune*, June 6, 1988.

[15]For example, see S. Davis, *Managing Corporate Culture* (Cambridge, MA: Ballinger, 1984); T. Deal and A. Kennedy, *Corporate Cultures* (Reading, MA: Addison-Wesley, 1982); Peters and Waterman, *In Search of Excellence*.

must be accomplished through a congruence among the elements of people, structure, and culture. For example, a decision to compete on innovation rather than price requires an appropriate formal structure and control system which then indicates the types of people required to accomplish the objectives and to fit the structure. The choice of a strategy also has significant implications for the information organization or culture; that is, the norms of the organization must help execute the strategy.

An illustration of the importance of fit between strategy, people, structure, and culture can be seen in the history of the three major Silicon Valley firms that manufacture integrated circuits. Although operating in the same product market, Intel, National Semiconductor, and Advanced Micro Devices has each pursued a different strategy that is reflected in their people, structures, and cultures. National Semiconductor has chosen to compete largely as a low-cost manufacturer. To do this, it emphasizes strict cost control, a functional organizational structure, and a culture emphasizing numbers, a lack of frills, and a certain ruthlessness that has earned its people the sobriquet of "animals of the valley." Intel, however, has chosen to compete on product innovation. It has a looser formal organization with a culture valuing collegial interaction and the development of new technologies and products. Advanced Micro Devices has chosen a marketing strategy offering very high quality products, often as second source. Its strength has been in its marketing, and its culture reflects the value placed on selling, service, and quality.

For a strategy to be successfully implemented, it requires an appropriate culture. When firms change strategies, and often structures, they sometimes fail because the underlying shared values do not support the new approach. For example, a large, integrated electronics firm with a very strong culture based on technical excellence decided to enter the word processing market. Although they already made equipment that could easily be used as a basis for a word processor, the culture that made them successful in the design and manufacture of satellites and other sophisticated equipment ultimately sabotaged their efforts to design a word processor. The firm's engineers had a strong ethic of "getting it right" and would not release the machine. The window of opportunity for entry into the market passed, leaving the firm with a $40 million write-off of their investment. The point is both simple and important. As firms grow and strategies change, the culture or social control system also needs to be realigned to reflect the new direction.

Culture and Commitment

Culture is critical in developing and maintaining levels of intensity and dedication among employees that often characterizes successful firms. This strong attachment is particularly valuable when the employees have knowledge that is instrumental to the success of the organization or when very high levels of motivation are required. When IBM bought ROLM, the critical resource was not the existing product line but the design and engineering expertise of ROLM's staff. A failure to gain the commitment of the employees during mergers and acquisitions can diminish or destroy the value of the venture. In contrast, a highly dedicated work force represents a significant competitive advantage. Under turbulent or changing conditions, relying on employees who wait to be told exactly what to do can be a liability.

How, then, do strong culture organizations develop intensity and commitment? A 20-year veteran of IBM was quoted in a *Wall Street Journal* article as saying, "I don't know what a cult is and what it is those bleary-eyed kids selling poppies really do, but I'm probably that deeply committed to the IBM company."[16] To understand this process, we need to consider what commitment is and how it is developed. By understanding the underlying psychology of commitment, we can then think about how to design systems to develop such an attachment among employees.

Organizational Commitment   What is meant by the term "organizational commitment"? It is typically conceived of as an individual's psychological bond to the organization, including a sense of job involvement, loyalty, and a belief in the values of the organization. There are three processes or stages of commitment: *compliance, identification,* and *internalization*.[17] In the first stage, *compliance,* a person accepts the influence of others mainly to obtain something from others, such as pay. The second stage is *identification* in which the individual accepts influence in order to maintain a satisfying, self-defining relationship. People feel pride in belonging to the firm. The final stage of commitment is *internalization* in which the individual finds the values of the organization to be intrinsically rewarding and congruent with personal values.

Conceiving of commitment as developing in this manner allows us to understand how a variety of organizations—ranging from cults to strong culture corporations—generate commitment among their members. In fact, these organizations can be categorized based on the type of commitment displayed by their members. Cults and religious organizations, for example, typically have members who have internalized the values of the organization and who become "deployable agents," or individuals who can be relied upon to go forth and proselytize.[18] Japanese organizations, Theory Z, and strong culture firms are characterized by members who have a strong identification with the organization. These employees identify with the firm because it stands for something they value. In typical corporations, members comply with directions but may have little involvement with the firm beyond self-interest; that is, there is no commitment with the firm beyond that of a fair exchange of effort for money and, perhaps, status.

HOW CULTURE IS DEVELOPED

How do people become committed to organizations? Why, for example, would someone choose to join a cult? How do firms such as NUMMI get the incredible levels of productivity from their employees (as one team member said, "I like the new system so much it scares me. I'm scared because it took me 18 years to realize that I blew it at GM. Now we have a chance to do things a different way.")? The answer to this puzzle is simultaneously simple and

---

[16]*The Wall Street Journal*, April 7, 1986.

[17]C. O'Reilly and J. Chatman, "Organizational Commitment and Psychological Attachment: The Effects of Compliance, Identification and Internalization on Prosocial Behavior," *Journal of Applied Psychology* 71 (1986), pp. 492–99.

[18]W. Appel, *Cults in America* (New York: Holt, Rinehart and Winston, 1983); D. Gerstel, *Paradise Incorporated: Synanon* (San Francisco: Presidio Press, 1982).

nonobvious. As Jerry Salancik has noted, "commitment is too easy," yet it relies on an understanding of human motivation that is counterintuitive.[19]

Constructing Social Realities

Most discussions of motivation assume a stable set of individual needs and values.[20] These are seen as shaping expectations, goals, and attitudes. In turn, these are presumed to guide behavior and people's responses to situations. In Maslow's theory, for instance, people are assumed to have a hierarchy of needs.[21] The managerial consequence of this view can be seen in our theories of job design in which jobs are supposed to be designed to take advantage of the desire of people to grow and self- actualize.[22] But are such theories correct? The empirical evidence is weak at best.[23] In spite of numerous efforts to demonstrate the effect of needs and personality, there is little support for the power of individual differences to predict behavior.

Consider the results of two experiments. In the first, Christian seminary students were approached and given one of two requests. Both asked them to extemporaneously address a visiting class in a discussion of the parable of the Good Samaritan. They were told to walk over to a classroom building to do this. In one condition they were informed that the class was already there and that they should hurry. In the other condition they were told that the class would arrive in several minutes. As they walked to the classroom, all subjects passed an old man (the "victim") dressed in shabby clothes and in obvious need of help. The experimenters were interested in what proportion of Christian seminarians thinking of the Good Samaritan would stop and help this person. Surprisingly, in the condition in which the subjects were told to hurry, only 30 percent paid any attention. Think about this. Seventy percent of a group of individuals with religious values who were training to be ministers failed to stop. Ninety-five percent of those who were not in a hurry stopped to help.

In another experiment, researchers observed when students using a campus restroom washed their hands. They discovered that when another person was visible in the restroom, 90 percent washed their hands. When no other person was visible, less than 20 percent did so.

What explains these and other findings? What often seems to account for behavior are the expectations of others. As individuals, we are very susceptible to the informational and normative influence of others. We pay attention to the action of others and learn from them. "In actuality, virtually all learning phenomena resulting from direct experience occur on a vicarious basis by observing other people's behavior and its consequences for them." We watch others and form expectations about how and when we should act.[24]

---

[19]G. Salancik, "Commitment Is Too Easy!" *Organizational Dynamics*, Summer 1977, pp. 62–80.

[20]For example, see F. Herzberg, B. Mausner, and B. Snyderman, *The Motivation to Work* (New York: John Wiley, 1959); A. Maslow, *Motivation and Personality* (New York: Harper & Row, 1970).

[21]Maslow, *Motivation and Personality*.

[22]For example, see J. R. Hackman and G. Oldham, *Work Redesign* (Reading, MA: Addison-Wesley, 1980).

[23]For example, see G. Salancik and J. Pfeffer, "A Social Information Processing Approach to Job Attitudes and Task Design," *Administrative Science Quarterly* 23 (1978), pp. 224–53.

[24]For example, see S. Milgram, *Obedience to Authority* (New York: Harper & Row, 1969); A. Bandura, *Social Learning Theory* (Englewood Cliffs, NJ: Prentice Hall, 1977).

Yet, we are not sensitive to how much of our world is really a social construction—one that rests on shared agreements. We often tend to underestimate the degree to which situations and the expectations of others can constrain and shape behavior. Strong situations—ones in which there are very clear incentives and expectations about what constitutes appropriate attitudes and behavior—can be very powerful. When we care what others think, the power of these norms or social expectations can be heightened.

Mechanisms for Developing Culture

How can cultures be developed and managed in organizations? All organizations—from cults to strong culture corporations—draw on the same underlying psychology and create situations characterized by strong norms that focus people's attention, provide clear guidance about what is important, and provide for group reinforcement of appropriate attitudes and behavior. Four common mechanisms are used to accomplish this. What varies across these organizations is not what is done but only the degree to which these mechanisms are used.

Participation   The first mechanism that is critical in developing or changing a culture are systems that provide for participation. These systems encourage people to be involved and send signals to the individual that he or she is valued. These may range from formal efforts such as quality circles and advisory boards to less formal efforts such as suggestion systems and opportunities to meet with top managers and informal social gatherings. What is important about these processes is that people are encouraged to make incremental choices and develop a sense of responsibility for their actions. In some cases, such as work design, the specific choices made may be less important for future success than the fact that people had the chance to make them.

From a psychological perspective, choice is often associated with commitment. When we choose of our own volition to do something, we often feel responsible.[25] When the choice is volitional, explicit, public, and irrevocable, the commitment is even more binding.[26] For instance, direct sales companies have learned that by getting the customer to fill out the order sheet, they can cut cancellations dramatically. A large number of psychological experiments have convincingly shown that participation can lead to both commitment and enjoyment, even when people are induced to engage in physically and emotionally stressful activities such as eating earthworms and becoming bone marrow donors.[27]

How do organizations use participation? Marc Galanter has documented how members of the Unification Church use processes of incremental commitment to recruit cult members.[28] Individuals are invited to dinner, convinced to spend the weekend for a seminar, and in some cases, induced to remain

---

[25]For example, see R. Caldini, *Influence: The New Psychology of Modern Persuasion* (New York: Quill, 1984).

[26]Salancik, "Commitment Is Too Easy!"

[27]For example, see I. Janis and L. Mann, *Decision Making: A Psychological Analysis of Conflict, Choice, and Commitment* (New York: Free Press, 1977).

[28]M. Galanter, "Psychological Induction into the Large Group: Findings from a Modern Religious Sect," *American Journal of Psychiatry* 137 (1980), pp. 1574–79.

permanently with their new found "friends." Interestingly, there is no evidence that people who join cults under these circumstances are suffering from any psychopathology. Religious organizations often use elaborate systems of incremental choice and participation leading to greater and greater involvement. Japanese-managed automobile companies in the United States also have elaborate systems of selection and orientation that rely heavily on these approaches, as do American "strong culture" firms.

Management as Symbolic Action   The second mechanism commonly seen in strong culture organizations is that of clear, visible actions on the part of management in support of the cultural values.[29] In organizations, participants typically want to know what is important. One way we gain this information is to carefully watch and listen to those above us. We look for consistent patterns. When top management not only says that something is important but also consistently behaves in ways that support the message, we begin to believe what is said. When the CEO of Xerox, David Kearns, began his quest for improved quality, there was some initial uncertainty about whether he meant it. Over time, as the message was repeated again and again, and as resources continued to be devoted to the quality effort, norms developed setting expectations about the role and importance of quality throughout the corporation.[30]

An important function of management is to provide interpretations of events for the organization's members. Without a shared meaning, confusion and conflict can result. Managers need to be sensitive to how their actions are viewed. Interpreting (or reinterpreting) history, telling stories, the use of vivid language, spending time, and being seen as visible in support of certain positions are all potential ways of shaping the organization's culture. This does not mean that managers need to be charismatic. However, managers need to engage in acts of "mundane symbolism." By this they can insure that important issues get suitable amounts of time, that questions are continually asked about important topics, and that the subject gets on the agenda and it is followed up.

The appropriate use of symbols and ceremonies is also important. When Jerry Sanders, CEO of Advanced Micro Devices, decided to shift the firm's strategy toward innovation, he not only made substantive changes in budget, positions, and organizational structure, he also used a symbol. As a part of the many talks he had with employees describing the need to change, Sanders would also describe how important it was to invest in areas that others could not easily duplicate—such as investing in proprietary products. He would describe how a poor farmer would always need a cash crop at the end of the year if he was to survive. But if he began to prosper, a smart farmer would begin to plant crops that others might not be able to afford—crops, for example, that took more than a year to come to fruition; crops like asparagus. The notion of asparagus became a visible and important symbol for change within AMD, even to the point where managers begin referring to revenues from new proprietary products as "being measured on asparagus."

---

[29]J. Pfeffer, "Management as Symbolic Action: The Creation and Maintenance of Organizational Paradigms," in L. Cummings and B. Staw, eds., *Research in Organizational Behavior*, 3 (Greenwich, CT: JAI Press, 1981).

[30]G. Jacobsen and J. Hillkirk, *Xerox: American Samurai* (New York: Collier Books, 1986).

Symbols are not a substitute for substance, and ceremonies cannot replace content. Rather, many of the substantive changes that occur in organizations, such as promotions or reorganizations, have multiple meanings and interpretations. Over time, people may lose a clear sense for what the superordinate goals are and why their jobs are important. In strong culture organizations, managers frequently and consistently send signals helping to renew these understandings. They do this by continually calling attention to what is important, in word and in action.

Information from Others   While clear messages from management are an important determinant of a culture, so too are consistent messages from co-workers. If control comes from the knowledge that someone who matters is paying attention, then the degree to which we care about our co-workers also gives them a certain control over us. Years ago, several researchers conducted an experiment in which subjects were placed in a room to complete a questionnaire. While they were doing this, smoke began to flow from an air vent. While 75 percent of the subjects who were alone responded by notifying the experimenter of a possible fire, only 38 percent did so when in the company of two other subjects. When these other two were confederates of the experimenter and deliberately said nothing, only 10 percent of the subjects responded. One conclusion from this and other similar experiments is that we often take our cue from others when we are uncertain what to do.

In organizations, during periods of crisis or when people are new to the situation, they often look to others for explanations of what to do and how to interpret events. Strong cultures are typically characterized by consensus about these questions. In these settings there are often attempts made to insure a consistency of understanding and to minimize any us-them attitudes between parts of the organization. For instance, strong culture firms often pride themselves on the equality of treatment of all employees. At Mars, all employees punch a time clock and no one has a private secretary. At Gore-Tex, Wal-Mart, Disney, and others there are no employees or managers, only associates, team members, and hosts. At NUMMI, Honda, and Nissan there are no private dining rooms for managers and both managers and workers often wear uniforms. In the Rajneesh Commune, everyone wore clothes with the color magenta.

The goal here is to create a strong social construction of reality by minimizing contradictory interpretations. In cults, this is often done by isolating the members from family and friends. Some religious organizations do this by encouraging extensive involvement in a variety of church activities and meetings. Japanese firms expect after-work socializing. At NUMMI, for instance, each work team is given a semiannual budget to be spent only on team-sponsored activities where the entire team participates. In corporations, 60-hour work weeks can also isolate people from competing interpretations. Some electronics firms in Silicon Valley have provided employee T-shirts with slogans such as "Working 80 hours a week and loving it." With this commitment of time, workers may be as isolated as if they had joined a cult.

Comprehensive Reward Systems   A final mechanism for promoting and shaping culture is the reward system, but not simply monetary rewards. Rather, these systems focus on rewards such as recognition and approval which can be given more frequently than money. These rewards also focus on the intrinsic aspects of the job and a sense of belonging to the organization. Recognition by your boss or co-workers for doing the right thing can be more potent in shaping behavior than an annual bonus. In the words of a popular management book, the trick is to catch someone doing something right and to reward it on the spot. While tokens such as scrolls or badges can be meaningless, under the right circumstances they can also be highly valued.

It is easy to desire one type of behavior while rewarding another. Often management professes a concern for quality while systematically rewarding only those who meet their goals, regardless of the quality. Innovation may be espoused but even the slightest failure is punished. At its simplest, people usually do what they are rewarded for and don't do what they're punished for. If this is true and to be taken seriously, then a simple analysis of what gets management's attention should give us a sense for what the culture supports. Who gets promoted? At 3M, one important aspect of success is to be associated with a new product introduction. If innovation is espoused, but doing things by-the-book is what is rewarded, it doesn't take a psychologist to figure out what the firm actually values. In fact, if there are inconsistencies between what top management says and what is actually rewarded, the likely outcome will be confusion and cynicism.

Managing Culture

Each of these can affect the development of a shared set of expectations. As shown in Figure 1, the process begins with words and actions on the part of the group's leaders. Even if no explicit statements are made, subordinates will attempt to infer a pattern. If management is credible and communicates consistently, members of the group may begin to develop consistent expectations about what is important. When this consensus is also rewarded, clear norms can then emerge.

Whether or not these norms constitute a desirable culture depends on the critical tasks to be accomplished and whether the formal control system provides sufficient leverage to attain these. If culture *is* important, four steps can help a manager understand how to manage it.

- Identify the strategic objectives of the unit. Once identified, specify the short-term objectives and critical actions that need to be accomplished if the strategic objectives are to be accomplished.
- Analyze the existing values and norms that characterize the organization. This can be done by focusing on what people in the unit feel is expected of them by their peers and bosses and what is actually rewarded. What does it take to get ahead? What stories are routinely told? Who are the people who exemplify the group? Look for norms that are widely shared and strongly felt.
- Once these are identified, look for norms that may hinder the accomplishment of critical tasks; norms that would help but are not currently present; and conflicts between what is needed and what is currently rewarded.

FIGURE 1

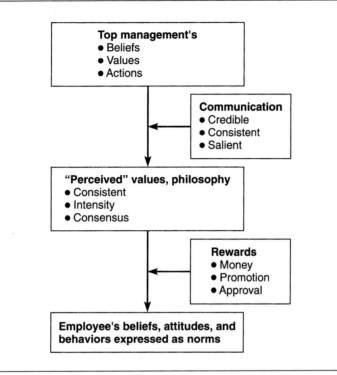

- Once these are identified, programs can be designed to begin to shape or develop the desired norms. These can draw upon the psychological mechanisms discussed previously.

The logic here is straightforward and links culture to those activities critical for the implementation of strategy and for generating widespread understanding and commitment among the organization's members. Obviously, these actions take time and management resources to accomplish. However, to ignore them is to ignore a social control system that may already be operating in the organization. The issue is whether this system is helping or hindering. Managers need to be sensitive to what the central organizational norms are and how they can affect them. To not be sensitive to these issues is to ignore the advice of a CEO who said, "We will either be a victim or a successful result of our culture."

P A R T

III

APPENDIX:
CASES IN STRATEGIC
MANAGEMENT

A Guide to Case Analysis

I keep six honest serving men
(They taught me all I knew);
Their names are What and Why and When;
And How and Where and Who.
Rudyard Kipling

In most courses in strategic management, students practice at being strategy managers via case analysis. A case sets forth, in a factual manner, the events and organizational circumstances surrounding a particular managerial situation. It puts readers at the scene of the action and familiarizes them with all the relevant circumstances. A case on strategic management can concern a whole industry, a single organization, or some part of an organization; the organization involved can be either profit seeking or not-for-profit. The essence of the student's role in case analysis is to *diagnose* and *size up* the situation described in the case and then to *recommend* appropriate action steps.

WHY USE CASES TO PRACTICE STRATEGIC MANAGEMENT

A student of business with tact
Absorbed many answers he lacked.
But acquiring a job,
He said with a sob,
"How does one fit answer to fact?"

The foregoing limerick was used some years ago by Professor Charles Gragg to characterize the plight of business students who had no exposure to cases.[1]

---

[1]Charles I. Gragg, "Because Wisdom Can't Be Told," in *The Case Method at the Harvard Business School*, ed. M. P. McNair (New York: McGraw-Hill, 1954), p. 11.

Gragg observed that the mere act of listening to lectures and sound advice about managing does little for anyone's management skills and that the accumulated managerial wisdom cannot effectively be passed on by lectures and assigned readings alone. Gragg suggested that if anything had been learned about the practice of management, it is that a storehouse of ready-made textbook answers does not exist. Each managerial situation has unique aspects, requiring its own diagnosis, judgment, and tailor-made actions. Cases provide would-be managers with a valuable way to practice wrestling with the actual problems of actual managers in actual companies.

The case approach to strategic analysis is, first and foremost, an exercise in learning by doing. Because cases provide you with detailed information about conditions and problems of different industries and companies, your task of analyzing company after company and situation after situation has the twin benefit of boosting your analytical skills and exposing you to the ways companies and managers actually do things. Most college students have limited managerial backgrounds and only fragmented knowledge about different companies and real-life strategic situations. Cases help substitute for actual on-the-job experience by (1) giving you broader exposure to a variety of industries, organizations, and strategic problems; (2) forcing you to assume a managerial role (as opposed to that of just an onlooker); (3) providing a test of how to apply the tools and techniques of strategic management; and (4) asking you to come up with pragmatic managerial action plans to deal with the issues at hand.

OBJECTIVES OF CASE ANALYSIS

Using cases to learn about the practice of strategic management is a powerful way for you to accomplish five things:[2]

1. Increase your understanding of what managers should and should not do in guiding a business to success.
2. Build your skills in conducting strategic analysis in a variety of industries, competitive situations, and company circumstances.
3. Get valuable practice in diagnosing strategic issues, evaluating strategic alternatives, and formulating workable plans of action.
4. Enhance your sense of business judgment, as opposed to uncritically accepting the authoritative crutch of the professor or "back-of-the-book" answers.
5. Gain in-depth exposure to different industries and companies, thereby gaining something close to actual business experience.

If you understand that these are the objectives of case analysis, you are less likely to be consumed with curiosity about "the answer to the case." Students who have grown comfortable with and accustomed to textbook statements of fact and definitive lecture notes are often frustrated when discussions about a case do not produce concrete answers. Usually, case discussions produce good

---

[2]Ibid., pp. 12–14; and D. R. Schoen and Philip A. Sprague, "What Is the Case Method?" in *The Case Method at the Harvard Business School*, ed. M. P. McNair, pp. 78–79.

arguments for more than one course of action. Differences of opinion nearly always exist. Thus, should a class discussion conclude without a strong, unambiguous consensus on what do to, don't grumble too much when you are *not* told what the answer is or what the company actually did. Just remember that in the business world answers don't come in conclusive black-and-white terms. There are nearly always several feasible courses of action and approaches, each of which may work out satisfactorily. Moreover, in the business world, when one elects a particular course of action, there is no peeking at the back of a book to see if you have chosen the best thing to do and no one to turn to for a provably correct answer. The only valid test of management action is *results*. If the results of an action turn out to be "good," the decision to take it may be presumed "right." If not, then the action chosen was "wrong" in the sense that it didn't work out.

Hence, the important thing for a student to understand in case analysis is that the managerial exercise of identifying, diagnosing, and recommending builds your skills; discovering the right answer or finding out what actually happened is no more than frosting on the cake. Even if you learn what the company did, you can't conclude that it was necessarily right or best. All that can be said is "here is what they did. . . ."

The point is this: *The purpose of giving you a case assignment is not to cause you to run to the library to look up what the company actually did but, rather, to enhance your skills in sizing up situations and developing your managerial judgment about what needs to be done and how to do it.* The aim of case analysis is for *you* to bear the strains of thinking actively, of offering your analysis, of proposing action plans, and of explaining and defending your assessments—this is how cases provide you with meaningful practice at being a manager.

PREPARING A CASE FOR CLASS DISCUSSION

If this is your first experience with the case method, you may have to reorient your study habits. Unlike lecture courses where you can get by without preparing intensively for each class and where you have latitude to work assigned readings and reviews of lecture notes into your schedule, *a case assignment requires conscientious preparation before class.* You will not get much out of hearing the class discuss a case you haven't read, and you certainly won't be able to contribute anything yourself to the discussion. What you have got to do to get ready for class discussion of a case is to study the case, reflect carefully on the situation presented, and develop some reasoned thoughts. Your goal in preparing the case should be to end up with what you think is a sound, well-supported analysis of the situation and a sound, defensible set of recommendations about which managerial actions need to be taken.

To prepare a case for class discussion, we suggest the following approach:

1. *Read the case through rather quickly for familiarity.* The initial reading should give you the general flavor of the situation and indicate which issue or issues are involved. If your instructor has provided you with study questions for the case, now is the time to read them carefully.

2. *Read the case a second time.* On this reading, try to gain full command of the facts. Begin to develop some tentative answers to the study questions your

instructor has provided. If your instructor has elected not to give you assignment questions, then start forming your own picture of the overall situation being described.

3. *Study all the exhibits carefully.* Often, the real story is in the numbers contained in the exhibits. Expect the information in the case exhibits to be crucial enough to materially affect your diagnosis of the situation.

4. *Decide what the strategic issues are.* Until you have identified the strategic issues and problems in the case, you don't know what to analyze, which tools and analytical techniques are called for, or otherwise how to proceed. At times the strategic issues are clear—either being stated in the case or else obvious from reading the case. At other times you will have to dig them out from all the information given.

5. *Start your analysis of the issues with some number crunching.* A big majority of strategy cases call for some kind of number crunching on your part. This means calculating assorted financial ratios to check out the company's financial condition and recent performance, calculating growth rates of sales or profits or unit volume, checking out profit margins and the makeup of the cost structure, and understanding whatever revenue-cost-profit relationships are present. See Table 1 for a summary of key financial ratios, how they are calculated, and what they show.

Use whichever tools and techniques of strategic analysis are called for. Strategic analysis is not just a collection of opinions; rather, it entails application of a growing number of powerful tools and techniques that cut beneath the surface and produce important insight and understanding of strategic situations. Every case assigned is strategy related and contains an opportunity to usefully apply the weapons of strategic analysis. Your instructor is looking for you to demonstrate that you know *how* and *when* to use the strategic management concepts presented earlier in the course. Furthermore, expect to have to draw regularly on what you have learned in your finance, economics, production, marketing, and human resources management courses.

7. *Check out conflicting opinions and make some judgments about the validity of all the data and information provided.* Many times cases report views and contradictory opinions (after all, people don't always agree on things, and different people see the same things in different ways). Forcing you to evaluate the data and information presented in the case helps you develop your powers of inference and judgment. Asking you to resolve conflicting information "comes with the territory" because a great many managerial situations entail opposing points of view, conflicting trends, and sketchy information.

8. *Support your diagnosis and opinions with reasons and evidence.* The most important things to prepare for are your answers to the question "Why?" For instance, if after studying the case you are of the opinion that the company's managers are doing a poor job, then it is your answer to "Why?" that establishes just how good your analysis of the situation is. If your instructor has provided you with specific study questions for the case, by all means prepare answers that include all the reasons and number-crunching evidence you can muster to support your diagnosis. *Generate at least two pages of notes!*

9. *Develop an appropriate action plan and set of recommendations.* Diagnosis divorced from corrective action is sterile. The test of a manager is always to convert sound analysis into sound actions—actions that will produce the

T A B L E   1   **A Summary of Key Financial Ratios, How They Are Calculated, and What They Show**

Ratio	How Calculated	What It Shows
Profitability Ratios		
1. Gross profit margin	$\dfrac{\text{Sales} - \text{Cost of goods sold}}{\text{Sales}}$	An indication of the total margin available to cover operating expenses and yield a profit.
2. Operating profit margin (or return on sales)	$\dfrac{\text{Profits before taxes and before interest}}{\text{Sales}}$	An indication of the firm's profitability from current operations without regard to the interest charges accruing from the capital structure.
3. Net profit margin (or net return on sales)	$\dfrac{\text{Profits after taxes}}{\text{Sales}}$	Shows aftertax profits per dollar of sales. Subpar-profit margins indicate that the firm's sales prices are relatively low or that its costs are relatively high, or both.
4. Return on total assets	$\dfrac{\text{Profits after taxes}}{\text{Total assets}}$ or $\dfrac{\text{Profits after taxes} + \text{Interest}}{\text{Total assets}}$	A measure of the return on total investment in the enterprise. It is sometimes desirable to add interest to aftertax profits to form the numerator of the ratio since total assets are financed by creditors as well as by stockholders; hence, it is accurate to measure the productivity of assets by the returns provided to both classes of investors.
5. Return on stockholders' equity (or return on net worth)	$\dfrac{\text{Profits after taxes}}{\text{Total stockholders' equity}}$	A measure of the rate of return on stockholders' investment in the enterprise.
6. Return on common equity	$\dfrac{\text{Profits after taxes} - \text{Preferred stock dividends}}{\text{Total stockholders' equity} - \text{Par value of preferred stock}}$	A measure of the rate of return on the investment which the owners of the common stock have made in the enterprise.
7. Earnings per share	$\dfrac{\text{Profits after taxes} - \text{Preferred stock dividends}}{\text{Number of shares of common stock outstanding}}$	Shows the earnings available to the owners of each share of common stock.
Liquidity Ratios		
1. Current ratio	$\dfrac{\text{Current assets}}{\text{Current liabilities}}$	Indicates the extent to which the claims of short-term creditors are covered by assets that are expected to be converted to cash in a period roughly corresponding to the maturity of the liabilities.
2. Quick ratio (or acid-test ratio)	$\dfrac{\text{Current assets} - \text{Inventory}}{\text{Current liabilities}}$	A measure of the firm's ability to pay off short-term obligations without relying on the sale of its inventories.
3. Inventory to net working capital	$\dfrac{\text{Inventory}}{\text{Current assets} - \text{Current liabilities}}$	A measure of the extent to which the firm's working capital is tied up in inventory.
Leverage Ratios		
1. Debt-to-assets ratio	$\dfrac{\text{Total debt}}{\text{Total assets}}$	Measures the extent to which borrowed funds have been used to finance the firm's operations.
2. Debt-to-equity ratio	$\dfrac{\text{Total debt}}{\text{Total stockholders' equity}}$	Provides another measure of the funds provided by creditors versus the funds provided by owners.

desired results. Hence, the final and most telling step in preparing a case is to develop an action agenda for management that lays out a set of specific recommendations on what to do. Bear in mind that proposing realistic, workable solutions is far preferable to casually tossing out off-the-top-of-your-head sug-

Ratio	How Calculated	What It Shows
3. Long-term debt-to-equity ratio	$$\frac{\text{Long-term debt}}{\text{Total shareholders' equity}}$$	A widely used measure of the balance between debt and equity in the firm's long-term capital structure.
4. Times-interest-earned (or coverage) ratio	$$\frac{\text{Profits before interest and taxes}}{\text{Total interest charges}}$$	Measures the extent to which earnings can decline without the firm becoming unable to meet its annual interest costs.
5. Fixed-charge coverage	$$\frac{\text{Profits before taxes and interest} + \text{Lease obligations}}{\text{Total interest charges} + \text{Lease obligations}}$$	A more inclusive indication of the firm's ability to meet all of its fixed-charge obligations.

Activity Ratios

1. Inventory turnover	$$\frac{\text{Sales}}{\text{Inventory of finished goods}}$$	When compared to industry averages, it provides an indication of whether a company has excessive or perhaps inadequate finished goods inventory.
2. Fixed assets turnover	$$\frac{\text{Sales}}{\text{Fixed Assets}}$$	A measure of the sales productivity and utilization of plant and equipment.
3. Total assets turnover	$$\frac{\text{Sales}}{\text{Total assets}}$$	A measure of the utilization of all the firm's assets; a ratio below the industry average indicates the company is not generating a sufficient volume of business, given the size of its asset investment.
4. Accounts receivable turnover	$$\frac{\text{Annual credit sales}}{\text{Accounts receivable}}$$	A measure of the average length of time it takes the firm to collect the sales made on credit.
5. Average collection period	$$\frac{\text{Accounts receivable}}{\text{Total sales} \div 365}$$ or $$\frac{\text{Accounts receivable}}{\text{Average daily sales}}$$	Indicates the average length of time the firm must wait after making a sale before it receives payment.

Other Ratios

1. Dividend yield on common stock	$$\frac{\text{Annual dividends per share}}{\text{Current market price per share}}$$	A measure of the return to owners received in the form of dividends.
2. Price-earnings ratio	$$\frac{\text{Current market price per share}}{\text{Aftertax earnings per share}}$$	Faster-growing or less-risky firms tend to have higher price-earnings ratios than slower-growing or more-risky firms.
3. Dividend payout ratio	$$\frac{\text{Annual dividends per share}}{\text{Aftertax earnings per share}}$$	Indicates the percentage of profits paid out as dividends.
4. Cash flow per share	$$\frac{\text{Aftertax profits} + \text{Depreciation}}{\text{Number of common shares outstanding}}$$	A measure of the discretionary funds over and above expenses that are available for use by the firm.

Note: Industry-average ratios against which a particular company's ratios may be judged are available in *Modern Industry* and *Dun's Reviews* published by Dun & Bradstreet (14 ratios for 125 lines of business activities), Robert Morris Associates' *Annual Statement Studies* (11 ratios for 156 lines of business), and the FTC-SEC's *Quarterly Financial Report* for manufacturing corporations.

gestions. Be prepared to argue why your recommendations are more attractive than other courses of action that are open.

As long as you are conscientious in preparing your analysis and recommendations, and as long as you have ample reasons, evidence, and arguments to support your views, you shouldn't fret unduly about whether what you've prepared is the right answer to the case. In case analysis there is rarely just one right approach or one right set of recommendations. Managing companies and devising and implementing strategies are not such exact sciences that there exists a single provably correct analysis and action plan for each strategic situation. Of course, some analyses and action plans are better than others; but, in truth, there's nearly always more than one good way to analyze a situation and more than one good plan of action. So, if you have done a careful and thoughtful job of preparing the case, don't lose confidence in the correctness of your work and judgment.

PARTICIPATING IN CLASS DISCUSSION OF A CASE

Classroom discussions of cases are sharply different from attending a lecture class. In a case class students do most of the talking. The instructor's role is to solicit student participation, keep the discussion on track, ask "Why?" often, offer alternative views, play the devil's advocate (if no students jump in to offer opposing views), and otherwise lead the discussion. The students in the class carry the burden for analyzing the situation and for being prepared to present and defend their diagnoses and recommendations. Expect a classroom environment, therefore, that calls for *your* size up of the situation, *your* analysis, what actions *you* would take, and why *you* would take them. Do not be dismayed if, as the class discussion unfolds, some insightful things are said by your fellow classmates that you did not think of. It is normal for views and analyses to differ and for the comments of others in the class to expand your own thinking about the case. As the old adage goes, "Two heads are better than one." So it is to be expected that the class as a whole will do a more penetrating and searching job of case analysis than will any one person working alone. This is the power of group effort, and its virtues are that it will help you see more analytical applications, let you test your analyses and judgments against those of your peers, and force you to wrestle with differences of opinion and approaches.

To orient you to the classroom environment on the days a case discussion is scheduled, we compiled the following list of things to expect:

1. Expect students to dominate the discussion and do most of the talking. The case method enlists a maximum of individual participation in class discussion. It is not enough to be present as a silent observer; if every student took this approach, there would be no discussion. (Thus, expect a portion of your grade to be based on your participation in case discussions.)

2. Expect the instructor to assume the role of extensive questioner and listener.

3. Be prepared for the instructor to probe for reasons and supporting analysis.

4. Expect and tolerate challenges to the views expressed. All students have to be willing to submit their conclusions for scrutiny and rebuttal. Each student needs to learn to state his or her views without fear of disapproval and to overcome the hesitation of speaking out. Learning respect for the views and approaches of others is an integral part of case analysis exercises. But there are times when it is OK to swim against the tide of majority opinion. In the practice of management, there is always

room for originality and unorthodox approaches. So while discussion of a case is a group process, there is no compulsion for you or anyone else to cave in and conform to group opinions and group consensus.

5. Don't be surprised if you change your mind about some things as the discussion unfolds. Be alert to how these changes affect your analysis and recommendations (in the event you get called on).

6. Expect to learn a lot from each case discussion; use what you learn to be better prepared for the next case discussion.

There are several things you can do on your own to be good and look good as a participant in class discussions:

- Although you should do your own independent work and independent thinking, don't hesitate before (and after) class to discuss the case with other students. In real life, managers often discuss the company's problems and situation with other people to refine their own thinking.

- In participating in the discussion, make a conscious effort to contribute, rather than just talk. There is a big difference between saying something that builds the discussion and offering a long-winded, off-the-cuff remark that leaves the class wondering what the point was.

- Avoid the use of "I think," "I believe," and "I feel"; instead, say, "My analysis shows . . . " and "The company should do . . . because. . . ." Always give supporting reasons and evidence for your views; then your instructor won't have to ask you "Why?" every time you make a comment.

- In making your points, assume that everyone has read the case and knows what it says; avoid reciting and rehashing information in the case—instead, use the data and information to explain your assessment of the situation and to support your position.

- Always prepare good notes (usually two or three pages' worth) for each case and use them extensively when you speak. There's no way you can remember everything off the top of your head—especially the results of your number crunching. To reel off the numbers or to present all five reasons why, instead of one, you will need good notes. When you have prepared good notes to the study questions and use them as the basis for your comments, *everybody* in the room will know you are well prepared, and your contribution to the case discussion will stand out.

PREPARING A WRITTEN CASE ANALYSIS

Preparing a written case analysis is much like preparing a case for class discussion, except that your analysis must be more complete and reduced to writing. Unfortunately, though, *there is no ironclad procedure for doing a written case analysis.* All we can offer are some general guidelines and words of wisdom—this is because company situations and management problems are so diverse that no one mechanical way to approach a written case assignment always works.

Your instructor may assign you a specific topic around which to prepare your written report. Or, alternatively, you may be asked to do a comprehensive written case analysis, where the expectation is that you will (1) *identify* all the pertinent issues that management needs to address, (2) perform whatever *analysis* and *evaluation* is appropriate, and (3) propose an *action plan* and set of *recommendations* addressing the issues you have identified. In going through the exercise of identify, evaluate, and recommend, keep the following pointers in mind.[3]

Identification   It is essential early on in your paper that you provide a sharply focused diagnosis of strategic issues and key problems and that you demonstrate a good grasp of the company's present situation. Make sure you can identify the firm's strategy (use the concepts and tools in Chapters 1–8 as diagnostic aids) and that you can pinpoint whatever strategy implementation issues may exist (again, consult the material in Chapters 9 and 10 for diagnostic help). Consult the key points we have provided at the end of each chapter for further diagnostic suggestions. Consider beginning your paper by sizing up the company's situation, its strategy, and the significant problems and issues that confront management. State problems/issues as clearly and precisely as you can. Unless it is necessary to do so for emphasis, avoid recounting facts and history about the company (assume your professor has read the case and is familiar with the organization).

Analysis and Evaluation   This is usually the hardest part of the report. Analysis is hard work! Check out the firm's financial ratios, its profit margins and rates of return, and its capital structure, and decide how strong the firm is financially. Table 1 contains a summary of various financial ratios and how they are calculated. Use it to assist in your financial diagnosis. Similarly, look at marketing, production, managerial competence, and other factors underlying the organization's strategic successes and failures. Decide whether the firm has core skills and competencies and, if so, whether it is capitalizing on them.

Check to see if the firm's strategy is producing satisfactory results and determine the reasons why or why not. Probe the nature and strength of the competitive forces confronting the company. Decide whether and why the firm's competitive position is getting stronger or weaker. Use the tools and concepts you have learned about to perform whatever analysis and evaluation is appropriate.

In writing your analysis and evaluation, bear in mind four things:

1. You are obliged to offer analysis and evidence to back up your conclusions. Do not rely on unsupported opinions, over-generalizations, and platitudes as a substitute for tight, logical argument backed up with facts and figures.

2. If your analysis involves some important quantitative calculations, use tables and charts to present the calculations clearly and efficiently. Don't just tack the exhibits on at the end of your report and let the reader figure out what they mean and why they were included. Instead,

---

[3]For some additional ideas and viewpoints, you may wish to consult Thomas J. Raymond, "Written Analysis of Cases," in *The Case Method at the Harvard Business School*, ed. M. P. McNair, pp. 139–63. Raymond's article includes an actual case, a sample analysis of the case, and a sample of a student's written report on the case.

in the body of your report cite some of the key numbers, highlight the conclusions to be drawn from the exhibits, and refer the reader to your charts and exhibits for more details.

3. Demonstrate that you have command of the strategic concepts and analytical tools to which you have been exposed. Use them in your report.

4. Your interpretation of the evidence should be reasonable and objective. Be wary of preparing a one-sided argument that omits all aspects not favorable to your conclusions. Likewise, try not to exaggerate or overdramatize. Endeavor to inject balance into your analysis and to avoid emotional rhetoric. Strike phrases such as "I think," "I feel," and "I believe" when you edit your first draft and write in "My analysis shows," instead.

Recommendations   The final section of the written case analysis should consist of a set of definite recommendations and a plan of action. Your set of recommendations should address all of the problems/issues you identified and analyzed. If the recommendations come as a surprise or do not follow logically from the analysis, the effect is to weaken greatly your suggestions of what to do. Obviously, your recommendations for actions should offer a reasonable prospect of success. High-risk, bet-the-company recommendations should be made with caution. State how your recommendations will solve the problems you identified. Be sure the company is financially able to carry out what you recommend; also check to see if your recommendations are workable in terms of acceptance by the persons involved, the organization's competence to implement them, and prevailing market and environmental constraints. Try not to hedge or weasel on the actions you believe should be taken.

By all means state your recommendations in sufficient detail to be meaningful—get down to some definite nitty-gritty specifics. Avoid such unhelpful statements as "the organization should do more planning" or "the company should be more aggressive in marketing its product." For instance, do not simply say "the firm should improve its market position" but state exactly how you think this should be done. Offer a definite agenda for action, stipulating a timetable and sequence for initiating actions, indicating priorities, and suggesting who should be responsible for doing what.

In proposing an action plan, remember there is a great deal of difference between being responsible, on the one hand, for a decision that may be costly if it proves in error and, on the other hand, casually suggesting courses of action that might be taken when you do not have to bear the responsibility for any of the consequences. A good rule to follow in making your recommendations is: *Avoid recommending anything you would not yourself be willing to do if you were in management's shoes.* The importance of learning to develop good judgment in a managerial situation is indicated by the fact that, even though the same information and operating data may be available to every manager or executive in an organization, the quality of the judgments about what the information means and which actions need to be taken does vary from person to person.[4]

---

[4]Gragg, "Because Wisdom Can't Be Told," p. 10.

It goes without saying that your report should be well organized and well written. Great ideas amount to little unless others can be convinced of their merit—this takes tight logic, the presentation of convincing evidence, and persuasively written arguments.

THE TEN COMMANDMENTS OF CASE ANALYSIS

As a way of summarizing our suggestions about how to approach the task of case analysis, we have compiled what we like to call "The Ten Commandments of Case Analysis." They are shown in Table 2. If you observe all or even most of these commandments faithfully as you prepare a case either for class discussion or for a written report, your chances of doing a good job on the assigned cases will be much improved. Hang in there, give it your best shot, and have some fun exploring what the real world of strategic management is all about.

TABLE 2   **The Ten Commandments of Case Analysis**

To be observed in written reports and oral presentations, and while participating in class discussions.

1. Read the case twice, once for an overview and once to gain full command of the facts; then take care to explore every one of the exhibits.

2. Make a list of the problems and issues that have to be confronted.

3. Do enough number crunching to discover the story told by the data presented in the case. (To help you comply with this commandment, consult Table 1 to guide your probing of a company's financial condition and financial performance.)

4. Look for opportunities to use the concepts and analytical tools you have learned earlier.

5. Be thorough in your diagnosis of the situation and make at least a one- or two-page outline of your assessment.

6. Support any and all opinions with well-reasoned arguments and numerical evidence; don't stop until you can purge "I think" and "I feel" from your assessment and, instead, are able to rely completely on "My analysis shows."

7. Develop charts, tables, and graphs to expose more clearly the main points of your analysis.

8. Prioritize your recommendations and make sure they can be carried out in an acceptable time frame with the available skills and financial resources.

9. Review your recommended action plan to see if it addresses all of the problems and issues you identified.

10. Avoid recommending any course of action that could have disastrous consequences if it doesn't work out as planned; therefore, be as alert to the downside risks of your recommendations as you are to their upside potential and appeal.

SUBJECT INDEX